MODERN
MACROECONOMICS

MODERN MACROECONOMICS

MAJOR CONTRIBUTIONS TO CONTEMPORARY THOUGHT

Panayotis G. Korliras
University of Pittsburgh and
Athens School of Economics
and Business Science

Richard S. Thorn
University of Pittsburgh

HARPER & ROW, PUBLISHERS
New York / Hagerstown / Philadelphia / San Francisco / London

Sponsoring Editor: John Greenman
Project Editor: Penny Schmukler
Designer: Emily Harste
Senior Production Manager: Kewal K. Sharma
Compositor: Syntax International Pte. Ltd.
Printer and Binder: Halliday Lithograph Corporation
Art Studio: J & R Technical Services Inc.

**MODERN
MACROECONOMICS:
MAJOR
CONTRIBUTIONS
TO CONTEMPORARY
THOUGHT**

Library of Congress Cataloging in Publication Data

Main entry under title:

Modern macroeconomics.

    1. Macroeconomics—Addresses, essays,
lectures.   I. Korliras, Panayotis G.   II. Thorn,
Richard S.
HB171.5.M669   339   78-14959
ISBN 0-06-043764-2

To Our Children

George and Athena
Bettina, Clifford, and Eric

Contents

Preface ix

PART ONE
**Consumption
and Investment**
1

Consumer Economics: A Survey 5
Robert Ferber

**Econometric Studies of Investment
Behavior: A Survey** 41
Dale W. Jorgenson

**Econometric Studies of Investment
Behavior: A Comment** 77
Robert Eisner

PART TWO
**Aggregate
Demand
Management
and Stabilization
Policies**
87

The Role of Monetary Policy 91
Milton Friedman

**Rational Expectations and the Theory of
Economic Policy** 103
Thomas J. Sargent and Neil Wallace

**The Monetarist Controversy or, Should We
Forsake Stabilization Policies?** 114
Franco Modigliani

PART THREE
**Inflation
and Unemployment**
135

Inflation: A Survey 139
David Laidler and Michael Parkin

**Excess Demand, Unemployment,
Vacancies, and Wages** 198
Bent Hansen

**Money-Wage Dynamics and the Labor
Market Equilibrium** 213
Edmund S. Phelps

Inflation and Unemployment 242
James Tobin

**Recent Developments in the Theory of
Inflation and Unemployment** 259
Robert J. Gordon

**PART FOUR
Disequilibrium
Macroeconomics
285**

**The Keynesian Counter-Revolution: A
Theoretical Appraisal 289**
Robert W. Clower

**Keynes and the Keynesians: A Suggested
Interpretation 305**
Axel Leijonhufvud

**Output, Employment, and Wages in the
Short-Run 312**
Robert M. Solow and Joseph E. Stiglitz

**A General Disequilibrium Model of Income
and Employment 327**
Robert J. Barro and Herschel I. Grossman

**A Disequilibrium Macroeconomic
Model 339**
Panayotis G. Korliras

**PART FIVE
Monetary
Growth
Models
355**

Money and Economic Growth 359
James Tobin

Monetary Growth Theory in Perspective 370
Jerome L. Stein

Effective Demand in the Long Run 390
Hugh Rose

**Money, Growth, and the Propensity to
Save 404**
Ronald I. McKinnon

Preface

The goal of this book is to introduce the advanced student of economics to the most significant recent developments in macroeconomics. It reviews the large and rapidly growing macroeconomic literature, and it concentrates on research findings of the last decade.

No branch of economics has undergone a more dramatic revolution than macroeconomics. In the early 1960s economists were congratulating themselves that major problems of economic stabilization had been solved and that they could safely turn their attention to problems of economic growth. But in the following decade we have witnessed the failure of Keynesian demand management policies and the birth of a new kind of inflation: stagflation. This has resulted in a renewed interest in classical economics, as well as the evolution of a new theoretical movement, disequilibrium economics. This movement strikes at the very heart of neoclassical economics—Walrasian general equilibrium.

Macroeconomics has been an exciting, if at times somewhat confusing, discipline in recent years. No survey volume, including this one, can adequately cover the total spectrum of recent developments, but we have tried to include every major new direction macroeconomics has taken.

All the articles in this book have been reprinted exactly as originally published, except for the inclusion of minor corrections supplied by their authors.

We are indebted to the original authors and publishers for their generous permission to reprint the articles contained in this volume. Kishore Kulkarni and Debbie Barran assisted us in assembling the manuscript and in checking references. Esther Zavos met her usual high standards of excellence when preparing the manuscript. Lastly we wish to express our appreciation to Harper & Row for its continued dedication to scholarly publishing.

P. K.
R. S. T.

PART ONE
Consumption and Investment

Classical economics did not require aggregate consumption and investment functions, only a theory of individual consumption and firm investment plus a theory of general equilibrium such as that provided by Walras to guarantee all the factors of production would be fully employed. If asked to draw up an aggregate consumption and investment theory, they probably would agree that consumption depended on income, the rate of interest, and custom and that investment depended on the rate of return on capital. The rate of interest was given a critical role in equating aggregate saving with aggregate investment so that the classical position could be summarized by the following equation:

$$S(Y, i) = I(i)$$

Alfred Marshall went even further and suggested that wealth also might be a factor in the consumption function, but neither he nor his followers pursued this avenue very far. While classical theory of saving and investment could be characterized as essentially a real theory, the key role played by the rate of interest permitted the savings and investment equilibrium to be related to financial markets. This possibility was expertly exploited by Knut Wicksell to develop a disequilibrium theory of business cycles by permitting the monetary rate of interest to differ from the real rate of interest.

The Keynesian revolution with its emphasis on the determinants of effective demand in the medium-run downplayed the role of the rate of interest in equating saving and investment and clearly defined an aggregate consumption function while retaining largely unchanged the classical investment function as developed by Irving Fisher with the following formulization:

$$S(Y) = I(i)$$

Consumption in this view was changed mainly by a change in income. The stability of the consumption function was a cornerstone of the Keynesian analysis. Monetary policy could not affect investment easily in the Keynesian world because of doubts about the elasticity of interest rates with respect to the money supply at low levels of interest rates and the interest rate elasticity of investment. Keynesians believed one must operate directly on consumption and this had to be accomplished largely through fiscal policy.

Three empirical facts, however, placed the simple Keynesian consumption function into question. Cross-sectional budget studies showed the marginal propensity to consume to decrease as income rose so that the marginal propensity to consume was less than the average propensity to consume. Long-run trend data, such as that developed by Kuznets, however, showed a constant marginal propensity to consume with respect to income so that the marginal propensity to consume and the average propensity to consume were equal. Further data over the business cycle showed that the average propensity to consume is smaller than average in periods of expansion and larger than average in periods of contraction, so that again the marginal propensity to consume seemed smaller than the average propensity to consume.

Lastly, economists concluded that the enormous error they made in forecasting a postwar slump was the result of their failure to take account of the large amount of liquid assets in the hands of consumers at the end of the war so that it seemed desirable to include liquid assets or some other wealth variable or variables in the consumption function.

In view of these well-established empirical facts, three main theories were developed to explain aggregate consumption: (1) the life cycle hypothesis of Ando-Modigliani, (2) the permanent income hypothesis of Friedman, and (3) the relative income hypothesis of Duesenberry. Keynes tried to capture much of the same effects explained by these theories by his suggestion that the marginal propensity to save was greater out of earned income than property income, but the life cycle hypothesis and the permanent income hypothesis provide an intellectually more satisfying explanation. Ferber examines the development and empirical testing of these three hypotheses. The life cycle hypothesis of Ando-Modigliani and the permanent income hypothesis of Friedman cannot be considered competing theories since they exhibit only small differences in their formal structure and explain in slightly different verbal terms the same objective process.

The life cycle hypothesis maintains that current consumption is not only affected by current income but also the present value of one's future expected income and net wealth, especially liquid wealth. It implies that individual consumption in any time period reflects a long-term plan to optimally allocate one's income between consumption and savings.

Further work has been done on investigating whether there are any long-run changes in the marginal propensity to consume, despite Kuznets findings, and what might possibly affect these changes. The life cycle hypothesis provides a handle on this problem. According to the life cycle hypothesis changes in the demographic composition of the population and institutional changes such as those in social security benefits should affect the long-run propensity to save: the former by a change in the proportions of the population in various phases of the consumption life cycle, and the latter by changing one's net wealth, in effect capitalizing future social benefits much like an annuity. The life cycle hypothesis and its variants have provided a useful analytical framework and major advance in the analysis of consumption.

In classical economics the determinant of investment demand was simply expected profit which was determined by innovation, anticipated demand, the cost of capital, and replacement demand. In the short run the rate of profit and interest rates were believed to be the dominant factors. Empirical studies have not found either the rate of profit or interest rates extremely important factors in the short or medium run. However, expected profits, expected changes in output, and past changes in output are so closely related that it is statistically difficult to disentangle the independent influence of each.

Changes in output seem to be the most important factor changing investment demand in the short and medium run. A theoretical explanation for this is given by the acceleration principle discovered independently by Aftalion, Bickerdike, Clark, and Hawtrey in the first decades of this century. The accelerator theory assumed that the capital stock would be adjusted to its desired level in the current period. This seemed obviously an extreme assumption and led to the development of a series of distributed lag models in which investment depends on past values of output:

$$I = f(Y_t, Y_{t-1}, \ldots)$$

Koyck showed that a model of this form is equivalent to an autoregressive model (which was christened the flexible accelerator) of the form

$$I = f(K_t, K_{t-1}, \ldots)$$

Much discussion has centered on the specification and regularity of the lag, whether it was degenerative or had some inverted U-shape form. Eisner and others pointed out that this model has both a formal and a theoretical resemblance to Friedman's permanent income consumption hypothesis. Empirical studies of the lag between output and the peak of induced investment have found it to be generally long-ranging from four to eight quarters.

The policy implications of the flexible accelerator investment models lead to a super Keynesianism. If neither investment nor consumption were affected significantly by the rate of interest in the short and medium term, only direct influences on effective demand could influence the level of employment. And indeed the early large-scale macroeconomic models of the economy contained no financial sector. Subsequent experience has shown that the inclusion of a financial sector improves forecasting performance, and most large-scale models now include a financial sector.

Many of the models discussed by Jorgenson contained either directly or indirectly financial elements but not in such a manner as to make one optimistic about the use of monetary policy for short-run stabilization. The interest inelasticity of investment demand rather than the Keynesian liquidity trap seems to favor fiscal policy as a short-run stabilizer.

The modern theory of investment demand also has placed greater emphasis on the determinants of replacement demand for investment and improving the specification of this demand.

Empirical studies have found with regularity that the returns to scale from capital investment appear to be constant. These results imply that the size of the firm under perfect competition is indeterminate.

In spite of the extensive theoretical and empirical investigations since the late 1940s, the theory of investment is one of the least understood areas of economics. The instability of investment still remains one of the principal causes of business cycles, and our inability to forecast investment behavior remains one of the major shortcomings of stabilization policies. Some economists have gone so far as to argue that investment behavior may not be completely explained rationally.

One cannot help but muse with Loamsby[1] that perhaps this is because the problem has been attacked with the wrong tools—profit maximization and equilibrium. Certainly economists can take little satisfaction from the present state of knowledge concerning the determinants of aggregate business investment.

[1] Brian J. Loamsby, *Choice, complexity and ignorance* (London: 1976), chap. 12.

Consumer Economics: A Survey

Robert Ferber

University of Illinois

This review attempts to synthesize recent currents of thought in consumer economics. The focus is on the determination of total consumption (and saving) rather than on the allocation of the total by categories of consumption. The latter, usually classified under the heading of consumer demand functions, is a major topic in itself, and is covered in some detail in a comprehensive recent review article by Alan Brown and Angus Deaton [31, 1972]. Hence, the emphasis in this review is on the macro aspects of consumer economics, but with attention to micro aspects insofar as they interrelate with the former or involve relevant topics from other social sciences or branches of economics that have received little attention by consumer economists.

1. INTRODUCTION

Section 2 is a review of general theories of the consumption function. The relation of these various theories to each other and especially the role of permanent income theories that came into vogue in the 1950s and the 1960s are covered in this section, including a review of the extensive empirical work that has sought to test these theories.

Section 3 of the paper considers the more recent work on the role of the *ceteris paribus* conditions of the consumption function and

Reprinted from the *Journal of Economic Literature*, 11:1303–1342 (1973), by permission of the author and the publisher (copyright by the American Economic Association).

their effects on consumer behavior. Special attention is given to the roles of attitudinal variables and of wealth variables in consumption because of the considerable attention that has been given to them in recent years. In addition, the burgeoning attention to the determinants of assets and of wealth has produced much interesting work on the relatively new topics of assets functions, the highlights of which are covered in Section 4.

Section 5 of the paper turns to recent advances in the economics literature that are in many ways extensions of received theory, in particular, the human capital approach and the growing interest in time allocation and in the view of the household as a producer. Implications of these recent advances for current theory are examined, and a number of studies under each of these subheadings are brought together and compared.

It would be remiss in a survey article of this type not to give attention to work in the other social sciences that may impinge and provide interesting insights on consumer economic behavior. In particular, attention is given in Section 6 to such relatively recent questions as decision-making within the consumer unit, the use of information and the role of reference groups in decision-making. Decision-making and the likely heterogeneity of consumer units are topics with potentially fundamental implications for consumer theory and hence are given special attention in this part of the paper. Finally, some concluding remarks are presented, with special reference to future directions for research.

2. GENERAL THEORIES OF THE CONSUMPTION FUNCTION

a. The Keynesian Approach

The concept of a consumption function seems to have had its genesis in J. M. Keynes' *General Theory.* Unlike the neoclassical economists who, in the consumer area, were mostly concerned with such micro questions as the meaning of utility and the relationship between the price of a product and the quantity demanded, Keynes was concerned primarily with such macroeconomic questions as how to deal with business fluctuations and the determination of the level of employment. The latter was said to depend on effective demand as represented by the sum of consumption expenditures and investment expenditures, with consumption dependent on the level of income and on the generalization that ". . . men are disposed, as a rule and on the average, to increase their consumption as their income increases, but not by as much as the increase in their income" [115, 1936, p. 96]. Based apparently on casual observation, Keynes advanced this proposition that the marginal propensity is less than the average propensity to consume, as a cornerstone of his general theory, assuming that it would enable the amount of consumption, and of saving, to be predicted for any given level of aggregate income. Known later as the absolute income hypothesis, this statement set off a virtual gold rush to translate it into empirical terms and to find "the consumption function," that is, the relation between aggregate consumption and aggregate income, holding other relevant variables constant. Numerous such studies were carried out, mostly regressing time series aggregates of consumption expenditures on aggregate disposable income and other variables, and clearly confirmed the existence of such a function.[1] The multiple correlation coefficient usually exceeded .95, the current income variable accounted for most of the variability in

consumption, and the marginal propensity to consume out of current income was less than the average propensity, both being less than unity.

The stability of the aggregate consumption function was, however, more of a question. A number of variables other than current income were found to affect consumption expenditures, so that the parameters of the "consumption function," like that of a demand schedule, could be highly sensitive to changes in such other variables as prices, expectations, and past income. Even slight changes in the marginal propensity to consume could produce substantial changes in the amount of aggregate saving, and thereby affect substantially the balance between saving and investment, and later experience showed that this happened not infrequently with changes in business conditions. Although highly satisfactory goodness-of-fit results were obtained (due, incidentally, in large measure to the fact that consumption expenditures comprise over 90 percent of disposable income), a question was raised about the adequacy of this absolute income variant of the consumption function for explaining aggregate consumption behavior, especially when these functions yielded very poor post-World War II predictions.

Another question about the adequacy of the absolute income hypothesis related to its inability to explain why the aggregate average propensity to consume had remained virtually constant since 1870, at least in the United States [82, Goldsmith, 1955; 123, Kuznets, 1952; 122, Kuznets, 1946, pp. 75–87], when cross-section data at various points in time indicated clearly that the marginal propensity declined as incomes rose. With sharply rising levels of aggregate income, one would expect the average propensity to decline over time.

b. Relative Income Hypothesis

The foundation of the absolute income hypothesis is that the propensity to consume is a function of the *level* of income. The foundation of the relative income hypothesis is that this propensity depends on *relative* income,

---

[1] An extensive list of these early studies will be found in Orcutt and Roy [165, 1949]. A synthesis of these studies to 1950 is contained in Ferber [66, 1962].

that is, income relative to some prior standard in the case of time series or relative to income of a reference group in the case of cross-section data.

The cross-section form of this hypothesis seems to have been first suggested by Dorothy Brady and Rose Friedman who suggested that the saving rate of an individual depends not on the level of his income but rather on his relative position on the income scale, namely:

$$s/y = a + b\frac{y}{\bar{y}}$$

where s and y represent individual saving and income, respectively, and $\bar{y}$ represents average income [27, 1947].

Further support for this hypothesis was provided about the same time by Franco Modigliani and by J. S. Duesenberry. The latter's support was primarily on a psychological plane, noting the tendency for people to emulate their neighbors and to strive for a continually higher standard of living. Moreover, once a higher standard of living was attained, people seek to maintain it even when incomes go down, whereas when incomes rise people try to move to a higher standard of living [51, 1949].

From a time series point of view, Duesenberry, as well as Modigliani independently [150, 1949], formulated and successfully tested the hypothesis that the aggregate saving rate was a function of the ratio of current income to the highest previous level of aggregate income, namely:

$$S/Y = a + b\frac{Y}{Y_o}$$

where Y_o represents the highest level of income previously attained (deflated for prices and population). On the basis of this formulation, therefore, the saving ratio over the long run is independent of the absolute level of income although it would vary from year to year in accordance with changes in the ratio of current income to previous peak income. Also worth noting is that, like the later permanent income hypothesis, this theory accepts the invariance of the consumption-income ratio to secular changes in income.

A variant of this formulation, by T. E. Davis, was that the past standard be previous peak consumption rather than previous peak income, because people become more adjusted to spending than to income [47, 1952]. W. S. Vickrey, among others, also noted that consumption expenditures are likely to be more stable than income and that the data estimates undoubtedly are less inaccurate [209, 1947].

Considerable evidence was marshalled in support of the relative income hypothesis in the late forties and early fifties; since then the main interest in general hypotheses seems to have shifted to permanent income formulations. On an aggregative level, Davis [47, 1952], Duesenberry [51, 1949], and Modigliani [150, 1949] showed that functions based on the relative income hypothesis provided at least as good statistical fits to the data as the various forms of the absolute income hypothesis. A similar finding was reported in an independent evaluation of the two approaches by Ferber [65, 1955]. At the micro level, Brady and Friedman used the relative income hypothesis to reconcile higher saving rates of village than city families, of farm than non-farm families, and geographical differences [27, 1947].

In addition, Duesenberry used this hypothesis in a similar manner [51, 1949], while Brady showed that family saving was a function not only of the level of family income but also of the income level of the community in which the family resided [26, 1952].

These findings do not, however, necessarily invalidate the absolute income hypothesis because a basic tenet of that hypothesis is the *ceteris paribus* assumption for all variables other than current income. Since on many of these earlier studies data on variables such as wealth were not available to enable the *ceteris paribus* assumption to be justified, there is no assurance that such other relevant variables were indeed held constant. Thus, James Tobin has shown that the smaller financial resources available to black than to white families can be used to explain the apparent failure of the absolute income hypothesis to explain black-white saving differentials, as earlier alleged by Duesenberry [202, 1951]. He also shows how the historical constancy of the saving ratio does not necessarily conflict with the absolute income hypothesis if the tremendous growth in wealth over time served to reduce the need for saving out of current income and hence acted to raise the propensity to consume as real income increased.

c. Permanent Income and Life Cycle Theories

The basic idea underlying these theories is that the consumer plans his expenditures not on the basis of the income received during the current period but rather on the basis of his long-run or lifetime income expectation. At one extreme, this is obvious, as Milton Friedman points out, since a person does not plan his expenditures for one day according to what income he expects to receive on that particular day [73, 1957]. Applied to the theory of the consumption function, the result is a hypothesis that the consumer plans his expenditures for a given period, whether it is a day or a year, on the basis of a longer run view of the resources that will be available to him. In a sense, these views reflect a return to the preKeynesian views of the importance of wealth and interest rates, as propounded by Irving Fisher for example, since permanent income represents the yield from human plus nonhuman wealth.

The two principal forms of the hypothesis were both developed in the fifties more or less independently, the permanent income hypothesis (PIH) by Milton Friedman, and the life cycle hypothesis (LCH) by Franco Modigliani and his associates. In many respects they are very similar but there are also some key differences. Both theories divide the current income of the consumer unit into permanent (y_p) and transitory components (y_t), and the same is true for PIH of consumption expenditures (c_p and c_t, respectively). The PIH assumes the absence of any correlation between y_t and y_p, between c_t and c_p, or between y_t and c_t. In the LCH also, no correlation is assumed between y_t and y_p, but over time y_t may add to y_p because to the extent it is invested, the yield on the investment raises permanent income.

In both cases, the key relationship is that permanent consumption, c_p, is a linear multiple, k, of permanent income, y_p. To Friedman, the multiple depends on the interest rate, on the ratio of nonhuman to total wealth and on a catch-all variable which includes age and tastes as major components. Modigliani accepts the same determining variables but allows the multiple to vary with time and stresses the age of the consumer unit.

In both formulations permanent income is obtained as the product of the estimated wealth of the consumer unit and a rate of return at which this wealth is discounted. Friedman puts more emphasis on estimating wealth on the basis of the flow of current and past incomes as a proxy for y_p whereas Modigliani puts more emphasis on current income plus nonhuman net worth for estimating household resources. In both approaches, consumption is defined to include the real consumption of goods and services rather than monetary expenditures; durables are expenditures only to the extent that they are depreciated in a particular period, not the amount spent for their acquisition. By either formulation, the central hypothesis is that the proportion of permanent income saved by the consumer unit is independent of its income in a particular period, and that transitory income has no (Friedman) or little (Modigliani) effect on current consumption.

In both models, an increase in real income may raise the saving ratio, in the PIH because this increases permanent income, and consumption, relative to their measured components. In the LCH the effect varies with the age of the household, being positive for younger households and negative for older, and retired, households. Modigliani [152, 1966] specifically allows for a positive secular relationship because of income growth due to both population increase and higher productivity.

While such hypotheses seem simple in theory, testing them gives rise to a great many empirical problems, primarily because of the difficulty of separating the permanent from the transitory components of income and of consumption. Partly for these reasons and partly because of the very rich nature of these hypotheses, a substantial literature has appeared since the late 1950s testing or making use of them. To abstract from this literature, the principal findings would seem to be the following:[2]

1. The concept of permanent income is an invaluable addition to our understanding of economic behavior. In his original work, Friedman had shown how this concept explained various apparent paradoxes of consumer economics, such as the consistency of the aggregate marginal propensity to consume over the last hundred years while incomes were rising with the cross-section marginal propensity declining as income rises [73, 1957, Ch. 5]. In addition, however, the concept has been found extremely useful in a wide variety of other studies and in other countries. Thus, Tang Hun Lee found that y_p is a more important determinant of the demand for housing in the United States than current income [135, 1964; 137, 1968], while a similar finding for total expenditures was reported for Chile by Roger Betancourt [18, 1971]. Similar support for the practical value of the concept has been provided, among others, by P. S. Laumas for Canada [130, 1969], by Michael Landsberger for Israel [127, 1970], and by R. Ramanathan for India [176, 1969]. The concept has also been extended to other areas of economics, as exemplified by Robert Eisner's use of it in investment analysis [58, 1967]. In another interesting application based on the life cycle hypothesis, W. H. Branson and A. K. Klevorick have shown that when consumption functions are estimated using permanent income variables there is strong

[2] The focus here is on the more recent studies. For a comprehensive review of the older studies as well as of Friedman's and Modigliani's own tests, see Mayer [147, 1972].

evidence of money illusion [28, 1969]. Moreover, from an aggregative forecasting point of view, G. D. Craig found that saving functions incorporating permanent income concepts were either the best or equal to the best of seven alternative hypotheses tested [40, 1970]. On the other hand, Nissan Liviatan has contended that cross-section data in Israel suggest that current income is the main concept of relevance to explaining consumption [143, 1965].

2. Nevertheless, the validity of a basic tenet of the permanent income hypothesis remains questionable: it is not at all clear that the permanent income elasticity of consumption is unity. Albert Ando and Franco Modigliani did find that "Consumption is in fact roughly homogeneous in income and assets" in annual time-series regressions on United States data for 1929–59 (excluding 1941–46) [6, 1963], as did Spiro [190, 1962]. Also, Eisner obtained an income elasticity of virtually 1.0 for 1950 cross-section data among city-size classes, but when occupation of head and age of head were used as instrumental variables the elasticities drop to the .8–.9 range [57, 1958]. An earlier study by Irwin Friend and I. B. Kravis [77, 1957] using occupation as a proxy for permanent income had yielded a clear correlation of the propensity to consume with average income of different occupations, counter to the PIH. Many other studies using regression models obtained an income elasticity clearly less than unity (usually about .9). This is true of Colin Wright [219, 1969], of Paul Taubman [196, 1965], and of Laumas and K. A. Mohabbat [131, 1972], all for the United States, of Betancourt for Chile [18, 1971], and Laumas for Canada [130, 1969]. Robert Holbrook and Frank Stafford suggested that several types of permanent income need to be distinguished, and demonstrated that the marginal propensity varies by type of income, from a maximum of .9 for husband's and wife's earnings to .35 for transfer income [93, 1971].

3. The assumed lack of effect of transitory income on current consumption receives mixed support from empirical tests. Analyses of two windfall payment situations—by R. Bird and R. Bodkin of onetime insurance dividends to American veterans [23, 1965], and by M. E. Kreinin of 1957–58 German restitution payments to Israeli residents [120, 1961]—found moderate expenditures from those receipts, and not only for durable goods, which might in large part be considered saving. Landsberger, using some of the same data as Kreinin and also later (1963–64) data on windfall payments in Israel, obtained low marginal propensities [127, 1970].

Yet, more general regression models have obtained indications of a strongly positive marginal propensity to consume out of y_t, in Canada of .45 [129, Laughhunn, 1969], and between .55 and .84 in the United States [131, Laumas and Mohabbat, 1972]. A marginal propensity to save out of y_t slightly above to that out of y_p was obtained by Taubman in analyzing cross-section data [196, 1965]. J. M. Holmes, in a time-series analysis of American data for 1905–51, found that y_t as well as y_p were statistically significant in explaining fluctuations in c_p [94, 1970].

On the other hand, in still another study of American time-series data, R. E. Smith [189, 1962] concludes that y_t is more important than y_p for explaining variations in durable goods expenditures and that windfall income accounts for most of the variation in purchases of durable goods. George Katona and Eva Mueller [113, 1968] also found that response to higher income in the United States in 1964–65 as a result of unexpected tax decrease went mostly for durables and saving but for other goods and services as well.

A recent time-series study by M. R. Darby [43, 1972] shows in an interesting fashion how transitory income is allocated among money, financial assets and durable goods,

with the fraction going into durable goods varying inversely with the ratio of "transitory" assets to permanent assets. The assertion by the author, however, that the study supports a zero effect of transitory income on consumption is hardly valid in view of the initial assumption that "All transitory income is assumed to be saved" (p. 928), not to mention a highly significant coefficient of .5 for transitory income in the one aggregate consumption function shown in the article.

Proponents of the permanent income hypothesis can argue that some nonzero marginal propensity out of transitory income is only to be expected to the extent that transitory income gives rise to higher permanent income, say, through interest on investment of such income, or through changes in expectations. Moreover, the type of data used can have a substantial effect on empirical estimates of marginal propensities; Taubman [197, 1968] obtained marginal propensities to save of any where between .3 and .6 for the United States depending on the saving series he used.

4. In addition, y_p and y_t may not be unrelated either. In his study, Holmes found a strong correlation between these two variables [94, 1970], as did Laumas and Mohabbat [131, 1972]. In time-series studies, such a relationship could be an artifact of the process of estimating y_p as a weighted moving average distributed lag of measured incomes, with y_t as the residual [56, Ebberler, 1973; 95, Holmes, 1971]. In fact, in a study of the determinants of durable goods purchases, Brian Motley argues that expected future income is actually a function of transitory income [156, 1969].

To sum up, as of the present time, the concept of permanent income seems to be firmly established as both operational and highly meaningful. Specific postulates of the permanent income hypothesis have not received much support from empirical tests but have led to modifications that may be simpler and more realistic. Thus, Irwin Friend and Paul Taubman have substituted the idea of "normal income" for "permanent income." They define normal income in terms of a trend or average of income in recent years in the case of time-series data [196, 1965] or as a function of key socioeconomic variables in the case of cross-section data [75, 1966], in each case the frame of reference, e.g., time horizon, varying with the particular problem. Their studies show that this approach yields meaningful results both for "normal income" effects and for transitory income effects, the latter defined as the difference between measured and "normal" incomes.

More recently, Thomas Mayer has suggested a compromise between the permanent income hypothesis and the relative income hypothesis, which "asserts that the income elasticity of consumption is greater for permanent income than for transitory income, but that it is neither unity for one nor zero for the other. It also claims that there is *some* lag in the consumption function but that this lag is substantially shorter than the lag found by Friedman or Modigliani" [147, 1972, pp. 45–46]. In his study, Mayer finds support for his "standard income" theory on the double grounds that the marginal propensity to consume out of transitory income is generally from 40 to 90 percent of that out of permanent or normal income, and that at least some lag effects on consumption appear to be very short.[3]

d. Stock Adjustment Theories

The view that economic behavior represents a continuous process of adjustment has become increasingly popular in the last 10 to 15 years. For a while, this view was manifested in two seemingly diverse ways. One approach was to view stocks in the form of tastes and habits which conditioned consumer behavior over a long period of years and which accounted to a large extent for the positive

[3] But Mayer admits that his results are very mixed on this point and that other types of lags may cover the entire life span of the household, e.g., [147, 1972, p. 356].

autocorrelation in consumer purchases of many nondurables and similar goods and services. Thus, once a person begins to smoke cigarettes he tends to continue to do so, and to consume cigarettes at a steady rate as the habit becomes more ingrained. Hence, the link between current and past purchases is habit formation, a view developed by both Duesenberry and Modigliani in their classic works on this subject [51, 1949; 150, 1949], as noted in an earlier section. This view was supported by work by T. M. Brown [32, 1952] on Canadian time-series data with a modification he suggested—that the decline of the effects of past habits in consumption is continuous and is not subject to a ratchet effect.

More recently, the theoretical role of habit formation on demand functions was explored by W. M. Gorman [84, 1967] and by R. A. Pollak [170, 1970], the latter using this concept to distinguish between long-run and short-run demand functions, something that Brown had also focused on. In an earlier empirical study covering time series data for 13 countries, H. S. Houthakker [100, 1965] had also noted that within country (time-series) regressions capture mostly short-run effects and between country (cross-section) regressions mostly long-run effects, and that theoretically as well as empirically the two types of elasticities were very different and should be treated as such.

The other view sought to explain why consumer purchases of many durables followed an opposite pattern—the purchase of, say, a refrigerator one quarter, or year, was not likely to be followed by another purchase of the same good in the next period. Incorporating the obvious elements of depreciation and obsolescence, this approach viewed stocks as a physical accumulation of goods desired by consumers which led to additional puchases as desired stocks of (for example) durables deviated from actual stocks. A simple form of this hypothesis would be:

$$S_t - S_{t-1} = \lambda(S_t^* - S_{t-1}) \quad \lambda > 0 \qquad \text{(a)}$$

where S_t is actual stock at time t and S_t^* is the desired stock. To the extent that the desired stock at t exceeds (is below) actual stock in the previous period, the consumer will be motivated to add to (subtract from) his actual stock by a multiple, λ, of this difference.[4] By postulating that S_t^* is a function of such observable variables as income and family size, and making the appropriate substitution, an equation is obtained whose parameters can then be estimated. This approach has proved successful in studying the demand for a wide variety of durable goods, as illustrated in the volume edited by A. C. Harberger [89, 1960] and in other studies by D. S. Huang for autos [102, 1963; 103, 1964], and by Wu for household durables [220, 1965].

Hence, on the one hand theory had given us a stock of psychological tastes and habits that accounted for positive autocorrelation in some purchases while on the other hand we had a stock of physical goods that accounted for negative autocorrelation in other types of purchases. In their epic study, Houthakker and L. D. Taylor (H-T) combined the two views in a single theory [101, 1970]. Their basic postulate is that current purchases depend on current as well as past values of the variables that determine consumer purchases and that these values are reflected in the current stock of the consumer. In simple form:

$$q_t = \alpha + \beta s_t + \gamma x_t \tag{b}$$

where q_t is purchases in period t, s_t is the stock and x_t is income, all at the micro level, and α, β, γ are parameters. β is the stock adjustment parameter: if β is positive, that product (category) is said to be influenced by habit purchases so that an increase in the stock leads to still more purchases; whereas if β is negative the stock adjustment effect is predominant and an increase in the stock serves to depress new purchases.

Like S_t^* in (a), s_t is not observable, but it is easily eliminated by relating the change in stock to purchases and to depreciation,

making the appropriate substitutions and solving, resulting in an equation relating change in purchases to purchases, change in income and income [101, Houthakker, 1970, Ch. 1]. (For estimation, H-T also add price terms to this equation.) H-T also present an alternate derivation based on a variant of (a) that leads to the same result.

Empirical tests provide strong support for the H-T model. In their study of American time-series expenditures by 82 categories, H-T find that the dynamic formulation including lagged income and expenditures (and sometimes lagged price), is superior almost invariably to the corresponding static formulation, and that of 65 expenditure categories for which the stock coefficient was estimated, the large majority, 46 (or 61 percent of expenditures) were positive, suggesting habit formation. Incorporation of the same approach in an additive dynamic model yields similarly favorable results for the Canadian time series, as well as for the American, but less favorable results for the Netherlands, and Sweden, especially for the Netherlands when many (16) consumption categories are used, which may violate the independence assumption underlying the model. The habit formation hypothesis also receives strong support from an analysis of Canadian time-series data by E. H. Oksanen [164, 1972] for major categories on consumption as well as in a study by Feng-Yao Lee [133, 1970] of income and expenditures in 28 Japanese cities between 1955 and 1968. In the latter study, the H-T model was judged superior to distributed lag and expected income models. Habit formation tended to be the predominant variable.

An extension of the habit formation hypothesis has been proposed by W. W. McMahon [148, 1971], who argues that two separate and distinct stock effects need to be taken into account in explaining consumer purchases—physical stocks and psychological stocks of tastes and habits. Rather than cancelling out the two effects, McMahon includes both types of stock variables in cross-sectional equations explaining variations principally in purchases of a wide

---

[4] While in an aggregative sense only positive values of the right-hand expression are allowed for individual consumers the term could also be negative, e.g., an older couple wanting to move to a smaller house after their children have left home.

variety of durables and financial holdings, and shows that such purchases tend to be associated positively with psychological stocks and negatively with physical stocks (including financial holdings as part of this category). In fact, Pollak had also suggested the two effects could be combined, because a fixed assumption of the habit formation model is that the effects of current purchases are not related to future preferences and future consumption, but this is hardly true of consumer durables, so that theoretically the habit adjustment coefficient should not be allowed to be negative [170, 1970, p. 761].

Apart from the recognized importance of stock effects, if one additional thing is clear from the theoretical and empirical work of the last 10–15 years, it is that consumer purchases are best explained in terms of a dynamic view of income. This may be some sort of permanent income concept, a distributed lag view of the world, or something else. However formulated, it is surprising to note how often the testable, and successful form of the hypothesis reduces to the inclusion of lagged consumption as the manifestation of income effects. Thus, R. D. Husby [104, 1970] uses such a variable to support the plausibility of nonlinear income effects, Arnold Zellner and M. S. Geisel [222, 1970] found this form to be quite effective, as did De-Min Wu [220, 1965]. In his extensive forecasting tests, Craig [40, 1970] finds that functions including lagged consumption are among the most accurate and that the combination of this approach and that of habit formation seems best. That is also what K. H. Young [221, 1972] finds in his study of the demand for air transportation. The significance of lagged consumption has already been demonstrated. Because it enters into so many different theories and interpretations, its meaning needs further exploration.

3. CETERIS PARIBUS VARIABLES

As in evident from the foregoing material, considerable progress has been made in incorporating tastes and other *ceteris paribus*

variables directly into the consumption function. Income and lagged consumption variables alone cannot reflect all the other diverse factors that affect consumption, and research on the identification and specification of these other factors has continued along many different lines. The principal factors are reviewed briefly in this section.

a. Wealth

In the life cycle and permanent income hypotheses, as discussed earlier wealth is a basic variable, serving as a basis for estimating permanent income. Many other studies have sought to include nonhuman wealth as a separate variable in a consumption function, and the growing availability of consumer wealth data is an irresistible attraction for empirical work.[5] This is especially so since the studies in the 1960s utilizing wealth variables serve to reinforce earlier findings [66, Ferber, 1962, pp. 40–43] that they influence consumer spending apart from income effects.

A major focus has been on components of wealth rather than on total wealth or net worth, though at least three studies were reported using the latter. In a time-series study of American data, M. K. Evans [59, 1967] obtained mixed results, a wealth variable being significant in a long-period (1929–62) consumption function but not in a post-World War II function. Ramanathan [176, 1969] found net worth to have a strong negative effect on the saving of Delhi households apart from an income effect.

Using the 1962–63 data from the Federal Reserve survey of family financial characteristics, Dorothy Projector [174, 1968] finds that net worth affects consumption but not fully in accordance with the life-cycle hypothesis of Modigliani and Ando. The fraction of net worth spent for consumption

---

[5] Just as funds availability tends to stimulate research on that particular subject, so data availability tends to promote the development of approaches using them, plus the fact that wealth in consumer economics has long been a major interest in itself.

tends to be higher for those in the 35–44 age group than in older ages. However, the coefficients of net worth, while statistically significant, are many times smaller than disposable income, the other independent variable in these regressions, though this is to be expected in view of the much larger magnitude of wealth than income. The net worth effect that Ando and Modigliani [6, 1963] obtained in a study of American data is similarly small and statistically significant, the coefficient ranging between .04 and .08, as did Modigliani [153, 1971] in a later study that included disposable income as one of the variables.

The two principal components of wealth whose effects on consumption have been studied individually are liquid assets and capital gains. Liquid assets seem to be an independent determinant of various types of expenditures, though they may also serve as a proxy for wealth, for permanent income, or as a reservoir for imminent purchases. Suites [194, 1963] noted that liquid assets were more important in aggregate consumption functions in the postwar period. Zellner, Huang and L. C. Chan [223, 1965] in a study of quarterly time series (1947–62) data for the United States, conclude that "imbalances in consumer liquid assets holdings exert a statistical and economically significant influence on consumption expenditures." Liquid asset holdings were found to influence durable goods expenditures in a study of cross-section data by J. A. Fisher [70, 1963] and to affect per capita consumption of nondurable goods and services in a time-series study of American data by P. L. Cheng [35, 1963]. In another American cross-section study, however, J. G. Cragg and R. S. Uhler, using a multinominal extension of a linear logit model, reported that a liquid assets variable was not significant in influencing car purchases [39, 1970]. The weight of the evidence so far, however, is in favor of including a liquid assets variable in a consumption function.

In the case of capital gains, J. J. Arena [7, 1965] concluded that they "had little or no impact on aggregate consumption, primarily because of the highly skewed distribution of stock ownership," based on annual and quarterly time-series regressions for 1946–64. However, using an improved set of estimates of capital gains and a model that allows for a distributed lag effect of capital gains, K. B. Bhatia [19, 1972] concludes, from time-series regressions for 1948–64 using a model based on the permanent income approach, that both accrued and realized capital gains affect consumption expenditures, the latter defined to include only the depreciation component of durable goods spending. The marginal propensity to consume out of either type of gains was about .06, highly significant statistically but far below the comparable values (.70 to .80) obtained for the income variable. In addition, the lag effect of capital gains on consumption seemed to be substantially longer than that of income.

As Bhatia has shown [20, 1973], capital gains may comprise substantial proportions of income, about 15 percent or more in the aggregate out of corporate stock holdings alone, and hence would seem to merit special attention in studies of consumption and saving functions. Their effects are likely to be very different from other types of financial resources, and may best be allowed for, separate from the usual income variables, as has been done in the Federal Reserve econometric model of the United States [139, de Leeuw, 1968].

A negative component of wealth, not surprisingly found to influence durable goods expenditures, is credit. Studies of cross-section data in the United States by Fisher [70, 1963] and by Maw Lin Lee [134, 1964] both found the probability of durable goods purchases to vary (positively) with use of credit. The latter also reported that the size of the purchase tended to increase with the use of credit but that credit users exhibited lower income elasticities than those paying all cash, i.e., past used credit influences current purchases. R. J. Ball and P. S. Drake [10, 1963] showed that variations in credit variables in England exerted major influence on durable goods spending during a period of credit restriction. Credit variables were also found important in explaining different types of consumer expenditures entering into the Brookings econometric mod[ ] of the United States [53, 1969].

To date, the most comprehensive attempt to obtain saving functions by category is a study by Lester Taylor [198] applying multiple regression techniques to quarterly Flow-of-Funds time-series data for 1954–70 to 14 different saving and asset components of those data, based on a model allowing for stock adjustment and for differences by age groups. Among the principal findings is the substantial effect of wealth on saving but varying with the type of wealth involved. Thus, the stock of durable goods is found to influence total saving, housing stock influences gross saving and gross investment, and holdings of corporate securities influence both saving (including durables) and consumption (the latter defined as the sum of expenditure for non-durables and services). Capital gains are found to have roughly twice as great an effect on savings as on consumption.

b. Interest Rates and Other Prices

The main findings on the significance of interest rates on consumer spending relate to durable goods. Thus, M. J. Hamburger [88, 1967] found from an analysis of quarterly data for 1953–64 that expenditures for autos as well as for other durables were influenced (negatively) by interest rates as well as by product prices.

Numerous studies of housing demands also found interest rates to be an important determining variable. In their study, Zellner, et al. [223, 1965] suggested that interest rates affect total consumption expenditures, and Colin Wright [218, 1967] documented this by finding a strong substitution effect between the yield on corporate bonds and the propensity to consume, from time-series regressions including permanent income and net worth as other independent variables. In a later study, however, Warren Weber [211, 1970] finds a positive relationship between the two variables; the income effect

of an interest rate change more than offsetting the substitution effect, though the model employed required a number of heroic assumptions (such as that future labor income is expected by the consumer to rise or decline at a constant rate).

In time-series studies of the demand for individual products, or consumption categories, prices of those and of competing products are naturally key variables; the lack of such data in many cross-section studies is a major shortcoming and very likely yields unwarrantedly high estimates of the effect of income and of other variables that may be closely and positively correlated with prices. A review of such studies is outside the scope of this article and would be a major task in itself. It is of interest to note here, however, that at least one study has found that both income and price elasticity estimates are affected by what prices are used for the category (food) but not by the type of price index [204, Tolley, 1969].

At the level of aggregate expenditures, the variables are invariably deflated by price indexes, on the plausible assumption that consumers are influenced by variables in "real" rather than monetary terms. Nevertheless, evidence continues to accumulate that this assumption is contrary to fact, and that consumers are subject to money illusion. If such illusion exists, Power [172, 1959] notes that one such effect in the face of rising prices would be for consumers to shift expenditures from the future to the present. In fact, this is what W. H. Branson and A. K. Klevorick [28, 1969] found, namely, a highly significant and positive coefficient of a price level variable with per capital real consumption as dependent and after including real income and real net worth.[6] After testing various alternative explanations, they come to the firm conclusion that, "in the short run the price level has an independent effect on real consumption due

[6] As a reader points out, however, studies of the demand function for money have found little evidence of money illusion.

to what is commonly called money illusion" [28, 1969, p. 846].

F. T. Juster and Paul Wachtel [108, 1972] distinguish between the effects of anticipated and unanticipated inflation, based on whether an index of expected price increases (from the University of Michigan Survey Research Center data) is or is not equal to the change in the Consumer Price Index. They conclude from quarterly time-series regressions covering different periods between 1954 and 1971 that anticipated inflation tends to increase total spending at the expense of saving while unanticipated inflation has the reverse effect. The uncertainty created by the latter situation is felt to partly explain the high saving rates in recent years [109, Juster, 1972].

c. Socioeconomic Variables

Every cross-section study of consumption functions tends to include a set of socioeconomic variables in addition to income, the usual criterion of selection being the very pragmatic one of throwing in all such variables available. In view of the large sample sizes, often in thousands, a subset if not all of these variables turn out to be significant, and there the matter is left to rest. As a rule, the focus of the study is on another question altogether, and the socioeconomic variables are added essentially for completeness of the model formulation. Other than the development of the life cycle concept roughly 20 years ago and its effect on expenditures and saving [66, Ferber, 1962], theorists seem to have neglected this topic.

Even studies focusing on the role of socioeconomic variables in the consumption function have been virtually nonexistent. One interesting exception is an attempt by R. Agarwals and J. Drinkwater [4, 1972] to use Canadian cross-section data to regress the marginal propensity to consume on socioeconomic factors, principally presence of a working wife, and then incorporate the resulting estimates as additional variables interacting with income in aggregate time-series consumption functions. The result is

sufficiently promising (moderately significant interaction effects) to warrant further attention to such approaches. One other attempt had been made to incorporate effects of socioeconomic variables in consumption functions, by V. G. Lippitt [142, 1959]. This method was tested on nine consumption categories by D. J. Laughhunn [129, 1969] and proved superior to a straight time-series model in three cases, about the same for three others, and worse for the remaining three.

A more recent attempt appears in the consumption-saving model developed by Sommermeyer and Bannink [189a, 1972] in which they interrelate sex, age, occupation and other demographic variables with economic variables, and show how key parameters depend on these noneconomic variables.

d. Regional Differences

Regional differences may exist in consumption after other relevant variables have been taken into account. K. S. Palda [168, 1967] found such differences in fitting Engel curves to 1959 survey data for 11 expenditure categories between two Canadian provinces. In a more extensive study, also for Canada, W. J. Gillen and A. Guccione [80, 1970] used generalized least squares to estimate time-series consumption functions for a number of provinces with very good results. In a very different approach on Indian survey data, N. Bhattacharya and B. Mahalanobis [21, 1967] utilized measures of concentration to find substantial regional disparities in per capita household consumption expenditures. How climatic and cultural factors act to bring about such differences, and even their extent, is clearly something for future study.

e. International Differences

If consumption functions differ among regions within a country, one would also expect differences among countries, and this phenomenon by now seems to be well documented. Indeed, a fair amount of work has been done over the past ten to fifteen years on international differences in consumption functions, partly to study this phenomenon in its own right and partly to test some of the theories of the consumption function on an international scale.

Sharp differences in the marginal propensity to save among countries were reported by D. W. Johnson and J. S. Y. Chiu [106, 1968] based on regressions of aggregate saving on income for each of 44 countries during the period 1950–61. Similar results were obtained when trend income was substituted for current income as a proxy for permanent income, results which led the authors to conclude that "there does not exist one true world saving function in which saving is a function of current income" [106, 1968, p. 333].

A somewhat similar point had been made by Houthakker [99, 1964], as noted earlier, in estimating demand elasticities for parts of 12 years (1948–1959) over 13 countries in which he concluded that there is no such thing as a single elasticity of demand; rather, the elasticity estimates from the within-country regressions were felt to capture mostly short-run effects while the elasticity estimates from the between-country regressions estimated mostly long-run effects. Differences among countries were also very pronounced, as found by a different specification in a study by Goldberger [81, 1970].

Permanent income concepts have also been applied to international data. Indeed, Houthakker attributed his findings in his study just cited to differences between short-run and long-run income changes rather than to distinctive characteristics of the countries. In another study covering 22 countries, Houthakker [99, 1964] reported that the marginal propensity to save out of "normal" income was approximately .08 on the average, based on time-series regressions with normal income estimated as the average income in that country for the entire period of observation. A similar result is reported by Friend and Taubman [78, 1966]: the overall marginal propensity to save out of normal income based on time-series regressions for 1953–60 for 22 countries is estimated at

between .06 and .07 (which the authors feel may be understated because of the procedures used) with a higher marginal propensity out of transitory income than out of normal income.

Testing the permanent income theory on budget data for various countries, Mayer [146, 1966] finds a negative correlation between permanent income and the propensity to consume, using average income for broad occupational groups as a measure of permanent income. He concludes that the marginal propensity to consume out of permanent income cannot be equal to the average propensity, contrary to the assumption of the permanent income theory. On the other hand, Balvir Singh and Helmar Drost [188, 1971] find support for the permanent income theory, as against an absolute income theory, from time-series regressions on 11 countries in that the marginal and average propensities to consume are approximately equal, at least by one of two estimation methods. They find considerable differences in the marginal propensities among countries, those with higher growth rates tending to have a lower marginal propensity to consume (though the causal effect might well be the other way).

Making use of the habit-formation hypothesis of Houthakker and Taylor, Subramanian Swamy [195, 1968] also finds substantial differences in estimates of time-series saving functions from one country to another. The parameters of the dynamic saving function are found to vary with the level of economic development of the country.

A somewhat different hypothesis is advanced by N. H. Leff [140, 1969] to explain why the saving-income ratio is higher in developed than in less developed countries. The explanation advanced by Leff is that "a country's aggregate savings rate is lower, *ceteris paribus*, to the extent that it has more dependents in its population" [140, 1969, p. 888]. Logarithmic linear regressions of the saving-income ratio on income and on variables measuring the proportion of dependents (both the very young and the very old), using individual countries as the observations, provide support for this hypothesis, with dependency variables being statistically significant and having the appropriate negative signs.

More broadly, the use of consumption functions in economic development and differences in consumption patterns and parameters among less developed countries were treated in a number of papers presented at a Conference in October 1973, in Hamburg, Germany, organized by a group of Latin American research institutes (Estudios Conjuntos Sobre Integracion Economica Latinoamericana) under the auspices of the Brookings Institute and the Institut für Iberoamerika-Kunde. It was by no means clear from the papers presented there that consumption theories based on conditions in the more developed countries are equally applicable to other countries.

f. Attitudes and Buying Plans

The great debate over the relative value of consumer attitudes versus buying plans seems to be turning out in favor of attitudes. In particular, the University of Michigan Survey Research Center (SRC) Index of Consumer Attitudes has been found in a number of studies to make net contributions to the explanation of the variation over time in consumer spending, especially for durable goods, after income and other variables have been taken into account. For the period 1952–61, Eva Mueller [159, 1963] reported that the attitudinal index made a net contribution even when a buying plans variable was included as well, while the latter lost significance. More recently, in time-series studies of the United States covering 1953–67, Juster and Wachtel [110, 1972] found that plans and anticipations variables alone provided about as good explanations of durables goods demand as income, prices and other objective variables, and that the combination of the two sets of variables was more effective than either set alone.

Roughly similar findings were obtained for Canada, where H. T. Shapiro and G. E. Angevine [186, 1969], studying quarterly 1960–66 data, showed that a composite attitudinal index similar to the SRC index was significant in explaining auto and other durable goods purchases even after including income and other variables. This index improved predictive accuracy for 1967, while a buying intentions variable was less effective. In West Germany, G. Poser and P. Hecheltjen [171, 1973] also found an attitudinal index highly significant in helping to predict both durables (including services) and nondurable expenditures.

While buying intentions data still may be more significant than attitudes on a cross-section basis, their value for prediction remains to be established. These data were collected until this year on a quarterly basis by the United States Bureau of the Census [207] and were modified in 1967 to refer to a scale of 11 subjective probabilities. However, except for the Juster-Wachtel study, the data have not been found of much net value for time-series prediction, which may possibly reflect our lack of knowledge how to use these data, as Juster and Wachtel have argued, but which has led the Census Bureau to discontinue collecting such data.

On the other hand, attitudinal indexes arc now incorporated in econometric forecasting models [52, 1965] though no specific study seems to have appeared concerning their value in this sense. Indeed their forecasting record is as yet by no means fully established. Thus, in one recent study S. W. Burch and H. O. Stekler [33, 1969] find that while the SRC attitudinal index improves goodness of fit substantially when added to a regression equation for consumer expenditures, their forecasting accuracy is not much better than that of two naive models. All major turns in expenditures were predicted by the equation but many at wrong dates and there were a number of false signals.

What makes an attitude index tick? The answer, to judge by extensive work by Gerald Adams [1, 1964], is the short-term business outlook, one of the five components of the index. Using principal components analysis, Adams reported much overlap among the attitude components, but the short-term business outlook was the key component in the index. For this reason, Adams felt that attitudes were more likely to be relevant for time-series analysis than for cross-section analysis, a point documented in a later study [2, 1965] in which comparisons of variances of both cross-section and time-series data revealed differences large enough to suggest that the two types of attitudes are entirely different.

To what extent might an attitude index simply be a proxy for other, more easily measurable, variables? The closest proxy so far seems to have been stock market prices, but even they were effective substitutes for only part of the (1952–62) period covered in a study by Friend and Adams [76, 1964]. In his recent study, Modigliani [153, 1971] considered stock prices preferable to attitudes on essentially *a priori* grounds.

Also, "attitudes are highly correlated with other cyclical indicators, particularly those relating to employment conditions," according to an analysis by Adams and E. W. Green [3, 1965] of 1955–63 time series using SRC data. Using current variables, a goodness of fit (R^2) as high as .85 was obtained, but attempts to predict attitudes using lagged variables were much less successful, with values of R^2 less than .6. In other words, the weight of the evidence as of this writing favors the by now classic observation of George Katona that attitudes make a net contribution to our understanding of economic behavior by supplementing our measures of ability to buy with a measure of willingness to buy.

g. Effects of Advertising

That advertising can influence sales of individual brands of a product is now well documented in the marketing literature. In a classic study, Palda [167, 1964] showed that sales of Lydia Pinkham's, the proprietary medicine, were strongly affected by cumulative advertising over the period 1907–60. In another relatively early quantitative analysis, L. G. Telser [200, 1962] found that advertising exerted substantial effects on the sales of the major cigarette companies

and of their main brands, and that these effects decreased just prior to World War II at a rate of 15–20 percent per year.

The growing adoption of econometric methods in marketing analysis has produced, among other things, an increasing body of evidence of the influence of advertising on sales. Two very good examples are by D. L. Weiss [212, 1968] showing how price and advertising interacted with each other in influencing the monthly brand shares of a food product, and by F. M. Bass [12, 1969], bringing out the elasticities and cross-elasticities between sales and advertising of filter and non-filter cigarettes.

On a more aggregative level, most discussions of the subject still seem to generate more heat than light. One exception was a regression study of advertising sales and price data for 85 industries in the United Kingdom by P. Doyle [50, 1968] that found the ratio of advertising to sales to decline with both higher sales and prices. An even more significant exception was the finding by L. D. Taylor and David Weiserbs [199, 1972] that inclusion of advertising outlays in a Houthakker-Taylor type of state adjustment aggregate consumption model for the period 1929–68 yielded a highly significant (positive) coefficient. Thus, while much work remains to be done, evidence seems to be accumulating that, whatever its merits, advertising affects consumer behavior in a variety of ways and at different levels of aggregation.

4. ASSETS FUNCTIONS

Assets, or wealth, have played a dual role in consumer economics in recent times. On the one hand, they have been considered in their more traditional role as potential determinants of consumption expenditures, as discussed in the preceding section. Second, and more recently, increasing attention has been given to asset characteristics and to the development of what is perhaps best termed asset functions. In these functions, wealth or one of its components is the dependent variable and the objective is to explain its fluctuations either over time or among consumer units in terms of a set of determining variables. In other words, asset functions are analogous to consumption functions, except that income does not necessarily play the key role it does in the latter case. As we shall see, the two topics are no longer as distinct as they once were because the permanent income theories, especially the life cycle hypothesis, have a great deal to say about wealth determination and have served as a basis for some of the sudies reviewed in this section.

This section deals with work relating to assets in this second role. The growing interest in such aspects is explained by the fact that assets data have become available only in the last 20 years, at least in the United States, and time series of any length even more recently. Thus, cross-section data on selected assets first began to be available in the late 1940s, from the Survey Research Center of the University of Michigan; and aggregative estimates for the nation back to the 1890s in the pioneering work of Raymond Goldsmith [82, 1955] during the 1950s and time-series data on individual asset categories from the Flow-of-Funds estimates of the Federal Reserve starting in 1959.[7]

The early studies established very quickly the suspected much more highly concentrated nature of asset ownership than of income. Thus, from what is probably the most extensive such cross-section study in the United States, the 1962–63 Federal Reserve Study of Family Financial Characteristics [174, Projector, 1968], it was noted that the highest 20 percent of wealth holders owned about 60 percent of the wealth; and less than 10 percent owned over two-thirds of all marketable securities. Similar degrees of concentration, also present in England, are by all indications far larger than could be accounted for by the accumulation of saving over one's lifetime [9, Atkinson, 1971]. Moreover, the

wealth of the wealthy is heavily concentrated in variable-dollar assets (securities, real estate, own business) [111, Katona, 1964], and since wealth elasticities (relative change in one asset to relative change in total assets) are the highest for these assets [173, Projector, 1965; 175, Projector, 1966],[8] increasing wealth tends to promote even greater concentration in particular assets.

Demand functions for total consumer assets or net worth have not been estimated too frequently, undoubtedly because of lack of data. However, at least two such studies can be reported for the United States in the 1960s. Jean Crockett and Friend [41, 1967] regressed net worth on disposable income for grouped data from the Federal Reserve 1962–63 survey data and also net worth on normal (5 year average) income and other variables from a panel of the Survey of Consumer Finances of the University of Michigan Survey Research Center. Their principal finding is "... that the long-run normal income elasticity of total net worth and the short-run normal income elasticity of total saving are substantially higher than one ...," a finding that contradicts a basic postulate of the permanent income hypothesis. (Mayer [146, 1966] had obtained a similar finding with other cross-section data.) They also find that lagged net worth and age of head are the primary determinants of current net worth, with income becoming significant if lagged net worth is omitted. Using more complete data from the Federal Reserve 1962–63 survey, Projector and G. S. Weiss [175, 1966] come to a roughly similar conclusion, namely, that income and age are the primary explanatory variables of net worth, and that the long-run normal income elasticity of net worth tends to exceed unity.

Demand functions for assets can in theory be derived in the same manner as demand functions for goods and services, as has been done by G. O. Bierwag and M. A. Grove [22, 1968]. Assuming an investor's utility depends on the expected value and on the

---

[7] This is the year when they first began to be published on a regular basis. The estimates go back to 1946 annually and to 1952 quarterly. Estimates for selected individual asset categories were available earlier from trade sources and from SEC sources but not on any consistent basis among assets and not always separately for the consumer sector.

[8] As a reader suggests, the much higher asset concentrations than those that might be expected from saving-income ratios may reflect inclusion of capital gains and bequests in assets.

variance of his net worth, they derive a set of Slutsky-type demand equations in which the change in the optimal quantity of an asset is related to net worth effects and asset substitution effects.

The estimation of assets functions has proceeded so far along two main lines, some studies focusing on one asset while others have tried to consider the demand for all assets by type of assets. Liquid assets have been the main focus of the former group, either savings deposits or demand deposits or both. Thus, in a national cross-section study of the determinants of various types of liquid asset holdings, Lee [136, 1964] found both current income and net worth statistically significant variables (as well as various socioeconomic variables), with the elasticity of the demand for money approximately unity for income and less than unity for net worth. In a cross-section study more restricted geographically, H. J. Claycamp [36, 1965] reported that psychological variables were more important than either socioeconomic or asset balance variables in discriminating between savings deposit owners in commercial banks and in savings and loan associations. In a very good summary of the empirical work to 1969, D. E. W. Laidler [124, 1969] concludes that the demand for money is affected by mostly short-term rates of interest and by wealth (or permanent income) rather than current income.

In a later application of the permanent income concept, S. B. Chase, Jr., [34, 1969] found permanent income as well as prices and interest rates to be principal determinants of American household demand for savings deposits over time. In another application of the same concept, J. H. David [44, 1971] also found changes in savings accounts to be influenced by changes in permanent income but in addition noted that changes in demand deposits were affected mainly by transitory income as well as by price changes and other factors.

Studies estimating the demand for several assets have either considered each type of asset individually or, more recently, as an interdependent joint system. The former approach is illustrated by (1952–62 semi-

annual) time-series regressions by Hamburger [87, 1968] for four asset categories (marketable bonds, life insurance reserves, time deposits in commercial banks, and time deposits in other institutions) by ordinary least squares using an independent variable in each case the other asset categories as well as wealth, income and various interest rates. Interest rates and total wealth were found to be highly significant, and income was asserted to have negligible effect. Hamburger also found that some of the assets were close substitutes for each other and that adjustment to change does not take place within a single period, which would indicate the need for a jointly-determined model. M. R. Darby [43, 1972], in his recent study, had also shown, at least for saving out of transitory income, that allocations to money, financial assets and durable goods purchases were interrelated.

One such model, a complete set of asset-demand functions, was derived from utility theory by Motley [157, 1970] and applied to quarterly American data for 1953–65 for four types of assets—demand deposits, savings deposits, real assets and debt. The exogenous variables included a measure of permanent income, as a weighted average of past incomes, and transitory income, as the ratio of current to permanent income. Both types of variables were statistically significant, the permanent income less so than the transitory measure and, as in the Hamburger study, Motley found considerable interdependence among the assets.

A still broader simultaneous equation approach was taken by Wachtel [210, 1972] who also tested a time-series joint determination model for four categories of assets, but with durables and consumption excluding durables as two of the four asset categories; the other two are liquid assets and consumer credit. Based on a partial adjustment approach, this model tries in effect to synthesize the problem of the allocation of wealth with that of income using quarterly 1953–67 Flow-of-Funds data, and finds that transitory income more than permanent income affects three of the four categories (all but consumption excluding durables) and that lagged forms of the asset variables are especially important for the same three of four categories, with the rate of adjustment of stocks to new levels varying substantially by asset category.

In his study of saving and asset functions, Taylor [198] found substantial differences in saving and asset propensities by age level as well as in the propensity to save and hold wealth out of transfer income compared to that out of labor income. Asset accumulation tended to be higher in the 20s and 40s than in the 30s and over-50 age groups, and was much higher out of transfer income than labor income; findings similar to those obtained by Robert Holbrook and Frank Stafford [93, 1971] that the propensity to consume varies by type of income.

This global joint determination approach may well represent the wave of the future. In general form, the consumer is faced with a fund of resources, which includes assets, current and expected future incomes as well as credit, and has to allocate this fund among expenditures, saving and asset forms in both the current period (an immediate decision) and in all future periods of his lifetime. The formulation becomes even more general if human capital is added to the fund of resources and use of time to the allocation alternatives, as is discussed in a later section. The problem is to develop models to explain consumer behavior in such a simultaneous manner taking into account the numerous alternatives (asset and spending possibilities) and the many uncertainties involved.

5. EXTENSIONS OF CONSUMER THEORY

Within the last 10 to 15 years, the theories that underlie consumer economics have been extended to a much broader range of topics that also relate to consumer behavior but which in the past have received little attention from economists. These topics are perhaps best classified under the heading of social welfare in its broadest sense, and include the formation of human capital, the use of time, the components of utility, and the demand for quasi-public goods. The theoretical base is in all cases that of utility theory, namely, the consumer is faced with a utility function which he attempts to maximize in the face of certain constraints on his ability to act. By including in the utility function the variable(s) under study and in the constraint function(s) these and other relevant variables and solving the resulting system, one or more equations are obtained that serve as the basis for obtaining empirical estimates of the key parameters. How this has been done in specific cases is illustrated in this section, which is too brief to do justice to the rapidly growing volume of work in this area but will, it is hoped, provide an idea of how such problems are being handled.

a. Human Capital

While considerable attention has been given over the years to the role of nonhuman capital in consumer behavior, and more recently to financial wealth, as noted in the preceding section, it has only been in the 1950s and 1960s that much consideration has been given to the uses of human capital and its effects. Though human capital as an economic concept was recognized many years earlier, at least as early as Marshall's time [116, 1968], it was not until the work of Gary Beck, T. W. Schultz and their colleagues that the analytical possibilities of this approach began to be realized. (See for example, 184, Schultz, 1962; for a number of earlier articles, see 117, Kiker, 1972.)

The basic theoretical apparatus was supplied by Becker [15, 1964], who utilized economic concepts to develop a theory of investment in human capital with a methodology of measuring the rate of return from such investment. Since this theory is well explained in a review article by Jacob Mincer [149, 1970] there is no need to repeat it here other than to stress its main implications for consumer economics. In particular, the rate of return on investment in human capital is based on the fundamental notion that the cost of doing so "equals the net earnings foregone by choosing to invest rather than choosing an activity requiring no investment" [15, Becker, 1964, p. 39]. Using this approach, rates of return from education are estimated; for college graduates the return is estimated at about 13 percent per year.

By this approach, human capital is another form of wealth entering into the consumption function, because life cycle changes in consumption necessarily depend on the age-wealth profile, and hence on investment in human capital. The age-wealth profile will be sharper for cohorts with more human capital; aggregate consumer debt is higher partly because of the secular increase in human capital; and the latter also serves to mitigate the positive effect of population growth on the rate of saving. These and other aspects of human capital are covered in a recent book by Schultz [183, 1971] though their full implications for consumption economics have yet to be developed.

b. The Allocation of Time

The attention given to investment in human capital has also served to focus consideration on the scarcity aspects of a basic input into this process—time—and has helped to establish the study of the allocation of time as a separate topic of economic analysis. Two examples are given here to illustrate this approach.

In a basic article, Becker [16, 1965] incorporates time into the theory of consumer choice on the assumption that households are producers as well as consumers of goods. The household produces a set of basic "commodities," Z_i, that enter directly into a utility function; these are commodities such as eating, going to a theatre, sleeping, working, etc. These commodities are produced by means of an appropriate combination of market goods (and services), X_i, and of time inputs, T_i. In other words, X_i and T_i are each vectors which enter as variables in the household production function.

$$Z_i = f_i(X_i, T_i)$$

The household seeks to maximize its utility function, $U = U(Z_1, \ldots, Z_m)$, subject to a budget constraint, $g(Z_1, \ldots, Z_m) - Z$, where Z defines the maximum resources available to it. This restraint can be subdivided into a goods constraint and a time constraint, though these are not independent and would seem best represented by a single function. The equilibrium condition for utility maximization is that the marginal utility of Z_i equal the sum of the marginal costs of using time and of using goods to produce Z_i.

By means of this framework, Becker shows that the treatment of time as another commodity rather than as a separate element called "leisure," as in J. M. Henderson and R. E. Quandt [90, 1958], has many direct applications, including an explanation of the secular decline in hours of work (primarily because of offsetting substitution effects of the higher productivity of work time and of consumption time coupled with the high income elasticity of demand for time-intensive commodities), the length and mode of commuting to work, and the relation between family size and income. A strong case is made for the collection of data on "full income," namely, money income plus income foregone by the use of time for other purposes, as a better basis for the study of economic behavior.

A second example is the use of utility theory by J. D. Owen [166, 1971] to develop a model for measuring the demand for leisure. His approach is to define a utility function that depends on the hours of leisure time (L), the quantity of recreational goods and services on the market (R), and the quantity of all other consumer goods (X). The consumer then seeks to maximize the utility function, $U = U(L, R, X)$, subject to the following two restraints:

1. Leisure hours (L) plus work hours (H) equal total hours (T), or:

   $$L + H = T$$

2. Earnings that could be made from leisure time ($P_L L$) plus actual earning (wH) equal total financial resources (F) for that period, or:

   $$P_L L + wH = P_L L + P_R R + P_X X = F$$

These yield demand equations for L and for R, each as a function of F, P_L, P_R, P_X. Applying the theory with some modifications to time-series full-employment peak data for 1900–61,[9] Owen obtains a positive elasticity (about .2) of leisure time with regard to relative wage rates, a negative elasticity with regard to the relative price of recreation, though only $-.03$, and a negative elasticity of R with regard to P_R. Overall, he concludes that about three-quarters of the rise in leisure time during this period was associated with increases in real hourly wages. In a more recent study, Rueben Gronau [86a, 1973] applies utility theory to explain time allocation among time working for pay, time working in the home and leisure time, separately by husband and wife, and shows that whether a wife is in the labor force depends on the value of her time in the absence of market opportunities in relation to her potential wage rate. The tendency for a husband to work for pay and for the wife to look after the home is shown to be a result of the comparative advantage of the members of the couple in the production of market goods and in the production of goods in the home.

c. The Utility of What?

The idea of the household as a producer was advanced by Margaret Reid approximately 40 years ago, though her focus was on the unpaid activities of household members that substitute for goods or services that could be obtained in the market [178, 1934, p. 11]. More recently, the general production approach as exemplified in the previous section in the development of theories on the allocation of time has also been used in an attempt to arrive at a more basic understanding of what is involved in utility maximization. That consumers buy goods not for the objects themselves but for the services they

provide has long been a maxim of consumer economics. An attempt to place this idea in a more formal theoretical framework has been made by Kevin Lancaster [125, 1966] who, in effect, looks on the household as an activity process trying to achieve certain ends. The approach taken by Lancaster is to link utility not to goods but to the components, or characteristics, of these goods. This approach rests on the "crucial assumption that goods possess, or give rise to, multiple characteristics in fixed proportions and that it is these characteristics, not goods themselves, on which the consumer's preferences are exercised." Accordingly, the consumer is faced with a transformation function, $z = f(x)$, that shows how a particular collection of goods, x, is transformed into a collection of characteristics, z. The objective of the consumer is to maximize the utility of z subject to the budget constraint, $px \le y$, where p is a vector of prices and y is income.

From a theoretical point of view, this approach offers some advantages, as Lancaster points out in a later work [126, 1971]. Thus, it explains more concretely why a consumer may be indifferent between goods that are seemingly quite different, say, a radio and a hi-fi set—to that consumer the two goods may be viewed as possessing similar sets of characteristics. Yet, a question arises whether this approach is really different from the long-standing view expressed by so many others that consumers value goods not for themselves but for the services they provide— these services are now transformed into explicit characteristics. From a practical point of view, the measurement of durable goods consumption in terms of service flows is one manifestation of this concept.

This idea has already taken hold in the development of so-called hedonic price indexes [85, Griliches, 1971], whereby prices are related by regression methods to the characteristics of those products. It is too soon, however, to discern how well the specific approach of Lancaster will take hold in the study of consumer behavior.

Another type of approach using household production functions is that of R. F. Muth

---

[9] Full employment estimates are needed for the model because it is only during such periods that consumers can be assumed to be exercising free choice as assumed by the model.

[160, 1966] who advances the hypothesis "that commodities purchased on the market by consumers are inputs into the production of goods within the household." What the household seeks to maximize, therefore, is utility from the goods and services it produces, subject to production functions relating these household goods to the "raw materials" and services purchased on the outside and to a budget restraint on available resources. A consequence of this approach that household demand for many goods and services is now a composite demand, and household labor becomes a major input in the home production function. Thus, the household demand for fuel is a composite of the derived demand for fuel for cooking and the derived demand for fuel for heating, and an understanding of the income elasticity for fuel depends on the separate income elasticities for final goods. The practical value of this approach, however, still has to be determined.

d. Demand for Quasi-Public Goods

The increasing social consciousness of economists has manifested itself in a number of ways, not the least of which has been the growing tendency to apply tools of economic analysis to studying the demand for goods and services partly in the public sector and for which, often, no clear market price may exist. Such is the case, for example, with such consumer "products" as education, health, public recreation and children. One general approach to this problem has been through the investment in, and returns from, human capital devoted to these activities; initially focusing on education, these studies have spread to cover other aspects of human capital. Another general approach has been essentially the same as used in the past with the private sector, namely, to derive a demand function either through the use of utility theory or by *a priori* reasoning. However, the specification and measurement of relevant variables, especially price variables, often requires considerable ingenuity. The study of Owen on the demand for recreation, described earlier, is a case in point.

A general theoretical framework for studying the demand for education was provided by H. E. Brazer and Martin David [29, 1962]. Illustrative of the more empirical studies on the demand for education is that by Harvey Golper and R. M. Dunn [83, 1969] who expressed college undergraduate enrollments in the United States for 1925–65 as a function of real income, number of high school graduates (with a four-year distributed lag) and a nonmarket variable such as size of the military forces. In a study with broader coverage, James Morgan, David, and others [154, 1962; 155, 1963] pinpointed, by multiple regressions of Survey Research Center cross-section family data, a wide number of determinants of education, principal among which were age. Estimates are given of the income associated with additional education at various age levels. In another study, G. S. Tolley and E. Olson [203, 1971] used a simultaneous equations approach on 1960 data for individual states to study the interrelation between income and education. Among other things, "nonhuman wealth is estimated to have twice as much effect on education expenditures as other forms of wealth" [203, 1971, p. 460]. Thus, they found rather paradoxically, that the elasticity of income with respect to education is only .07 whereas that of education with respect to income was .8.

The human capital approach has also been used to study the demand for education, and a comparison with the older approach is provided by Mary Jean Bowman [25, 1962]. A good example of how the two approaches interrelate is illustrated in a recent study by Michael Grossman [86, 1972] in which a model for the demand for health is constructed on the premise "that health can be viewed as a durable capital stock that produces an output of healthy time" [86, 1972, p. 223]. Individuals are assumed to inherit an initial stock of health that depreciates with age and can be increased by investment. Their utility function over time depends on their consumption of health services and of other commodities in each period, with two sets of production functions, one for investment in the production of health and one for investment in the production of other commodities.

Although this model contains some drastic assumptions (such as that age of death is predicted with certainty), Grossman shows how it can serve to explain health outlays in terms of economic theory, such as that the demand for health and medical care should be positively correlated with one's wage rate, and that this demand is also correlated positively with education to the extent that the latter increases the efficiency of gross investments in health. The biological process of aging is thus represented in economic terms, for these factors "raise the price of health capital and cause individuals to substitute away from future health until death is 'chosen'" [86, 1972, p. 240]. In other words, at a certain stage death occurs because it is too expensive to go on living!

Fertility is another topic on which economists have begun to train their tools of demand analysis. One such model that has stimulated much additional work on this subject has been developed by Becker [14, 1960]. Using the theory of the demand for consumer durables as a framework, he derives a demand function for children as a function of tastes, income, costs, knowledge and uncertainty. He points out, among other things, that by this theory, a rise in income should increase both the quantity and the quality of children desired, cyclical fluctuations in birth rates should be less than for durable goods purchases (initial costs of the former are relatively much less), and fertility of farm families would be expected to be higher than that of urban families (the former have a comparative cost advantage).

A number of economic analyses of fertility have been undertaken since then, notably the attempts by R. A. Easterlin [55, 1969], Deborah Freedman [71, 1963], N. K. Namboodiri [161, 1972], T. P. Schultz [181, 1969], and Schultz and Marc Nerlove [182, 1970]. Indicative of the growing interest in applying the tools of economic analysis to problems of fertility and population planning is the publication of a special supplement of

the *Journal of Political Economy* on this subject [185, 1973]. As Schultz notes in the introduction to that issue, the rational of this approach is no longer to accept size of population as exogenous but rather to attempt to explain in economic terms what accounts for changes in population and in birth rates. The human capital approach serves as a cornerstone for such an explanation, the basic view being that people invest in human beings (children) analogous to the manner in which they invest in themselves and in nonhuman wealth, a major determinant of the allocation of these investment expenditures being the cost of human time. The time variable becomes one input, with other "commodities," into a generalized household production function used by the family for deciding how to allocate its time and other resources in the production of children as well as of other "outputs." Social as well as economic variables can be incorporated into such a model which, in its most general form, would provide a description (or prediction) of the lifetime behavior of the household.

The study of poverty is another area to which demand analysis has been applied. Thus, C. T. Brehm and T. R. Saving [30, 1964], in a study of general assistance payments (G.A.P.), take the approach that "the demand for G.A.P. can be treated as a special case of the traditional theoretical treatment of the demand for leisure." Setting up demand functions on this basis and estimating parameters from annual cross-section regressions for 1951–59 with individual states as observations, they find that the frequency of such payments is related to the amount of the payment, the unemployment rate and the nonfarm employment rate (the latter a proxy for the ease of getting on the G.A.P. rolls), all of which leads them to conclude that "G.A.P. recipients are like the remainder of consumers in that they react to economic incentives" [30, 1964, p. 1018]. In a similar study, L. C. Thurow [201, 1967] finds that variations in the proportion of low-income families among states in 1960 can be explained in terms of the quality of the labor force, the industrial structure of the state, the amount of farming and labor force participation.

6. CONSIDERATIONS FROM OTHER SOCIAL SCIENCES[10]

The growing interest in consumer behavior has stimulated a great deal of work on this subject in other social sciences. Partly because of the broadening scope of the work in economics, as noted earlier, and partly because of the nature of this other work, an awareness of these studies can be very useful to economists. While it is impossible to do justice to all such work in this brief section, an attempt is made to convey some of the ways in which this work overlaps economics with reference to three key areas, namely, decision-making, the search for information, and the role of reference groups.

a. Decision-making

Goals and decision processes are two cornerstones of consumer behavior which have received considerable attention in other social sciences while being treated largely as givens in consumer economics, though in very different ways. Thus, goals are invariably assumed *a priori* to consist of some sort of maximizing or optimizing behavior, depending on the theoretical model postulated; while decision processes are implicitly considered to be an intermediate step between goals and behavior that is of little consequence in itself. The findings from these other subject areas would seem to indicate a need for re-examining these assumptions, particularly with reference to the following questions:

Do families have financial goals or plans? To judge by scattered studies in home economics, an appreciable proportion do not have clear financial goals or plans in the

sense of clearly enunciated programs for allocation of income or acquisition of assets. Thus, R. R. Honey and W. M. Smith, Jr., [98, 1952] report that over 40 percent of the students in home economics courses reported that their parents did not have any financial plan. In a study of financial management practices of 426 farm families in Pennsylvania, Honey [96, 1957] reports that a major source of dissatisfaction was lack of a financial plan. J. M. Phelan and R. R. Ruef [169, 1961] report that clearly enunciated goals and financial plans were much more common among Indiana farmers in younger families, those better educated, and in families where the wife was in a professional or managerial occupation.

Where financial goals and plans did exist, J. H. Crow [42, 1961] found that such plans were mainly concerned with financial security and increases in the level of living, with strong indications of close relationships among goals, concepts of financial security and financial management practices. For example, families strongly oriented toward financial security were also more likely to be concerned with job security and were strongly disinclined to go into debt.

That differing goals and plans can lead to very different behavior was highlighted in a case study by R. C. Freeman and J. M. Due [72, 1961] of two farm families over 23 years, showing how the different goals of these families led to strikingly different expenditure and saving patterns over the years.

While this evidence is largely based on purposive samples, the fact remains that these as well as other studies suggest that many families do not have such goals in any conscious sense. Moreover, where such goals do exist they may lead to very different forms of economic behavior.[11] That such goals and

---

[10] This section is based heavily on the author's paper [67].

[11] A cooperative study of financial security among rural families in nine North Central states was undertaken by agricultural experiment stations in the 1950s and 1960s that produced a number of reports on this question. A general description of this research program and a list of these studies is provided in [48, DeHuff, 1964].

plans are more likely to be reported by younger families is in accord with the permanent income and life cycle hypotheses of consumer behavior, but it is not clear that the optimizing behavior contained in these theories would be supported on any wide basis (except if it could be demonstrated that families unconsciously act in accord with these hypotheses regardless of the existence of such goals).

How are decisions made? From a theoretical point of view, the framework advanced about 15 years ago by J. G. March and H. A. Simon [144, 1958]—based on the sequential steps of awareness, search for alternatives and acquisition of information, deliberation, and choice—has stood up very well. Even here, however, considerable controversy exists regarding the applicability of this sequence to different types of families. Substantial evidence has accumulated that a large proportion of consumer purchases are unplanned in the sense that no specific decision is made to consummate the purchase, nor does the purchase have to be made on account of necessity. Such behavior seems to characterize from 20 to 30 percent of major durable goods purchases [64, Ferber, 1955; 112, Katona, 1954–55] to approximately half of items purchased in supermarkets [54, DuPont de Nemours and Co., 1945, 1949, 1954, 1959; 214, West, 1951].

To be sure, the possibility of a purchase may have been considered implicitly at some earlier time by the purchaser or by the family itself. Also, it could be argued that even impulse purchases in a supermarket represent rational economic behavior to the extent that, as H. Stern [191, 1962] has pointed out, this behavior gives the shopper an opportunity to adjust to special deals and to unanticipated opportunities encountered in the store (such as noticing only in the store that the item exists). Nevertheless, these findings raise questions as to whether purchases are made in a rational manner, and the extent to which purchases represent the culmination of a deliberate decision-making process, even allowing for the possibility that habit formation may enter into the choice of frequently purchased articles. The families among whom such deliberate decision-making does take place are more likely to be the better educated, in the middle-income range, younger and with heads who are in professional or managerial occupations [54, DuPont de Nemours and Co., 1945, 1949, 1954, 1959; 112, Katona, 1954–55].

Even in the case of financial decisions, careful decision-making may not be common. Once more, the only evidence seems to be from scattered studies in home economics. In one such case, P. K. Schomaker [180, 1961] reports that financial problems were recognized in a sample of 100 farm families about half the time only as a result of necessity. In another study of New York farm families, L. C. Dix [49, 1957] found that only a third of the sample seemed to consciously use decision-making steps. Although this evidence is again based on purposive samples, their nature suggests that, if anything, decision-making of this sort in the general population may be even less frequent.

Who makes decisions? Whether it is women's liberation or some other reason, the traditional patriarchal system of economic decisions seems a relic of the past. Among young married families, the wife is as likely as the husband to be making the financial and spending decisions, as noted in farm family studies in Wisconsin [216, Wilkenberg, 1958] and Pennsylvania [97, Honey, 1959], as well as among rural couples in New York [213, Wells, 1959]. The same was found in the more extensive urban studies of Wolgast [217, 1958], H. Sharp and P. Mott [187, 1956], and Ferber and F. M. Nicosia [69, 1972], where, at least with regard to money management, joint husband-wife decisions characterized about 30 percent of the couples, with husbands and wives splitting this responsibility about equally in the remaining cases. Moreover, family roles in spending decisions vary greatly not only with the nature of the product, as documented, among others, by P. D. Converse and C. M. Crawford [37, 1949], Carla Van Syckle [208, 1951], H. L.

Davis [45, 1970] and L. J. Jaffe and H. Senft [105, 1966]; but decision roles in the purchase of one product may be very different from those for another [46, Davis, 1970].

What determines family roles in spending and saving behavior? The principal socio-economic variables appear to be youth, education and income. Thus, among rural couples in New York State, H. L. Wells [213, 1959] found that responsibilities for money management were more likely to be shared if the couple had been married recently. In the study reported earlier by Schomaker [180, 1961], involvement of the wife in financial decisions was much more frequent among families with younger heads, and where the husband and wife had more education.

Studies of influence over spending decisions come to similar conclusions, as is supported by S. G. Barton [11, 1955], Converse and Crawford [37, 1949], Van Syckle [208, 1951], Wolgast [217, 1958] and Sharp and Mott [187, 1956]. The one major modification is that spending decisions on goods used primarily by a single member are most likely to be influenced by that individual, even if the individual is a teenager as noted by M. Gibbs [79, 1963].

After examining a number of empirical studies on decision-making, Komarovsky concludes that "there is greater autonomy with regard to expenditures at the bottom and at the top of the socioeconomic hierarchy than among the middle classes" [119, 1961, p. 260]. In an evaluation of decision-making from a family living point of view, Bernard Farber [60, 1964, pp. 199–200] finds that joint decision-making is much more likely to exist if the marriage is a satisfactory one, especially when age and education of the couple are held constant.

There is no doubt that the changing role of women in society has greatly affected family roles. Thus, in their panel data on young married couples, Ferber and Nicosia [69, 1972] find that saving decisions are reported as being made on a joint basis by approximately four-fifths of the couples. It

would be hard to imagine finding such a high proportion of joint decisions in a corresponding sample, say, 40 years ago. Moreover, if the wife is working she is much more likely to be involved in the family finances or to be making key decisions herself.

A basic consideration in evaluating what determines family roles is that a purchase may involve many decisions, not one, and husband-wife roles may vary substantially with the type of decision. Thus, Davis [46, 1970] in Quebec City found that the relative influence of various family members in seven different types of auto purchase decisions (when, where, how much, make, etc.) varied substantially within the family. In another study, Davis [45, 1970] found that decision roles in the purchase of a car were not related to decision roles in the purchase of furniture.

Do family roles make any difference to economic behavior? This is a key question, for if family spending and saving behavior are independent of which family member makes or influences decisions, the latter is hardly relevant for economic models. While available evidence is highly fragmentary, such evidence as exists suggests that the identity of the influencing family member does indeed make a difference. To quote from a recent study on the identity and influence of the "family financial officer" (FFO—the individual that exerts major control over family finances), Ferber and Lee [68, 1972] conclude, from multivariate analysis of panel data, that, "if the husband is the FFO, the couple is likely to save a higher proportion of its income and to have a higher proportion of its gross assets in variable dollar form, that is, in the form of real estate and negotiable securities. Auto purchases also tend to be less frequent. . . ."

b. The Role of Information

While economists have established a theoretical basis for the role of information in consumer behavior, researchers in other fields—sociology, home economics, marketing—have been establishing empirically that information uses vary substantially in all sorts of ways and do affect market behavior. To a large extent, the work in these two different sets of subject areas supplement each other though often carried out independently. Some of these interrelations are brought out in this brief review.

A theoretical basis for the value of information was provided by George Stigler [192, 1961], who advanced the general principle that the search for information will be carried to the point where the cost of search is equal to the expected marginal return. As extensions of this principle, he inferred that search behavior on the part of consumers will rise with the cost of the product, with the geographic size of the market and with the proportion of experienced (repetitive) buyers in the market. Advertising, especially of price information, was cited as a means of eliminating ignorance and of reducing search costs for many possible buyers all at once. Though Stigler seems to have tested these hypotheses only on the labor market [193, 1962], J. U. Farley [61, 1964] added some more generalizations from the point of view of the consumer, particularly that amount of search will depend on expected gain, relative to information acquisition costs, and that heavy users of a product are more likely to engage in search processes than light users, seeking especially lower prices.

Phillip Nelson [162, 1970] extended the economic theory to cover search for information in relation to quality of goods, distinguishing between "search goods" (those for which price and quality information is best obtained prior to purchasing the goods, such as trying on a dress or suit) and "experience goods" (where information is best obtained on the basis of purchase experience, e.g., food products). Though his inferences and empirical tests dealt primarily with business structure and operations, he did find support for the idea that consumers were likely to seek more advice on experience goods than search goods (a conclusion that belies the author's selection of terms), and to seek more different brands for search goods than for experience goods.

A key determinant of information search which marketing researchers have stressed, and which might have been expected of economists, is uncertainty (though referred to more often as risk in other subject areas). Combining survey work with laboratory experiments, D. F. Cox and others at the Harvard Business School amassed an impressive body of evidence to support the notion that, "the nature and amount of risk will define consumer information needs" [38, 1967, p. 613]. That consumers seek information to reduce risk or eliminate uncertainty is by now widely documented in the marketing literature and would seem to constitute an essential determinant of information seeking. An economics approach to quantifying the effects of quality on markets is illustrated in the study by G. A. Akerlof [5, 1970], who shows that if both quality and uncertainty are variable enough, a market may cease to exist.

Still another key determinant, this one established by rural sociologists and home economists, is the novelty of the product. Information seeking is especially high for new products, notably consultation of the mass media. The media are of main relevance in becoming aware of new products, while word-of-mouth and personal influence seem to have substantial effects at the information-gathering purchase-decision stages [13, Beal, 1957; 145, Mason, 1964]. Whatever the sources, uncertainty rather than risk (in the sense of an estimable probability distribution of, say, failure) is the main problem facing consumers with most new products,[12] and information search activity seems to be much higher for such products than would otherwise be justified by such factors as cost and durability.

As might be expected, people engaging in search activity are more likely to be younger, better educated and at higher income levels [179, Roberts, 1963]. (For a reverse sort of confirmation, see [206, Uhl, 1970].) More-

---

[12] The extent to which a product is really "new" is a relevant question, frequently discussed in marketing circles, but which need not be considered here.

over, knowledge and search activity of different products seem to be positively correlated, at least for food and textiles [91, Henell, 1953].

At least one finding on consumer search behavior is not easily reconcilable with utility theory, namely, that more search and more information does not necessarily produce more satisfaction with the ultimate purchase [163, Newton, 1969]. Is ignorance really bliss? Or does it reflect lower aspirations? Or both?

c. Reference Groups

The role of reference groups in consumer behavior has by no means been ignored by economists, as is evident from the earlier discussion of the relative income hypotheses. Much less attention has been given to this factor by economists in recent years despite the growing documentation from other disciplines of its relevance and characteristic effects.

The principal medium by which reference groups transmit their influence seems to be by word-of-mouth. This has been demonstrated by, to name a few, the social psychologist, Kurt Lewin [141, 1947], in a laboratory situation relating to diet changes; by sociologists Elihu Katz and P. F. Lazarsfeld [114, 1955] on product choice and media use; by sociologist-journalist William H. Whyte, Jr., [215, 1954] on the clustering of window air conditioners by block; and by marketing researcher J. G. Udell [205, 1966] on purchase of small appliances. At least one study found that such influence may vary considerably with the product. Thus, F. S. Bourne [24, 1957] found that group influence on housewives was much higher in their choosing of socially conspicuous products (such as beer or cigarettes) than of other products.

Who are these reference groups? Friends seem to be predominant, as distinct from relatives and strangers, even if the latter are specialists. Thus, in her study of financial decision-making, Schomaker [180, 1961] found that friends were consulted 88 percent

of the time, relatives 38 percent, and outside experts 22 percent (more than one answer was allowed), with all these percentages higher for younger and better-educated families. S. P. Feldman and M. C. Spencer [62, 1971] found that in choosing a physician and medical services, newcomers to an area tended to rely heavily on friends, neighbors or recent acquaintances in the same socioeconomic class; while G. D. Bell [17, 1967] reported that many new car buyers tended to bring along a "purchase pal" to assist them in making the purchase decision, usually a friend, neighbor or relative.

Especially interesting have been relatively recent attempts to pinpoint generalized opinion leaders, i.e., those who set the pace in changing market behavior. In terms of social structure, they were noted by Eva Mueller [158, 1958] to be generally the younger, better-educated, married and higher-income groups. Unfortunately, however, the more recent, more highly focused studies, such as by C. W. King and J. L. Summers [118, 1970], suggest that the people who are opinion leaders in one product area are not necessarily the opinion leaders in other areas.

If such groups could be pinpointed, an interesting recursive system of reference group influence could be tested by adapting the so-called two-step flow hypothesis to market behavior. Originally proposed by Lazarsfeld and his colleagues in a voter study [132, 1948], the hypothesis states that initially information flows through impersonal channels to opinion leaders who, by their behavior and by word-of-mouth, influence others. The hypothesis was supported by Johan Arndt [8, 1968] in a study of a new food product but has yet to be tested on any broad scale.

7. FUTURE DIRECTIONS

As should be evident from the foregoing pages, a great deal of information about consumer economic behavior has been uncovered in recent years. New analytical approaches have opened up while others have lost some of their lustre. The concept of permanent, or normal, income, the stock-habit adjustments mechanism, international comparisons of consumption and saving functions, dynamic relationships, and the determinants of human and nonhuman capital, have occupied a major part of the stage during this period. Multi-equation econometric models of an economy incorporating one or more consumption functions are no longer a novelty, e.g., [139, de Leeuw, 1968; 92, Hickman, 1972]. Concomitantly, econometric and statistical estimation methods have become much more sophisticated, with a growing emphasis on Bayesian estimation procedures, methods of pooling estimates from different data sets, estimation of lag effects, and use of equation systems. At times, unfortunately, it is not clear whether a method has been developed to solve a substantive problem or whether a problem has been created to suit the method.

Yet, a major consequence of this great amount of work has been the growing realization of how little is known about consumer behavior and of the need for much more work to fill the many gaps in present knowledge. Specific directions for future research have been noted on the previous pages, and need not be repeated here. More useful would seem to be a few brief final comments on the general directions such future work is likely to take. There would seem to be at least five. They are not necessarily in order of importance:

Unification of the different theories of the consumption function. Each of the theories reviewed in Section 2 seems to "work" under some circumstances. No one is superior to the others in all circumstances, though some are more frequently superior than others. The evidence would seem to point to the desirability of combining the unique features of each in a more general theory, but how to do this remains to be determined. Any such theory would have to allow for the effects on consumption (and on saving) of both human and nonhuman capital.

Development of a theory for the role of ceteris paribus variables, particularly socio-economic factors, in consumption. This is being done, to some extent, as in the incorporation of tastes through a habit formation hypothesis. Still, socioeconomic variables remain the stepchildren of consumption theory. They are invariably introduced as the extra, though essential, ingredient—like pouring salt on french fries—with no theoretical basis except to highlight other relationships (and using what variables of this type are available).

Incorporation of knowledge about consumer behavior from other social sciences. Most consumption economists seem to have reacted to the growing popularity and usefulness of interdisciplinary approaches by, if anything, drawing blinders about their eyes even more tightly lest they be contaminated by other disciplines. Many of these other studies have not been at the same level of sophistication as some in economics. Nonetheless, they are of great relevance to consumer economics and suggest variables and types of data collection, which may lead to more meaningful analysis.

Determination of human and nonhuman capital, including the interrelation of the two categories. Studies so far have focused on one or the other, with notable progress in the study of human capital. The further development of the theoretical basis of each may well rest to a large extent on the integration of the two types of capital, for to a large extent each is both a supplement and a substitute for the other, depending on the circumstances.

Application of consumer economics analysis to the public sector. Much work of this type has already been started, as noted in Section 5. In view of the growing importance of the public sector, it is clear that only the surface has been scratched. Thus, the approach to date has been to study the demand for one quasi-public good at a time, e.g., education or health or fertility. Since many of these quasi-public goods are interrelated (on the supply side as well as on the demand side), a logical extension would be to consider demands for a number of such goods simultaneously.

A final comment. Probably the major limitation of many of these past studies, as well as of studies that need to but cannot be done, is the lack of relevant data. The principal and growing need is for data relating the spending, saving, and asset behavior (both human and nonhuman) of the same consumer units to factors such as use of time and family composition and socioeconomic characteristics. These data should relate to the same units over many time periods, so that changes in behavior can be pinpointed and temporal differences segregated from intergenerational differences.[13] While the obtaining of such data may seem utopian to survey researchers, economists, and policy makers, the need for "lifetime" panel data of this sort is growing and would permit far more powerful tests of theories than is now possible.

References

1. Adams, F. G., "Consumer Attitudes, Buying Plans, and Purchases of Durable Goods: A Principle Components, Time Series Approach," *Review of Economics and Statistics,* 46:347–355 (1964).
2. _____, "Prediction with Consumer Attitudes: The Time Series Cross-Section Paradox," *Review of Economics and Statistics,* 47:367–378 (1965).
3. _____, and Green, E. W., "Explaining and Predicting Aggregative Consumer Attitudes," *International Economic Review,* 6:275–293 (1965).
4. Agarwals, R., and Drinkwater, J., "Consumption Functions with Shifting Parameters Due to Socioeconomic Factors," *Review of Economics and Statistics,* 54:89–96 (1972).
5. Akerlof, G. A., "The Market for 'Lemons': Qualitative Uncertainty and the Market Mechanism," *Quarterly Journal of Economics,* 84:488–500 (1972).
6. Ando, A., and Modigliani, F., "The 'Life Cycle' Hypothesis of Saving: Aggregate Implications and Tests," *American Economic*

Review, 53:55–84 (1963); also "Correction," 54:111–112 (1964).
7. Arena, J. J., "Postwar Stock Market Changes and Consumer Spending," *Review of Economics and Statistics,* 47:379–391 (1965).
8. Arndt, J., "A Test of the Two-Step Flow in Diffusion of a New Product," *Journal Quarterly,* 45:457–465 (1968).
9. Atkinson, A. B., "The Distribution of Wealth and Individual Life-Cycle," *Oxford Economic Papers,* 23:239–254 (1971).
10. Ball, R. J., and Drake, P. S., "The Impact of Credit Control on Consumer Durable Spending in the United Kingdom, 1957–1961," *Review of Economic Studies,* 30:181–194 (1963).
11. Barton, S. G., "The Life Cycle and Buying Patterns," in L. H. Clark (ed.), *The Life Cycle and Consumer Behavior* (New York: New York University Press, 1955).
12. Bass, F. M., "A Simultaneous Equation Regression Study of Advertising and Sales of Cigarettes," *Journal of Marketing Research,* 6:291–300 (1969).
13. Beal, G. M., and Rogers, E. M., "Information Sources in the Adoption Process of New Fabrics," *Journal of Home Economics,* 49:630–634 (1957).
14. Becker, G. S., "An Economic Analysis of Fertility," in *Demographic and Economic Change in Developed Countries* (Princeton: Princeton University Press for National Bureau Economic Research, 1960).
15. _____, *Human Capital* (New York: National Bureau of Economic Research, 1964).
16. _____, "A Theory of the Allocation of Time," *Economic Journal,* 75:493–517 (1965).
17. Bell, G. D., "Self-Confidence, Persuasibility and Cognitive Dissonance among Automobile Buyers," in D. F. Cox [38, 1967].
18. Betancourt, R., "The Normal Income Hypothesis in Chile," *Journal of American Statistical Association,* 66:258–263 (1971).
19. Bhatia, K. B., "Capital Gains and the Aggregate Consumption Function," *American Economic Review,* 62:866–879 (1972).
20. _____, "The Estimation of Accrued Capital Gains on Individuals' Corporate Stock Holdings," *Journal of American Statistical Association,* 68:55–62 (1973).
21. Bhattacharya, N., and Mahalanobis, B., "Regional Disparities in Household Consumption in India," *Journal of American Statistical Association,* 62:143–161 (1967).

[13] The need for special data has been expressed in a number of sources in recent years, for example, see [74, Friend; 147, Mayer, 1972].

22. Bierwag, G. O., and Grove, M. A., "Slutsky Equations for Assets," *Journal of Political Economy*, 76:114–127 (1968).

23. Bird, R. C., and Bodkin, R. G., "The National Service Life Insurance Dividends of 1950 and Consumption: A Further Test of the 'Strict' Permanent-Income Hypothesis," *Journal of Political Economy*, 73:499–515 (1965).

24. Bourne, F. S., "Group Influence in Marketing and Public Relations," in R. Likert and S. P. Hayes (eds.), *Some Applications of Behavioral Research* (Paris, France: UNESCO, 1957).

25. Bowman, M. J., "Human Capital: Concepts and Measures," in S. J. Mushkin (ed.), *Economics of Higher Education* (Washington, D.C.: U.S. Department of Health, Education, and Welfare, 1962).

26. Brady, D. S., "Family Saving in Relation to Changes in the Level and Distribution of Income," in *Studies in Income and Wealth*, vol. 15 (New York: National Bureau Economic Research, 1952).

27. _____ and Friedman, R., "Savings and the Income Distribution," in *Studies in Income and Wealth* vol. 10 (New York: National Bureau Economic Research, 1947).

28. Branson, W. H., and Klevorick, A. K., "Money Illusion and the Aggregate Consumption Function," *American Economic Review*, 59:832–850 (1969).

29. Brazer, H. E., and David, M., "Social and Economic Determinants of the Demand for Education," in S. J. Mushkin (ed.), *Economics of Higher Education* (Washington, D.C.: U.S. Department of Health, Education, and Welfare, 1962).

30. Brehm, C. T., and Saving, T. R., "The Demand for General Assistance Payments," *American Economic Review*, 54:1002–1018 (1964).

31. Brown, A., and Deaton, A., "Survey in Applied Economics: Models of Consumer Behavior," *Economic Journal*, 82:1145–1236 (1972).

32. Brown, T. M., "Habit Persistence and Lags in Consumer Behavior," *Econometrica*, 20:355–371 (1952).

33. Burch, S. Q., and Stekler, H. O., "The Forecasting Accuracy of Consumer Attitude Data," *Journal of American Statistical Association*, 64:1225–1233 (1969).

34. Chase, S. B., Jr., "Household Demand for Savings Deposits, 1921–1965," *Journal of Finance*, 24:643–658 (1969).

35. Cheng, P. L., "Consumption of Nondurable Goods and Contractual Commitment of Disposable Income," *Review of Economics and Statistics*, 45:254–263 (1963).

36. Claycamp, H. J., "Characteristics of Owners of Thrift Deposits in Commercial Banks and Savings and Loan Associations," *Journal of Marketing Research*, 2:163–170 (1965).

37. Converse, P. D., and Crawford, C. M., "Family Buying: Who Does It? Who Influences It?" *Current Economic Comment*, 11:38–50 (1949).

38. Cox, D. F. (ed.) Risk Taking and Information Handling in Consumer Behavior (Boston: Harvard University Graduate School of Business, 1967).

39. Cragg, J. G., and Uhler, R. S., "The Demand for Automobiles," *Canadian Journal of Economics*, 3:386–406 (1970).

40. Craig, G. D., "Predictive Accuracy of Quarterly and Annual Aggregate Savings Functions," *Journal of American Statistical Association*, 65:1131–1145 (1970).

41. Crockett, J., and Friend, I., "Consumer Investment Behavior," in R. Ferber (ed.), *Determinants of Investment Behavior* (New York: National Bureau of Economic Research, 1967).

42. Crow, J. H., "Financial Management in Relation to Family Values and Concepts of Financial Security," unpublished Ph.D. thesis (Cornell University, 1961).

43. Darby, M. R., "The Allocation of Transitory Income Among Consumers' Assets," *American Economic Review*, 62:928–941 (1972).

44. David, J. H., "Means of Payment and Liquid Savings of Households," *European Economic Review*, 2:303–336 (1971).

45. Davis, H. L., "Determinants of Martial Roles in Consumer Purchase Decisions," unpublished working paper (Graduate School of Business, University of Chicago, 1970).

46. _____, "Dimensions of Marital Roles in Consumer Purchase Decision-Making," *Journal of Marketing Research*, 7:168–177 (1970).

47. Davis, T. E., "The Consumption Function as a Tool for Prediction," *Review of Economics and Statistics*, 34:270–277 (1952).

48. De Huff, Elizabeth (Willis), *Famility Financial Security* (Ames, Iowa: Iowa State Agricultural and Home Economics Experiment Station Report 36, 1964).

49. Dix, L. C., "Decision-Making in the Farm Family," unpublished master's thesis (Cornell University, 1957).

50. Doyle, P., "Advertising Expenditures and Consumer Demand," *Oxford Economic Papers* (NS) 30:394–416 (1968).

51. Duesenberry, J., *Income, Saving, and the Theory of Consumer Behavior* (Cambridge, Massachusetts: Harvard University Press, 1949).

52. _____, Fromm, G., Klein, L. R., and Kuh, E. (eds.), *The Brookings Quarterly Econometric Model of the United States* (Chicago: Rand-McNally, 1965).

53. _____, et al., *The Brookings Model: Some Further Results* (Chicago: Rand-McNally, 1969).

54. Du Pont de Nemours and Co., *Consumer Buying Habit Studies* (Wilmington, Delaware: author, 1945, 1959, 1954, 1959).

55. Easterlin, R. A., "Toward a Socioeconomic Theory of Fertility," in S. J. Behrman (3d.), *Fertility and Family Planning* (Ann Arbor: University of Michigan Press, 1969).

56. Ebberler, D. H., "Permanent Component of a Series," *Journal of American Statistical Association* 68:343–347 (1972).

57. Eisner, R., "The Permanent Income Hypothesis: Comment," *American Economic Review*, 57:363–390 (1967).

58. _____, "A Permanent Income Theory for Investment: Some Empirical Explorations," *American Economic Review*, 57: 363–390 (1967).

59. Evans, M. K., "The Importance of Wealth in the Consumption Function," *Journal of Political Economy*, 75:335–351 (1967).

60. Farber, B., *Family Organization and Interaction* (San Francisco: Chandler Publishing Co., 1964).

61. Farley, J. U., "'Brand Loyalty' and the Economics of Information," *Journal of Business of the University of Chicago*, 27: 370–381 (1964).

62. Feldman, S. P., and Spencer, M. C., "The Effect of Personal Influence in the Selection of Consumer Services," in Holloway; Mittelstaedt, and Venkatesan (eds), *Consumer Behavior, Contemporary Research in Action* (Boston: Houghton Mifflin Co., 1971).

63. Ferber, R., "A Study of Aggregate Consumption Functions," *Technical Paper 8* (New York: National Bureau of Economic Research, 1953).

64. _____, *Factors Influencing Durable Goods Purchases* (Urbana, Illinois: University of Illinois Bureau of Economic Business Research, 1955).

65. _____, "The Accuracy of Aggregate Savings Functions in the Postwar Years," *Review of Economic Statistics*, 37:134–148 (1955).

66. _____, "Research on Household Behavior," *American Economic Review*, 52:19–63 (1962).

67. _____, "Family Decision-Making and Economic Behavior," in E. Sheldon (ed.), *Family Economic Behavior: Problems and Prospects* (New York: J. B. Lippincott, 1973).

68. _____, and Lee, L. C., "Husband-Wife Influence in Family Financial Economic Behavior," unpublished working paper (University of Illinois, College of Commerce and Business Administration, 1972).

69. _____, and Nicosia, F. M., "Newly Married Couples and their Asset Accumulation Decisions," in *Human Behavior in Economic Affairs: Essays in Honor of George Katona* (Amsterdam: North Holland Publishing Co., 1972).

70. Fisher, J. A., "Consumer Durable Goods Expenditures, with Major Emphasis on the Role of Assets, Credit, and Intentions," *Journal of American Statistical Association*, 58: 648–657 (1963).

71. Freedman, D., "The Relation of Economic Status to Fertility," *American Economic Review*, 53:414–426 (1963).

72. Freeman, R. C., and Due, J. M., "Influence of Goals on Family Financial Management," *Journal of Home Economics*, 53:448–452 (1961).

73. Friedman, M., *A Theory of the Consumption Function* (Princeton: National Bureau of Economic Research, 1957).

74. Friend, I., "Mythology in Finance," *Working Paper* (Wharton School, University of Pennsylvania, 1–72)

75. _____, "The Propensity to Save in India," in P. S. Lakanathan (ed.), *Economic Development: Issues and Policies* (1966).

76. _____, and Adams, F. G., "The Predicitive Ability of Consumer Attitudes, Stock Prices and Non-Attitudinal Variables," *Journal of American Statistical Association*, 59:987–1005 (1964).

77. _____, and Kravis, I. B., "Consumption Patterns and Permanent Income," *American Economic Review*, 47:536–655 (1057).

78. _____, and Taubman, P., "The Aggregate Propensity to Save: Some Concepts and Their Application to International Data," *Review of Economics and Statistics*, 48:113–123 (1966).

79. Gibbs, M., "Decision-Making Procedures by Young Consumers," *Journal of Home Economics*, 55:359–360 (1963).

80. Gillen, W. J., and Guccione, A., "The Estimation of Postwar Regional Consumption in Canada," *Canadian Journal of Economics*, 3:276–290 (1970).

81. Goldberger, A. S., and Gamaletsos, T., "A Cross-Country Comparison of Consumer Expenditure Patterns," *European Economic Review*, 1:357–400 (1970).

82. Goldsmith, R., *A Study of Saving in the United States*, vol. 1 (Princeton: Princeton University Press, 1955).

83. Golper, H., and Dunn, R., M., Jr., "A Short-run Demand Function for Higher Education in the U.S.," *Journal of Political Economy*, 77:765–777 (1969).

84. Gorman, W. M., "Tastes, Habits, and Choices," *International Economic Review*, 8:218–222 (1967).

85. Griliches, Z. (ed.), *Price Indexes and Quality Change: Studies in New Methods of Measurement*, Price Statistics Committee, Federal Reserve Board (Cambridge, Massachusetts: Harvard University Press, 1971).

86. Gronau, R., "The Intra-family Allocation of Time: Value of the Housewives' Time," *American Economic Review*, 53:634–651 (1973).

86a. Grossman, M., "On the Concept of Health Capital and the Demand for Health," *Journal of Political Economy*, 80:223–255 (1972).

87. Hamburger, M. J., "Household Demand for Financial Assets," *Econometrica*, 36:97–118 (1968).

88. _____, "Interest Rates and the Demand for Consumer Durable Goods," *American Economic Review*, 57:1131–1153 (1967).

89. Harberger, A. C. (ed.), *The Demand for Durable Goods* (Chicago: University of Chicago Press, 1960).

90. Henderson, J. M., and Quandt, R. E., *Microeconomic Theory* (New York: McGraw-Hill, 1958).

91. Henell, O., *Marketing Aspects of Housewives' Knowledge of Goods* (Goteborg, Sweden: Institute for Marketing and Management Research, 1953).

92. Hickman, B. (ed.), *Econometric Models of Cyclical Behavior* (New York: National Bureau of Economic Research, 1972).

93. Holbrook, R., and Stafford, F., "The Propensity to Consume Separate Types of Income: A Generalized Permanent Income Hypothesis," *Econometrica*, 39:1–22 (1971).

94. Holmes, J. M., "A Direct Test of Friedman's Permanent Income Theory," *Journal of American Statistical Association*, 65:1159–1162 (1970).

95. _____, "A Condition for Independence of Permanent and Transitory Components of a Series," *Journal of American Statistical Association*, 66:13–15 (1971).

96. Honey, R. R., "Family Financial Management Experiences," *Research Publication 141* (Pennsylvania State University, School of Home Economics, 1959).

97. _____, Britton, V., and Hotchkiss, A. S., "Decision-Making in the use of Family Financial Resources," *Research Publication 163* (Pennsylvania State University, School of Home Economics, 1959).

98. _____, and Smith, W. M., Jr. "Family Financial Management Experiences as Reported by 179 College Students, *Research Publication 113* (Pennsylvania State University, School of Home Economics, 1952).

99. Houthakker, H. S., "Some Determinants of Saving in Developed and Underdeveloped Countries," *Proceedings of International Economics Association* (Vienna, 1964).

100. _____, "New Evidence on Demand Elasticities," *Econometrica*, 33:277–288 (1965).

101. _____, and Taylor, L. D., *Consumer Demand in the United States*, 2nd ed. (Cambridge: Harvard University Press, 1970).

102. Huang, D. S., "Initial Stock and Consumer Investment in Automobiles," *Journal of American Statistical Association*, 58:789–798 (1963).

103. _____, "Discrete Stock Adjustment: The Case of Demand for Automobiles," *International Economic Review*, 5:46–62 (1964).

104. Husby, R. D., "A Nonlinear Consumption Function Estimated from Time-Series and Cross-Section Data," *Review of Economics and Statistics*, 52:76–79 (1970).

105. Jaffe, L. J., and Senft, H., "The Roles of Husbands and Wives in Purchasing Decisions," in Adler and I. Crespi (eds.), *Attitude Research at Sea* (Chicago: American Marketing Association, 1966).

106. Johnson, D. W., and Chiu, J. S. Y., "The Saving-Income Relation in Underdeveloped and Developed Countries," *Economic Journal*, 78:321–333 (1968).

107. Johnson, T., "Returns from Investment in Human Capital," *American Economic Review*, 60:546–560 (1970).

108. Juster, F. T., and Wachtel, P., "Inflation and

the Consumer," *Brookings Papers on Eco-Economic Activity*, 1:71–114 (1972).

109. _____, and Wachtel, P., "A Note on Inflation and the Saving Rate," *Brookings Papers on Economic Activity*, 3:765–778 (1972).

110. _____, and Wachtel, P., "Anticipatory and Objective Models of Durable Goods Demand," *American Economic Review*, 62:564–579 (1972).

111. Katona, G., and Lansing, J. B., "The Wealth of the Wealthy," *Review of Economics and Statistics*, 46:1–13 (1964).

112. _____, and Mueller, E., "A Study of Purchase Decisions," in L. H. Clark (ed.), *Consumer Behavior: The Dynamics of Consumer Reaction* (New York: New York University Press, 1954–1955).

113. _____, and Mueller, E., *Consumer Response to Income Increases* (Washington, D.C.; Brookings Institution, 1968).

114. Katz, E., and Lazarsfeld, P. F., *Personal Influence* (Glencoe, Illinois: Free Press, 1955).

115. Keynes, J. M., *The General Theory of Employment, Interest, and Money* (London: Macmillan Co., 1936).

116. Kiker, B. F., "Marshall on Human Capital: Comment," *Journal of Political Economy*, 76:1088–1090 (1968).

117. _____ (ed.), *Investment in Human Capital* (Columbia, South Carolina: University of South Carolina Press, 1972).

118. King, C. W., and Summers, J. L., "Overlap of Opinion Leadership Across Consumer Product Categories," *Journal of Marketing Research*, 7:43–50 (1970).

119. Komarovsky, M., "Class Differences in Family Decision-Making and Expenditures," in N. N. Foote (ed.), *Household Decision-Making* (New York: New York University Press, 1961).

120. Kreinin, M. E., "Windfall Income and Consumption-Additional Evidence," *American Economic Review*, 51:388–390 (1961).

121. _____, and Lininger, C. A., "Ownership and Purchases of New Cars in the U.S.," *International Economic Review*, 4:310–324 (1963).

122. Kuznets, S., *National Product Since 1869* (New York: National Bureau of Economic Research, 1946).

123. _____, "Proportion of Capital Formation to National Product," *American Economic Review*, 42:507–526 (1952).

124. Laidler, D. E. W., *The Demand for Money* (Scranton, Pennsylvania: International Textbook Co., 1969).

125. Lancaster, K., "A New Approach to Consumer Theory," *Journal of Political Economy*, 74:132–157 (1966).

126. _____, *Consumer Demand; A New Approach* (New York: Columbia University Press, 1971).

127. Landsberger, M., "The Life Cycle Hypothesis—A Reinterpretation and Empirical Test," *American Economic Review*, 60:175–183 (1970).

128. _____, "Consumer Discount Rate and the Horizon: New Evidence," *Journal of Political Economy*, 79:1346–1359 (1971).

129. Laughhunn, D. J., *On the Predictive Value of Combining Cross-Section and Time-Series Data in Empirical Demand Studies* (Urbana, Illinois: University of Illinois Bureau of Economic Business Research, 1969).

130. Laumas, P. S., "A Test of the Permanent Income Hypothesis," *Journal of Political Economy*, 77:857–861 (1969).

131. _____, and Mohabbat, J. A., "The Permanent Income Hypothesis; Evidence from Time-Series Data," *American Economic Review*, 42:730–734 (1972).

132. Lazarsfeld, P. F., Berelson, B., and Gaudet, H., *The People's Choice* (New York: Columbia University Press, 1948).

133. Lee, Feng-Yao, "Estimation of Dynamic Demand Relations from a Time Series of Family Budget Data," *Journal of American Statistical Association*, 65:586–597 (1970).

134. Lee, Maw Lin, "Income, Income Change, and Durable Goods Demand," *Journal of American Statistical Association*, 59:1194–1202 (1964).

135. Lee, T. H., "The Stock Demand Elasticities of Non-farm Housing," *Review of Economic Statistics*, 46:82–90 (1964).

136. _____, "Income, Wealth and the Demand for Money; Some Evidence from Cross-Section Data," *Journal of American Statistical Association*, 59:747–762 (1964).

137. _____, "Housing and Permanent Income," *Review of Economics and Statistics*, 50:480–490 (1968).

138. De Leeuw, F., "The Demand for Housing: A Review of Cross-Section Evidence," *Review of Economics and Statistics*, 52:1–10 (1971).

139. _____, and Gramlich, E., "The Federal Reserve-MIT Econometric Model," *Federal Reserve Bulletin*, 54:11–40 (1968).

140. Leff, N. H., "Dependency Rates and Savings Rates," *American Economic Review*, 59:886–896 (1969).

141. Lewin, K., "Group Decision and Social Change," in H. Newcomb et al. (eds.),

Readings in Social Psychology (New York: Henry Holt, 1947).

142. Lippitt, V. G., *Determinants of Consumer Demand for House Furnishings and Equipment* (Cambridge: Harvard University Press, 1959).

143. Liviatan, N., "Estimates of Distributed Lag Consumption Functions from Cross-Section Data," *Review of Economics and Statistics*, 47: 44–53 (1965).

144. March, J. G., and Simon, H. A., *Organizations* (New York: Wiley, 1958).

145. Mason, R. G., "The Use of Information Sources in the Process of Adoption," *Rural Sociology*, 29:40–52 (1964).

146. Mayer, T., "The Propensity to Consume Permanent Income," *American Economic Review*, 56:1158–1177 (1966).

147. _____, *Permanent Income, Wealth, and Consumption: A Critique of the Permanent Income Theory, the Life-Cycle Hypothesis, and Related Theories* (Berkeley and Los Angeles: University of California Press, 1972).

148. McMahon, W. W., "Dynamic Interdependence in Consumer Stocks, Tastes, and Choices," unpublished manuscript (College of Commerce and Business Administration, University of Illinois, 1971).

149. Mincer, J., "The Distribution of Labor Incomes: A Survey with Special Reference to the Human Capital Approach," *Journal of Economic Literature*, 8:1–26 (1970).

150. Modigliani, F., "Fluctuations in the Saving-Income Ration: A problem in Economic Forecasting," *Studies in Income and Wealth*, vol. 11 (New York: National Bureau of Economic Research, 1949).

151. _____, and Ando, A., "Tests of the Life Cycle Hypothesis of Savings: Comments and Suggestions," *Bulletin of Oxford University Institute of Statistics*, 19:99–124 (1957).

152. _____, "The Life-Cycle Hypothesis of Saving, the Demand for Wealth, and the Supply of Capital," *Social Research*, 33:160–217 (1966).

153. _____, "Monetary Policy and Consumption," in *Consumer Spending and Monetary Policy: The Linkages* (Boston: Federal Reserve Bank of Boston, 1971).

154. Morgan, J., Martin D., Cohen, W., and Brazer, H., *Income and Welfare in the United States* (New York: McGraw-Hill, 1962).

155. _____, and Martin, D., "Education and Income," *Quarterly Journal of Economics*, 77: 423–437 (1963).

156. Motley, B., "Consumer Investment, Expecta-
tions, and Transitory Income," *Western Economic Journal*, 7:223–229 (1969).

157. _____, "Household Demand for Assets: A Model of Short-Run Adjustments," *Review of Economic Statistics*, 52:236–241 (1970).

158. Mueller, E., "Desire for Innovations in Household Goods," in L. H. Clark (ed.), *Consumer Behavior: Research on Consumer Reactions* (New York: Harper, 1958).

159. _____, "Ten Years of Consumer Attitude Surveys: Their Forecasting Record," *Journal of American Statistical Association*, 58:899–917 (1963).

160. Muth, R. F., "Household Production and Consumer Demand Functions," *Econometrica*, 34:699–708 (1966).

161. Namboodiri, N. K., "Some Observations on the Economic Framework for Fertility Analysis," *Population Studies*, 26:185–206 (1972).

162. Nelson, P., "Information and Consumer Behavior," *Journal of Political Economy*, 78:311–329 (1970).

163. Newton, A. E., and Gilmore, D. L., "Consumer Behavior in Carpet Purchasing," *Journal of Home Economics*, 61:110–113 (1969).

164. Oksanen, E. H., "Testing an Aggregate Consumption Model for Canada," *Canadian Journal of Economics*, 5:96–109 (1972).

165. Orcutt, G. H., and Roy, A. D., *A Bibliography of the Consumption Function* (Cambridge University, Department of Applied Economics, 1949).

166. Owen, J. D., "The Demand for Leisure," *Journal of Political Economy*, 79:56–76 (1971).

167. Palda, K. S., *The Measurement of Cumulative Advertising Effects* (Englewood Cliffs, New Jersey: Prentice-Hall, 1964).

168. _____, "Comparison of Consumer Expenditures in Quebec and Ontario," *Canadian Journal of Economics and Political Science*, 33:16–26 (1967).

169. Phelan, J. M., and Ruef, R. R., "Values expressed and Realized in Family Financial Plans," *Research Publication 176* (Pennsylvania State University, School of Home Economics, 1961).

170. Pollak, R. A., "Habit Formation and Dynamic Demand Functions," *Journal of Political Economy*, 78:745–763 (1970).

171. Poser, G., and Hecheltjen, P., "The Use of Anticipatory Data in a Quarterly Econometric Model of the Federal Republic of Germany's Economy," unpublished manuscript (Darmstadt, West Germany: Technische Hochschule, 1973).

172. Power, J. H., "Price Expectations, Money Illusion and the Real-Balance Effect," *Journal of Political Economy*, 67:131–143 (1959).

173. Projector, D. S., "Consumer Asset Preferences," *American Economic Review*, 55:227–251 (1965).

174. _____, *Survey of Changes in Family Finances* (Washington, D.C., Federal Reserve Board, 1968).

175. _____, and Weiss, G. S., *Survey of Financial Characteristics of Consumers* (Washington, D.C.; Federal Reserve Board, 1966).

176. Ramanathan, R., "An Econometric Exploration of Indian Saving Behavior," *Journal of American Statistical Association*, 64:90–101 (1969).

177. _____, "Measuring the Permanent Income of a Household: An Experiment in Methodology," *Journal of Political Economy*, 79:177–185 (1971).

178. Reid, M., *Economics of Household Production* (New York: Wiley, 1934).

179. Roberts, J. B., *Sources of Information in Food Buying Decisions* (Lexington: *Kentucky Agricultural Experiment Station Bulletin*, vol. 85 (1963).

180. Schomaker, P. K., "Financial Decision-Making as Reported by 100 Farm Families in Michigan," unpublished Ph.D. thesis (Michigan State University, 1961).

181. Schultz, T. P., "An Economic Model of Family Planning and Fertility," *Journal of Political Economy*, 77:153–180 (1969).

182. _____, and Nerlove, M., *Love and Life Between Censuses: A Model of Family Decision-Making in Puerto Rico, 1950–1960* (Santa Monica: Rand Corporation, 1970).

183. Schultz, T. W., *Investment in Human Capital* (New York: The Free Press, 1971).

184. _____ (ed।)., "Reflections on Investment in Man," *Journal of Political Economy*, 70:1962.

185. _____ (ed.), "The Value of Children: An Economic Perspective," *Journal of Political Economy*, 81:S2–S13 (1973).

186. Shapiro, H. T., and Angevine, G. E., "Consumer Attitudes, Buying Intentions and Expenditures—An Analysis of the Canadian Data," *Canadian Journal of Economics*, 2:230–249 (1969).

187. Sharp, H., and Mott, P., "Consumer Decisions in the Metropolitan Family," *Journal of Marketing*, 21:149–156 (1956).

188. Singh, B., and Drost, H., "An Alternative Econometric Approach to the Permanent Income Hypothesis: An International Comparison," *Review of Economic Statistics*, 53:326–334 (1971).

189. Smith, R. E., "The Demand for Durable Goods: Permanent of Transitory Income," *Journal of Political Economy*, 70:500–504 (1962).

189a. Somermeijer, W. H., and Bannink, R., *A Consumption-Savings Model and Its Applications* (Amsterdam: North Holland, 1972).

190. Spiro, A., "Wealth and the Consumption Function," *Journal of Political Economy*, 70:339–354 (1962).

191. Stern, H., "The Significance of Impulse Buying Today," *Journal of Marketing*, 26:59–62 (1962).

192. Stigler, G., "The Economics of Information," *Journal of Political Economy*, 69:213–225 (1961).

193. _____, "Information in the Labor Market," *Journal of Political Economy*, 70(2):94–105 (1962).

194. Suits, D. B., "The Determinants of Consumer Expenditure: A Review of Present Knowledge," in *Commission on Money and Credit, Impacts of Monetary Policy* (Englewood Cliffs, New Jersey. Prentice-Hall, 1963).

195. Swamy, S., "A Dynamic Personal Savings Function and Its Long-Run Implications," *Review of Economics and Statistics*, 50:111–116 (1968).

196. Taubman, P., "Permanent and Transitory Income Effects," *Review of Economics and Statistics*, 47:38–43 (1965).

197. _____, "Personal Saving: A Time Series Analysis of Three Measures of the Same Conceptual Series," *Review of Economics and Statistics*, 50:125–129 (1968).

198. Taylor, L. D., "Saving of U.S. Households: Evidence from the Quarterly Flow of Funds," unpublished manuscript (New York: National Bureau of Economic Research).

199. _____, and Weiserbs, D., "Advertising and the Aggregate Consumption Function," *American Economic Review*, 62:642–655 (1972).

200. Telser, L. G., "Advertising and Cigarettes," *Journal of Political Economy*, 70:471–499 (1962).

201. Thurow, L. C., "The Causes of Poverty," *Quarterly Journal of Economics*, 81:39–57 (1967).

202. Tobin, J.; "Relative Income, Absolute Income, and Saying," in *Money Trade and Economic Growth, Essays in Honor of John Henry Williams* (New York: 1951).

203. Tolley, G. S., and Olson, E., "The Interde-

pendence Between Income and Education," *Journal of Political Economy*, 79:460–480 (1971).

204. _____; Wang, Y., and Fletcher, R. G., "Re-examination of the Time-Series Evidence on Food Demand," *Econometrica*, 37:695–705 (1969).

205. Udell, J. G., "Prepurchase Behavior of Buyers of Small Electrical Appliances," *Journal of Marketing*, 30:50–52 (1966).

206. Uhl, K., Andurs, R., and Paulsen, L., "How Are Laggards Different? Empirical Inquiry," *Journal of Marketing Research*, 7:51–54 (1970).

207. U.S. Bureau of the Census, *Consumer Buying Indicators* (Current Population Reports, Series P-65).

208. Van Syckle, C., "Practices Followed by Consumers in Buying 'Large Expenditures' Items of Clothing, Furniture, and Equipment," *Bulletin 222* (East Lansing: Michigan State Agricultural Experiment Station, 1951).

209. Vickrey, W. S., "Resource Distribution Patterns and the Classification of Families," in *Studies in Income and Wealth*, vol. 10 (New York: National Bureau of Economic Research, 1947).

210. Wachtel, P., "A Model of Interrelated Demand for Assets by Households," *Annual Economics Society Measures*, 1:129–140 (1972).

211. Weber, W., "The Effect of Interest Rates on Aggregate Consumption," *American Economic Review*, 60:591–600 (1970).

212. Weiss, D. L., "Determinants of Market Share," *Journal of Marketing Research*, 5:290–295 (1968).

213. Wells, H. L., "Financial Management Practices of Young Families," *Journal of Home Economics*, 51:439–444 (1959).

214. West, C. J., "Results of a Two Year Study of Impulse Buying," *Journal of Marketing*, 15:362–363 (1951).

215. Whyte, W. H., Jr., "The Web of Word of Mouth," *Fortune* (1954).

216. Wilkenberg, E. A., "Joint Decision-Making in Farm Families as a Function of Status and Role," *American Social Review*, 23:187–192 (1958).

217. Wolgast, E. H., "Do Husbands or Wives Make the Purchasing Decisions," *Journal of Marketing*, 23:151–158 (1958).

218. Wright, C., "Some Evidence on the Interest Elasticity of Consumption," *American Economic Review*, 57:850–854 (1967).

219. _____, "Estimating Permanent Income: A Note," *Journal of Political Economy*, 77:845–850 (1969).

220. Wu, De-Min, "An Empirical Analysis of Household Durable Goods Expenditures," *Econometrica*, 33:761–780 (1965).

221. Young, K. H., "A Synthesis of Time Series and Cross Section Analyses: Demand for Air Transportation Service," *Journal of American Statistical Association*, 67:560–566 (1972).

222. Zellner, A., and Geisel, M. S., "Analysis of Distributed Lag Models with Application to Consumption Function Estimation," *Econometrica*, 38:865–888 (1970).

223. _____, Huang, D. S., and Chan, L. C., "Further Analysis of the Short-Run Consumption Function with Emphasis on the Role of Liquid Assets," *Econometrica*, 33:571–581 (1965).

Econometric Studies of Investment Behavior: A Survey

Dale W. Jorgenson

Harvard University

1. INTRODUCTION

In this paper the reader will find a review of econometric studies of investment in fixed capital. A review of these studies through 1953 was given in 1957 by J. Meyer and E. Kuh [86], and a detailed review through 1960 was presented by R. Eisner and R. H. Strotz in 1963 [36]. In this review we concentrate on recent research on time series of investment expenditures for individual firms and industries. Our point of departure is the flexible accelerator model of investment originated by H. B. Chenery [13, 1952] and L. M. Koyck [74, 1954]. In this model attention is focused on the time structure of the investment process. The desired level of capital is determined by long-run considerations. Changes in desired capital are transformed into actual investment expenditures by a geometric distributed lag function—the specification of desired capital has been the subject of a wide variety of alternative theories; the alternative theories do agree on the validity of the flexible accelerator mechanism.

Denoting the actual level of capital by K and the desired level by K^+, capital is adjusted toward its desired level by a constant proportion of the difference between desired and actual capital,

$$K_t - K_{t-1} = [1 - \lambda][K_t^+ - K_{t-1}]. \qquad (1)$$

Alternatively, actual capital may be represented as a weighted average of all past levels of desired capital,

$$K_t = [1 - \lambda] \sum_{\tau=0}^{\infty} \lambda^{\tau} K_{t-\tau}^+, \qquad (2)$$

with geometrically declining weights. We refer to the latter form of the flexible accelerator as a distributed lag function relating the actual level of capital to past desired levels of capital. The flexible accelerator model was originally propounded as an alternative to the accelerator model of J. M. Clark [14, 1917]. In the accelerator model, the adjustment coefficient $1 - \lambda$ is taken to be unity, so that actual capital is equal to desired capital, and net investment is proportional to the change in desired capital,

$$K_t - K_{t-1} = K_t^+ - K_{t-1}^+.$$

In Clark's accerator model desired capital is proportional to output. The accelerator model with adjustment coefficient $1 - \lambda$ equal to unity was rejected in tests by S. Kuznets, J. Tinbergen, H. B. Chenery, L. M. Koyck, and B. Hickman [78, Kuznets, 1935; 103, Tinbergen, 1938; 13, Chenery, 1952; 74, Koyck, 1954 and 56, Hickman, 1957].

A second alternative to Clark's accelerator model is that investment depends on the level of profits; this theory of investment was

Reprinted from the *Journal of Economic Literature*, 9:1111–1147 (1971), by permission of the authors and the publisher (copyright by the American Economic Association).

first proposed by Tinbergen [103, 1938 and 104, 1939] and subsequently developed by Klein [70, 1950 and 71, 1951]. Two alternative rationalizations of this theory have been offered. First, Tinbergen argues [104] that realized profits measure expected profits: "It is almost a tautology to say that investment is governed by profits expectations." Secondly, the rate of investment may be constrained by the supply of funds. In the strong version of this theory the financial constraint operates at all times (the cost of funds schedule becomes highly inelastic where internal funds are exhausted). In a weaker version of the theory the financial constraint operates at low rates of capacity utilization, while extreme pressure on capacity may result in the use of outside sources of finance [86, Meyer and Kuh, 1957, pp. 190–208; 3, Anderson, 1964; 85, Meyer and Glauber, 1964; 76, Kuh, 1963 and 22, Duesenberry, 1958]. Within the framework provided by the flexible accelerator model all three determinants of investment—output, internal funds, and the cost of external finance—may be included as determinants of the desired level of capital.

The flexible accelerator mechanism may be transformed into a complete theory of investment behavior by adding a specification of the desired level of capital and a model of replacement investment. By accounting definition, the change in capital from period to period is equal to gross investment less replacement investment. The flexible accelerator provides an explanation of change in capital, but not of gross investment. The choice of a model of replacement is important since replacement investment predominates in total investment expenditures, at least at the aggregate level [77, Kuznets, 1961].[1] The geometric mortality distribution has been widely adopted for empirical work; for this distribution replacement is proportional to actual capital stock [57, Hickman, 1965; 59, Jorgenson, 1963 and 60, Jorgenson, 1965]. Under this assumption the change in

capital stock may be written:

$$K_t - K_{t-1} = A_t - \delta K_{t-1}, \tag{3}$$

where A is gross investment and δ is the rate of replacement, a fixed constant. Combining the geometric model of replacement with the flexible accelerator model of net investment, we obtain a model of investment expenditures:

$$A_t = [1 - \lambda][K_t^+ - K_{t-1}] + \delta K_{t-1}. \tag{4}$$

In this model the adjustment coefficient for replacement investment is equal to unity. The speed of adjustment for gross investment is much more rapid than the speed of adjustment for net investment.

Alternative econometric models of investment behavior differ in the determinants of the desired level of capital, in characterization of the time structure of the investment process, and in treatment of replacement investment. In the flexible accelerator model of Chenery and Koyck, desired capital is proportional to output, as in the rigid accelerator of Clark. In alternative models of investment behavior, desired capital depends on capacity utilization, internal funds, the cost of external finance, and other variables. In reviewing alternative models of investment behavior our first objective is to describe and evaluate the selection of the determinants of the desired level of capital in each of the studies under review.

In the flexible accelerator model of Chenery and Koyck, the time structure of the investment process is characterized by a geometric distributed lag function. Actual capital is a distributed lag function of desired capital with geometrically declining weights. This characterization has been modified by Chenery so that desired capital is proportional to lagged output; the best fitting lag may be determined by comparing different lags with regard to goodness of fit. Koyck has modified the geometric distributed lag function so that the first weight may be determined as a separate parameter with successive weights declining geometrically,

$$K_t = \alpha K_t^+ + [1 - \alpha][1 - \lambda] \sum_{\tau=0}^{\infty} \lambda^\tau K_{t-\tau-1}^+.$$

---

[1] Capital consumption has dominated gross capital formation for the economy as a whole since 1919.

The geometric distributed lag function may be extended by allowing additional weights to be determined as separate parameters or by making desired capital a function of the lagged values of its determinants. In reviewing models of investment behavior our second objective is to describe and evaluate alternative representations of the time structure of the underlying investment process.

Finally, models of investment behavior differ in their treatment of replacement investment. If replacement is proportional to capital stock, the underlying mortality distribution for investment goods is geometric. Change in capital stock is equal to gross investment less a constant proportion of capital stock, so that capital stock is a weighted sum of past gross investments with geometrically declining weights,

$$K_t = \sum_{\tau=0}^{\infty} (1 - \delta)^\tau A_{t-\tau}.$$

An internally consistent model of replacement investment based on proportionality between replacement investment and capital stock requires a measure of capital stock based on the geometric mortality distribution. Furthermore, duality between acquisition of investment goods and the time rental value of capital requires the incorporation of depreciation into the cost of capital. Our final objective in reviewing alternative models of investment behavior is to describe and evaluate the treatment of replacement investment.

2. INVESTMENT BY INDIVIDUAL FIRMS

2.1. Introduction

The first part of this review is devoted to studies of investment behavior by individual U.S. manufacturing firms. We focus attention on studies of time series on investment expenditures; time series analysis requires a detailed representation of the time structure of the investment process. These results can be compared directly with results from studies of industry groups. Time series studies of investment by individual firms have been completed by Eisner [30, 1967], Y. Grunfeld [49, 1960], Jorgenson and C. D. Siebert [65, 1968 and 64, 1968], and Kuh [76, 1963]. Cross section studies have been carried out by P. J. Dhrymes and M. Kurz [20, 1967], J. J. Diamond [21, 1962], Eisner [26, 1960; 29, 1962; 27, 1963; 25, 1964 and 30, 1967], Kuh [76, 1963], Meyer and Glauber [85, 1964, Chapters 2, 3, 5 and 6], and Mueller [97, 1967].

2.2. Kuh's Capital Stock Growth

Kuh's study of time series on investment by individual firms compares two models of investment behavior. The first is closely related to the flexible accelerator model of Chenery and Koyck with desired capital proportional to sales. The second is analogous to the flexible accelerator with desired capital proportional to profits. A third model with desired capital a function of both sales and profits is included in the comparisons. Kuh's principal conclusions [76, 1963, p. 213] are based on comparisons of the alternative models: "Since the major objective is to improve understanding of dynamic time series behavior, it should be pointed out that no matter how the contrasts are drawn from time series, the acceleration sales model is superior to the internal fund flow, profit model."

In formulating the profits model Kuh points out [76, p. 208] that " ... the expectational hypothesis for profits cannot, and perhaps should not, be distinguished from the sales level or capacity accelerator hypothesis. The main candidate variable for the expectational hypothesis is simply net income after tax, a secondary candidate being gross operating profit. Both variables will have strong correlations with the level of sales." The alternative rationale for the profits theory of investment is that the rate of investment is constrained by the supply of funds. The basic premise of this version of the profits theory is that the supply of funds schedule rises sharply at the point where internal funds are exhausted. Kuh employs retained earnings plus depreciation as a measure of profits; his results suggest that sales rather than internal funds determine the level of desired capital.

Kuh's version of the flexible accelerator treats desired capital as proportional to sales (or profits), lagged sales, or an average of sales and lagged sales. The weights associated with desired capital decline geometrically [76, pp. 7–16]. Within Kuh's study, estimates from time series and cross sections conflict. Estimates from a first difference model are dissimilar from the corresponding results for other treatments of the time structure.[2] These results suggest that the geometric distributed lag function employed by Kuh results in a mis-specification of the time structure of the investment process.

In Kuh's model for gross investment replacement investment is proportional to capital stock [76, p. 296]. The implied mortality distribution for investment goods, including retirements and the decline in efficiency of existing capital goods, is geometric. Kuh measures capital stock as cumulated gross investment less retirements, each deflated by an appropriate investment goods price index [76, pp. 64–74]. Decline in efficiency of existing capital goods is ignored in measuring capital stock, which is inconsistent with Kuh's treatment of replacement investment.

2.3. Grunfeld's Study of Corporate Investment

An alternative attack on the use of profits as a determinant of desired capital has been made by Y. Grunfeld. He incorporates lagged profits into a flexible accelerator model and finds [49, Grunfeld, 1960, p. 219] that the partial correlation of profits and investment, given capital stock, is insignificant: "Our results do not confirm the hypothesis that profits are a good measure of those expected profits that will tend to induce investment expenditures. The observed simple correlation between investment and profits seems to be due to the fact that profits are just

another measure of the capital stock of the firm. . . . " Similar results are obtained for the stock of liquid assets and the current level of profits.

Grunfeld suggests that discounted future earnings less the costs of future additions to capital provide a better measure of expected profits than current realized profits. In Grunfeld's theory desired capital is proportional to the value of the firm's outstanding securities. Grunfeld justifies this theory on the grounds that stock market participants have as much information about future earnings as the managers of firms. In addition, participants in the stock market have strong economic incentives to make accurate forecasts of future earnings. The partial correlation of the value of the firm and investment, given capital stock, is significant [49, p. 233]. Multiplying the value of the firm by the corporate bond rate to measure expected profits, Grunfeld finds that "The over-all power of the value of the firm to explain investment seems to be nearly identical to the combined powers of the expectations variable and the rate of interest" [49, p. 241].

The representation of the time structure of the investment process employed by Grunfeld is identical to that of Kuh.[3] Grunfeld, like Kuh, assumes that replacement investment is proportional to capital stock or that the mortality distribution for investment goods is geometric. He measures capital as cumulated gross investment less depreciation, each deflated by an appropriate investment goods price index. The initial level of capital is set equal to zero in 1935. Accounting depreciation throughout the period of Grunfeld's study, 1935–1954, is based on the straight-line method, which is inconsistent with a geometric mortality distribution for investment goods [49, pp. 217–18]. Nonetheless, Grunfeld's measurement of capital stock is an improvement over Kuh's since deflated accounting depreciation provides a better approximation to replacement requirements than deflated retirements.

---

[2] See below, section 4.3.

[3] See above, section 2.2.

2.4. Eisner's Permanent Income Theory for Investment

The first permanent income model of investment considered by Eisner employs the ratio of investment to gross fixed assets as an independent variable and the rate of growth of sales, the ratio of profits to gross fixed assets, and the ratio of depreciation to gross fixed assets for a single year as independent variables. The depreciation variable is constant across time series observations for a given firm and may be regarded as the constant term in the time series regression for each firm. Unlike Grunfeld and Kuh, Eisner imposes the assumption that parameters other than the constant term in the regression are the same for all firms. Profits and the rate of growth of sales are both significant determinants of desired capital in the firm time series regressions for the period 1955–62 [30, 1967, p. 374]. The proportion of the firm time series variance explained by Eisner's model for this period is .055.

Eisner considers an alternative model of investment for individual firms for the period 1960–62. This alternative model includes two additional independent variables representing the market value of the firm introduced by Grunfeld and the rate of return. To be more precise, the additional independent variables are the ratio of the market value of the firm to net worth plus depreciation reserve plus bonded indebtedness, and the ratio of profits after taxes plus depreciation plus interest to the market value of the firm. The results for firm time-series change dramatically with the addition of these two variables. Only profits and the rate of return appear as significant determinants of desired capital. Desired capital is positively related to profits and negatively related to the rate of return [30, p. 378].

Eisner's results for the period 1960–62 directly contradict his results for the period 1955–62, based on a less complete model, incorporating all of the same variables (except for market value of the firm and the rate of return). The results for the period 1960–62 also contradict the model underlying Eisner's extensive earlier analysis of investment by individual firms. The earlier analysis is based on models incorporating change in sales as the principal determinant of investment behavior [20, 1967; 21, 1962; 26, 1960; 29, 1962; 27, 1963; 25, 1964 and 30, 1967]. Upon empirical testing, Eisner's model for the period 1960–62 effectively reduces to the model proposed by Grunfeld. The profits variables represent profit expectations; the rate of return represents the cost of external finance. In Grunfeld's model profit expectations are represented by the product of the value of the firm and the corporate bond rate; the cost of external finance is represented by the corporate bond rate. The product of Eisner's rate of return and the value of the firm is profits after taxes plus depreciation plus interest. Profits after taxes are a significant explanatory variable in Eisner's model.

Eisner's distributed lag function consists of a finite weighted average of past rates of growth of sales, profits, rates of return, and market values of the firm. Although seven lagged terms in the rate of growth of sales are included in the regressions, only two lagged terms in each of the other variables are included. In effect, investment is a weighted average of current and lagged values of profits and the rate of return [30, 1967, p. 378]. Replacement investment is treated as proportional to gross capital stock; no attempt is made to correct book values of gross capital stock for variations in the acquisition cost of investment goods [30, pp. 370–71]. The use of gross capital stock is inconsistent with the geometric mortality distribution for investment goods assumed by Eisner.

This review of Eisner's permanent income model of investment is limited to firm time series results. Only these results are comparable to those for the other studies of firm behavior included in this review. Eisner presents regressions for cross sections of firms and for industry time series and cross sections. His own analysis of the results attempts to relate differences in estimates of the factors affecting investment "to differing permanent and transitory components in the relevant variances and covariances [30, 1967, p. 386]." A detailed summary of this analysis is presented by Eisner in his 1967 work [30, pp. 386–87].

2.5. Jorgenson and Siebert's Theory of Optimal Capital Accumulation

Jorgenson and Siebert considered two models of corporate investment behavior based on an optimal time path for capital accumulation. Optimal accumulation implies a theory of the rate of return; this theory has been developed by Modigliani and Miller [89, 1958; 94, 1959; 91, 1961; 92, 1963; 88, 1963; 90, 1965; 95, 1966; 96, 1967 and 93, 1969]. In the Modigliani-Miller theory the cost of capital is shown to be independent of the financial structure of the firm or of dividend policy; this view contrasts sharply with the theory of the cost of capital underlying the liquidity theory of investment behavior. In the liquidity theory the supply schedule is horizontal up to the point at which internal funds are exhausted and vertical at that point.

In the Modigliani-Miller theory the appropriate cost of capital for investment decisions is a weighted average of the expected return to equity and the return to debt. The return to equity is measured in two alternative ways: first, capital gains on assets held by the firm may be regarded as transitory, so that return to equity is measured excluding capital gains. Second, capital gains on assets may be regarded as part of the return to investment so that return to equity includes capital gains. The first model studied by Jorgenson and Siebert, referred to as Neoclassical I, includes capital gains. The second model, referred to as Neoclassical II, excludes capital gains [65, 1968, p. 1130].

In both models considered by Jorgenson and Siebert, desired capital is proportional to the ratio of the value of output to the price of capital services. The price of capital services depends on the price of investment goods, the rate of return, the rate of depreciation, the rate of growth of the price of investment goods, and the tax structure. The objective of the firm is to maximize its market value; maximization of market value is implied by maximization of profit at every point of time, where profit is defined as net revenue on current account less the rental value of capital services.

The version of the flexible accelerator employed by Jorgenson and Siebert treats net investment as a distributed lag function of changes in desired capital. The weights associated with changes in desired capital are approximated by the weights in a rational distributed lag function [65, 1968, p. 1128]. This class of distributed lag functions includes the geometric distributed lag function and generalizations of it proposed by Koyck as special cases. Jorgenson and Siebert choose the best-fitting rational distributed lag function for each model of investment they consider.

In the Jorgenson-Siebert models for gross investment, replacement is proportional to capital stock, so the implied mortality distribution for capital goods is geometric. Capital stock is measured by a perpetual inventory method with declining balance replacement. Gross investment in constant prices is interpolated between initial and terminal estimates of net capital stock from balance sheet data [65, 1968, p. 1129]. For the geometric mortality distribution, the rate of replacement is equal to the rate of depreciation; this common rate is employed in estimating capital stock and in measuring the price of capital services.

Jorgenson and Siebert find that a model of optimal capital accumulation, incorporating capital gains on assets held by the firm, performs best [65, pp. 1142–43 and 64, 1968]. They have also compared the performance of models based on optimal capital accumulation with corresponding models based on the acceleration principle—like those employed by Kuh and Eisner, internal liquidity, like those employed by Grunfeld and Kuh, and expected profits, employed by Grunfeld and Eisner. The overall ranking for postwar data is:

1. Neoclassical I.
2. Neoclassical II.
3. Expected Profits.
4. Accelerator.
5. Liquidity.

This ranking corresponds with that of Kuh for the Accelerator and Liquidity models, with Grunfeld for Expected Profits and Liquidity models, and with Eisner for Expected Profits and Accelerator models.

3. INVESTMENT BY INDUSTRY GROUPS

3.1. Introduction

The second part of our review is devoted to studies of investment behavior by industry groups within American manufacturing. In reviewing these studies we concentrate on econometric models of investment behavior for two-digit industries within U.S. manufacturing. Results consistent across industries are difficult to achieve by consideration of a wide range of alternative specifications and selection of the best fitting among them. Studies of quarterly data on investment by industry groups from the OBE-SEC Survey have been made by Anderson [3, 1964], Eisner [29, 1962 and 31, 1965], Evans [37, 1967], Jorgenson and Stephenson [67, 1967; 68, 1967 and 66, 1969], Meyer and Glauber [85, 1964, Chapters 4 and 7], and Resek [98, 1966]. Studies of annual data have been made by Bourneuf [10, 1964] and Hickman [57, 1965]. Studies of annual or quarterly data for aggregates such as total manufacturing have been made by Anderson [2, 1967, pp. 413–25], Bischoff [9, 1969; 8, 1970 and 41, 1971, pp. 61–130], Coen [16, 1968; 17, 1969 and 15, 1971], de Leeuw [79, 1962], Eckstein [24, 1965], Eisner [32, 1969; 28, 1969 and 33, 1970], Eisner and Nadiri [34, 1968 and 35, 1968], Greenberg [42, 1964], Griliches and Wallace [48, 1965], Hall and Jorgenson [51, 1967; 52, 1969 and 53, 1971], Hammer [54, 1964], Jorgenson [59, 1963 and 60, 1965], Klein and Taubman [73,

1971], Lintner [80, 1967], Schramm [100, 1970], and Thurow [102, 1969]. Studies of cross sections of industries have been made by G. J. Stigler [101, 1963].

In assessing the determinants of the desired level of capital in studies of investment by individual industry groups, we divide the studies into two categories. In the first group of studies, Anderson, Bourneuf, Evans, Meyer and Glauber, and Resek, each determinant enters the regression function determining investment expenditures as a single variable. To appraise the results we can test each of the proposed determinants for significance. Where several determinants enter the regression function, this appraisal requires simultaneous hypothesis testing. An appropriate technique for this purpose is Scheffé's S-method. In this method critical regions for each of the hypotheses are set simultaneously so as to control the overall level of significance at a predetermined level. This method is discussed in detail by Scheffé [99, 1959] and compared with the alternative and incorrect method of applying ordinary critical regions for each individual hypothesis when several hypotheses are tested simultaneously. In the second group of studies—those of Eisner, Hickman, and Jorgenson and Stephenson—some determinants of investment expenditures enter the regression function as a number of separate variables, representing different lagged values of the same variable. Scheffé's S-method can not be used to appraise the overall significance of all of the lagged values of each variable. For this purpose a direct comparison of the performance of alternative models is useful.

3.2. Anderson's Corporate Finance and Fixed Investment

We first consider W. H. L. Anderson's model of investment behavior. The rationale for Anderson's model has been developed by Duesenberry. Duesenberry's theory of investment is characterized by Anderson as

... a restatement of the neoclassical position that investment is determined by the intersection of the marginal efficiency schedule with the marginal cost of funds schedule. The marginal efficiency schedule, Duesenberry argues, shifts about primarily in response to changes in the rate of utilization of existing capacity. The marginal cost of funds schedule shifts about in response to changes in the degree of financial risk as well as to changes in the market cost of funds [3, 1964, p. 37].

The determinants of desired capital in Anderson's model include three relatively standard elements—pressure on capacity, profits, and interest rates—and three novel ones—stocks of government securities held at the beginning of the period, accrued tax liability at the end of the period, and long-term debt capacity [3, pp. 70–71]. Pressure on capacity is measured by the difference between actual sales and previous maximum sales, taken as a measure of productive capacity. Long-term debt capacity is defined as the difference between 18 percent of total assets and outstanding long-term debt at the beginning of the period. Debt capacity represents the availability of unused borrowing ability, whereas government securities and tax liability represent available liquidity and the need for liquid assets. Anderson omits replacement investment from his model altogether.

Anderson divides the time structure of the investment process into three components. One part is a lag between changes in the determinants of investment behavior and changes in the expectations about these variables. Alternatively, expectations may be determined by a trend plus some constant proportion of the deviation of the actual variable from trend [3, pp. 62–63]. This is the expectations mechanism used in the analysis of investment by two-digit industry groups. The second part of the time structure is a lag from a change in the expected values of determinants of desired capital to the actual decision to invest. Anderson identifies the final decision with the appropriation of funds [3, pp. 65–69] and treats the decision lag as a fixed parameter to be estimated from the data. Finally, there is a lag

from the investment decision to actual expenditures, that is, from appropriations to actual investment.

Anderson determines the lag from appropriations to expenditures empirically from data on appropriations and investment. The fitted lag distribution assigns equal weights to appropriations lagged one through four periods, so that the average lag is two and a half quarters [3, p. 68]. As a consequence of this empirical finding, Anderson represents the underlying determinants of investment as moving four-quarter averages of quarterly data. For two-digit industries, "In all cases but three, the best decision lag seemed to be three quarters, the lag which [also] yielded the best results for aggregate manufacturing" [3, p. 113]. For the total investment process, a three-quarter decision lag implies a lag of five and a half quarters plus the lag from actual to expected values of the determinants of desired capital.

For a more formal version of Anderson's model, including his specification of the determinants of investment and of the time structure of the investment process, let investment in current prices be $q_{At}A_t$ where q_{At} is the price of investment goods and A_t the quantity of investment expenditures; the model takes the form:

$$
\begin{aligned}
q_{At}A_t = \beta_0 &+ \beta_1 t + \beta_2 (\overline{S - S_{\max}})_{t-3} \\
&+ \beta_3 \overline{RED}_{t-3} + \beta_4 \overline{G}_{t-3} \\
&+ \beta_5 \overline{T}_{a,t-3} + \beta_6 \overline{K}_{DL,T-3} \\
&+ \beta_7 i'_{t-3} + \beta_8 Q_1 + \beta_9 Q_2 \\
&+ \beta_{10} Q_3 + \epsilon_t.
\end{aligned} \tag{5}
$$

In this model a bar over a variable ($^-$) indicates a moving average for four quarters beginning with the quarter indicated (e.g., $t-3$) and extending backward. The variable t is a time trend, $S - S_{\max}$ corresponds to pressure on capacity, where S is sales and $S_{\max}$ is its previous maximum value, RED is gross retained profits, the sum of retained earnings and depreciation expense, and i' is the Treasury bill yield. The time trend is introduced to account for difference between actual and expected values of the determinants of investment expenditures. The other three variables represent the effects of capacity utilization, profit, and the interest rate. The variable G is the stock of government securities held at the beginning of the period, T_a is accrued tax liability at the end of the period, and K_{DL} is long-term debt capacity. These variables represent the effects of the need for liquidity and the riskiness of borrowing. The variables Q_1, Q_2, and Q_3 are seasonal dummy variables equal to one in the corresponding quarter and zero otherwise.

To appraise Anderson's empirical findings [3, 1964, pp. 108–16] we can test each of the proposed determinants of investment expenditures for significance by means of Scheffé's S-method. The results are given in Table 1. These results suggest that the explanatory variables may be divided into three groups. Capacity utilization $S - S_{max}$ and the interest rate i' are clearly significant determinants of investment. The capacity utilization variable is significantly different from zero in 5 of 13 industries; this variable has an incorrect sign for only one industry group. The interest rate is significantly different from zero in 6 of 13 industries; this variable has the wrong sign for three industry groups. The second set of explanatory variables—debt

capacity K_{DL}, government securities G, and tax liability T_a includes variables that are barely significant as determinants of investment. Debt capacity is significant for four industry groups, but has the wrong sign for one of these groups. Government securities is significant for three industry groups, not significant with the right sign for six, and not significant with the wrong sign for four. Tax liability is significant for only two industry groups. None of these results is out of line with the null hypothesis that the corresponding coefficients are equal to zero. Internal funds RED is clearly insignificant as a determinant of investment decisions; it has the wrong sign for 6 of the 13 industry groups and is significantly different from zero for one of these groups.

3.3. Meyer and Glauber's Accelerator-Residual Funds Model

The determinants of investment expenditures in the model employed by Meyer and Glauber for analyzing data on investment by industry groups include capacity utilization, profits, interest rates, and the percentage change in the price of common stocks [85, 1964, pp. 139–54]. Pressure on capacity is measured by the ratio of the Federal Reserve Board (FRB) index of industrial production to the McGraw-Hill capacity series, interpolated from annual benchmarks using the OBE-SEC series on investment in the manufacturing sector. The profits variable is essentially the same as that employed by Anderson, profits after taxes minus dividends plus depreciation expense. The interest rate is Moody's AAA industrial bond rate rather than the Treasury Bill rate employed by Anderson [85, p. 46]. The theoretical basis of the model is similar to that proposed by Anderson and Duesenberry. The cost of funds schedule is assumed to depend on the availability of internal funds, as well as on the cost of external finance as reflected in the bond rate, and the percentage rate of change of stock prices. Meyer and Glauber, like Anderson, omit replacement investment from their model.

TABLE 1

Significance of Determinants of Investment Expenditures, Anderson Model, Thirteen Industry Groups, 1949I–1958IV

($F_{.05;6,29} = 2.43$, $S = 3.8$)

Determinant	Significant Coefficients		Insignificant Coefficients	
	Right Sign	Wrong Sign	Right Sign	Wrong Sign
$S - S_{max}$	5		7	1
RED		1	7	5
G	3		6	4
T_a	2		9	2
K_{DL}	3	1	7	2
i'	6		4	3

Source: Anderson [3, 1964, pp. 108–16].

Meyer and Glauber use a geometric lag to describe the time structure of the investment process as a whole. For each independent variable a separate fixed lag is determined; for example, profits are lagged one quarter, whereas the bond rate is lagged three quarters. The total average lag for the variables lagged one quarter—profits, capacity utilization, and stock prices—is estimated at 8.7 quarters for total manufacturing. The average lag for the interest rate, lagged three quarters, is 10.7 quarters [85, p. 153]. Because of the choice of two quarters, rather than one quarter, as the lag for investment expenditures as a dependent variable, the shape of the lag distribution is rather peculiar. Change in profits, capacity utilization, or stock prices has no impact for one quarter. The impact in the second quarter is .207 of the long-run effect of the determinants of investment on the actual level of expenditures. There is then a one-quarter gap with no impact, followed by an impact of .164, and so on, with zero effects and geometrically declining effects for alternate quarters. Meyer and Glauber characterize each two-digit industry of manufacturing by this type of lag distribution.

A formal version of the Meyer-Glauber model, where A_t represents investment in constant prices, is:

$$A_t = \beta_0 + \beta_1(T - V)_{t-1} + \beta_2 C^M_{t-1}$$
$$+ \beta_3 r_{t-3} + \beta_4 \left(\frac{\Delta SP}{SP} \right)_{t-1}$$
$$+ \beta_5 A_{t-2} + \beta_6 Q_1 + \beta_7 Q_2$$
$$+ \beta_8 Q_3 + \epsilon_t. \qquad (6)$$

The variable $T - V$ is net profit plus depreciation expense less dividends; it corresponds to Anderson's RED. The variable C^M is the ratio of production to capacity, where production is measured by the FRB index of industrial production and capacity by the McGraw-Hill capacity index. The variable r is Moody's corporate bond rate; SP is Standard and Poor's index of the prices of 425 industrials; $\Delta SP/SP$ is the percentage

rate of change of this price index. The variables Q_1, Q_2, and Q_3 are seasonal dummy variables, as in Anderson's model.

To appraise the empirical findings of Meyer and Glauber, it would be desirable to employ the same procedure as for Anderson's model, namely, to test each of the proposed determinants of investment for significance by means of Scheffé's S-method. Unfortunately, Meyer and Glauber do not report standard errors for their fitted regression coefficients [85, 1964, pp. 155 and 157]. However, they do report coefficients that have the wrong sign and coefficients that have the right sign and are statistically significant by "conventional" t-tests at one-tailed levels of significance of .05 and .01. These levels of significance are, of course, inappropriate where more than one coefficient in a regression is tested for significance [99, 1959, p. 80]. The level of significance of the test criterion for the S-method corresponding to Meyer and Glauber's "conventional" one-tailed level of significance of .01 is greater than .10. The results are tabulated in Table 2. The number of significant coefficients of the right sign is, of course, over-stated relative to the number presented for the Anderson model in Table 1. Nevertheless, a number of conclusions stand out. Net profits plus depreciation less dividends $T - V$ is the only clearly sig-

TABLE 2

Significance of Determinants of Investment Expenditures, Meyer-Glauber Model, Thirteen Industry Groups, 1950I–1958IV

$(F_{> .10; 4, 27} = 1.92, S = 2.8)$

| Determinant | Coefficient Right Sign | | Coefficient Wrong Sign |
	Signif- icant	Insignif- icant	
$T - V$	7	5	1
C^M	3	7	3
r	3	8	2
$\Delta SP/SP$	1	8	4

Source: Meyer and Glauber [85, 1964, Tables VII-5 and VII-6, pp. 155 and 157].

nificant determinant of investment included in the Meyer-Glauber model. Capacity utilization C_M and the interest rate r are barely significant. The change in stock prices $\Delta SP/SP$ is clearly insignificant. These results are diametrically opposed to the results of Anderson.

3.4. Resek's Study of Investment

A third econometric model of investment expenditures based on Duesenberry's theory of investment is that of Robert Resek. In the Resek model the determinants of investment expenditures include output, change in output, the rate of interest, a measure of debt capacity, and an index of stock prices [98, 1966, p. 325]. The dependent variable is gross investment, deflated by a price index for investment goods and divided by capital stock. Output and change in output are divided by capital stock, but the other determinants of investment enter the regression directly. Replacement investment is assumed to be proportional to capital stock, so the rate of replacement is incorporated into the constant term in the regression. Capital stock is measured by the declining balance method so Resek's treatment of replacement is internally consistent [98, p. 327]. The debt capacity variable depends on the ratio of debt less retained earnings to the assets of the firm [98, pp. 323–24]. This variable provides an alternative measure of debt capacity to that employed by Anderson. Retained earnings enter the determination of debt capacity but are not included as a separate variable.

Resek employs a fixed lag distribution for all variables entering the model of investment behavior [98, pp. 325–27]. The weights in this lag distribution are taken directly from a regression of investment expenditures on capital appropriations fitted by Almon [1, 1965]. This treatment of the lag structure is similar to Anderson's, but Anderson includes separate lags from the determinants of desired capital to investment decisions, from decisions to capital appropriations, and from appropriations to actual expenditures.

Anderson finds that the expectations lag is one quarter and that a decision lag of three quarters provides the best fitting investment function. The average lag from appropriations to investment expenditures is two and a half quarters for all industries in Anderson's study. The average lag from appropriations to investment expenditures generally falls between two and a half and three quarters in Almon's study; the weights are determined separately for each industry [1, Almon and 98, Resek, p. 329]. Resek employs Almon's weights with all variables lagged one quarter; in effect, he assumes that expectations and decision lags are one quarter. This assumption is directly contradicted by Anderson's results, implying that Resek's characterization of the time structure of the investment process is invalid.

Resek presents three alternative models for determination of investment expenditures; a formal version of the best-fitting model is.

$$\frac{A_t}{K_t} = \beta_0 + \beta_1 Q_1 + \beta_2 Q_2 + \beta_3 Q_3$$

$$+ \beta_4 \frac{(\Delta 0)_{L,t}}{K_t} + \beta_5 r_{L,t}$$

$$+ \beta_6 \left[\frac{1}{M - \dfrac{D - F}{A}} \right]_{L,t}$$

$$+ \beta_7 SP_{L,t} + \epsilon_t. \tag{7}$$

In this model the subscript L refers to a moving average of the corresponding variable with Almon weights. The variable $\Delta 0$ is change in output over four quarters, where output is measured as the FRB index of industrial production. The variable r is the interest rate, measured by Moody's AAA industrial bond rate as in the Meyer-Glauber model. The variable $(D - F)/A$ is debt capacity, measured from the FTC—SEC *Quarterly Financial Report* and M is a constant. The variable SP is the SEC stock price index for the industry [98, p. 332]. The variables Q_1, Q_2 and Q_3 are seasonal dummy variables as in the Anderson and Meyer-Glauber models.

To appraise Resek's empirical findings we

employ the same procedure as for Anderson's model. The results are given in Table 3. The interest rate r and stock price SP are clearly significant determinants of investment expenditures. Change in output $\Delta 0$ is somewhat less significant but the null hypothesis that the corresponding coefficients are all equal to zero is clearly rejected. The debt capacity variable is significant with the wrong sign in two industries and significant with the right sign in four industries. This variable is of marginal significance in the explanation of investment behavior. In general, Resek's results appear to corroborate Anderson's findings rather than those of Meyer and Glauber. Debt capacity has little or no role to play in explaining investment behavior. The rate of interest and the price of corporate securities, associated with the costs of external funds, are significant determinants of investment behavior. Change in output plays an important role in determining the level of investment.

3.5. Evans' Study of Investment

A fourth study of investment behavior based on Duesenberry's theory of investment is that

TABLE 3
Significance of Determinants of Investment Expenditures, Resek Model, Thirteen Industry Groups, 1953I–1962IV

$(F_{.05;4,32} = 2.67, S = 3.3)$

Determinant	Significant Coefficients		Insignificant Coefficients	
	Right Sign	Wrong Sign	Right Sign	Wrong Sign
$\Delta 0/K$	5		7	1
r	8		4	1
$M - \dfrac{1}{\dfrac{D-F}{A}}$	4	2	5	2
SP	8		3	2

Source: Resek [98, 1966, Table 4, p. 332].

of M. K. Evans. The determinants of investment in the Evans model include capacity utilization, capital stock, sales, cash flow, and the interest rate [37, 1967, pp. 153–55]. Capacity utilization is measured as the Wharton School capacity index; this index is calculated from the FRB index of industrial production, as follows:

... the method involves marking off cyclical peaks for each of thirty component indexes of the Federal Reserve Board's Index of Industrial Production and then fitting linear segments between successive peaks. Between the present time period and the last established peak, the previous line segment is extrapolated at its established slope unless the index in the present period exceeds the extrapolated trend line. In this case a new slope is computed by fitting a new linear line segment from the last cyclical peak to the present value of the index [72, Klein and Preston, 1967, p. 34].

This procedure is similar to that involved in computing Anderson's $S - S_{\max}$ variable, except that capacity is extrapolated linearly from previous peak output rather than set equal to sales at the previous peak. Cash flow is measured as profits after taxes plus depreciation less dividends, which is identical to the cash flow variable employed by Meyer and Glauber. The interest rate is Moody's AAA bond rate. Cash flow is deflated by the investment goods price index. Sales are deflated by the wholesale price index excluding farm commodities.

Evans assumes that replacement is proportional to the average of capital stock lagged five and six quarters [37, 1967, p. 153]. This assumption implies that the decline in efficiency of investment goods is zero until five quarters have elapsed and that relative efficiency is $1 - \delta/2$ in the fifth quarter, $1 - \delta$ in the sixth quarter, $1 - 3\delta/2$ in the seventh quarter, and so on. No justification for this relative efficiency function is offered by Evans. Capital stock is measured by deflating net fixed assets by a price index of investment goods. No effort is made to correct book values of gross fixed assets or accumulated depreciation allowances for variations in the cost of acquisition of investment goods. Accounting depreciation is not calculated on the basis of the mortality distribution for investment goods assumed by Evans, so his treatment of replacement investment is internally inconsistent.

Evans employs a double distributed lag model based on the geometric distributed lag function. In terms of desired capital, the lag structure may be represented in the form:

$$K_t + \frac{\lambda_1}{2} \sum_{\tau=0}^{\infty} \lambda_0^\tau [K_{t-\tau-5} + K_{t-\tau-6}]$$

$$= \lambda_2 \sum_{\tau=0}^{\infty} \lambda_0^\tau K_{t-\tau-1}^+ + \left[\frac{1 - \lambda_0 + \lambda_1 - \lambda_2}{2} \right]$$

$$\cdot \sum_{\tau=0}^{\infty} \lambda_0^\tau [K_{t-\tau-5}^+ + K_{t-\tau-6}^+],$$

or:

$$K_t - \lambda_0 K_{t-1} + \frac{\lambda_1}{2} [K_{t-5} + K_{t-6}]$$

$$= \lambda_2 K_{t-1}^+ + \left[\frac{1 - \lambda_0 + \lambda_1 - \lambda_2}{2} \right]$$

$$\cdot [K_{t-5}^+ + K_{t-6}^+].$$

Adding replacement investment this relationship becomes:

$$I_t = \lambda_2 K_{t-1}^+ + \left[\frac{1 - \lambda_0 + \lambda_1 - \lambda_2}{2} \right]$$

$$\cdot [K_{t-5}^+ + K_{t-6}^+] + [\lambda_0 - 1]K_{t-1}$$

$$+ \left[\frac{\delta - \lambda_1}{2} \right] [K_{t-5} + K_{t-6}],$$

where δ is the rate of replacement. If K^+ involves an unknown parameter, the parameters λ_1 and δ cannot be identified from this relationship. It is impossible to analyze Evans' distributed lag function without further information.

Evans substitutes capacity utilization for the terms in K_{t-1}^+ and K_{t-1}. He makes desired capital in the term $K_{t-5}^+ + K_{t-6}^+$ a linear function of sales, cash flow, and the interest rate. Denoting $K_{t-5}^+ + K_{t-6}^+$ by K_{56}^+, and so on, a formal version of the Evans model may be represented as follows:

$$A_t = \beta_0 + \beta_1 Cp_1 + \beta_2 S_{56}$$
$$+ \beta_3 K_{56} + \beta_4 L_{56} + i_{56}, \qquad (8)$$

where Cp_1 is capacity utilization lagged once, S_{56} is the sum of sales lagged five and six periods, K_{56} is the sum of similarly lagged capital stock, L_{56} is the sum of lagged cash flow, and i_{56} is the sum of lagged interest rates [37, Evans, 1967, p. 156]. Capacity utilization Cp is the Wharton School capacity index, sales S and cash flow L are taken from the SEC-FTC *Quarterly Financial Report*, capital K is a book value computed from the same data, and i is Moody's AAA corporate bond rate, the interest rate employed by Meyer and Glauber and by Resek.

To appraise Evans' results, we employ the same procedure as for the Anderson and Resek models; the results are presented in Table 4. From this table it is clear that sales and capacity utilization are significant determinants of desired capital. Capacity utilization Cp is significant for 9 of the 13 industry groups and has the wrong sign for only one. Sales S is a significant variable for six industries and also has only one wrong sign. Capital stock K, measured as the book value of net fixed assets deflated by the current price index for investment goods, is significant for four industries; the sign is positive for two of these industry groups and negative for two. The sign of the coefficient of capital stock depends on the relative magnitude of the rate

TABLE 4

Significance of Determinants of Investment Expenditures, Evans Model, Thirteen Industry Groups, 1949I–1963IV

$(F_{.05;5,54} = 2.39, S = 3.5)$

Determinant	Significant Coefficients		Insignificant Coefficients	
	Right Sign	Wrong Sign	Right Sign	Wrong Sign
Cp	9		3	1
K	2	2	6	3
S	6		6	1
L	3		6	4
i	3		7	3

Source: Evans [37, 1967, Table 1, p. 156].

of replacement δ and the adjustment coefficient λ_1. If replacement requirements predominate, the coefficient of capital stock has a positive sign; we take this sign to be the right one. Alternatively, if the adjustment coefficient predominates, the coefficient of capital stock is negative. Cash flow L and the interest rate i are barely significant as determinants of investment expenditures. Each one is significant for only three industry groups; wrong signs occur for the coefficients of cash flow in four industries and for the interest rate in three industries. Upon empirical testing the Evans model reduces to an ordinary flexible accelerator with desired capital proportional to output.

3.6. Eisner's Accelerator Model

We have reviewed the application of Eisner's model of investment to time series data for individual firms. We next review Eisner's study of investment behavior for industry groups. The determinants of investment include changes in sales, changes in profits, and, for replacement investment, level of capital stock. Investment net of replacement equals a weighted average of past changes in output. Changes in profits are introduced as a possible representation of changes in "the expected profitability of investment" [31, Eisner, 1965, p. 97]. In an earlier study the relationship of this model to the theory of the firm is characterized by Eisner as follows:

... The acceleration principle whose manifestations we shall note and investigate is not the simple first or second order difference equation frequently presented, presumably in the interest of pedagogical clarity. Rather, we have in mind a world of risk and uncertainty in which business firms strive to maximize the mathematical expectation of some monotonic increasing function of expected future profit, subject to a production function with decreasing marginal returns to each factor and positive cross partial derivatives. This means, in particular, that for a firm initially in equilibrium it pays to increase the stock of capital for permanent or certainly expected increases in demand for output [26, 1960, p. 1].

Eisner treats the time structure of investment behavior as a modification of Koyck's

distributed lag function, with weights determined arbitrarily for the first lagged values of profits and sales and then declining geometrically [29, 1962, p. 198]. He has applied the complete model to data from the OBE-SEC Survey for total durable and total nondurable manufacturing industries for the realization of investment expenditures, given anticipations. He has also applied similar models to annual investment expenditure data from the McGraw-Hill Survey for industry groups [26, p. 11]. For this annual data he characterizes the investment process time structure by a finite distributed lag function.

Eisner's specification of the determinants of investment expenditures and of the time structure of the investment process for quarterly time series is the following:

$$
\begin{aligned}
A_t = \beta_0 &+ \beta_1 \Delta S_{t-1} + \beta_2 \Delta S_{t-2} \\
&+ \beta_3 \Delta P_{t-1} + \beta_4 \Delta P_{t-2} + \beta_5 A_{t-1} \\
&+ \beta_6 K_t + \epsilon_t.
\end{aligned} \tag{9}
$$

In this model ΔS is change in sales, ΔP is change in profits, K is capital stock at the beginning of the period. The lagged value of investment expenditures is introduced to represent the effects of changes in sales and profits lagged more than two periods; the weights associated with these changes decline geometrically. Sales are deflated by the wholesale price index for each industry group and profits are deflated by the price index of investment goods. Capital stock is measured by the declining balance method so that Eisner's treatment of replacement investment in the study of industry groups, unlike his treatment in the study of individual firms, is internally consistent. No overall appraisal of Eisner's model on the basis of results for individual industry groups can be made because Eisner has fitted the model only for realizations of investment expenditures and only for the totals of durable and nondurable manufacturing industries [31, 1965, p. 105]. For these groupings only one of the four coefficients associated with change in profits exceeds its standard error. After empirical testing, Eisner's model reduces to the flexible accelerator of Chenery and Koyck.

3.7. Hickman's Study of Investment

The determinants of investment behavior in Hickman's model are output, capital stock, wage rate, rental price of capital, price of output and a time trend [57, 1965, pp. 28–32]. Hickman employs a logarithmic form of the flexible accelerator, similar to that used by Koyck,

$$\ln K_t = \sum_{\tau=0}^{\infty} \lambda_0^{\tau}[\lambda_1 \ln K_{t-\tau}^+ + \lambda_2 \ln K_{t-\tau-1}^+$$
$$+ (1 - \lambda_0 - \lambda_1 - \lambda_2) \ln K_{t-\tau-2}^+].$$

In Koyck's form of the distributed lag function $1 - \lambda_0 - \lambda_1 - \lambda_2 = 0$ and $\lambda_2 = 1 - \lambda_0 - \lambda_1$. Hickman distinguishes between an expectations lag in the determination of desired capital and an adjustment lag between actual and desired capital; assuming a constant rate of adjustment, he identifies the two lags separately [57, 1965, pp. 36–38]. Hickman makes the logarithm of desired capital a linear homogeneous function of output and a price ratio. The price ratio is taken, alternatively, as the wage rate divided by the rental price of capital and the rental price of capital divided by the price of output. The model is completed by adding a time trend. The model is fitted to annual data for 1949–60, a total of twelve annual observations. As many as eight coefficients are determined from these data— three output terms, three price terms, the coefficient of the time trend and a constant term.

A formal version of the model used by Hickman to analyze data for individual industry groups within manufacturing is:

$$\ln K_t - \ln K_{t-1}$$
$$= \beta_0 + \beta_1 T + \beta_2 (\ln Y_t - \ln K_{t-1})$$
$$+ \beta_3 (\ln Y_{t-1} - \ln K_{t-1})$$
$$+ \beta_4 (\ln Y_{t-2} - \ln K_{t-1})$$
$$+ \beta_5 \ln P_t + \beta_6 \ln P_{t-1}$$
$$+ \beta_7 \ln P_{t-2} + \epsilon_t, \qquad (10)$$

where Y is output, K is capital stock, P is a price ratio, and T a time trend. Capital stock is estimated by Hickman using declining balance replacement or, equivalently, a geometric mortality distribution. Output is measured

as real gross product originating in each industry, estimated by the OBE. The price of output is the price index implicit in nominal and real gross product originating, as estimated by the OBE. The rental price of capital services is the product of the investment goods price index and the sum of interest and depreciation rates. The depreciation rate is a constant equal to the replacement rate; the interest rate is Moody's AAA industrial bond rate. The wage rate is employee compensation per man-hour as estimated by Charles Schultze [57, 1965, pp. 42–44]. After a comparison of alternative possible specifications, Hickman's model, like that of Eisner, reduces to the flexible accelerator model of Chenery and Koyck. Except for the presence of a third lagged term in output, the lag specification is the same as that employed by Koyck [57, 1954, pp. 54–56].

3.8. Bourneuf's Study of Capacity and Investment

The determinants of investment behavior in Bourneuf's model are limited to output and capacity [10, 1964, p. 609]. A formal version of this model is:

$$A_t = \beta_0 + \beta_1 (C_{t-1} - Y_{t-1})$$
$$+ \beta_2 C_{b,t} + \beta_3 \Delta Y_t + \epsilon_t,$$

where C is average capacity during the period, C_b capacity at the beginning of the period and Y is output. Output is measured by the Federal Reserve Board index of industrial production, and capacity is measured by the McGraw-Hill capacity index for each industry [10, pp. 608–09]. Capacity at the beginning of the period C_b is intended to adjust for the effect of replacement investment. The lag structure implicit in this relationship can be brought out by letting $A_t - \beta_2 C_{b,t}$ represent net investment. Then:

$$\Delta K_t = \beta_0 + \beta_3 Y_t - (\beta_1 + \beta_3) Y_{t-1}$$
$$+ \frac{\beta_1}{\alpha} K_{t-1}, \qquad (11)$$

where $\alpha = K/C$, the ratio of capital stock to capacity. This relationship is an arithmetic version of Koyck's flexible accelerator.

The relationship described above is fitted to annual data for 13 industry groups, 1950–61 [10, pp. 617–18]. To appraise the results we employ Scheffé's S-method as before; tests of significance are given in Table 5. The difference between capacity and output is a highly significant determinant of investment expenditures with significant coefficients with the right sign for 7 of the 13 industries. Capacity at the beginning of the period, representing replacement requirements generated by existing capital stock, is also significant as a determinant of investment with significant coefficients with the right sign in 5 of the 13 industries. Only the change in output is barely significant as a determinant of investment. These results substantiate the conclusions of Anderson, Resek, Evans, Eisner, and Hickman that capacity utilization is an important determinant of investment expenditures.

3.9. Jorgenson and Stephenson's Study of Investment

The final study of investment by industry groups to be included in our survey is that of Jorgenson and Stephenson [67, 1967]. We have reviewed the application of models based on optimal capital accumulation to time series data for individual firms by Jorgenson and Siebert. The model employed in analyzing time series data for industry groups by Jorgenson and Stephenson corresponds to the Jorgenson-Siebert model, Neoclassical II; capital gains are regarded as transitory so return to equity is measured excluding capital gains.

The Jorgenson-Stephenson model takes the form:

$$A_t = \beta_0 + \beta_1 \Delta \left(\frac{pQ}{c}\right)_{t-4} + \beta_2 \Delta \left(\frac{pQ}{c}\right)_{t-5}$$
$$+ \beta_3 \Delta \left(\frac{pQ}{c}\right)_{t-6} + \beta_4 \Delta \left(\frac{pQ}{c}\right)_{t-7}$$
$$+ \beta_5 (A - \delta K)_{t-1} + \beta_6 (A - \delta K)_{t-2}$$
$$+ \beta_7 K_t + \epsilon_t.$$

In this model pQ is gross value added in current prices; c is the price of capital services, defined as:

$$c = q \left[\frac{1-uv}{1-u} + \frac{1-uw}{1-u}r\right],$$

where q is the price of investment goods, δ the rate of replacement, r the cost of capital, u the tax rate, v the proportion of depreciation deductible from income for tax purposes, and w the proportion of the cost of capital deductible from income. Capital stock at the beginning of the period K is estimated from investment data, using a perpetual inventory method based on declining balance replacement. The value of output is taken to be gross value added in each industry; components of value added and the tax structure are taken from the U.S. national income and product accounts, distributed by quarterly data from the SEC-FTC *Quarterly Financial Report*. The cost of capital is the ratio of return to capital net of depreciation to the market value of the firm [67, p. 218].

Jorgenson, J. Hunter, and M. I. Nadiri have compared the performance of the Jorgenson-Stephenson model with that of the Anderson, Eisner and Meyer-Glauber models for quarterly data on investment expenditures for fifteen two-digit industry groups within manufacturing for the period 1949–64 [62, 1970 and 63, 1970]. The Eisner model effec-

TABLE 5
Significance of Determinants of Investment Expenditures, Bourneuf Model, Thirteen Industry Groups, 1950–1961

$(F_{.05;3,8} = 4.07, S = 3.5)$

	Significant Coefficients		Insignificant Coefficients	
Determinant	Right Sign	Wrong Sign	Right Sign	Wrong Sign
$C - Y$	7		5	1
C_b	5		7	1
ΔY	3		7	2

Source: Bourneuf [10, 1964, Table 4, pp. 617–18].

tively reduces to the flexible accelerator of Chenery and Koyck; similarly, the Bourneuf, Evans, and Hickman models are essentially versions of the flexible accelerator model with desired capital proportional to output. The Anderson, Meyer-Glauber, and Resek models incorporate internal funds, the cost of external funds, and capacity utilization as determinants of investment expenditures. In the Meyer-Glauber model only internal funds emerge as a significant determinant of investment. In the Anderson and Resek models only capacity utilization and the cost of external funds are significant.

Among the models compared by Jorgenson, Hunter, and Nadiri, the best explanation of investment behavior for individual industry groups is provided by the Jorgenson-Stephenson model [62, 1970, pp. 206–09]. This model is superior to the Anderson and Meyer-Glauber models for fourteen of fifteen industry groups and to the Eisner model for eleven of fiften groups. The second-ranking model is the Eisner model; it is superior to the Meyer-Glauber model for twelve of fifteen industry groups and to the Anderson model for all fifteen groups. Finally, the Meyer-Glauber model is superior to the Anderson model for eleven of the fifteen groups. In terms of the models of investment behavior for individual firms, these results may be summarized as follows:

1. Neoclassical
2. Accelerator
3. Liquidity

This ranking coincides with that for individual firms based on the results of Jorgenson and Siebert [65, 1968, pp. 1142–43].

4. SUMMARY AND CONCLUSION

4.1. Summary

The main features of econometric models of investment behavior included in our survey are summarized in Table 6. We can compare alternative models with respect to determinants of desired capital, the time structure of the investment process, and the

treatment of replacement investment. Models of investment behavior differ substantially in all three respects. For each model the data and time period of the study are given in the first column of Table 6. This information is followed by a list of the determinants of desired capital, by a characterization of the time structure of the investment process, and by a description of the treatment of replacement investment.

4.2. Determinants of Desired Capital

The determinants of the desired level of capital may be divided into three groups: 1) capacity utilization, represented by the ratio of output to capacity, the difference between output and capacity, change in output, sales less previous peak of sales, and so on; 2) internal finance, represented by the flow of internal funds, the stock of liquid assets, debt capacity, and accrued tax liability; 3) external finance, represented by interest rates, rates of return, stock prices, the market value of the firm. Our first objective is to evaluate the role of these groups of variables in the explanation of investment behavior.

Capacity utilization appears as a highly significant determinant of the desired capital in most of the studies we have considered. Measures of capacity utilization appearing as significant determinants of investment include Anderson's measure of sales less previous peak sales, Bourneuf's difference between the FRB index of industrial production and the McGraw-Hill capacity index, and the Wharton School capacity index employed by Evans. The level of real output may be regarded as a measure of capacity utilization in a relationship also including capital stock. Measures of output employed in this way include deflated sales as employed by Kuh, Hickman's real gross product originating, Resek's change in the FRB index of industrial production, and the change in deflated sales employed by Eisner in the study of industry groups.

Only the Meyer-Glauber measure of capacity utilization, based on the ratio of the FRB index to the McGraw-Hill capacity

TABLE 6

Comparison of Alternative Investment Functions

	Data and Time Period	Determinants of Desired Capital	Time Structure of Investment Process	Replacement Investment
		A. Individual Firms, Annual Observations		
Eisner	McGraw-Hill data on plant and equipment expenditures, deflated by an implicit price deflator for producers, durable equipment and non-residential construction, 1955–62.	Change in sales, deflated by industry wholesale price index; profits, deflated by investment price index; depreciation; rate of return; value of the firm.	Finite distributed lag function.	Replacement rate proportional to depreciation charges divided by gross fixed assets.
Grunfeld	Moody's data on gross additions to plant and equipment plus maintenance and repairs, deflated by an implicit price deflator for producers' durable equipment, 1935–54.	Value of the firm, deflated by the implicit price deflator for gross national product; Moody's AAA corporate bond rate.	Geometric distributed lag function.	Replacement proportional to net capital stock.
Jorgenson-Siebert	Moody's data on gross additions to plant and equipment, deflated by an implicit deflator for producers' durable equipment and non-residential construction, 1937–63.	Gross value added in current prices; price of investment goods; depreciation; rate of return; rate of growth of the price of investment goods; tax structure.	Rational distributed lag function.	Replacement proportional to net capital stock.
Kuh	Moody's data on gross additions to plant and equipment, deflated by an implicit price deflator for producers' durable equipment and non-residential construction, 1935–55.	Sales and retained earnings plus depreciation, deflated by investment price index.	Geometric distributed lag function.	Replacement proportional to gross capital stock.
		B. Industry Groups, Annual Observations		
Bourneuf	OBE-SEC data on plant and equipment expenditures, deflated by an implicit price deflator for producers' durable equipment and non-residential construction, 1950–61.	FRB index of industrial production; McGraw-Hill capacity index.	Weight of first value of output (FRB index) arbitrary; remaining weights declining geometrically.	Replacement proportional to capacity.

58

TABLE 6
(*Continued*)

	Data and Time Period	Determinants of Desired Capital	Time Structure of Investment Process	Replacement Investment
Hickman	OBE-SEC data on plant and equipment expenditures, deflated by Boeckh construction cost index for plant and wholesale price index for producer finished goods for equipment, 1949–60.	Gross product originating in constant prices; price of capital services; wage rate; implicit price deflator for gross product originating.	Weight of first two values of output (gross product) and price ratio arbitrary; remaining weights declining geometrically.	Replacement proportional to net capital stock.

C. Industry Groups, Quarterly Observations

	Data and Time Period	Determinants of Desired Capital	Time Structure of Investment Process	Replacement Investment
Anderson	OBE-SEC data on plant and equipment expenditures, undeflated, not seasonally adjusted; quarterly dummy variables included as independent variables; first quarter, 1949, to fourth quarter, 1958.	Sales less previous maximum sales; retained earnings plus depreciation; stocks of government securities; accrued tax liability; debt capacity; Treasury bill rate.	Four quarter moving average of each of the determinants used as independent variables; time trend included to represent lag in expectations; decision lag taken to be fixed.	Omitted.
Eisner	OBE-SEC data on plant and equipment expenditures, deflated by an implicit deflator for producers, durable equipment and non-residential construction, adjusted for seasonal variations; third quarter, 1948, to fourth quarter, 1960.	Change in sales, deflated by industry wholesale price index; change in profits, deflated by investment price index.	Weight of first values of change in sales and change in profits arbitrary; remaining weights declining geometrically.	Replacement proportional to net capital stock.
Evans	OBE-SEC data on plant and equipment expenditures, deflated by an implicit deflator for producers' durable equipment and non-residential construction, adjusted for seasonal variations; first quarter, 1949, to fourth quarter, 1963.	Sales, deflated by wholesale price index excluding farm commodities; Wharton index of capacity utilization; retained earnings plus depreciation, deflated by investment price index; Moody's AAA corporate bond rate.	Three-parameter rational distributed lag function.	Replacement proportional to average of net capital stock lagged five and six quarters.

59

TABLE 6
(*Continued*)

	Data and Time Period	Determinants of Desired Capital	Time Structure of Investment Process	Replacement Investment
Jorgenson-Stephenson	OBE-SEC data on plant and equipment expenditures, deflated by an implicit deflator for producers' durable equipment and non-residential structures, adjusted for seasonal variations; first quarter, 1949, to fourth quarter, 1960.	Gross value added in current prices; price of investment goods; depreciation, rate of return; tax structure.	Rational distributed lag functions.	Replacement proportional to net capital stock.
Meyer-Glauber	OBE-SEC data on plant and equipment expenditures, deflated by an implicit deflator for producers' durable equipment and non-residential construction, not seasonally adjusted; quarterly dummy variables included as independent variables; first quarter, 1950, to fourth quarter, 1958.	Capacity utilization—ratio of FRB index of industrial production to McGraw-Hill capacity index; retained earnings plus depreciation, deflated by investment price index; Moody's AAA corporate bond rate; change in Standard and Poor's stock price index.	Weights alternately zero and declining geometrically.	Omitted.
Resek	OBE-SEC data on plant and equipment expenditures, deflated by an implicit deflator for producers' durable equipment and non-residential construction, not seasonally adjusted; quarterly dummy variables included as independent variables; first quater, 1953, to fourth quarter, 1962.	Change in FRB index of industrial production; debt capacity; Moody's AAA corporate bond rate; SEC industry stock price index.	Finite distributed lag function, weights determined from regression of expenditures on appropriations.	Replacement proportional to net capital stock.

index, fails to appear as a significant determinant of desired capital. This finding conflicts sharply with that of Bourneuf, who finds that the difference between these variables is highly significant. Change in deflated sales does not appear as a significant determinant of desired capital in Eisner's time series study for individual firms. This finding conflicts with Eisner's results for time series of industry groups.

Capacity utilization or output provides the only significant determinant of desired capital for several of the models of investment behavior included in our survey. These models include Kuh's model of firm time series and the models of Bourneuf, Eisner, Evans, and Hickman for industry groups. All of these models reduce to the flexible accelerator model of Chenery and Koyck with desired capital proportional to output. The most important difference between the models of investment proposed by Eisner, Evans, and Hickman and the models of Bourneuf, Chenery, Koyck, and Kuh is in the characterization of the time structure of the investment process. We will discuss alternative characterizations of the time structure in more detail below.

The studies of individual firms by Grunfeld and by Jorgenson and Siebert and the study of industry groups by Jorgenson and Stephenson are the only studies we have reviewed that do not include capacity utilization or real output as a possible explanatory variable. The Jorgenson-Siebert and Jorgenson-Stephenson models embody a description of technology based on a Cobb-Douglas production function or, equivalently, a CES production function with constant returns to scale and elasticity of substitution equal to unity. Real output enters together with the ratio of its price to the price of capital services. The Grunfeld model does not include real output as a determinant of investment behavior.

A flexible accelerator model with desired capital proportional to output embodies a specialization of the description of technology based on the CES production function [4, 1961]. This specialization corresponds to a description of technology with constant returns to scale and elasticity of substitution equal to zero. For a CES production function with zero elasticity of substitution, the capital-output ratio is constant and the determinants of investment do not include the prices of output or capital services. The production function is characterized by fixed technical coefficients; the fixed coefficients production function was originally employed by Chenery and Koyck in deriving the flexible accelerator model of investment behavior.

Evidence on the form of the production function based on direct estimation of the production function is presented by P. Zarembka for two-digit manufacturing industries for 1957 and 1958 [108, 1970 and 109, 1969]. Zarembka first tests the hypothesis that the elasticity of substitution and the scale parameter are the same for the two years. This hypothesis is accepted; proceeding conditionally, Zarembka tests the hypotheses that the scale parameter is equal to unity and that the elasticity of substitution is equal to unity. Both hypotheses are accepted, so the CES production function reduces to the Cobb-Douglas with constant returns to scale. Z. Griliches has carried out a similar study for 1958; the hypothesis that distribution, efficiency and scale parameters are the same for all industry groups is employed in Griliches' study [45, 1967; 46, 1967 and 47, 1968]. This hypothesis is inconsistent with the evidence [61].

Attempts have been made to estimate the degree of returns to scale and the elasticity of substitution from marginal productivity conditions for labor and capital by Dhrymes [19, 1965] and by Eisner and Nadiri [34, 1968]. The results suggest increasing returns, invalidating the model of production employed by Dhrymes [19, p. 364] and by Eisner and Nadiri [34, p. 373]. Equality between the marginal product of labor and the real wage, and between the marginal product of capital and the real rental, are neither necessary nor sufficient for profit maximization under increasing returns. The results of Eisner and Nadiri have been traced to an error in the stochastic specification of their model by Bischoff [9, 1969, p. 358].[4] Bischoff finds that the residuals in their distributed lag function are serially correlated, so their estimates of the elasticity of substitution and degree of returns to scale are inconsistent [9, p. 359].[5] When this error is corrected the hypotheses that the elasticity of substitution and the degree of returns to scale are equal to unity are not rejected [9, Table 2]; the CES production function reduces to Cobb-Douglas form with constant returns to scale.

The hypothesis of constant returns to scale is consistent with estimates of the scale parameter from the CES production function. This hypothesis can also be tested by analysis of data from engineering studies, growth of firms by size of firm, and the size distribution of firms. Under constant returns to scale the optimal policy for capital accumulation determines labor-output and capital-output ratios and the rate of growth of the firm is independent of size. Bain's analysis of evidence from engineering studies supports the conclusion that returns to scale at the firm level are increasing up to a firm size equal to the minimum optimal size of plant; beyond that point plant economies of scale are constant; there are no economies of multi-plant operation [5, 1956, pp. 68–82 and 6, 1969]. This evidence corroborates the findings from econometric studies of the CES production function that the degree of returns to scale is equal to unity.

Under constant returns to scale the rate of growth of capital is independent of size of firm. An extensive study of rates of growth of assets for the one thousand largest manufacturing firms in the United States for the period 1946 to 1955 has been made by Hymer and Pashigian [58, 1962]. Their conclusion is that rate of growth of assets is independent of size of firm [58, p. 558]. Independence of the rate of growth of assets and firm size implies that the relative size distribution of firms is stable over time. This implication is consistent with evidence on concentration ratios in American manufacturing industries over the period 1947–63 [69, 1968, p. 241].[6] The evidence on growth of firms by size and the size distribution of firms further corroborates the findings from econometric studies of the CES production function that returns to scale are constant.

Zarembka has presented evidence on the elasticity of substitution from direct estimation of the CES production function. Given constant returns to scale as a maintained hypothesis, further evidence on the elasticity of substitution can be obtained from estimation of parameters of the marginal productivity conditions for labor and capital. Zarembka has estimated the elasticity of substitution from the marginal productivity condition for labor for cross section observations by states for two-digit manufacturing industries in 1957 and 1958. He first tests the hypothesis that the elasticity of substitution is the same for the two years. This hypothesis is accepted; proceeding conditionally, Zarembka tests the hypothesis that the elasticity of substitution is equal to unity [108, 1970, p. 49]. This hypothesis is also accepted so the CES production function reduces to the Cobb-Douglas form. Griliches has analyzed data similar to Zarembka's for 1957 and 1958. He tests the hypothesis that the elasticity of substitution is equal to unity [46, 1967, p. 292]. Again, the hypothesis is accepted, validating the Cobb-Douglas form of the production function.

F. W. Bell and P. J. Dhrymes have attempted to estimate the elasticity of substitution from data on capital input and its rental price [7, 1965 and 19, 1965]. If the output-capital ratio is regressed on the rental price of capital, the estimated elasticity of substitution is below estimates from a regression of the output-labor ratio on the wage rate. The estimates from labor data agree

---

[4] The results labeled "c_1" in Bischoff's Table 1 are for the data employed by Eisner and Nadiri.

[5] This erroneous specification is used by Eisner [28, 1969]; his estimates are also inconsistent.

[6] The concentration measures are ratios of the value of shipments for the four largest, eight largest, and twenty largest firms in each four-digit industry to the value of shipments for the industry.

with direct estimates of the production function, but the estimates from capital data do not. An obvious explanation of this apparent discrepancy is that marginal conditions with no costs of adjustment or gestation lags are appropriate for labor but not for capital. The marginal product of labor is equal to the real wage, but the marginal product of capital enters a distributed lag investment function of the type fitted by Bischoff. Bischoff's estimates of the elasticity of substitution are consistent with direct estimates of the production function. For cross section estimates of the production function and the marginal productivity condition for labor and time series estimates of a distributed lag investment function incorporating the marginal productivity condition for capital, the evidence is consistent with an elasticity of substitution equal to unity and with constant returns to scale.

The assumption of constant returns to scale that underlies the fixed coefficients production function is consistent with the evidence we have reviewed on the description of technology. The second assumption underlying the fixed coefficients production function, that the elasticity of substitution is equal to zero, is directly contradicted by the evidence we have reviewed [61]. The fixed coefficients description of technology is implicit in the models of investment behavior employed by Bourneuf, Evans, Hickman, and Kuh. For Evans, Hickman, and Kuh this characterization emerges as the result of a comparison among alternative specifications of the investment function. The fixed coefficients description of technology has been employed by Eisner in the study of investment by individual firms and industry groups extending over a period of 15 years [30, 1967; 26, 1960; 29, 1962; 27, 1963; 25, 1964; 31, 1965; 32, 1969; 28, 1969 and 33, 1970]. The assumptions of constant returns and elasticity of substitution equal to unity employed by Jorgenson, Siebert, and Stephenson are consistent with the evidence we have reviewed.

We now turn to determinants of desired capital other than output and capacity utilization. These determinants may be divided into two groups—internal finance and external finance. Variables associated with internal finance do not appear as significant determinants of desired capital in any model that also includes output as a significant determinant. Cash flow variables employed by Anderson and Evans are not significant as determinants of investment; essentially the same variable appears as the only significant determinant in the Meyer-Glauber model. The results of Anderson and Evans contradict those of Meyer and Glauber. Kuh's study of time series for individual firms provides a direct comparison of models based on sales and models based on cash flow. The sales models are superior in all time series comparisons. Other measures of internal finance employed by Anderson—stocks of government securities, accrued tax liability, debt capacity—are not significant as determinants of desired capital. Resek's measure of debt capacity is also not significant.

Among variables associated with external finance, the interest rate appears as a significant determinant of desired capital in the Anderson and Resek models. The interest rate is barely significant in the Evans and Meyer-Glauber models. An index of stock prices is highly significant in the Resek model; the rate of change of this index is not significant in the Meyer-Glauber model. With the exception of the Meyer-Glauber model, variables measuring the cost of external finance play a more important role than variables representing internal finance. External finance variables are, however, definitely subordinate to variables associated with output. External finance appears as a significant determinant of desired capital only in models such as the Anderson and Resek models, with output a highly significant determinant.

We have already observed that Grunfeld's study of investment by individual firms does not include output or capacity utilization as a possible determinant of desired capital. In this model desired capital is proportional to the market value of the firm. Another model studied by Grunfeld is equivalent in performance to the market value model. Desired capital depends on the interest rate, the product of the interest rate, and the market value of the firm. This product plays the role of output in other models of investment. Output, represented by the product of the interest rate and the market value of the firm, is the most significant determinant of desired capital; the cost of external funds, represented by the interest rate, is also significant but definitely subordinate to output. Similarly, in Eisner's model for firm time-series, profits play the role of output, and the rate of return measures the cost of external finance.

Our overall conclusion is that where internal finance variables appear as significant determinants of desired capital, they represent the level of output. Where both output and cash flow are included as possible determinants, only one is a significant determinant. The preponderance of evidence clearly favors output over cash flow.[7]

The studies by Jorgenson and Siebert of investment by individual firms, and by Jorgenson and Stephenson of investment by industry groups, include the cost of external finance as part of the price of capital services. In both studies the cost of external finance is measured as a weighted average of the rate of return on equity and the rate of interest on debt. In the Jorgenson-Siebert study the rate of return on equity is measured in two alternative ways—including and excluding capital gains on assets as part of the return to equity. The cost of external finance enters the price of capital services along with the price of capital goods, depreciation, the rate of growth of the price of investment goods, and variables representing the tax structure. In the Jorgenson-Stephenson study the rate of return on equity is measured excluding capital gains on assets.

The findings on the role of internal and external finance we have reviewed directly contradict the basic premise of the theory of finance propounded by Meyer and Kuh

[86, 1957] and by Duesenberry [22, 1958]. In this theory the cost of internal funds is below the cost of external funds. The schedule representing the supply of funds to the firm is discontinuous at the point where internal funds are exhausted. Dividend policy and financial structure are important determinants of the cost of capital and of investment behavior. Interpreting the cash flow variable in the Meyer-Glauber model as representing output, which does not otherwise appear as a significant determinant of desired capital, there is no evidence to support the theory of finance of Meyer, Kuh, and Duesenberry. Desired capital is independent of cash flow, holdings of liquid assets, and debt capacity. This evidence implies that the cost of capital is independent of the availability of internal funds. Independence of the cost of capital and financial policies determining dividend payments and financial structure is, of course, the principal conclusion of the Modigliani-Miller theory of finance [89, 1958; 94, 1959; 91, 1961; 92, 1963; 88, 1963; 90, 1965; 95, 1966; 96, 1967 and 93, 1969].

From the point of view of the Modigliani-Miller theory of finance, the representation of the cost of external finance in most econometric studies of investment behavior is seriously incomplete. First, many econometric studies employ the rate of interest on debt as the cost of capital. The corporate bond rate is used as a cost of capital by Evans, Grunfeld, Hickman, Meyer and Glauber, and Resek. Anderson uses the Treasury bill rate. The cost of capital is not equal to the corporate bond rate so long as equity is included in the financial structure of the firm.

Among the studies we have reviewed, only the studies of individual firms by Eisner, and by Jorgenson and Siebert, and the studies of industry groups by Jorgenson and Stephenson and by Resek include measures of the cost of debt and the cost of equity. Secondly, only Eisner, Hickman, Jorgenson and Siebert, and Jorgenson and Stephenson have included depreciation with the cost of capital in the price of capital services. Only

---

[7] This conclusion corroborates the results of Kuh [76, 1963, p. 213].

measures of depreciation by Hickman, Jorgenson and Siebert, and Jorgenson-Stephenson are consistent with the mortality distribution for investment goods that underlies the corresponding measures of capital stock. Only the Jorgenson-Siebert and Jorgenson-Stephenson measures take account of the tax structure. The appropriate cost of capital is a before-tax rate. Eisner measures the rate of return on equity after taxes. Finally, only the Jorgenson-Siebert measure takes account of capital gains. This completes our evaluation of the determinants of desired capital.

4.3. The Time Structure of the Investment Process

The time structure of the investment process has been represented by finite, geometric, and rational distributed lag functions. Finite distributed lag functions are employed by Eisner in studying individual firms and by Resek in studying industry groups. Geometric distributed lag functions are employed without modification by Grunfeld and Kuh. The geometric distributed lag scheme employed by Koyck, with the first weight arbitrary and the remaining weights declining geometrically, has been used by Bourneuf and Eisner in studying investment by industry groups. Hickman has used a similar scheme with the first two weights arbitrary; a closely related distributed lag function is employed by Anderson. Jorgenson and Siebert and Jorgenson and Stephenson employ rational distributed lag functions that include the geometric distributed lag functions used by Koyck and Hickman as special cases.

The characterization of average lags in the investment process from finite, geometric, and rational distributed lag functions can be compared with extensive survey studies of lags between decisions to invest and the start of construction, and between the start of construction and completion made by Thomas Meyer [83, 1960; 82, 1958 and 84, Mayer and Sonenblum, 1955]. Mayer's survey evidence is based on the

study of new industrial plants and plant additions in the United States started in 1954 and 1955. A questionnaire was sent to individual companies, requesting information on lags between drawing of plans, the final decision to build, and the placing of the first significant order to the start of construction [83]. Very extensive studies of the lag from start of construction to completion had been made earlier from data on complete plants from the period of the Korean War and World War II; the two sets of results are very similar [83, p. 130 and 84]. A frequency distribution of lags in invesment projects is given in Table 7. Weighting these results by size of project, Mayer obtains average lags from the drawing of plans to start of construction of six months or two quarters, from placing of first significant order to start of construction of two months, and from start of construction to completion of 15 months or five quarters [83, p. 128]. An unweighted mean for complete plants from start of construction to completion is 11 months, which coincides with the estimate of this lag by Mayer and Sonenblum from data for the period of the Korean War [83, p. 132]. The difference between weighted and unweighted means is explained by a positive correlation between time required for completion and size of plant [83, p. 128]. Mayer obtains a total lag from decision and completion of seven quarters [83, p. 128].[8]

Comparing Mayer's survey results with estimates of average lags from finite distributed lag functions, we find that Eisner's distributed lag functions for individual firms reduce to functions of current and lagged values of profits and the rate of return. The resulting average lags are less than one year in length, which is inconsistent with findings from survey evidence. Weights in the distributed lag functions of Anderson and Resek are partly determined from regressions of investment expenditures on investment appropriations. The distributed lag function

[8] R. E. Krainer [75, 1968] conducted a detailed study of 25 projects in the automobile industry and found results similar to those of Mayer.

TABLE 7

Distribution of Lags in Completion of Investment Projects

	Quarters	Number of Plants	Percent
Drawing of plans to start of construction	0	.8	11
	1	21	29
	2	21	29
	3	10	14
	4 and over	12	17
Total		72	100
Placing of first significant order to start of construction	0	42	54
	1	19	25
	2	12	16
	3 and over	4	5
Total		77	100
Start of construction to completion	2 and under	14	16
	3	24	27
	4	33	37
	5	5	6
	6	6	7
	7 and over	8	9
Total		90	100

Source: Mayer [83, 1960; Table 2, p. 130].

from appropriations to investment estimated by Almon is employed with an additional lag of one quarter as the distributed lag from investment decisions to actual expenditures by Resek. Anderson permits additional lags from the determinants of desired capital to expectations and from expectations to appropriations. Anderson estimates the sum of these lags to be four quarters in length, contradicting Resek's implicit assumption that the lag is one quarter. Our conclusion is that the finite distributed lag functions employed by Resek, like those of Eisner, lead to underestimates of the average lags underlying the investment process.

Mayer's survey results may be compared with Koyck's estimates of the average lag from a geometric distributed lag function. Koyck's model may be represented in the form:

$$\ln K_t = \alpha \ln Y_t + (1 - \alpha - \lambda) \ln Y_{t-1} + \lambda \ln K_{t-1},$$

where Y_t is production and K_t is capacity. Within manufacturing, Koyck's estimates of average lags are 10.20 years for cement, 29.94 years for open hearth blast furnaces, and 5.26 years for petroleum refining.[9] It should be noted that Koyck's pioneering study of investment was completed before Mayer's survey results became available.

A detailed analysis of lag structures estimated from models closely related to Koyck's has been carried out by Kuh in his study of individual firms [76, 1963]. Alternative models employed by Kuh include the first difference model,

$$\Delta A_t = \lambda \beta \, \Delta X_t + (\delta - \lambda) \, \Delta K_t,$$

where A_t is the level of investment, X_t sales, and δ the rate of replacement, the levels

[9] The average lags are for direct estimates under constant returns to scale. The direct estimates are given by Koyck [74, 1954, pp. 99, 104, 106].

model,

$$A_t = \lambda\beta X_t + (\delta - \lambda)K_t,$$

the lagged model,

$$A_t = \lambda\beta X_{t-1} + (\delta - \lambda)K_t,$$

and the average model,

$$A_t = \lambda\beta\tfrac{1}{2}(X_t + X_{t-1}) + (\delta - \lambda)K_t.$$

Average lags for each model estimated from time series are given in Table 8.[10]

TABLE 8

Average Lags for Sixty Manufacturing Firms, Estimated by Kuh

Model	a. $\hat{\lambda} - \hat{\delta}$	b. λ	c. Average Lag (Years)
First difference	.1638	.2033	3.92
Levels	.0010	.0405	23.69
Lagged	−.0040	.0355	28.17
Average	.0150	.0545	17.85

Source: Kuh [76, 1963, Table 9.1, pp. 294–95].

Kuh's estimates for time series data coincide roughly with Koyck's estimates; both sets of results conflict sharply with Mayer's survey evidence.[11] The conflict in evidence implies that the geometric distributed lag function employed by Koyck and by Kuh is mis-specified. This argument has been formalized by Griliches [44, 1967]. If the geometric distributed lag function is applied where a less restrictive form of distributed lag function is appropriate, the omitted variables have the effect of biasing the estimated average lag upward very substantially [44, pp. 36–38].

Koyck's flexible accelerator model of

investment behavior has been modified by Hickman to incorporate an additional lagged term in output [57, 1965, pp. 32–41]. The model employed by Hickman is:

$$\ln K_t = \alpha \ln Y_t + \beta \ln Y_{t-1}$$
$$+ (l - \alpha - \beta - \lambda) \ln Y_{t-2}$$
$$+ \lambda \ln K_{t-1}.$$

Hickman fits this model to annual data on capital stock K_t and real output Y_t, dropping coefficients in the distributed lag function that are not significant. Estimates of the parameters of Hickman's model and average lags derived from these parameters are presented in Table 9. The addition of a third term in real output is required for five of the 13 industry groups analyzed by Hickman. Hickman's estimates of the average lag are much lower than those of Koyck. All of Hickman's estimates for manufacturing industries are below the lowest of Koyck's estimate of 5 years for petroleum

TABLE 9

Average Lags for Thirteen Two-Digit Industries, U.S. Manufacturing, Estimated by Hickman

Industry Group	a. $\hat{\alpha}$	b. $\hat{\beta}$	c. 1-$\hat{\alpha}$-$\hat{\beta}$-$\hat{\lambda}$	d. Average Lag (Years)
Primary metals	.1297	.2383	.1110	2.05
Machinery	.1508	.0975		3.42
Motor vehicles	.1132	.1859		2.96
Transportation equipment	.2715	.0369	.3232	1.67
Stone, clay, and glass	.1837	.0663	.0012	3.25
Other durables	.2597	.1224		1.94
Food and beverages	.0029	.3343		2.96
Textiles	.1577	.1832	.0278	2.36
Paper	.1685	.2321		2.08
Chemicals	.1317	.3477	.1826	1.59
Petroleum	.1503	.2639		2.05
Rubber	.2085	.2342		1.79
Other non-durables	.0816	.2488		2.78

Source: Hickman [57, 1965, Tables 4 and 5, pp. 54–56].

[10] Estimates of the average lags are based on the depreciation adjusted capital stock slope; the capital stock slopes are estimated from the "B-regression" results. The annual depreciation rate used in this adjustment is .0395 [76, Kuh, 1963, Table 9.1, pp. 294–95, 296].

[11] Koyck's estimates for manufacturing range from 20 to 120 quarters; Kuh's estimates range from 16 to 115 quarters. Mayer's estimate is seven quarters.

refining. Although Hickman's estimates appear to be somewhat higher than the average lags suggested by Mayer's survey evidence, the bias is reduced very substantially relative to the estimates of Koyck and Kuh. Our conclusion is that the modified geometric distributed lag functions employed by Hickman provide an adequate representation of the investment process, but that the geometric distributed lag functions used by Koyck and Kuh do not.

Meyer and Glauber employ a lag scheme with weights alternatively zero and declining geometrically. This pattern of weights appears to be highly implausible. Evans employs a lag scheme with geometrically declining weights for both dependent and independent variables. The rate at which weights decline is the same for both sets of variables. This pattern of weights also appears to be implausible.

To complete our evaluation of alternative characterizations of the time structure of the investment process, we consider estimates of average lags from rational distributed lag functions by Jorgenson and Siebert for annual data on investment by individual firms and by Jorgenson and Stephenson for quarterly data for industry groups. Jorgenson and Siebert select the best-fitting lag distribution from rational distributed lag functions of the form:

$$\Delta K_t = \gamma_0 \, \Delta K_t^+ + \gamma_1 \, \Delta K_{t-1}^+ + \gamma_2 \, \Delta K_{t-3}^+ - \omega_1 \, \Delta K_{t-1} - \omega_2 \, \Delta K_{t-2},$$

where:

$$\gamma_0 + \gamma_1 + \gamma_2 = 1 - \omega_1 - \omega_2.$$

Average lags estimated for 1949–63 and for 1937–41, 1949–63 for the Neoclassical I model are given in Table 10 [65, 1968, p. 1145]. Jorgenson and Stephenson select the best-fitting lag distribution from functions of the form:

$$\Delta K_t = \sum_{\tau=0}^{7} \gamma_\tau \Delta K_{t-\tau}^+ - \omega_1 \Delta K_{t-1} - \omega_2 \Delta K_{t-2},$$

where:

$$\sum_{\tau=2}^{7} \gamma_\tau = 1 + \omega_1 + \omega_2.$$

TABLE 10

Average Lags for Fifteen U.S. Manufacturing Firms Estimated by Jorgenson and Siebert

Firm	Average Lag (Years)	
	1949–63	*1937–41, 1949–63*
General Motors	1.01	2.17
Goodyear	.32	.63
American Can	3.15	2.74
Pittsburgh Plate Glass	1.49	2.06
U.S. Steel	1.61	1.18
General Electric	1.61	1.55
Reynolds Tobacco	2.12	2.62
Du Pont	1.00	1.00
Anaconda	1.80	1.42
Standard Oil, N. J.	.83	.50
International Paper	.45	1.44
Westinghouse Air Brake	.37	.68
International Business Machines	.48	.47
Swift	1.09	1.51
Westinghouse Electric	2.37	2.64

Source: 1949–63: Jorgenson and Siebert, [65, 1968, Table 6, p. 1145]. 1937–41, 1949–63: Siebert, personal communication.

Average lags estimated for the period 1949, first quarter to 1950, fourth quarter, are given in Table 11 [68, 1967, pp. 21–22].

The results of Jorgenson and Stephenson for industry groups are similar to those of Hickman; both sets of estimates are somewhat higher than Mayer's survey estimate. The results of Jorgenson and Siebert for individual firms vary more widely than results for industry groups. On the whole their estimates of average lags for individual firms are lower than estimates for industry groups and agree more closely with Mayer's survey results. Our overall conclusion is that the rational distributed lag functions employed by Hickman and by Jorgenson and Siebert for annual data and by Jorgenson and Stephenson for quarterly data provide satisfactory representations of the time structure of the investment process. In

TABLE 11
Average Lags for Fifteen Two-Digit Industries,
U.S. Manufacturing, Estimated
by Jorgenson and Stephenson

Industry Group	Average Lag (Years)
Primary metals	2.27
Primary nonferrous metals	2.06
Electrical machinery	1.76
Non-electrical machinery	1.77
Motor vehicles	2.68
Nonautomotive	2.20
Stone, clay, and glass	1.95
Other durables	1.69
Food and beverages	2.19
Textiles	2.06
Paper	2.82
Chemicals	1.77
Petroleum	1.93
Rubber	1.50
Other nondurables	1.50

Source: Jorgenson and Stephenson [68, 1967; Table 2, pp. 21–22].

these studies the typical shape of the lag distribution is first rising and then falling; in the geometric lag distribution the lag coefficients are always falling. This may help to account for the pronounced difference in empirical results for studies based on the geometric distribution and studies based on generalizations of this distribution. This completes our evaluation of alternative representations of the time structure.

4.4. Replacement Investment

Except for Evans' study of investment by industry groups, studies that includes replacement investment explicitly employ the geometric mortality distribution for investment goods. Eisner, Grunfeld, Jorgenson and Siebert, and Kuh employ this distribution in the study of investment by individual firms. Bourneuf, Eisner, Hickman, Jorgenson and Stephenson, and Resek employ this distribution in the study of investment by industry groups. Bourneuf, like Chenery and Koyck, employs capacity as a measure of capital stock. Implicitly, Bourneuf assumes that the capital-capacity ratio is constant. The studies of Anderson and Meyer and Glauber do not include replacement investment.

The geometric mortality distribution implies that replacement is proportional to capital stock. It also implies that capital stock is a weighted sum of past gross investments with geometrically declining weights. An internally consistent model of replacement investment based on the proportionality of replacement and capital stock requires a measure of capital stock that employs the geometric mortality distribution [57, Hickman, 1965; 59, Jorgenson, 1963; 60, Jorgenson, 1965]. The studies of industry groups by Eisner, Hickman, Jorgenson and Stephenson, and Resek and the study of individual firms by Jorgenson and Siebert are internally consistent and employs an appropriate measure of capital stock.[12]

In the study of investment by individual firms, Eisner and Kuh assume that replacement is proportional to gross capital stock, an unweighted sum of past gross investments net of retirements. This assumption is inconsistent with a geometric mortality distribution for capital goods. Eisner makes no attempt to revalue acquisitions and retirements for changes in the price of acquisition of investment goods. Kuh revalues both acquisitions and retirements.

Grunfeld assumes that replacement is proportional to net capital stock, gross capital stock less accumulated depreciation. Both acquisitions of investment goods and depreciation are revalued to correct for changes in the price of acquisition of investment goods. Accounting depreciation during the period considered by Grunfeld is based on the straight line method rather than the declining balance method implied by the geometric mortality distribution for investment goods.

[12] Eisner and Resek use the capital stock data of Jorgenson and Stephenson. Hickman employs his own estimates.

Evans' study employs the assumption that replacement investment is proportional to the average of capital stock held five and six quarters earlier. This assumption is not tested. Capital stock is measured as net capital stock, which is inconsistent with the mortality distribution for investment goods employed in Evans' model of replacement investment. Net capital stock in each period is deflated by the investment goods price index. Evans, like Eisner, does not attempt to correct acquisitions of investment goods for past changes in the price of acquisition.

Although the geometric mortality distribution is commonly employed in the estimation of replacement requirements, relatively little direct evidence is available on the validity of this distribution. Meyer and Kuh have studied the "echo effect" in analyzing data for individual firms [86, 1957, pp. 91–100]. An extreme form of the "echo effect" is associated with a periodic mortality distribution, resulting in a periodic distribution of replacements and periodic cycles of replacement investment [39, Feller, 1957, pp. 290–93]. A weaker form of the echo effect is associated with relatively high values of the replacement distribution at particular ages. This is the form of the echo effect tested by Meyer and Kuh. The age of a firm's capital equipment is measured by accumulated depreciation reserves divided by gross fixed assets at the beginning of the period. Firms are divided into 15 industry groups within manufacturing, corresponding roughly to two-digit industries [86, 1957, pp. 209–32]. The dependent variable is gross investment divided by gross fixed assets on the grounds ". . . that since replacement investment is included in gross investment the net impact of the echo effect should be ascertainable even when using gross investment as the dependent variable—although perhaps not as precisely as would be desirable" [86, p. 93].

Meyer and Kuh employ a profit model and a sales model to explain gross investment. In regressions for averages of annual data over the period 1946–50, the age variable is significant in both models for only one industry group—Vehicles and Suppliers; age

is significantly negative for this industry, suggesting high rates of replacement for low ages of capital goods [86, pp. 255–56]. For other industry groups the age variable is both positive and negative with small negative values predominating. Age is significantly negative for Light Chemicals in the sales model but not in the profits model. The proportion of significant results—3 out of 30 regressions—is not out of line with the null hypothesis that the echo effect plays no role in the determination of investment for individual firms.

M. S. Feldstein and D. K. Foot have attempted to construct a model of replacement investment based on estimates of replacement investment from the McGraw-Hill Survey and estimates of capital stock from the Department of Commerce [38, 1971]. The capital stock estimates imply separate estimates of replacement investment, so the two bodies of data employed by Feldstein and Foot are mutually inconsistent. They assume that replacement as a proportion of gross capital stock depends on variables such as cash flow and capacity utilization. The hypothesis that the replacement rate depends on cash flow or capacity utilization is inconsistent with the perpetual inventory method used by the Department of Commerce in estimating capital stock.

Feldstein and Foot attempt to test the hypothesis that the replacement rate is constant. This hypothesis would be true only if the replacement rate is calculated as the ratio of replacement investment to capital stock, and only if capital stock is estimated by the declining balance method. Under these circumstances the test proposed by Feldstein and Foot is superfluous since the average replacement rate is constant by definition. We conclude that Feldstein and Foot have not successfully avoided the necessity for direct observation of both replacement investment and capital stock in a test of the model of replacement they propose. Perpetual inventory estimates of capital stock such as the estimates of the Department of Commerce cannot be employed in such a test.

An alternative approach to the empirical study of mortality distributions is through the analysis of used equipment prices. Data on used equipment prices are limited to readily movable assets. A study of price data for farm tractors is reported by Griliches [43, 1960] and studies of price data for automobiles are presented by P. Cagan [12, 1965] and F. Wykoff [107, 1970]. A much more intensive study of price data for pick-up trucks is given by Hall [50, 1971]. Used equipment prices, like prices for acquisition of new equipment, are equal to the sum of future rental prices weighted by the relative efficiency of the capital good over its remaining lifetime. For geometric decline in efficiency the acquisition prices decline geometrically with age. We now review the evidence on decline in relative efficiency from data on used equipment prices.

Studies of prices of acquisition of new and used capital goods reveal a sharp drop between the price of new equipment and the price of used equipment. The obvious explanation is that prices of new equipment are "list" prices paid by relatively few purchasers. The actual prices paid vary over a model year, declining as a new model year approaches; this variation is omitted from the observed list prices. The prices of used equipment are based on actual transactions and vary over the year [43, 1960, p. 198]. From an examination of prices of used farm tractors, ages one to 13, for ten different points of time during the years 1937–58, Griliches concludes: "The data point to a declining balance [geometric] depreciation model, with a rate somewhat higher in the 1930's than in the 1950's" [43, p. 198]. Wykoff's findings for used automobiles, ages one to seven, for five different points of time during the years 1950–68, are similar [107, 1970, pp. 171–72]: "After the first year cars do appear to decay exponentially [geometrically]." Cagan also finds that geometric depreciation provides a satisfactory approximation [12, 1965, pp. 225–26].

Hall studied data for second-hand pick-up trucks, ages one to six, for the years 1961–67. He concludes [50, 1971] that: "... the geo-

metric [mortality distribution] function is probably a reasonable approximation for many purposes. Certainly, there are no grounds for believing that any very serious error has been comitted by using a geometric deterioration function in calculating capital stock." We conclude that Hall's study of the mortality distribution for pick-up trucks supports the conclusions of Cagan, Griliches, and Wykoff for automobiles and farm tractors. The geometric mortality distribution explains the behavior of used equipment prices for all three types of capital goods. The empirical evidence from studies of equipment prices supports the findings of Meyer and Kuh from an analysis of replacement requirements. This completes our evaluation of models of replacement investment.

4.5. Conclusion

The point of departure for the large body of empirical research on investment behavior during the past decade has been the flexible accelerator model of Chenery and Koyck. This model has been gradually modified and extended under the impact of new empirical findings, but its basic outlines have found substantial empirical support. Desired capital is determined by long-run considerations; changes in desired capital are translated into investment expenditures by a distributed lag function. This model provides an explanation of net investment in all of the empirical studies we have reviewed.

Alternative models of investment behavior differ substantially in the determinants of desired capital. The empirical evidence now available provides a means of discriminating among competing hypotheses on the basis of their performance. First, real output emerges as the most important single determinant of investment expenditures. Considered as a competing model of investment, the profits or liquidity model of Tinbergen and Klein is definitely inferior. A second important determinant of investment is the availability of finance. The introduction of financial considerations with variations in output necessitates substantial modification of the flexible accelerator model of Chenery and Koyck.

Financial considerations can be introduced into a model of investment expenditures in two forms: internal funds or liquidity and external funds or the cost of capital. These two alternative formulations are associated with the theories of finance of Duesenberry and Meyer and Kuh and of Modigliani and Miller, respectively. The evidence clearly favors the Modigliani-Miller theory. Internal liquidity is not an important determinant of investment, given the level of output and the cost of external funds.

A second extension of the flexible accelerator model necessitated by empirical evidence is the incorporation of replacement requirements. A model of replacement investment based on the geometric mortality distribution is used in all empirical studies that incorporate replacement explicitly. This model has important implications for the measurement of capital stock and the associated rental price. Capital stock is measured in a way that is inconsistent with the geometric mortality distribution in many of the studies of investment we have reviewed.

The durable goods model is characterized by price-quantity duality. This duality provides a means of integrating financial and real determinants of desired capital into a model of producer behavior. The implications of the durable goods model for measurement of the price of capital services have been developed only recently. In all but a few studies we have reviewed, the cost of capital services is measured in a way that fails to reflect the underlying durable goods model. The price side of the durable goods model has been extended recently to incorporate details of the tax structure, providing a direct link between economic policy and the determinants of investment expenditures [7a, 1971, pp. 15, 51–53].

Given the validity of the model for durable capital goods that underlies aggregate capital stock, a subsidiary problem is the validity of the geometric mortality distribution. Direct tests of the corresponding models of replacement requirements and capital goods prices support the geometric distribution. A

test of the validity of the durable-goods model itself would require a well defined alternative theory of replacement that does not employ an aggregate measure of capital. A corresponding theory of the cost of the use of durable equipment would also be required.

Chenery and Koyck employed the geometric distributed lag function in representing the time structure of the investment process. The empirical evidence we have reviewed suggests that the resulting estimates of average lags are biased upward very substantially. Rational distributed lag functions employed by Anderson, Hickman, Jorgenson and Siebert, and Jorgenson and Stephenson produce estimates of the average lags consistent with survey evidence on the lag structure; for manufacturing, the average lag between the determinants of investment and actual expenditures is from one and a half to two years. The average lag varies among industries and among firms and, of course, among projects within a firm.

In the study of investment behavior the most important current problem is the integration of the time structure of the investment process into the representation of technology. Models retaining the durable goods model of capital and augmenting the production function with internal adjustment costs have been proposed by Lucas [81, 1967], Uzawa [106, 1969], and Treadway [105, 1969]. These models of technology may be approximated by distributed lag investment functions. An important secondary problem is the time structure of financial determinants of investment; Bischoff [7a] has suggested that real output and the cost of capital should have separate lag structures in the determination of investment expenditures.

At a more basic level the most important open question in the study of investment is the integration of uncertainty into the theory and econometrics of investment. The Modigliani-Miller theory of finance underlying recent studies of investment already incorporates some aspects of uncertainty. A more thoroughgoing integration would require the simultaneous determination of production, investment, financial policy, and security prices. This ambitious goal appears to be well within the range of existing economic theory and econometric technique.

In the past decade the econometric study of investment behavior has developed from empirical comparisons of alternative determinants to increasingly explicit theories of producer behavior. Investment research has been an important area for the development and testing of new models of production and finance. It has been the principal area for the development of new econometric techniques for representation of the time structure of economic behavior. The implications of the new approach to the study of investment are far from exhausted.

References

1. Almon, S. "The Distributed Lag between Capital Appropriations and Expenditures," *Econometrica*, Jan. 1965, *33*(1), pp. 178–196.

2. Anderson, W. H. L. "Business Fixed Investment: A Marriage of Fact and Fancy" in Ferber, R., ed. *Determinants of investment behavior*. Universities-National Bureau Conference Series, No. 18. New York: Columbia University Press for the National Bureau of Economic Research, 1967.

3. _____, *Corporate finance, and fixed investment, an econometric study*. Boston: Division of Research, Graduate School of Business Administration, Harvard University, 1964.

4. Arrow, K. J.; Chenery, H. B.; Minhas, B. S. and Solow, R. M. "Capital-Labor Substitution and Economic Efficiency," *Rev. Econ. Statist.*, Aug. 1961, *43*(3), pp. 225–50.

5. Bain, J. S. *Barriers to new competition*. Cambridge: Harvard University Press, 1956.

6. _____, "Survival-Ability as a Test of Efficiency," *Amer. Econ. Rev.*, May 1969, *59*(2), pp. 99–104.

7. Bell, F. W. "A Note on the Empirical Estimation of the CES Production Function with the Use of Capital Data," *Rev. Econ. Statist.*, Aug. 1965, *47*(3), pp. 328–330.

7a. Bischoff, C. W. "The Effect of Alternative Lag Distributions" in Fromm, G., ed. *Tax incentives and capital spending*. Washington, D.C.: Brookings Institution, 1971.

8. _____, "A Model of Nonresidential Construction in the United States," *Amer. Econ. Rev.*, May 1970, *60*(2), pp. 10–17.

9. _____, "Hypothesis Testing and the Demand for Capital Goods," *Rev. Econ. Statist.*, Aug. 1969, *51*(3), pp. 354–368.

10. Bourneuf, A. "Manufacturing Investment, Excess Capacity and the Rate of Growth of Output," *Amer. Econ. Rev.*, Sept. 1964, *54*(5), pp. 607–625.

11. Brown, M. *The theory and empirical analysis of production*. Studies in Income and Wealth, Vol. 31. New York: Columbia University Press, 1967.

12. Cagan, P. "Measuring Quality Changes and the Purchasing Power of Money: An Exploratory Study of Automobiles," *National Banking Rev.*, Dec. 1965, *3*, pp. 217–236.

13. Chenery, H. B. "Overcapacity and the Acceleration Principle," *Econometrica*, Jan. 1952, *20*(1), pp. 1–28.

14. Clark, J. M. "Business Acceleration and the Law of Demand: A Technical Factor in Economic Cycles," *J. Polit. Econ.*, March 1917, *25*(1), pp. 217–235.

15. Coen, R. M. "The Effect of Cash Flow on the Speed of Adjustment" in Fromm, G., ed. *Tax incentives and capital spending*. Washington, D.C.: Brookings Institution, 1971.

16. _____, "Effects of Tax Policy on Investment in Manufacturing," *Amer. Econ. Rev.*, May 1968, *58*(2), pp. 200–211.

17. _____, "Tax Policy and Investment Behavior: Comment," *Amer. Econ. Rev.*, June 1969, *59*(3), pp. 370–377.

18. Commission on Money and Credit. *Impacts of monetary policy*. Englewood Cliffs, N.J.: Prentice-Hall, 1964.

19. Dhrymes, P. J. "Some Extensions and Tests for CES class of Production Functions," *Rev. Econ. Statist.*, Nov. 1965, *47*(4), pp. 357–366.

20. Dhrymes, P. J. and Kurtz, M. "Investment, Dividends, and External Finance Behavior of Firms," in Ferber, R., ed. *Determinants of investment behavior*. Universities-National Bureau Conference Series, No. 18. New York: Columbia University Press for the National Bureau of Economic Research, 1967.

21. Diamond, J. J. "Further Development of a Distributed Lag Investment Function," *Econometrica*, Oct. 1962, *30*(4), pp. 788–800.

22. Duesenberry, J. S. *Business cycles and economic growth*. New York: McGraw-Hill, 1958.

23. Duesenberry, J. S.; Fromm, G.; Klein, L. R. and Kuh, E., eds. *The Brookings quarterly*

model of the United States. Amsterdam: North-Holland, 1965.

24. Eckstein, O. "Manufacturing Investment and Business Expectations: Extensions of de Leeuw's Results," *Econometrica*, April 1965, *33*(2), pp. 420–424.

25. Eisner, R. "Capital Expenditures, Profits and the Acceleration Principle" in *Models of income determination.* Studies in Income and Wealth, Vol. 28. Princeton: Princeton University Press, 1964.

26. _____, "A Distributed Lag Investment Function," *Econometrica*, Jan. 1960, *28*(1), pp. 1–29.

27. _____, "Investment: Fact and Fancy," *Amer. Econ. Rev.*, May 1963, *53*(2), pp. 237–246.

28. _____, "Investment and the Frustrations of Econometricians," *Amer. Econ. Rev.*, May 1969, *59*(2), pp. 50–64.

29. _____, "Investment Plans and Realizations," *Amer. Econ. Rev.*, May 1962, *52*(2). pp. 190–203.

30. _____, "A Permanent Income Theory for Investment," *Amer. Econ. Rev.*, June 1967, *57*(3), pp. 363–390.

31. _____, "Realization of Investment Anticipations" in Duesenberry, J.; Fromm, G.; Klein, L. R. and Kuh, E., eds. *The Brookings quarterly model of the United States.* Amsterdam: North Holland, 1965.

32. _____, "Tax Policy and Investment Behavior: Comment," *Amer. Econ. Rev.*, June 1969, *59*(3), pp. 378–387.

33. _____, "Tax Policy and Investment Behavior: Further Comment," *Amer. Econ. Rev.*, Sept. 1970, *60*(4), pp. 746–752.

34. Eisner, R. and Nadiri, M. I. "Investment Behavior and the Neo-Classical Theory," *Rev. Econ. Statist.*, August 1968, *50*(3), pp. 369–382.

35. _____, "Neoclassical Theory of Investment Behavior: A Comment," *Rev. Econ. Statist.*, May 1970, *52*(2), pp. 216–222.

36. Eisner, R. and Strotz, R. H. "Determinants of Business Investment" in Commission on Money and Credit, *Impacts of monetary policy.* Prentice-Hall: Englewood Cliffs, N.J., 1963.

37. Evans, M. K. "A Study of Industry Investment Decisions," *Rev. Econ. Statist.*, May 1967, *49*(2), pp. 151–164.

38. Feldstein, M. S. and Foot, D. K. "The Other Half of Gross Investment: Replacement and Modernization Expenditures," *Rev. Econ. Statist.*, Feb. 1971, *53*(1), pp. 49–58.

39. Feller, W. *An introduction to probability theory and its applications,* Vol. I. 2nd ed. New York: Wiley and Sons, 1957.

40. Ferber, R. *Determinants of investment behavior.* Universities-National Bureau Conference Series, No. 18. New York: Columbia University Press for the National Bureau of Economic Research, 1967.

41. Fromm, G. *Tax incentives and capital spending.* Washington, D.C.: Brookings Institution, 1971.

42. Greenberg, E. "A Stock Adjustment Investment Model," *Econometrica*, July 1964, *32*(3), pp. 339–357.

43. Griliches, Z. "The Demand for Durable Input: U.S. Farm Tractors, 1921–57" in Harberger, A. C., ed. *The demand for durable goods.* Chicago: University of Chicago Press, 1960.

44. _____, "Distributed Lags, A Survey," *Econometrica*, Jan. 1967, *35*(1), pp. 16–19.

45. _____, "More on CES Production Functions," *Rev. Econ. Statist.*, Nov. 1967, *49*(4), pp. 608–610.

46. _____, "Production Functions in Manufacturing: Some Preliminary Results" in Brown, M., ed. *The theory and empirical analysis of production.* Studies in Income and Wealth, Vol. 31. New York: Columbia University Press, 1967.

47. _____, "Production Functions in Manufacturing: Some Additional Results," *Southern Econ. J.*, Oct. 1968, *35*(2), pp. 151–156.

48. Griliches, Z. and Wallace, N. "The Determinants of Investment Revisited," *Int. Econ. Rev.*, Sept. 1965, *6*(3), pp. 311–329.

49. Grunfeld, Y. "The Determinants of Corporate Investment" in Harberger, A. C., ed. *The demand for durable goods.* Chicago: University of Chicago Press, 1960.

50. Hall, R. E. "The Measurement of Quality Change from Vintage Price Data" in Griliches, Z., ed. *Price indexes and quality change.* Cambridge: Harvard University Press, 1971.

51. Hall, R. E. and Jorgenson, D. W. "Tax Policy and Investment Behavior," *Amer. Econ. Rev.*, June 1967, *57*(3), pp. 391–414.

52. _____, "Tax Policy and Investment Behavior: Reply and Further Results," *Amer. Econ. Rev.*, June 1969, *59*(3), pp. 388–401.

53. _____, "Application of the Theory of Optimum Capital Accumulation" in Fromm, G., ed. *Tax incentives and capital spending.* Washington, D.C.: Brookings Institution, 1971.

54. Hammer, F. S. *The demand for physical capital: Application of a wealth model.* Englewood Cliffs, N.J.: Prentice-Hall, 1964.

55. Harberger, A. C., ed. *The demand for durable goods*. Chicago: University of Chicago Press, 1960.

56. Hickman, B. "Capacity, Capacity Utilization, and the Acceleration Principle" in *Problems of capital formation*. Studies in Income and Wealth, Vol. 19. Princeton: Princeton University Press, 1957.

57. _____, *Investment demand and U.S. economic growth*. Washington, D.C.: The Brookings Institution, 1965.

58. Hymer, S. and Pashigian, P. "Firm Size and Rate of Growth," *J. Polit. Econ.*, Dec. 1962, *70*(6), pp. 556–569.

59. _____, "Capital Theory and Investment Behavior," *Amer. Econ. Rev.*, May 1963, *53*(2), pp. 247–259.

60. Jorgenson, D. W. "Anticipations and Investment Behavior" in Duesenberry, J. S.; Fromm, G.; Klein, L. R. and Kuh, E., eds. *The Brookings quarterly model of the United States*. Amsterdam: North Holland, 1965.

61. _____, "Investment Behavior and the Production Function" (unpublished).

62. Jorgenson, D. W.; Hunter, J. and Nadiri, M. I. "A Comparison of Alternative Econometric Models of Corporate Investment Behavior," *Econometrica*, March 1970, *38*(2), pp. 187–212.

63. _____, "The Predictive Performance of Econometric Models of Quarterly Investment Behavior," *Econometrica*, March 1970, *38*(2), pp. 213–224.

64. Jorgenson, D. W. and Siebert, C. D. "A Comparison of Alternative Theories of Corporate Investment Behavior," *Amer. Econ. Rev.*, Sept. 1968, *58*(4), pp. 681–712.

65. _____, "Optimal Capital Accumulation and Corporate Investment Behavior," *J. Polit. Econ.*, Nov.-Dec. 1968, *76*(6), pp. 1123–1151.

66. Jorgenson, D. W. and Stephenson, J. A. "Anticipations and Investment Behavior in U.S. Manufacturing, 1947–1960," *J. Amer. Statist. Assoc.*, March 1969, *64*(325), pp. 67–87.

67. _____, "Investment Behavior in U.S. Manufacturing, 1947–1960," *Econometrica*, April 1967, *35*(2), pp. 169–220.

68. _____, "The Time Structure of Investment Behavior in U.S. Manufacturing, 1947–1960." *Rev. Econ. Statist.*, Feb. 1967, *49*(1), pp. 16–27.

69. Kamerschen, D. R. "Market Growth and Industry Concentration," *J. Amer. Statist. Assoc.*, March 1968, *63*(321), pp. 228–41. 241.

70. Klein, L. R. *Economic fluctuations in the United States, 1921–1941*. Cowles Commission for Research in Economics, Monograph No. 11. New York: John Wiley and Sons, 1950.

71. _____, "Studies in Investment Behavior" in *Conference on business cycles*. Universities-National Bureau Conference Series, No. 2. New York: Columbia University Press for the National Bureau of Economic Research, 1951.

72. Klein, L. R. and Preston, R. S. "Some New Results in the Measurement of Capacity Utilization," *Amer. Econ. Rev.*, March 1967, *57*(1), pp. 34–58.

73. Klein, L. R. and Taubman, P. "Estimating Effects within a Complete Econometric Model," in Fromm, G., ed. *Tax incentives and capital spending*. Washington, D.C.: Brookings Institution, 1971.

74. Koyck, L. M. *Distributed lags and investment analysis*. Amsterdam: North-Holland, 1954.

75. Krainer, R. E. "The Time Profile of Capital Accumulation in the Automobile Industry," *J. Polit. Econ.*, Sept.–Oct. 1968, *76*(5), pp. 1049–1957.

76. Kuh, E. *Capital stock growth: A micro-econometric approach*. Amsterdam: North-Holland, 1963.

77. Kuznets, S. *Capital in the American economy*. Princeton: Princeton University Press, 1961.

78. _____, "Relation between Capital Goods and Finished Products in the Business Cycle" in *Economic Essays in Honor of Wesley Clair Mitchell*. New York: Columbia University Press, 1935.

79. De Leeuw, F. "The Demand for Capital Goods by Manufacturers: A Study of Quarterly Time Series," *Econometrica*, July 1962, *30*(3), pp. 407–423.

80. Lintner, J. "Corporation Finance: Risk and Investment" in Ferber, R., ed. *Determinants of investment behavior*. Universities-National Bureau Conference Series, No. 18. New York: Columbia University Press for the National Bureau of Economic Research, 1967.

81. Lucas, R. E., Jr. "Adjustment Costs and the Theory of Supply," *J. Polit. Econ.*, August 1967, *75*(4), pp. 321–334.

82. Mayer, T. "The Inflexibility of Monetary Policy," *Rev. Econ. Statist.*, Nov. 1958, *40*(4), pp. 358–374.

83. _____, "Plant and Equipment Lead Times," *J. Bus.*, April 1960, *33*(2), pp. 127–132.

84. Mayer, T. and Sonenblum, S. "Lead Times for Fixed Investment," *Rev. Econ. Statist.*, August 1955, *37*(3), pp. 300–304.

85. Meyer, J. and Glauber, R. *Investment decisions, economic forecasting, and public policy.* Boston: Division of Research, Graduate School of Business Administration, Harvard University, 1964.

86. Meyer, J. and Kuh, E. *The Investment decision.* Cambridge, Mass.: Harvard University Press, 1957.

87. [Mitchell, Wesley Clair.] *Economic essays in honor of Wesley Clair Mitchell.* New York: Columbia University Press, 1935.

88. Modigliani, F. and Miller, M. H. "Corporate Income Taxes and the Cost of Capital: A Correction," *Amer. Econ. Rev.,* June 1963, *53*(3), pp. 433–443.

89. _____, "The Cost of Capital, Corporation Finance, and the Theory of Investment," *Amer. Econ. Rev.,* June 1958, *48*(3), pp. 261–297.

90. _____, "The Cost of Capital, Corporation Finance and the Theory of Investment: A Reply," *Amer. Econ. Rev.,* June 1965, *55*(3), pp. 524–527.

91. _____, "Dividend Policy, Growth, and the Valuation of Shares," *J. Bus.,* Oct. 1961, *34*(4), pp. 411–433.

92. _____, "Dividend Policy and Market Valuation: A Reply," *J. Bus.,* Jan. 1963, *36*(1), pp. 112–119.

93. _____, "Reply to Heins and Sprenkle," *Amer. Econ. Rev.,* Sept. 1969, *59*(4), pp. 592–595.

94. _____, "Reply to Rose and Durand," *Amer. Econ. Rev.,* Sept. 1959, *49*(4), pp. 655–659.

95. _____, "Some Estimates of the Cost of capital to the Electric Utility Industry, 1954–1957," *Amer. Econ. Rev.,* June 1966, *56*(3), pp. 333–391.

96. _____, "Some Estimates of the Cost of Capital to the Electric Utility Industry, 1954–1957: Reply," *Amer. Econ. Rev.,* Dec. 1967, *57*(5), pp. 1288–1300.

97. Mueller, D. C. "The Firm Decision Process: An Econometric Investigation," *Quart. J. Econ.,* Feb. 1967, *81*(322), pp. 58–87.

98. Resek, R. W. "Investment by Manufacturing Firms: A Quarterly Time Series Analysis of Industry Data," *Rev. Econ. Statist.,* August 1966, *48*(3), pp. 322–333.

99. Scheffé, H. *The analysis of variance.* New York: John Wiley and Sons, 1959.

100. Schramm, R. "The Influence of Relative Prices, Production Conditions and Adjustment Costs on Investment Behavior," *Rev. Econ. Stud.,* July 1970, *37*(3), pp. 361–376.

101. Stigler, G. J. *Capital and rates of return in manufacturing.* Princeton: Princeton University Press, 1963.

102. Thurow, L. C. "A Disequilibrium Neoclassical Investment Function," *Rev. Econ. Statist.,* Nov. 1969, *51*(4), pp. 431–435.

103. Tinbergen, J. "Statistical Evidence on the Acceleration Principle," *Economica,* May 1938, *5*(2), pp. 164–176.

104. _____, "A Method and its Application to Investment Activity" in *Statistical testing of business cycle theories.* Vol. I. Geneva: League of Nations, 1939.

105. Treadway, A. B. "On Rational Entrepreneurial Behavior and the Demand for Invesment," *Rev. Econ. Stud.,* April 1969, *36*(106), pp. 227–239.

106. Uzawa, H. "Time Preference and the Penrose Effect in a Two-Class Model of Economic Growth," *J. Polit. Econ.,* July–August 1969, *77*(4), pp. 628–652.

107. Wykoff, F. "Capital Depreciation in the Postwar Period: Automobiles," *Rev. Econ. Statist.,* May 1970, *52*(2), pp. 168–172.

108. Zarembka, P. "On the Empirical Relevance of the CES Production Function," *Rev. Econ. Statist.,* Feb. 1970, *52*(1), pp. 47–53.

109. Zarembka, P. and Chernicoff, H. "Further Results on the Empirical Relevance of the CES Production Function." Institute of International Studies, Technical Report No. 29. Berkeley: University of California, 1969.

Econometric Studies of Investment Behavior: A Comment

Robert Eisner

Northwestern University

I. INTRODUCTION—FRAMEWORK OF ANALYSIS

In an attempt to offer a systematic presentation of a number of the vast set of studies in investment generally subsequent to those reviewed by Meyer and Kuh [51] and Eisner and Strotz [24], Dale W. Jorgenson, in his recent "Econometric Studies of Investment Behavior: A Survey" [40], has understandably sought some broad framework for analysis. The framework he has chosen is, largely, his own approach to the study of investment. This approach projects three main elements in an investment function: 1) determination of desired capital stocks; 2) an adjustment process over time whereby investment (positive or negative) moves the existing capital stock toward its (changing) desired levels; and 3) a decay or depreciation function which indicates how much of gross capital expenditures will be absorbed in mere replacement of existing capital. Jorgenson examines the various studies in terms of their contributions to these three aspects of the subject. But within his framework of analysis, certain of Jorgenson's particular positions loom large and concerns of others, where not rejected, are frequently ignored. The purpose of this paper is to review some of the same studies from a rather different point of view. If my remarks seem to focus unduly on issues and on work in which I have been personally involved, I hope this may be attributed to my own limitations of time and space and that others will find the opportunity to enlarge the discussion in other directions where that seems appropriate.[1]

II. DETERMINANTS OF DESIRED CAPITAL

The desired capital stock should depend upon expected future output, expectations of the future production function, and current and expected future prices.[2] Most studies, including Jorgenson's, have taken some presumed function of current and past rates of output as proxies for expected future output, with little consideration of the question of stability or even existence of such a function. But if "real output emerges as the most important single determinant of investment expenditures," as Jorgenson concludes (p. 1141), what must be fundamental is the relation between ex post changes in demand and changes in the expectation of future output. One approach to dealing with this is to recognize that where business decision-

1. One such contribution is now provided in L. R. Klein [47].

2. More generally, abandoning implicit as well as explicit assumptions of perfect competition, desired capital stock should depend upon production functions and supply and demand functions for inputs and outputs, as perceived by business decisions-makers.

Reprinted from the *Economic Inquiry*, 12:91–103 (1974), by permission of the authors and the publisher (copyright by the Western Economic Association).

makers have reason to view changes in demand as "permanent," altering significantly their perception of expected future demand and output, investment should be more affected than where changes in demand are viewed as largely transitory. Jorgenson's consideration of expectational relations in estimates of the role of demand, capacity, or the accelerator is limited to the cryptic sentences (p. 116):

Eisner presents regressions for cross sections of firms and for industry time series and cross sections. His own analysis of the results attempts to relate differences in estimates of the factors affecting investment "to differing permanent and transitory components in the relevant variances and covariances [18, 1967, p. 386]." A detailed summary of this analysis is presented by Eisner in his 1967 work [18, pp. 386–87].

Jorgenson ignores in his survey (and in his own work) the critical issue of the relation between the various parameters of current price and their relevant expected future values. How much a change in present rates of interest and business taxation, depreciation allowances, or equipment credits will affect investment must surely depend upon how such changes relate to expectations of future values of these variables. By tying all of these factors into one pre-specified composite "c, the rental price of capital," Jorgenson tethers expectations and assumes identical effects on investment from all changes in c whether from interest rates, corporate taxes, accelerated depreciation, or credits or allowances on equipment or investment in general. This was called into question by Eisner [20]. Feldstein and Flemming [26], working with British data, have most recently reported major, apparently intertemporal substitution effects of changing investment allowances which were not to be found in other elements of the "rental price of capital."

A critical assumption employed by Jorgenson in generating the desired demand for capital is the Cobb-Douglas production function, or the special case of the constant-elasticity-of-substitution production function with constant returns to scale and unitary

elasticity of substitution. Now the Cobb-Douglas production function is a simple and therefore useful tool in many kinds of analysis, but it does have some very particular properties. Jorgenson adds to these properties the perfect-competition assumptions of prices equal to marginal costs and marginal net revenue products equal to marginal factor costs, along with implicitly assumed elasticities of price expectations equal to unity. On this basis he generates investment functions with the striking parameter of elasticity of demand for capital with respect to a change in its relative price[3] equal to unity.

An aggregate investment function built on such foundations has some major implications for monetary and fiscal policy and the general issue of the maintenance of full employment. For it implies, contrary to several decades of Keynesian thinking, that relatively modest changes in interest rates or certain tax parameters may have substantial effects upon investment. Jorgenson's own policy-oriented work [32, 33, 34 and 39, for example] has indeed stressed this.

Jorgenson cites a number of studies, generally based on cross sections, which purport to show that the unitary-elasticity-of-substitution, Cobb-Douglas assumptions are acceptable. He ignores a substantial body of estimates, particularly from time series, which point to an elasticity of substitution considerably below unity. These, cited by Nerlove [54], include estimates of Kravis; Arrow, Chenery, Minhas and Solow; Diwan; Kendrick-Sato; Brown-de Cani; Kendrick; Ferguson; and David-Van de Klundert. Lucas has found "time series estimates of elasticity of substitution . . . well below cross-sectional estimates" and concludes "that for time series applications of substitution elasticities, time series estimates should be preferred" [49, pp. 265, 267]. And Harberger, summarizing the Lucas study, pointed to "strong biases in the direction of an estimated elasticity of unity in cross section estimates" and added, "Lucas' con-

3. The ratio of price of output to rental price of capital.

clusion is that rather than ranging around unity as the cross-section studies suggest, the elasticities of substitution between labor and capital in most manufacturing industries are probably well below unity, with 0.4 or 0.5 as the regression measure of their central tendency" [35, pp. 7, 8]. And there have been still other recent papers by Chetty [7] and Evans [25] also indicating estimates of elasticities of substitution distinctly less than the value of unity assumed by Jorgenson.[4]

Jorgenson does not consider the substantial gap between the technical elasticity of substitution in the production function and the price elasticity of demand for capital. This critical latter question may be tackled by direct, unconstrained estimates of the investment function which leave open the composite of underlying production functions, competitive relations and expectations which generate them. This was done by Eisner and Nadiri [22] using Jorgenson data and essentially a Jorgenson formulation, and by Coen [10]. The results pointed to estimates of the price elasticity of demand for capital considerably closer to zero than to unity, contradicting a basic maintained hypothesis of the Jorgenson model.

Jorgenson's comment, ignoring Coen's similar findings with a quite different method of estimation, is "The results of Eisner and Nadiri have been traced to an error in the stochastic specification of their model by Bischoff [4, 1969, p. 358]. Bischoff finds that the residuals in their distributed lag function are serially correlated, so their estimates of the elasticity of substitution and degrees of return to scale are inconsistent [4, p. 359]" (p. 1131).

This assertion, taken from a Jorgenson-Stephenson comment [46] on the original Eisner-Nadiri paper, is surprising in view of the Eisner-Nadiri response [23, 1970] to which Jorgenson had offered no rejoinder. This pointed out: 1) The so-called "error in the stochastic specification of their model" consisted almost precisely (except for a logarithmic transformation which is not here at issue) of the specification that Jorgenson had used in all of his own work on investment; 2) re-estimation utilizing the specification suggested by Bischoff resulted in confirmation of the original Eisner-Nadiri findings.[5]

It may be added that, despite a deservedly extensive discussion of Hickman's work [36], except for the cryptic statement, "After a comparison of alternative possible specifications, Hickman's model, like that of Eisner, reduces to the flexible accelerator model of Chenery and Koyck" (p. 1126), Jorgenson does not point out that Hickman's findings of very low price elasticity of demand for capital are consistent with the Eisner-Nadiri results. And Jorgenson also ignores the further, similar findings by Coen [11] presented in a paper and conference in which Jorgenson was involved as a co-contributor [34].

---

4. Jorgenson also ignores Thurow's report [56, p. 432] that, working with the Jorgenson investment function, "When the cost-of-capital variable was held constant at its median value, turning the model into a simple acceleration model, the model worked slightly better," and Thurow's inference from work with his own "disequilibrium" investment function that, "If the world were really represented by a CES production function rather than a Cobb-Douglas production function, a low elasticity of substitution might explain observed behavior. The elasticity of substitution would, however, have to be less than 0.1" (p. 434).

And nowhere in his survey does Jorgenson mention that his investment function with his assumption of a Cobb-Douglas production function generates implausibly low estimates of the capital coefficient [Jorgenson and Stephenson, 44, p. 215, cited by Eisner and Nadiri, 22, p. 375, fn. 26], in the neighborhood of .11 [Hall and Jorgenson, 32, p. 400, Table 2, cited by Eisner, 20, p. 381] instead of the .25 and .33 generally found in direct estimates of Cobb-Douglas production functions, or the .35 which Jorgenson elsewhere felt confirmed by the data [38, especially p. 471, cited by Eisner, 20, p. 381, fn. 5].

5. It is only with his own curiously defined rental price of capital variable estimated to fit a similar investment function that Bischoff derives estimates of the price elasticity of capital demand close to unity. It may be added that Bischoff has abandoned the assumption that the price elasticity of demand for capital is always identically equal to unity in some of his own later work on investment.

III. THE TIME STRUCTURE OF THE INVESTMENT PROCESS

In his survey of distributed lag functions which measure the dynamic response of investment to its determinants, Jorgenson barely touches on the basic question of whether there is a single, stable structure of lags for all factors affecting investment. In one brief reference, he states, "Bischoff [5] has suggested that real output and the cost of capital should have separate lag structures in the determination of investment expenditures" (p. 1142). But this has been a recurring theme in Bischoff's work for several years (including the paper of Bischoff's [4] cited earlier), and has also been considered by Eisner and Nadiri [22 and 23]. Coen [11] found cash flow to be positively related to the speed of adjustment of capital stock and Nadiri and Rosen [52] have fit the estimation of the investment function into the broader context of interrelated factor demand functions and the adjustment of the various stocks of factors to changing relative prices and demands for output. Coen and Hickman have explored the implications of imposing common production function parameters on demand functions for both labor and capital [12]. Eisner [20] and particularly Feldstein and Flemming [26] have raised serious questions as to whether speed of adjustment can properly be taken as identical for changes in the various components of the price of capital.

After stating that "Finite distributed lag functions are employed by Eisner in studying individual firms"[6] (p. 1134) Jorgenson declares:

We find that Eisner's distributed lag functions for individual firms reduce to functions of current and lagged values of profits and the rate of return. The resulting average lags are less than one year in length, which is inconsistent with findings from survey evidence. . . . Our conclusion is that the finite

distributed lag functions employed by Resek, like those by Eisner, lead to underestimates of the average lags underlying the investment process (pp. 1135–6).

But the only case where my work reduces "to functions of current and lagged values" of variables is in regard to the realizations function [14, 17], where I am explaining not the determinants of capital expenditures but rather merely the difference between expenditures and anticipated expenditures. Here, of course, we should look mainly to changes in underlying determinants which have occurred since the anticipations were formulated or expressed, and the lags should be short. In my various works with individual firm and industry data, time series and cross sections, the average lags are found to be substantial, running to several years, and as large or larger than those usually estimated by Jorgenson. Working with annual data, I have generally found significantly positive coefficients of past sales changes going back over six years.

There is indeed no reason for "the finite distributed lag function" to lead to underestimates of the average lag. My freely estimated, finite distributed lag function (a special case of Jorgenson's rational lag distribution with the denominator function equal to unity) may easily extend back far enough, given sufficient observations, to capture all of the most delayed determinants of investment, and that without any constraint as to the form of the "tail" of the distribution. Infinite lag functions such as Jorgenson's and finite lag functions such as Almon's [1] have been found particularly useful where a shortage of observations placed a premium on economy in the number of parameters to be estimated. Working with literally thousands of individual firm observations of annual data, I was able to estimate finite and long distributed lag functions directly by least squares. The Almon estimator may better be used for finite and long distributed lag functions where the number of observations is small. In neither case should readers or researchers conclude that finite distributed lag functions necessarily "lead

6. Also employed by Eisner in his estimates from industry group annual observations, which Jorgenson does not include in his tabular comparison of alternative investment functions or related discussion.

to underestimates of the average lags underlying the investment process."[7]

IV. REPLACEMENT INVESTMENT

Another of Jorgenson's maintained hypotheses is a "geometric mortality distribution for investment goods" (p. 1138). He gives the impression that this is a necessary condition for the proportionality of replacement expenditures to capital stock[8] and argues that both the geometric mortality distribution and proportional replacement exist.[9] He also declares that "an internally consistent model of replacement investment based on the proportionality of replacement and capital stock requires a measure of capital stock that employs the geometric mortality distribution" (p. 1139).

It may first be observed that a geometric mortality distribution or exponential decay in "efficiency" of capital goods, in Jorgenson's terminology [e.g., 41, pp. 266–83], is not necessary for proportional replacement. The distribution of mortality or decay, by way of counter-example, might be rectangular with a range equal to the time period of the sine function which described the path of actual capital expenditures around some constant

exponential rate of growth. Replacement as a ratio of capital stock would then be a constant of magnitude determined by the average length of life of capital and the rate of growth.

But more importantly, there is little evidence that the rate of depreciation is precisely geometric or that the replacement rate is a constant proportion of capital stock. Jorgenson's objection to the finding by Feldstein and Foot [27] that the replacement rate is not constant is without substance. For Jorgenson objects that Feldstein and Foot do not estimate their capital stock by the declining balance method, but in fact the differences in the values of capital stock occasioned by the use of other measures (such as those employed by Feldstein and Foot and those employed by me [21]) are not sufficient or of a nature to explain the observed variation in the replacement ratio.[10] In his survey Jorgenson fails to cite previous criticism [22] of conclusions in his own work that estimation of a positive coefficient of capital stock in an investment function implies that replacement is in fact proportional.[11] He also writes that "Eisner makes no attempt to revalue acquisitions and retirements for changes in the price of acquisition of investment goods" (p. 1139),

7. Jorgenson elsewhere refers to "a modification of Koyck's distributed lag function, with weights determined arbitrarily for the first lag values ... and then declining geometrically," this with regard to Eisner on p. 1124 and again similarly on pp. 1134–5, referring to Bourneuf, Eisner and Hickman. It is difficult to know what Jorgenson understands or means to signify by the term "arbitrarily." The initial weights are actually estimated. And the method is hardly a "modification" of the Koyck function, as it was originally suggested by Koyck. See, for example, [48, (111, 11.1), p. 69], much of Koyck's earlier analytical development, and his subsequent empirical analysis. Again, this is merely another special case of the Jorgenson rational lag function, this time with only one lagged term in the denominator function.

8. "A model of replacement investment based on the geometrical mortality distribution is used in all empirical studies that incorporate replacement explicitly" (pp. 1141–1142).

9. "Direct tests of the corresponding models of replacement requirements and capital goods prices support the geometric [mortality] distribution" (p. 1142).

10. Indeed, both Feldstein and Foot and Eisner [21] find statistically significant determinants of the variability of replacement expenditures in such variables as profits and the utilization of capacity, which would be difficult to reconcile with the view that the variability in the replacement ratio is fully accountable to errors in the measurement of capital.

11. Jorgenson was incorrect in asserting that "If replacement is not proportional to capital stock, there is no reason for capital stock to appear in the [gross investment] regression with a non-zero coefficient" [37, p. 75], and then claiming confirmation of proportional replacement on the basis of significantly positive regression estimates of the coefficient of capital stock. For as Eisner and Nadiri point out [22, p. 380]: "... the expected value of δ [the capital stock coefficient] would be positive if there were any kind of positive relation between gross capital expenditures and capital stock, however far from a proportionate one. Proper tests of proportionality would entail a search for nonlinearities, which could hardly be ruled out a priori unless the regression fit were perfect.

ignoring Eisner's report of analysis based on such attempts at revaluation [18, pp. 384–6]. I had in fact shown that "results are not found to differ sharply from those shown . . . where gross fixed assets were not price deflated" [18, p. 384].

While alleging inconsistencies in the work of others on replacement investment, Jorgenson does not mention in his survey the significant inconsistency between his figure of .02730 [45, p. 21, Table 2], used for depreciation in total manufacturing to make capital stock figures consistent with benchmarks and intermediate capital expenditures, and his own regression estimate of .01935 which he reports with Stephenson [44, p. 189]. The contradiction may of course be explained precisely by the hypothesis that replacement is not proportional to capital stock and that the error in specification leads to this discrepancy.

It might also be noted that while Jorgenson cites the work of a number of others including Hall [31], who finds "the geometric [mortality distribution] function . . . probably a reasonable approximation for many purposes, he ignores the similar work of Ramm [55], who also worked with used vehicle data; Ramm's results point to a monotonically rising sequence, from .209 to .389, for the average ratio of depreciation to capital stock for automobiles aged zero years to six years. There is also other recent work by Mendelowitz [50] which points to very low and possibly even negative initial depreciation followed by a hump and than a decline. I do not claim any definitive word on this matter but merely call attention to Jorgenson's selective presentation of the evidence.

V. SOME MISLEADING RENDITIONS

At one point, Jorgenson proclaims, "Profits after taxes are a significant variable in Eisner's model" (p. 1115). This is a curious reading, quite out of the context of the main body of my work. For I have emphasized that it is the expected profits on investment and not current or past profits which should prove significant in investment. In a considerable series of reports [13, 15 and 16

inter alia] of cross section analyses over the years, I have shown that when other variables measuring the pressure of demand on capacity are introduced, past and current profits lose their explanatory power. I did report evidence that, perhaps because small firms may suffer from imperfect capital supply markets, profits have some role in smaller firms capital expenditures. And I also found that in individual firm time series data, as Jorgenson reports, profits are a "significant explanatory variable." But I interpret the juxtaposition of very low profits coefficients in cross section regressions and fairly high ones in time series relations as "evidence . . . consistent with the hypothesis that past profits play some significant role in the timing of capital expenditures but do not affect its long run average" [18, p. 386].

In his discussion of "Eisner's permanent income theory for invesment" Jorgenson unaccountably focuses on one particular model for the years 1960–62 where information as to market value of the firm was available. Jorgenson declares:

Eisner's results for the period 1960–62 directly contradict his results for the period 1955–62, based on a less complete model. . . . Upon empirical testing, Eisner's model for the period 1960–62 effectively reduces to the model proposed by Grunfeld [30]. The profits variables represent profit expectations; the rate of return represents the cost of external finance (p. 1115).

Jorgenson here interprets coefficients of profits variables and rates of return quite differently from the author of the work. My own view is that the rate-of-return variable, defined as the ratio of gross profits to the market value of the firm, measured essentially the inverse of the profit expectations which underlie market value. As I wrote originally:

With regard to the variables measuring rate of return (r), it was thought that in a regression already including profits, their coefficients would prove negative. For when profit expectations are higher than current profits, the value of the firm would be relatively higher, and the current rate of return lower, while with generally high profit expectations, the marginal efficiency of investment would probably be greater and capital expenditures higher [18, pp. 378–9].

I also suggested that "higher profits co-efficients in the time series relations may have reflected some of the role of replacement investment which is postponed until the year when profits are relatively higher" [18, p. 375].

Why Jorgenson interprets the 1960–62 results as contradicting those for 1955–62 is hard to fathom. The sum of the sales change coefficients for the 1955–62 data was .244, with a standard error of .045, hence significantly positive [18, p. 374]. For the 1960–62 regressions with the additional rate of return variables, the sum of the sales change variables was .140, not significantly different from zero in view of the standard error of .162 with the substantially smaller number of observations and the additional, possibly somewhat collinear rate-of-return variables. Clearly, however, the difference between .244 in the larger sample and .140 with a standard error of .162 in the smaller sample is not statistically significant.[12] What is more, past changes of sales in my formulation are always proxies for changes in expected future demand. There is nothing contradictory in having a "rate of return" variable, which reflects the market valuation of expected future sales and earnings, pick up some of this proxy role of past sales changes.[13]

12. This may be seen roughly by noting that if we could assume the samples were independent with zero covariance in the estimates, we would have a difference of .244 − .140 = .104 with a standard error of

$$\sqrt{(.045)^2 + (.162)^2} = .168$$

13. Apparently again looking only at the 1960–62 results, Jorgenson incorrectly reports, "Change in deflated sales does not appear as a significant determinant of desired capital in Eisner's time series study for individual firms. This finding conflicts with Eisner's results for time series of industry groups" (p. 1130). But as already noted the sum of the deflated sales change coefficients was a highly significant .244 with a standard error of .045 in Eisner firm time series (p. 374) and indeed .276 with a standard error of .042 in regressions with different capital stock and average sales deflators. The industry time series sum of sales change coefficients was, it is true, a higher .477 (standard error of .195, p. 373) but this was hardly a contradiction in the Eisner model which looked for higher coefficients in more "permanent" industry variance than in data for individual firms.

The Jorgenson survey is uneven in the way of its criticism, explicit and implicit. In regard to "Eisner's permanent income theory for investment," for example, Jorgenson observes (accurately enough). "The proportion of the firm time series variance explained by Eisner's model for this period [1955–62] is .055" (p. 1115). He fails to remind the reader either that unlike the Jorgenson models, this Eisner model did not employ lagged values of the dependent variable, or that Eisner's dependent variable was capital expenditures divided by gross fixed assets, which tended to rule out possible explanation of the bulk of variance related to size or trend picked up in many other models. Jorgenson also failed to observe that the same Eisner model when applied to observations in which investment and other variables are deflated by immediately preceding values of capital stock (or average sales in the case of sales changes) yielded a coefficient of determination of .253 in the firm time series, and .648 in industry time series where random disturbances for individual firms apparently wash out [18, Table 5, p. 380].

The Jorgenson survey fails to be critical of Jorgenson. Thus in presenting "Jorgenson and Stephenson's study of investment," Jorgenson again reports as one of the elements in his measure of the price of capital services the variable "v the proportion of depreciation deductible from income for tax purposes" (p. 1127). But that formulation was shown by Coen [8 and 9] to be in error, and was corrected by Coen and by Hall, and was indeed used in its correct form in later work by Hall and Jorgenson as "z the present value of the depreciation deduction on one dollar's investment" [32, p. 393].

The presentation of comparisons of models merits comment. Jorgenson cites one paper by Jorgenson, Hunter, and Nadiri [42] for the conclusion that the ranking of models they consider is: 1) Jorgenson-Stephenson, 2) Eisner, 3) Meyer-Glauber, and 4) Anderson. This ranking is based on goodness of fit to post-war data. Meyer and Glauber and Anderson actually have considerably greater reason to complain here than I, in that the comparisons quite ignored the fact that their models could not benefit from first order autocorrelation of the dependent variable and were hence clearly foredoomed to defeat in comparisons with the Eisner model, which included one immediately lagged value of the dependent variable, and the Jorgenson-Stephenson model which had two![14] It might be added that the so called "Eisner model" in this case was a version of my realization function equations containing only two lagged values of the independent variables, hardly a relation to be used in explaining actual capital expenditures.

Further, it should be pointed out that Jorgenson reported these results of the Jorgenson, Hunter and Nadiri article relating to goodness of fit but did not cite results in the companion article by Jorgenson, Hunter and Nadiri [43] on, "The Predictive Performance of Econometric Models of Quarterly Investment Behavior." Here the test of predictive performance was made to rest on the issue of structural stability as between relations estimated with data from 1949 to 1960 and relations for data for 1961 through 1964. Jorgenson, Hunter and Nadiri then concluded, "On the basis of our test for structural change we can rank the four econometric models of investment behavior with regard to stability over time: (i) Eisner, (ii) Jorgenson-Stephenson, (iii) Meyer-Glauber, and (iv) Anderson" (p. 223).

I would hardly make any claims on this basis for that version of the "Eisner model" as against Jorgenson's or anybody else's. As I have remarked before [19], estimation of investment functions is a tricky and difficult business and the best posture for any of us in that game is one of humility.

VI. CONCLUSION

I have not attempted in this comment to resurvey the vast literature of econometric studies of investment. I may however focus upon a few notes that emerge from the consideration of Jorgenson's much more substantial effort.

1. Critical parameters of the "neo-classical model" remain uncertain. In particular there is evidence that the price elasticity of the demand for capital is not uniformly equal to unity and that replacement expenditures are not an invariant ratio of capital. Variables in some way measuring expected growth in demand for output retain prime place among determinants of capital expenditures.

2. The speed of adjustment of investment to changes in its determinants has not been established as either uniform or constant. There is considerable evidence that investment expenditures respond at different rates to changes in output and the components of the price of capital. In particular, it is doubtful that rates of response to changes in capital goods prices, interest rates, tax depreciation, and investment credits and allowances are identical. Rates of response of expenditures for capital may also be importantly interrelated to changes in the demand and supply of other factors.

3. Intertwined and largely unresolved in all of the econometric work is the critical issue of expectations. Investment must ultimately depend upon business expectations of future values and parameters of key variables and functions. Yet almost all of our work involves current and past proxies for the relevant unobserved expectations. Major progress in discerning reliable and stable investment functions will require facing up to and illuminating the fundamental relations between past, present and future.

References

1. S. Almon, "The Distributed Lag Between Capital Appropriations and Expenditures," *Econometrica*, 33(1), pp. 178–196 (Jan. 1965).
2. W. H. L. Anderson, "Business Fixed Investment: A Marriage of Fact and Fancy" in R. Ferber ed. *Determinants of Investment Behavior*. Universities-National Bureau Conference Series, No. 18. New York: Columbia University Press for the National Bureau of Economic Research, (1967).

14. The version of the Meyer-Glauber employed included only investment lagged *two* quarters and the Anderson model had no lagged values of the dependent variable.

3. _____, *Corporate Finance, and Fixed Investment, An Econometric Study*. Boston: Division of Research, Graduate School of Business Administration, Harvard University (1964).

4. C. W. Bischoff, "Hypothesis Testing and the Demand for Capital Goods. *Rev. Econ. Statist.*, *51*(3), pp. 354–368 (Aug. 1969).

5. _____, "The Effect of Alternative Lag Distributions," in [29].

6. A. Bourneuf, "Manufacturing Investment, Excess Capacity and the Rate of Growth of Output," *Amer. Econ. Rev. 54*(5), pp. 607–625 (Sept. 1964).

7. V. K. Chetty, "Pooling of Time Series and Cross Section Data," *Econometrica 36*, pp. 279–290 (Apr. 1968).

8. R. M. Coen, "Accelerated Depreciation, The Investment Tax Credit and Investment Decisions," presented to the December 1965 meetings of the Econometric Society.

9. _____, "Effects of Tax Policy on Investment in Manufacturing," *Amer. Econ. Rev. 58*(2), pp. 200–211 (May 1968).

10. _____, "Tax Policy and Investment Behavior: Comment." *Amer. Econ. Rev. 59*(3), pp. 370–377 (June 1969).

11. _____, "The Effect of Cash Flow on the Speed of Adjustment" in [29].

12. R. M. Coen and B. G. Hickman, "Constrained Joint Estimating of Factor Demand and Production Functions," *Rev. Econ. Statist.* pp. 287–300 (Apr. 1970).

13. R. Eisner," A Distributed Lag Investment Function," *Econometrica 28*(1), pp. 1–29 (Jan. 1960).

14. _____, "Investment Plans and Realizations," *Amer. Econ. Rev. 52*(2), pp. 190–203 (May 1962).

15. _____, "Investment: Fact and Fancy," *Amer. Econ. Rev. 53*(2), pp. 237–246 (May 1963).

16. _____, "Capital Expenditures, Profits and the Acceleration Principle" in *Models of Income Determination*. Studies in Income and Wealth, Vol. 28, Princeton: Princeton University Press (1964).

17. _____, "Realization of Investment Anticipations" in J. Duesenberry; G. Fromm; L. R. Klein, and E. Kuh, eds. *The Brookings Quarterly Model of the United States*. Amsterdam: North Holland (1965).

18. _____, "A Permanent Income Theory for Investment," *Amer. Econ. Rev. 57*(3), pp. 363–390 (June 1967).

19. _____, "Investment and the Frustrations of Econometricians," *Amer. Econ. Rev. 59*(2), pp. 50–64 (May 1969).

20. _____, "Tax Policy and Investment Behavior: Comment," *Amer. Econ. Rev. 59*(3), pp. 378–387 (June 1969).

21. _____, "Components of Capital Expenditures: Replacement and Modernization Versus Expansion," *Rev. of Econ. and Statist. 54*(3), pp. 297–305 (Aug. 1972).

22. R. Eisner, and M. I. Nadiri, "Investment Behavior and the Neo-Classical Theory," *Rev. Econ. Statist. 50*(3), pp. 369–382 (Aug. 1968).

23. _____, "Neo-classical Theory of Investment Behavior: A Comment," *Rev. Econ. Statist. 52*(2), pp. 216–222 (May 1970).

24. R. Eisner and R. H. Strotz, "Determinants of Business Investment" in Commission on Money and Credit, *Impacts of Monetary Policy*. Prentice-Hall: Englewood Cliffs, N.J., (1963).

25. M. K. Evans, "A Further Study of Industry Investment Functions," Discussion Paper No. 93, Department of Economics, University of Pennsylvania, Philadelphia, (1965).

26. M. S. Feldstein and J. S. Flemming, "Tax Policy, Corporate Saving and Investment Behavior in Britain," *Rev. Econ. Stud. 38*(116), pp. 415–434 (Oct. 1971).

27. M. S. Feldstein and D. K. Foot, "The Other Half of Gross Investment: Replacement and Modernization Expenditures," *Rev. Econ. Statist. 53*(1), pp. 49–58 (Feb. 1971).

28. F. M. Fisher, "Discussion," in [29], pp. 243–255.

29. G. Fromm, ed., *Tax Incentives and Capital Spending*. Washington, D.C.: Brookings Institution, (1971).

30. Y. Grunfeld, "The Determinants of Corporate Investment" in A. C. Harberger ed. *The Demand for Durable Goods*. Chicago: University of Chicago Press, (1960).

31. R. E. Hall, "The Measurement of Quality Change from Vintage Price Data" in Z. Griliches, ed., *Price Indexes and Quality Change*. Cambridge: Harvard University Press (1971).

32. R. E. Hall and D. W. Jorgenson, "Tax Policy and Investment Behavior," *Amer. Econ. Rev. 57*(3), pp. 391–414 (June 1967).

33. _____, "Tax Policy and Investment Behavior: Replay and Further Results," *Amer. Econ. Rev. 59*(3), pp. 388–401 (June 1969).

34. _____, "Application of the Theory of Optimum Capital Accumulation" in [29].

35. A. C. Harberger and M. J. Bailey, eds., *The Taxation of Income from Capital*. Washington, D.C.: Brookings Institution (1969).

36. B. Hickman, *Investment Demand and U.S.*

Economic Growth. Washing, D.C.: Brookings Institution, (1965).

37. D. W. Jorgenson, "Anticipations and Investment Behavior," in J. S. Dusenberry, E. Kuh, G. Fromm, and L. R. Klein, eds., *The Brookings Quarterly Econometric Model of the United States*. Chicago: Rand-McNally, (1965) pp. 35–94.

38. _____, "Comment" on Eisner, "Capital and Labor in Production: Some Direct Estimates," in M. Brown, ed., *The Theory and Empirical Analysis of Production*, NBER Studies in Income and Wealth, Vol. 31, New York (1967).

39. _____, Statement on Asset Depreciation Range System before U.S. Treasury Department, (March 18, 1971).

40. _____, "Econometric Studies of Investment Behavior: A Survey," *Jour. of Econ. Lit.* 9(4), pp. 1111–1147 (Dec. 1971).

41. L. R. Christensen and D. W. Jorgenson, "Measuring Economic Performance in the Private Sector," in M. Moss, ed., *Measurement of Economic and Social Performance*. Studies in Income and Wealth, No. 38, New York: National Bureau of Economic Research, pp. 233–338 (1973).

42. D. W. Jorgenson, J. Hunter and M. I. Nadiri, "A Comparison of Alternative Econometric Models of Corporate Investment Behavior," *Econometrica* 38(2), pp. 187–212 (Mar. 1970).

43. _____, "The Predictive Performance of Econometric Models of Quarterly Behavior," *Econometrica*, 38(2), pp. 213–224 (Mar. 1970).

44. D. W. Jorgenson and J. A. Stephenson, "Investment Behavior in U.S. Manufacturing, 1947–1960," *Econometrica*, 35(2), pp. 169–220 (Apr. 1967).

45. _____, "The Time Structure of Investment Behavior in U.S. Manufacturing, 1947–1960," *Rev. Econ. Statist.* 49(1), pp. 16–27 (Feb. 1967).

46. _____, "Issues in the Development of the Neo-Classical Theory of Investment Behavior," *Rev. Econ. Statist.* 51, pp. 346–353 (Aug. 1969).

47. L. R. Klein, "Issues in Econometric Studies of Investment Behavior," *Jour. of Econ. Lit.*, Vol. 12 (March 1974).

48. L. M. Koyck, *Distributed Lags and Investment Analysis*. Amsterdam: North Holland, (1954).

49. R. E. Lucas, "Labor-Capital Substitution in U.S. Manufacturing" in [35], A. C. Harberger and M. J. Bailey, eds., *The Taxation of Income from Capital*. Washington, D.C.: Brookings Institution pp. 223–274 (1969).

50. A. I. Mendelowitz, "The Measurement of Economic Depreciation," *1970 Business and Economic Statistics Section, Proceedings of the American Statistical Association*, pp. 140–148.

51. J. Meyer and R. Glauber, *Investment Decisions, Economic Forecasting, and Public Policy*. Boston: Division of Research, Graduate School of Business Administration, Harvard University, 1964.

52. J. Meyer and E. Kuh, *The Investment Decision*. Cambridge: Harvard University Press, (1957).

53. M. I. Nadiri and S. Rosen, "Interrelated Factor Demand Functions," *Amer. Econ. Rev. 59*, pp. 457–471 (1969).

54. M. Nerlove, "Recent Empirical Studies of the CES and Related Production Functions," in M. Brown, ed., *The Theory and Empirical Analysis of Production*, Studies in Income and Wealth. No. 31. New York: Columbia University Press, pp. 55–122 (1967).

55. W. Ramm, "Measuring the Services of Household Durables: The Case of Automobiles," *1970 Business and Economic Statistics Section, Proceedings of the American Statistical Association*, pp. 148–158.

56. L. C. Thurow, "A Disequilibrium Investment Function," *Rev. Econ. Statist. 51*(4), pp. 431–435 (Nov. 1969).

Prior to Keynes' *General Theory of Employment, Interest and Money,* stabilization policies consisted largely of monetary policies designed to moderate the business cycle. Basically they relied on low interest rates and credit availability to stimulate investment demand. Keynes shifted the emphasis of stabilization policies to fiscal policies designed to increase aggregate effective demand, relying on the income multiplier and acceleration effects to stimulate an increase in economic activity.

Prior to Keynes economists generally believed that complete stabilization of the economy was not possible and that recessions might be necessary to correct imbalances in the economy in order to return to an equilibrium growth path. Keynes offered a more attractive alternative by suggesting that recessions might be eliminated through correct demand management policies, relying principally on discretionary fiscal policies. The classical view of the business cycle was revived in a more doctrinaire and theoretically articulated form by Milton Friedman and has been enshrined as the monetarist view of stabilization policy.

That there was no classical policy counterpart to Keynes in Anglo-Saxon economics (underconsumptionist theories only presented the problem) may be explained in part by the small role of government expenditure before World War I. Federal government expenditures were only 1.8 percent of GNP in 1914 in the United States and quantitatively important fiscal effects did not seem to be a practical possibility.

The monetarists have argued that there is little that discretionary stabilization policies can do to improve the stability of the economy. Furthermore they have argued that any trade-off between unemployment and inflation is a short-run phenomenon and that any attempt to lower the ''natural'' rate of unemployment will only result in inflation without lasting effects on employment. To permanently lower the rate of unemployment below the natural rate, they argue, would require continuously accelerating inflation. The theoretical reasoning underlying this argument is discussed in Part Three of this book.

Aside from maintaining there was a floor on the rate of unemployment set by institutional and real factors, Milton Friedman has argued that the lags relating discretionary monetary policy to the desired economic goals were so long and so variable as to make a discretionary monetary policy difficult, if not impossible, to conduct.

PART TWO
Aggregate Demand Management and Stabilization Policies

He went on to demonstrate that relatively small errors in estimating the length of these lags could lead to destabilizing effects. Friedman, in fact, attributes much of the postwar economic instability to shocks administered by a discretionary monetary policy.

Friedman's contention that the lags involved in discretionary monetary and fiscal policy are long and variable has been hotly contested by the Keynesians who have marshaled large amounts of empirical evidence designed to show that the lags are sufficiently short and stable so as to permit an effective stabilization policy. Most large econometric models of the U.S. economy now include monetary variables with a distributed lag structure.

Finally, the monetarists have attacked the relative efficiency of fiscal policy, arguing that its immediate expansionary impact is offset by a subsequent negative effect so that after a few quarters it has a zero, or even negative, cumulative impact as a result of the "crowding out effect." This latter effect maintains that a government deficit financed by the sale of government securities to the public will raise interest rates to such a degree as to discourage private investment sufficiently to offset the expansionary effects of the increase in government expenditure. This criticism, however, cuts two ways since it seems that the characteristics of fiscal policy described by Friedman may be desirable in many circumstances where one would like to administer a sharp boost to aggregate expenditure and then, when the private sector responds via accelerator effects, remove the stimulus.

The monetarists' solution to the policy problem is to set the rate of growth of the money supply, suitably defined, in accordance with the expected long-run growth rate potential of the economy. They argue that this on balance will achieve the best stabilization policy possible given the hypothesized stability of the relevant economic relationships. Lucas has pointed out that any stabilization rule, such as the monetarists', is suboptimal since it disregards feedback effects. Lucas, nevertheless, supports the idea of employing a monetary rule but for very different reasons. He argues that even if the economic relationships of the system are stable and the policy instruments are potent, a discretionary stabilization policy may not be possible. If economic policy-makers behave rationally, then these rational rules of behavior will become known and will be taken into account by economic agents in making their decisions. In short, the economic behavior of the economic authorities becomes endogeneous to the decision-making process of individual decision-makers and the authorities lose their ability to influence economic targets.

In practice, the approach of Lucas suggests that it would be possible to construct a model of the way the Federal Reserve and Congress would react to various states of the economy and that one could identify the operative model of the economy that each policy-maker was employing to make his policy decisions—a tall order. Lucas's criticism, however, is relevant, if not absolute. Furthermore, it may well turn out that in such a system as envisaged by Lucas the actions of private agents are stabilizing rather than destabilizing so that all economic authorities ever need do is announce the rules under which they will operate. While they would not be able to employ feedback to correct their rule, there is nothing to prevent the authorities from announcing that they will continue to change their rules until they achieve the desired targets. There is no a priori reason why this type of rational behavior will be destabilizing. On the contrary, if there was general agreement on the economic model the authorities were employing, rational behavior on the part of individual agents acting on the endogenous behavior of the economic authorities might produce a stable economy.

The Keynesian reply to the essentially classical counterattack of the monetarists is that if demand management policies are not good, they also cannot be all that bad since the world has experienced an unparalleled rate of economic growth and stability in the postwar period under essentially discretionary stabilization policies. Modigliani offers essentially a Keynesian reply to the monetarists that challenges almost every point of their argument. However, after having read both the Keynesian and monetarist arguments, one feels that underlying all the theoretical fencing and hurling of empirical counterexamples lies a "gut" feeling about the inherent instability of the economy. The monetarist believes that the economy's self-righting properties are rapid and that the best one can do is stand out of the way. The Keynesians believe the self-equilibrating properties of the economy are sluggish and need a helping hand. This difference of sentiment leads to different conclusions drawn from the same set of facts.

A good example of this is the differing attitude toward fiscal policy. The monetarist downplays its importance because after its initial stimulative effect it reverses itself and nets out close to zero. The Keynesians do not dispute the facts but look at the possibility that the initial stimulus will give rise to favorable multiplier and accelerator effects that might become self-sustaining.

Recent experience has been very trying to both Keynesians and monetarists. The economy has not shown snappy self-righting properties, nor has it responded well to discretionary policy instruments. Modigliani speculates that the reason for this may have been the supply source of the recent shocks which have been experienced and which have been dealt with essentially demand management policies. Such supply-side shocks may indeed call for different stabilization policy rules, not exclusively relying on aggregate demand management. The theory for designing such a policy has been slow in developing.

Politically, discretionary stabilization policy seems to be here to stay; people will insist on calling the doctor even if no cure is available.

The Role of Monetary Policy*
Milton Friedman
University of Chicago

There is wide agreement about the major goals of economic policy: high employment, stable prices, and rapid growth. There is less agreement that these goals are mutually compatible or, among those who regard them as incompatible, about the terms at which they can and should be substituted for one another. There is least agreement about the role that various instruments of policy can and should play in achieving the several goals.

My topic for tonight is the role of one such instrument—monetary policy. What can it contribute? And how should it be conducted to contribute the most? Opinion on these questions has fluctuated widely. In the first flush of enthusiasm about the newly created Federal Reserve System, many observers attributed the relative stability of the 1920s to the System's capacity for fine tuning—to apply an apt modern term. It came to be widely believed that a new era had arrived in which business cycles had been rendered obsolete by advances in monetary technology. This opinion was shared by economist and layman alike, though, of course, there were some dissonant voices. The Great Contraction destroyed this naive attitude. Opinion swung to the other extreme. Monetary policy was a

Reprinted from the *American Economic Review*, 58:1–17 (1968), by permission of the author and the publisher (copyright by the American Economic Association).

* Presidential address delivered at the Eightieth Annual Meeting of the American Economic Association, Washington, D.C., December 29, 1967.

string. You could pull on it to stop inflation but you could not push on it to halt recession. You could lead a horse to water but you could not make him drink. Such theory by aphorism was soon replaced by Keynes' rigorous and sophisticated analysis.

Keynes offered simultaneously an explanation for the presumed impotence of monetary policy to stem the depression, a nonmonetary interpretation of the depression, and an alternative to monetary policy for meeting the depression and his offering was avidly accepted. If liquidity preference is absolute or nearly so—as Keynes believed likely in times of heavy unemployment—interest rates cannot be lowered by monetary measures. If investment and consumption are little affected by interest rates—as Hansen and many of Keynes' other American disciples came to believe—lower interest rates, even if they could be achieved, would do little good. Monetary policy is twice damned. The contraction, set in train, on this view, by a collapse of investment or by a shortage of investment opportunities or by stubborn thriftiness, could not, it was argued, have been stopped by monetary measures. But there was available an alternative—fiscal policy. Government spending could make up for insufficient private investment. Tax reductions could undermine stubborn thriftiness.

The wide acceptance of these views in the economics profession meant that for some two decades monetary policy was believed by all but a few reactionary souls to have been rendered obsolete by new economic knowledge. Money did not matter. Its only role was the minor one of keeping interest rates low, in order to hold down interest payments in the government budget, contribute to the "euthanasia of the rentier," and maybe, stimulate investment a bit to assist government spending in maintaining a high level of aggregate demand.

These views produced a widespread adoption of cheap money policies after the war. And they received a rude shock when these policies failed in country after country, when central bank after central bank was forced to give up the pretense that it could indefinitely keep "the" rate of interest at a low level. In this country, the public denouement came with the Federal Reserve-Treasury Accord in 1951, although the policy of pegging government bond prices was not formally abandoned until 1953. Inflation, stimulated by cheap money policies, not the widely heralded postwar depression, turned out to be the order of the day. The result was the beginning of a revival of belief in the potency of monetary policy.

This revival was strongly fostered among economists by the theoretical developments initiated by Haberler but named for Pigou that pointed out a channel—namely, changes in wealth—whereby changes in the real quantity of money can affect aggregate demand even if they do not alter interest rates. These theoretical developments did not undermine Keynes' argument against the potency of orthodox monetary measures when liquidity preference is absolute since under such circumstances the usual monetary operations involve simply substituting money for other assets without changing total wealth. But they did show how changes in the quantity of money produced in other ways could affect total spending even under such circumstances. And, more fundamentally, they did undermine Keynes' key theoretical proposition, namely, that even in a world of flexible prices, a position of equilibrium at full employment might not exist. Henceforth, unemployment had again to be explained by

rigidities or imperfections, not as the natural outcome of a fully operative market process.

The revival of belief in the potency of monetary policy was fostered also by a re-evaluation of the role money played from 1929 to 1933. Keynes and most other economists of the time believed that the Great Contraction in the United States occurred despite aggressive expansionary policies by the monetary authorities—that they did their best but their best was not good enough.[1] Recent studies have demonstrated that the facts are precisely the reverse: the U.S. monetary authorities followed highly deflationary policies. The quantity of money in the United States fell by one-third in the course of the contraction. And it fell not because there were no willing borrowers—not because the horse would not drink. It fell because the Federal Reserve System forced or permitted a sharp reduction in the monetary base, because it failed to exercise the responsibilities assigned to it in the Federal Reserve Act to provide liquidity to the banking system. The Great Contraction is tragic testimony to the power of monetary policy—not, as Keynes and so many of his contemporaries believed, evidence of its impotence.

In the United States the revival of belief in the potency of monetary policy was strengthened also by increasing disillusionment with fiscal policy, not so much with its potential to affect aggregate demand as with the practical and political feasibility of so using it. Expenditures turned out to respond sluggishly and with long lags to attempts to adjust them to the course of economic activity, so emphasis shifted to taxes. But here political factors entered with a vengeance to prevent prompt adjustment to presumed need, as has been so graphically illustrated in the months since I wrote the first draft of this talk. "Fine tuning" is a marvelously evocative phrase in this electronic age, but it has little resemblance to

---

[1] In [2], I have argued that Henry Simons shared this view with Keynes, and that it accounts for the policy changes that he recommended.

what is possible in practice—not, I might add, an unmixed evil.

It is hard to realize how radical has been the change in professional opinion on the role of money. Hardly an economist today accepts views that were the common coin some two decades ago. Let me cite a few examples.

In a talk published in 1945, E. A. Goldenweiser, then Director of the Research Division of the Federal Reserve Board, described the primary objective of monetary policy as being to "maintain the value of Government bonds. ... This country" he wrote, "will have to adjust to a $2\frac{1}{2}$ per cent interest rate as the return on safe, long-time money, because the time has come when returns on pioneering capital can no longer be unlimited as they were in the past" [4, p. 117].

In a book on *Financing American Prosperity*, edited by Paul Homan and Fritz Machlup and published in 1945, Alvin Hansen devotes nine pages of text to the "savings-investment problem" without finding any need to use the words "interest rate" or any close facsimile thereto [5, pp. 218–27]. In his contribution to this volume, Fritz Machlup wrote, "Questions regarding the rate of interest, in particular regarding its variation or its stability, may not be among the most vital problems of the postwar economy, but they are certainly among the perplexing ones" [5, p. 466]. In his contribution, John H. Williams—not only professor at Harvard but also a long-time adviser to the New York Federal Reserve Bank—wrote, "I can see no prospect of revival of a general monetary control in the postwar period" [5, p. 383].

Another of the volumes dealing with postwar policy that appeared at this time, *Planning and Paying for Full Employment*, was edited by Abba P. Lerner and Frank D. Graham [6] and had contributors of all shades of professional opinion—from Henry Simons and Frank Graham to Abba Lerner and Hans Neisser. Yet Albert Halasi, in his excellent summary of the papers, was able to say, "Our contributors do not discuss the question of money supply. ... The contributors make no special mention of credit policy

to remedy actual depressions. ... Inflation ... might be fought more effectively by raising interest rates. ... But ... other anti-inflationary measures ... are preferable" [6, pp. 23–24]. *A Survey of Contemporary Economics*, edited by Howard Ellis and published in 1948, was an "official" attempt to codify the state of economic thought of the time. In his contribution, Arthur Smithies wrote, "In the field of compensatory action, I believe fiscal policy must shoulder most of the load. Its chief rival, monetary policy, seems to be disqualified on institutional grounds. This country appears to be committed to something like the present low level of interest rates on a long-term basis" [1, p. 208].

These quotations suggest the flavor of professional thought some two decades ago. If you wish to go further in this humbling inquiry, I recommend that you compare the sections on money—when you can find them—in the Principles texts of the early postwar years with the lengthy sections in the current crop even, or especially, when the early and recent Principles are different editions of the same work.

The pendulum has swung far since then, if not all the way to the position of the late 1920s, at least much closer to that position than to the position of 1945. There are of course many differences between then and now, less in the potency attributed to monetary policy than in the roles assigned to it and the criteria by which the profession believes monetary policy should be guided. Then, the chief roles assigned monetary policy were to promote price stability and to preserve the gold standard; the chief criteria of monetary policy were the state of the "money market," the extent of "speculation" and the movement of gold. Today, primacy is assigned to the promotion of full employment, with the prevention of inflation a continuing but definitely secondary objective. And there is major disagreement about criteria of policy, varying from emphasis on money market conditions, interest rates, and the quantity of money to the belief that the state of employment itself should be the proximate criterion of policy.

I stress nonetheless the similarity between the views that prevailed in the late 'twenties and those that prevail today because I fear that, now as then, the pendulum may well have swung too far, that, now as then, we are in danger of assigning to monetary policy a larger role than it can perform, in danger of asking it to accomplish tasks that it cannot achieve, and, as a result, in danger of preventing it from making the contribution that it is capable of making.

Unaccustomed as I am to denigrating the importance of money, I therefore shall, as my first task, stress what monetary policy cannot do. I shall then try to outline what it can do and how it can best make its contribution, in the present state of our knowledge—or ignorance.

I. WHAT MONETARY POLICY CANNOT DO

From the infinite world of negation, I have selected two limitations of monetary policy to discuss: (1) It cannot peg interest rates for more than very limited periods; (2) It cannot peg the rate of unemployment for more than very limited periods. I select these because the contrary has been or is widely believed, because they correspond to the two main unattainable tasks that are at all likely to be assigned to monetary policy, and because essentially the same theoretical analysis covers both.

Pegging of Interest Rates

History has already persuaded many of you about the first limitation. As noted earlier, the failure of cheap money policies was a major source of the reaction against simple-minded Keynesianism. In the United States, this reaction involved widespread recognition that the wartime and postwar pegging of bond prices was a mistake, that the abandonment of this policy was a desirable and inevitable step, and that it had none of the disturbing and disastrous consequences that were so freely predicted at the time.

The limitation derives from a much misunderstood feature of the relation between money and interest rates. Let the Fed set out to keep interest rates down. How will it try to do so? By buying securities. This raises their prices and lowers their yields. In the process, it also increases the quantity of reserves available to banks, hence the amount of bank credit, and, ultimately the total quantity of money. That is why central bankers in particular, and the financial community more broadly, generally believe that an increase in the quantity of money tends to lower interest rates. Academic economists accept the same conclusion, but for different reasons. They see, in their mind's eye, a negatively sloping liquidity preference schedule. How can people be induced to hold a larger quantity of money? Only by bidding down interest rates.

Both are right, up to a point. The *initial* impact of increasing the quantity of money at a faster rate than it has been increasing is to make interest rates lower for a time than they would otherwise have been. But this is only the beginning of the process not the end. The more rapid rate of monetary growth will stimulate spending, both through the impact on investment of lower market interest rates and through the impact on other spending and thereby relative prices of higher cash balances than are desired. But one man's spending is another man's income. Rising income will raise the liquidity preference schedule and the demand for loans; it may also raise prices, which would reduce the real quantity of money. These three effects will reverse the initial downward pressure on interest rates fairly promptly, say, in something less than a year. Together they will tend, after a somewhat longer interval, say, a year or two, to return interest rates to the level they would otherwise have had. Indeed, given the tendency for the economy to overreact, they are highly likely to raise interest rates temporarily beyond that level, setting in motion a cyclical adjustment process.

A fourth effect, when and if it becomes operative, will go even farther, and definitely mean that a higher rate of monetary expansion will correspond to a higher, not lower, level of interest rates than would otherwise have prevailed. Let the higher rate of monetary growth produce rising prices, and let the public come to expect that prices will continue to rise. Borrowers will then be willing to pay and lenders will then demand higher interest rates—as Irving Fisher pointed out decades ago. This price expectation effect is slow to develop and also slow to disappear. Fisher estimated that it took several decades for a full adjustment and more recent work is consistent with his estimates.

These subsequent effects explain why every attempt to keep interest rates at a low level has forced the monetary authority to engage in successively larger and larger open market purchases. They explain why, historically, high and rising nominal interest rates have been associated with rapid growth in the quantity of money, as in Brazil or Chile or in the United States in recent years, and why low and falling interest rates have been associated with slow growth in the quantity of money, as in Switzerland now or in the United States from 1929 to 1933. As an empirical matter, low interest rates are a sign that monetary policy *has been* tight—in the sense that the quantity of money has grown slowly; high interest rates are a sign that monetary policy *has been* easy—in the sense that the quantity of money has grown rapidly. The broadest facts of experience run in precisely the opposite direction from that which the financial community and academic economists have all generally taken for granted.

Paradoxically, the monetary authority could assure low nominal rates of interest—but to do so it would have to start out in what seems like the opposite direction, by engaging in a deflationary monetary policy. Similarly, it could assure high nominal interest rates by engaging in an inflationary policy and accepting a temporary movement in interest rates in the opposite direction.

These considerations not only explain why monetary policy cannot peg interest rates; they also explain why interest rates are such a misleading indicator of whether monetary

policy is "tight" or "easy." For that, it is far better to look at the rate of change of the quantity of money.[2]

Employment as a Criterion of Policy

The second limitation I wish to discuss goes more against the grain of current thinking. Monetary growth, it is widely held, will tend to stimulate employment; monetary contraction, to retard employment. Why, then, cannot the monetary authority adopt a target for employment or unemployment—say, 3 per cent unemployment; be tight when unemployment is less than the target; be easy when unemployment is higher than the target; and in this way peg unemployment at, say, 3 per cent? The reason it cannot is precisely the same as for interest rates—the difference between the immediate and the delayed consequences of such a policy.

Thanks to Wicksell, we are all acquainted with the concept of a "natural" rate of interest and the possibility of a discrepancy between the "natural" and the "market" rate. The preceding analysis of interest rates can be translated fairly directly into Wicksellian terms. The monetary authority can make the market rate less than the natural rate only by inflation. It can make the market rate higher than the natural rate only by deflation. We have added only one wrinkle to Wicksell—the Irving Fisher distinction between the nominal and the real rate of interest. Let the monetary authority keep the nominal market rate for a time below the natural rate by inflation. That in turn will raise the nominal natural rate itself, once anticipations of inflation become widespread, thus requiring still more rapid inflation to hold down the market rate. Similarly, because of the Fisher effect, it will

[2] This is partly an empirical not theoretical judgment. In principle, "tightness" or "ease" depends on the rate of change of the quantity of money supplied compared to the rate of change of the quantity demanded excluding effects on demand from monetary policy itself. However, empirically demand is highly stable, if we exclude the effect of monetary policy, so it is generally sufficient to look at supply alone.

require not merely deflation but more and more rapid deflation to hold the market rate above the initial "natural" rate.

This analysis has its close counterpart in the employment market. At any moment of time, there is some level of unemployment which has the property that it is consistent with equilibrium in the structure of *real* wage rates. At that level of unemployment, real wage rates are tending on the average to rise at a "normal" secular rate, i.e., at a rate that can be indefinitely maintained so long as capital formation, technological improvements, etc., remain on their long-run trends. A lower level of unemployment is an indication that there is an excess demand for labor that will produce upward pressure on real wage rates. A higher level of unemployment is an indication that there is an excess supply of labor that will produce downward pressure on real wage rates. The "natural rate of unemployment," in other words, is the level that would be ground out by the Walrasian system of general equilibrium equations, provided there is imbedded in them the actual structural characteristics of the labor and commodity markets, including market imperfections, stochastic variability in demands and supplies, the cost of gathering information about job vacancies and labor availabilities, the costs of mobility, and so on.[3]

You will recognize the close similarity between this statement and the celebrated Phillips Curve. The similarity is not coincidental. Phillips' analysis of the relation between unemployment and wage change is deservedly celebrated as an important and original contribution. But, unfortunately, it contains a basic defect—the failure to distinguish between *nominal* wages and *real* wages—just as Wicksell's analysis failed to distinguish between *nominal* interest rates and *real* interest rates. Implicitly, Phillips wrote his article for a world in which everyone anti-cipated that nominal prices would be stable and in which that anticipation remained unshaken and immutable whatever happened to actual prices and wages. Suppose, by contrast, that everyone anticipates that prices will rise at a rate of more than 75 per cent a year—as, for example, Brazilians did a few years ago. Then wages must rise at that rate simply to keep real wages unchanged. An excess supply of labor will be reflected in a less rapid rise in nominal wages than in anticipated prices,[4] not in an absolute decline in wages. When Brazil embarked on a policy to bring down the rate of price rise, and succeeded in bringing the price rise down to about 45 per cent a year, there was a sharp initial rise in unemployment because under the influence of earlier anticipations, wages kept rising at a pace that was higher than the new rate of price rise, though lower than earlier. This is the result experienced, and to be expected, of all attempts to reduce the rate of inflation below that widely anticipated.[5]

To avoid misunderstanding, let me emphasize that by using the term "natural" rate of unemployment, I do not mean to suggest that

[3] It is perhaps worth noting that this "natural" rate need not correspond to equality between the number unemployed and the number of job vacancies. For any given structure of the labor market, there will be some equilibrium relation between these two magnitudes, but there is no reason why it should be one of equality.

[4] Strictly speaking, the rise in nominal wages will be less rapid than the rise in anticipated nominal wages to make allowance for any secular changes in real wages.

[5] Stated in terms of the rate of change of nominal wages, the Phillips Curve can be expected to be reasonably stable and well defined for any period for which the *average* rate of change of prices, and hence the anticipated rate, has been relatively stable. For such periods, nominal wages and "real" wages move together. Curves computed for different periods or different countries for each of which this condition has been satisfied will differ in level, the level of the curve depending on what the average rate of price change was. The higher the average rate of price change, the higher will tend to be the level of the curve. For periods or countries for which the rate of change of prices varies considerably, the Phillips Curve will not be well defined. My impression is that these statements accord reasonably well with the experience of the economists who have explored empirical Phillips Curves.

Restate Phillips' analysis in terms of the rate of change of real wages—and even more precisely, anticipated real wages—and it all falls into place. That is why students of empirical Phillips Curves have found that it helps to include the rate of change of the price level as an independent variable.

it is immutable and unchangeable. On the contrary, many of the market characteristics that determine its level are man-made and policy-made. In the United States, for example, legal minimum wage rates, the Walsh-Healy and Davis-Bacon Acts, and the strength of labor unions all make the natural rate of unemployment higher than it would otherwise be. Improvements in employment exchanges, in availability of information about job vacancies and labor supply, and so on, would tend to lower the natural rate of unemployment. I use the term "natural" for the same reason Wicksell did—to try to separate the real forces from monetary forces.

Let us assume that the monetary authority tries to peg the "market" rate of unemployment at a level below the "natural" rate. For definiteness, suppose that it takes 3 per cent as the target rate and that the "natural" rate is higher than 3 per cent. Suppose also that we start out at a time when prices have been stable and when unemployment is higher than 3 per cent. Accordingly, the authority increases the rate of monetary growth. This will be expansionary. By making nominal cash balances higher than people desire, it will tend initially to lower interest rates and in this and other ways to stimulate spending. Income and spending will start to rise.

To begin with, much or most of the rise in income will take the form of an increase in output and employment rather than in prices. People have been expecting prices to be stable, and prices and wages have been set for some time in the future on that basis. It takes time for people to adjust to a new state of demand. Producers will tend to react to the initial expansion in aggregate demand by increasing output, employees by working longer hours, and the unemployed, by taking jobs now offered at former nominal wages. This much is pretty standard doctrine.

But it describes only the initial effects. Because selling prices of products typically respond to an unanticipated rise in nominal demand faster than prices of factors of production, real wages received have gone down—through real wages anticipated by employees went up, since employees implic-

itly evaluated the wages offered at the earlier price level. Indeed, the simultaneous fall *ex post* in real wages to employers and rise *ex ante* in real wages to employees is what enabled employment to increase. But the decline *ex post* in real wages will soon come to affect anticipations. Employees will start to reckon on rising prices of the things they buy and to demand higher nominal wages for the future. "Market" unemployment is below the "natural" level. There is an excess demand for labor so real wages will tend to rise toward their initial level.

Even though the higher rate of monetary growth continues, the rise in real wages will reverse the decline in unemployment, and then lead to a rise, which will tend to return unemployment to its former level. In order to keep unemployment at its target level of 3 per cent, the monetary authority would have to raise monetary growth still more. As in the interest rate case, the "market" rate can be kept below the "natural" rate only by inflation. And, as in the interest rate case, too, only by accelerating inflation. Conversely, let the monetary authority choose a target rate of unemployment that is above the natural rate, and they will be led to produce a deflation, and an accelerating deflation at that.

What if the monetary authority chose the "natural" rate—either of interest or unemployment—as its target? One problem is that it cannot know what the "natural" rate is. Unfortunately, we have as yet devised no method to estimate accurately and readily the natural rate of either interest or unemployment. And the "natural" rate will itself change from time to time. But the basic problem is that even if the monetary authority knew the "natural" rate, and attempted to peg the market rate at that level, it would not be led to a determinate policy. The "market" rate will vary from the natural rate for all sorts of reasons other than monetary policy. If the monetary authority responds to these variations, it will set in train longer term effects that will make any monetary growth path it follows ultimately consistent with the rule of policy. The actual course of monetary growth will be analogous to a random walk, buffeted this way and that by the forces that produce temporary departures of the market rate from the natural rate.

To state this conclusion differently, there is always a temporary trade-off between inflation and unemployment; there is no permanent trade-off. The temporary trade-off comes not from inflation per se, but from unanticipated inflation, which generally means, from a rising rate of inflation. The widespread belief that there is a permanent trade-off is a sophisticated version of the confusion between "high" and "rising" that we all recognize in simpler forms. A rising rate of inflation may reduce unemployment, a high rate will not.

But how long, you will say, is "temporary"? For interest rates, we have some systematic evidence on how long each of the several effects takes to work itself out. For unemployment, we do not. I can at most venture a personal judgment, based on some examination of the historical evidence, that the initial effects of a higher and unanticipated rate of inflation last for something like two to five years; that this initial effect then begins to be reversed; and that a full adjustment to the new rate of inflation takes about as long for employment as for interest rates, say, a couple of decades. For both interest rates and employment, let me add a qualification. These estimates are for changes in the rate of inflation of the order of magnitude that has been experienced in the United States. For much more sizable changes, such as those experienced in South American countries, the whole adjustment process is greatly speeded up.

To state the general conclusion still differently, the monetary authority controls nominal quantities—directly, the quantity of its own liabilities. In principle, it can use this control to peg a nominal quantity—an exchange rate, the price level, the nominal level of national income, the quantity of money by one or another definition—or to peg the rate of change in a nominal quantity—the rate of inflation or deflation, the rate of growth or decline in nominal national income, the rate of growth of the quantity of money. It cannot

use its control over nominal quantities to peg a real quantity—the real rate of interest, the rate of unemployment, the level of real national income, the real quantity of money, the rate of growth of real national income, or the rate of growth of the real quantity of money.

II. WHAT MONETARY POLICY CAN DO

Monetary policy cannot peg these real magnitudes at predetermined levels. But monetary policy can and does have important effects on these real magnitudes. The one is in no way inconsistent with the other.

My own studies of monetary history have made me extremely sympathetic to the oft-quoted, much reviled, and as widely misunderstood, comment by John Stuart Mill. "There cannot . . . ," he wrote, "be intrinsically a more insignificant thing, in the economy of society, than money; except in the character of a contrivance for sparing time and labour. It is a machine for doing quickly and commodiously, what would be done, though less quickly and commodiously, without it: and like many other kinds of machinery, it only exerts a distinct and independent influence of its own when it gets out of order" [7, p. 488].

True, money is only a machine, but it is an extraordinarily efficient machine. Without it, we could not have begun to attain the astounding growth in output and level of living we have experienced in the past two centuries—any more than we could have done so without those other marvelous machines that dot our countryside and enable us, for the most part, simply to do more efficiently what could be done without them at much greater cost in labor.

But money has one feature that these other machines do not share. Because it is so pervasive, when it gets out of order, it throws a monkey wrench into the operation of all the other machines. The Great Contraction is the most dramatic example but not the only one. Every other major contraction in this country has been either produced by monetary disorder or greatly exacerbated by monetary disorder. Every major inflation has been produced by monetary expansion—mostly to meet the overriding demands of war which have forced the creation of money to supplement explicit taxation.

The first and most important lesson that history teaches about what monetary policy can do—and it is a lesson of the most profound importance—is that monetary policy can prevent money itself from being a major source of economic disturbance. This sounds like a negative proposition: avoid major mistakes. In part it is. The Great Contraction might not have occurred at all, and if it had, it would have been far less severe, if the monetary authority had avoided mistakes, or if the monetary arrangements had been those of an earlier time when there was no central authority with the power to make the kinds of mistakes that the Federal Reserve System made. The past few years, to come closer to home, would have been steadier and more productive of economic well-being if the Federal Reserve had avoided drastic and erratic changes of direction, first expanding the money supply at an unduly rapid pace, then, in early 1966, stepping on the brake too hard, at the end of 1966, reversing itself and resuming expansion until at least November, 1967, at a more rapid pace than can long be maintained without appreciable inflation.

Even if the proposition that monetary policy can prevent money itself from being a major source of economic disturbance were a wholly negative proposition, it would be none the less important for that. As it happens, however, it is not a wholly negative proposition. The monetary machine has gotten out of order even when there has been no central authority with anything like the power now possessed by the Fed. In the United States, the 1907 episode and earlier banking panics are examples of how the monetary machine can get out of order largely on its own. There is therefore a positive and important task for the monetary authority—to suggest improvements in the machine

that will reduce the chances that it will get out of order, and to use its own powers so as to keep the machine in good working order.

A second thing monetary policy can do is provide a stable background for economy—keep the machine well oiled, to continue Mill's analogy. Accomplishing the first task will contribute to this objective, but there is more than that. Our economic system will work best when producers and consumers, employers and employees, can proceed with full confidence that the average level of prices will behave in a known way in the future—preferably that it will be highly stable. Under any conceivable institutional arrangements, and certainly under those that now prevail in the United States, there is only a limited amount of flexibility in prices and wages. We need to conserve this flexibility to achieve changes in relative prices and wages that are required to adjust to dynamic changes in tastes and technology. We should not dissipate it simply to achieve changes in the absolute level of prices that serve no economic function.

In an earlier era, the gold standard was relied on to provide confidence in future monetary stability. In its heyday it served that function reasonably well. It clearly no longer does, since there is scarce a country in the world that is prepared to let the gold standard reign unchecked—and there are persuasive reasons why countries should not do so. The monetary authority could operate as a surrogate for the gold standard, if it pegged exchange rates and did so exclusively by altering the quantity of money in response to balance of payment flows without "sterilizing" surpluses or deficits and without resorting to open or concealed exchange control or to changes in tariffs and quotas. But again, though many central bankers talk this way, few are in fact willing to follow this course—and again there are persuasive reasons why they should not do so. Such a policy would submit each country to the vagaries not of an impersonal and automatic gold standard but of the policies—deliberate or accidental—of other monetary authorities.

In today's world, if monetary policy is to provide a stable background for the economy it must do so by deliberately employing its powers to that end. I shall come later to how it can do so.

Finally, monetary policy can contribute to offsetting major disturbances in the economic system arising from other sources. If there is an independent secular exhilaration—as the postwar expansion was described by the proponents of secular stagnation—monetary policy can in principle help to hold it in check by a slower rate of monetary growth than would otherwise be desirable. If, as now, an explosive federal budget threatens unprecedented deficits, monetary policy can hold any inflationary dangers in check by a slower rate of monetary growth than would otherwise be desirable. This will temporarily mean higher interest rates than would otherwise prevail—to enable the government to borrow the sums needed to finance the deficit—but by preventing the speeding up of inflation, it may well mean both lower prices and lower nominal interest rates for the long pull. If the end of a substantial war offers the country an opportunity to shift resources from wartime to peacetime production, monetary policy can ease the transition by a higher rate of monetary growth than would otherwise be desirable—though experience is not very encouraging that it can do so without going too far.

I have put this point last, and stated it in qualified terms—as referring to major disturbances—because I believe that the potentiality of monetary policy in offsetting other forces making for instability is far more limited than is commonly believed. We simply do not know enough to be able to recognize minor disturbances when they occur or to be able to predict either what their effects will be with any precision or what monetary policy is required to offset their effects. We do not know enough to be able to achieve stated objectives by delicate, or even fairly coarse, changes in the mix of monetary and fiscal policy. In this area particularly the best is likely to be the enemy of the good. Experience suggests that the path of wisdom is to use monetary policy explicitly to offset other disturbances only when they offer a "clear and present danger."

III. HOW SHOULD MONETARY POLICY BE CONDUCTED?

How should monetary policy be conducted to make the contribution to our goals that it is capable of making? This is clearly not the occasion for presenting a detailed "Program for Monetary Stability"—to use the title of a book in which I tried to do so [3]. I shall restrict myself here to two major requirements for monetary policy that follow fairly directly from the preceding discussion.

The first requirement is that the monetary authority should guide itself by magnitudes that it can control, not by ones that it cannot control. If, as the authority has often done, it takes interest rates or the current unemployment percentage as the immediate criterion of policy, it will be like a space vehicle that has taken a fix on the wrong star. No matter how sensitive and sophisticated its guiding apparatus, the space vehicle will go astray. And so will the monetary authority. Of the various alternative magnitudes that it can control, the most appealing guides for policy are exchange rates, the price level as defined by some index, and the quantity of a monetary total—currency plus adjusted demand deposits, or this total plus commercial bank time deposits, or a still broader total.

For the United States in particular, exchange rates are an undesirable guide. It might be worth requiring the bulk of the economy to adjust to the tiny percentage consisting of foreign trade if that would guarantee freedom from monetary irresponsibility—as it might under a real gold standard. But it is hardly worth doing so simply to adapt to the average of whatever policies monetary authorities in the rest of the world adopt. Far better to let the market, through floating exchange rates, adjust to world conditions the 5 per cent or so of our resources devoted to international trade while reserving monetary policy to promote the effective use of the 95 per cent.

Of the three guides listed, the price level is clearly the most important in its own right. Other things the same, it would be much the best of the alternatives—as so many distinguished economists have urged in the past. But other things are not the same. The link between the policy actions of the monetary authority and the price level, while unquestionably present, is more indirect than the link between the policy actions of the authority and any of the several monetary totals. Moreover, monetary action takes a longer time to affect the price level than to affect the monetary totals and both the time lag and the magnitude of effect vary with circumstances. As a result, we cannot predict at all accurately just what effect a particular monetary action will have on the price level and, equally important, just when it will have that effect. Attempting to control directly the price level is therefore likely to make monetary policy itself a source of economic disturbance because of false stops and starts. Perhaps, as our understanding of monetary phenomena advances, the situation will change. But at the present stage of our understanding, the long way around seems the surer way to our objective. Accordingly, I believe that a monetary total is the best currently available immediate guide or criterion for monetary policy—and I believe that it matters much less which particular total is chosen than that one be chosen.

A second requirement for monetary policy is that the monetary authority avoid sharp swings in policy. In the past, monetary authorities have on occasion moved in the wrong direction—as in the episode of the Great Contraction that I have stressed. More frequently, they have moved in the right direction, albeit often too late, but have erred by moving too far. Too late and too much has been the general practice. For example, in early 1966, it was the right policy for the Federal Reserve to move in a less expansionary direction—though it should have done so at least a year earlier. But when it moved, it went too far, producing the sharpest change in the rate of monetary growth of the postwar era. Again, having

gone too far, it was the right policy for the Fed to reverse course at the end of 1966. But again it went too far, not only restoring but exceeding the earlier excessive rate of monetary growth. And this episode is no exception. Time and again this has been the course followed—as in 1919 and 1920, in 1937 and 1938, in 1953 and 1954, in 1959 and 1960.

The reason for the propensity to overreact seems clear: the failure of monetary authorities to allow for the delay between their actions and the subsequent effects on the economy. They tend to determine their actions by today's conditions—but their actions will affect the economy only six or nine or twelve or fifteen months later. Hence they feel impelled to step on the brake, or the accelerator, as the case may be, too hard.

My own prescription is still that the monetary authority go all the way in avoiding such swings by adopting publicly the policy of achieving a steady rate of growth in a specified monetary total. The precise rate of growth, like the precise monetary total, is less important than the adoption of some stated and known rate. I myself have argued for a rate that would on the average achieve rough stability in the level of prices of final products, which I have estimated would call for something like a 3 to 5 per cent per year rate of growth in currency plus all commercial bank deposits or a slightly lower rate of growth in currency plus demand deposits only.[6] But it would be better to have a fixed rate that would on the average produce moderate inflation or moderate deflation, provided it was steady, than to suffer the wide and erratic perturbations we have experienced.

Short of the adoption of such a publicly stated policy of a steady rate of monetary growth, it would constitute a major improvement if the monetary authority followed the

[6] In an as yet unpublished article on "The Optimum Quantity of Money," I conclude that a still lower rate of growth, something like 2 per cent for the broader definition, might be better yet in order to eliminate or reduce the difference between private and total costs of adding to real balances.

self-denying ordinance of avoiding wide swings. It is a matter of record that periods of relative stability in the rate of monetary growth have also been periods of relative stability in economic activity, both in the United States and other countries. Periods of wide swings in the rate of monetary growth have also been periods of wide swings in economic activity.

By setting itself a steady course and keeping to it, the monetary authority could make a major contribution to promoting economic stability. By making that course one of steady but moderate growth in the quantity of money, it would make a major contribution to avoidance of either inflation or deflation of prices. Other forces would still affect the economy, require change and adjustment, and disturb the even tenor of our ways. But steady monetary growth would provide a monetary climate favorable to the effective operation of those basic forces of enterprise, ingenuity, invention,

hard work, and thrift that are the true springs of economic growth. That is the most that we can ask from monetary policy at our present stage of knowledge. But that much—and it is a great deal—is clearly within our reach.

References

1. Ellis, H. S., ed., *A Survey of Contemporary Economics*. Philadelphia 1948.
2. Friedman, Milton, "The Monetary Theory and Policy of Henry Simons," *Jour. Law and Econ.*, Oct. 1967, *10*, 1–13.
3. _____, *A Program for Monetary Stability*. New York 1959.
4. Goldenweiser, E. A., "Postwar Problems and Policies," *Fed. Res. Bull.*, Feb. 1945, *31*, 112–121.
5. Homan, P. T., and Machlup, Fritz, ed., *Financing American Prosperity*. New York 1945.
6. Lerner, A. P., and Graham, F. D., ed., *Planning and Paying for Full Employment*. Princeton 1946.
7. Mill, J. S., *Principles of Political Economy*, Bk. III, Ashley ed. New York 1929.

Rational Expectations and the Theory of Economic Policy*

Thomas J. Sargent and Neil Wallace

University of Minnesota

Reprinted from the *Journal of Monetary Economics*, 2:169–183 (1976), by permission of the authors and the publisher (copyright by the North-Holland Publishing Company).

* This paper is intended as a popular summary of some recent work on rational expectations and macroeconomic policy. To make the main points simple, the paper illustrates things by using simple ad hoc, linear models. However, the ideas cannot really be captured fully within this restricted framework. The main ideas we are summarizing are due to Robert E. Lucas, Jr., and were advanced by him most elegantly in the context of a stochastic general equilibrium model [see Lucas (1972a)]. Lucas's paper analyzes policy questions in what we regard to be the proper way, namely, in the context of a consistent general equilibrium model. The present paper is a popularization that fails to indicate how Lucas's neutrality propositions are derived from a consistent general equilibrium model with optimizing agents. It is easy to overturn the 'neutrality' results that we derive below from an ad hoc structure by making ad hoc changes in that structure. The advantage of Lucas's model is that ad hockeries are given much less of a role and, consequently, the neutrality proposition he obtains is seen to be a consequence of individual agents' optimizing behavior. In summary, this paper is not intended to be a substitute for reading the primary sources, mainly Lucas (1972a, 1972b, 1973, forthcoming).

There is no longer any serious debate about whether monetary policy should be conducted according to rules or discretion. Quite appropriately, it is widely agreed that monetary policy should obey a rule, that is, a schedule expressing the setting of the monetary authority's instrument (e.g. the money supply) as a function of all the information it has received up through the current moment. Such a rule has the happy characteristic that in any given set of circumstances, the optimal setting for policy is unique. If by remote chance, the same circumstances should prevail at two different dates, the appropriate settings for monetary policy would be identical.

The central practical issue separating monetarists from Keynesians is the appropriate form of the monetary policy rule. Milton Friedman has long advocated that the monetary authority adopt a simple rule having no feedback from current and past variables to the money supply. He recommends that the authority cause the money supply to grow at some rate of x percent per year without exception. In particular, the Fed ought not to try to 'lean against the wind' in an effort to attenuate the business cycle.

Within the context of macroeconometric models as they are usually manipulated, Friedman's advocacy of a rule without feedback seems indefensible. For example, suppose that a variable y_t, which the authority is interested in controlling, is described by the stochastic difference equation,

$$y_t = \alpha + \lambda y_{t-1} + \beta m_t + u_t, \tag{1}$$

where u_t is a serially independent, identically distributed random variable with variance σ_u^2 and mean zero; m_t is the rate of growth of the money supply; and α, λ and β are parameters. The variable y_t can be thought of as the unemployment rate or the deviation of real GNP from 'potential' GNP. This equation should be thought of as the reduced form of a simple econometric model.

Suppose that the monetary authority desires to set m_t in order to minimize the variance over time of y_t around some desired level y^*. It accomplishes this by appropriately choosing the parameters g_0 and g_1 in the feedback rule,

$$m_t = g_0 + g_1 y_{t-1}. \tag{2}$$

Substituting for m_t from (2) into (1) gives

$$y_t = (\alpha + \beta g_0) + (\lambda + \beta g_1) y_{t-1} + u_t. \tag{3}$$

From this equation the steady-state mean of y is given by

$$E(y) = (\alpha + \beta g_0)/[1 - (\lambda + \beta g_1)], \tag{4}$$

which should be equated to y^* in order to minimize the variance of y around y^*. From (3) the steady-state variance of y around its mean (and hence around y^*) is given by

$$\text{var } y = (\lambda + \beta g_1)^2 \text{ var } y + \sigma_u^2$$

or

$$\text{var } y = \sigma_u^2/[1 - (\lambda + \beta g_1)^2] \tag{5}$$

The monetary authority chooses g_1 to minimize the variance of y, then chooses g_0 from eq. (4) to equate $E(y)$ to y^*. From eq. (5), the variance of y is minimized by setting $\lambda + \beta g_1 = 0$, so that g_1 equals $-\lambda/\beta$. Then from eq. (4) it follows that the optimal setting of g_0 is $g_0 = (y^* - \alpha)/\beta$. So the optimal feedback rule for m_t is

$$m_t = (y^* - \alpha)/\beta - (\lambda/\beta) y_{t-1}. \tag{6}$$

Substituting this control rule into (1) gives

$$y_t = y^* + u_t,$$

which shows that application of the rule sets y_t equal to y^* plus an irreducible noise. Notice that application of the rule eliminates all serial correlation in y, since this is the way to minimize the variance of y. Use of rule (6) means that the authority always expects to be on target, since its forecast of y_t at time $t - 1$ is

$$\hat{y}_t = \alpha + \lambda y_{t-1} + \beta m_t,$$

which under rule (6) equals y^*.

Friedman's x-percent growth rule in effect sets g_1 equal to zero. So long as λ is not zero, that rule is inferior to the feedback rule (6).

This example illustrates all of the elements of the usual proof that Friedman's simple x-percent growth rule is suboptimal. Its logic carries over to larger stochastic difference equation models, ones with many more equations and with many more lags. It also applies where criterion functions have more variables. The basic idea is that where the effects of shocks to a goal variable (like GNP) display a stable pattern of persistence (serial correlation), and hence are predictable, the authority can improve the behavior of the goal variable by inducing offsetting movements in its instruments.

The notion that the economy can be described by presumably a large system of stochastic difference equations with fixed parameters underlies the standard Keynesian objections to the monism of monetarists who argue that the monetary authority should ignore other variables such as interest rates and concentrate on keeping the money supply on a steady growth path. The view that, on the contrary, the monetary authority should 'look at (and respond to) everything,' including interest rates, rests on the following propositions:[1] (a) the economic structure is characterized by extensive simultaneity, so that shocks that impinge on one variable, e.g. an interest rate, impinge also on most others; (b) due to lags in the system, the effects of shocks on the endogenous variables are distributed over time, and so are serially correlated and therefore somewhat predictable; and (c) the 'structure' of these lags is constant over time and does not depend on how the monetary authority is behaving. These propositions imply that variables that the authority observes very frequently, e.g. daily, such as interest rates, carry information useful for revising its forecasts of future value of variables that it can't observe as often, such as GNP and unemployment. This follows because the same shocks are affecting both the observed and the unobserved variables, and because those shocks have effects that persist. It follows then from (c) that the mone-

---

[1] See Kareken, Muench, and Wallace (1973) for a detailed presentation of this view.

tary authority should in general revise its planned setting for its policy instruments each time it receives some new and surprising reading on a variable that is determined simultaneously with a variable, like GNP or unemployment, that it is interested in controlling. Such an argument eschewing a simple x-percent growth rate rule in favor of 'looking at everything' has been made by Samuelson (1970):

'... when I learned that I has been wrong in my beliefs about how fast M was growing from December, 1968 to April, 1969, this news was just one of twenty interesting items that had come to my knowledge that week. And it only slightly increased my forecast for the strength of aggregate demand at the present time. That was because my forecasts, so to speak, do not involve "action at a distance" but are loose Markov processes in which a broad vector of current variables specify the "phase space" out of which tomorrow's vector develops. (In short, I knowingly commit that most atrocious of sins in the penal code of the monetarists—I pay a great deal of attention to all dimensions of "credit conditions" rather than keeping my eye on the solely important variable M/M.)
... often, I believe, the prudent man or prudent committee can look ahead six months to a year and with some confidence predict that the economy will be in other than an average or "ergodic" state. Unless this assertion of mine can be demolished, the case for a fixed growth rate for M, or for confining M to narrow channels around such a rate, melts away.

These general presumptions arise out of what we know about plausible models of economics and about the findings of historical experience.'[2]

There can be little doubt about the inferiority of an x-percent growth rule for the

[2] Perhaps the 'look at everything' view goes some way toward rationalizing the common view that policy ought not to be made by following a feedback rule derived from an explicit, empirically estimated macroeconometric model. It might be argued that the models that have been estimated omit some of the endogenous variables that carry information about the shocks impinging on the system as a whole. If the authority has in mind an a priori model that assigns those variables an important role, it is appropriate for it to alter its policy settings in response to new information about those variables. Perhaps this is what some people mean by 'discretion,' although we aren't sure.

money supply in a system satisfying proportions (a), (b), and (c) above. A reasonable disagreement with the 'look at everything, respond to everything' view would seemingly have to stem from a disbelief of one of those three premises. In particular, proposition (c) asserting the invariance of lag structures with respect to changes in the way policy is conducted would probably not be believed by an advocate of a rule without feedback.

Thus, returning to our simple example, a critical aspect of the proof of the suboptimality of Friedman's rule is clearly the assumption that the parameters α, λ, and β of the reduced form (1) are independent of the settings for g_0 and g_1 in the feedback rule. Macroeconometric models are almost always manipulated under such an assumption. However, Lucas (forthcoming) has forcefully argued that the assumption is inappropriate, and that the parameters of estimated reduced forms like (1) in part reflect the policy responses in operation during the periods over which they are estimated. This happens because in the reduced forms are embedded the responses of expectations to the way policy is formed. Changes in the way policy is made then ought not to leave the parameters of estimated reduced forms unchanged.

To illustrate this point while continuing without our example, suppose that our reduced form (1) has been estimated during some sample period and suppose that it comes from the 'structure:'

$$y_t = \xi_0 + \xi_1(m_t - E_{t-1}m_t) + \xi_2 y_{t-1} + u_t, \tag{7}$$

$$m_t = g_0 + g_1 y_{t-1} + \epsilon_t, \tag{8}$$

$$E_{t-1}m_t = g_0 + g_1 y_{t-1}. \tag{9}$$

Here ξ_0, ξ_1, and ξ_2 are fixed parameters; ϵ_t is a serially independent random term with mean zero. We assume that it is statistically independent of u_t. Eq. (8) governed the money supply during the estimation period. The variable $E_{t-1}m_t$ is the public's expectation of m_t as of time $t-1$. According to (9), the public knows the monetary authority's feedback rule and takes this into account in forming its expectations. According to eq. (7), unantici- pated movements in the money supply cause movements in y, but anticipated movements do not. The above structure can be written in the reduced form

$$y_t = (\xi_0 - \xi_1 g_0) + (\xi_2 - \xi_1 g_1) y_{t-1}$$
$$+ \xi_1 m_t + u_t, \qquad (10)$$

which is in the form of (1) with $\alpha = (\xi_0 - \xi_1 g_0)$, $\lambda = (\xi_2 - \xi_1 g_1)$ and $\beta = \xi_1$. While the form of (10) is identical with that of (1), the coefficients of (10) are clearly functions of the control parameters, the g's, that were in effect during the estimation period.

Suppose now that the monetary authority desires to design a feedback rule to minimize the variance of y around y^* under the assump- tion that the public will know the rule it is using and so use the currently prevailing g's in (8) in forming its expectations, rather than the old g's that held during the estimation period. The public would presumably know the g's if the monetary authority were to an- nounce them. Failing that, the public might be able to infer the g's from the observed behavior of the money supply and other vari- ables. In any case, on the assumption that the public knows what g's the authority is using, α and λ of eq. (1) come to depend on the authority's choice of g's. This fundamentally alters the preceding analysis, as can be seen by substituting $g_0 + g_1 y_{t-1}$ for m_t in (10) to arrive at

$$y_t = (\xi_0 - \xi_1 g_0) + (\xi_2 - \xi_1 g_1) y_{t-1}$$
$$+ \xi_1(g_0 + g_1 y_{t-1}) + u_t$$

or

$$y_t = \xi_0 + \xi_2 y_{t-1} + u_t + \xi_1 \epsilon_t. \qquad (11)$$

According to (11), the stochastic process for y_t does not even involve the parameters g_0 and g_1. Under different values of g_0 and g_1, the public's method of forming its expecta- tions is also different, implying differences in the values of α and λ in (1) under different policy regimes. In our hypothetical model, the resulting differences in α and λ just offset the differences in g_0 and g_1, leaving the behavior

of y identical as a result. Put somewhat dif- ferently, our old rule 'set $g_1 = -\lambda/\beta$' can no longer be fulfilled. For on the assumption that the public uses the correct g's in forming its expectations, it implies

$$g_1 = -\lambda/\beta = (\xi_1 g_1 - \xi_2)/\xi_1 = g_1 - \xi_2/\xi_1$$

or

$$0 = -\xi_2/\xi_1,$$

which is an equality not involving the g's, and one that the monetary authority is powerless to achieve. The rule '$g_1 = -\lambda/\beta$' in no way restricts g_1.

The point is that estimated reduced forms like (1) or (10) often have parameters that depend partly on the way unobservable ex- pectations of the public are correlated with the variables on the right side of the equation, which in turn depends on the public's percep- tion of how policymakers are behaving. If the public's perceptions are accurate, then the way in which its expectations are formed will change whenever policy changes, which will lead to changes in the parameters α and λ of the reduced-form equation. It is consequently improper to manipulate that reduced form as if its parameters were invariant with respect to changes in g_0 and g_1. According to this argument, then, the above 'proof' of the infer- iority of a rule without feedback is fallacious. The argument for the 'look at everything, re- spond to everything' view is correspondingly vitiated.

The simple model above is one in which there is no scope for the authority to conduct countercyclical policy by suitably choosing g_0 and g_1 so as to minimize the variance of y. Indeed, one choice of the g's is as good as another, so far as concerns the variance of y, so that the authority might as well set g_1 equal to zero, thereby following a rule without feed- back. It seems, then, that our example con- tains the ingredients for constructing a more general defense of rules without feedback. These ingredients are two: first, the author- ity's instrument appears in the reduced form for the real variable y only as the discrepancy of the instrument's setting from the public's prior expectation of that setting; and second, the public's psychological expectation of the setting for the instrument equals the objective mathematical expectation conditioned on data available when the expectation was formed. The first property in part reflects a homogeneity of degree zero of supply with respect to prices and expected prices, the natural unemployment rate hypothesis. But it also derives partly from the second property, which is the specification that the public's expectations are 'rational,' that is, are formed using the appropriate data and objective probability distributions.

The natural rate hypothesis posits that fully anticipated increases in prices have no effects on the rate of real economic activity, as indexed for example by the unemployment rate. A Phillips Curve that obeys the natural rate hypothesis can be written as

$$p_t - p_{t-1} = \phi_0 + \phi_1 U_t + {}_{t-1}p_t^*$$
$$- p_{t-1} + \epsilon_t, \quad \phi_1 < 0, \qquad (12)$$

or

$$p_t - {}_{t-1}p_t^* = \phi_0 + \phi_1 U_t + \epsilon_t, \qquad (13)$$

where U_t is the unemployment rate, p_t is the log of the price level, ${}_{t-1}p_t^*$ is the log of the price level that the public expects to prevail at time t as of time $t - 1$, and ϵ_t is a random term. According to (12), the Phillips Curve shifts up by the full amount of any increase in expected inflation. That implies, as indicated by eq. (13), that if inflation is fully anticipated, so that $p_t = {}_{t-1}p_t^*$, then the unemployment rate is unaffected by the rate of inflation, since (13) becomes one equation,

$$0 = \phi_0 + \phi_1 U_t + \epsilon_t,$$

that is capable of determining the unemployment rate independently of the rate of inflation.

As Phelps (1972) and Hall (forthcoming) have pointed out, in and of itself, the natural rate hypothesis does not weaken the logical foundations for 'activist' Keynesian macroeconomic policy, i.e. rules with feedback. This fact has prompted some to view the natural rate hypothesis as an intellectual curiosity,

having but remote policy implications.[3] To illustrate, we complete the model by adding to (13) a reduced form aggregate demand schedule and an hypothesis about the formation of expectations. We subsume 'Okun's Law' in the former and assume it takes the form

$$p_t = am_t + bx_t + cU_t, \quad c > 0, \qquad (14)$$

where m_t is the log of the money supply, the authority's instrument; and x_t is a vector of exogenous variables that follows the Markov scheme $x_t = \delta x_{t-1} + u_t$, u_t being a vector of random variables. For price expectations, we posit the ad hoc, in general 'irrational' scheme,

$$_{t-1}p_t^* = \lambda p_{t-1}, \qquad (15)$$

where λ is a parameter. Using (13)–(15), we can easily solve for unemployment as a function of m_t and x_t,

$$U_t = [\phi_0 - a(m_t - \lambda m_{t-1}) - b(x_t - \lambda x_{t-1})$$
$$+ c\lambda U_{t-1} + \epsilon_t]/(c - \phi_1). \qquad (16)$$

It follows that the current setting for m_t affects both current and future values of unemployment and inflation. Given that the authority wishes to minimize a loss function that depends on current and future unemployment and perhaps inflation, the choice of m_t is a nontrivial dynamic optimization problem, the solution to which can often be characterized as a control rule with feedback. The optimal policy rule will depend on all of the parameters of the model and on the parameters of the authority's loss function. The policy problem in this context has been studied by Hall and Phelps. The authority can improve the characteristics of the fluctuations in unemployment and inflation by setting m so as to offset disturbances to the x's.

In this system, if the authority has a 'humane' loss function that assigns regret to unemployment and that discounts the future somewhat, the authority should to some extent exploit the tradeoff between inflation and

---

[3] For example, see the remarks attributed to Franco Modigliani in *Brookings Papers on Economic Activity* 2 (1973, p. 480).

unemployment implied by (14) and (16). As Hall (forthcoming) has emphasized, the authority is able to do this by fooling people:

... the benefits of inflation derive from the use of expansionary policy to trick economic agents into behaving in socially preferable ways even though their behavior is not in their own interests. ... The gap between actual and expected inflation measures the extent of the trickery. ... The optimal policy is not nearly as expansionary when expectations adjust rapidly, and most of the effect of an inflationary policy is dissipated in costly anticipated inflation.

Hall has pinpointed the source of the authority's power to manipulate the economy. This can be seen by noting that removing the assumption that the authority can systematically trick the public eliminates the implication that there is an exploitable tradeoff between inflation and unemployment in *any* sense pertinent for making policy. The assumption that the public's expectations are 'rational' and so equal to objective mathematical expectations accomplishes precisely this. Imposing rationality amounts to discarding (15) and replacing it with

$$_{t-1}p_t^* = E_{t-1}p_t, \tag{17}$$

where E_{t-1} is the mathematical expectation operator conditional on information known at the end of period $t - 1$. If (17) is used in place of (15), eq. (16) must be replaced with[4]

$$U_t = [a(m_t - E_{t-1}m_t) + b(x_t - E_{t-1}x_t) \\ - \epsilon_t]/(\phi_1 - c) - \phi_0/\phi_1. \tag{18}$$

---

[4] Using (17), compute E_{t-1} of both sides of (13) and subtract the result from (13) to get

$$p_t - {_{t-1}}p_t^* = \phi_1(U_t - E_{t-1}U_t) + \epsilon_t. \tag{i}$$

Perform the same operation on (14) to get

$$p_t - {_{t-1}}p_t^* = a(m_t - E_{t-1}m_t) + b(x_t - E_{t-1}x_t) \\ + c(U_t - E_{t-1}U_t). \tag{ii}$$

Solve (i) for $(U_t - E_{t-1}U_t)$ and substitute the result into (ii) to get

$$(1 - c/\phi_1)(p_t - {_{t-1}}p_t^*) = a(m_t - E_{t-1}m_t) - (c/\phi_1)\epsilon_t \\ + b(x_t - E_{t-1}x_t). \tag{iii}$$

Upon substituting the implied expression for $(p_t - {_{t-1}}p_t^*)$ into (13), we get (18).

To solve the model for U_t, it is necessary to specify how the authority is behaving. Suppose we assume that the authority uses the feedback rule,

$$m_t = G\theta_{t-1} + \eta_t, \tag{19}$$

where θ_{t-1} is a set of observations on variables dated $t - 1$ and earlier, and η_t is a serially uncorrelated error term obeying $E[\eta_t|\theta_{t-1}] = 0$; G is a vector conformable with θ_{t-1}.

If the rule is (19) and expectations about m are rational, then

$$E_{t-1}m_t \equiv Em_t|\theta_{t-1} = G\theta_{t-1}, \tag{20}$$

since $E[\eta_t|\theta_{t-1}] = 0$. So we have

$$m_t - E_{t-1}m_t = \eta_t. \tag{21}$$

Substituting from (21) into (18) we have

$$U_t = [a\eta_t + b(x_t - E_{t-1}x_t) - \epsilon_t]/(\phi_1 - c) \\ - \phi_0/\phi_1. \tag{22}$$

Since the parameters G of the feedback rule don't appear in (22), we can conclude that the probability distribution of unemployment is independent of the values chosen for G. The distribution of the random, unpredictable component of m, which is η, influences the distribution of unemployment but there is no way in which this fact provides any logical basis for employing a rule with feedback. The η's have a place in (22) only because they are unpredictable noise. On the basis of the information in θ_{t-1}, there is no way that the η's can be predicted, either by the authority or the public.

In this system, there is no sense in which the authority has the option to conduct countercyclical policy. To exploit the Phillips Curve, it must somehow trick the public. But by virtue of the assumption that expectations are rational, there is no feedback rule that the authority can employ and expect to be able systematically to fool the public. This means that the authority cannot expect to exploit the Phillips Curve even for one period. Thus, combining the natural rate hypothesis with the assumption that expectations are rational transforms the former from a curiosity with perhaps remote policy implications into an hypothesis with immediate and drastic implications about the feasibility of pursuing countercyclical policy.[5]

As indicated above, by a countercyclical policy we mean a rule with feedback from current and past economic variables to the authority's instrument, as in a regime in which the authority 'leans against the wind.' While the present model suggests reasons for questioning even the possibility of a successful countercyclical policy aimed at improving the behavior of the unemployment rate or some closely related index of aggregate activity, the model is compatible with the view that there is an optimal rule for the monetary authority, albeit one that need incorporate no feedback. Such an optimal rule could be determined by an analysis that determines the optimal rate of expected inflation, along the lines of Bailey (1956) or Tobin (1967). If there is an optimal expected rate of inflation, it seems to imply restrictions on the constant and trend terms (and maybe the coefficients on some slowing moving exogenous variables like the labor force) of a rule for the money supply, but is not a cause for arguing for a feedback rule from endogenous variables to the money supply. The optimal rate of inflation, if there is one, thus has virtually no implications for the question of countercyclical policy. Furthermore, there is hardly any theoretical agreement about what the optimal rate of expected inflation is, so that it seems to be a weak reed for a control rule to lean on.

The simple models utilized above illustrate the implications of imposing the natural rate and rational expectations hypotheses in interpreting the statistical correlations summarized by the reduced forms of macroeconometric models, reduced forms that capture the correlations between monetary and fiscal variables on the one hand, and various real variables on the other hand. What is there to recommend these two hypotheses? Ordinarily, we impose two requirements on an economic model: first that it be consistent with the theoretical core of economics-optimizing behavior within a coherent general equilibrium framework; and second, that it not be refuted by observations. Empirical studies have not turned up much evidence that would cause rejection at high confidence levels of models incorporating our two hypotheses.[6] Furthermore, models along these lines seem to be the only existing ones consistent with individuals' maximizing behavior that are capable of rationalizing certain important correlations, such as the Phillips Curve, that exist in the data and are summarized by the reduced forms of macroeconometric models. The key feature of models that imply our hypotheses has been described by Lucas (1973): 'All formulations of the natural rate theory postulate rational agents, whose decisions depend on *relative* prices only, placed in an economic setting in which they cannot distinguish relative from general price movements.' Their inability separately to identify relative and overall nominal price changes is what gives rise to reduced forms like (1). But their rationality implies that only the surprise components of the aggregate demand variables enter. And this has the far reaching policy implications described above.

Several reasons can be given for using the hypotheses of rational expectations. An important one is that it is consistent with the findings that large parts of macroeconometric models typically fail tests for structural change (essentially versions of Chow tests).[7] As eq. (10) illustrates, if expectations are rational and properly take into account the way policy instruments and other exogenous variables evolve, the coefficients in certain representations of the model (e.g. reduced forms) will change whenever the processes governing

---

[5] The original version of such a 'neutrality' result is due to Lucas (1972a). His formulation is much deeper and more elegant than the one here, since his procedure is to start from individual agents' objectives and their information and then to investigate the characteristics of general equilibria. Less elegant formulations of neutrality results are in Sargent (1973) and Sargent and Wallace (1975).

[6] See Lucas (1973) and Sargent (1976, forthcoming) for empirical tests of the natural rate hypothesis.

[7] For example, see Muench et al. (1974).

those policy instruments and exogenous variables change. A major impetus to work on rational expectations is thus that it offers one reason, but probably not the only reason, that macroeconometric models fail tests for structural change. Indeed, the hypothesis of rational expectations even offers some hope for explaining how certain representations of the model change out of the sample.

A second reason for employing the hypothesis of rational expectations is that in estimating econometric models it is a source of identifying restrictions. The usual method of modeling expectations in macroeconometric models—via a distributed lag on the own variable—leaves it impossible to sort out the scalar multiplying the public's expectations from the magnitude of the weights in the distributed lag on own lags by which expectations are assumed to be formed. Therefore, the coefficients on expectations are generally underidentified econometrically. The way out of this has usually been to impose a unit sum on the distributed lag whereby expectations are formed. The problem is that this is an ad hoc identifying restriction with no economic reason to recommend it. It is generally incompatible with the hypothesis of rational expectations, which can be used to supply an alternative identifying restriction.[8]

A third reason for using the rational expectations hypothesis is that it accords with the economist's usual practice of assuming that people behave in their own best interests. This is not to deny that some people are irrational and neurotic. But we have no reason to believe that those irrationalities cause *systematic and predictable* deviations from rational behavior that a macroeconomist can model and tell the monetary authority how to compensate for. In this regard, it should be noted that the rational expectations hypothesis does not require that people's expectations equal conditional mathematical expectations, only that they equal conditional mathematical expectations plus what may be a very large random term (random with respect to the conditioning information). Thus we need only assume, for example, that

$$_{t-1}p_t^* = E_{t-1}p_t + \phi_t, \tag{18a}$$

where $E_{t-1}\phi_t = 0$, and ϕ_t is a random 'mother-in-law' term allowing for what may be very large random deviations from rationality. It is easy to verify that all of our results about countercyclical policy go through when (18a) is assumed. Therefore, in the context of the natural rate hypothesis, random deviations from perfectly rational expectations buy the monetary authority no leverage in making countercyclical policy. To be able to conduct a countercyclical policy, there must be systematic deviations from rational expectations which the monetary authority somehow knows about and can predict.

A fourth reason for adopting the hypothesis of rational expectations is the value of the questions it forces us to face. We must specify exactly the horizon over which the expectations are cast and what variables people are assumed to see and when, things that most macroeconometric models are silent on. In doing policy analysis under rational expectations, we must specify whether a given movement in a policy variable was foreseen beforehand or unforeseen, an old and important distinction in economics, but one that makes no difference in the usual evaluations of policy made with macroeconometric models.

Although the imposition of the natural rate and rational expectations hypotheses on reduced-form equations like (1) has allowed us to state some important results, such reasoning is no substitute for analysis of the underlying microeconomic models. Manipulation of such reduced forms even under the interpretation given by eqs. (7)–(9), which imposes the natural rate and rational expectations hypotheses, can be misleading because it leaves implicit some of the dependencies between parameters and rules. (For example, the 'structure' consisting of (7)–(9) is itself a reduced form suggested by Lucas (1973), some of whose parameters depend on the variance of ϵ_t in (8).) Also, a welfare analysis using such

---

[8] See Lucas (1972b, 1973) and Sargent (1971).

a model can be misleading because it requires adoption of an ad hoc welfare criterion, like the 'humane' loss function described above. In general, such a loss function is inconsistent with the usual welfare criterion employed in models with optimizing agents—Pareto optimality.

Finally, we want to take note of a very general implication of rationality that seems to present a dilemma. Dynamic models that invoke rational expectations can be solved only by attributing to the agents whose behavior is being described a way of forming views about the dynamic processes governing the policy variables. Might it not be reasonable at times to attribute to them a systematically incorrect view? Thus suppose an economy has been operating under one rule for a long time when secretly a new rule is adopted. It would seem that people would learn the new rule only gradually as they acquired data and that they would for some time make what from the viewpoint of the policy-maker are forecastable prediction errors. During this time, a new rule could be affecting real variables.

A telling objection to this line of argument is that new rules are not adopted in a vacuum. Something would cause the change—a change in administrations, new appointments, and so on. Moreover, if rational agents live in a world in which rules can be and are changed, their behavior should take into account such possibilities and should depend on the process generating the rule changes. But invoking this kind of complete rationality seems to rule out normative economics completely by, in effect, ruling out freedom for the policymaker. For in a model with completely rational expectations, including a rich enough description of policy, it seems impossible to define a sense in which there is any scope for discussing the optimal design of policy rules. That is because the equilibrium values of the endogenous variables already reflect, in the proper way, the parameters describing the authorities prospective subsequent behavior, including the probability that this or that proposal for reforming policy will be adopted.

Thus, suppose that a policy variable x_t is described by the objective probability distribution function,

$$\text{Prob}[x_{t+1} < F|Y_t, Z_t]$$
$$= G[F, Y_t, Z_t; g_1, \ldots, g_p], \quad (23)$$

where $Y_t = [y_t, y_{t-1}, \ldots]$ is a set of observations on current and past values of an endogenous variable, or vector of endogenous variables y; and where $Z_t = [z_t, z_{t-1}, \ldots]$ is a set of observations on current and past values of a list of n exogenous variables and disturbances z_t^i, $i = 1, \ldots, n$. The probability distribution has p parameters $g_1, \ldots, g_p$.

The probability distribution in (23) represents a very general description of the prospects about policy. It obviously can describe a situation in which policy is governed by a deterministic feedback rule, in which case the probability distribution collapses to a trivial one. The probability distribution in (23) can also model the case in which the monetary authority follows a feedback rule with random coefficients, coefficients that themselves obey some probability law. This situation is relevant where the monetary authority might consider changing the feedback rule from time to time for one reason or another. The probability distribution (23) can also model the case in which policy is in part simply random. The parameters $[g_1, \ldots, g_p]$ determine the probability function (23) and summarize all of the factors making up the objective prospects for policy. Policy settings appear to be random drawings from the distribution given in (23).

Now consider a rational expectations, structural model for y_t leading to a reduced form,

$$y_t = h(x_t, x_{t-1}, \ldots, Z_t, E_t y_{t+1}), \quad (24)$$

where $E_t y_{t+1}$ is the objective expectation of y_{t+1} conditioned on information observed up through time t. The Z_t's are assumed to obey some probability distribution functions,

$$\text{Prob}[z_{t+1}^1 < H^1, z_{t+1}^2 < H^2, \ldots, z_{t+1}^n < H^n|Z_t]$$
$$= F[H^1, H^2, \ldots, H^n, Z_t].$$

A final form solution for the model is represented by an equation of the form

$$y_t = \phi(x_t, x_{t-1}, \ldots, Z_t; \overline{g}), \qquad (25)$$

with the property that

$$E_t y_{t+1} = \iint \phi(x_{t+1}, x_t, \ldots, Z_{t+1}; \overline{g}) \, dG \, dF,$$

so that the expectation of y_{t+1} equals the prediction from the final form. The parameters $\overline{g} = [g_1, \ldots, g_p]$ turn out to be parameters of the final form (25), which our notation is intended to emphasize. Those parameters make their appearance in (25) via the process of eliminating $E_t y_{t+1}$ from (24) by expressing it in terms of the x's and Z's. The parameters of F also are embedded in ϕ for the same reason. That is, the function ϕ must satisfy the equation

$$\phi(x_t, x_{t-1}, \ldots, Z_t; \overline{g})$$

$$= h\left[x_t, x_{t-1}, \ldots, Z_t, \right.$$

$$\left. \iint \phi(x_{t+1}, x_t, \ldots, Z_{t+1}; \overline{g}) \, dG \, dF \right],$$

in which the parameters of F and G make their appearance by virtue of the integration with respect to G and F.

The final form (25) formally resembles the final forms of the usual macroeconometric models without rational expectations. But there is a crucial difference, for in (25) there are no parameters that the authority is free to choose. The parameters in the vector $\overline{g}$ describe the objective characteristics of the policy-making process and cannot be changed. They capture all of the factors that determine the prospects for policy. The authority in effect makes a random drawing of x from the distribution described by (23). The persons on the committee and staffs that constitute the authority 'matter' in the sense that they influence the prospects about policy and so are represented by elements of $\overline{g}$. But the authority has no freedom to influence the parameters of the final form (23), since the objective prospects that it will act wisely or foolishly are known to the public and are properly embedded in the final form (25).

The conundrum facing the economist can be put as follows. In order for a model to have normative implications, it must contain some parameters whose values can be chosen by the policymaker. But if these can be chosen, rational agents will not view them as fixed and will make use of schemes for predicting their values. If the economist models the economy taking these schemes into account, then those parameters become endogenous variables and no longer appear in the reduced-form equations for the other endogenous variables. If he models the economy without taking the schemes into account, he is not imposing rationality.

References

Bailey, M., 1956, The welfare cost of inflationary finance, Journal of Political Economy 64, April.

Hall, R. G., 1976, The Phillips Curve and macroeconomic policy, in: K. Brunner, ed., The Phillips Curve and labor markets, Journal of Monetary Economics, supplement.

Kareken, J. H., T. Muench and N. Wallace, 1973, Optimal open market strategy: The use of information variables, American Economic Review, March.

Lucas, R. E., Jr., 1972a, Expectations and the neutrality of money, Journal of Economic Theory 4, April, 103–124.

Lucas, R. E., Jr., 1972b, Econometric testing of the natural rate hypothesis, in: O. Eckstein, ed., The econometrics of price determination conference, sponsored by the Board of Governors of the Federal Reserve System and Social Science Research Council.

Lucas, R. E., Jr., 1973, Some international evidence on output-inflation tradeoffs, American Economic Review 63, June.

Lucas, R. E., Jr., 1976, Econometric policy evaluation: A critique, in: K. Brunner, ed., The Phillips Curve and labor markets, Journal of Monetary Economics, supplement.

Muench, T., A. Rolnick, N. Wallace, and W. Weiler, 1974, Tests for structural change and prediction intervals for the reduced forms of two structural models of the U.S.: The FRB-MIT and Michigan Quarterly models, Annals of Economic and Social Measurement 3, no. 3.

Phelps, E. S., 1972, Inflation policy and unemployment theory (Norton, New York).

Samuelson, P. A., 1930, Reflections on recent federal reserve policy, Journal of Money, Credit, and Banking, February.

Sargent, T. J., 1971, A note on the accelerationist controversy, Journal of Money, Credit, and Banking, August.

Sargent, T. J., 1973, Rational expectations, the real rate of interest, and the natural rate of unemployment, Brookings Papers on Economic Activity 2.

Sargent, T. J. and N. Wallace, 1975, Rational expections, the optimal monetary instrument, and optimal money supply rule, Journal of Political Economy, March–April.

Sargent, T. J., A classical macroeconometric model for the United States, Journal of Political Economy, forthcoming.

Tobin, J., 1967, Notes on optimal monetary growth, Journal of Political Economy, supplement.

The Monetarist Controversy or, Should We Forsake Stabilization Policies?

Franco Modigliani*

M.I.T.

In recent years and especially since the onset of the current depression, the economics profession and the lay public have heard a great deal about the sharp conflict between "monetarists and Keynesians" or between "monetarists and fiscalists." The difference between the two "schools" is generally held to center on whether the money supply or fiscal variables are the major determinants of aggregate economic activity, and hence the most appropriate tool of stabilization policies.

My central theme is that this view is quite far from the truth, and that the issues involved are of far greater practical import. There are in reality no serious analytical disagreements between leading monetarists and leading nonmonetarists. Milton Friedman was once quoted as saying, "We are all Keynesians, now," and I am quite prepared to reciprocate that "we are all monetarists"—if by monetarism is meant assigning to the stock of money a major role in determining output and prices. Indeed, the list of those who have long been monetarists in this sense is quite extensive, including among others John Maynard Keynes as well as myself, as is attested by my 1944 and 1963 articles.

Reprinted from the *American Economic Review*, 69:1–19 (1977), by permission of the author and the publisher (copyright by the American Economic Association).

* Presidential address delivered at the eighty-ninth meeting of the American Economic Association, Atlantic City, New Jersey, September 17, 1976.

In reality the distinguishing feature of the monetarist school and the real issues of disagreement with nonmonetarists is not monetarism, but rather the role that should probably be assigned to stabilization policies. Nonmonetarists accept what I regard to be the fundamental practical message of *The General Theory:* that a private enterprise economy using an intangible money *needs* to be stabilized, *can* be stabilized, and therefore *should* be stabilized by appropriate monetary and fiscal policies. Monetarists by contrast take the view that there is no serious need to stabilize the economy; that even if there were a need, it could not be done, for stabilization policies would be more likely to increase than to decrease instability; and, at least some monetarists would, I believe, go so far as to hold that, even in the unlikely event that stabilization policies could on balance prove beneficial, the government should not be trusted with the necessary power.

What has led me to address this controversy is the recent spread of monetarism, both in a simplistic, superficial form and in the form of growing influence on the practical conduct of economic policy, which influence, I shall argue presently, has played at least some role in the economic upheavals of the last three years.

In what follows then, I propose first to review the main arguments bearing on the *need* for stabilization policies, that is, on the likely extent of instability in the absence of such policies, and then to examine the issue of the supposed destabilizing effect of pursuing stabilization policies. My main concern will be with instability generated by the traditional type of disturbances—demand shocks. But before I am through, I will give some consideration to the difficult problems raised by the newer type of disturbance—supply shocks.

I. THE KEYNESIAN CASE FOR STABILIZATION POLICIES

A. The General Theory

Keynes' novel conclusion about the need for stabilization policies, as was brought out by the early interpreters of *The General Theory* (for example, John Hicks, the author, 1944), resulted from the interaction of a basic contribution to traditional monetary theory—liquidity preference—and an unorthodox hypothesis about the working of the labor market—complete downward rigidity of wages.

Because of liquidity preference, a change in aggregate demand, which may be broadly defined as any event that results in a change in the market clearing or equilibrium rate of interest, will produce a corresponding change in the real demand for money or velocity of circulation, and hence in the real stock of money needed at full employment. As long as wages are perfectly flexible, even with a constant nominal supply, full employment could and would be maintained by a change of wages and prices as needed to produce the required change in the real money supply—though even in this case, stability of the price level would require a countercyclical monetary policy. But, under the Keynesian wage assumption the classical adjustment through prices can occur only in the case of an increased demand. In the case of a decline, instead, wage rigidity prevents the necessary increase in the real money supply and the concomitant required fall in interest rates. Hence, if the nominal money supply is constant, the initial equilibrium must give way to a new stable one, characterized by

lower output and by an involuntary reduction in employment, so labeled because it does not result from a shift in notional demand and supply schedules in terms of real wages, but only from an insufficient real money supply. The nature of this equilibrium is elegantly captured by the Hicksian *IS-LM* paradigm, which to our generation of economists has become almost as familiar as the demand-supply paradigm was to earlier ones.

This analysis implied that a fixed money supply far from insuring approximate stability of prices and output, as held by the traditional view, would result in a rather unstable economy, alternating between periods of protracted unemployment and stagnation, and bursts of inflation. The extent of downward instability would depend in part on the size of the exogenous shocks to demand and in part on the strength of what may be called the Hicksian mechanism. By this I mean the extent to which a shift in *IS*, through its interaction with *LM*, results in some decline in interest rates and thus in a change in income which is smaller than the original shift. The stabilizing power of this mechanism is controlled by various parameters of the system. In particular, the economy will be more unstable the greater the interest elasticity of demand for money, and the smaller the interest responsiveness of aggregate demand. Finally, a large multiplier is also destabilizing in that it implies a larger shift in *IS* for a given shock.

However, the instability could be readily counteracted by appropriate stabilization policies. Monetary policy could change the nominal supply of money so as to *accomodate* the change in real demand resulting from shocks in aggregate demand. Fiscal policy, through expenditure and taxes, could *offset* these shocks, making full employment consistent with the initial nominal money stock. In general, both monetary and fiscal policies could be used in combination. But because of a perceived uncertainty in the response of demand to changes in interest rates, and because changes in interest rates through monetary policy could meet difficulties and substantial delays related to expectations (so-called liquidity traps), fiscal policy was regarded as having some advantages.

B. The Early Keynesians

The early disciples of the new Keynesian gospel, still haunted by memories of the Great Depression, frequently tended to outdo Keynes' pessimism about potential instability. Concern with liquidity traps fostered the view that the demand for money was highly interest elastic; failure to distinguish between the short- and long-run marginal propensity to save led to overestimating the long-run saving rate, thereby fostering concern with stagnation, and to underestimating the short-run propensity, thereby exaggerating the short-run multiplier. Interest rates were supposed to affect, at best, the demand for long-lived fixed investments, and the interest elasticity was deemed to be low. Thus, shocks were believed to produce a large response. Finally, investment demand was seen as capriciously controlled by "animal spirits," thus providing an important source of shocks. All this justified calling for very active stabilization policies. Furthermore, since the very circumstances which produce a large response to demand shocks also produce a large response to *fiscal* and a small response to *monetary* actions, there was a tendency to focus on fiscal policy as the main tool to keep the economy at near full employment.

C. The Phillips Curve

In the two decades following *The General Theory*, there were a number of developments of the Keynesian system including dynamization of the model, the stress on taxes versus expenditures and the balanced budget multiplier, and the first attempts at estimating the critical parameters through econometric techniques and models. But for present purposes, the most important one was the uncovering of a "stable" statistical relation between the rate of change of wages and the rate of unemployment, which has since come to be known as the Phillips curve. This relation, and its generalization by Richard Lipsey to allow for the effect of recent inflation, won wide acceptance even before an analytical underpinning could be provided for it, in part because it could account for the "puzzling" experience of 1954 and 1958, when wages kept rising despite the substantial rise in unemployment. It also served to dispose of the rather sterile "cost push"— "demand pull" controversy.

In the following years, a good deal of attention went into developing theoretical foundations for the Phillips curve, in particular along the lines of search models (for example, Edmund Phelps et al.). This approach served to shed a new light on the nature of unemployment by tracing it in the first place to labor turnover and search time rather than to lack of jobs as such: in a sense unemployment is all frictional—at least in developed countries. At the same time it clarified how the availability of more jobs tends to reduce unemployment by increasing vacancies and thus reducing search time.

Acceptance of the Phillips curve relation implied some significant changes in the Keynesian framework which partly escaped notice until the subsequent monetarists' attacks. Since the rate of change of wages decreased smoothly with the rate of unemployment, there was no longer a unique Full Employment but rather a whole family of possible equilibrium rates, each associated with a different rate of inflation (and requiring, presumably, a different long-run growth of money). It also impaired the notion of a stable underemployment equilibrium. A fall in demand could still cause an initial rise in unemployment but this rise, by reducing the growth of wages, would eventually raise the real money supply, tending to return unemployment to the equilibrium rate consistent with the given long-run growth of money.

But at the practical level it did not lessen the case for counteracting lasting demand disturbances through stabilization policies rather than by relying on the slow process of wage adjustment to do the job, at the

cost of protracted unemployment and instability of prices. Indeed, the realm of
stabilization policies appeared to expand in
the sense that the stabilization authority had
the power of choosing the unemployment rate
around which employment was to be stabilized, though it then had to accept the
associated inflation. Finally, the dependence
of wage changes also on past inflation forced
recognition of a distinction between the
short- and the long-run Phillips curve, the
latter exhibiting the long-run equilibrium
rate of inflation implied by a *maintained*
unemployment rate. The fact that the long-
run tradeoff between unemployment and
inflation was necessarily less favorable than
the short-run one, opened up new vistas of
"enjoy-it-now, pay-later" policies, and even
resulted in an entertaining literature on the
political business cycle and how to stay in
the saddle by riding the Phillips curve (see
for example, Ray Fair, William Nordhaus).

II. THE MONETARISTS' ATTACK

A. The Stabilizing Power of the Hicksian Mechanism

The monetarists' attack on Keynesianism
was directed from the very beginning not at
the Keynesian framework as such, but at
whether it really implied a need for stabilization. It rested on a radically different empirical assessment of the value of the parameters controlling the stabilizing power of the
Hicksian mechanism and of the magnitude
and duration of response to shocks, given a
stable money supply. And this different
assessment in turn was felt to justify a radical
downgrading of the *practical relevance* of the
Keynesian framework as distinguished from
its *analytical validity*.

Liquidity preference was a fine contribution to monetary theory but in practice
the responsiveness of the demand for money,
and hence of velocity, to interest rates, far
from being unmanageably large, was so small
that according to a well-known paper by
Milton Friedman (1969), it could not even
be detected empirically. On the other hand,

the effect of interest rates on aggregate
demand was large and by no means limited
to the traditional fixed investments but quite
pervasive. The difficulty of detecting it empirically resulted from focusing on a narrow
range of measured market rates and from the
fact that while the aggregate could be counted
on to respond, the response of individual
components might not be stable. Finally,
Friedman's celebrated contribution to the
theory of the consumption function (1957)
(and my own work on the life cycle hypothesis
with Richard Brumberg and others, reviewed
by the author, 1975) implied a very high
short-run marginal propensity to save in
response to transient disturbances to income
and hence a small short-run multiplier.

All this justified the conclusion that (i)
though demand shocks might qualitatively
work along the lines described by Keynes,
quantitatively the Hicks mechanism is so
strong that their impact would be *small* and
transient, provided the stock of money was
kept on a steady growth path; (ii) fiscal
policy actions, like other demand shocks,
would have *minor* and *transitory* effects on
demand, while changes in money would
produce *large* and *permanent* effects on money
income; and, therefore, (iii) the observed
instability of the economy, which was anyway
proving moderate as the postwar period
unfolded, was most likely the result of the
unstable growth of money, be it due to misguided endeavors to stabilize income or to
the pursuit of other targets, which were
either irrelevant or, in the case of balance of
payments goals, should have been made
irrelevant by abandoning fixed exchanges.

B. The Demise of Wage Rigidity and the Vertical Phillips Curve

But the most serious challenge came in
Friedman's 1968 Presidential Address, building on ideas independently put forth also by
Phelps (1968). Its basic message was that,
despite appearances, wages were in reality
perfectly flexible and there was accordingly
no involuntary unemployment. The evidence
to the contrary, including the Phillips curve,

was but a statistical illusion resulting from failure to differentiate between price changes and *unexpected* price changes.

Friedman starts out by reviving the Keynesian notion that, at any point of time, there exists a unique full-employment rate which he labels the "natural rate." An unanticipated fall in demand in Friedman's competitive world leads firms to reduce prices and also output and employment along the short-run marginal cost curve—unless the nominal wage declines together with prices. But workers, failing to judge correctly the current and prospective fall in prices, misinterpret the reduction of nominal wages as a cut in *real* wages. Hence, assuming a positively sloped supply function, they reduce the supply of labor. As a result, the effective real wage rises to the point where the resulting decline in the demand for labor matches the reduced supply. Thus, output falls not because of the decline in demand, but because of the entirely voluntary reduction in the supply of labor, in response to erroneous perceptions. Furthermore, the fall in employment can only be temporary, as expectations must soon catch up with the facts, at least in the absence of new shocks. The very same mechanism works in the case of an increase in demand, so that the responsiveness of wages and prices is the same on either side of the natural rate.

The upshot is that Friedman's model also implies a Phillips-type relation between inflation, employment or unemployment, and past inflation—provided the latter variable is interpreted as a reasonable proxy for expected inflation. But it turns the standard explanation on its head: instead of (excess) employment causing inflation, it is (the unexpected component of) the rate of inflation that causes excess employment.

One very basic implication of Friedman's model is that the coefficient of price expectations should be precisely unity. This specification implies that whatever the shape of the short-run Phillips curve—a shape determined by the relation between expected and actual price changes, and by the elasticity of labor

supply with respect to the perceived real wage—the long-run curve *must be vertical.*

Friendman's novel twist provided a fresh prop for the claim that stabilization policies are not really needed, for, with wages flexible, except possibly for transient distortions, the Hicksian mechanism receives powerful reinforcement from changes in the real money supply. Similarly, the fact that full employment was a razor edge provided new support for the claim that stabilization policies were bound to prove destabilizing.

C. The Macro Rational Expectations Revolution

But the death blow to the already badly battered Keynesian position was to come only shortly thereafter by incorporating into Friedman's model the so-called rational expectation hypothesis, or *REH*. Put very roughly, this hypothesis, originally due to John Muth, states that rational economic agents will endeavor to form expectations of relevant future variables by making the most efficient use of all information provided by past history. It is a fundamental and fruitful contribution that has already found many important applications, for example, in connection with speculative markets, and as a basis for some thoughtful criticism by Robert Lucas (1976) of certain features of econometric models. What I am concerned with here is only its application to macro-economics, or *MREH*, associated with such authors as Lucas (1972), Thomas Sargent (1976), and Sargent and Neil Wallace (1976).

The basic ingredient of *MREH* is the postulate that the workers of Friedman's model hold rational expectations, which turns out to have a number of remarkable implications: (i) errors of price expectations, which are the only source of departure from the natural state, cannot be avoided but they can only be short-lived and random. In particular, there cannot be persistent unemployment above the natural rate for this would simply high serial correlation between the successive errors of expectation, which is inconsistent with rational expectations; (ii) any attempts to stabilize the economy by means of stated monetary or fiscal rules are bound to be totally ineffective because their effect will be fully discounted in rational expectations; (iii) nor can the government successfully pursue *ad hoc* measures to offset shocks. The private sector is already taking care of any anticipated shock; therefore government policy could conceivably help only if the government information was better than that of the public, which is impossible, by the very definition of rational expectations. Under these conditions, *ad hoc* stabilization policies are most likely to produce instead further destabilizing shocks.

These are clearly remarkable conclusions, and a major *re*discovery—for it had all been said 40 years ago by Keynes in a well-known passage of *The General Theory:*

If, indeed, labour were always in a position to take action (and were to do so), whenever there was less than full employment, to reduce its money demands by concerted action to whatever point was required to make money so abundant relatively to the wage-unit that the rate of interest would fall to a level compatible with full employment, we should, in effect, have monetary management by the Trade Unions, aimed at full employment, instead of by the banking systems.

[p. 267]

The only novelty is that *MREH* replaces Keynes' opening "if" with a "since."

If one accepts this little amendment, the case against stabilization policies is complete. The economy is inherently pretty stable—except possibly for the effect of government messing around. And to the extent that there is a small residual instability, it is beyond the power of human beings, let alone the government, to alleviate it.

III. HOW VALID IS THE MONETARIST CASE?

A. The Monetarist Model of Wage Price Behavior

In setting out the counterattack it is convenient to start with the monetarists' model of price and wage behavior. Here one must distinguish between the model as such and a specific implication of that model, namely that the long-run Phillips curve is vertical, or, in substance, that, in the long run, money is neutral. That conclusion, by now, does not meet serious objection from nonmonetarists, at least as a first approximation.

But the proposition that other things equal, and given time enough, the economy will eventually adjust to any indefinitely maintained stock of money, or nth derivative thereof, can be derived from a variety of models and, in any event, is of very little practical relevance, as I will argue below. What is unacceptable, because inconsistent with both micro and macro evidence, is the specific monetarist model set out above and its implication that all unemployment is a voluntary, fleeting response to transitory misperceptions.

One may usefully begin with a criticism of the Macro Rational Expectations model and why Keynes' "if" should not be replaced by "since." At the logical level, Benjamin Friedman has called attention to the omission from *MREH* of an explicit learning model, and has suggested that, as a result, it can only be interpreted as a description not of short-run but of long-run equilibrium in which no agent would wish to recontract. But then the implications of *MREH* are clearly far from startling, and their policy relevance is almost nil. At the institutional level, Stanley Fischer has shown that the mere recognition of long-term contracts is sufficient to generate wage rigidity and a substantial scope for stabilization policies. But the most glaring flaw of *MREH* is its inconsistency with the evidence: if it were valid, deviations of unemployment from the natural rate would be small and transitory—in which case *The General Theory* would not have been written and neither would this paper. Sargent (1976) has attempted to remedy this fatal flaw by hypothesizing that the persistent and large fluctuations in unemployment reflect merely corresponding swings in the natural rate itself. In other words, what happened to the United States in the 1930's was a severe attack of contagious laziness! I can only say that, despite Sargent's ingenuity, neither I nor, I expect, most others at least of the nonmonetarists' persuasion are quite ready yet to turn over the field of economic fluctuations to the social psychologist!

Equally serious objections apply to Friedman's modeling of the commodity market as a perfectly competitive one—so that the real wage rate is continuously equated to the *short-run* marginal product of labor—and to his treatment of labor as a homogenous commodity traded in an auction market, so that, at the going wage, there never is any excess demand by firms or excess supply by workers. The inadequacies of this model as a useful formalization of present day Western economies are so numerous that only a few of the major ones can be mentioned here.

Friedman's view of unemployment as a voluntary reduction in labor supply could at best provide an explanation of variations in labor force—and then only under the questionable assumption that the supply function has a significantly positive slope—but cannot readily account for changes in unemployment. Furthermore, it cannot be reconciled with the well-known fact that *rising* unemployment is accompanied by a fall, not by a *rise* in quits, nor with the role played by temporary layoffs to which Martin Feldstein has recently called attention. Again, his competitive model of the commodity market, accepted also in *The General Theory*, implies that changes in real wages, adjusted for long-run productivity trend, should be significantly negatively correlated with cyclical changes in employment and output and with changes in money wages. But as early as 1938, John Dunlop showed that this conclusion was rejected by some eighty years of British experience and his results have received some support in more recent tests of Ronald Bodkin for the United States and Canada. Similar tests of my own, using quarterly data, provide striking confirmation that for the last two decades from the end of the Korean War until 1973, the association

of trend adjusted real compensation of the private nonfarm sector with either employment or the change in nominal compensation is prevailingly positive and very significantly so.[1]

This evidence can, instead, be accounted for by the oligopolistic pricing model—according to which price is determined by *long-run* minimum average cost up to a mark-up reflecting entry-preventing considerations (see the author, 1958)—coupled with some lags in the adjustment of prices to costs. This model implies that firms respond to a change in demand by endeavoring to adjust output and employment, without significant changes in prices relative to wages; and the resulting changes in available jobs have their initial impact not on wages but rather on unemployment by way of layoffs and recalls and through changes in the level of vacancies, and hence on the length of average search time.

If, in the process, vacancies rise above a critical level, or "natural rate," firms will endeavor to reduce them by outbidding each other, thereby raising the rate of change of wages. Thus, as long as jobs and vacancies remain above, and unemployment remains below, some critical level which might be labeled the "noninflationary rate" (see the

---

[1] Thus, in a logarithmic regression of private nonfarm hourly compensation deflated by the private nonfarm deflator on output per man-hour, time, and private nonfarm employment, after correcting for first-order serial correlation, the latter variable has a coefficient of .17 and a t-radio of 5. Similar though less significant results were found for manufacturing. If employment is replaced by the change in nominal compensation, its coefficient is .40 with a t-radio of 6.5. Finally, if the change in compensation is replaced by the change in price, despite the negative bias from error of measurement of price, the coefficient of this variable is only $-.09$ with an entirely insignificant t-ratio of .7. The period after 1973 has been omitted from the tests as irrelevant for our purposes, since the inflation was driven primarily by an exogenous price shock rather than by excess demand. As a result of the shock, prices, and to some extent wages, rose rapidly while employment and real wages fell. Thus, the addition of the last two years tends to increase spuriously the positive association between real wages and employment, and to decrease that between real wages and the change in nominal wages or prices.

author and Lucas Papademos, 1975), wages and prices will tend to accelerate. If, on the other hand, jobs fall below, and unemployment rises above, the noninflationary rate, firms finding that vacancies are less than optimal—in the limit the unemployed queuing outside the gate will fill them instantly—will have an incentive to reduce their relative wage offer. But in this case, in which too much labor is looking for too few jobs, the trend toward a sustained decline in the rate of growth of wages is likely to be even weaker than the corresponding acceleration when too many jobs are bidding for too few people. The main reason is the nonhomogeneity of labor. By far the largest and more valuable source of labor supply to a firm consists of those already employed who are not readily interchangeable with the unemployed and, in contrast with them, are concerned with protecting their earnings and not with reestablishing full employment. For these reasons, and because the first to quit are likely to be the best workers, a reduction of the labor force can, within limits, be accomplished more economically, not by reducing wages to generate enough quits, but by firing or, when possible, by layoffs which insure access to a trained labor force when demand recovers. More generally, the inducement to reduce relative wages to eliminate the excess supply is moderated by the effect that such a reduction would have on quits and costly turnover, even when the resulting vacancies can be readily filled from the ranks of the unemployed. Equally relevant are the consequences in terms of loss of morale and good will, in part for reasons which have been elaborated by the literature on implicit contracts (see Robert Gordon). Thus, while there will be some tendency for the rate of change of wages to fall, the more so the larger the unemployment—at least in an economy like the United States where there are no overpowering centralized unions—that tendency is severely damped.

And whether, given an unemployment rate significantly and persistently above the noninflationary level, the rate of change of wages would, eventually, tend to turn nega-

tive and decline without bound or whether it would tend to an asymptote is a question that I doubt the empirical evidence will ever answer. The one experiment we have had—the Great Depression—suggests the answer is negative, and while I admit that, for a variety of reasons, that evidence is muddied, I hope that we will never have the opportunity for a second, clean experiment.

In any event, what is really important for practical purposes is not the long-run equilibrium relation as such, but the speed with which it is approached. Both the model sketched out and the empirical evidence suggest that the process of acceleration or deceleration of wages when unemployment differs from the noninflationary rate will have more nearly the character of a crawl than of a gallop. It will suffice to recall in this connection that there was excess demand pressure in the United States at least from 1965 to mid-1970, and during that period the growth of inflation was from some 1.5 to only about 5.5 percent per year. And the response to the excess supply pressure from mid-1970 to early 1973, and from late 1974 to date was equally sluggish.

B. The Power of Self-Stabilizing Mechanisms: The Evidence from Econometric Models

There remains to consider the monetarists' initial criticism of Keynesianism, to wit, that even without high wage flexibility, the system's response to demand shocks is small and short-lived, thanks to the power of the Hicksian mechanism. Here it must be acknowledged that every one of the monetarists' criticisms of early, simpleminded Keynesianism has proved in considerable measure correct.

With regard to the interest elasticity of demand for money, post-Keynesian developments in the theory of money, and in particular, the theoretical contributions of William Baumol, James Tobin, Merton Miller, and Daniel Orr, point to a modest value of around one-half to one-third, and empirical studies (see for example, Stephen

Goldfeld) are largely consistent with this prediction (at least until 1975!). Similarly, the dependence of consumption on long-run, or life cycle, income and on wealth, together with the high marginal tax rates of the postwar period, especially the corporate tax, and leakages through imports, lead to a rather low estimate of the multiplier.

Last but not least, both theoretical and empirical work, reflected in part in econometric models, have largely vindicated the monetarist contention that interest effects on demand are pervasive and substantial. Thus, in the construction and estimation of the MIT-Penn-Social Science Research Council (*MPS*) econometric model of the United States, we found evidence of effects, at least modest, on nearly every component of aggregate demand. One response to money supply changes that is especially important in the *MPS*, if somewhat controversial, is via interest rates on the market value of all assets and thus on consumption.

There is, therefore, substantial agreement that in the United States the Hicksian mechanism is fairly effective in limiting the effect of shocks, and that the response of wages and prices to excess demand or supply will also work *gradually* toward eliminating largely, if not totally, any effect on employment. But in the view of nonmonetarists, the evidence overwhelmingly supports the conclusion that the *interim* response is still of significant magnitude and of considerable duration, basically because the wheels of the offsetting mechanism grind slowly. To be sure, the first link of the mechanism, the rise in short-term rates, gets promptly into play and heftily, given the low money demand elasticity; but most expenditures depend on long-term rates, which generally respond but gradually, and the demand response is generally also gradual. Furthermore, while this response is building up, multiplier and accelerator mechanisms work toward amplifying the shock. Finally, the classical mechanism—the change in real money supply through prices—has an even longer lag because of the sluggish response of wages to excess demand.

These interferences are supported by simulations with econometric models like the *MPS*. Isolating, first, the working of the Hicksian mechanism by holding prices constant, we find that a 1 percent demand shock, say a rise in real exports, produces an impact effect on aggregate output which is barely more than 1 percent, rises to a peak of only about 2 percent a year later, and then declines slowly toward a level somewhat over 1.5 percent.

Taking into account the wage price mechanism hardly changes the picture for the first year because of its inertia. Thereafter, however, it becomes increasingly effective so that a year later the real response is back at the impact level, and by the end of the third year the shock has been fully offset (thereafter output oscillates around zero in a damped fashion). Money income, on the other hand, reaches a peak of over 2.5, and then only by the middle of the second year. It declines thereafter, and tends eventually to oscillate around a *positive* value because normally, a demand shock requires eventually a change in interest rates and hence in velocity and money income.

These results, which are broadly confirmed by other econometric models, certainly do not support the view of a highly unstable economy in which fiscal policy has powerful and everlasting effects. But neither do they support the monetarist view of a highly stable economy in which shocks hardly make a ripple and the effects of fiscal policy are puny and fast vanishing.

C. The Monetarist Evidence and the St. Louis Quandary

Monetarists, however, have generally been inclined to question this evidence. They countered at first with tests bearing on the stability of velocity and the insignificance of the multiplier, which, however, as indicated in my criticism with Albert Ando (1965), must be regarded as close to worthless. More recently, several authors at the Federal Reserve Bank of St. Louis (Leonall Andersen,

Keith Carlson, Jerry Lee Jordan) have suggested that instead of deriving multipliers from the analytical or numerical solution of an econometric model involving a large number of equations, any one of which may be questioned, they should be estimated directly through "reduced form" equations by relating the change in income to current and lagged changes in some appropriate measure of the money supply and of fiscal impulses.

The results of the original test, using the current and but four lagged values of M^1 and of high Employment Federal Expenditure as measures of monetary and fiscal impulses, turned out to be such as to fill a monetarist's heart with joy. The contribution of money, not only current but also lagged, was large and the coefficients implied a not unreasonable effect of the order of magnitude of the velocity of circulation, though somewhat higher. On the other hand, the estimated coefficients of the fiscal variables seemed to support fully the monetarists' claim that their impact was both small and fleeting: the effect peaked in but two quarters and was only around one, and disappeared totally by the fourth quarter following the change.

These results were immediately attacked on the ground that the authors had used the wrong measure of monetary and fiscal actions, and it was shown that the outcome was somewhat sensitive to alternative measures; however, the basic nature of the results did not change, at least qualitatively. In particular, the outcome does not differ materially, at least for the original period up to 1969, if one replaces high employment outlays with a variable that might be deemed more suitable, like government expenditure on goods and services, plus exports.

These results must be acknowledged as disturbing for nonmonetarists, for there is little question that movements in government purchases and exports are a major source of demand disturbances; if econometric model estimates of the response to demand disturbances are roughly valid, how can they be so grossly inconsistent with the reduced form estimates?

Attempts at reconciling the two have taken several directions, which are reviewed in an article coauthored with Ando (1976). Our main conclusion, based on simulation techniques, is that when income is subject to substantial shocks from many sources other than monetary and fiscal, so that these variables account for only a moderate portion of the variations in income (in the United States, it has been of the order of one-half to two-thirds), then the St. Louis reduced form method yields highly unstable and unreliable estimates of the true structure of the system generating the data.

The crucial role of unreliability and instability has since been confirmed in more recent work of Daniel O'Neill in his forthcoming thesis. He shows in the first place that different methods of estimation yield widely different estimates, including many which clearly overstate the expenditure and understate the money multipliers. He further points out that, given the unreliability of the estimates resulting from multicollinearity and large residual variance, the relevant question to ask is not whether these estimates differ from those obtained by structural estimation, but whether the *difference is statistically significant;* that is, larger than could be reasonably accounted for by sampling fluctuations.

I have carried out this standard statistical test using as true response coefficients those generated by the *MPS* model quoted earlier.[2] I find that, at least when the test is based on the largest possible sample—the entire post-Korean period up to the last two very disturbed years—the difference is totally insignificant when estimation is in level form (F is less than one) and is still not significant at the 5 percent level, when in first differences.

This test resolves the puzzle by showing that there really is no puzzle: the two alter-

---

[2] For the purpose of the test, coefficients were scaled down by one-third to allow for certain major biases in measured government expenditure for present purposes (mainly the treatment of military procurement on a delivery rather than work progress basis, and the inclusion of direct military expenditure abroad).

native estimates of the expenditure multipliers are not inconsistent, given the margin of error of the estimates. It implies that one should accept whichever of the two estimates is produced by a more reliable and stable method, and is generally more sensible. To me, those criteria call, without question, for adopting the econometric model estimates. But should there be still some lingering doubt about this choice, I am happy to be able to report the results of one final test which I believe should dispose of the reduced form estimates—at least for a while. Suppose the St. Louis estimates of the expenditure multiplier are closer to God's truth than the estimates derived through econometric models. Then it should be the case that if one uses their coefficients to forecast income beyond the period of fit, these forecasts should be appreciably better than those obtained from a forecasting equation in which the coefficients of the expenditure variable are set equal to those obtained from econometric models.

I have carried out this test, comparing a reduced form equation fitted to the period originally used at St. Louis, terminating in 1969 (but reestimated with the lastest revised data) with an equation in which the coefficients of government expenditure plus exports were constrained to be those estimated from the *MPS*, used in the above *F*-test. The results are clear cut: the errors using the reduced form coefficient are not smaller but on the average substantially *larger* than those using *MPS* multipliers. For the first four years, terminating at the end of 1973, the St. Louis equation produces errors which are distinctly larger in eight quarters, and smaller in but three, and its squared error is one-third larger. For the last two years of turmoil, both equations perform miserably, though even here the *MPS* coefficients perform just a bit better. I have repeated this test with equations estimated through the first half of the postwar period, and the results are, if anything, even more one-sided.

The moral of the story is pretty clear. First, reduced form equations relying on just two exogenous variables are very unreliable for the purpose of estimating structure, nor are they particularly accurate for forecasting, though per dollar of research expenditure they are surprisingly good. Second, if the St. Louis people want to go on using this method and wish to secure the best possible forecast, then they should ask the *MPS* or any other large econometric model what coefficients they should use for government expenditure, rather than trying to estimate them by their unreliable method.

From the theory and evidence reviewed, we must then conclude that opting for a constant rate of growth of the nominal money supply can result in a stable economy only in the absence of significant exogenous shocks. But obviously the economy has been and will continue to be exposed to many significant shocks, coming from such things as war and peace, and other large changes in government expenditure, foreign trade, agriculture, technological progress, population shifts, and what not. The clearest evidence on the importance of such shocks is provided by our postwar record with its six recessions.

IV. THE RECORD OF STABILIZATION POLICIES: STABILIZING OR DESTABILIZING

A. Was Postwar Instability Due to Unstable Money Growth?

At this point, of course, monetarists will object that, over the postwar period, we have *not* had a constant money growth policy and will hint that the observed instability can largely be traced to the instability of money. The only way of meeting this objection squarely would be, of course, to rerun history with a good computer capable of calculating 3 percent at the helm of the Fed.

A more feasible, if less conclusive approach might be to look for some extended periods in which the money supply grew fairly smoothly and see how the economy fared. Combing through our post-Korean War history, I have been able to find just two stretches of several years in which the growth of the money stock was relatively stable, whether one chooses to measure stability in terms of percentage deviations from a constant growth or of dispersion of four-quarter changes. It may surprise some that one such stretch occurred quite recently and consists of the period of nearly four years beginning in the first quarter of 1971 (see the author and Papademos, 1976). During this period, the average growth was quite large, some 7 percent, but it was relatively smooth, generally well within the 6 to 8 percent band. The average deviation from the mean is about .75 percent. The other such period lasted from the beginning of 1953 to the first half of 1957, again a stretch of roughly four years. In sharp contrast to the most recent period, the average growth here is quite modest, only about 2 percent; but again, most four-quarter changes fell well within a band of two percentage points, and the average deviation is again .7. By contrast, during the remaining 13-year stretch from mid-1957 to the end of 1970, the variability of money growth was roughly twice as large if measured by the average deviation of four quarter changes, and some five times larger if measured by the percentage deviation of the money stock from a constant growth trend.

How did the economy fare in the two periods of relatively stable money growth? It is common knowledge that the period from 1971 to 1974, or from 1972 to 1975 if we want to allow a one-year lag for money to do its trick, was distinctly the most unstable in our recent history, marked by sharp fluctuations in output and wild gyrations of the rate of change of prices. As a result, the average deviation of the four-quarter changes in output was 3.3 percent, more than twice as large as in the period of less stable money growth. But the first stretch was also marked by well above average instability, with the contraction of 1954, the sharp recovery of 1955, and the new contraction in 1958, the sharpest in postwar history except for the present one. The variability of output is again 50 percent larger than in the middle period.

To be sure, in the recent episode serious exogenous shocks played a major role in the development of prices and possibly output, although the same is not so readily apparent for the period 1953 to 1958. But, in any event, such extenuating circumstances are quite irrelevant to my point; for I am not suggesting that the stability of money was the major cause of economic instability—or at any rate, not yet! All I am arguing is that (i) there is no basis for the monetarists' suggestion that our postwar instability can be traced to monetary instability—our most unstable periods have coincided with periods of relative monetary stability; and (ii) stability of the money supply is not enough to give us a stable economy, precisely because there are exogenous disturbances.

Finally, let me mention that I have actually made an attempt at rerunning history to see whether a stable money supply would stabilize the economy, though in a way that I readily acknowledge is much inferior to the real thing, namely through a simulation with the *MPS*. The experiment, carried out in cooperation with Papademos, covered the relatively quiet period from the beginning of 1959 to the introduction of price-wage controls in the middle of 1971. If one eliminates all major sources of shocks, for example, by smoothing federal government expenditures, we found, as did Otto Eckstein in an earlier experiment, that a stable money growth of 3 percent per year does stabilize the economy, as expected. But when we allowed for all the historical shocks, the result was that with a constant money growth the economy was far from stable—in fact, it was distinctly less stable than actual experience, by a factor of 50 percent.

B. The Overall Effectiveness of Postwar Stabilization Policies

But even granted that a smooth money supply will not produce a very stable world and that there is therefore room for stabilization policies, monetarists will still argue that we should nonetheless eschew such policies. They claim, first, that allowing for unpredictably variable lags and unforseeable future shocks, we do not know enough to successfully design stabilization policies, and second, that the government would surely be incapable of choosing the appropriate policies or be politically willing to provide timely enforcement. Thus, in practice, stabilization policies will result in destabilizing the economy much of the time.

This view is supported by two arguments, one logical and one empirical. The logical argument is the one developed in Friedman's Presidential Address (1968). An attempt at stabilizing the economy at full employment is bound to be destabilizing because the full employment or natural rate is not known with certainty and is subject to shifts in time; and if we aim for the incorrect rate, the result must perforce be explosive inflation or deflation. By contrast, with a constant money supply policy, the economy will automatically hunt for, and eventually discover, that shifty natural rate, wherever it may be hiding.

This argument, I submit, is nothing but a debating ploy. It rests on the preposterous assumption that the only alternative to a constant money growth is the pursuit of a very precise unemployment target which will be adhered to indefinitely no matter what, and that if the target is off in the second decimal place, galloping inflation is around the corner. In reality, all that is necessary to pursue stabilization policies is a rough target range that includes the warranted rate, itself a range and not a razor edge; and, of course, responsible supporters of stabilization policies have long been aware of the fact that the target range needs to be adjusted in time on the basis of forseeable shifts in the warranted range, as well as in the light of emerging evidence that the current target is not consistent with price stability. It is precisely for this reason that I, as well as many other nonmonetarists, would side with monetarists in strenuous opposition to recent proposals for a target unemployment rate rigidly fixed by statute (although there is nothing wrong with Congress committing itself and the country to work toward the eventual achievement of some target unemployment rate

through *structural* changes rather than aggregate demand policies).

Clearly, even the continuous updating of targets cannot guarantee that errors can be avoided altogether or even that they will be promptly recognized; and while errors persist, they will result in some inflationary (or deflationary) pressures. But the growing inflation to which Friedman refers is, to repeat, a crawl not a gallop. One may usefully recall in this connection the experience of 1965–70 referred to earlier, with the further remark that the existence of excess employment was quite generally recognized at the time, and failure to eliminate it resulted overwhelmingly from political considerations and not from a wrong diagnosis.[3]

There remains then only the empirical issue: have stabilization policies worked in the past and will they work in the future? Monetarists think the answer is negative and suggest, as we have seen, the misguided attempts at stabilization, especially through monetary policies, are responsible for much of the observed instability. The main piece of evidence in support of this contention is the Great Depression, an episode well documented through the painstaking work of Friedman and Anna Schwartz, although still the object of dispute (see, for example, Peter Temin). But in any event, that episode while it may attest to the power of money, is irrelevant for present purposes since the contraction of the money supply was certainly not part of a comprehensive stabilization program in the post-Keynesian sense.

When we come to the relevant postwar period, the problem of establishing the success

---

[3] Friedman's logical argument against stabilization policies and in favor of a constant money growth rule is, I submit, much like arguing to a man from St. Paul wishing to go to New Orleans on important business that he would be a fool to drive and should instead get himself a tub and drift down the Mississippi: that way he can be pretty sure that the current will eventually get him to his destination; whereas, if he drives, he might make a wrong turn and, before he notices he will be going further and further away from his destination and pretty soon he may end up in Alaska, where he will surely catch pneumonia and he may never get to New Orleans!

or failure of stabilization policies is an extremely taxing one. Many attempts have been made at developing precise objective tests, but in my view, none of these is of much value, even though I am guilty of having contributed to them in one of my worst papers (1964). Even the most ingenious test, that suggested by Victor Argy, and relying on a comparison of the variability of income with that of the velocity of circulation, turns out to be valid only under highly unrealistic restrictive assumptions.

Dennis Starleaf and Richard Floyd have proposed testing the effectiveness of stabilization by comparing the stability of money growth with that of income growth, much as I have done above for the United States, except that they apply their test to a cross section of industrialized countries. They found that for a sample of 13 countries, the association was distinctly positive. But this test is again of little value. For while a negative association for a given country, such as suggested by my U.S. test, does provide some weak indication that monetary activism helped rather than hindered, the finding of a positive association across countries proves absolutely nothing. It can be readily shown, in fact, that, to the extent that differential variability of income reflects differences in the character of the shocks—a most likely circumstance for their sample—successful stabilization also implies a positive correlation between the variability of income and that of money.

But though the search for unambiguous quantitative tests has so far yielded a meager crop, there exists a different kind of evidence in favor of Keynesian stabilization policies which is impressive, even if hard to quantify. To quote one of the founding fathers of business cycle analysis, Arthur Burns, writing in 1959, "Since 1937 we have had five recessions, the longest of which lasted only 13 months. There is no parallel for such a sequence of mild—or such a sequence of brief—contractions, at least during the past hundred years in our country" (p. 2). By now we can add to that list the recessions of 1961 and 1970.

There is, furthermore, evidence that very similar conclusions hold for other industrialized countries which have made use of stabilization policies; at any rate that was the prevailing view among participants to an international conference held in 1967 on the subject, "Is the business cycle obsolete?" (see Martin Bronfenbrenner, editor). No one seemed to question the greater postwar stability of all Western economies—nor is this surprising when one recalls that around that time business cycle specialists felt so threatened by the new-found stability that they were arguing for redefining business cycles as fluctuations in the *rate of growth* rather than in the *level* of output.

It was recognized that the reduced severity of fluctuations might in part reflect structural changes in the economy and the effect of stronger built-in stabilizers, inspired, of course, by the Keynesian analysis. Furthermore, the greater stability in the United States, and in other industrialized countries, are obviously not independent events. Still, at least as of the time of that conference, there seemed to be little question and some evidence that part of the credit for the greater stability should go to the conscious and on balance, successful endeavor at stabilizing the economy.

V. THE CASE OF SUPPLY SHOCKS AND THE 1974–76 EPISODE

A. Was the 1974 Depression Due to Errors of Commission or Omission?

In pointing out our relative postwar stability and the qualified success of stabilization policies, I have carefully defined the postwar period as ending somewhere in 1973. What has happened since that has so tarnished the reputation of economists? In facing this problem, the first question that needs to be raised is whether the recent combination of unprecedented rates of inflation as well as unemployment must be traced to crimes of commission or omission. Did our monetary and fiscal stabilization policies misfire, or did we instead fail to use them?

We may begin by establishing one point that has been blurred by monetarists' blanket indictments of recent monetary policy: the virulent explosion that raised the four-quarter rate of inflation from about 4 percent in 1972 to 6.5 percent by the third quarter of 1973, to 11.5 percent in 1974 with a peak quarterly rate of 13.5, can in no way be traced to an excessive, or to a disorderly, growth of the money supply. As already mentioned, the average rate of money growth from the beginning of 1970 to the second half of 1974 was close to 7 percent. To be sure, this was a high rate and could be expected sooner or later to generate an undesirably high inflation—but how high? Under any reasonable assumption one cannot arrive at a figure much above 6 percent. This might explain what happened up to the fall of 1973, but not from the third quarter of 1973 to the end of 1974, which is the really troublesome period. Similarly, as was indicated above, the growth of money was reasonably smooth over this period, smoother than at any other time in the postwar period, staying within a 2 percent band. Hence, the debacle of 1974 can just not be traced to an erratic behavior of money resulting from a misguided attempt at stabilization.

Should one then conclude that the catastrophe resulted from too slavish an adherence to a stable growth rate, forsaking the opportunity to use monetary policy to stabilize the economy? In one sense, the answer to this question must in my view be in the affirmative. There is ample ground for holding that the rapid contraction that set in toward the end of 1974, on the heels of a slow decline in the previous three quarters, and which drove unemployment to its 9 percent peak, was largely the result of the astronomic rise in interest rates around the middle of the year. That rise in turn was the unavoidable result of the Fed's stubborn refusal to accommodate, to an adequate extent, the exogenous inflationary shock due to oil, by letting the money supply growth exceed the 6 percent rate announced at the beginning of the year. And this despite repeated warnings about that

unavoidable result (see, for example, the author 1974).

Monetarists have suggested that the sharp recession was not the result of too slow a monetary growth throughout the year, but instead of the declaration that took place in the last half of 1974, and early 1975. But this explanation just does not stand up to the facts. The fall in the quarterly growth of money in the third and fourth quarters was puny, especially on the basis of revised figures now available: from 5.7 percent in the second to 4.3 and 4.1—hardly much larger than the error of estimate for quarterly rates! To be sure, in the first quarter of 1975 the growth fell to .6 percent. But, by then, the violent contraction was well on its way—between September 1974 and February 1975, industrial production fell at an annual rate of 25 percent. Furthermore, by the next quarter, monetary growth had resumed heftily. There is thus no way the monetarist proposition can square with these facts unless their long and variable lags are so variable that they sometimes turn into substantial leads. But even then, by anybody's model, a one-quarter dip in the growth of money could not have had a perceptible effect.

B. What Macro Stabilization Policies Can Accomplish, and How

But recognizing that the adherence to a stable money growth path through much of 1974 bears a major responsibility for the sharp contraction does not per se establish that the policy was mistaken. The reason is that the shock that hit the system in 1973–74 was not the usual type of demand shock which we gradually learned to cope with, more or less adequately. It was, instead, a supply or price shock, coming from a cumulation of causes, largely external. This poses an altogether different stabilization problem. In particular, in the case of demand shocks, there exists in principle an ideal policy which avoids all social costs, namely to offset completely the shock thus, at the same time, stabilizing employment and the price level. There may be disagreement as to whether this target can be achieved and how, but not about the target itself.

But in the case of supply shocks, there is no miracle cure—there is no macro policy which can both maintain a stable price level and keep employment at its natural rate. To maintain stable prices in the face of the exogenous price shock, say a rise in import prices, would require a fall in all domestic output prices; but we know of no macro policy by which domestic prices can be made to fall except by creating enough slack, thus putting downward pressure on wages. And the amount of slack would have to be substantial in view of the sluggishness of wages in the face of unemployment. If we do not offset the exogenous shock completely, then the initial burst, even if activated by an entirely transient rise in some prices, such as a once and for all deterioration in the terms of trade, will give rise to further increases, as nominal wages rise in a vain attempt at preserving real wages; this secondary reaction too can only be cut short by creating slack. In short, once a price shock hits, there is no way of returning to the initial equilibrium except after a painful period of both above equilibrium unemployment and inflation.

There are, of course, in principle, policies other than aggregate demand management to which we might turn, and which are enticing in view of the unpleasant alternatives offered by demand management. But so far such policies, at least those of the wage-price control variety, have proved disappointing. The design of better alternatives is probably the greatest challenge presently confronting those interested in stabilization. However, these policies fall outside my present concern Within the realm of aggregate demand management, the only choice open to society is the cruel one between alternative feasible paths of inflation and associated paths of unemployment, and the best the macro-economist can offer is policies designed to approximate the chosen path.

In light of the above, we may ask: is it conceivable that a constant rate of growth of the money supply will provide a satisfactory response to price shocks in the sense of giving rise to an unemployment-inflation path to which the country would object least?

C. The Monetarist Prescription: Or, Constant Money Growth Once More

The monetarists are inclined to answer this question affirmatively, if not in terms of the country's preferences, at least in terms of the preferences they think it should have. This is evidenced by their staunch support of a continuation of the 6 percent or so rate of growth through 1974, 1975 and 1976.

Their reasoning seems to go along the following lines. The natural rate hypothesis implies that the rate of inflation can change only when employment deviates from the natural rate. Now suppose we start from the natural rate and some corresponding steady rate of inflation, which without loss of generality can be assumed as zero. Let there be an exogenous shock which initially lifts the rate of inflation, say, to 10 percent. If the Central Bank, by accommodating this price rise, keeps employment at the natural rate, the new rate of 10 percent will also be maintained and will in fact continue forever, as long as the money supply accommodates it. The only way to eliminate inflation is to increase unemployment enough, above the natural rate and for a long enough time, so that the cumulated reduction of inflation takes us back to zero. There will of course be many possible unemployment paths that will accomplish this. So the next question is: Which is the least undesirable?

The monetarist answer seems to be—and here I confess that attribution becomes difficult—that it does not make much difference because, to a first approximation, the cumulated amount of unemployment needed to unwind inflation is independent of the path. If we take more unemployment early, we need to take less later, and conversely. But then it follows immediately that the specific path of unemployment that would be generated by a constant money growth is, if not better, at least as good as any other. Corollary: a constant growth of money is a satisfactory answer to supply shocks just as it is to demand shocks—as well as, one may suspect, to any other conceivable illness, indisposition, or disorder.

D. Why Constant Money Growth Cannot Be the Answer

This reasoning is admirably simple and elegant, but it suffers from several flaws. The first one is a confusion between the price level and its rate of change. With an unchanged constant growth of the nominal money stock, the system will settle back into equilibrium not when the rate of inflation is back to zero but only when, in addition, the price level itself is back to its initial level. This means that when inflation has finally returned back to the desired original rate, unemployment cannot also be back to the original level but will instead remain above it as long as is necessary to generate enough deflation to offset the earlier cumulated inflation. I doubt that this solution would find many supporters and for a good reason; it amounts to requiring that none of the burden of the price shock should fall on the holder of long-term money fixed contracts—such as debts—and that all other sectors of society should shoulder entirely whatever cost is necessary to insure this result. But, if, as seems to be fairly universally agreed, the social target is instead to return the system to the original rate of inflation—zero in our example—then the growth of the money supply cannot be kept constant. Between the time the shock hits and the time inflation has returned to the long-run level, there must be an additional increase in money supply by as much as the price level or by the cumulant of inflation over the path.

A second problem with the monetarists' argument is that it implies a rather special preference function that depends only on cumulated unemployment. And, last but not least, it requires the heroic assumption that the Phillips curve be not only vertical in the long run but also linear in the short run, an assumption that does not seem consistent with empirically estimated curves. Dropping this last assumption has the effect that, for any given social preference, there will be in general a unique optimal path. Clearly, for this path to be precisely that generated by a constant money growth, would require a miracle—or some sleight of the invisible hand!

Actually, there are grounds for holding that the unemployment path generated by a constant money growth, even if temporarily raised to take care of the first flaw, could not possibly be close to an optimal. This conclusion is based on an analysis of optimal paths, relying on the type of linear welfare function that appears to underlie the monetarists' argument, and which is also a straightforward generalization of Okun's famous "economic discomfort index." That index (which according to Michael Lovell appears to have some empirical support) is the sum of unemployment and inflation. The index used in my analysis is a weighted average of the cumulated unemployment and cumulated inflation over the path. The weights express the relative social concern for inflation versus unemployment.

Using this index, it has been shown in a forthcoming thesis of Papademos that, in general, the optimum policy calls for raising unemployment at once to a certain critical level and keeping it there until inflation has substantially abated. The critical level depends on the nature of the Phillips curve and the relative weights, but does not depend significantly on the initial shock—as long as it is appreciable. To provide an idea of the order of magnitudes involved, if one relies on the estimate of the Phillips curve reported in my joint paper with Papademos (1975), which is fairly close to vertical and uses Okun's weights, one finds that (i) at the present time, the noninflationary rate of unemployment corresponding to a 2 percent rate of inflation can be estimated at 5.6 percent, and (ii) the optimal response to a large exogenous price shock consists in increasing unemployment from 5.6 to only about 7 percent. That level is to be maintained until inflation falls somewhat below 4 percent; it should then be reduced slowly until inflation gets to 2.5 (which is estimated to take a couple of years), and rapidly thereafter. If, on the other hand, society were to rate inflation twice as costly as unemployment, the initial unemployment rate becomes just over 8 percent, though the path to final equilibrium is then shorter. These results seem intuitively sensible and quantitatively reasonable, providing further justification for the assumed welfare function, with its appealing property of summarizing preferences into a single readily understandable number.

One important implication of the nature of the optimum path described above is that a constant money growth could not possibly be optimal while inflation is being squeezed out of the system, regardless of the relative weights attached to unemployment and inflation. It would tend to be prevailingly too small for some initial period and too large thereafter.

One must thus conclude that the case for a constant money growth is no more tenable in the case of supply shocks than it is in the case of demand shocks.

VI. CONCLUSION

To summarize, the monetarists have made a valid and most valuable contribution in establishing that our economy is far less unstable than the early Keynesians pictured it and in rehabilitating the role of money as a determinant of aggregate demand. They are wrong, however, in going as far as asserting that the economy is sufficiently shockproof that stabilization policies are not needed. They have also made an important contribution in pointing out that such policies might in fact prove destabilizing. This criticism has had a salutary effect on reassessing what stabilization policies can and should do, and on trimming down fine-tuning ambitions. But their contention that postwar fluctuations resulted from an unstable money growth or that stabilization policies decreased raher than increased stability just does not stand up to an impartial examination

of the postwar record of the United States and other industrialized countries. Up to 1974, these policies have helped to keep the economy reasonably stable by historical standards, even though one can certainly point to some occasional failures.

The serious deterioration in economic stability since 1973 must be attributed in the first place to the novel nature of the shocks that hit us, namely, supply shocks. Even the best possible aggregate demand management cannot offset such shocks without a lot of unemployment together with a lot of inflation. But, in addition, demand management was far from the best. This failure must be attributed in good measure to the fact that we had little experience or even an adequate conceptual framework to deal with such shocks; but at least from my reading of the record, it was also the result of failure to use stabilization policies, including too slavish adherence to the monetarists' constant money growth prescription.

We must therefore, categorically reject the monetarist appeal to turn back the clock forty years by discarding the basic message of *The General Theory*. We should instead concentrate our eflorts in an endeavor to make stabilization policies even more effective in the future than they have been in the past.

References

Andersen, L. C. and Carlson, K. M., "A Monetarist Model for Economic Stabilization," *Fed. Reserve Bank St. Louis Rev.*, Apr. 1970, *52*, 7–25.
_____ and Jordan, J. L., "Monetary and Fiscal Action: A Test of Their Relative Importance in Economic Stabilization," *Fed. Reserve Bank St. Louis Rev.*, Nov. 1968, *50*, 11–23.
Argy, V., "Rules, Discretion in Monetary Management, and Short-Term Stability," *J. Money, Credit, Banking*, Feb. 1971, *3*, 102–122.
Baumol, W. J., "The Transactions Demand for Cash: An Inventory Theoretic Approach," *Quart. J. Econ.*, Nov. 1952, *66*, 545–556.
Bodkin, R. G., "Real Wages and Cyclical Variations in Employment: A Reexamination of the Evidence," *Can. J. Econ.*, Aug. 1969, *2*, 353–174.
Bronfenbrenner, Martin, *Is the Business Cycle Obsolete?*, New York 1969.

Burns, A. F., "Progress Towards Economic Stability," *Amer. Econ. Rev.*, Mar. 1960, *50*, 1–19.

Dunlop, J. T., "The Movement of Real and Money Wage Rates." *Econ. J.*, Sept. 1938, *48*, 413–434.

Eckstein, O. and Brinner, R., "The Inflation Process in the United States," in Otto Eckstein, ed., *Parameters and Policies in the U.S. Economy*, Amsterdam 1976.

Fair, R. C., "On Controlling the Economy to Win Elections," unpub. paper, Cowles Foundation 1975.

Feldstein, M. S., "Temporary Layoffs in the Theory of Unemployment," *J. Polit. Econ.*, Oct. 1976, *84*, 937–957.

Fischer, S., "Long-term Contracts, Rational Expectations and the Optimal Money Supply Rule," *J. Polit. Econ.*, forthcoming.

Friedman, B. M., "Rational Expectations Are Really Adaptive After All," unpub. paper, Harvard Univ. 1975.

Friedman, Milton, *A Theory of the Consumption Function*, Princeton 1957.

———, "The Role of Monetary Policy," *Amer. Econ. Rev.*, Mar. 1968, *58*, 1–17.

———, "The Demand for Money: Some Theoretical and Empirical Results," in his *The Optimum Quantity of Money, and Other Essays*, Chicago 1969.

——— and Schwartz, A., *A Monetary History of the United States 1867–1960*, Princeton 1963.

Goldfeld, S., "The Demand for Money Revisited," *Brookings Papers*, Washington 1973, *3*, 577–646.

Gordon, R. J., "Recent Developments in the Theory of Inflation and Unemployment," *J. Monet. Econ.*, Apr. 1976, *2*, 185–219.

Hicks, J. R., "Mr. Keynes and the "Classics"; A Suggested Interpretation," *Econometrica*, Apr. 1937, *5*, 147–59.

John Maynard Keynes, *The General Theory of Employment, Interest and Money*, New York 1935.

Lipsey, R. G., "The Relation Between Unemployment and the Rate of Change of Money Wage Rates in the United Kingdom, 1862–1957: A Further Analysis," *Economica*, Feb. 1960, *27*, 1–31.

Lovell, M., "Why Was the Consumer Feeling So Sad?," *Brookings Papers*, Washington 1975, *2*, 473–479.

Lucas, R. E., Jr., "Econometric Policy Evaluation: A Critique," *J. Monet. Econ.*, suppl. series, 1976, *1*, 19–46.

———, "Expectations and the Neutrality of Money," *J. Econ. Theory*, Apr. 1972, *4*, 103–124.

Miller, M., and Orr, D., "A Model of the Demand for Money by Firms," *Quart. J. Econ.*, Aug. 1966, *80*, 413–435.

Modigliani, F., "Liquidity Preference and the Theory of Interest and Money," *Econometrica*, Jan. 1944, *12*, 45–88.

———, "New Development on the Oligopoly Front," *J. Polit. Econ.*, June 1958, *66*, 215–33.

———, "The Monetary Mechanism and Its Interaction with Real Phenomena," *Rev. Econ. Statist.*, Feb. 1963, *45*, 79–107.

———, "Some Empirical Tests of Monetary Management and of Rules versus Discretion," *J. Polit. Econ.*, June 1964, *72*, 211–245.

———, "The 1974 Report of the President's Council of Economic Advisers: A Critique of Past and Prospective Policies," *Amer. Econ. Rev.*, Sept. 1974, *64*, 544–577.

———, "The Life Cycle Hypothesis of Saving Twenty Years Later," in Michael Parkin, ed., *Contemporary Issues in Economics*, Manchester 1975.

——— and Ando, A., "The Relative Stability of Monetary Velocity and the Investment Multiplier," *Amer. Econ. Rev.*, Sept. 1965, *55*, 693–728.

——— and ———, "Impacts of Fiscal Actions on Aggregate Income and the Monetarist Controversy: Theory and Evidence," in Jerome L. Stein, ed., *Monetarism*, Amsterdam 1976.

——— and Brumberg, R., "Utility Analysis and the Consumption Function: Interpretation of Cross-Section Data," in Kenneth Kurihara, ed., *Post-Keynesian Economics*, New Brunswick 1954.

——— and Papademos, L., "Targets for Monetary Policy in the Coming Years," *Brookings Papers*, Washington 1975, *1*, 141–165.

——— and ———, "Monetary Policy for the Coming Quarters: The Conflicting Views," *New Eng. Econ. Rev.*, Mar./Apr. 1976, 2–35.

Muth, J. F., "Rational Expectations and the Theory of Price Movements," *Econometrica*, July 1961, *29*, 315–335.

Nordhaus, W. D., "The Political Business Cycle," *Rev. Econ. Stud.*, Apr. 1975, *42*, 169–190.

Okun, A. M., "Inflation: Its Mechanics and Welfare Costs," *Brookings Papers*, Washington 1975, *2*, 351–390.

O'Neill, D., "Directly Estimated Multipliers of Monetary and Fiscal Policy," doctoral thesis in progress, M.I.T.

Papademos, L., "Optimal Aggregate Employment Policy and Other Essays," doctoral thesis in progress, M.I.T.

Phelps, Edmond S., "Money-Wage Dynamics and Labor-Market Equilibrium," *J. Polit. Econ.*, July/Aug. 1968, *76*, 678–711.

_____ et al., *Microeconomic Foundations of Employment and Inflation Theory*, New York 1970.

Phillips, A. W., "The Relation Between Unemployment and the Rate of Change of Money Wages Rates in the United Kingdom, 1861–1957," *Economica*, Nov. 1958, *25*, 283–299.

Sargent, T. J., "A Classical Macroeconomic Model for the United States," *J. Polit. Econ.*, Apr. 1976, *84*, 207–237.

_____ and Wallace, N., "'Rational' Expectations, the Optimal Monetary Instruments, and the Optimal Money Supply Rule," *J. Polit. Econ.*, Apr. 1975, *83*, 241–257.

Starleaf, D. and Floyd, R., "Some Evidence with Respect to the Efficiency of Friedman's Monetary Policy Proposals," *J. Money, Credit, Banking*, Aug. 1972, *4*, 713–722.

Temin, Peter, *Did Monetary Forces Cause the Great Depression?*, New York 1976.

Tobin, James, *Essay in Economics: Vol. 1, Macroeconomics*, Chicago 1971.

The most vexing problem confronting economic policy-makers in the seventies was the appearance of "stagflation." The coexistence of inflation and involuntary unemployment was not envisaged by either classical theory or the Keynesian theory. The initial short-lived experience with stagflation in the United States in the late fifties gave rise to a wave of "cost-push" theories of inflation. When stagflation became more than a passing phenomenon in the early seventies the neglect of economists concerning aggregate supply conditions in the face of the Keynesian-inspired emphasis on the determination of effective aggregate demand was thrown into sharp relief. The hasty attempts that were made to remedy this deficiency are recorded in the selections that follow. This new wave of theorizing has not coalesced sufficiently, however, to offer any clear guidance to economic policy-makers, and this must be considered a theoretical problem of the highest priority.

Economists were a little better prepared to deal with the problem of full employment and inflation. The theoretical discussion centered around the existence or nonexistence of the "Philips curve," an empirical and theoretical relationship that had been discussed by Irving Fisher in 1926 and by Keynes in *The General Theory*. Here the theory of the determination of the general level of wages was found inadequate to explain the actual behavior of wages and prices.

The development of employment and inflationary theory followed two general paths in the sixties and early seventies. One was to reflect on the microeconomic basis of inflation, concentrating on the behavior of the participants in the labor market, and the other was to formalize the idea of "disequilibrium." The earlier cost-push theories, and even *The General Theory* itself, contained many disequilibrium elements that were never formally integrated into the general analysis. According to the post-Keynesian macroeconomic theory, unemployment, at a given level of money wages, is due to the possibility that the level of aggregate effective demand may not provide to the labor-employing firms enough proceeds to justify the full employment of the available labor force.

The differential attribution of unemployment to the level of aggregate demand and the level of money wages and the identification of the respective importance of these two causes

PART THREE
Inflation and Unemployment

under different economic conditions continue to broadly characterize contemporary employment theory. However, if there is some agreement among economists on the role of aggregate demand, there is much less agreement on what labor market behavior is consistent with less than full employment macroeconomic equilibrium. Inflation is variously attributed to both demand and supply factors, expressed in the traditional distinction between "demand-pull" and "cost-push" (and "mark-up") types of inflation.

The lengthy survey by Laidler and Parkin discusses the vast literature on inflation without exhausting the field. Their survey appeared almost simultaneously with a number of other surveys,[1] and its principal characteristic is that the authors expressly lean toward the monetarist doctrine that inflation is always a monetary phenomenon caused by more rapid increases in the quantity of money than in output. Compared with the early sixties survey by Bronfenbrenner and Holzman, the Laidler and Parkin survey is indicative of the rise of monetarism during the last decade. The opponents to the monetary explanation of inflation argue that the monetary authorities are often accommodating the inflationary tendencies caused by social or political factors or by the system's inability or unwillingness to accept the consequences of sluggish productivity growth. Keynes in the General Theory had argued that "the long-term stability or instability of prices will depend on the strength of the upward trend of the wage-unit (or, more precisely, of the cost-unit) compared with the rate of increase in the efficiency of the productive system" (p. 309). For the monetarists, however, it is monetary accommodation which finally permits inflation to occur and run its course.

In evaluating the monetary explanation of inflation, one has to ponder two fundamental questions. First, within a general macroeconomic framework, is the supply of money an endogenous or an exogenous variable? An exogenous money supply means that it can

be controlled by the monetary authorities. In practice the authorities can change at will only the monetary base, but the latter will have predictable effects on the total money via the stable behavioral functions of the commercial banks, since the monetary base constitutes the banks' reserves. An endogenous money supply means that it cannot be effectively controlled by the monetary authorities. The behavioral functions of the commercial banks are unstable, and the money supply is determined at levels appropriate to the needs of business.

These positions concerning the exogeneity and the endogeneity of the money supply can be traced back to the respective positions taken by the English "Currency School" and "Banking School" in the early nineteenth century debates. The issue is still unresolved both theoretically and empirically, although any synthesis of the two positions essentially leads to a denial of the exogeneity argument.[2]

Second, we have the question as to whether or not a monetary nonaccommodation, leading to a dampening of aggregate demand, can cure inflation without causing a prolonged recession. At the theoretical level Kaldor argued that the source of inflationary pressures are money wage increases in response to rising profits. Since one cannot have rising production without rising profits, it follows that a monetary restriction can only succeed in stopping inflation if it also brings to a halt the growth process.[3] At the empirical level one can rarely find historical episodes when a monetary restriction did not cause at least a minor recession. On the whole it can be said that what is missing from a general theory of inflation is a "political economy of inflation," which would force one to reflect on the nature and interrelations among the various economic and political constraints imposed upon the monetary authorities' freedom to combat inflation.

Inflation and unemployment used to be thought of as polar cases. Keynes had repudiated this simplistic view by saying that any "increase in effective demand will, generally speaking,

[1] J. Trevithick and C. Mulvey, *The Economics of inflation* (New York: Wiley, 1975). Haberler, G., "Some Currently Suggested Explanations and Cures for Inflation," in Brunner, K., and Meltzer, A. (eds.), *Institutional Arrangements and the Inflation Problem* (Amsterdam: North Holland, 1976), pp. 143–177.

[2] F. Modigliani, "The Monetary Mechanism and its Interaction with Real Phenomena," *Review of Economics and Statistics*, 45:79–107 (1963).

[3] N. Kaldor, "Economic Growth and the Problem of Inflation," *Economica*, 26:212–226, 287–298 (1959). Reprinted in his *Essays on Economic Policy*, vol. 1 (New York: Norton, 1965), pp. 166–199.

spend itself partly in increasing the quantity of employment and partly in raising the level of prices. Thus, instead of constant prices in conditions of unemployment, and of prices rising in proportion to the quantity of money in conditions of full employment, we have in fact a condition of prices rising gradually as employment increases" (*The General Theory*, p. 296). The idea that inflation and unemployment can coexist and be inversely related to each other was to be rediscovered in the 1960s, following the publication of the empirical findings by A. W. Phillips, which suggested an inverse relationship between observed rates of unemployment and inflation, now generally referred to as the "Phillips curve." To examine the phenomenon of the Phillips curve became the pervasive concern of modern theories of unemployment and inflation.

Following Phillip's discovery there was a flurry of publications, mostly empirical, demonstrating that a Phillips curve does or does not exist and attempting to integrate this into general macroeconomic theory. At the theoretical level the analytical link between market behavior and the empirical observations was provided by a notion of "excess supply" such that money wages (and prices too) increase when there exists an excess of the number of unfilled job vacancies over the number of unemployed workers. Building on this base, which introduces the idea that nonmarket-clearing or "disequilibrium" is the foundation of a Phillips curve "theory," Bent Hansen presented a systematic explanation of the Phillips curve phenomenon, enriched by such concepts as "spontaneous wage changes" and inflationary expectations. In a certain way Hansen's paper marks the culmination of the "older generation" of Phillips curve theories, which left unanswered two fundamental theoretical questions: First, what are the cause of disequilibrium, or what are the essential operational properties of an economy in which unfilled vacancies coexist with unemployment? Second, what are the determinants of "spontaneous wage changes" and of expectations, and what would be the implications of introducing in the analysis an endogenous expectations mechanism exhibiting some degree of adaptation or "learning," especially when expectations are not fulfiled?

The answer to these questions marks the emergence of the "new wave" of Phillips curve

theories, whose classic statement can be found in the 14-author volume *Microeconomic Foundations of Employment and Inflation Theory*. This new approach is often associated with the work by E. S. Phelps, who in a subsequent book extended the ideas expressed in the above volume to its policy conclusions.[4] According to the "new wave" theories, any kind of disequilibrium is the outcome of decision-making under conditions of incomplete information and uncertainty. This is the source of behavior based on expectations that will very often be "wrong" and thus frustrated. Individual economic agents (firms, workers, etc.) behave in a rational way according to their own expectations so that they are always in a state of "equilibrium" in the sense that what they are doing is voluntary, regardless of whether their decisions lead to employment or not or to selling their product or not. The economy as a whole, however, may be in a state of disequilibrium when any divergence between expectations and the actual state of the economy generates money wage and price level changes. A macroeconomic equilibrium is then defined as a situation where aggregate supply is equal to aggregate demand and also where the observed frequency of wage and job offers is identical to the workers' subjective probability distribution of expected wage and job offers.

To this state of macroequilibrium there corresponds a rate of unemployment that depends upon the technological, demographic, and institutional parameters of the economy and which cannot be permanently altered by means of aggregate demand management policies. This "equilibrium rate of unemployment" is consistent with any rate of wage and price changes as long as that rate is fully anticipated. A negatively sloped Phillips curve can exist only when expectations are not fulfiled, and in that case the actual rate of unemployment can be different from the "natural" rate. When expectations are fulfiled, the Phillips curve will be vertical or, in other words, the equilibrium behavior of economic agents will imply just the natural rate of unemployment, regardless of the rate of inflation that is fully anticipated. This is the Phelps-Friedman "natural rate theory," whose policy implications are discussed in the

[4] E. S. Phelps, *Inflation Policy and Unemployment Theory* (New York: Norton, 1972).

debate presented in the previous section of this book.

The "new wave" Phillips curve theories have been criticized with respect to some obvious shortcomings. From an analytical point of view, this approach can only explain such types of unemployment as "speculative," "wait," and "search" unemployment, to borrow from Phelps's typology based on "motives." But all such unemployment is voluntary. In fact, this approach fails to explain involuntary unemployment, especially in the form of layoffs. Furthermore, there is evidence that most laid-off workers do not engage in speculative search activity, looking for alternative jobs, but instead wait to be recalled by their previous employer, living on income derived from unemployment compensation.[5] What seems to make the "new wave" theories unable to explain the phenomenon of layoffs is probably their exclusive emphasis of microeconomic behavior in an atomistic and perfectly competitive framework. Such a disequilibrium framework is obviously not consistent with Keynesian theory, where any degree of money wage rigidity was due to the unions' reluctance to see the relative wage structure change as not being in their favor.

Keynes's own explanation may appear *ad hoc* or based on his perception of what union behavior was at his time. Of course, what is true is that layoffs (and involuntary unemployment in general) cannot be explained without some degree of money wage rigidity. It recently has been argued that wage rigidity may be the outcome of rational choice for both individual workers and unions, to the extent that they prefer the certainty of a constant money wage (accompanied by the probability of temporary layoffs) over the uncertainty involved in having to look for different jobs every time they do not

get what they expect. The fundamental reason for preferring such fixed-wage (explicit or implicit) contractual arrangements is that workers are risk-averse and cannot minimize their risks as easily as the owners of nonhuman wealth.[6] These "contract models" make a significant contribution toward a rational theory of wage rigidity and layoffs, and we should soon see their generalization and integration into a genuine macroeconomic framework.

Finally, it must be noted that during the last 5 to 10 years the observed rates of unemployment and inflation in most western nations suggest a positively sloped Phillips curve. We still lack an adequate analysis of this phenomenon, despite a few attempts. For Kaldor[7] this reflects a structural change in the economy, accompanied by an increasing predominance of the manufacturing sector where prices are cost-determined and not necessarily market-clearing. To this he adds what Hicks calls "wage resistance," that is, unwillingness to accept real wage reductions even when the economy is sluggishly growing. On the other hand, Friedman[8] interprets this phenomenon to the economic agents' getting the habit of expecting higher inflation rates as a sort of hedging against the increasing unpredictability of the state of the economy. He argues that current institutional arrangements do not permit the agents to become fully insulated against unforeseen inflation (as would be the case with indexation). The erratic shifts in inflationary expectations very often cause situations which severely test the ability of the authorities to stabilize the economy, in view of the political constraints associated with the high unemployment rates necessary to break the inflationary expectations.

[5] M. Feldstein, "The importance of Temporary Layoffs: An Empirical Analysis," *Brookings Papers on Economic Activity*, pp. 725–745 (1975). *Brimmer, R. E.*, "The Death of the Phillips Curve Reconsidered," *Quarterly Journal of Economics*, 91: 389–418 (1977).

[6] See the references to Azariadis (1975a), M. N. Bailey (1974), and D. F. Gordon (1974) listed in the bibliography of R. J. Gordon's survey.
[7] N. Kaldor, "Inflation and Recession in the World Economy," *Economic Journal*, 86:703–714 (1976).
[8] M. Friedman, "Nobel Lecture: Inflation and Unemployment," *Journal of Political Economy*, 85:451–472 (1977).

Inflation: A Survey
David Laidler and Michael Parkin

University of Western Ontario

1. INTRODUCTION

Inflation is a process of continuously rising prices, or equivalently, of a continuously falling value of money. Its importance stems from the pervasive role played by money in a modern economy. A continuously falling value of pins, or of refrigerators, or of potatoes would not be regarded as a major social problem, important though it might be for the people directly engaged in the production and sale of those goods. The case of money is different precisely because the role that it plays in co-ordinating economic activity ensures that changes in its value over time impinge upon the well-being of everyone.

Money is a means of exchange, a store of value, and a unit of account. The ability of an asset to act as a store of value is a necessary precondition to its fulfilling the role of a means of exchange. Hence, a falling value of money detracts from its desirability as a store of value and begins to affect for the worse the efficiency of the mechanism of exchange in a market economy. Money's role as a unit of account stems from its use as a means of exchange, and in this role too it is undermined by inflation. In particular its usefulness as a unit of account in transactions involving deferred payments is vitiated. Inflation thus has a potentially serious effect on credit markets.[1]

Inflation is, then, fundamentally a monetary phenomenon. Some would go further and agree with Friedman that "*Inflation is always and everywhere a monetary phenomenon* . . . and can be produced only by a more rapid increase in the quantity of money than in output" (Friedman, 1970, p. 24). Whilst few would deny that inflation is a monetary phenomenon in the sense that we have described, or in the sense that it is *accompanied* by a rise in the quantity of money, many would deny that its origins are monetary. Rather they would agree with Hicks that "our present troubles are not of a monetary character and are not to be cured by monetary means", and that whilst "it was true in the old days that inflation was a monetary matter; prices rose because the supply of money was greater than the demand for it . . . money is now a mere counter, which is supplied by the banking system (or by the government

[1] Accounts of the social role of money were at one time a commonplace in the textbook literature. Developments in the so-called "new micro economics" which deal with behavior in conditions of imperfect information have led to a revival of interest in this branch of analysis (cf., for example, Brunner and Meltzer, 1971; Feldman, 1973; Ostroy, 1973; Starr, 1972; Nichans, 1969; Laidler, 1974). Note that Alchian & Klein (1973) regard the effect of inflation on asset prices as sufficiently important for them to propose that conventional price indices in which asset prices are relatively unrepresented are inappropriate as bases for measuring inflation.

Reprinted from the *Economic Journal,* 85:741–809 (1975), by permission of the authors and the publisher (copyright by the Royal Economic Society, published by Cambridge University Press).

through the banking system) just as it is required" (Hicks, 1975, p. 17). Some would go even further and agree with Harrod that the "new wage-price explosion is altogether unprecedented . . . the causes [of which] are sociological [and] first cousins to the causes of such things as student unrest" (Harrod, 1972, p. 44). It is virtually impossible in surveying a problem area as important as that of inflation, and one which generates such divergent views as those just cited, to be entirely fair to all positions. We have tried to be fair, but we are conscious that many will feel that we have not succeeded. We should declare at the outset, therefore, that, in terms of the alternative views cited above, we find ourselves in broad agreement with Friedman.

Since a large element in the debate on inflation centres on the direction of causation between money and prices it may seem natural to organize a survey of the literature around the traditional cost-push versus demand-pull distinction. The distinction is central to much of the literature surveyed here, but we have not, for several reasons, used it as a basis for our exposition. We find the distinction to be, first, imprecise—this imprecision being all too evident from the quotation with which Bronfenbrenner and Holzman (1963) began an earlier survey on this topic:[2] "The economic stalactite of inflated demand has met a sociological stalagmite of up-thrusting claims; when the stalactite and stalagmite meet and fuse in an icy kiss—I hope there is no geologist present to tell me that I am talking through my hat—nobody on earth can be quite sure where the one ends and the other begins" (Robertson, 1961). Secondly, the distinction implies that inflation can be analyzed by examining separately the supply and demand sides of product and factor markets and investigating the

forces making for shifts in functional relationships in all four areas. We do not believe that this way of looking at things accords well with the structure of much modern analysis of inflation. The role of excess demand as a proximate determinant of rising wages or prices lies at the centre of such analysis, but much of the analysis of the process of rising wages and prices is quite independent of whether the *source* of excess demand is a supply side or a demand side shift. Another major ingredient of modern theory is inflationary expectations and such expectations can influence both the supply and demand sides of both factor and product markets. It is helpful to distinguish between supplyside and demandside factors when analyzing a single micro-market, but the interdependence of aggregate demand and supply is a central feature of modern macro-economics. Since inflation is a phenomenon affecting the whole economy, we find the cost-push/demand-pull distinction analytically unhelpful as a device for classifying those developments in inflation theory that are grounded in macro-economics.

We have found the distinction between equilibrium, or perfectly anticipated inflation, and disequilibrium, or imperfectly anticipated inflation, more useful. Much recent work, particularly of a theoretical nature, on monetary explanations of inflation concentrates on the former, but clearly all the interesting and important practical questions concern macroeconomic disequilibrium in which inflation is imperfectly anticipated: inflation can only be perfectly anticipated in any actual economy if all people and organizations (e.g., Trade Unions, Trade Associations) hold the same expectations, since otherwise some expectations are bound to be wrong. The interaction of prices and wages with excess demand, unemployment, inventory changes and the like, when expectations and realizations are different, is an important element in the subject matter of modern short-run macroeconomics. Analysis of such problems goes back through the work of Keynes (1936) and Hayek (1933) to Fisher (1911) and

---

[2] A further earlier survey of inflation is Johnson (1963). Books which contain a large element of survey material but which also stand as major contributions to the subject at the time of their publication are Brown (1955) and Wilson (1961) as well as the I.E.A. conference proceedings edited by Hague (1962).

Wicksell (1898). When expectations are not fulfilled the burden of adjustment falls partly on quantities of employment, output, and inventories, and partly on prices. Study of the behavior of wage and price setters and their role in the transmission process of monetary and fiscal impulses to price and quantity decisions provides a necessary micro-foundation for macro-analysis and has attracted much attention recently. Discussion of the relevant literature takes up a large part of this survey. In surveying this literature, we also examine theories and evidence on the role of sociological or cost-push influences on inflation.

Much modern literature has returned to an older tradition in monetary theory in recognizing that inflation is not, except in particular circumstances, a purely national phenomenon. Fixed exchange rates link countries together in a monetary union within which each country shares a common inflationary experience. The analysis of inflation in such a world has to be conducted at the level of the monetary union and not at the level of the individual nation state. As we shall see, the analysis of inflation as an international phenomenon is well developed for a world of fixed exchange rate countries but is still in its infancy as regards the behavior of economies linked by temporarily rigid (or "jumping") exchange rates or by "dirty floating" rates.

These then are the main themes of our survey. We begin with an account of recent developments in the mainly theoretical analysis of fully anticipated inflation. Then we go on to deal with wage and price setting behavior in situations of less than fully anticipated inflation, showing how such micro-analysis may be incorporated into a "complete" macro-model of disequilibrium inflation. We next turn attention to inflation as an international phenomenon, after which, in the final substantive section of our survey, we deal with the consequences of inflation.

The reader will notice certain omissions from the list of topics that might have found a place in a survey such as this. First, we have hardly touched upon the extensive literature on inflation in less developed countries. Many

of the issues involved in that literature are, of course, the same as those that arise in the context of the British or American economies, whence most of the applied work we discuss is drawn, but the interaction of inflation with the process of economic development provides an extra theme in literature on developing countries that requires expertise in development economics if justice is to be done to it. This expertise is possessed by neither of us, and since a survey article specifically on inflation in less developed countries by Kirkpatrick & Nixon (1975) already exists, we consciously chose to avoid dealing with this literature.

Our other major omission concerns explicit discussion of policy towards inflation as a separate topic. A good deal of policy discussion is, of course, implicit in the work that follows, and our omission is not as blatant as it might seem at first sight. Even so, policy aspects of the literature are relatively down-played in what follows, and for two reasons. First, a good deal of literature on anti-inflation policy, particularly in the context of the British economy, has been concerned with so-called "prices and incomes" policies, and one of us has only recently been involved in the preparation of a survey of that literature.[3] Secondly, and more important, in the process of preparing this survey we became painfully aware of an important gap in the literature in the area of what we might term the "political economy" of inflation; although, of course, much policy discussion in the post-war years did center on political aspects of choice, which was sometimes considered to be constrained by a stable inflation—employment trade-off. The literature that we survey has a great deal to say about, and much light to shed upon, the behavior of price and wage setters. It also has a great deal to say about how monetary and fiscal policy affects that behavior. It does not have a great deal to say about why the particular policies which so often lead to inflation are pursued. A survey of the political economy of inflation

---

[3] Cf. Parkin, Sumner and Jones (1972).

will have to await the generation of literature to be surveyed, but it is within the context of this, as yet unwritten, literature, that we would expect to find the fundamental issues involved in the design of policy towards inflation being clearly defined. As yet, in our judgment, they have not been.

2. THE QUANTITY THEORY AND PERFECTLY ANTICIPATED INFLATION

Though it has been under persistent challenge, the quantity theory of money has, in one form or another, dominated the literature on inflation for the greater part of the last three hundred years.[4] We therefore begin with an account of the post-war developments of this tradition as they impinge on the economics of inflation. The phrase "quantity theory of money" has two distinct meanings, and we use it here in its traditional sense to refer to a body of doctrine about the relationship between the money supply and the general price level, rather than in its more recent and narrow sense, to refer to a theory of the demand for money; although we shall see in due course that it is only in this latter sense that the quantity theory survives as a useful component of inflation theory.

The most attractive feature of the quantity theory as a theory of the price level is the simplicity that arises from its being a particular application of the tools of supply and demand to the problem of determining a particular price, in this case the price of money in terms of goods, or to use the more familiar inverse concept, the general price level of goods in terms of money.[5] Certain

preconditions must be met if supply and demand analysis is to be useful. First, the factors affecting the demand curve must be independent of those affecting the supply curve. Secondly, if price variations are to be attributed to supply curve shifts, as indeed they are in this particular application, the demand for money must be a stable function of rather few factors which in turn must remain relatively constant over time.

In the classical and neo-classical economic analyses with which the history of the quantity theory is inextricably bound, these conditions were assumed to be met. The demand for money was viewed as being proportional to the general price level or, equivalently, as being a demand for real money balances. With the determinants of the demand for real balances held constant and the demand for nominal money required to be equal to its nominal supply, the general price level was uniquely determined and proportional to the nominal money supply; in turn the percentage rate of inflation was equal to the percentage rate of change of the nominal money supply.[6] The determinants of the demand for real balances in neo-classical economics were the volume of real transactions, or the level of real income or even perhaps wealth—there is considerable ambiguity here—and occasionally, but not with any central importance being accorded to it, some measure of the opportunity cost of holding money.[7] The values of these variables were, according to neo-classical theory, determined by real factors such as population growth, technical change, productivity and

---

[4] The first explanation of inflation in terms of monetary expansion seems to have been due to Jean Bodin, the seventeenth-century French philosopher, but it was the work of David Hume that established the dominance of the quantity theory in British economics. Viner (1937), particularly chapter VI, is still an excellent source on the development of the quantity theory tradition.

[5] Pigou (1917) provides the most accessible account of the quantity theory cast in these terms.

[6] We implicitly assume zero real growth here. In a growing economy it is necessary to allow for the effect of growing real income on the demand for real balances. Also one should distinguish between the effects of growing *per capita* income on the one hand and growing population, *per capita* real income held constant, on the other. There is no reason why the aggregate demand for real balances should respond in the same fashion to aggregate growth coming from these two sources.

[7] On the importance (or lack thereof) of the opportunity cost of holding money in the demand for money function in pre-Keynesian monetary theory, see Patinkin (1974).

thrift. Not only were these arguments few in number and independent of the money supply; they were also assumed to change so slowly over time that they could be regarded as constant for the purpose of analyzing movements in the price level. In short, there was a completely real theory of allocation and distribution and a completely monetary theory of the price level—neutral money and the classical dichotomy.

The depressions of the 1920s and 1930s and concurrent developments in economic theory thoroughly undermined this view of the world. The central problem for monetary economics ceased to be the determination of the level or rate of change of prices and became instead the determination of the level of real income and employment. Variations in the money supply were accorded a role in influencing those variables, the classical dichotomy was given up, and the independence of the demand for real balances and the money supply, essential to the usefulness of the quantity theory, as a theory of the price level, was destroyed. Nevertheless, Keynes accorded the quantity theory validity as a special case of his "General Theory" applicable to a situation of pure inflation and full employment.[8] It is perhaps not surprising, therefore, that when the behavior of the price level again became a central concern for policy after the second world war, there should be a revival of interest in the quantity theory.

This revival began in 1956 with the publication of *Studies in the Quantity Theory of Money*. In his introductory essay Friedman set out a theory of the demand for money and not a theory of the determination of prices, but work inspired by that essay was concerned with the role of money in generating inflation. However, the new quantity theory led to a more sophisticated theory of inflation than the pre-*General Theory* version. Though the opportunity cost of holding money played a role in pre-Keynesian discussions of the demand for money, that role was peripheral. Friedman's theoretical essay, however (in contrast to some of his later empirical work),

laid stress on this matter, so much so that some writers have argued that this essay, far from reviving an earlier approach, represents a major contribution to the Keynesian tradition in monetary theory.[9] Specifically, he pointed out that a positive rate of inflation represented a negative yield on money balances and hence had a role to play in determining the demand for money. He thus predicted an inverse relationship between the demand for real money balances and the inflation rate.

Since a decision to hold money must be taken with respect to the future, it is the expected rate of inflation over some time-horizon that is relevant here rather than the actual rate that prevails at a particular instant. Even if we assume the constancy of other variables in the demand for money function, such as real income and the real interest rate, it is only permissible, in terms of the quantity theory as modified by Friedman, to predict that the rate of inflation will vary in proportion to the rate of monetary expansion if the expected rate of inflation is constant. It is hardly reasonable to suppose that the expected rate of inflation can be independent of the actual rate, so that the independence of the supply and demand sides of the market for money balances, essential to the traditional monetary analysis of inflation, begins to break down.

This problem would not undermine our ability to analyze inflation in terms of the supply and demand for money if the expected inflation rate remained constant over time, and it is usual to take it that this would be the case if the realized rate were to turn out to be

[8] See Keynes (1936), pp. 304–6.
[9] On this matter see Patinkin (1969). For Friedman's views on the same issue see Friedman (1972). In his famous empirical paper on the demand for money (1959) Friedman appeared to play down the importance of the opportunity cost of holding money in the empirical demand function. However, subsequent work by Friedman (1966) and Laidler (1966) showed Friedman's (1959) results to be misleading and established the empirical importance of the opportunity cost of holding money for the behaviour of velocity.

equal to the expected rate.[10] If we did have such a state of affairs and if variations in the other arguments in the demand for money function—for example, real income and the real interest rate—could be ignored, we would predict proportionality between a given rate of monetary expansion and the rate of inflation. If the rate of monetary expansion then increased, we could also predict that, were the rate of inflation to increase by the same amount, and were this higher rate of inflation to be correctly anticipated, then there would be no forces in the system to cause the inflation rate to vary further. The inflation rate would have attained a new equilibrium value.

However, it is logically impossible that such a new equilibrium inflation rate could be established instantaneously when the rate of monetary expansion increases. The expected inflation rate affects the demand for money: if it rises, the demand for real balances falls. The higher is the *rate of change* of the nominal money supply, the higher will be the equilibrium *rate of inflation*. Hence for a given *level* of the nominal money supply the higher must be the equilibrium *price level*. Thus, if a new equilibrium inflation rate is to be established the rate of monetary expansion is increased, inflation must proceed for some time at a greater than equilibrium rate.[11] But is the dynamic process which governs the behavior of the inflation rate when it is out of equilibrium such as to ensure that the new equilib-

rium is reached? The predictions of the quantity theory about the proportionality of the equilibrium inflation rate to the rate of monetary expansion (given no change in real output, etc.) are of little practical interest if the equilibrium inflation rate in question is an unstable one. To put the same issue in another way, implicit in the interrelationship between the actual and expected inflation rates and the demand for money is the logical possibility of a "flight from money" leading to a self-generating and explosive inflationary process.

Though formulated in a different way, this problem was investigated by Keynes (1923) and by Bresciani-Turroni (1937), both of whom concluded that an explosive flight from money had not *in and of itself* been responsible for any of the particular inflations that they studied. The more recent literature has strengthened this conclusion. Friedman's analysis of the expected inflation rate as an argument in the demand for money function showed how this potential property of the inflationary process related to the general theory of the demand for money. Cagan formulated a specific version of the demand for money function and a specific hypothesis about the formulation of inflationary expectations in terms of which econometric techniques could be brought to bear on the matter. Not that less formal analysis was superseded by Cagan's work: his results are heavily dependent upon the particular way in which he relates the expected to the actual inflation rate, while econometric techniques are particularly exacting in their data requirements. To give but two examples: Lerner (1956) in his study of the Confederacy and Patinkin

---

[10] This is not a point that can be taken for granted. It is not necessarily reasonable to suppose that, if individuals have made a correct forecast of a variable, they have no incentive to change that forecast in the future. They may well have other information apart from the value of the variable itself that would affect their expectations about it. Nevertheless so much of the literature on the influence of inflationary expectations on the demand for money rests on the assumption that equality of the actual and expected inflation rates implies no incentive to revise expectations as time passes that we maintain this assumption in the discussion that follows. We also follow the literature in assuming that economic agents behave as if they held their expectations with complete certainty and that they hold the same expectation about the inflation rate regardless of the time horizon considered.

[11] Note that the above analysis is carried out on the assumption that the only monetary change at work here is an increase in the rate of expansion of the nominal money stock. The problem of the transition to a new equilibrium can in principle be avoided by cutting the *level* of the money stock to its new equilibrium value by a partial demonetisation of existing money at the same time as its rate of change is increased. Such a conceptual experiment is useful when analysing certain problems concerned with the role of money in growth models. It is a device used, for example, by Foley and Sidrauski (1971).

(1972*b*) in his study of Israel both took a more traditional approach in discovering tha⁺ the inflations in question had not been self-generating.

Nevertheless, Cagan's paper posed and dealt with questions about the role of money in generating inflation with altogether more rigor than had previously been applied and produced results that have had applications far beyond the bounds of an exclusively monetary approach to inflation. Cagan confined his study to hyper-inflations where, he argued, fluctuations in the price level and the inflation rate swamped those in real income or the rate of return on capital goods. Hence he formulated a demand for real balances function in which the only argument was the expected inflation rate. Further, he postulated that the expected inflation rate adapted to the actual rate by being revised in proportion to the ratio of the actual to the expected inflation rate. Cagan chose a semi-logarithmic form for his demand for money function and his model can therefore be written as

$$m - p = -\alpha \dot{p}^e, \ d\dot{p}^e/dt = \beta(\dot{p} - \dot{p}^e)$$

where *m* is the logarithm of nominal money balances, and *p* is the logarithm of the price level, $\dot{p}$ the percentage inflation rate and the superscript *e* refers to the expected value of the inflation rate. Cagan shows that a self-generating inflation is impossible if the product of the parameters α and β is less than unity.[12] Thus econometric estimates of these

two parameters provide vital evidence on the stability of the inflationary process.

Cagan estimated his model using data on seven hyper-inflations and was not able to reject the hypothesis that the stability conditions were satisfied. Thus he strengthened the conclusions reached less formally by Keynes and Bresciani-Turroni. A large number of subsequent studies of "rapid" inflationary episodes have produced results broadly consistent with Cagan's. For example, studies of Argentina (Diz, 1970), Chile (Deaver, 1970), China (Hu, 1971), Brazil (Silveira, 1973*a*), Brazil and South Korea (Campbell, 1970), Turkey (Akyuz, 1973) all confirm that the sensitivity of the demand for money to the expected rate of inflation and the sensitivity of the expected inflation rate to the actual rate are both small enough to rule out a self-generated flight from money. Moreover, the sensitivity of the demand for money to the expected inflation rate in these countries seems to be of the same order of magnitude as that observed in other countries, such as the United States and Britain, when other measures of the opportunity cost of holding money, such as bond and bill rates, are used. This fact lends further strength to these conclusions about the stability of the inflationary process.[13]

Now the foregoing analysis tells us that the rate of inflation has a stable equilibrium value if the rate of monetary expansion is constant. Further, if real income were constant, then that equilibrium value would be the rate of monetary expansion. We have the old quantity theory result then, but it was not obtained by the old quantity theory methods. It has proved impossible to maintain the assumption that one factor at least

[12] Cagan's model produces a first order differential equation. Dutton (1971*b*) and Akyuz (1973) set out a difference equation version of Cagan's model that is second order and converges on a new equilibrium inflation rate with a time path that may, with plausible parameter values, be cyclical. One difficulty with Cagan's model is that it simultaneously has the money market always in equilibrium and real income given at full employment. Nevertheless, the actual inflation rate can depart from the expected rate. One might have thought that excess demand would be required for the latter effect, but none appears in the model (cf. Section 5 below). Note that Goldman (1972) modifies Cagan's model by dropping the assumption that the money market is always in equilibrium and finds its dynamic properties considerably altered by this modification. This problem might better be treated in terms of a "complete" model of inflation.

[13] Note that this is rather a broad generalization drawn from a wide variety of empirical tests which on the whole did not attempt simply to replicate Cagan's results with other data. A tabular summary of much of the evidence on the interest elasticity of demand for money is to be found in the Bank of England (1970). The elasticity of demand for real balances with respect to the expected inflation rate, or with respect to short term nominal interest rates, seems almost universally to lie between 0 and −0.5.

underlying the demand for money function—
the expected rate of inflation—can be treated
as independent of supply side factors. The
key contribution of the revived quantity
theory is to show that analysis which treats
the demand function for real balances as
independent of the behavior of the money
supply is both theoretically and empirically
inadequate. In the long run the demand for
real balances varies with the rate of change
of the nominal money stock because that
rate of change affects the actual and hence
the expected rate of inflation. The question
immediately arises as to whether the opportunity cost of holding real balances in the
only variable on the demand side of the
money market affected by the behavior of
the nominal money supply. Could the level
of real income also be affected?

The work which we have considered so
far has treated the behavior of real income
as exogenous. This assumption has been
repeatedly questioned by work within the
quantity theory tradition. In particular, it
came in for a great deal of attention in the
post-war literature on the integration of
monetary and value theory. Such well-known
contributions as those of Brunner (1951),
Patinkin (1956), Archibald and Lipsey (1958),
Clower and Burstein (1960) and Modigliani
(1963) all dealt with the circumstances in
which a change in the level of the money
stock would change only the price level
leaving the values of real variables unaltered.
An important insight of this literature was
highlighted by Marty (1964). He argued that
the existence of monetary disequilibrium
must imply the existence of disequilibrium
vis-à-vis all assets and vis-à-vis consumption
plans as well; that the demand for real money
balances must be looked upon as interdependent with all other aspects of economic
agents' utility-maximizing choices and in
particular with those involving the allocation
of consumption over time. Now if different
rates of inflation (expected and actual) imply
different rates of return to real balances and
hence provide economic agents with incentives to rearrange their portfolios, it follows
immediately that, even if all real variables

have equilibrium values that are independent
of the *level* of the nominal money supply,
there is no reason to suppose that those
equilibrium values are independent of its
rate of change.

A voluminous literature has dealt with
this problem. To survey it fully would take
us deeply into the fields of monetary theory
and the theory of economic growth, but it
will suffice to sketch its salient features.[14]
First, virtually all the analysis has been
carried out in the framework of the neoclassical growth model initially developed by
Swan (1956) and Solow (1956), despite the
fact that, formally speaking, such models
deal with a single output economy with
continuous full employment in which it is
hard to conceive of money having any role
to play. In such a model, if technical change is
ignored, the long-run rate of growth of real
income is determined uniquely by the rate of
growth of the labor force, this being fixed
exogenously. Thus, the equilibrium inflation
rate in such a model is still given by the
quantity theory formula of the rate of monetary expansion minus the product of the income elasticity of demand for real balances
and the rate of growth of real income.

However, if a neo-classical model of the
equilibrium level of the capital–output ratio,
and hence the equilibrium level of real
income, are determined by savings behavior,
and are susceptible to influence by the
inflation rate along lines already sketched out
above. The particular results generated here
depend critically upon the assumptions made
about savings behavior. Tobin (1965), for
example, assumes *per capita* real savings to
be a function of *per capita* real disposable
income. When money is included in the model
its real rate of expansion adds to disposable

<hr/>

[14] This literature whose major features are surveyed
by Dornbusch & Frenkel (1973) has close links to that
on the so-called "optimum quantity of money" problem
(cf. Friedman (1969) and Feige and Parkin (1971) for
key contributions here). It is also closely related to the
work on the "inflationary tax" on cash balances with
which we deal in Section 6 below. See Burmeister and
Phelps (1971) for a paper that explicitly recognizes and
exploits the interrelatedness of these problems.

income in a form that cannot be consumed but must be saved. Hence Tobin argues that an economy with money in it will grow at a lower capital-output ratio and a lower level of real income than a non-money economy. Johnson (1967a) argues that the utility yield on real balances should be included in disposable income as an item that must be consumed, and hence that the effect of introducing money (and of varying the rate of monetary expansion in a money economy) is ambiguous. There are virtually as many theoretical results in this literature as there are *a priori* plausible assumptions about the determinants of savings behaviour, but the almost universal result is that money is non-neutral. Variations in the inflation rate and hence in the rate of nominal monetary expansion do influence real variables.[15]

The lesson of the literature on money in growth models for those approaching the problem of inflation by way of the quantity theory of money is straightforward. It is not just that behavior on the supply and demand sides of the money market is interdependent; rather an analysis of that interdependence, even when only situations of long-run equilibrium are being considered, requires the construction and investigation of a complete general equilibrium model of the economy (albeit perhaps a highly aggregated one). Thus the most appealing feature of the old quantity theory tradition, namely that it enabled inflation to be treated as a problem susceptible to analysis with the tools of

partial equilibrium supply and demand analysis, is totally undermined.

The one central feature of the quantity theory approach which is not undermined by the above analysis is the one insisted on by Friedman, that the quantity theory be formulated not as a theory of the price level but as a theory of the demand for money. It is crucial therefore to examine this feature of the quantity theory and ask whether its basic assumptions concerning the demand for money are supported or rejected by the empirical evidence. Those assumptions, as we have already noted, are that the demand for money is a demand for real balances and depends in a stable and predictable manner on the level of real income (or wealth) and on one or more opportunity cost (interest rate or expected inflation rate) variables. If such a demand function is a feature of actual economies then, although the price level cannot be determined simply by analyzing the supply for and demand for money, the money market will, nevertheless, play a crucial part in a more complete and general analysis.

We have already cited evidence above about the stability of the demand for money function in conditions of rapid inflation, but Cagan's (1956) results are of little relevance to economies in which output fluctuations cannot be ignored. Although the other studies cited above (p. 748) do take output variations into account in generating their results, that evidence is drawn, by and large, from economies having relatively simple financial systems. It has been argued, notably by the Radcliffe Committee (1959) that for economies with sophisticated financial systems in which there exists a wide spectrum of assets of varying degrees of liquidity, the demand for money function will be much less stable.

There is, however, an overwhelming body of evidence against this general proposition, which has already been surveyed elsewhere (e.g., Laidler, 1969a; Bank of England, 1970). Even, indeed particularly, for economies as sophisticated as the United States or Britain, the aggregate demand for real money balances can be thought of as depending upon

---

[15] An exception arises in models of the type pioneered by Sidrauski (1967) in which the behaviour of the real side of the economy is kept independent of that of the money stock by making the marginal product of capital independent of the stock of real balances, and by maintaining it equal to an exogenously given rate of time preference. It is easy to be misled into believing that non-neutrality is introduced by explicit consideration of real growth. This is not the case. The key factor is that variations in the rate of monetary expansion affect the rate of inflation and that the latter variable is one of the relative prices affecting the allocative decisions of economic agents. Money can easily be shown to be potentially non-neutral in the special case of an economy with a zero growth rate (cf. Laidler, 1969b).

some measure of aggregate real income, and, with a rather low elasticity, upon the level of nominal interest rates, variations in which are thought of as capturing variations in both real interest rates and in inflationary expectations. More detailed and specific studies of the degree of substitutability between those assets usually classified as money— say the deposit liabilities of the commercial banking system—and other financial assets have consistently found the extent of such substitutability to be rather low. This matter has been extensively studied for the United States, and Feige (1974) provides a survey of the relevant literature. For the United Kingdom, less work has been done, but the study by Barrett Gray and Parkin (1975) suggests that the United Kingdom is no different from the United States in this respect.

It has been suggested by Kaldor (1970) that the apparent empirical stability of the demand for money relationship and the low degree of substitutability between money and other assets is the result of the supply of money being a passive variable in the economic system that simply adjusts to demand. He argues that if the monetary authorities were to pursue a policy of actively controlling the money supply, then the potential for an unstable demand for money function implicit in the structure of the financial system would soon manifest itself. As far as the United States is concerned, the evidence is strongly against this view. The studies of Friedman and Schwartz (1963) and Cagan (1965) carefully investigate the determination of the money supply in the United States using the techniques of the historian as much as those of the econometrician. They show that, although in certain episodes the supply of money did respond passively to demand, in most cases the direction of causation was clearly from supply side factors to demand side factors. Moreover, the same stable demand for money function can be shown to have existed under both types of monetary policy regime.

For Britain we have less evidence, but the institution of a new approach to monetary control in 1971 that lays greater emphasis on controlling monetary aggregates than did

earlier methods promises to provide us with an important body of evidence on this question. So far we are aware of only one study on this question that exploits this new evidence (Artis and Lewis, 1975) and it produces results consistent with the proposition that the stability of the demand for money function in Britain survived the change in monetary policy regimes. Artis and Lewis do, however, argue that different econometric means must be adopted to measure the parameters of the demand for money function after 1971.

In short, there is every reason to believe that the stable demand for money function on which the quantity theory literature relies so heavily does exist over a wide variety of economies and financial systems. Thus, this literature is of considerable practical relevance. Changes in the quantity of money must, given the existence of a stable demand for money function, lead to changes in the values of some or all the arguments of the demand function. The form of those changes, and in particular the relative effects in the short-run adjustment process on real income (and hence employment) on the one hand and prices on the other cannot be predicted by the quantity theory.

The literature on such short-run problems has resolved around the so-called "Phillips Curve." As that literature has developed it has become increasingly apparent that the Phillips curve is no more capable of providing, by itself, a complete analysis of inflation than is the modern quantity theory of money. It provides a theory of labor market behaviour (and if extended to deal with price inflation, of goods market behaviour) but it is by now clear that in order to understand the short-run characteristics of the inflationary process it is necessary to analyze the interaction of markets, including labor, goods and money markets, in the context of a complete general equilibrium, or rather disequilibrium, system. Before we can go on to discuss the problems involved in achieving such a synthesis, however, we must first discuss the salient features of the literature on wage and price behavior, and it is to that task that we now turn.

3. WAGE AND PRICE SETTING BEHAVIOR AND EXPECTATIONS

The original stimulus, in the 1950s, for work on wage and price setting behavior was the need to extend in an important direction the then widely accepted post-Keynesian framework for dealing with macroeconomic issues. That framework, enshrined in the Hicks (1937)–Hansen (1953) IS–LM model, treated the money wage rate (and in some versions the price level) as exogenous. It seemed natural and important, therefore, to extend that framework by explaining wage and price behavior. How useful the framework might remain would, of course, depend crucially on the nature of the extension. Such an extension could take several forms, only one of which would leave the framework completely intact. This would be when wages and prices were completely independent of the stage of aggregate demand, the central variable determined by the IS–LM model. In this case, inflation being determined by non-economic, institutional social and political factors, monetary and fiscal policy could, according to the model be used to achieve any desired level of aggregate demand and real income. At the opposite extreme, if wage and price inflation could be shown to depend *only* on excess demand, then only by analyzing the interaction of the determinants of aggregate demand and of wage and price change could the rate of inflation and the level of real income (and employment) be understood. This would still be so even if, in addition to excess demand, inflation expectations also influenced wage and price change, provided such expectations themselves depended only on the previous history of inflation. In such a case, an explicit dynamic model of the evolution of real income and prices would be required to analyze inflation. Inflation and real income at any moment would depend not just on current demand creation policies, but also on their previous history. Of course, it was possible that an intermediate, more eclectic, position, would be a better representation of the facts than either of the two extremes just postulated with demand, inflation expecta-

tions, as well as socio-political and institutional factors proximately affecting the rate of wage and price change.

In the light of above remarks it will be clear that the literature surveyed in this section is central to the problem of discriminating amongst competing hypotheses about the inflationary process around which much of the current policy debate resolves. First, we survey the literature on wage determination, then price determination and finally, since it features centrally in both of these areas, the determinants of inflation expectations.

The seminal contributions to the literature on wage inflation were empirical.[16] Brown (1955), Parkinson (1958), Phillips (1958), Klein and Ball (1959), Dicks-Mireaux and Dow (1959), Lipsey (1960), Dicks-Mireaux (1961) and Ball (1962) for the United Kingdom, and Bowen (1960a), Samuelson and Solow (1960) Bhatia (1961), Bodkin (1966) and Perry (1964) for the United States all found an inverse relationship between the rate of wage change and the unemployment rate.[17] Phillips, whose name more than the others has been attached to that relation, made a particularly impressive contribution. He found that an inverse relation between wage change and unemployment derived from data for the United Kingdom for the period 1861–1913 could predict almost exactly the relationship between those two variables for the period between 1951 and 1957. However, as Knowles and Winsten (1959), Routh (1959) and Griffin (1962) were quick to point out, this gave a somewhat misleading

[16] Although Brown (1955) was the first to draw a scatter diagram showing the relation between wage change and unemployment, Irving Fisher (1926) seems to have been the first to discover and empirically investigate the basic idea. Also, it featured in the early econometric models of Tinbergen (1951) and Klein and Goldberger (1955).

[17] Similar findings for other countries are to be found in Kaliski (1964) and Reuber (1964) for Canada; Watanabe (1966) for Japan; Hancock (1966), Higgins (1973), Jonson et al. (1975), Nevile (1970), Parkin (1973b) and Pitchford (1968) for Australia; Gallaway, Koshall and Chapin (1970) for South Africa; Koshal and Gallaway (1971) for Germany; Modigliani and Tarantelli (1973) for Italy.

impression of the nature of the stylized facts about the relation between wage change and unemployment. Those stylized facts for the United Kingdom[18] had four features, to which recent experience has added a fifth. First, there is a weak inverse correlation between wage change and unemployment.[19] Secondly, for the 19th century there are well-defined anti-clockwise loops in the relationship. (For any given level of unemployment, the rate of wage change was higher if unemployment was falling and lower if unemployment was rising.) Thirdly, in the post-second world war period the loops are still present but are clockwise. Fourthly, for the inter-war years the relation between wage change and unemployment is so weak as to be barely discernible. Fifthly, in the late 1960s and 1970s there has been a tendency for wage inflation and unemployment either to rise together or for wage inflation to rise independently of the unemployment rate. It is this latest development which has led many to search for an explanation for a "new inflation."

Theoretical work on wage inflation up to the middle 1960s focused on the negative correlation between wage change and unemployment and on the anti-clockwise loops. The first attempt was that of Lipsey (1960),[20] whose central idea was that the Phillips curve derives from two behavioral relations: first, a positive relation between wage change and excess demand for labor and second an inverse (and non-linear) relation between excess demand and unemployment as well as the rate of change of unemployment. The

existence of a wage reaction function was justified by appeal to Walrasian *tâtonnement* but the hypothesis about the relation between excess demand and unemployment was novel and, therefore, given a fuller explanation.

Any change in the unemployment rate is equal to the difference between the quit rate and the hiring rate. Lipsey assumed the quit rate to be constant and hiring to respond positively both to the number of people looking for jobs (unemployment) and the number of jobs available (vacancies). Since excess demand for labour is by definition equal to the difference between vacancies and unemployment, the hiring rate depends positively on the unemployment rate and the level of excess demand. The rate of change of unemployment will thus vary inversely with both the unemployment rate and excess demand, from which the existence of an inverse relation between excess demand, unemployment and its rate of change immediately follows. Combining this with the wage reaction function yields the proposition that the rate of wage change will be an inverse function of both the unemployment rate and its rate of change, thus generating an (on average) downward sloping relation between wage change and unemployment and an anti-clockwise loop configuration as unemployment moves through a cycle.[21] Phelps (1968) derived the same basic relation in a more general way and one which has a more appealing micro-economic foundation. In his analysis each firm sets its wage offer

[18] The stylized facts for the United States and the other major countries are broadly the same as for the United Kingdom in the post-war period but, with the exception of the United States, little is known about other countries' wage and unemployment behavior for earlier periods.

[19] Lipsey reports the simple correlation between wage change and the best fitting non-linear form of unemployment as 0.64 for the period 1862–1913.

[20] Alternative theories of the Phillips curve may be found in Sargan (1964), Kuska (1966), Corry and Laidler (1967), Kuh (1967) and Hansen (1970). Also an attack on the conventional theory has been presented by Holmes and Smyth (1970).

[21] It is interesting to note that Lipsey (1960) did not present the above analysis as an explanation for the loops. All the analysis is there in an extended footnote (footnote 1, p. 15) but its implications for the loops were not drawn out by Lipsey. Instead he used an aggregation argument starting from the proposition that the national labor market was made up of a number of micro labor markets each with its own "Phillips curve." As unemployment across the micro labor markets, whilst when the economy was moving from a slump to a boom, there would be an increase in dispersion. It follows from the non-linearity of the micro Phillips relation that the larger is the dispersion, the higher is the average rate of wage change. Hence with Lipsey's assumption anti-clockwise loop would be generated as an aggregation phenomenon.

so as to achieve a wage relative to its expectation of the market average wage which depends upon the average unemployment and vacancy rates and the firm's own vacancy rate. Vacancies are in turn shown to depend on the level and rate of change of unemployment.

Lipsey's theory of the Phillips curve cannot explain the large fluctuations in wage change relative to unemployment during the inter-war years or the tendency for there to be an upward sloping relation with clockwise loops in the post-war years. These facts raise questions about the stability of the inflation unemployment trade off and about whether it is more than a short-run phenomenon. Phelps's (1968) approach, as well as that of Friedman (1968), suggests that there is one systematic factor giving rise to shifts in the short-run wage change—unemployment trade off which not only ensures that in the long run the trade off disappears but which also gives rise to the possibility of clockwise loops about an inverse relationship in the short run. The central idea of both Friedman and Phelps is the same. Both argue in effect that Lipsey's basic money-wage reaction function is an incomplete specification of the forces that make for money-wage change. They suggest (with different underlying stories) that the rate of money-wage change will be equal to the expected rate of inflation plus some adjustment for excess demand.

Friedman's argument is that it is *real* wages and not money wages which respond to excess demand. If that is so then *money* wages will respond both to excess demand and to expected changes in prices, in the latter case with a coefficient of unity. Phelps's analysis, briefly described above, leads firms to change their wage offers by the amount they expect other firms to change theirs, provided they are happy with their relative market positions. However, if a firm has an excess demand for labor (excessive vacancies) it will raise its wages by more than it expects others to be raising theirs and conversely for an excess supply. Thus, if all firms taken together have an excess demand for labor, wages will be raised on average by more than each firm is expecting the others to raise theirs. Thus, averaging over all firms, the rate of wage change will equal the expected rate of wage change plus an adjustment for excess demand. Both Phelps's and Friedman's explanations are identical in a world of zero productivity growth and easy to reconcile provided one recognizes that in the Friedman formulation the time path of the real wage will depend on productivity growth. Both hypotheses are capable of generating clockwise loops in a wage change–unemployment space, and can thus account for periods of positive correlation between the two variables, so long as inflation expectations are generated by some simple distributed lag function of previous inflation. A full analysis of these matters is provided by Brechling (1968).

More rigorous choice-theoretic analyses of the Phillips relation have been provided by Lucas and Rapping (1969), Alchian (1960), Mortensen (1970), Gordon and Hynes (1970) and Gronau (1971). Each of these studies views the short-run Phillips curve as a short-run labor supply function and ignores involuntary unemployment arising from lay-offs. They also reverse the direction of causation between the variables postulated by Lipsey and Phelps, and return to Fisher's (1926) original interpretation, under which the causation is viewed as running from inflation to unemployment. However, in agreement with Friedman and Phelps, the analyses predict instability in the short-run relation between the variables and the absence of a long-run inflation-employment trade off. Lucas and Rapping develop a two-period analysis of a utility maximizing household which supplies labor as a function of the actual and expected level of both money and wages and prices. Unemployment is the difference between the supply of labor and the amount demanded by profit maximizing firms. They show that these two propositions taken together imply a short-run inverse relation between inflation and unemployment.

Alchian provides a general theoretical analysis of the causes of resource (human and non-human) unemployment which, in broad terms, is similar to Mortensen's specific labor market analysis. The latter studies household job search under conditions of uncertainty. There are three types of households: those who are unemployed, those who are employed and deciding whether or not to quit their jobs in order to become unemployed searchers, and, third, those who are employed and deciding whether or not to quit their present job to take up a new job immediately. The household has in mind a wage which it believes with certainty it could obtain after a certain period of search. It also faces a concrete wage offer (or existing wage), and has to decide whether or not to accept the offer (or retain the job which provides the existing wage in the case of an employed person) or to remain (become) unemployed in order to seek a better wage. The household compares the present value of the income that it would obtain by accepting a job at a low wage with that of waiting (for a presumed known period) in order to obtain a job with a higher wage. The model predicts that the higher is the actual rate of wage change relative to the expected rate of wage change the fewer people will be unemployed and searching for a job. In addition, with a minimum of contrivance, Mortensen shows that the resulting relation between wage change and unemployment (for a given level of expected wage change) will not only be inverse but will also display anti-clockwise loops. He further shows that the equilibrium unemployment rate is independent of the rate of inflation.

Wages are determined in both the Lucas and Rapping and Mortensen models as a result of the interaction of the supply (Phillips curve) and demand sides of the labor market. Lucas and Rapping have a neo-classical demand for labor function. Mortensen has firms who choose a time path for wages to maximize their present values subject to an assumed Phillips curve labor supply constraint. Both models are incomplete in the sense that they hold expectations constant, but they do emphasize that the relevant expectations in the Phillips relation are those of workers and not those of firms.

The great difficulty with all this analysis in that it treats *all* unemployment as voluntary. Workers always voluntarily quit to search for better jobs and choose to remain unemployed until they have found their expected wealth (or utility) maximizing offer. Lay-offs are ignored and their satisfactory explanation is clearly an important problem area for further research. Whether the qualitative conclusions of these models concerning the relationships between the actual and expected rates of wage change and unemployment will survive an adequate incorporation of involuntary lay-offs is, at this stage, an open question.

The theoretical arguments outlined above all deal with atomistically competitive markets. Theoretical work has also been done on monopolistic markets in which trade unions and monopolistic firms set wages. Much of this literature has been surveyed by De Menil (1971). He points out that whilst a variety of different bargaining models could be applied to the wage determination process their varying assumptions all lead to certain common results. The fixed threat game models of Nash (1950, 1953), Raiffa (1953) and Bishop (1963) and the non-game theoretic approaches of Zeuthen (1930), Harsanyi (1966), Hicks (1932), Foldes (1964), Cross (1965, 1966) and Coddington (1966, 1968) have in common the prediction of maximization of the gains from trade and a sharing of those gains in proportion to the relative marginal disutility that each party could and would, but never does, inflict upon the other. In addition these models all predict that the rate of wage change thus determined will be homogeneous of degree one in all money prices which are assumed to be relevant. Which other prices are deemed relevant depends upon the detail of the analysis in question but could include product price and the price of labor in the competitive sector as well as taxes. The homogeneity prediction is also found in Johnston's (1972) model. Here only the firm takes an active part in the wage setting process.

None of these monopolistic models leads directly to the same detailed predictions as the competitive models, but there is no obvious conflict between them. The rate of unemployment is a natural variable to use as an indicator of the relative bargaining strengths of the two parties and expected inflation variables have an identical role to play in both competitive and monopolistic markets. A theoretical basis for the relation between wage change and unemployment may thus be derived either from competitive or monopolistic analysis but in either case the prediction is that the relationship will be crucially influenced by some expected rate of inflation.[22] Furthermore, both approaches predict that the coefficient on the expected rate of inflation in the wage inflation equation will be unity. This implies that equilibrium situations in which the actual and expected rates of inflation are equal will all have the same unemployment rate regardless of the rate of inflation. How dependent these conclusions are on the—often unstated—assumptions that all economic agents hold the same expectations, and act as if they did so with perfect certainty, remains to be seen. They do, however, imply that, if inflation expectations are formed solely on the basis of past values of the actual rate of inflation, there will be a long-run trade off between *not the level of but the rate of change of the rate of inflation* and the *level of unemployment*.

The unemployment rate at which these models generate a stationary rate of inflation may be called an equilibrium rate in the sense that it is the rate which rules when expectations are fulfilled and therefore (on the model's assumptions) unchanging. This equilibrium unemployment rate is independent of the steady state inflation rate and often called the "natural" unemployment rate. However, it will not in general be constant. Its level depends upon a number of factors that might well vary. This is brought out very clearly for example by Mortensen's analysis in which the "natural" rate depends positively upon the degree of dispersion of wage offers, the rate at

which new workers enter the labor force and the frequency with which employed workers consider quitting to search for a better job, negatively upon the frequency with which an employed worker receives an offer and ambiguously on the frequency with which an unemployed worker receives an offer.[23] Tobin (1972) has suggested that it is probably misleading to regard the natural unemployment rate as involving only voluntary search unemployment since dispersion across labour markets will mean that when there is no inflationary pressure on wages there is still an excess of unemployment over vacancies. There is a substantial literature on the role of dispersion in affecting the position of the short-run inflation-unemployment trade off and hence, by implication, the "natural" unemployment rate, and this subject is taken up below in more detail.

Phelps' (1972) discussion of the determination of the natural unemployment rate suggests that inflation may be non-netural, that it may affect real rates of interest and real after-tax wages, by substituting the inflation tax for income tax, and thereby affect the equilibrium amount of consumption, leisure and search unemployment. He also suggests that the relationship in question may display "hysteresis," the equilibrium unemployment rate at any time depending on the previous path of inflation and unemployment. Akerlof (1969) and Stephens (1974) go even further and show that, in models where wages and prices are changed at fixed intervals, the "natural" unemployment rate might (on their assumptions) depend *positively* on the rate of inflation. It is clear from these pieces of analysis that it cannot be taken for granted on theoretical grounds that the size of the steady inflation unemployment rate is a constant or that no long-run unemployment-inflation trade off exists. The factors which determine

[22] The expected rate of inflation of wages in the case of Phelps, of prices in the case of Friedman and of a variety of non-union wage variables and product prices in the case of monopolistic models.

[23] The reason for this counter-intuitive result is that an increase in the frequency of job offers to unemployed workers is assumed to (a) raise the job acceptance rate which lowers the "natural" unemployment rate and (b) lower the cost of search unemployment which raises the "natural" rate. The net effect cannot be assigned a priori.

the natural unemployment rate as well as the nature of the long-run trade off between inflation and unemployment require further theoretical and particularly empirical investigation.

Empirical studies which have tested some form of the expectation-excess demand model of wage inflation abound. Broadly speaking, they show that the basic model is consistent with data taken from the United States (Brechling, 1968; Lucas and Rapping, 1969; Gordon, 1971; Nordhaus, 1972b; Turnovsky and Wachter, 1972), Canada (Kaliski, 1972; Vanderkamp, 1972; Turnovsky, 1972), the United Kingdom (Parkin, Sumner & Ward, 1975; McCallum, 1975), Australia, (Parkin, 1973b), and the aggregate "Group of Ten" countries (Duck et al., 1975). The size of the coefficient on the expected rate of inflation is not always unity as predicted by so many theoretical models but there are grounds for questioning many of the estimates in question. These grounds are discussed in detail below where we consider inflation expectations.

Most empirical studies of wage inflation have examined the effects on wages of factors other than excess demand and inflation expectations. In some studies these factors are seen as merely modifying the wage inflation-unemployment trade off, but in others the very existence and usefulness of the concept of an unemployment-wage inflation trade off is denied. First, we will deal with work which is entirely within the spirit of the expectations-excess demand model already discussed and then go on to examine work critical of that approach.

Recent empirically oriented studies by Gordon (1973) and Parkin et al. (1975) have suggested that a fully developed expectations hypothesis would have the rate of wage change depend upon the *expected* rates of change of all variables that affect the excess demand for labor. Phelp's "expected rate of wage change" is of course a variable which subsumes all such factors. However, it is possible to be more explicit and recognize that the expected rate of wage change will depend upon expected changes in such variables as payroll taxes, income taxes, foreign and domestic wholesale prices as well as domestic retail prices. Foreign price changes would be especially important in a fixed exchange rate open economy where they would have a direct and immediate effect upon the value of the marginal product of domestic labor and therefore on money wages. Such a line of argument does, however, imply that many difficult problems associated with measuring such expectations would be encountered in empirical work.

An important branch of the literature on wage inflation (still within the excess demand-expectations framework) deals with the effects of aggregation on observed relationships between variables. This issue was raised by Lipsey in his discussion of the Phillips curve loops. Data on industrial and regional unemployment make it possible to investigate the effects on average wage change of the structure of unemployment. These matters have been investigated by examining regional Phillips curves (Cowling and Metcalf (1967); Thirlwall (1969, 1970); Metcalf (1971); MacKay and Hart (1974) for the United Kingdom and Albrecht (1966); Kaun (1965); Kaun and Spiro (1970) for the United States) and by explicit aggregation over regional data (Archibald (1969), Thomas and Stoney[24] (1971), Archibald, Kemmiss and Perkins (1974) for the United Kingdom, and Brechling (1973) for the United States). The central idea which emerges from Archibald's 1969 work is that the variance of the distribution of unemployment either between regions or industries should appear systematically to influence national average wage inflation.

Although Archibald's 1969 paper seemed to find evidence of this effect and expressed some optimism concerning the possibility of improving the overall short-run inflation-unemployment trade off by policies designed to reduce regional dispersion in unemployment rates his optimism may have been premature. First, at the empirical level, both Hines (1972) and in a subsequent paper Archibald et al. (1974) conclude that "for

---

[24] See also the exchange between Sharot (1973) and Thomas (1973).

the post-war period at least, the aggregation or 'structuralist' hypothesis is poorly supported."[25] Secondly, even if it could be shown that the aggregate trade off depended on the structure of unemployment, it would be wrong to conclude that dispersion minimization was the way to achieve the best possible trade off. Burns (1972) has shown that it is micro Phillips curve slope equalization and not dispersion minimization which is required to achieve the best possible trade off. In the light of the estimates of the slopes of regional Phillips curves in the cases cited above (provided those slopes could be projected outside the sample range (see Leslie, (1973)), dispersion minimization would actually worsen the United Kingdom aggregate short-run trade off. A recent paper by Thomas (1974) on an industry cross-section study shows there to be important slope differences between industries thereby giving potential additional weight to Burns's point.

In addition to dealing with explicit aggregation, Brechling (1973) Thomas and Stoney (1971) and Mulvey and Trevithick (1974) have considered the possibility of transmission of wage change from "leading sectors" through to the rest of the economy. This hypothesis seems to work well. Using American data, Brechling found evidence for a transmission from leading sectors to the rest of the economy where the leading sector was defined as the high wage sector. Working with the United Kingdom data, Stoney and Thomas found a similar effect, but they defined the leading sector as that with the lowest unemployment rate.[26] Using data for Ireland, Mulvey and Trevithick find transmission from a "key" occupational sector.

A variety of other labor-market structural hypotheses have been advanced, most comprehensively perhaps, by Holt (1970b). In empirical work using United States data, Perry (1970) suggests that changes in the sex

and age composition of the labor force have affected the Phillips curve during the 1960s; Gordon (1971) casts some doubt on the importance of those considerations and suggests instead that unemployment dispersion and hidden unemployment are better indicators of changing labor market tightness; Packer and Park (1973) use a variable which is designed to measure distortion in the relative wage structure and find a significant role for that and Flanagan (1973) investigates the role of the duration of unemployment.

A related problem concerns the selection of the most appropriate labor-market excess demand pressure variable. All the early studies, with the exception of Dicks-Mireaux (1961), and most of the more recent studies used the recorded unemployment rate. Dicks-Mireaux used an index of excess demand (cf. Dow and Dicks-Mireaux, 1958) based on unemployment and vacancies. Taylor (1970) calculated, and used in earnings equations, a measure of unemployment which included estimates of hoarded labor. Simler and Tella (1968) used a "labor reserves" variable based on variations in participation rates. For most of the time, the relationship between the alternative measures is sufficiently stable for a choice between them not to be too crucial. However, recently there have been some shifts in the relationship between unemployment and vacancies and there is room for some debate about alternative proxies for excess demand.[27]

None of the work surveyed so far challenges the basic notion of a short-run trade off between inflation and unemployment with inflation expectations removing or at least weakening the trade off in the long run. Several investigators have taken the view, however, that the short-run trade off is at best not a very useful concept and at worst totally misleading. The most influential of these have argued instead that trade union pushfulness is a crucial independent force in the determination of the rate of wage change. Early

[25] Archibald et al. (1974), p. 156.
[26] There is probably no difference between these two since for the United Kingdom the lowest unemployment region, London and the South East, is also the highest wage region.

[27] See Bowers, Cheshire and Webb (1970), Foster (1973, 1974), Gujarati (1972a, b), MacKay (1972), MacKay and Reid (1972), Taylor (1970, 1972, 1974).

work on this problem (Morton, 1950; Bronfenbrenner, 1950; Lapkin, 1950; Slichter, 1954; Christenson, 1954; Gallaway, 1958) was mainly concerned with establishing the conditions under which wage push could lead to a sustained inflation and offering guesses as to whether it was or was not a major source of inflation.

The most systematic early study of the role of wage push via union strength is Hines (1964). He postulated that the rate of wage change depends directly upon union pushfulness and that union pushfulness itself can be measured (proxied) by the rate of change of the percentage of the labor force which is unionized (union density). The proxying of pushfulness with density change is justified on the assumption that militancy manifests itself simultaneously in wage negotiations and in union recruiting. If this is true, even though no direct causal link is postulated between the rate of change of density and the rate of wage change, we should observe a positive correlation between the two and might interpret that evidence as indicating the independent effects of trade union militancy on the rate of wage change. In studies for the United Kingdom by Hines (1964, 1968, 1969, 1971) and in a United States study by Ashenfelter, Johnson and Pencavel (1972) such a correlation was found.

However, Stoney and Thomas (1970) pointed out that Hines's 1964 model is dynamically unstable, while the legitimacy of using density change as a proxy for militancy has been attacked on several fronts. Purdy and Zis (1974) argue, on the basis of an analysis of the objectives of and constraints on union behavior, that the change in density cannot be regarded as a useful proxy for militancy. They point out (1973) that there is at least one other plausible explanation for any positive correlation between union density change and wage change—an explanation for which they find a good deal of empirical support. Purdy and Zis note that there are two sources of density change: that assumed by Hines resulting from a step up in recruiting effort, but also passive changes resulting from reallocation of the labor force away from sectors of the economy with low union densities towards

those with high ones. In the extreme case there could be a reallocation from those with no unionization to those with closed-shop union structures. If the highly unionized sectors are the high-wage sectors then there will be a correlation between the rate of change of average earnings (but not of the wage-rate index) and the rate of change of union density for reasons completely independent of union strength or militancy.

The Purdy and Zis view is in line with the analysis of Holt (1970a) who develops a theoretical model of wage determination for the union sector and the non-union sector and then aggregates the two. For Holt union behavior simply determines an equilibrium union wage relative to the non-union wage. Aggregation over union and non-union workers brings in the rate of change in union density as one of the variables in the aggregate wage inflation relation but purely as a result of aggregation. This is also the view taken by Thomas (1974). Further, despite Hines's assertions to the contrary, the change in union density is correlated with the level of economic activity and hence may to some extent be working as a proxy variable for labor market demand pressure (see Purdy and Zis, 1973).

An alternative and in some respects superior method of investigating the role of trade unions, but a method which is more applicable to the United States than to the United Kingdom, is to divide the economy into unionized and non-unionized sectors and separately study the determinants of wage inflation in each sector. This has been done by Pierson (1968), Throop (1968) and Hamermesh (1970). Broadly speaking, these studies conclude that the wage change–unemployment trade off is present in both sectors but is steeper and therefore less important in the union sector. Hamermesh (1972a) goes even further and disaggregates the economy on the basis both of degree of unionization and degree of concentration in product markets.[28] This work strengthens the conclusion that

[28] See also Eagly (1965), Gustman (1972) and Hamermesh (1972b).

monopolized sectors are less responsive to market pressures, as measured by the unemployment rate, than are competitive sectors. However, these authors do not attempt to study whether changes in militancy play a role: the presence of monopoly is simply assumed to affect the position of the short-run trade off between wage inflation and unemployment and this leads to the prediction that the equilibrium unemployment rate will depend (in a way that has not been investigated) on the degree of monopoly power that is present in the economy as a whole.

An alternative measure of union pushfulness suggested by Taylor (1972), Knight (1972), Godfrey (1971) and Godfrey and Taylor (1973) is the volume of strike activity. They report a positive correlation between strikes and wage change. In contrast, Johnston and Timbrell (1973) and Ward and Zis (1974) report that they can find no robust correlation here. The problem of interpreting such correlation (or lack of it) is even greater than in the case of changes in union density. First, the models of wage determination which incorporate strike activity (see, for example, Johnston, 1972) do not offer predictions about the sign of the relationship between the two variables. Secondly, like the Hines variable, strikes are well correlated with the level of economic activity (and hence inversely correlated with unemployment) (Ashenfelter and Johnston, 1969; Pencavel, 1970). Hence it may be the case that strikes are another possible proxy variable for labor-market demand pressure. Thirdly, it might be argued that strikes are the outcome of mismatched expectations about inflation rates held by employers and workers. It is entirely plausible that such mismatching increases as the rate of inflation increases and hence produces a positive correlation between strikes and wage change entirely independently of push or militancy. Fourthly, there is a tendency for wage changes and strikes to be seasonal in character; hence a correlation which ignores the seasonal nature of these relaionships is likely to overstate the correlation between the two. Those studies which find a strong correlation are

quarterly (Godfrey) or semi-annual (Taylor), whilst those which find little or no correlation are annual (Johnston and Timbrell and Ward and Zis). Fifthly, there are three alternative measures of strike activity not always closely correlated with each other (see Ward and Zis, 1974) and the investigator thus has scope to indulge in data mining in order to choose that definition which best suits his purpose.

A third possible way of measuring union militancy arises from the postulate that unions become more militant when profits are high and therefore push for higher money wages the higher the rate of profit. This matter has been investigated by Lipsey and Steuer (1961), who found little cross-section correlation between wage change and profits in the United Kingdom. In contrast, Bhatia (1961) and Perry (1964) in time-series studies of the United States do find a role for a profit variable. The correlation between profits and demand pressure is strong enough however to make it impossible to interpret this result as showing effects of militancy as opposed to those of excess demand.

A further proposition about wage determination which challenges the universality of the short-run relationship between inflation and unemployment is that direct controls on wages either shift or flatten the relationship. The evidence on this for the United Kingdom is fairly clear. It suggests that whilst the short-run relation between wage change and unemployment appears to be less stable when wages controls are operating, the average wage inflation over the control period is not significantly different from what would be predicted in the absence of controls (see Parkin and Sumner, 1972). Evidence from the United States is less clear but seems best interpreted as indicating at most only a slight effect from controls (see Perry, 1967, 1969, 1970, 1972; Alexander, 1971; Anderson, 1969; Wachter, 1969; Throop, 1969; Ackley, 1972; Bosworth, 1972; Fiedler, 1972; Gordon, 1972; Weidenbaum, 1972; Parkin, 1973b). Furthermore, no study of wage controls in the United States has suggested anything other than a modification of an otherwise well-determined wage inflation–unemployment relation. There is no suggestion that the relationship disappears in their presence.[29]

The view that the rate of wage change is largely independent of the state of excess demand but nevertheless the crucial central determinant of the overall rate of price inflation is widely held. It follows from the proposition that wage change depends upon the degree of "frustration" of wage negotiators and those whom they represent. This idea is closely related to the concept of "relative deprivation" introduced by Runciman (1966). It is argued that people come to feel "relatively deprived" with the rate of growth of their own real incomes is low relative to expectations, these being based on their own earlier experience and on observations of other people's real incomes. Attempts to improve their position will involve members of the labor force trying to increase their money wages at a rate they judge will put them in the desired real position. However, the economy's capacity to provide real income is limited by available resources and technology and may, from time to time, lag behind the desired rate of growth of real wages. It should be apparent that this hypothesis either requires that people suffer from money illusion or is in all essentials equivalent to the expectations hypothesis already discussed.

Models based on the notion of income claims adding up to more than the real output of the economy, but not relying explicitly on "frustration," can be found in the work of Turvey (1951) and Pitchford (1957, 1961, 1963). These authors simply assume a rigid structure of relative income claims which over-exhaust output. A related set of hypotheses concerning wage inflation is put forward by Balogh (1970), Harrod (1972), Jones (1972), Wiles (1973), Marris (1972), Baxter (1973) and Turner and Jackson (1970) and Hicks (1974), all of whom advance versions of the idea that the rate of wage change is an essentially sociological matter.

Detailed propositions vary between authors and take in such matters as a rigid link between wage change and productivity growth in the faster-growing sector of the economy spreading to the rest of the economy (Turner and Jackson, 1970; Jones, 1972), the general moral climate (Wiles, 1973; Harrod, 1972; Marris, 1972) or inconsistent notions about the fairness of the structure of relative wages (Hicks, 1974). A related idea first advanced by Reddaway[30] (1965, 1966) and later by Phelps-Brown (1971) is that confidence in the government's capacity and willingness to maintain full employment leads organized labor to behave as if there was a highly inelastic demand for labor over a range of wage variation which has been progressively widening and hence to an institutionally generated inflation rate.

Testing all these competing hypotheses about the determination of wage inflation and discriminating amongst them is, as we have seen above, no easy matter. However, the weight of the available evidence leads us tentatively to accept some variant of the expectations excess demand view of wage inflation and to reject the sociological and other push hypotheses. The econometric studies cited above using post-war data up to the middle of the 1960s all agree that during that period there was an inverse relation between the rate of wage change and unemployment.[31] Those studies that use data coming up to the early 1970s and which allow for the role of inflationary expectations continue to find a negative relation between the rate of wage change and unemployment.[32]

[29] For a non-quantitative survey of the evidence on a large number of countries see Ulman and Flanagan (1971).

[30] Written in 1957 at the request of the then newly established Council on Prices, Productivity and Incomes.
[31] Especially Phillips (1958), Klein and Ball (1958), Lipsey (1960), Dicks-Mireaux (1961), Samuelson and Solow (1960), Bhatia (1961), Perry (1964), Brechling (1968), Cowling and Metcalf (1967), Taylor (1970), Simler and Tello (1968), Purdy and Zis (1973), as well as the literature on the "income policy debate" surveyed in Parkin, Sumner and Jones (1972).
[32] These (cited above) are Brechling (1968), Lucas and Rapping (1969), Gordon (1972), Nordhaus (1972b), Turnovsky and Wachter (1972), Vanderkamp (1972), Turnovsky (1972), Parkin (1973b), Parkin et al. (1975), Duck et al. (1975), McCallum (1975).

Differences in the measure of unemployment used as an indicator of labor market demand pressure appear on the basis of the studies cited to be of secondary importance as far as their results are concerned. The role of inflationary expectations is clear and significant and in the studies by Vanderkamp (1972), Parkin (1973a), Duck et al. (1975), Parkin et al. (1975) and MacCallum (1975) the estimated coefficient of the effect of a change in inflation expectations on the actual rate of wage change is not significantly different from unity, thereby implying no long-run trade off between inflation and unemployment.[33] The roles of the rate of change of and dispersion of unemployment in generating wage inflation have, as we have seen, been harder to pin down.[34]

As to direct taxes, the work of Gordon (1972) and (with a bargaining theoretical justification) Johnston and Timbrell (1973) suggests that they play an important role. The rate of wage change is positively correlated with some definitions of the volume of strike activity but not others.[35] It is also correlated with changes in union density.[36] However, the interpretation of those correlations is at best ambiguous. As we have seen, some theoretical analyses imply either a causation that runs from wages to density and not vice versa or that the correlation is an aggregation phenomenon. Tests of the "frustration"[37] version of the sociological explanation of variations in the rate of wage inflation and of the power of incomes policies[38] have produced negative results. It has proved difficult to formulate testable

versions of the other sociological explanations and they remain untested. Wage leadership models perform[39] well but they leave open the question as to what determines the rate of wage change in the leading sector.[40] Such models may well be interpreted as complementary to excess demand and inflation expectations models, telling us about the details of the transmission of wage inflation through the economy, rather than being alternatives to them.

So much for studies of wage inflation. We now turn to discuss work on the proximate determinants of price inflation. Two questions have dominated the literature on this matter. First: does excess demand exert an independent upward pressure on prices, particularly of manufactures, or does its influence come entirely through its effect upon factor prices, particularly wages, and hence upon costs? Second: inasmuch as prices respond to cost changes, do they respond to changes in actual costs or to changes in some normalized or expected cost measure?[41]

Walrasian price-level dynamics postulates a *tâtonnement* process in which an "as if" auctioneer calls a random set of prices, contemplates the excess demands and supplies that these generate and adjusts prices in proportion to excess demands until the market clearing set of prices has been found. At that point, but not before, trading takes place. In such a world we would never observe excess demands and equilibrium product prices would adjust in proportion to changes in marginal cost. At the other extreme, some recent Keynesian work [Clower (1965); Barro and Grossman (1971)] drops the fiction of the auctioneer and introduces the "as if" assumption that prices are completely rigid so that

---

[33] In the Vanderkamp (1972), Parkin (1973b) and Duck et al. (1975) studies, inflation expectations were proxied by a distributed lag on past inflation; Parkin et al. (1975) used estimates based on surveys and McCallum used the future actual rate of inflation as a proxy for a "rational" expectation.

[34] See especially Archibald et al. (1974).

[35] See Taylor (1972), Knight (1972), Godfrey (1971), Johnston and Timbrell (1973), Ward and Zis (1974).

[36] See Hines (1964, 1968, 1969, 1971), Ashenfelter, Johnson and Pencavel (1972), Purdy and Zis (1973).

[37] The only test available appears to be that by Nordhaus (1972b) and is entirely negative.

[38] See Parkin and Sumner (eds.) (1972).

[39] Brechling (1973), Thomas and Stoney (1971) and also Eatwell, Llewellyn and Tarling (1974).

[40] Brechling and Thomas and Stoney imbed their models in an excess demand framework whilst Eatwell et al. leave the question open of what determines the inflation rate in the leading sector.

[41] A third question which has been raised but not answered is: do monopolistic firms exert an independent push on prices in a similar manner to that in which it is suggested that trade unions affect wages?

all disequilibrium adjustments involve quantities only. In this world, we would observe excess demands, but price changes would not occur, let alone be related to excess demand.

The modern theory of price-setting behavior (part of which is usefully surveyed by Nordhaus (1972a)) owes much to a basic insight of Arrow (1959). Since in a perfectly competitive equilibrium all firms are price takers, a theory of price *setting* must be based on an analysis of monopolistic or quasi-monopolistic behavior; in disequilibrium *all* firms must be quasi-monopolistic even if in equilibrium they would be operating in competitive markets. Following Arrow's lead, Phelps and Winter (1970) and Barro (1972a) have developed explicit dynamic models of price setting. Phelps and Winter's analysis is similar to that employed by Mortensen in analyzing wage setting. The key assumptions are that the firm is an expected-present-value maximizer facing a dynamic demand function which determines the rate of change of its sales as a function of its own product price relative to the market average price for the product. In equilibrium, when the firm's own price is equal to the market average, it maintains a constant level of sales. Barro deals with an expected present value maximizing monopolist who faces a stochastic demand function and introduces an explicit cost of price adjustment. His firm trades off this cost against the expected profits lost through maintaining a disequilibrium price. In the Phelps-Winter model there is no explicit cost of price change, but, because the rate of flow of consumers from the rest of the market to the firm in question is a function of its price relative to the market average (or for operational purposes the firm's expectation of that average), there is an implicit cost to price adjustment. The present value-maximizing time path for the firm's price gradually approaches the market average price, thereby stabilizing its market share. The rate of price adjustment is a function of *both* the difference between actual and expected average price and the actual and expected equilibrium quantity. This Phelps-Winter model also predicts homogeneity of degree one of the rate of

price adjustment with respect to the expected rate of inflation.

Barro specifies the demand for a firm's output as depending only on its own price. In his model aggregation over individual firms yields the proposition that the rate of price change will be a positive function of market excess demand. Clearly if he made demand depend on own price relative to the general price level, then the expected rate of change of the general price level would also appear as a determinant of actual price change and with a coefficient of unity satisfying the usual homogeneity conditions.

These recent theoretical developments in price dynamics have not yet had an impact on empirical work. Most estimated price equations are based on some variant of a mark-up model sometimes allowing the mark-up to vary with excess demand, sometimes making the mark-up relate to actual costs and sometimes to "normal" costs.

The earliest United Kingdom empirical studies assumed no role for excess demand in price equations. Work by Dow (1956), Klein and Ball (1959), Dicks-Mireaux (1961), Neild (1963) and Godley and Rowe (1964) all postulated that price changes were determined by changes in labor costs and some measure of import prices. In addition, Dicks-Mireaux used a productivity variable, Klein and Ball indirect tax changes, while Neild and Godley and Rowe added a lagged dependent variable to the equation.[42] Subsequent work has however included excess demand, as well as factor price changes, among the explanatory variables and has found that it played a role in explaining price change. Papers by Rushdy and Lund (1967), McCallum (1970, 1974), Solow (1969) and Brechling (1972) all find positive and statistically significant coefficients on a variety of alternative excess demand variables. The studies by Rushdy and

[42] Price equations used in studies, forming part of the "incomes policy" debate, by Lipsey and Parkin (1970) and Burrows and Hitiris (1972), were based essentially on the Dicks-Mireaux model, and hence did not examine the effects of excess demand.

Lund and McCallum used the Dow-Dicks-Mireaux (1958) index, Solow used an index of capacity utilization calculated by Paish (1962) while Brechling used the difference between real national product and a quadratic trend. In addition to excess demand, Rushdy and Lund used wage and import price changes; McCallum the lagged dependent variable; Solow, unit labor cost changes and the expected rate of inflation, and Brechling import price changes only.

In the light of these studies, it seemed to be well established that excess demand exerted an upward pressure on prices independently of changes in factor prices and hence costs, but Godley and Nordhaus (1972) presented results which challenged that consensus. They advanced the "normal" cost hypothesis, according to which prices respond to changes in "normal" costs and are independent of excess demand. By de-cycling factor price and productivity changes they computed a time series for "normal costs" and then, using that series along with ten alternative measures of excess demand in ten alternatively specified price equations (i.e., 100 equations in all) found only *one* significant positive coefficient on excess demand. They thus concluded in favor of the normal cost hypothesis that excess demand has no independent role to play in determining price behavior.

This conclusion appears to be mistaken for a variety of reasons, of which we mention three. First, in ninety of their regressions, Godley and Nordhaus specified the rate of price change as depending on *changes* in excess demand. This is an incorrect specification: it is at odds both with the usual theory of price setting and with earlier empirical work which had found the *level* of excess demand to be important. Secondly, of the remaining equations, only three use a goods market variable to measure excess demand, and all of those yield positive coefficients with *t*-statistics greater than one (though under 1.4). Thirdly, even in their "preferred" equation, the coefficient on price changes predicted from normal cost changes, which should be unity if the normal cost hypothesis is to be accepted, is 0.6 and significantly less than

unity. This constitutes a refutation of the normal cost hypotheses.

Also relevant to the interpretation of all the empirical work on price determination is the fact that actual unit cost changes fall during booms and rise in recessions. Prices move pro-cyclically but with less amplitude. There is a fundamental difficulty here in identifying the separate effects of actual cost changes, "normal" cost changes and excess demand. When actual costs are combined with excess demand both variables are significant; the use of "normal" costs necessarily leaves a smaller role for excess demand to play.

Price equations for the United States by Kuh (1959), Schultze and Tryon (1965), Fromm and Taubman (1968), Perry (1966), Klein and Evans (1967), Solow (1968), Eckstein and Fromm (1968), Gordon (1972) and Andersen and Carlson (1970) are extensively surveyed by Nordhaus (1972a) and a duplicate discussion is not required here. It is sufficient to note that with the exception of Kuh's equation for the corporate output deflator and Schultze and Tryon's durable manufacturing wholesale price index equation, all United States price equations display significant excess demand effects. Moreover, in a review of the role of demand in generating price changes, De Menil (1974) confirms this conclusion as does a recent disaggregated study by Ripley and Segal (1973). It is worth noting that the United States literature abounds with arbitrarily mis-specified price equations in which *levels* of price rather than rates of change of prices are regressed on the level of excess demand. In such cases, the excess demand coefficient, as would be expected, is often insignificant (see especially Schultze and Tryon, 1965). Finally, studies by the OECD (1970) and Ball and Duffy (1972) covering, with some duplication, twelve major countries also find the role of excess demand to be significant along with unit labor costs and import prices in all cases except France.

Whether or not prices respond to excess demand independently of cost changes is not relevant to the overall existence of a short-run trade off between the rate of inflation and excess demand. This trade off will exist if either product prices or factor prices or both are responsive to excess demand since no one disputes that cost (factor price) changes affect product prices. It is an almost universal finding that prices respond to cost changes, a major element of which is wage change. Wages in turn, as we have seen, are usually found to be responsive to excess demand as well as to other variables, sometimes including current or expected price changes. By taking the wage and price equations together, it is possible to obtain quasi-reduced form relations which make both price and wage changes functions of excess demand and expected inflation, as well as of other exogenous variables which might appear in either structural equation.

Whether or not the quasi-reduced form price setting equation displays a partial long-run trade off between inflation and excess demand depends on the combined effects of inflation expectations on wage change and of wage changes on price changes. Most models for which such a quasi-reduced form relationship has been explored (mainly for the large-scale econometric models evaluated and compared by Hymans in Eckstein (ed.) (1972)) suggest that, even in the long run, there is a trade off between inflation and unemployment. The models in question invariably use a distributed lag relationship in actual inflation rates to generate the expected rate of inflation with weights restricted to sum to unity and declining geometrically. The estimated coefficient of the expected rate of inflation (as so defined) on the actual inflation rate is less than unity.

In the small-scale United States model constructed by the Federal Reserve Bank at St Louis, Andersen and Carlson (1972), no long-run inflation-unemployment trade off is present but the model imposes rather than estimates that result. In the case of the Canadian RBX_2 model, Helliwell et al. (1971), no long-run trade off is present, while in a study which directly estimates a quasi-reduced form price equation for twenty countries, Cross and Laidler (1975) find a statistically significant role for excess demand in thirteen individual cases and no evidence of a long-run trade off in any country. The

key reason advanced by Cross and Laidler for the failure of so many earlier studies to generate a no-long-run trade off (or "natural rate") result is their inadequate allowance for the influence of foreign inflation on expectations of domestic inflation. In six of the seven cases for which the excess demand variable did not take a coefficient significantly different from zero, the coefficient was nevertheless positive. Moreover, all seven cases were small very open economies (e.g., Ireland, Belgium, Norway) and Cross and Laidler argued that, in these cases, imported inflation was swamping any purely domestic influence on the inflation rate.

The "natural rate" hypothesis is further strengthened by the results of ingenious tests devised by Lucas (1973) (see also Lucas (1972a)). He shows that if there exists a long-run trade off then there should be a (cross-section) relationship between the variance of real output about its trend. If no long-run trade off exists, no such relationship should be found. Using data for a cross-section of eighteen countries he shows the "natural rate" hypothesis to perform better than the alternative stable trade off view. Cagan (1968) attempts to test the "natural rate" hypothesis for the United States and United Kingdom using long-run average time series data and again concludes that the long-run trade off hypothesis is rejected by the data.

The *expected* rate of inflation plays a crucial role in many of the models of the proximate determinants of the *actual* rate of inflation of both wages and prices outlined above. It also influences the opportunity cost of holding (non-interest-bearing) money and therefore features centrally in the quantity theory analysis of perfectly anticipated inflation. In view of the central importance of inflation expectations, it is not surprising that this topic has generated a large literature in its own right. Three questions arise in connection with expectations. First, what precisely is the expected rate of inflation, is this unique variable or may several measures of it coexist? And if they do, what consequences flow from differences between expectations? Secondly, how may expectations be measured (or proxied)? Third, how are expectations formed?

The first question has only received passing treatment in the literature. Expectations can vary over at least three important dimensions. First, different individuals and other agents will, in general, form different expectations of the same variable over the same future time horizon: this means that some expectations are bound to prove wrong, which is contrary to the assumptions made in analyzing fully anticipated inflation. Second, different price indices will be relevant to different decisions and to different individuals: and expectations about, say, consumer prices and capital goods prices may differ significantly. Third, the time horizon over which an expectation is formed will depend on the problem for whose solution it is necessary to form the expectation, and the same person may easily have very different expectations about the course of prices over, for example, the next year and the next decade. In addition to these differences concerning individuals, indices and time horizons, expectations are seldom held with complete certainty and there will be variability concerning the degree of confidence with which any expectation is held. Except *en passant* none of these problems appear to have been addressed and it seems to us that their exploration will be a fruitful area for future work.[43] Until this work is done, one cannot know how far the conclusions which have been reached in much of the literature depend on the (usually unstated) assumptions that expectations are held with complete certainty and that a single inflation expectation is adequate for all purposes.

Much of the early empirical literature which made use of inflation expectations treated the other two questions as if they were one by making an untested assumption about how expectations are formed and then

used that assumption as an auxiliary hypothesis in wage or price equations. The most common such assumption, first introduced by Cagan (1956), and followed in empirical work by many others,[44] is that inflation expectations adjust by a constant fraction of the difference between the most recently recorded actual inflation rate and the previously formed expectation.[45] This intuitively appealing idea of "error learning" or "adaptive expectations," as Cagan's hypothesis is interchangeably called, was shown by Muth (1960) to provide an optimal forecast (in the sense of minimum mean square error) for a time series the first difference of which is a first order moving average process. Implicit here, and explicit in much literature in the field of mathematical statistics, popularized among economists by Box and Jenkins (1970), is the proposition that the optimal (minimum mean square error) forecast for a time series in general depends on the particular form of the stochastic process which characterizes the series being forecast. Rose (1972) showed that provided the series being forecast could be described by an ARIMA (auto-regressive integrated moving average) process then there remains an "error learning" interpretation for the optimal forecast, but that in general the current period forecast would be revised by a weighted average of *all* previous erros, not just by a fraction of the last one.

A second approach to the problem of expectations, also started by Muth (1961), is that of "rational expectations." The idea here is that expectations are formed such that they "depend, in a proper way, on the same things that economic theory says actually determine that variable" (Sargent and Wallace, 1973, p. 328).[46] Such an approach is

---

[43] A study which has considered multiple expectations is Parkin et al. (1975). One which has used as a central feature of its analysis the variability across individuals is Carlson and Parkin (1975) and one which has considered alternative forecast horizons is Rose (1972).

[44] See the works referred to in footnotes 31–40.

[45] In terms of a difference equation, $\Delta^2 p^e = \lambda(\Delta p - \Delta p^e_{-1})$, where $p = \log$ of price level, $\Delta =$ difference operator, λ constant fraction, superscript $e =$ expectations, subscript $-1 =$ time lag. Cagan used a continuous time formulation, $dp^e/dt = \lambda(p - p^e)$.

[46] In addition to Muth's seminal paper and Sargent and Wallace, see also Brock (1972) and, for a monetarist analysis of the essential ideas, Walters (1971).

probably better suited to a characterization of expectation formation in the very long run. In the short run, it seems more likely that expectations will be based on cruder forecasting procedures which, even if optimal (in a minimum mean square error sense) are capable of being systematically wrong. Moreover, if expectations are to be formed "rationally" it is important that those forming them be able to forecast government policy. This point poses a very serious problem for the advocates of "rational expectations." Lucas (1972a, b) shows, in a paper that abstracts from this type of problem, that even if expectations are formed rationally, because it is not possible for agents to distinguish absolute from relative price changes, a systematic deviation of output from its full equilibrium level would still follow a monetary disturbance.

A third approach to expectations is grounded in Bayesian statistics and the relationship between a Bayesian approach and "adaptive expectations" has been investigated by Turnovsky (1969).[47] He shows that, whilst a Bayesian forecast of a time series has an adaptive expectations interpretation, the speed with which expectations adapt to experience when a Bayesian approach to forecasting is taken will not, in general, be constant and will depend on the nature of the time series being forecast.

Most empirical studies of wage and price determination using inflation expectations have made use of the simple error learning hypothesis. Models incorporating that hypothesis have typically performed well in the sense that they have provided an overall explanatory power of wage or price change that would be regarded as adequate. However, they often generate a coefficient on the expected rate of inflation, predicted by theory to be unity, which is significantly less than unity. About half of the recent studies that have used this expectations hypothesis, have generated a coefficient significantly different from unity.[48] One possible reason for this is

suggested by Sargent (1971). He shows that, if it is assumed that the rate of inflation is a stationary autoregressive process, then for expectations of inflation to be optimal forecasts, they should be formed as a weighted average of past inflation with the weights summing to less than unity.[49] The error learning hypothesis measures expectations as a weighted average of past inflation where the weights decline geometrically and sum to unity. Thus, if inflation is indeed a stationary autoregressive process, and if expectations are in fact formed optimally, to model expectations as being formed by an error learning process, this procedure will in general impart a downward bias of unknown magnitude to the estimate of the response of actual to expected inflation. If expectations are not formed optimally then nothing can be said *a priori* about the interpretation of such an estimate. This analysis would not, of course, apply to the formation of expectations about the level of the inflation rate if its rate was secularly increasing (but it might well apply to the formation of expectations about its rate of acceleration).

There is a general problem here, and it is simply stated: it is not possible to identify the coefficient relating actual to expected inflation without having an independent measure of inflation expectations.[50] One possible

---

[47] See also Aoki (1967) and Raiffa and Schlaifer (1961).

[48] Recent studies which in some forms examined obtained coefficients of unity are Nordhaus (1972b), Turnovsky (1972), Parkin (1973b), Vanderkamp (1972), Laidler (1973a), MacKay and Hart (1974). Those which obtain coefficients of less than unity are Parkin (1970), Nordhaus (1972b), Toyoda (1972) and Turnovsky (1972). Those listed twice found coefficients of unity in some cases but not in others. Solow (1969) found values of coefficients on expected inflation of less than unity but, on the sum of expected inflation and unit cost changes, the relevant sum not significantly less than unity.

[49] This conclusion has been generalized and shown to apply to any ARIMA process by Gray (1975).

[50] A special case of this is shown by Saunders and Nobay (1972). Using Parkin's (1970) United Kingdom wage equation they show that the replacement of the standard adaptive expectation model with an alternative but single parameter rational distributed lag function leads to the same reduced form parameter estimates but changes the interpretation of the coefficient relating expected to actual inflation.

independent measure of the expected rate of inflation is the difference between *equilibrium* nominal and real rates of interest. However, in order to use that difference, which no one disputes would measure a unique expected rate of inflation for the economy if everyone dealt in the bond market and held identical expectations, it is necessary to observe both the equilibrium nominal and real rates. Setting aside the far from trivial question of our ability to identify equilibrium values of variables, nominal rates are market phenomena and therefore are observable but real rates are not usually observable. To overcome this problem an untested assumption about the real rate has to be made. The most common is that the real rate is a constant (which reflects real productivity and thrift) plus a random element uncorrelated with the expected rate of inflation. As Sargent (1972) points out, this assumption does not hold up in a simple Keynesian model and may well not hold in a wider class of models. In fact the real rate will move systematically with inflation and take a considerable length of time to return to its equilibrium level after a disturbance. Thus, using a nominal-real interest rate difference rather than some form of error learning to measure the expected inflation rate merely replaces one untested assumption with another, raises new problems in the process, and brings us no closer to being able to identify the relation between actual and expected inflation.

The foregoing problems have led some investigators to attempt directly to estimate inflation expectations but such work is in its infancy.[51] Livingstone has obtained quantitative data on inflation expectations of United States businessmen and business economists by using survey techniques. However, when his series is used in wage equations (Turnovsky, 1970; Turnovsky and Wachter, 1972) it performs little differently from the actual rate of inflation both in terms of its

coefficient, which is less than unity, and its overall contribution to explanatory power. Lack of success with this variable should perhaps not be too surprising in view of the highly specialized and hence potentially unrepresentative nature of the people whose expectations Livingston was able to obtain by his survey. Carlson and Parkin (1975) have devized a method for deriving an estimate of the expected rate of inflation from a time series of *qualitative* survey data generated by asking people whether they believe certain prices will rise, fall or stay the same over some specific future period. If one knows what proportions of the population expect prices to rise, stay the same, or fall, and is willing to make sufficiently strong assumptions about the nature of the distribution of expectations across individuals, an estimate of the mean expected inflation rate can be derived for the population covered, though this estimate obviously depends on the nature of the assumptions made and on the accuracy of the respondents' statements as a reflection of their genuine expectations. Data drawn from Gallup Poll surveys of households and Confederation of British Industry surveys of business firms have been used to compute expected inflation rates for United Kingdom retail prices, domestic wholesale prices and export prices. When all three of these are used in an excess demand expectation wage inflation equation by Parkin et al. (1975) these series produce the predicted value of unity as the sum of the coefficients on the three expected rates of inflation variables and display significantly better explanatory power than the previous quarter's actual rate of inflation.

The availability of directly measured inflation expectations makes it possible to do more than discover the effects of expected on actual inflation. It also permits the investigation of hypotheses about the formation of expectations. Carlson and Parkin (1975) using the Gallup data described above find that a second-order error learning process (i.e., expectations adjust to the preceding two errors) with allowance for exchange-rate changes gave a plausible explanation of

[51] Some of the earliest attempts to use survey techniques to discover how people learn about prices are those by Behrend (1964, 1966).

expectations formation in the British economy on a monthly basis from 1960 to 1973. They also found inflation expectations to be more strongly correlated with the previous expectation than with the most recently announced past actual inflation rate.

A common procedure in the literature on inflation (see especially Eckstein (ed.), 1972) is to combine the three relations which determine wages behavior, price behavior and expected price behavior, in order to produce a quasi-reduced form which generates the short-run and long-run trade offs between inflation and unemployment, or more completely, the interrelated dynamic time paths of these variables. The drawback of this approach is that it treats excess demand as if it were exogenous to the inflationary process. This is not the case; the full properties of the interactions between inflation and unemployment can only be analyzed properly by broadening the framework to deal with models in which endogenous aggregate demand is influenced by fiscal and monetary policy. To the literature that deals with such models we now turn.

4. "COMPLETE" SHORT-RUN MODELS OF INFLATION, OUTPUT AND EMPLOYMENT

At the end of our survey of recent developments in the quantity theory approach to inflation we pointed out that, since changes in the rate of monetary expansion bring about changes in real income, a complete analysis of disequilibrium inflation requires an analysis of the interaction of the money market with markets for goods and services and labor. The work on wage and price setting behavior and expectation formation which we have just surveyed is equally partial in that it examines wage and price setting behavior and their inter-action, given some, as if exogenous, state of excess (or deficient) demand. We now need to bring these two elements in the analysis of inflation together into a "complete" macroeconomic model of inflation, income and employment determination. In this section, however, we deal

only with closed economies, and international problems are introduced in the next one.

The simplest post-Keynesian macroeconomic models that dominate the pages of a generation of elementary and intermediate textbooks do not determine the price level at all but analyze the effects of monetary and fiscal policy changes on the levels of real output and employment. It would be wrong, however, to conclude that such fixed price-level models can shed no light on an inflationary economy. Developed from a well-specified choice-theoretic foundation, such models as those of Clower (1965) and Barro and Grossman (1971) give considerable insights into the working of an economy in which markets are characterized by excess demand but whose inflation is suppressed. For example, analyzing such an economy, Barro and Grossman (1974) derive the interesting result that generalized excess demand combined with rigid wages and prices will, like deficient demand, lead to a less than full employment volume of economic activity. Furthermore, in their model either excess demand or supply can prevail even if the *real* wage is equal to its equilibrium value.

A more complex Keynesian model commonly advanced as an interpretation of the model implicit in the *General Theory* (Hicks, 1937; Modigliani, 1944; Patinkin, 1956), takes the money wage rate as given and then determines, along with output and employment, the price *level*. The latter variable, however, is of secondary interest. The effects of monetary and fiscal policy changes on real output and employment are still the focus of the model. Some work uses this model to examine the dynamics of the price level (e.g., Patinkin) but only analyzes movements between two equilibrium price *levels*. It does not examine inflation as a continuing process.

Although mainstream post-Keynesian macroeconomics represents a major advance in our understanding of fluctuations in real output and employment, as far as inflation analysis is concerned, it is a retrogression from the earlier Keynes of the *Tract* (1923) and from the Wicksellian tradition (Wicksell, 1898). This earlier tradition, presented in modern terms by Patinkin (1956) and Laidler (1972) had, as the focus of its attention, the determination of the price level and its rate of change. The Wicksellian economy never departed from full employment, however, and it is understandable that such analysis was widely regarded as having been discredited by the 1920s and 1930s. Nevertheless the influence of Wicksell on Scandinavian economists has been persistent; they have never lost the message that inflation needs to be analyzed and explained in terms of a complete macroeconomic model. They have not, however, achieved a convincing integration of the Wicksellian and Keynesian traditions in monetary theory for their analysis of inflation has always been for a fully employed economy (see, for example, Hansen, 1951, 1957; Paunio, 1961). Analysis of simultaneous inflation and unemployment in a macromodel has been achieved only relatively recently with the continuing development of large-sacle econometric models (such as the FMP, Brookings, etc., models for the United States and the London Business School model for the United Kingdom)[52] and of small-scale, highly aggregative models (in some cases empirical and others analytical) the best-known examples of which are those of Andersen and Carlson (1970, 1972), Ball (1964), Brunner *et al.* (1973), Brunner and Meltzer (1972, 1973), Laidler (1973*a*), Lucas (1972*b*), McCallum (1973), Petersen, Lerner & Lusk (1971), Sargent (1972, 1973), Stein (1974), Vanderkamp (1975) and Williamson (1970). Such models are capable of analyzing the simultaneous determination of both the inflation rate and the level of economic activity.

Although these models differ considerably among themselves in their degrees of aggregation and even in aspects of their basic specification, their essential structure can nevertheless be understood in terms of three sets of relationships which interact to determine the inflation rate, the expected inflation

[52] For a survey of large-scale models which is slanted towards the treatment of inflation see Eckstein (ed.) (1972).

rate and the state of demand (or excess demand). First there is an equation, or group of equations which may be used to produce a single quasi-reduced form equation, which specifies the proximate determinants of the rate of inflation as being excess demand, inflation expectations and, possibly, other *exogenous* variables, i.e.,

$$\Delta p = \alpha(L)x + \beta(L)\Delta p^e + \gamma(L)Z, \qquad (1)$$

where x is excess demand, Δp is the actual rate of inflation, Δp^e is the expected rate of inflation, Z is a vector of exogenous variables and where $\alpha(L)$, etc., indicate general distributed lag relationships. Second, there is a relationship which specifies how inflation expectations are generated. This may relate expectations purely to the past behavior of prices or to other exogenous variables as well, i.e.,

$$\Delta p^e = \lambda(L)\Delta p + \kappa(L)Z. \qquad (2)$$

Third, there is an equation (or again a number of equations reducible to one quasi-reduced form equation) which specifies the proximate determinants of excess demand as being the stock of real money balances, fiscal policy variables and the expected rate of inflation, as well perhaps as other exogenous variables. Such an equation, with m the log. of the nominal money stock, p the log. of the price level and f as a vector of fiscal policy variables, may be thought of as the solution to a dynamic IS–LM type system combined with an aggregate supply analysis, i.e.,

$$x = \delta(L)(m - p) + \phi(L)\Delta p^e + \mu(L)f + \psi(L)Z. \qquad (3)$$

For an exogenously given time path of monetary expansion rates (Δm) and fiscal policy (f) and for given paths of the exogenous variables (Z), the above three equations will produce time paths for the actual and expected inflation rates and for excess demand. Models of the general class described by the above three equations can nevertheless differ in many details. The more important differences here are their long-run inflation–unemployment trade off properties, and the relative weights which they give to the effects of monetary and fiscal policy on excess demand. Whatever their differences in these respects, however, all the major models produce a response to monetary and/or fiscal policy changes which first affects real output and employment and only subsequently, and often with very long lags, affects the rate of inflation. The specific empirical estimates of some of the more important large-scale United States models and evaluations of time paths of inflation and output (or unemployment) on well defined policies have been extensively surveyed in Eckstein (ed.) (1972).

It is only in the context of a complete model such as that set out in highly aggregative form in (1), (2) and (3) that the full necessary and sufficient conditions for the nonexistence or otherwise of the long-run inflation–unemployment trade off can be established. Essentially what is required for no long-run trade off is that equation (3) be a correct specification of the way in which money affects demand (i.e. that equation must ·be homogeneous of degree zero in money magnitudes); that the effects of inflation expectations on actual inflation in equation (1) be homogeneous of degree one; and that, in the long run, expectations be unbiased. These results, established in Gray and Parkin (1974) but intuitively obvious, are apparently different from those suggested by Turnovsky (1974). There is, however, no conflict here. Turnovsky shows with the aid of a complete macro model that the impact effect of an *exogenous* change in expectations on actual inflation will not in general be proportional. This proposition is true in terms of the model set out above and has nothing to do with the existence or otherwise of a long-run inflation–unemployment trade off.

An insight into the working of the class of models set out above can be obtained (though not of course a quantitatively accurate one) by considering the behavior generated by a simple, special case of the general framework. Such a model, has been developed by Laidler (1973a) and may be set out as follows:[53]

$$\Delta p = \alpha x_{-1} + \Delta p^e_{-1}, \tag{4}$$

$$\Delta p^e = \lambda \, \Delta p + (1 - \lambda) \, \Delta p^e_{-1}, \tag{5}$$

$$\Delta x = \delta(\Delta m - \Delta p). \tag{6}$$

In this model, Δp is the inflation rate over the current time period (Laidler suggests a year in his exposition), x_{-1} is the average level of excess demand (measured as the log. of the ratio of actual to trend output) over the previous year, Δp^e is the expectation of inflation held, as if with certainty, by all economic agents at the end of the previous period about the current period and Δm is the rate of change of the nominal money stock.

Although this very simple model ignores many features which would be present in an actual economy, it enables us to see how a model which is extremely "monetarist" in its assumptions about the influence of fiscal policy and in its long-run properties, nevertheless is capable of generating unemployment as well as inflation in response to a change in the rate of monetary expansion. One may get a feel for how this model behaves in general by considering the following experiment. Suppose the economy is initially in a full equilibrium with the actual and expected rates of inflation equal to each other and to the percentage rate of monetary expansion,[54] i.e., $\Delta p_0 = \Delta p^e_0 = \Delta m_0$.

In this situation, of course, excess demand will be zero. This state of affairs is depicted as holding during the interval from t_0 to t_1 in Fig. 1. At t_1 let the rate of monetary expansion fall but then maintain a new lower level for ever as shown by the steep drop in the line labelled Δm_*. At that instant there will be a fall in excess demand (that is the creation of excess supply) of an amount given by δ times the change in the rate of monetary expansion. After a delay of one time interval,

[53] See Laidler (1973a), pp. 371, equations (1)–(3).
[54] This formulation abstracts from real growth. It is, however, extremely simple to adapt the analysis to fluctuations of the economy about a rising trend and Laidler's paper contains such an analysis.

FIGURE I

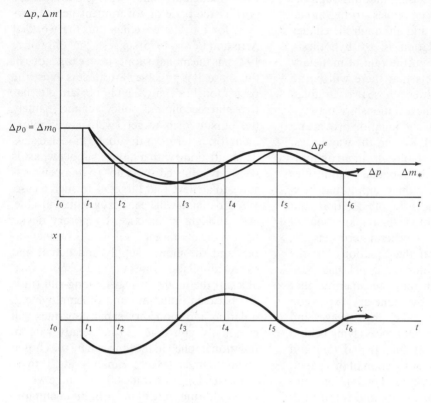

the inflation rate will fall by $\alpha\delta$ times the change in the rate of monetary expansion. This change in the inflation rate will, for the purpose of the intuitive diagrammatic analysis, be presumed to be less than the change in the rate of the monetary expansion. Immediately after the point t_1 the inflation rate exceeds the rate of monetary expansion and hence real balances are falling. Falling real balances will generate additional excess supply through equation (6) so that by t_2 the inflation rate will have fallen via equation (4) to equal the rate of monetary expansion. At that point, via equation (6) excess demand will begin to turn around. Between t_2 and t_3 real balances are rising since the rate of inflation is below the rate of monetary expansion. However, inflationary expectations, which, by equation (5), are lagged behind the actual rate of inflation, will be above the actual rate and excess demand will continue to be negative although falling towards zero. At t_3 actual

and expected inflation are equal to each other and excess demand is zero. However at t_3 the stock of real balances is increasing since both the actual and expected inflation rates are now below the rate of monetary expansion. This growth in real balances leads to positive excess demand and with excess demand increasing the actual and expected inflation rates continue to increase. Once more, as excess demand rises the actual rate of inflation eventually overtakes the rate of monetary expansion and real balances again begin to fall. Excess demand will also turn down again at this point and reaches zero at t_5 when the expected rate of inflation has caught up with the actual rate. The actual and expected inflation rates and excess demand will continue to cycle in a damped fashion towards a full equilibrium in which excess demand is zero and the actual and expected inflation rates are equal to the lower rate of monetary expansion.

It is worth emphasising that although the model just analyzed embodies strong "monetarist" assumptions and although the change in the rate of inflation is, by hypothesis, caused by a change in the rate of monetary expansion, it predicts that there will be no close correlation between those two variables. Observations on the relationship between monetary expansion and inflation provide no test of such a model. Rather, the way to test such a model is to establish from an analysis of the behavior of the monetary authorities whether or not the money supply has been controlled independently of inflation and excess demand, and to estimate equations of the type specified in general terms as (1), (2) and (3) above. If the equations "fit the facts" and if the money supply has been exogenous, then it may be inferred that inflation is caused by monetary expansion and transmitted via the price, wage and expectations adjustment process lying behind equations (1) and (2) [or (4) and (5)] and surveyed in the previous section of this paper.

Of course, the extreme assumptions embodied in equations (4), (5) and (6) are not offered by anyone as a complete characterization of inflation. However, a series of empirical papers by Duck et al. (1975), Gray, Ward and Zis (1975) and Parkin et al. (1975) which apply components of the model to the aggregate economy of the "Group of Ten" countries (as an approximation to the closed world economy) show that they fit the broad facts of "Group of Ten" inflation very closely in the period from the mid 1950s to 1971, while Laidler's initial (1973) study showed the model to fit United States experience in the 1952–70 period rather well.

The main problem with the above analysis is, of course, the assumed exogeneity of the money supply. The work of Friedman and Schwartz (1963), Cagan (1965) and Sims (1972) suggests that this is a reasonable enough assumption to make about the United States economy, in the sense that causation has primarily run from money to income and prices rather than vice versa over most time periods, an important exception being in the post-second-world-war years when monetary policy was geared to supporting the price of government debt. However, for the United Kingdom, the work of Artis and Lewis (1975) suggests that only since 1971 has the money supply been exogenous in this sense. It is possible nevertheless to use the basic model to analyze an important alternative macroeconomic policy regime, namely the pursuit of a target level of unemployment (or, in terms of the above model, excess demand) along with a money supply which is passively adjusted so as not to hamper measures to achieve that target.[55] In such a case, excess demand will be the exogenous variable, even though, in practice, temporary deviations from its target level would be inevitable, and the money supply and actual and expected inflation rates the endogenous variables. If the model displays a long-run trade off between inflation and unemployment, inflation and monetary expansion rates will eventually converge to the steady rate of inflation implied in the long run by the chosen unemployment (excess demand) rate. If there is no such long-run trade off then there will be no equilibrium rate of inflation; if unemployment is set below its equilibrium level there will be well-defined time paths for the rate of inflation and the rate of monetary expansion but the variables will eventually explode towards infinity. Whether or not one talks about inflation being "caused" by monetary expansion in this latter case seems to us to be semantic for, if the wage and price setting process does in fact respond only to the previous history of excess demand (as assumed in a strong form in equations (4) and (5)) then whether or not the money supply *has* been exogenous is irrelevant to the more important question of inferring what would happen *if* the money supply *were* made exogenous. "Exogenous" is used here not in the sense of the government being free to pick any rate of monetary expansion independently of its fiscal policy, exchange rate and interest rate policy or independently of the wider social

---

[55] This appears to be a predominant view of the way U.K. monetary policy has been conducted, at least until recently, and a view with which we concur.

and political implications of these policies, but in the narrow technical sense of conducting all its policies so as to ensure that the main line of causation stems from money to output and prices rather than vice versa. If policy is endogenous in the sense that the money supply and fiscal policy respond in part to output and prices then there are, of course, simultaneous equation problems in estimating the wage and price setting equations and the demand for money and policy response supply of money equation but these are not insuperable.[56]

So far, in this review of complete short-run models of inflation, we have focused on a monetary "demand pull" view of the inflationary process to the neglect of the sociological "push" views. This focus and bias is in part a reflection of the weight of the literature and in part, perhaps, a reflection of our own views. For the most part, the literature has presented sociological forces as proximate determinants of wage and price setting behavior and has not analyzed them in the context of a complete macroeconomic system. We have already referred to this work in the previous section. However, two important and influential analyses of sociologically generated inflation, those by Phelps-Brown (1971) and Hicks (1974), have been cast explicitly in the framework of a complete although informal macroeconomic system. Both see the adoption of full employment demand management policies as a crucial factor in the inflation explosion of recent years. In this respect, there is a similarity between the Phelps-Brown and Hicks positions on the one hand and the alternative, exogenous excess demand interpretation of the monetarist model described and analyzed above. However, there are differences of substance here, for both Phelps-Brown and Hicks not only argue that the money supply has been endogenous but also argue crucially that even if it could in fact be made exogenous, in the sense used above, it would fail to control

inflation. This conclusion follows from their views that a removal of fear of unemployment (Phelps-Brown) and increasingly inconsistent ideas about equity (Hicks) have led money wages to rise almost independently of the state of excess demand for labor and without any systematic relationship to inflationary expectations.[57] Both view variations in the unemployment rate within politically feasible boundaries as being virtually without direct effect on the inflation, though they might have some influence on the outcome of political negotiations between trade unions and government. If they are correct then control of the money supply would moderate inflation only marginally and at the expense of totally unacceptable rises in the unemployment rate. Whether or not they are correct, however, is impossible to say. Their views derive from general observations of the course of events and not from any econometric or statistical analysis. However, an idea ought not to be dismissed because it has not been, and perhaps cannot be, subjected to *quantitative* testing. *Qualitative* evidence is still evidence. Nor should a line of thought be ignored because it is not yet sufficiently developed for its proponents to be able clearly to state what evidence, either qualitative or quantitative, would, if presented to them, cause them to change their views. At this stage, no final judgment can be passed on the views of Hicks and Phelps-Brown. All that we can do to evaluate their empirical relevance is to refer the reader back to the vast empirical literature on wage and price setting behavior reviewed in the preceding section of this paper and to the conclusions which we drew from that literature and to note that, with Brunner et al. (1973) and Brunner (1974), we regard evidence of a systematic influence of excess demand on wage inflation in recent years as making it difficult to give primary emphasis

[57] As part of his analysis, Hicks makes use of what he terms the flexprice-fixprice distinction. It seems to us that the expectations augmented excess demand framework encompasses both of these. A flexprice market is one in which prices respond very quickly to excess demand whilst a fixprice market has a more sluggish response.

[56] There is already a growing empirical literature which has estimated monetary and fiscal policy response functions; see Reuber (1964), Fisher (1970), Nobay (1974), Pissarides (1972).

to sociological factors as proximate determinants of the inflation rate.

In the present state of the debate an eclectic position such as we described earlier (p. 753) appeals to many, with excess demand and inflationary expectations being combined with sociological and political factors into a multi-cause explanation of inflation. We would not adopt such a position ourselves if what is implied is that socio-political factors are important proximate determinants of wage and price inflation rates and hence that orthodox fiscal and monetary policies would not bring inflation under control without a permanent and large increase in the unemployment rate.

However socio-political factors do seem to us to be of crucial importance in understanding why governments pursue, either actively or passively, inflationary monetary and fiscal policies. The development of what may be termed a "political economy" of inflation is in its infancy. One possibility is that inflation is used as a tax, though it is hard to see why so many governments would have sought to gather extra revenue in this way at the end of the 1960s. It seems to us to be more plausible to look at events in terms of the use of demand management policies to raise the level of employment, and to maintain low real interest rests both on government debt and on certain politically sensitive private debt instruments, notably mortgages. Instability in inflation rates may be partly explicable in terms of the government's ability to extract a greater inflation tax with unanticipated inflation (Sjaastad, 1975) or, more plausibly in the context of the developed world, in terms of election frequency and the time horizon of Governments (Nordhaus, 1975). Literature on the social and political causes of inflationary monetary policy is however, in its infancy in comparison with that on its economic consequences.

Although we have characterized the models discussed in this section as "complete" an important sense in which they are "incomplete" is their neglect of international aspects of the generation and transmission of inflation. There is a long and important literature on this topic to which we now turn.

5. INTERNATIONAL ASPECTS OF INFLATION

Whether the generation of inflation is viewed as primarily a monetary phenomenon, or as primarily a sociological or socio-psychological one, the framework of the analysis applied to its explanation in individual countries has all too frequently been that of an economy operating in isolation. It is now widely recognized that this will not do and, on all sides of the debate about inflation, increasing attention has been given to placing the problem in an international setting.

The extension of the monetary analysis of inflation to an international setting is relatively easy precisely because the quantity theory of money was originally developed quite explicitly to deal with monetary phenomena in the context of a world made up of a number of open economies. The relative neglect of international factors in the monetary- and macroeconomics in the 1940s and 1950s ran strongly counter to the quantity theory tradition. Bodin, after all, was concerned to explain a Europe-wide inflation in terms of the import of precious metals from the New World, while Hume developed the quantity theory not in isolation but as a vital component of his attack on mercantilist theories of the balance of trade. Thus, modern analysis of the monetary economics of an open economy pioneered in English language literature by Polak (e.g. 1957), who built on a long-standing tradition in Dutch monetary economics, and developed by Mundell, Johnson and their associates, represents not so much a new departure as a return to older ways of thinking.[58] The way in which money and prices interact on a world-wide basis

[58] De Jong (1973) gives a useful brief account of the development of monetary economics in the Netherlands. Mundell's contribution to this field is to be found in its most accessible form in (1968) and (1971). Johnson (1972) and (1973) contain much original material, but they are also extensive surveys to which the reader who is seeking a more comprehensive account of the literature on the monetary theory of the balance of payments than we have space for here should refer. In addition, volumes edited by Claassen and Salin (1972) and Connolly and Swoboda (1973) contain major contributions to this particular field.

depends critically upon the nature of international monetary institutions, and since the Bretton Woods system of fixed exchange rates between more or less convertible national currencies was in force until 1971, it is hardly surprising that the great majority of recent work has taken just such a framework as its starting point. In a world of fixed exchange rates the closed economy of the quantity theory models we have discussed earlier, in which the time path of prices is determined in the long run by the time path of the money supply, is not an individual country. Its appropriate empirical analogue is the aggregate of all those individual countries that are linked to one another by fixed exchange rates. Thus the relevant money supply, as far as the determination of prices is concerned, is the sum of the domestic money supplies of each national economy (converted to a common unit at the fixed exchange rates); its time path is determined as a result of the combined monetary policies of the individual countries. Thus, the monetary analysis of inflation described earlier becomes applicable at the level of the world economy.

Given this background the analysis of the relationship between money and the inflation rate in one particular country is viewed as having to do not with the causative mechanism of inflation in the economy as a whole but with the process whereby inflationary impulses are transmitted to a particular region of the economy. As far as long-run equilibrium is concerned, the predictions of the monetary approach are quite clear cut. If the world economy was always in full long-run equilibrium, any one country would be facing a level and structure of interest rates determined for it on world capital markets, and facing a price level and inflation rate (fully anticipated) also determined for it on world markets. It could operate at full employment only by conforming to these. Thus, domestic monetary policy would influence the domestic inflation rate in the long run only to the extent that domestic monetary expansion or contraction influenced the rate of change of the world money supply and hence the rate of change of world prices. Domestic monetary policy in any individual country would have

its main long-run effects not on that country's inflation rate but on its balance of payments.

A particular country's money supply is equal, by accounting identity, to the sum of its stock of foreign exchange reserves and the stock of credit extended by the banking system to domestic borrowers. The foreign-exchange reserves may be influenced to some extent by the floating of Government long-term loans abroad or by other types of intervention in the capital market, but the more important monetary policy variables potentially under the control of domestic authorities are the stock of domestic credit extended and its rate of change, the rate of domestic credit expansion. If the demand for nominal money is a stable function of real income, the price level, the level of real interest rates and the expected rate of inflation, then in the long run all its arguments are determined on world markets. If, in a particular country, the supply and demand for money are to be kept in equilibrium, it is the money supply that must adjust to accommodate demand and not the arguments in the demand for money that must adjust to accommodate supply. Thus, the rate of change of foreign exchange reserves must vary to eliminate any discrepancies between the rate of domestic credit expansion and the rate of change of the demand for money, but the rate of change of reserves is precisely the so-called "balance on official settlements" definition of the balance of payments.[59]

Now if we analyze the behavior of a small open fixed exchange rate economy in this way, we can establish its long-run properties if the world economy stays in full long-run equilibrium but we leave many important questions about the short run unanswered. Morever, the correspondence of the predictions of this

[59] This is not to say that this definition of the balance of payments is in any way essentially more "correct" than any other, but only that it is the relevant one as far as the analysis of money and inflation in an open economy is concerned. The balance on official settlements does after all represent the net purchases of foreign currencies that a central bank has to make to maintain the parity of its own currency. Note that recent work by Brunner (1975) has adapted the well-known Brunner-Meltzer (1972) analytic schema to the level of the world economy.

long-run analysis of the facts of the last decade or so is crude indeed. A step up in the rate of change of the world's money supply, mainly originating in the United States, in the mid-1960s did indeed accompany a world-wide acceleration of national inflation rates. Nevertheless major discrepancies between the inflation rates experienced by different countries persisted throughout the period in question and these divergences need explaining.

Changes in tariffs or in non-tariff barriers to trade could explain these divergences, but most recent work on these problems places at the centre of the analysis the awkward but apparently fruitful distinction between the determination of the prices of tradeable goods on the one hand and of non-tradeables on the other, a distinction which corresponds to that made in the "Nordic" literature between the output of the "exposed" and "sheltered" sectors of an economy. Non-tradeables are simply those items which, because they must be consumed at the point of production, have only a domestic market. The argument is that it is not the overall price level, but only the price level of tradeable goods that is determined on world markets. The behavior of the non-tradeables is related to world-wide happenings, of course, but only indirectly. To the extent that the tradeable and non-tradeable sectors of an economy compete for labor, world price level trends will be transmitted through the labor market to the non-tradeable sector, while to the extent that the division of domestic aggregate demand between tradeables and non-tradeables is related to their relative prices, there is another route whereby world-wide factors impinge upon the market for non-tradeables.

However, there is no reason to expect that the inflation rates in the two sectors will be the same even in the long run. If technical change in the two sectors is different in character then the possibility of the marginal productivity schedules of labor shifting at different rates arises. For given output mixes, and for a given rate of wage inflation, rates of price inflation will differ in such circumstances. They will also differ if, in a growing economy, the division of aggregate demand between the output of the two sectors changes over time. But if inflation rates differ between these two sectors, and if the overall domestic inflation rate is an average of the two then we have ample scope for any one country's inflation rate to differ from that ruling in the rest of the world, and to differ persistently.[60]

Even abstracting entirely from these matters, the process of transmitting changes in the world inflation rate through the labor market into changes in the inflation rate for non-tradeables is likely to be subject to time lags; the domestic inflation rate thus can differ from that ruling in the rest of the world while such adjustment is taking place. There is no reason to suppose that the lags in question will be sufficiently short as to be negligible. The time that must elapse for an economy fully to adjust to a new inflation rate is thought by some economists (notably Friedman; cf. 1968) to be more appropriately measured in decades than in years.[61]

We have so far said nothing about the interaction of inflation and unemployment in an international context. To the extent that the problem is to explain their interaction on a world-wide basis, there may be no particular difficulty. One of the more remarkable features of recent economic history has been the way in which employment fluctuations have been as closely synchronized across national

[60] The so-called Nordic model of inflation lays considerable stress on productivity growth differentials between sectors. Note that, although this model does not have anything to say about the monetary aspects of inflation in an open economy its structure is in no way inconsistent with that of a model that takes these factors into account. For one account of this Nordic model see Edgren, Faxen and Odhner (1969).

[61] Parkin (1974) explains discrepancies between the domestic inflation rate and that ruling elsewhere in the world solely in terms of lags of this sort, producing a model of a small open economy which in long-run equilibrium has the world inflation rate but in which the short-run inflation rate can deviate from its steady state value because the inflation rate in the non-tradeable sector takes time to catch up with that ruling in the tradeables sector. There is no necessary inconsistency between Parkin's model and the Nordic model because there is no reason why it could not be elaborated to deal with a situation in which productivity growth rates differed between sectors.

boundaries as have fluctuations in the inflation rate. It may well be that the closed
economy analysis of this problem dealt with
earlier can fruitfully be applied at the level of
the world economy.[62] However, as yet there
is very little literature on the role played by
fluctuations in income and employment in a
particular economy in the transmission of
world-wide variations in inflation and unemployment rates into that particular economy.
This surely is one of the more interesting
problem areas currently in need of further
research effort.[63]

Even more important, we need work on
the operation of a system of flexible exchange
rates in an inflationary environment. All the
analysis discussed so far in this section has
been cast against the background of a system
of fixed exchange rates between convertible
currencies. Such a system ceased to operate
in 1971. Though there is a substantial historical literature on flexible exchange rates
arising from the debates of the era of the
Revolutionary and Napoleonic Wars, and
from those of the 1930s, no systematic study
of the operation of flexible exchange rates in
an inflationary context is available in recently
published literature.[64] This gap in knowledge

at present detracts considerably from the
confidence with which the monetary approach can be applied to contemporary policy
problems. The usual approach taken is to
argue that an open economy operating a
flexible exchange rate may be analyzed "as if"
it were a closed economy. Even if this is
correct, it is not clear what differences are
made by the fact that we have a system, not of
completely flexible rates, but rather of man-
aged floating.

The last few pages have dealt with international aspects of inflation in terms of a
predominantly monetary interpretation of
the phenomenon. As we have already noted
above, there exists a strong school of thought,
particularly among British economists, that
the roots of the current inflation are to be
found in sociological and socio-psychological
forces. It would be quite misleading to suppose that only monetary economists have
noticed the international character of recent
inflation. As long ago as 1970, for example,
OECD drew attention to this aspect of the
problem but offered an explanation of it that
rested more on a growth in the importance of
factors leading to social conflict than on a
world-wide monetary expansion.[65] In terms
of such an explanation one channel for the
transmission of inflationary impulses across
national boundaries is a "demonstration
effect." Workers in one country become more

---

[62] The paper by Duck et al. (1975) presents results
that suggest that an expectations augmented Phillips
curve can successfully account for the interaction of
unemployment and wage inflation rates for data aggregated over a number of countries, but a great deal more
work is required before we can treat this result as
anything more than tentative.

[63] Papers by Laidler (1975b) and Scarfe (1973) are
the only ones of which we are aware that attempt to deal
with this problem on a theoretical level. Laidler builds
upon Parkin's (1972) model and upon his own (1973)
closed economy model (see above) by making fluctuations in income and employment an integral part of the
mechanism whereby changes in the inflation rate in the
world economy are transmitted through the tradeables
sector to that for non-tradeables. Scarfe focuses on the
inflation-unemployment trade off in an open economy
and analyses the manner in which the adoption of flexible
exchange rates enhances the domestic authorities' control over these variables.

[64] The early nineteenth-century literature did deal
with the operation of flexible exchange rates in an
inflationary environment and is dealt with by Viner
(1973), chapters III, IV. More recent work was largely
carried out against the background of deflation and its

relevance in the context of inflation has not been fully
developed in the literature. We do not have space to
carry out this task here. Note, though, that there was a
school of thought that regarded perverse speculation
against the currencies in question as being an important
cause of the post-first world war hyperinflations. Cagan's
(1956) evidence that domestic monetary expansion was
the key factor in these episodes has undermined this
view and it is now usually accepted that the depreciation
. of these currencies was the consequence and not the
cause of the domestic inflations that it accompanied.

[65] OECD (1970). See also Marris (1972). As we have
already noted above, a sociological explanation of
inflation is a natural partner to the view that so-called
"prices and incomes policies" are required to deal with
inflation. When combined with an hypothesis that
sociological factors are at work on a world-wide scale,
the policy application becomes one of internationally
co-ordinated prices and incomes policies, an implication
that was not altogether missed by OECD.

"militant" in their wage demands; this is noticed by workers in other countries who also become more militant. Hence, the forces leading to cost inflation become world-wide in their operation. This is not the only channel of international transmission consistent with the sociological view. Some adherents of the sociological approach—for example, Hicks (1974)—regard goods-market as opposed to labor-market behavior as being amenable to economic analysis. Thus they view pricing behavior in world-wide goods markets, particularly for food and commodities, as being another channel whereby inflation spreads through the international economy. In this respect, their views do not significantly differ from those of the "monetarists."

Proponents of sociological explanations make much use of the "international demonstration effect." Though it is an intuitively appealing idea that relatively "docile" workers in one country might become more "militant" as a result of learning about the activities of a more "aggressive" labor force elsewhere, is it not equally plausible that "militant" workers might learn from the example of "docile" neighbors? It seems to us that demonstration effects can go both ways, and until it is explained why in the late 1960s the example of, say, the French and Italian labor forces should have more influence on the international scene than that of the Germans or the Americans, we do not really have an explanation of the international transmission of inflationary impulses at all. All we have is a description of one aspect of inflation as it manifests itself on the international level.

6. THE REDISTRIBUTIVE CONSEQUENCES OF INFLATION

At the very outset of this survey we noted that the major reason for paying particular attention to the problem of inflation lay in its consequences.[66] These consequences mainly involve the distribution of income and wealth and it is convenient for purposes of exposition to divide such redistribution up into two categories: that which takes place within the private sector of the economy and that which takes place between the private sector and the government. We will begin by considering the matter of redistribution within the private sector. Analysis here has concentrated on two hypotheses, one concerning wages lag and the other concerning debtor–creditor relationships. In discussing the redistributive consequence of inflation it is, of course, vital to distinguish between inflation that is fully anticipated and inflation that is imperfectly anticipated. If by anticipated we mean not only that a particular rate of inflation is expected by everybody but also that the expectation in question has been acted upon by all concerned, then a fully anticipated inflation can, by definition, have no distributive consequences in the private sector.[67] All bargains, be they about wages or about borrowing and lending must, on these assumptions, be fully adjusted for inflation in such a way as to ensure that their outcome in real terms is just what it would have been at a fully anticipated zero rate of inflation. The hypotheses about the distributional consequences of inflation with which we are concerned here, therefore, involve the analysis of imperfectly anticipated inflation.

The literature on these hypotheses has been somewhat self-contained, and not without reason. Until recently, most theoretical analysis on inflation dealt with fully anticipated inflation; it was therefore impossible to connect up empirical work on the distributive consequences of imperfectly anticipated inflation with much of the available inflation theory. In consequence, the relevant literature has tended to be heavily empirical with very little theoretical foundation. We have already noted that more recent work, such as that

[66] In preparing this section of the paper we have benefited greatly from having access to a draft survey paper (Foster, 1975).

[67] We owe this distinction to Mr Foster, who notes that inflationary redistribution must therefore depend not only on the characteristics of economic agents but also on the characteristics of the assets and liabilities that they hold.

which has incorporated versions of the expectations augmented Phillips curve into complete macro-economic models of the inflationary process, may be looked upon as attempting, among other things, to analyse the evolution of an inflationary process where the various relevant inflation rates are not fully anticipated. The development of theoretical work along these lines brings with it the hope that future studies of the distributive consequences of inflation will be much more integrated with relevant theoretical work on inflation than they have been in the past, but such developments have hardly yet taken place. It is not difficult, though, to point to worthwhile lines of investigation.

Let us consider the wages lag hypothesis first of all. It is yet another aspect of the literature on inflation that may be traced back to David Hume. It states that, when inflation is taking place, price rises tend to run ahead of increases in money wages, so that real wages are lower than would be the case with stable prices. In the fully employed economy always assumed in Classical analysis, a lower real wage rate means a lower real wage bill and hence a greater share of a given level of real output going to profits. This in turn means a higher saving (and investment) rate and hence more real growth.[68] Early empirical work of Mitchell (e.g., 1908) on the Greenback era, that of Hamilton (e.g. 1934) on sixteenth- and seventeenth-century Europe, and that of Hansen (1925) on the post-first-world-war inflation in the United States seemed to give a great deal of empirical support to this hypothesis. Hamilton's work in particular was taken up by Keynes (cf. vol. II of the *Treatise*), who laid great stress

on the capacity of what he termed "profit inflation" to generate economic growth.

More recent empirical work has seriously undermined the wage lag hypothesis. Studies by Alchian and Kessel (1959), Kessel and Alchian (1960) and Felix (1956) argued that earlier work had made insufficient allowance for the effects of factors other than inflation on the time path of wages, while Hamilton's results in particular were shown to be highly sensitive to small changes in the time period employed in his tests (cf. Kessel and Alchian, 1960). Later work, mainly on post-second-world-war United States data (e.g., Bach and Ando, 1957; Bach and Stephenson, 1974; Conard, 1964; Phelps, 1961) but including a study using spectral methods to analyze long runs of British and U.S. data (Cargill, 1969), has produced such mixed results that the only safe conclusion about the wage lag hypothesis must be that it postulates a phenomenon which is certainly not universal, but which may from time to time have happened.[69]

This is all very unsatisfactory and it is easy enough to see why. The wage-lag hypothesis involves the proposition that, during inflation, price adjustment precedes wage adjustment. As we have seen earlier, it has only been in the last decade that we have had work on wage and price formation which recognizes that these variables are fixed endogenously to the economic system as part of the activity of firms and households rather than being given by some anonymous "market force" or "auctioneer." One implication of this work must be that the effects of unemployment on income distribution should be an integral part of any study of inflation's consequences, and this fact has been recognized by Scitovsky and Scitovsky (1964) and, more recently, by Nordhaus (1973). However, we have not yet had any rigorous micro analysis of the way in which wage and price setting behavior are carried on together and interact with one another. We have not had such analysis at the level of the individual firm or industry,

---

[68] In Classical economics, of course, the labor force was typically assumed to do no saving. To square this implication of the wage lag hypothesis with more modern approaches to economic theory one would have to postulate a higher saving rate out of profits than out of wages. Moreover, neo-classical growth theory of the type discussed in an earlier section of this paper would have a higher saving rate produce a higher capital-output ratio and a higher level of income rather than a higher growth rate unless there was some embodied technical progress included in the model.

[69] Foster (1975) gives a fuller account of these studies than we have space for here.

let alone for the economy as a whole.[70] We need such analysis in order to provide us with predictions about the circumstances in which we might expect wages to lag behind prices (or vice versa) and until we get it, it is difficult to believe that we are likely to see further progress with empirical work on the wage lag hypothesis.

The debtor–creditor hypothesis has generated more definite results, but here too there is room for a good deal more work; again, in our judgment it is theoretical rather than empirical work that is required. The hypothesis tells us that, if interest rates on assets denominated in terms of money are not fully adjusted to the rate of inflation, then during inflation creditors lose and debtors gain. As early as 1896 Irving Fisher suggested that inflationary expectations would exert a powerful influence on the level of nominal interest rates and produced empirical evidence consistent with this hypothesis.[71] Recent inflationary experience has led to a revival of interest in Fisher's hypothesis and evidence favorable to it has been generated by studies of United States data by Gibson (1960) and Yohe and Karnowsky (1969). Feldstein and Chamberlain (1973) combined Fisher's hypothesis with the Keynesian liquidity preference approach to interest rate determination, and as far as the United States long-term

rate of interest is concerned found that inflationary expectations exerted an important influence on it, particularly after 1967. A recent study by Silveira (1973*b*) of Brazil shows that expectations heavily influenced bank lending rates there despite legal constraints upon such rates.

Nevertheless, even though there is abundant evidence that inflationary expectations do drive nominal interest rates upwards, it is evident that this does nothing to compensate holders of long-term loans issued before the outset of more rapid inflation. Moreover if we ask how long it takes for rates to change sufficiently to compensate fully for a change in the inflation rate, the answer implicit in all this evidence, at least as far as the United States is concerned, is somewhere in the region of two decades. If this is the case, then there is ample scope for inflation to redistribute wealth from creditors to debtors in the interim, and of course if inflation continuously accelerates the adjustment is always incomplete. Two questions are raised by such a conclusion: who are the debtors and creditors in question, and why do interest rates take so long to adjust?

Overwhelmingly, the losers from inflation appear to be households, and, within the household sector, losses seem to concentrate on the rich and the poor. Middle income groups, having more nominal debt than those at either extreme of the wealth distribution, are less affected (cf. Bach and Stephenson, 1974). There is some suggestion that, in adjusting to inflation, the rich react more quickly than the poor (cf. Tait, 1967) so that they lose relatively less by it. In the private sector, the main gainers from inflation are non-financial corporations, although by no means all corporation are in the position of having more nominal liabilities than assets. The evidence on these matters is, however, overwhelmingly based on United States data and it is not clear to what extent one may generalize from it to other economies.[72]

---

[70] It will already be apparent from our account of the so-called "new microeconomics" (pp. 756-7 above) that studies of wage determination (e.g., Mortensen, 1970) take price behavior for granted, and that those of price setting (e.g., Phelps and Winter, 1970) take wage behavior for granted. The need to integrate these separate pieces of analysis is widely recognized.

[71] Although such authorities as Keynes (1936), pp. 142–3, and Harrod (1969, 1971) have argued that inflationary expectations drive down the real rate of interest rather than raise the nominal rate. Steindl (1973) builds on Mundell's (1963) analysis of the influence of inflation on the real rate of interest and argues that the effect of anticipated inflation on the real interest rate cannot be predicted *a priori*. Sargent (1973) produces a model in which rising prices and high interest rates go together as a result of being jointly determined by other factors rather than because of the effects of inflationary expectations. In a later (though earlier published) paper (1972) Sargent does incorporate inflationary expectations into his analysis. This later paper is discussed below.

[72] Once more the reader is referred to Foster (1975) for a fuller account of all this work.

Why interest rates fail fully to adjust to inflation is a question of considerable analytic interest. There can be two, by no means mutually exclusive, reasons for such failure: first, some or all economic agents can fail to form correct expectations of inflation and second, markets can fail to adjust in such a way as to reflect fully changed expectations. We have already seen above when dealing with the expectations augmented Phillips curve that there is abundant evidence that expectations do indeed lag significantly behind events; this factor must then certainly be part of the answer to the question under discussion here. However, it is implausible to argue that the public take between one and three decades fully to adjust their expectations of inflation to experience, and that is what one would have to believe if he looked to sluggish expectations as the only source of the slowness of interest rates to adjust. Moreover, such an argument would appear to be inconsistent with the evidence generated in Phillips curve type studies, where the lags of expectations behind experience are much shorter.[73] However, the relevant period over which expectations must be formed when setting an interest rate on a long-term loan is much longer than that involved in striking a wage bargain. It is quite plausible that the same agents might adjust their expectations of inflation over the next twenty years at a much slower rate than their expectation of the next twelve months' inflation.

Nevertheless, slow market adjustment probably has an important role to play in explaining the slow adaptation of nominal interest rates to inflation. Sargent's (1972) work on a complete macro model of the inflationary process is largely constructed to demonstrate the possibility of this. He notes that one would only expect inflationary expectations necessarily to be fully reflected in the difference between nominal and real

interest rates when the capital market was in full equilibrium and then shows, in the context of a macroeconomic model based on the IS–LM framework, that interdependence between markets might require that the whole economy be in equilibrium before this result was achieved. Sargent's paper thus focuses, more clearly than any other work of which we are aware, on the interdependence of the short-run dynamics of the inflationary process usually analyzed in the context of the inflation-unemployment trade off literature, and the distributional questions hitherto treated in a quite separate branch of the literature, and might be expected to open up an interesting line for future research.[74]

So far we have dealt with the redistributive consequences of inflation within the private sector, but Bach and Stephenson (1974) in particular provide striking evidence that the main gainer from recent inflation is government. In discussing the issues involved here it is once again important to distinguish between perfectly and imperfectly anticipated inflation. The government gains from inflation in three ways. First, inflation reduces the real value of government interest bearing

[73] Sargent (1973) shows that, using a first-order error-learning mechanism, the length of the learning process implicit in United States interest rate data is indeed to be measured in decades. We have discussed the results generated by Phillips curve type studies above.

[74] We must not leave the discussion of the behavior of nominal interest rates in inflationary conditions without referring to the work of Allais (1974) on this matter. He argues that the nominal interest rate in fact reflects what he terms "the psychological rate of interest," essentially the rate of time preference, and postulates that this variable is determined by a weighted sum of past volumes of money expenditure with weights declining as one goes into the past. This postulate of Allais is but one aspect of a body of work in money economics, only part of which is available in English (cf. Allais, 1966, 1969), which provides an alternative interpretation of a great deal of empirical evidence to that given by orthodox monetary theory. Like Cagan (1969) these authors find Allais' work difficult to understand. It seems to have no price theoretic foundations, while the empirical predictions that it makes are often difficult to distinguish from those of a more orthodox approach. Nevertheless, at the very least Allais does seem to have provided us with an empirical "law" which describes with considerable accuracy a large body of data. It would be quite wrong to dismiss his work on the grounds that it is difficult to understand and heretical. Work on comparing his theories and their predictions with those of the prevailing orthodoxy in monetary economics is thus badly needed.

debt.[75] The redistributive mechanism here is exactly the same as that involved in the redistribution between debtors and creditors in the private sector and needs no special analysis. As inflation becomes anticipated, upward pressure is placed on the interest rate that the government must pay on new borrowings. Resistance to this tendency involves government in switching its borrowing away from the public to the central bank and hence in generating further monetary expansion. This feedback from an existing inflation to the rate of monetary expansion, and thence to further inflation, gets considerable attention in so-called "monetarist" analyses of the inflationary process, analyses which stress the ultimate futility of attempts to keep nominal interest rates at low levels during inflation.

The second source of government gain from inflation is its influence on the real volume of tax payments. Regulations for taxation of income, capital gains, and business profits are usually drawn up on the assumption of price level stability. Hence, as far as income taxation is concerned, allowable deductions are defined in nominal terms while marginal tax rates are progressive with respect to nominal rather than real income. Capital gains taxation is levied upon nominal capital gains rather than real gains, while, as far as corporate taxation is concerned, appreciation of inventories is frequently treated as yielding profits on a par with any other source of corporate income. In all three cases, a rising price level increases the real burden of taxes even if there is no increase in the real value of the base upon which taxation is levied; against this, if payment of taxes is not legally due for a year or more after the middle of the reference year, the real value of the payment is seriously reduced by inflation. The last few years have seen widespread popular discussion of these fac-

tors and of schemes to deal with the problems they raise. In particular various schemes for "indexing" tax structures have been canvassed. However, these problems have received little attention in professional economics literature, perhaps because they seem to raise no new theoretical problems.[76] As far as the professional literature on accounting is concerned matters are different, for the tax treatment of nominal gains arising from inflation is just one of the many problems that face accountants in devising helpful conventions for providing and processing information about incomes, both private and business, in an inflationary situation.[77]

The third means whereby inflation redistributes income between the public and government arises from the "tax" that *anticipated* inflation levies on holdings of that part of the non-interest bearing money stock which is the liability of government. This matter has received a good deal of attention recently because the tools with which it can be analyzed are precisely those developed by adherents of the modern version of the quantity theory of money, but the analysis of inflation as a tax on cash balances also appeared in the pre-*General Theory* literature (cf. for example chapter 3 of Keynes's *Tract*). The analysis in question starts from the simple proposition that the issue of money is a source of revenue to the issuer. If no interest is paid on money holdings, and if, at a given anticipated rate of inflation, there is a given demand for real balances on the part of the public then, in order to maintain their real balances constant the public must continually acquire new nominal balances. Nominal balances must increase at the rate of inflation, and the issuer of money can obtain a stream of real resources in exchange for these nom-

---

[75] Keynes laid considerable stress on this particular redistributive consequence of inflation (cf. for example his discussion of post-world war monetary policy in France in the preface to the French edition of *The Tract*).

[76] But there have been pamphlets such as Giersch et al. (1974) that deal quite extensively with this matter. Note also that the *National Institute Economic Review* for November 1974 contained some discussion of indexation by Page and Trollope.

[77] For an example of the relevant literature in accounting cf. Carsberg, Hope and Scapens (forthcoming).

inal balances.[78] Since high powered money is a government liability, increases in the stock of high-powered money represent a source of government revenue.

The value of the resources thus acquired is equal to the product of the inflation rate and the stock of real high-powered money balances held and is exactly equivalent to the revenue arising from levying a tax on the ownership of (or equivalently on consuming the services of) any durable good. It is possible to apply the conventional Marshallian welfare analysis of indirect taxation to this aspect of inflation and such analysis was first applied to this problem by Bailey (1956), who, utilizing Cagan's estimates of the parameters of the demand for money function, constructed empirical measures of the welfare costs of various rates of inflation.

In comparing these welfare costs to the revenue obtained from inflationary finance, Bailey found them to be relatively high in the cases analyzed and concluded that, by the usual standards applied to judging the efficiency of indirect taxation, an inflationary tax on cash balances was inefficient. Subsequent work along these lines has tended to confirm Bailey's initial conclusion, and Pesek's (1960) work on the distributional consequences of taxing cash balances by inflation added further weight to this argument. He showed that such a tax seemed to fall more heavily on the relatively poor than would likely alternative sources of revenue such as sales or income taxes. We find Waud's (1970) argument, that if money-wage rigidity is causing unemployment, then perfectly anticipated inflation can increase welfare by increasing employment, an unconvincing counter to Bailey's position, since in a world in which all price changes are fully anticipated, it is hard to see why there should be

wage rigidity in the first place. An analysis of the welfare consequences of imperfectly anticipated inflation which could be used as a basis for dealing with the problem posed by Waud has not, as far as we are aware, been worked out.

Barro (1970, 1972b) developed a sophisticated version of the Baumol–Tobin inventory approach to the transactions demand for money in which the payments period was made an endogenous variable, and was able to give the rather vague notion of the "welfare cost" of inflation more concrete meaning by relating it to the amount of extra time and trouble devoted to trading both between money and interest earning assets and between money and goods. He also suggested that the implementation of the inflationary tax was likely to be, and in the particular cases he studied has been, unstable. If there is a revenue maximizing rate of inflation, and if this is exceeded, then the likely response of a government which does not understand the mechanisms at work in inflation would be to increase the rate of monetary expansion in an attempt to increase its revenue—a self-defeating and inherently unstable reaction.[79]

Now the analysis discussed so far begs the question of what it is that the government actually does with the revenue raised by an inflationary tax.[80] The implicit assumption is that it is redistributed to the community

[78] There are two implicit assumptions here. First, zero real growth is assumed. The consequences of taking account of growth are dealt with below. Second, it is assumed that in the absence of monetary expansion the nominal interest rate would be zero. This point is also taken up below.

[79] Note that the "instability" here lies in the reactions of the monetary authorities rather than in the behaviour of the public vis-à-vis money holdings. Thus, it is of a different type to that investigated by Cagan (1956) and discussed above (Section 2). Note that Dutton (1971a), in a model of Argentinian inflation, made the rate of monetary expansion an endogenous variable generated by the government's need to satisfy a budget constraint and found that such an hypothesis had considerable explanatory power.

[80] It also ignores the fact that variations in the inflation rate might affect the real rate of interest. Phelps (1965) investigates this matter, showing that fiscal policy might be used to offset this effect of using monetary policy to impose an inflationary tax.

for current consumption. However, it seems frequently to be the case, particularly in less-developed countries, that the main purpose of levying taxes, inflationary taxes included, is to finance development program. Mundell (1965) and Marty (1967) have analyzed, albeit with highly abstract models that incorporate the assumption of perfectly anticipated inflation, some of the issues involved here, for they treat the transfer of resources from the public to the government that is brought about by the inflationary tax as also being a transfer from current consumption to growth generating capital formation. However, their work in no way strengthens the case for inflationary finance. The extra growth generated by the inflation tax, both in terms of income and in terms of government revenue, turns out, given their assumptions, to be small in relation to the costs involved in generating it.

The work of Mundell and Marty studies a potential effect of revenue raising by money creation on an endogenous growth rate. There are also interesting questions to be raised about whether the existence of exogenous growth affects any of the conclusions to be drawn about the revenue raising capacity of inflation. There are potentially heavy overlaps here, of course, with the literature on the role of money in neo-classical growth models. A number of papers (e.g., Tower, 1971; Friedman, 1971; Marty, 1973; Cathcart, 1974) have explicitly addressed questions of the type just raised, and have shown that analysis that abstracts from exogenous growth might be misleading. If real income is constant the government can use it powers of money creation to raise revenue only by generating inflation. However, if real income is growing over time, so is the demand for real balances. The government can obtain revenue simply by meeting the growth in demand for real balances without recourse to any inflation. With a given growth rate in real income, and a given income elasticity of demand for real balances, the amount of revenue raised in this way will depend upon the ratio to real income in which the public hold real balances, but this ratio of course depends inversely upon the

rate of inflation. This analysis shows that, when this extra source of revenue from money creation is considered, there is even a logical possibility that the revenue maximizing rate of inflation might actually be negative given certain, not necessarily implausible parameter values of the demand for money function. The reduction in the real balances to income ratio brought about by inflation subtracts more from the government's ability to raise revenue than can be obtained from levying the inflationary tax on the stock of real balances actually held at any moment.

Even this analysis is incomplete, though. It assumes that the only source of revenue to the monetary authority is that which actually accrues from the creation of new nominal balances. But, even if the rate of monetary expansion was zero, the stock of non-interest-bearing high-powered money held by the public is, from the point of view of the monetary authorities, an alternative to having interest-bearing debt outstanding. Thus, the interest they save by having non-interest-bearing high-powered money among their liabilities may be regarded as contributing to their revenue. If this point, due to Auernheimer (1974) and Phelps (1973), is accepted, then the authorities' revenue from the right to issue money is better measured as the nominal interest rate times the real high-powered money stock outstanding than as the rate of monetary expansion times the real money stock. Once again, the effect of this further refinement of the analysis of the influence of money creation on the authorities' revenue is to reduce the rate of inflation compatible with revenue maximization. Thus the case for an inflationary tax as a means of raising revenue, already weakened by Bailey and Barro's work, is further weakened by the Friedman–Marty and Auernheimer–Phelps results. In the light of all this, it is hard indeed to defend rapid anticipated inflation as a satisfactory form of taxation.

7. CONCLUSIONS

The literature we have surveyed is so diffuse that we are precluded by its very nature from ending this article with any neatly drawn and definitive conclusions. Nevertheless, certain broad themes have run through our discussion, and we shall end our essay by drawing the reader's attention explicitly to them. In doing so we shall highlight what seem to us to be the important unsolved problems in the area. As we shall see, there are important linkages between these problems.

Inflation would not be a problem worth studying if it did not have serious social consequences. We have now seen that the inflationary process can produce important effects on the distribution of income and wealth and on the level of real income and employment. When inflation is not fully anticipated then contracts drawn up in money terms, whether between borrowers and lenders or between employers and employees, yield unexpected and (by at least one party) undesired results. Thus the effectiveness of money as a social institution which facilitates trade and enables contracts to be framed more easily is undermined by unanticipated inflation. Even perfectly anticipated inflation could have adverse consequences, as we have seen, but we would judge these resource allocation effects to be of relatively minor importance compared to the effects on distribution and employment of poorly anticipated variations in the inflation rate.

Here then is an important theme to emerge from the literature: the need to distinguish between fully and less than fully anticipated inflation. If inflation was fully anticipated by all parties the economy could operate consistently at full employment, and there would be no redistribution of income and wealth except between the holders of non-interest-bearing cash balances and those whose liabilities include such balances. The effects on economic welfare of such inflation seem amendable to analysis with the tools of conventional microeconomics. When inflation is poorly anticipated, employment can fluctuate away from its long-run equilibrium level, and apparently arbitrary redistributions of income and wealth take place.

Moreover, in this case, there are no tools available to economists to analyze the welfare effects.

Thus we have an important unsolved problem. The analysis of anticipated inflation needs to be so conducted that it covers all the varying extents to which inflation may be anticipated, including unequal expectations and lack of certainty about them. We do not pretend to know how such integration is to be achieved, but a much clearer idea than we have at present of the way in which economic agents form expectations, and of the way in which they change their behavior in the light of changed expectations, will be required before we can expect to get very far with this problem. It is notable that, in the context of the analysis of inflation, expectations—even if erroneous—are usually treated as if held with certainty, or it is assumed that any variance in expectations does not influence behavior. There exists a well-developed analysis, based on probability theory, of individual behavior in the face of risk elsewhere in our subject and there surely are gains to be had from applying this analysis to aspects of the problem of inflation. This at least would be our view, but there are many economists, notably Davidson (1972) and Shackle (1955), who would presumably regard the application of such analysis as misconceived (though possibly better than assuming all expectations to be held with certainty). They would stress that *uncertainty* in the Knightian sense as opposed to risk lay at the root of the problem. Certainly an analysis of behavior of this kind would provide an interesting alternative to the approach based on probability. There can be no guarantee *ex ante* as to which line of work will prove more fruitful, as a means of replacing the widespread assumption (often unstated) that people's actions are the same as if their expectations were held with certainty.

Analysis of the consequences of inflation is, by its very nature, inevitably concerned with the role of money in the economic system. Inflation is, after all, a sustained fall in the value of money, and as we said at the outset, must be regarded as a fundamentally monetary phenomenon for this reason alone. It does not follow from this that inflation's causes are also inherently monetary, but the evidence which we have cited on the stability of the demand for money function, particularly that generated under inflationary conditions, and the evidence which we have cited on the responsiveness of the inflation rate to excess demand, lends considerable weight to the proposition that sustained expansion of the money supply at a rate in excess of the product of the growth rate of real income and the real income elasticity of demand for money is both a necessary and sufficient condition for sustained inflation.

This, of course, should not be read as implying that only variations in the money supply can have effects on the level of aggregate demand. Swings in business confidence of the type postulated by Wicksell and Keynes can certainly exert an independent influence on aggregate demand, as can fiscal policies. However, we would argue that increases or decreases in aggregate demand from such sources will have only short lived effects on the rate of change of prices unless they also lead to changes in the rate of monetary expansion. But of course they can do just that in certain institutional circumstances, and it may be difficult in practice (for example) to reduce the rate of monetary expansion unless fiscal changes are made. It is the essence of Wicksellian analysis that any attempt to hold down interest rates in the face of an upswing in business confidence will lead to money creation and sustained inflation. It is central to modern work on the role of the government budget constraint in the money supply process that an expansionary fiscal policy met by borrowing from the central bank will result in sustained monetary expansion (cf., for example, Christ (1968), Brunner and Meltzer (1972), Kaldor (1970)). In the light of this work the question as to whether monetary expansion is a unique "cause" of inflation seems to us to be one mainly of semantics, and one that distracts attention from another, more important

theme to emerge from our survey, namely that analysis of the inflationary process must involve the study of the whole economic system and not just of one or two markets in isolation. The quantity theory of money might provide one with hypotheses about the behavior of the money market in the inflationary process, and the Phillips curve with hypotheses about the labor market, but precisely because inflation involves changes in the value of money, its analysis must deal with all markets in which money serves as a means of exchange and a unit of account. That, at least in a developed economy, must mean virtually all markets. The theoretical analysis of fully anticipated inflation in a growing economy recognizes this, as does the recent work on what we have termed "complete" models of imperfectly anticipated inflation. As we have seen, work in the latter field is very much in its infancy. We have already noted that progress here is likely to rely on further work on the way in which inflationary expectations interact with economic agents' decisions. Here, we would argue, lies the key to constructing an integrated analysis of the causes and consequences of imperfectly anticipated inflation, a task which must be accomplished before we can expect to see the production of an analytic framework in terms of which all types of inflation can be analyzed.

If excessive monetary expansion is a necessary and sufficient condition for sustained inflation, this immediately raises important problems in the analysis of the control of inflation. In developed economies at least the quantity of money is under the control of government, or would be if the government so desired. Why then has it not been controlled recently? How might governments be persuaded to bring monetary expansion under control and to lengthen the time horizon for their monetary policy decisions? These questions are representative of a large group of unsolved problems in the theory of inflation, problems on which the literature we have surveyed casts only a little light. The theoretical literature on the welfare costs of fully anticipated inflationary finance provides a powerful set of arguments against inflation from the point of view of both the government and the community at large. The monetary theory of the balance of payments tells us that a small open economy will find it impossible in the long run to make independent decisions about its money supply or price level while maintaining a fixed exchange rate. This is helpful when it comes to describing, for example, what happened in most economies before 1971, but it does not help us to understand why it happened. Countries which did not like the inflationary pace were not *forced* to maintain fixed exchange rates. But if we do not know why governments generate (or permit) inflation, how can we produce arguments that might persuade them to act against it?

The theoretical arguments against perfectly anticipated inflation are strong indeed, as we have shown above. Thus the prevalence of inflation can only be explained by postulating that Governments believe that there are gains from imperfectly anticipated inflation, or losses from reducing the inflation rate in such a way that the change is not anticipated. Nor is such a view hard to justify in the light of existing literature. First, gains accrue to governments from the effects of inflation on tax revenue and on the value of government debt outstanding, and these are, as we have seen, properly classified as gains from imperfectly anticipated inflation. Moreover, we have also seen that an integral part of the mechanism whereby an imperfectly anticipated inflation accelerates is a fall in unemployment. The gain here, if gain it be, lasts only so long as inflation is unanticipated and hence arises before economic agents perceive the costs involved in achieving it. The same analysis of course leads to the conclusion that slowing down an existing inflation rate imposes costs in terms of higher unemployment before the benefits of such a policy are perceived. Such arguments probably go a long way to explaining the inflationary bias of recent economic policy. Certain observers (e.g., Phelps, 1967, 1972)

have argued along these lines, and have gone so far as to argue that, once inflation is under way, it might be better to live with it than to cure it.

However, such analysis is tentative, and for a very good reason. Though Phelps (1972) in popularizing the ideas first set out in (1967) actually subtitled his book "The Cost Benefit Approach to Monetary Planning," the fact remains that we have no body of analysis analogous to Marshallian or Paretian welfare economics that permits us to discuss coherently the costs and benefits of imperfectly anticipated inflation. We do not even know what an appropriate measure of economic welfare might consist of when we deal with situations in which the outcomes of actions differ from those initially planned. Are we concerned with costs and benefits perceived *ex ante*, or *ex post*? When inflation is imperfectly anticipated these differ.

Once more then we return to what has been the constant theme of this concluding section of our survey. Until we have a much more fully articulated analysis of the formation of expectations and of the interaction of expectations formation and the behavior of economic agents it is hard to see how we are going to make any significant further progress in understanding inflation. On the other hand, significant progress in this problem area would have implications far beyond the confines of the economics of inflation.

References

The books and articles listed below are those actually referred to in the text. A more complete bibliography of the literature on inflation, prepared by Geoffrey Hilliard, Andrew Horsman, Linda Ward and Robert Ward is available as a University of Manchester Inflation Workshop Discussion Paper, which may be obtained by writing (enclosing 50p or $ equivalent) to the Secretary, Inflation Workshop, Department of Economics, University of Manchester, Manchester 13.

Abbreviations

AEA   American Economic Association
AEP   *Australian Economic Papers*

AER (p & p)	*American Economic Review* (papers and proceedings)
BOEQB	*Bank of England Quarterly Bulletin*
BOUIES	*Bulletin of the Oxford University Institute of Economics and Statistics*
CJE	*Canadian Journal of Economics*
CJEPS	*Canadian Journal of Economics and Political Science*
EJ	*Economic Journal*
FRB	Federal Reserve Board
IER	*International Economic Review*
JASA	*Journal of the American Statistical Association*
JES	*Journal of Economic Studies*
JET	*Journal of Economic Theory*
JMCB	*Journal of Money, Credit and Banking*
JME	*Journal of Monetary Economics*
JOF	*Journal of Finance*
JPE	*Journal of Political Economy*
LBR	*Lloyds Bank Review*
NIER	*National Institute Economic Review*
OBES	*Oxford Bulletin of Economics and Statistics*
OECD	Organisation for Economic Co-operation and Development
OEP	*Oxford Economic Papers*
QJE	*Quarterly Journal of Economics*
RE Stats	*Review of Economics and Statistics*
RE Studs	*Review of Economic Studies*
SAJOE	*South African Journal of Economics*
SEJ	*Southern Economic Journal*
SJPE	*Scottish Journal of Political Economy*
YBESR	*Yorkshire Bulletin of Economic and Social Research*
YEE	*Yale Economic Essays*

Ackley, G. (1972). "Observations on Phase II and Wage Controls." *Brookings Papers*, no. 1, pp. 173–190.

AEA & Royal Economic Society. (1965) *Surveys of Economic Theory*. Vol. 1. *Money, Interest and Welfare*. London: Macmillan; New York: St Martin's Press.

Akerlof, G. A. (1969). "Relative Wages and the Rate of Inflation." *QJE*, vol. 83(3), no. 332, pp. 353–374.

Akyuz, Y. (1973). *Money and Inflation in Turkey 1950–1968*. Political Science Monograph, no. 361. Ankara: Ankara U.P.

Albrecht, W. P. (1966). "The Relationship Between Wage Changes and Unemployment in Metropolitan and Industrial Labor Markets," *YEE*, vol. 6(2), pp. 279–342.

Alchian, A. A. (1970). In Phelps, E. S. et al. "Information Costs, Pricing and Resource Unemployment."

_____ and Kessel, R. A. (1959). "Redistribution of Wealth Through Inflation." *Science*, no. 130 (Sept.), pp. 535–539.

_____, and Klein, B. (1973). "On a Correct Measure of Inflation." *JMCB*, vol. 5(1), pp. 173–191.

Alexander, A. J. (1971). "Prices and the Guideposts: The Effects of Government Persuasion on Individual Prices." *R.E. Stats*, vol 53(1), pp. 67–75.

Aliber, R. Z. (ed.), (1974). *National Monetary Policies and the International Financial System*. Chicago, Ill. University of Chicago Press.

Allais, M. (1966). "A Restatement of the Quantity Theory of Money." *AER*, vol. 56(5), pp. 1123–1157.

_____, (1969). "Growth and Inflation." *JMCB*, vo. 1(3), pp. 355–426.

_____, (1974). "The Psychological Rate of Interest." *JMCB*, vol. 6(3), pp. 285–331.

Andersen, L. C. and Carlson, K. M. (1970). "A Monetarist Model for Economic Stabilization," *FRB of St Louis Review*, vol. 52(4), pp. 7–25.

_____, (1972). In Eckstein, O. (ed.). "An Econometric Analysis of the Relation of Monetary Variables to the Behaviour of Prices and Unemployment."

Anderson, P. (1969). "Wages and the Guideposts: Comment." *AER*, vol 59(3), pp. 351–354.

Aoki, M. (1967). *Optimisation of Stochastic Systems*. New York: Academic Press.

Archibald, G. C. (1969). "The Phillips Curve and the Distribution of Unemployment." *AER (p & p)*, vol. 59(2), pp. 124–134.

_____, Kemmiss, R. and Perkins, J. W. (1974). In Laidler, D. E. W. and Purdy, D. L. (eds.). "Excess Demand for Labour, Unemployment and the Phillips Curve."

_____, and Lipsey, R. G. (1958). "Monetary and Value Theory: A Critique of Large and Patinkin." *R.E. Studs*, vol. 26(69), pp. 1–22.

Arrow, K. (1959). "Towards a Theory of Price Adjustment." In Abramovitz, M. (ed.), *The Allocation of Economic Resources*. Stanford: Stanford U.P.

Artis, M. J. and Lewis, M. K. (1975). "The Demand for Money in the U.K. 1963–1973." *Manchester School* (forthcoming).

Ashenflter, O. C. and Johnson, G. E. (1969). "Bargaining Theory, Trade Unions and Industrial Strike Activity." *AER*, vol. 59(1), pp. 35–49.

_____, and Pencavel, J. H. (1972). "Trade Unions

and the Rate of Change of Money Wage Rates in United States Manufacturing Industry." *RE Studs*, vol. 39(1), no 117, pp. 27–54.

Auernheimer, L. (1974). "The Honest Government's Guide to Inflationary Finance " *JPE*, vol. 82(3), pp. 598–606.

Bach, G. L. and Ando, A. (1957). "The Redistributional Effects of Inflation." *RE Stats*, vol 39(1), pp. 1–13.

———, and Stephenson, J. B. (1974). "Inflation and the Redistribution of Wealth." *RE Stats*, vol. 56(1), pp. 1–13.

Bailey, M. J. (1956). "The Welfare Cost of Inflationary Finance." *JPE*, vol. 64(2), pp. 93–110.

Ball, R. J. (1962). "The Prediction of Wage-Rate Changes in the United Kingdom Economy 1957–1960." *EJ*, vol. 72(285), pp. 27–44.

———, (1964). *Inflation and the Theory of Money*. Chicago, Ill.: Aldine Publishing Co.

———, and Duffy, M. (1972). In Eckstein, O. (ed.). "Price Formation in European Countries."

Balogh, T. (1970). *Labour and Inflation*. London: The Fabian Society.

Bank of England (1970). "The Importance of Money." *BOEQB*, vol 10(2), pp. 159–198.

Barret, R. J., Gray, M. R. and Parkin, J. M. (1975). "The Demand for Financial Assets by the Personal Sector of the U.K. Economy." In Renton, G. A. (ed.), *Modelling the Economy*. London: Heinemann Educational (for SSRC).

Barro, R. J. (1970). "Inflation, the Payments Period and the Demand for Money." *JPE*. vol. 78(6), pp. 1228–1263.

———, (1972a). "A Theory of Monopolistic Price Adjustment." *RE Studs*, vol. 39(1), no. 117, pp. 17–26.

———, (1972b). "Inflationary Finance and the Welfare Cost of Inflation." *JPE*, vol. 80(5), pp. 978–1001.

———, and Grossman, H. I. (1971). "A General Disequilibrium Model of Income and Employment." *AER*, vol. 61(1), pp. 82–93.

———, (1974). "Suppressed Inflation and the Supply Multiplier." *RE Studs*, vol. 41(1), no 125, pp. 87–104.

Baxter, J. L. (1973). "Inflation in the Context of Relative Deprivation and Social Justice." *SJPE*, vol. 20(3), pp. 262–282.

Behrend, H. (1964). "Price and Incomes Images and Inflation." *SJPE*, vol. 11(2), pp. 85–103.

———, (1966). "Price Images, Inflation and National Incomes Policy." *SJPE*, vol. 13(3), pp. 273–296.

Bhatia, R. J. (1961). "Unemployment and the Rate of Change of Money Earnings in the U.S. 1900–

1958." *Economica* (NS), vol. 28(111), pp. 286–296.

Bishop, R. L. (1963). "Game Theoretic Analyses of Bargaining." *QJE*, vol. 77(4), no. 309, pp. 559–602.

Bodkin, R. G. (1966). *The Wage-Price-Productivity Nexus*. Philadelphia, Pa. University of Pennsylvania Press.

Bosworth, B. (1972). "Phrase II: The U.S. Experiment with an Income Policy." *Brookings Papers*. no. 2, pp. 343–383.

Bowen, W. G. (1960a). *Wage Behaviour in the Postwar Period: An Empirical Analysis*. Princeton, N. J.: Princeton U.P.

Bowers, J. K., Cheshire, P. C. and Webb, A. E. (1970). "The Change in the Relationship Between Unemployment and Earnings Increases." *NIER*, no. 54, pp. 44–63.

Box, G. E. P. and Jenkins, G. H. (1970). *Time Series Analysis: Forecasting and Control*. New York: Holden Day.

Brechling, F. P. R. (1968). "The Trade-Off Between Inflation and Unemployment." *JPE*, vol. 76(4), pp. 712–737.

———, (1972). In Parkin, J. M. and Summer, M. T. (eds.). "Some Empirical Evidence on the Effectiveness of Prices and Income Policies." Ch. 2, pp. 30–47.

———, (1973). "Wage Inflation and The Structure of Regional Unemployment." (Reprinted in Laidler, D. E. W. & Purdy, D. L. (eds.) 1974.) *JMCB*, vol. 5(1), pp. 355–379.

Bresciani-Turroni, C. (1968). *The Economics of Inflation: A Study of Currency Depreciation in Postwar Germany*. New York: Kelly (earlier editions 1931, 1937).

Brock, W. (1972). "On Models of Expectations That Arise From Maximisation Behavior of Economic Behavior Over Time." *JET*, vol. 5(3), pp. 348–376.

Bronfenbrenner, M. (1950). "Trade Unions, Full Employment and Inflation-Comment." *AER*, vol. 40(5), pp. 622–624.

———, and Holzman, F. D. (1963). "A Survey of Inflation Theory." *AER*, vol. 53(4), pp. 593–661. (Reprinted in AEA and Royal Economic Society, 1965.)

Brown, A. J. (1955). *The Great Inflation, 1939–1951*. London: Oxford U.P.

Brunner, K. (1951). "Inconsistency and Indeterminacy in Classical Economics." *Econometrica*, vol. 19(2), pp. 152–173.

———, (1974). In Aliber, R. Z. (ed.). "Monetary Management, Domestic Inflation, and Imported Inflation."

————, (1975). In Parkin, J. M. and Zis, G. (eds.). "A Fisherian Analysis of World Inflation."

————, Fratianni, M., Jordan, J. L., Meltzer, A. H., and Neumann, M. J. M. (1973). "Fiscal and Monetary Policies in Moderate Inflation." *JMCB*, vol. 5(1), pp. 313–353.

————, and Meltzer, A. H. (1971). "The Uses of Money: Money in the Theory of an Exchange Economy." *AER*, vol. 61(5), pp. 784–805.

————, (1972). "Money, Debt and Economic Activity." *JPE*, vol. 80(5), pp. 951–977.

————, (1973). "Mr Hicks and the Monetarists." *Economica* (NS), vol. 40 (no. 157), pp. 44–59.

————, (eds.) (1975). *Proceedings of the Conference on Wage and Price Controls at Rochester University, New York, October* (1973).

Burmeister, E. and Phelps, E. S. (1971). "Money, Public Debt, Inflation and Real Interest." *JMCB*, vol. 3(2), pp. 153–182.

Burns, M. E. (1972). "Regional Phillips Curves: A Further Note." *BOUIES*, vol. 34(3), pp. 295–307.

Burrows, P. and Hitiris, T. (1972). "Estimating the Impact of Incomes Policy." *Bulletin of Economic Research*, 24(1), vol. pp. 42–51. (Reprinted in Parkin, J. M. and Sumner, M. T. (eds.) 1972.)

Cagan, P. (1956). In Friedman, M. (ed.). "The Monetary Dynamics of Hyperinflation."

————, (1965). *Determinants and Effects of Money 1870–1960*. New York: Columbia U. P. (for NBER).

————, (1968). In Rousseas, S. W. (ed.). "Theories of Mild, Continuing Inflation: A Critique and Extension."

————, (1969). "Allais' Monetary Theory: Interpretation and Comment." *JMCB*, vol. 1(3), pp. 427–432.

Campbell, C. D. (1970). In Meiselman, D. (ed.). "The Velocity of Money and the Rate of Inflation: Recent Experiences in South Korea and Brazil."

Cargill, T. F. (1969). "An Empirical Investigation of the Wage-Lag Hypothesis." *AER*, vol. 59(5), pp. 806–816.

Carlson, J. A. and Parkin, J. M. (1975). "Inflation Expectations." *Economica*, (NS) vol. 42(166), pp. 123–138.

Carsberg, B. V., Hope, A. J. B. and Scapens, R. W. (eds.). (Forthcoming.) *Studies in Accounting for Inflation*. Manchester: Manchester U.P.

Cathcart, C. D. (1974). "Monetary Dynamics, Growth and the Efficiency of Inflationary Finance." *JMCB*, vol. 6(2), pp. 169–190.

Christ, C. F. (1968). "A Simple Macroeconomic Model With a Government Budget Constraint." *JPE*, vol. 76(1), pp. 53–67.

Christenson, C. L. (1954). "Variations in the Inflationary Force of Bargaining." *AER* (*p & p*), vol. 44(2), pp. 347–362.

Claassen, E. and Salin, P. (eds.) (1972). *Stabilisation Policies in Interdependent Economies*. Amsterdam: North-Holland.

Clayton, G., Gilbert, J. C. and Sedgwick, R. (eds.) (1971). *Monetary Theory Policy in the 1970's*. London: Oxford U.P.

Clower, R. W. (1965). In Hahn, F. H. and Brechling, F. P. R. (eds.). "The Keynesian Counter-Revolution: A Theoretical Appraisal." (Reprinted in part in Clower, R. W. (ed.) (1969).)

————, (ed.) (1969). *Monetary Theory*. Harmondsworth: Penguin Education.

————, Burstein, M. L. (1960). "On the Invariance of Demand for Cash and Other Assets." *RE Studs*, vol. 28(57), pp. 32–36.

Coddington, A. (1966). "A Theory of the Bargaining Process: Comment." *AER*, vol. 56(3), pp. 522–530 (reprinted in Coddington, A., 1968).

————, (1968). *Theories of the Bargaining Process*. London: Allen & Unwin.

Commission on Money and Credit. (1964). *Inflation, Growth and Unemployment*. Englewood Cliffs, N.J.: Prentice-Hall.

Conard, J. W. (1964). In Commission on Money and Credit. "The Causes and Consequences of Inflation."

Connolly, M. B. and Swoboda, A. K. (1973). *International Trade and Money*. London: Allen & Unwin.

Corry, B. A. and Laidler, D. E. W. (1967). "The Phillips Relation: A Theoretical Explanation." *Economica* (NS), vol. 34(134), pp. 189–197.

Cowling, K. and Metcalf, D. (1967). "Wage-Unemployment Relationships: A Regional Analysis for the U.K. 1960–1965." *BOUIES* 29(1), pp. 31–39.

Cross, J. G. (1965). "A Theory of the Bargaining Process." *AER*, vol. 55(1), pp. 67–94.

————, (1966). "A Theory of the Bargaining Process—Reply." *AER*, vol. 56(3), pp. 630–633.

Cross, R. B. and Laidler, D. E. W. (1975). In Parkin, J. M. and Zis, G. (eds.). "Inflation, Excess Demand and Expectations in Fixed Exchange Rate Open Economies: Some Preliminary Empirical Results."

Davidson, P. (1972). *Money and the Real World*. London: Macmillan.

Deaver, J. V. (1970). In Meiselman, D. (ed.). "The Chilean Inflation and the Demand for Money."

Dicks-Mireaux, L. A. (1961). "The Inter-Relationship Between Cost and Price Changes, 1945–1959: A Study of Inflation in Postwar Britain." *OEP* (NS), vol. 13(3), pp. 267–292.

_____, and Dow, J. C. R. (1959). "The Determinants of Wage Inflation in the United Kingdom, 1946–1956," *Journal of the Royal Statistical Society*, series A (General), vol. 122(2), pp. 145–184.

Diz, A. C. (1970). In Meiselman, D. (ed.). "Money and Prices in Argentina, 1935–1962."

Dornbusch, R. and Frenkel, J. A. (1973). "Inflation and Growth: Alternative Approaches. *JMCB*, vol. 5(1), pt. 1, pp. 141–156.

Dow, J. C. R. (1956). "Analysis of the Generation of Price Inflation." *OEP* (NS), vol. 8(3), pp. 252–301.

_____, and Dicks-Mireaux, L. A. (1958). "The Excess Demand for Labour." *OEP* (NS), vol. 10(1), pp. 1–33.

Duck, N. W., Parkin, J. M., Rose, D. and Zis, G. (1975). In Parkin, J. M. and Zis, G. (eds.). "The Determination of the Rate of Change of Wages and Prices in the Fixed Exchange Rate World Economy: 1956–1970."

Dutton, D. S. (1971*a*). "A Model of Self-Generating Inflation: The Argentine Case." *JMCB*, vol. 3(2), pt. 1, pp. 245–262.

_____, (1971*b*). "The Demand for Money and the Price Level." *JPE*, vol. 79(5), pp. 1161–1170.

Eagly, R. V. (1965). "Market Power as an Intervening Mechanism in Phillips Curve Analysis." *Economica* (NS), vol. 32(125), pp. 48–64.

Eatwell, J., Llewellyn, J. and Tarling, R. (1974). "Money Wage Inflation in Industrial Countries." *RE Studs*, vol. 61(4), no. 128, pp. 515–523.

Eckstein, O. (ed.) (1972). *The Econometrics of Price Determination, Conference*. Washington, D.C.: Board of Governors of the Federal Reserve System and the S.S.R.C.

_____, and Fromm, G. (1968). "The Price Equation." *AER*, vol 58(5), pt. 1, pp. 1159–1184.

Edgren, G., Faxen, K. O. and Odhner, G. E. (1969). "Wages, Growth and the Distribution of Income." *Swedish Journal of Economics*, vol. 71(3), pp. 133–160.

Feige, E. L. (1974). In Johnson, H. G. and Nobay, A. R. (eds.). "Alternative Temporal Cross-Section Specifications of the Demand for Demand Deposits."

_____, and Parkin, J. M. (1971). "The Optimal Quantity of Money, Bonds, Commodity Inventories and Capital." *AER*, vol. 61(3), pt. 1, pp. 335–349.

Feldman, A. M. (1973). "Bilateral Trading Pro-

cesses, Pairwise Optimality and Pareto Optimality." *RE Studs*, vol. 40(4), no. 124, pp. 463–473.

Feldstein, M. and Chamberlain, G. (1973). "Multimarket Expectations and the Rate of Interest." *JMCB*, vol. 5(4), pp. 873–902.

Felix, D. (1956). "Profit Inflation and Industrial Growth: The Historic Record and Contemporary Analogies." *QJE*, vol. 70(3), no. 320, pp. 441–463.

Fiedler, E. R. (1972). "The Price–Wage Stabilisation Program." *Brookings Papers*, no. 1, pp. 199–206.

Fisher, D. (1970). "The Instruments of Monetary Policy and the Generalized Trade-Off Function for Britain, 1955–1968." *Manchester School*, vol. 38(3), pp. 209–222.

Fisher, I. (1896). "Appreciation and interest." *AEA Publications, Series Three* (II), Aug., pp. 331–442.

_____, (1911). *The Purchasing Power of Money*. New York: Macmillan. (Latest edition, A. M. Kelly, New York, 1963.)

_____, (1926). "A Statistical Relation Between Unemployment and Price Changes." *International Labour Review* (reprinted as "I Discovered the Phillips Curve," *JPE*, vol. 81(2), pt. 1, Mar./Apr. 1973), pp. 496–502.

Flanagan, R. J. (1973). "The U.S. Phillips Curve and International Unemployment Rate Differentials." *AER*, vol. 63(1), pp. 114–131.

Foldes, L. (1964). "A Determinate Model of Bilateral Monopoly." *Economica* (NS), vol. 31(121), pp. 117–131.

Foley, D. K. and Sidrauski, M. (1971). *Monetary and Fiscal Policy in a Growing Economy*. New York: Macmillan.

Foster, J. I. (1973). "The Behaviour of Unemployment and Unfilled Vacancies: Great Britain 1958–1971—A Comment." *EJ*, vol. 83(329), pp. 192–201.

_____, (1974). In Laidler, D. E. W. and Purdy, D. L. (eds). "The Relationship Between Unemployment and Vacancies in Great Britain (1958–1972): Some Further Evidence."

_____, (1975). "The Redistributive Effects of Inflation—Questions and Answers." University of Manchester. Inflation Workshop Discussion Paper, no. 7504.

Friedman, M. (ed.) (1956). *Studies in the Quantity Theory of Money*. Chicago, Ill.: University of Chicago Press.

_____, (1959). "The Demand for Money–Some Theoretical and Empirical Results." *JPE*, vol. 67(4). pp. 327–351.

_____, (1966). "Interest Rates and the Demand for Money." *Journal of Law and Economics*, vol. 9 (reprinted in Friedman, M. 1969).

_____, (1968). "The Role of Monetary Policy." *AER*, vol. 58(1), pp. 1–17.

_____, (1969). *The Optimum Quantity of Money.* Chicago, Ill.: Aldine Press.

_____, (1970). *The Counter-Revolution in Monetary Theory.* London: *IEA* (for Wincott Foundation) Occasional Paper, no. 33.

_____, (1971). "Government Revenue From Inflation." *JPE*, vol. 79(4), pp. 846–856.

_____, (1972). "Comments on the Critics." *JPE*, vol. 80(5), pp. 906–950.

_____, and Schwartz, A. J. (1963). *A Monetary History of the United States, 1867–1960.* Princeton, N.J.: Princeton U.P. (For N.B.E.R.)

Fromm, G. and Taubman, P. (1968). *Policy Simulations With an Econometric Model.* Washington, D.C.: The Brookings Institution.

Gallaway, L. E. (1958). "The Wage-Push Inflation Thesis, 1950–1957." *AER*, vol. 48(5), pp. 967–972.

_____, Koshal, R. K. and Chapin, G. L. (1970). "The Relationship Between the Rate of Change in Money Wage Rates and Unemployment Levels in South Africa." *SAJOE*, vol. 38(4), pp. 367–373.

Gibson, W. (1970). "Price Expectations Effects on Interest Rates." *JOF*, March.

Giersch, H. *et al.* (1974). *Essays on Inflation and Indexation.* Washington, D.C.: American Enterprise Institute for Public Policy Research.

Godfrey, L. (1971). In Johnson, H. G. and Nobay, A. R. (eds.). "The Phillips Curve: Incomes Policy and Trade Union Effects." (Abridged and Amended in Parkin, J. M. and Sumner, M. T. (eds.), 1972.)

_____, and Taylor, J. (1973). "Earnings Changes in the U.K. 1954–1970: Excess Labor Supply, Expected Inflation and Union Influence." *BOUIES*, vol. 35(3), pp. 197–216.

Godley, W. A. H. and Nordhaus, W. D. (1972). "Pricing in the Trade Cycle." *EJ*, vol. 82(327), pp. 853–882.

_____, and Rowe, D. A. (1964). "Retail and Consumer Prices." *NIER* (30), pp. 44–57.

Goldman, S. M. (1972). "Hyperinflation and the Rate of Growth in the Money Supply." *JET*, vol. 5(2), pp. 250–257

Gordon, D. F. and Hynes, A. (1970). In Phelps, E. S. *et al.* "On the Theory of Price Dynamics."

Gordon, R. J. (1971). "Inflation in Recession and Recovery." *Brookings Papers*, no. 2, pp. 385–421.

_____, (1973). "The Response of Wages and Prices to the First Two Years of Controls." *Brookings Papers*, no. 3, pp. 765–779.

Gray, M. R. (1975). "Inflation Expectations and the Accelerationist Controversy." University of Manchester Inflation Workshop Discussion Paper, no. 7507 (mimeo).

_____, and Parkin, J. M. (1974). "Discriminating Between Alternative Explanations of Inflation." University of Manchester Inflation Workshop Discussion Paper, no. 7414 (mimeo).

_____, Ward, R. and Zis, G. (1975). In Parkin, J. M. and Zis, G. (eds.). "World Demand for Money." (Forthcoming.)

Griffin, K. B. (1962). "A Note on Wages, Prices and Unemployment." *BOUIES*, vol. 24(3), pp. 379–385.

Gronau, R. (1971). "Information and Frictional Unemployment." *AER*, vol. 61(3), pt. 1, pp. 290–301.

Gujarati, D. (1972a). "The Behaviour of Unemployment and Unfilled Vacancies: Great Britain, 1958–1971." *EJ*, 82(325), pp. 195–204.

_____, (1972b). "A Reply to Mr Taylor." *EJ*, vol. 82(328), pp. 1365–1368.

Gustman, A. (1972). "Wage Bargains and the Phillips Curve—Re-examination." *QJE*, vol 86(2), no. 343, pp. 332–338.

Hague, D. C. (ed.) (1962). *Inflation.* London: Macmillan.

Hahn, F. H. and Brechling, F. P. R. (eds.) (1965). *The Theory of Interest Rates.* London: Macmillan.

Hamermesh, D. S. (1970). "Wage Bargains, Threshold Effects, and the Phillips Curve." *QJE*, vol. 84(3), no. 336, pp. 501–517.

_____, (1972a), "Wage Bargains, Threshold Effects, and the Phillips Curve: Reply." *QJE*, vol. 86(2), no. 343, pp. 339–341.

_____, (1972b), "Market Power and Wage Inflation." *SEJ*, vol. 39(2), pp. 204–212.

Hamilton, E. J. (1934). *American Treasure and the Price Revolution in Spain, 1501–1650.* Cambridge, Mass.

Hancock, K. J. (1966). "Earnings Drift in Australia." *Journal of Industrial Relations*, vol. 8(2), pp. 128–157 (reprinted in Isaac, J. E. and Ford, G. W. (eds.), 1967).

Hansen, A. H. (1925). "Factors Affecting the Trend in Real Wages." *AER*, vol. 15(1), pp. 27–42.

_____, (1953). *A Guide to Keynes.* New York: McGraw-Hill.

Hansen, B. (1951). *A Study in the Theory of Inflation.* London: Macmillan.

_____, (1957). In Dunlop, J. T. (ed.). "Full Employment and Wage Stability." (Reprinted 1966.)

———, (1970). "Excess Demand, Unemployment, Vacancies and Wages." *QJE*, vol. 84(1), no. 334, pp. 1–23.

Harrod, R. F. (1969). *Money*. London:Macmillan.

———, (1971). In Clayton, G., Gilbert, J. C. and Sedgwick, R. (eds.). Discussant's Comments on Paper by M. Friedman.

———, (1972). In Hinshaw, R. (ed.). "The Issues: Five Views."

Harsanyi, J. C. (1966). "Approaches to the Bargaining Problem Before and After the Theory of Games: A Critical Discussion on Zeuthen, Hicks and Nash." *Econometrica*, vol. 24(2), pp. 144–157.

Hayek, F. A. (1933). *Monetary Theory and the Trade Cycle*. London: Jonathan Cape.

Helliwell, J. F. *et al.* (1971). *The Structure of RDX2*. Bank of Canada Staff Research Papers, no. 7 (2 parts).

Hicks, J. R. (1932). (2nd ed., 1963.) *The Theory of Wages*. London: Macmillan.

———, (1937). "Mr Keynes and the 'Classics': A Suggested Interpretation." *Econometrica*, vol. 5(2), pp. 147–159.

———, (1974). *The Crisis in Keynesian Economics*. Oxford: Blackwell.

———, (1975). "The Permissive Economy." In *Crisis '75 . . . ?* IEA Occasional Paper Special, no. 43, London: IEA.

Higgins, C. I. (1973). "A Wage-Price Sector for a Quarterly Australian Model." In Powell, A. A. and Williams, R. A. (eds.).

Hines, A. G. (1964). "Trade Unions and Wage Inflation in the United Kingdom, 1893–1961." *RE Studs*, vol. 31(3), no. 88, pp. 221–252.

———, (1968). "Unemployment and the Rate of Change of Money Wage Rates in the United Kingdom 1862–1963: A Reappraisal." *RE Stats*, vol. 50(1), pp. 60–67.

———, (1969). "Wage Inflation in the United Kingdom 1948–1962: A Disaggregated Study." *EJ*, vol. 79(313), pp. 66–89.

———, (1971). In Johnson, H. G. and Nobay, A. R. "The Determinants of the Rate of Change of Money Wage Rates and the Effectiveness of Incomes Policy."

———, (1972). "The Phillips Curve and the Distribution of Unemployment." *AER*, vol. 62(1), pp. 155–160.

Hinshaw, R. (ed.) (1972). *Inflation as a Global Problem*. London: Johns Hopkins Press.

Holmes, J. M. and Smyth, D. J. (1970). "The Relationship Between Unemployment and the

Excess Demand for Labour: an Examination of the Theory of the Phillips Curve." *Economica* (NS), vol. 37(147), pp. 311–314.

Holt, C. C. (1970*a*). In Phelps, E. S. *et al.*, "Job Search, Phillips' Wage Relation and Union Influence: Theory and Evidence."

———, (1970*b*). In Phelps, E. S. *et al.* "How Can the Phillips Curve be Moved to Reduce Both Inflation and Unemployment?"

Hu, T-W. (1971). "Hyper-Inflation and the Dynamics of the Demand for Money in China, 1945–1949." *JPE*, vol. 79(1), pp. 186–195.

Hymans, S. H. (1972). In Eckstein, O. (ed.). "Prices and Price Behaviour in Three Econometric Models."

———, (1963). "A Survey of Theories of Inflation." *Indian Economic Review*, vol. 6(4). (Reprinted in Johnson, H. G., 1967*b*.)

Johnson, H. G. (1967*a*). In Johnson, H. G. "Money in a Neo-Classical One-Sector Growth Model."

———, (1967*b*). *Essays in Monetary Economics*. London: Allen and Unwin.

———, (1972). "Inflation and the Monetarist Controversy." Amsterdam: North-Holland.

———, (1973). "Secular Inflation and the International Monetary System." *JMCB*, vol. 5(1), pt. II, pp. 509–520.

Johnson, H. G. and Nobay, A. R. (eds.) (1971). *The Current Inflation*. London: Macmillan.

———, (1974). (eds.). *Issues in Monetary Economics*. London: Oxford U.P.

Johnson, J. (1972). "A Model of Wage Determination Under Bilateral Monopoly." *EJ*, vol. 82(327), pp. 837–852 (reprinted in Laidler, D. E. W. and Purdy, D. (eds.), 1974).

———, and Timbrell, M. C. (1973). "Empirical Tests of a Bargaining Model of Wage Rate Determination." *Manchester School*, vol. 41(2), pp. 141–167 (reprinted in Laidler, D. E. W. and Purdy, D. (eds.), 1974).

Jones, A. (1972). *The New Inflation: The Politics of Prices and Incomes*. London: Penguin Books and Andre Deutsch.

De Jong, F. J. (1973). *Developments of Monetary Theory in the Netherlands*. Rotterdam: Rotterdam U.P.

Jonson, P. D., Mahar, K. L. and Thompson, G. J. (1975). "Earnings and Award Wages in Australia." Reserve Bank of Australia discussion paper.

Kaldor, N. (1970). "The New Monetarism." *LBR*, no. 97, pp. 1–18.

Kaliski, S. F. (1964). "The Relation Between Unemployment and the Rate of Change of Money Wages in Canada." *IER*, vol. 5(1), pp. 1–33.

———, (1972). *The Trade-Off Between Inflation and Unemployment: Some Explorations of the Recent Evidence for Canada*. Ottawa: Economic Council of Canada Special Study, no. 22.

Kaun, D. E. (1965). "Wage Adjustments in the Appalachian States." *SEJ*, vol. 32(2), pp. 127–136.

———, and Spiro, M. H. (1970). "The Relation Between Wages and Unemployment in U.S. Cities 1955–1965," *Manchester School*, no. 38(1), pp. 1–14.

Kessel, R. A. and Alchian, A. A. (1960). "The Meaning and Validity of the Inflation-Induced Lag of Wages Behind Prices." *AER*, vol. 50(1), pp. 43–66.

Keynes, J. M. (1923). *A Tract on Monetary Reform*. London: Macmillan.

———, (1930). *A Treatise on Money*. Vol. II. *The Applied Theory of Money*. London: Macmillan.

———, (1936). *The General Theory of Employment, Interest and Money*. London: Macmillan.

Kirkpatrick, C. H. and Nixson, F. I. (1974). "The Origins of Inflation in Less Developed Countries." University of Manchester Inflation Workshop Discussion Paper, no. 7413 (mimeo).

Klein, L. R. and Ball, R. J. (1959). "Some Econometrics of the Determination of the Absolute Level of Wages and Prices." *EJ*, vol. 69(275), pp. 465–482.

———, and Evans, M. K. (1967). *The Wharton Econometric Forecasting Model*. Philadelphia, Pa.: University of Pennsylvania Press.

———, and Goldberger, A. S. (1955). *An Econometric Model of the United States 1929–1952*. Amsterdam: North-Holland.

Knight, K. G. (1972). "Strikes and Wage Inflation in British Manufacturing Industry 1950–1968." *BOUIES*, vol. 35(3), pp. 281–294.

Knowles, K. G. J. C. and Winsten, C. B. (1959). "Can the Level of Unemployment Explain Changes in Wages?" *BOUIES*, vol. 21(2), pp. 113–120.

Koshal, R. K. and Gallaway, L. E. (1971). "The Phillips Curve for West Germany." *Kyklos*, vol. 24(2), pp. 346–349.

Kuh, E. (1959). "Profits, Mark-Ups and Productivity: an Examination of Corporate Behaviour Since 1947." Study Paper no. 15, Studies of Employment, Growth and Price Levels, Washington, D.C.: U.S. Joint Economic Committee.

———, (1967). "A Productivity Theory of Wage Levels—An Alternative to the Phillips Curve." *RE Studs*, vol. 34(4), no. 100, pp. 333–360.

Kuska, E. A. (1966). "The Simple Analytics of the Phillips Curve." *Economica* (NS), vol. 33(132), pp. 462–467.

Laidler, D. E. W. (1966). "The Rate of Interest and the Demand for Money—Some Empirical Evidence." *JPE*, vol. 74(6), pp. 545–555.

———, (1969a). *The Demand for Money: Theories and Evidence*. Scranton, Pa.: International Textbook Co.

———, (1969b). "Money, Wealth and Time Preference in a Stationary Economy." *CJE*, vol. 2(4), pp. 526–535.

———, (1972). "On Wicksell's Theory of Price-Level Dynamics." *Manchester School*, vol. 40(2), pp. 125–144 (reprinted in Laidler, D. E. W., 1975).

———, (1973a). "The Influence of Money on Real Income and Inflation: A Simple Model With Some Empirical Tests for the United States, 1953–1972." *Manchester School*, vol. 41(4), pp. 367–395 (reprinted in Laidler, D. E. W., 1975).

———, (1974). "Information, Money and the Macroeconomics of Inflation." *Swedish Journal of Economics*, vol. 76(1), pp. 27–42 (reprinted in Laidler, D. E. W., 1975).

———, (1975a). *Essays on Money and Inflation*. Manchester and Chicago: Manchester U.P. and Chicago U.P.

———, (1975b). "Price and Output Fluctuations in an Open Economy." In Laidler, D. E. W. (1975a).

———, and Purdy, D. (eds.) (1974). *Labour Markets and Inflation*. Manchester and Toronto: Manchester U.P. and Toronoto U.P.

Lapkin, D. T. (1950). "Trade Unionism, Full Employment and Inflation—Comment." *AER*, vol. 40(4), pp. 625–627.

Lerner, E. (1956). In Friedman, M. (ed.). "Inflation in the Confederacy, 1861–1865."

Leslie, D. G. (1973). "A Note on the Regional Distribution of Unemployment." *OBES*, vol. 35(3), pp. 233–237.

Lipsey, R. G. (1960). "The Relationship Between Unemployment and the Rate of Change of Money Wage Rates in the U.K. 1862–1957: A Further Analysis." *Economica* (NS), vol. 27(105), pp. 1–31.

———, and Parkin, J. M., (1970). "Incomes Policy: A Reappraisal." *Economica* (NS), vol. 37(146), pp. 115–138 (reprinted in Parkin, J. M. and Summer, M. T. (eds.), 1972).

———, and Steuer, M. D. (1961). "The Relation Between Profits and Wage Rates." *Economica* (NS), vol. 28(110), pp. 137–155.

Lucas, R. E. Jr. (1972*a*). In Eckstein, O. (ed.). "Testing the Natural Rate Hypothesis."

———, (1972*b*). "Expectations and the Neutrality of Money." *JET*, vol. 4(2), pp. 103–124.

———, (1973). "Some International Evidence on Output-Inflation Trade Offs." *AER*, vol. 63(3), pp. 326–334.

———, and Rapping, L. A. "Price Expectations and the Phillips Curve." *AER*, vol. 59(3), June (1969), pp. 342–350 (reprinted in Phelps, E. S. *et al.*, 1970).

MacKay, D. I. (1972). "Redundancy and Re-Engagement: A Study of Car Workers." *Manchester School*, vol. 40(3), pp. 295–312.

———, and Hart, R. A. (1974). "Wage Inflation and the Phillips Relationship." *Manchester School*, vol. 42(2), pp. 136–161.

———, and Reid, G. L. (1972). "Redundancy, Unemployment and Manpower Policy." *EJ*, vol. 82(328), pp. 1256–1272.

Marris, S. (1972). In Claassen, E. and Salin, P. (eds.). "World Inflation—Panel Discussion."

Marty, A. L. (1964). "The Real Balance Effect: An Exercise in Capital Theory." *CJEPS*, vol. 30(3), pp. 360–367.

———, (1967). "Growth and the Welfare Cost of Inflationary Finance." *JPE*, vol. 75(1), pp. 71–76.

———, (1973). "Growth, Satiety and the Tax Revenue From Money Creation." *JPE*, vol. 81 (5), pp. 1136–1152.

McCallum, B. T. (1970). "The Effect of Demand on Prices in British Manufacturing: Another View." *RE Studs*, vol. 37(1), no. 109, pp. 147–155.

———, (1973). "Freidman's Missing Equation; Another Approach." *Manchester School*, vol. 41(3), pp. 311–328.

———, (1975). "Rational Expectations and the Natural Rate Hypothesis: Some Evidence for the United Kingdom." *Manchester School*, vol. pp. 55–67.

Meiselman, D. (ed.). (1970). *Varieties of Monetary Experience*. Chicago, Ill.: University of Chicago Press.

De Menil, G. (1971). *Bargaining, Monopoly Power versus Union Power*. Cambridge, Mass.: M.I.T. Press.

———, (1974). "Aggregate Price Dynamics." *RE Stats*, vol. 51(2), pp. 129–141.

Metcalf, D. (1971). "The Determination of Earnings Changes: A Regional Analysis for the U.K., 1960–1968." *IER*, vol. 12(2), pp. 273–282.

Mitchell, W. C. (1908). *Gold, Prices and Wages Under the Greenback Standard*. Berkeley, Calif.

Modigliani, F. (1944). "Liquidity Preference and the Theory of Interest and Money." *Econometrica*, vol. 12(1), pp. 45–88.

———, (1963). "The Monetary Mechanism and Its Interaction with Real Phenomena." *RE Stats*, vol. 45(1), pt. II (Suppl.), pp. 79–107.

———, and Tarantelli, E. (1973). "A Generalization of the Phillips Curve for a Developing Country." *RE Studs*, vol. 40(2), no. 122, pp. 203–224.

Mortensen, D. T. (1970). "Job Search, the Duration of Unemployment and the Phillips Curve." *AER*, vol. 60(5), pp. 847–862, reprinted in Phelps, E. S. *et al.* (1970).

Morton, W. A. (1950). "Trade Unionism, Full Employment and Inflation." *AER*, vol. 40(1), pp. 13–39.

Mulvey, C. and Trevithick, J. A. (1974). "Some Evidence on the Wage Leadership Hypothesis." *SJPE*, vol. 21(1), pp. 1–12.

Mundell, R. A. (1963). "Inflation and Real Interest." *JPE*, vol. 71(3), pp. 280–283.

———, (1965). "Growth, Stability and Inflationary Finance." *JPE*, vol. 73(2), pp. 97–109.

———, (1968). *International Economics*. New York: Macmillan.

———, (1971). *Monetary Theory: Inflation, Interest and Growth in the World Economy*. Pacific Palisades, Calif.: Goodyear Publishing Co.

Muth, J. F. (1960). "Optimal Properties of Exponentially Weighted Forecasts." *JASA*, vol. 55 (290), pp. 299–306.

———, (1961). "Rational Expectations and the Theory of Price Movements." *Econometrica*, vol. 29(3), pp. 315–335.

Nash, J. F. Jr. (1950). "The Bargaining Problem." *Econometrica*, vol. 18(2), pp. 155–162.

———, (1953). "Two Person Co-Operative Games." *Econometrica*, vol. 21(1), pp. 128–40.

Neild, R. R. (1963). *Pricing and Employment in the Trade Cycle*. London: Cambridge U.P. (for N.I.E.S.R.).

Nevile, J. W. (1970). *Fiscal Policy in Australia: Theory and Practice*. Melbourne: Cheshire.

Niehans, J. (1969). "Money in a Static Theory of Optimal Payment Arrangements." *JMCB*, vol. 1(4), pp. 706–726.

Nobay, A. R. (1974). In Johnson, H. G. and Nobay, A. R. (eds.). "A Model of the United Kingdom Monetary Authorities' Behaviour 1959–1969."

Nordhaus, W. D. (1972*a*). In Eckstein, O. (ed.). "Recent Developments in Price Dynamics."

———, (1972*b*). "The World-Wide Wage Explosion." *Brookings Papers*, no. 2, pp. 431–463.

———, (1973). "The Effects of Inflation on the Distribution of Economic Welfare." *JMCB*, vol. 5(1), pt. II, pp. 465–504.

———, (1975). "Political Business Cycle." *RE Studs* (forthcoming).

OECD (1970). *Inflation: The Present Problem.* Paris: OECD.

Ostroy, J. M. (1973). "The Information Efficiency of Monetary Exchange." *AER*, vol. 63(4), pp. 597–610.

Packer, A. H. and Park, S. H. (1973). "Distortions in Relative Wages and Shifts in the Phillips Curve." *RE Stats*, vol. 55(1), pp. 16–22.

Page, S. A. B. and Trollope, S. (1974). "An International Survey of Indexing and its Effects." *NIER* (70), pp. 46–59.

Paish, F. W. (1962). *Studies in an Inflationary Economy—The United Kingdom, 1948–1961*, 2nd ed. (1966). London: Macmillan.

Parkin, J. M. (1970). "Incomes Policy: Some Further Results on the Rate of Change of Money Wages." *Economica* (NS), vol. 37(148), pp. 386–401 (reprinted in Parkin, J. M. and Sumner, M. T. (eds.), 1972).

———, (1973a). "The 1973 Report of the President's Council of Economic Advisers: A Critique." *AER*, vol. 63(4), pp. 535–545.

———, (1973b). "The Short Run and Long Run Trade-Off Between Inflation and Unemployment in Australia." *AEP*, vol. 12, pp. 127–144.

———, (1974). In Aliber, R. Z. (ed.). "Inflation, the Balance of Payments, Domestic Credit Expansion and Exchange Rate Adjustments."

———, and Sumner, M. T. (eds.). (1972). *Incomes Policy and Inflation*. Manchester and Toronto: Manchester U.P. and Toronto U.P.

———, Sumner, M. T. and Jones, R. A. (1972). In Parkin, J. M. and Sumner, M. T. (eds.). "A Survey of the Econometric Evidence of the Effects of Incomes Policy on the Rate of Inflation."

———, Sumner, M. T. and Ward, R. (1975). In Brunner, K. and Meltzer, A. H. (eds.). "The Effects of Excess Demand, Generalised Expectations and Wage-Price Controls on Wage Inflation in the U.K." (Forthcoming.)

———, and Zis, G. (eds.). (1975). *Inflation in the World Economy.*

Parkinson, J. R. (1958). "Wage Stability and Employment." *SJPE*, vol. 5(2), pp. 85–98.

Patinkin, D. (1956). *Money, Interest and Price—an Integration of Monetary and Value Theory.* Evanston, Ill.: Row Peterson (2nd ed., New York: Harper and Row).

———, (1969). "The Chicago Tradition, the Quantity Theory and Friedman." *JMCB*, vol. 1(1), pp. 46–70 (reprinted in Patinkin, D, 1972a).

———, (1972a). *Studies in Monetary Economics.* New York: Harper and Row.

———, (1972b). In Patinkin, D. "Monetary and Price Developments in Israel, 1949–1953."

———, (1974). In Johnson, H. G. and Nobay, A. R. (eds.). "Keynesian Monetary Theory and the Cambridge School."

Paunio, J. J. (1961). *A Study in the Theory of Open Inflation.* Helsinki: Bank of Finland.

Pencavel, J. H. (1970). "An Investigation into Industrial Strike Activity in Britain." *Economica* (NS), vol. 37(147), pp. 239–256.

Perry, G. L. (1964). "The Determinants of Wage Rate Changes and the Inflation-Unemployment Trade-Off for the United States." *RE Studs*, vol. 31(4), no. 88, pp. 287–308.

———, (1966). *Unemployment, Money Wage Rates and Inflation.* Cambridge, Mass.: M.I.T. Press.

———, (1967). "Wages and the Guideposts." *AER*, vol. 57(4), pp. 897–904.

———, (1969). "Wages and the Guideposts—Reply." *AER*, vol. 59(3), pp. 365–370.

———, (1970). "Changing Labor Markets and Inflation." *Brookings Papers*, no. 3, pp. 411–441.

———, (1972). "Controls and Income Shares." *Brookings Papers*, *no.* 1, pp. 191–194.

Pesek, B. P. (1960). "A Comparison of the Distributional Effects of Inflation and Taxation." *AER*, vol. 50(2), pp. 147–153.

Petersen, D. W., Lerner, E. M. and Lusk, E. J. (1971). "The Response of Prices and Incomes to Monetary Policy: an Analysis Based Upon a Differential Phillips Curve." *JPE*, vol. 79(4), pp. 857–866.

Phelps, E. S. (1961). "A Test For the Presence of Cost Inflation." *YEE*, vol. 1.

———, (1965). "Anticipated Inflation and Economic Welfare." *JPE*, vol. 73(1), pp. 1–17.

———, (1967). "Phillips Curves, Expectations of Inflation and Optimal Unemployment Over Time." *Economica* (NS), vol. 34(135), pp. 254–281.

Phelps, E. S. (1968). "Money Wage Dynamics and Labour Market Equilibrium." *JPE*, vol. 76(4), pt. II, pp. 678–711. (Amended reprint in Phelps, E. S. *et al.* (1970).)

———, (1972). *Inflation Policy and Unemployment Theory: The Cost-Benefit Approach to Monetary Planning.* New York: W. W. Norton & Co.

———, (1973). "Inflation in a Theory of Public Finance." *Swedish Journal of Economics*, vol. 75, pp. 67–82.

———, *et al.* (1970). *The Microeconomic Founda-*

tions of Employment and Inflation Theory. New York: W. W. Norton & Co.

————, and Winter, S. G. Jr. (1970). In Phelps, E. S. *et al.* "Optimal Price Policy Under Atomistic Competition."

Phelps-Brown, E. H. (1971). "The Analysis of Wage Movements Under Full Employment." *SJPE*, vol. 18(3), pp. 233–243.

Phillips, A. W. (1958). "The Relationship Between Unemployment and the Rate of Change of Money Wage Rates in the U.K. 1861–1957." *Economica* (NS), vol. 25(100), pp. 283–299.

Pierson, G. (1968). "The Effect of Union Strength on the U.S., Phillips Curve." *AER*, vol. 58(4), pp. 456–467.

Pigou, A. C. (1917). "The Value of Money." *QJE*, vol. 32(1), pp. 38–65.

Pissarides, C. A. (1972). "A Model of British Macroeconomic Policy, 1955–1969." *Manchester School*, vol. 40(3), pp. 245–259.

Pitchford, J. D. (1956/7). "Cost and Demand Elements in the Inflationary Process." *RE Studs* 24(64), pp. 139–148.

————, (1961). "The Inflationary Effects of Excess Demand for Goods and Excessive Real-Income Claims." *OEP* (NS), vol. 13(1), pp. 59–71.

————, (1963). *A Study of Cost and Demand Inflation*. Amsterdam: North Holland.

————, (1968). "An Analysis of Price Movements in Australia, 1947–1968." *AEP*, vol. 7(2), pp. 111–135.

Polak, J. J. (1957/8). "Monetary Analysis of Income Formation and Payments Problems." *IMF Staff Papers*, vol. 6, pp. 1–50.

Powell, A. A. and Williams, R. A. (eds.). (1973). *Econometric Studies of Macro and Monetary Relations*. Amsterdam: North-Holland.

Purdy, D. L. and Zis, G. (1973). "Trade Unions and Wage Inflation in the U.K.: A Reappraisal." In Parkin, J. M. (ed.), *Essays in Modern Economics.* London: Longmans (reprinted in Laidler, D. E. W. and Purdy, D. L. (eds.), 1974).

————, (1974). In Laidler, D. E. W. and Purdy, D. L. (eds.). "On the Concept and Measurement of Union Militancy."

Radcliffe Committee (1959). *Report on the Working of the Monetary System*. London: H.M.S.O.

Raiffa, H. (1953). "Arbitration Schemes for Generalised Two Person Games." In Kuhn, H. W. and Tucker, A. W. (eds.), *Contributions to the Theory of Games II.* Princeton, N.J.: Princeton U.P.

————, and Schlaifer, R. (1961). *Applied Statistical Decision Theory*. Boston, Mass.: Harvard Business School.

Reddaway, W. B. (1965). "Reasons for Rising Prices." University of Cambridge, Department of Applied Economics, Reprint Series, no. 230. London: Cambridge U.P.

————, (1966). "Rising Prices for Ever?" *LBR*, no. 81, pp. 1–15.

Reuber, G. L. (1964). "The Objectives of Canadian Monetary Policy, 1949–1961: Empirical 'Trade-Offs' and the Reaction Function of the Authorities." *JPE*, vol. 72(2), pp. 109–132.

Ripley, F. C. and Segal, L. (1973). "Price Determination in 395 Manufacturing Industries." *RE Stats*, vol. 53(3), pp. 263–271.

Robertson, D. H. (1961). *Growth, Wages, Money*. London: Cambridge U.P.

Rose, D. E. (1972). "A General Error-Learning Model of Expectations Formation." University of Manchester Inflation Workshop Discussion Paper, no. 7210 (mimeo).

Rousseas, S. W. (ed.). (1968). *Proceedings of a Symposium on Inflation: its Causes, Consequences and Control*. Wilton, Conn.: The Calvin K. Kazanjian Economics Foundation Inc.

Routh, G. (1959). "The Relationship Between Unemployment and the Rate of Change of Money Wage Rates in the U.K. 1861–1957: Comment." *Economica* (NS), vol. 26(104), pp. 299–315.

Runciman, W. G. (1966). *Relative Deprivation and Social Justice*. London: Routledge & Kegan Paul.

Rushdy, F. and Lund, P. J. (1967). "The Effect of Demand on Prices in British Manufacturing Industry." *RE Studs*, vol. 34(3), no. 99, pp. 361–373.

Samuelson, P. A. and Solow, R. M. (1960). "Analytical Aspects of Anti-Inflation Policy." *AER* (*p & p*), vol. 50(2), pp. 177–194.

Sargan, J. D. (1964). "Wages and Prices in the United Kingdom." In Hart, P. E., Mills, G. and Whittaker, J. K. (eds.). *Econometric Analysis for National Economic Planning.* London: Butterworths.

Sargent, T. J. (1971). "A Note on the 'Accelerationist' Controversy." *JMCB*, vol. 3(3), pp. 721–725.

————, (1972). "Anticipated Inflation and the Nominal Rate of Interest." *QJE*, vol. 86(2), no. 343, pp. 212–225.

————, (1973). "Interest Rates and Prices in the Long Run." *JMCB*, vol. 5(1), pt. II, pp. 385–449.

Sargent, T. J. and Wallace, N. (1973). "Rational Expectations and the Dynamics of Hyperinflation." *IER*, vol. 14(2), pp. 328–350.

Saunders, P. G. and Nobay, A. R. (1972). In Parkin,

J. M. and Sumner, M. T. (eds.). "Price Expectations, the Phillips Curve and Incomes Policy."

Scarfe, B. L. (1973). "A Model of the Inflation Cycle in a Small Open Economy." *OEP* (NS), vol. 25(2), pp. 192–203.

Schultze, C. L. and Tryon, J. L. (1965). "Prices and Wages." In Duesenberry, J. S. *et al. The Brookings Quarterly Econometric Model of the U.S.* Chicago: Rand McNally.

Scitovsky, T. and Scitovsky, A. A. (1964). "Inflation vs. Unemployment—Examination of Their Effects." In Commission on Money and Credit.

Shackle, G. L. S. (1955). *Uncertainty in Economics and Other Reflections.* London: Cambridge U.P.

Sharot, T. (1973). "Unemployment Dispersion as a Determinant of Wage Inflation in the United Kingdom 1925–1966. A Note." *Manchester School*, vol. 4(3), pp. 225–228.

Sidrauski, M. (1967). "Rational Choice and Patterns of Growth in a Monetary Economy." *AER* (*p & p*), vol. 57(2), pp. 534–544.

Silveira, A. M. (1973*a*). "The Demand for Money: The Evidence from the Brazilian Economy." *JMCB*, vol. 5(1), pt. I, pp. 113–140.

———, (1973*b*). "Interest Rates and Rapid Inflation: The Evidence from the Brazilian Economy." *JMCB*, vol. 5(3), pp. 794–805.

Simler, N. J. and Tella, A. (1968). "Labour Reserves and the Phillips Curve." *RE Stats*, vol. 50(1), pp. 32–49.

Sims, C. A. (1972). "Money, Finance, and Causality." *AER*, vol. 62(4), pp. 540–552.

Sjaastad, L. (1975). In Parkin, J. M. and Zis, G. (eds.), "Why Stable Inflations Fail."

Slichter, S. H. (1954). "Do Wage-Fixing Arrangements in the American Labour Market Have an Inflationary Bias?" *AER* (*p & p*), vol. 44(2), pp. 322–346.

Solow, R. M. (1956). "A Contribution to the Theory of Economic Growth." *QJE*, vol. 70(1), no. 278, pp. 65–94.

———, (1968). In Rousseas, S. (ed.). "Recent Controversies on the Theory of Inflation: An Eclectic View."

———, (1969). *Price Expectations and the Behaviour of the Price Level.* Manchester: Manchester U.P.

Starr, R. M. (1972). "Exchange in Barter and Money Economies." *QJE*, vol. 86(2), pp. 290–302.

Stein, J. L. (1974). "Unemployment, Inflation and Monetarism." *AER*, vol. 64(5), pp. 867–887.

Steindl, F. G. (1973). "Price Expectations and Interest Rates." *JMCB*, vol. 5(4), pp. 939–949.

Stephens, J. K. (1974). "A Note on Non-Synchronous Decisions and the Phillips Curve." *JES*, vol. 6(1/2) pp. 19–64.

Swan, T. W. (1956). "Economic Growth and Capital Accumulation." *ER*, vol. 32 (163), pp. 334–361.

Tait, A. A. (1967). "A Simple Test of the Redistributive Nature of Price Changes for Wealth Owners in the U.S. and U.K." *RE Stats*, vol. 49(4), pp. 651–655.

Taylor, J. (1970). "Hidden Unemployment, Hoarded Labour, and the Phillips Curves." *SEJ*, vol. 37(1), pp. 1–16.

———, (1972). In Parkin, J. M. and Sumner, M. T. (eds.). "Incomes Policy, the Structure of Unemployment and the Phillips Curve: the United Kingdom Experience, 1953–1970."

———, (1975). In Parkin, J. M. and Nobay, A. R., *Contemporary Issues in Economics.* "Wage Inflation, Unemployment and the Organised Pressure for Higher Wages in the U.K. 1961–1971." Manchester: Manchester. U.P.

Thirlwall, A. P. (1969). "Demand Disequilibrium in the Labour Market and Wage Rate Inflation in the United Kingdom." *YBESR*, vol. 21(1), pp. 65–76.

———, (1970). "Regional Phillips Curves." *BOUIES*, vol. 32(1), pp. 19–32.

Thomas, R. L. (1973). "Unemployment Dispersion as a Determinant of Wage Inflation in the United Kingdom, 1925–1966: Reply." *Manchester School*, vol. 41(3), pp. 229–234.

———, (1974). In Laidler, D. E. W. & Purdy, D. L. (eds.). "Wage Inflation in the U.K.—A Multi-Market Approach."

———, and Stoney, P. J. M. (1970). "A Note on the Dynamic Properties of the Hines Inflation Model." *RE Studs*, vol. 37(2), no. 110, pp. 286–294.

———, (1971). "Unemployment Dispersion as a Determinant of Wage Inflation in the United Kingdom, 1925–1966." *Manchester School*, vol. 39(2), pp. 83–116 (reprinted in Parkin, J. M. and Sumner, M. T. (eds.), 1972).

Throop, A. W. (1968). "The Union Non–Union Wage Differential and Cost-Push Inflation." *AER*, vol. 58(1), pp. 79–99.

———, (1969). "Wages and the Guideposts: Comment." *AER*, vol. 59(3), pp. 358–365.

Tinbergen, J. (1951). "An Economic Policy for 1936." In *Business Cycles in the United Kingdom, 1870–1914.* Amsterdam: North-Holland.

Tobin, J. (1965). "Money and Economic Growth." *Econometrica*, vol. 33(4), pp. 671–684.

———, (1972). "Inflation and Unemployment." *AER*, vol. 62(1), pp. 1–18.

Tower, E. (1971). "More on the Welfare Cost of Inflationary Finance." *JMCB*, vol. 3(4), pp. 850–860.

Toyoda, T. (1972). "Price Expectations and the Short Run and Long Run Phillips Curves in Japan, 1956–1968." *RE Stats*, vol. 54(3), pp. 267–274.

Turner, H. A. and Jackson, D. A. S. (1970). "On the Determination of the General Wage Level— A World Analysis: Or 'Unlimited Labour Forever'." *EJ*, vol. 80(320), pp. 827–849.

Turnovsky, S. J. (1969). "A Bayesian Approach to the Theory of Expectations." *JET*, vol. 1, pp. 220–227.

———, (1970). "Empirical Evidence on the Formation of Price Expectations." *JASA*, vol. 65, pp. 1441–1454.

———, (1972). "The Expectations Hypothesis and the Aggregate Wage Equation: Some Empirical Evidence for Canada." *Economica* (NS), vol. 39(153), pp. 1–17.

———, (1974). "On the Role of Inflationary Expectations in a Short-Run Macro-Economic Model." *EJ*, vol. 84(334), pp. 317–337.

———, and Wachter, M. L. (1972). "A Test of the Expectations Hypothesis Using Directly Observed Wage and Price Expectations." *RE Stats*, vol. 54(1), pp. 47–54.

Turvey, R. (1951). "Some Aspects of the Theory of Inflation in a Closed Economy." *EJ*, vol. 61(243), pp. 531–543.

Ulman, L. and Flanagan, R. J. (1971). *Wage Restraint: A Study of Incomes Policies in W. Europe*. Los Angeles, London: University of Los Angeles Press.

Vanderkamp, J. (1972). "Wage Adjustment, Productivity and Price Change Expectations." *RE Studs*, vol. 39(1), no. 117, pp. 61–72.

———, (1975). "Inflation: A Simple Friedman Theory With a Phillips Twist." *JME*, vol. 1(1), pp. 117–122.

Viner, J. (1937). *Studies in the Theory of International Trade*. New York, London: Harper Bros.

Wachter, M. L. (1969). "Wages and the Guideposts: Comment." *AER*, vol. 59(3), pp. 354–358.

Walters, A. A. (1971). "Consistent Expectations, Distributed Lags and the Quantity Theory." *EJ*, vol. 81(322), pp. 273–281.

Ward, R. and Zis, G. (1974). "Trade Union Militancy as an Explanation of Inflation: an International Comparison." *Manchester School*, vol. 42(1), pp. 44–65.

Watanabe, T. (1966). "Price Changes and the Rate of Change of Money Wage Earnings in Japan, 1955–1962." *QJE*, vol. 80(1), no. 318, pp. 31–47.

Waud, R. N. (1970). "Inflation, Unemployment and Economic Welfare." *AER*, vol. 60(4), pp. 631–641.

Weidenbaum, M. L. (1972). "New Initiatives in National Wage and Price Policy." *RE Stats*, vol. 54(3) pp. 213–234.

Wicksell, K. (1962). *Interest and Prices*. London: Cass Reprint of Economics Classics. (First published, 1898: First English Edition, 1936.)

Wiles, P. (1973). "Cost Inflation and the State of Economic Theory." *EJ*, vol. 83(330), pp. 377–398.

Williamson, J. (1970). "A Simple Neo-Keynesian Growth Model." *RE Studs*, vol. 37(2), no. 110, pp. 157–171.

Wilson, T. (1961). *Inflation*. Oxford: Blackwell; Cambridge, Mass.: Harvard U.P.

Yohe, W. P. and Karnosky, D. S. (1969). "Interest Rates and Price Level Changes 1952–1969." *FRB* of St Louis Review, vol. 51(12).

Zeuthen, F. (1930). *Problems of Monopoly and Economic Warfare*. London: Routledge.

Excess Demand, Unemployment, Vacancies, and Wages

Bent Hansen

University of California, Berkeley

The discussion about wage determination has, in later years, concentrated upon the Phillips curve and has been concerned partly with its statistical basis, and partly with the theoretical rationale for postulating a stable relationship between money wage changes and the rate of unemployment. It is usually taken for granted that there exists a basic, underlying relationship between the state of demand and supply in the labor market, or, more precisely, between the excess demand for labor and the rate of change of money wages, and that the Phillips relation is a secondary, or derived, relationship which exists only by virtue of some kind of relationship between the state of excess demand and the rate of unemployment. This was made clear already in the initial discussion of this problem by Phillips himself and R. G. Lipsey.[1] Some of the ingredients necessary for formulating this relationship more precisely have actually been available since the appearance of J. C. R. Dow and L. A. Dicks-Mireaux's studies of excess demand for labor and wages in Britain.[2] The solution of the problem hinges upon the relation between vacancies and unemployment, which, at least at the conceptual level, was clarified in an important contribution by C. Holt and M. David.[3] Still, there are some missing links to be filled in and some assumptions to be specified in order to establish the connection between demand and supply theory and the Phillips relation and to disclose all that is needed to put the Phillips relation on a sound theoretical basis—if this is possible at all. The following formal exposition tries to serve this purpose. The discussion is concerned with theoretical problems, but some of the conclusions have a bearing upon the empirical studies of money wage determinants.

I shall first develop a simple macro theory for the average rate of wage change based on assumptions fetched from ordinary neoclassi-

Reprinted from the Quarterly Journal of Economics, 84:1–23 (1970), by permission of the author and publisher (copyright by the President and Fellows of Harvard College, published by John Wiley and Sons, Inc.)

[1] A. W. Phillips, "The Relation Between Unemployment and the Rate of Change of Money Wage Rates in the United Kingdom, 1861–1957," Economica, XXVI (Nov. 1958), and R. G. Lipsey, "The Relation Between Unemployment and the Rate of Change of Money Wage Rates in the United Kingdom, 1862–1957," Economica, XXVII (Feb. 1960), and several other contributions.

[2] J. C. R. Dow and L. A. Dicks-Mireaux, "The Excess Demand for Labour. A Study of Conditions in Great Britain, 1946–56," Oxford Economic Papers, N. S. 10 (Feb. 1958); and L. A. Dicks-Mireaux and J. C. R. Dow, "The Determinants of Wage Inflation: United Kingdom, 1946–56," Journal of the Royal Statistical Society, Series A (General), Part II, 1959.

[3] Charles C. Holt and Martin H. David, "The Concept of Job Vacancies in a Dynamic Theory of the Labor Market," in The Measurement and Interpretation of Job Vacancies, N.B.E.R. (New York: Columbia University Press, 1966).

cal demand and supply theory. To this theory I shall then add the notion of spontaneous wage changes, the phenomenon which ultimately is responsible for income inflation, cost inflation, or whatever you want to call it. Thereafter, we proceed to the derivation of the Phillips curve. First, we apply a relationship between vacancies and unemployment which was first discussed by Dow and Dicks-Mireaux[4] and later by R. A. Gordon[5] and others and was used by these authors for defining and measuring the degree of frictional (structural) disequilibrium of the labor market; second, we shall draw upon the results of Holt and David in order to discuss the short-term dynamics of this relationship.

I. NEOCLASSICAL MACRO THEORY FOR MONEY WAGE CHANGES

In Walrasian neoclassical demand and supply theory, it is usually assumed that the rate of change of the price of a good is determined by the excess demand for the good in question. Applied to the determination of money wages, this means that we can write, say:

$$\frac{\Delta w_i}{w_i(t)} = k_i \frac{q_i^x(t)}{q_i(t)}, \quad k_i > 0, \tag{1}$$

where $w(t)$ denotes money wage rate, $q^x(t)$ excess demand for labor, $q(t)$ supply of labor, while i as a subscript indicates the ith submarket for labor, and t is time. Δw_i is $= w_i(t + 1) - w_i(t)$. k is a constant, the wage flexibility or response coefficient which may differ as between submarkets. What should be meant by a submarket will be discussed below. Equation (1) thus says that the rate of increase of the money wage rate in each particular labor submarket is proportional to the rate of excess demand (over total supply in the submarket).

Consider, then, the Laspeyres wage index where t is put $= 0$:

[4] Op. cit., pp. 20 ff.
[5] Robert Aaron Gordon, *The Goal of Full Employment* (New York: John Wiley ∴ Sons, Inc., 1967), p. 80.

$$W(1) = \frac{\Sigma w_i(1)q_i(0)}{\Sigma w_i(0)q_i(0)}, \tag{2}$$

$W(0) = 1$. We have, then, directly:[6]

$$W(1) = 1 + \frac{\Sigma \Delta w_i q_i(0)}{\Sigma w_i(0)q_i(0)}, \tag{3}$$

or, inserting (1):

$$\Delta W = \frac{\Sigma k_i q_i^x(0)w_i(0)}{\Sigma q_i(0)w_i(0)}. \tag{4}$$

Assuming $k_i = k$, and choosing the units of measurement so that all $w_i(0) = 1$, we get, finally:

$$\Delta W = k \frac{\Sigma q_i^x(0)}{\Sigma q_i(0)} = k \frac{\Sigma q_i^x(0)}{N(0)} = kr^x(0), \tag{5}$$

where $N(0)$ is the total labor force and r^x may be called the average rate of excess demand in the labor market as a whole. r^x may be positive or negative. The derived macro relationship is thus similar to the postulated micro relationships: the rate of wage change is a linear, increasing function of the rate of excess demand; and money wages are constant when the rate of excess demand is zero.

II. NEOCLASSICAL WAGE THEORY WITH SPONTANEOUS WAGE CHANGE AND ADDITIONAL WAGE DETERMINANTS

Let us then add the possibility of *spontaneous wage changes*.[7] We shall speak about spontaneous wage change if money wages change (increase) even though excess demand is zero.

The full line in Figure I through the origin depicts the relation (1). The dashed line is a money wage relation with spontaneous wage change: with excess demand at zero, the rate of wage increase will be ω_i. The upward shift

[6] Bent Hansen, *A Study in the Theory of Inflation* (London: Allen and Unwin, 1951), pp. 221 ff.
[7] J. M. Keynes was probably the first one to notice the importance of spontaneous wage changes for inflation; see *A Treatise on Money* (London: Macmillan, 1930), Vol. I, Ch. 11.

FIGURE 1

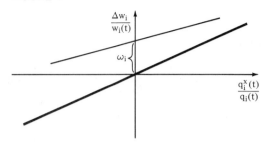

of the relation may be related to the bargaining power of the unions. This helps us, through comparison with the rate of increase of labor productivity, to define wage (or cost) inflation in an unambiguous way. The only problem is that the relation may not shift parallel upward, in which case the degree of spontaneous wage change and, hence, the degree of wage (or cost) inflation will be dependent upon the level of excess demand.[8]

[8] Swedish labor economists, in particular Rudolf Meidner and Gösta Rehn, have always maintained that although the (Swedish) unions shift the relation upward in the sense that, at zero excess demand, the rate of money wage change will be positive, they also make the relation less steep so that, indeed, at high excess demand, the rate of wage increase will even be smaller than in an unorganized market. They base their view on personal experience from wage negotiations. Considering the behavior of prices in other markets with imperfect competition, this sounds, of course, perfectly reasonable, with the only qualification that, whereas in commodity markets imperfect competition tends to make prices sticky, in the labor market it tends to make wage *increases* sticky. This is, on the other hand, a somewhat esoteric matter because we can never observe (1) and (1') simultaneously for the same submarket. A given submarket is either competitive or not.

On the assumption, however, that in competitive circumstance k_1 is the same for all submarkets, differences in the k_1's actually observed might be ascribed to differences in union strength and behavior.

In a study of Canadian wages, J. Vanderkamp ("Wages and Price Level Determination: An Empirical Model for Canada." *Economica*, N.S., XXXIII, No. 130, May 1966) found that the unorganized labor market responds less to changes in unemployment than wages in the organized market. This points in the opposite direction to the Swedish "experience." But, of course, without unions, the competitive k_1 of the organized market might be even higher. Who will ever know?!

Unfortunately, neoclassical theory has little to say about the determinants of the price-flexibility coefficients.

We have now, instead of (1):

$$\frac{\Delta w_i}{w_i(0)} = k_i \frac{q_i^x(0)}{q_i(0)} + \omega_i, \qquad k_i \text{ and } \omega_i > 0 \quad (1')$$

and, assuming $k_i = k$ and $\omega_i = \omega$, we derive as before from (2):

$$\Delta W = kr^x(0) + \omega. \qquad (5')$$

Once more we obtain a macro relation similar to the micro relations shown in Figure I. At zero overall excess demand, the average wage rate will increase, and the increase will be larger the larger is the rate of excess demand. The assumption $\omega_i = \omega$ is not essential for (5'). If we drop this assumption, the constant term will be replaced by $\Sigma \omega_i q_i^o / N^o$, i.e., a weighted average of ω_i. The assumption $k_i = k$ is much more essential; we shall return to it below.

We notice that q_i^x / q_i and r^x may be lagged, and that other determinants of money wage changes can be entered into the micro relations[9] in order to arrive at the kind of relations which have been tested empirically without changing the main line of the argument. If, for instance, the rate of price change,[10] or the rate of average wage change, lagged, enter the micro relations, they will appear in the macro relation in a similar way. If the average (macro) rate of wage increase appears unlagged in the micro relations, it will disappear in the macro relation, but will affect the coefficients on the right-hand side. And there is no particular problem involved in letting the current rate of price increase appear on the right-hand side in the micro relations; if expectations are geared to the current rate of price change this is a simple way of introducing expectations in the functions.[11]

[9] A natural extension of the simple neoclassical relation, equation (1), is to let all excess demands, or rates of price change, enter the equation as determinants of the rate of price change.

[10] Dicks-Mireaux and Dow, op. cit. p. 147.

[11] M. Friedman, "The Role of Monetary Policy," *The American Economic Review*, LVIII. No. 1 (March 1968), and E. S. Phelps, "Money-Wage Dynamics and Labor-Market Equilibrium," *The Journal of Political Economy*, Vol. 76, No. 4, Part II (July/August 1968).

III. VACANCIES AND UNEMPLOYMENT AND EXCESS DEMAND

If each submarket is *homogeneous* and *frictionless* within itself so that it will have either underemployment (excess supply) or job vacancies (excess demand), the sum Σq_i^x can be written $\Sigma^+ q_i^x - \Sigma^- q_i^x$, where $+$ indicates positive and $-$ negative excess demand (i.e., excess supplies). The idea is simply that for each submarket the demand and supply situation can be described by ordinary well-behaved demand and supply curves, and that actual employment is equal to supply when the wage rate is below its equilibrium rate and equal to demand when the wage rate is above the equilibrium. It is implied that there exists an equilibrium wage rate which just clears the market completely so that actual employment is equal to both supply and demand. $\Sigma^+ q_i^x$ is thus the sum of all job vacancies; $\Sigma^- q_i^x$ is the sum of all unemployed. Defining the (average) rate of vacancies as (leaving out the time indication) $v = \Sigma^+ q_i^x / N$, and the (average) rate of unemployment, $u = \Sigma^- q_i^x / N$, we can then write (5') as:

$$\Delta W = k(v - u) + \omega. \tag{5''}$$

The notion of homogeneous, frictionless submarkets is not easy to carry over to empirically observable submarkets, however. Even if it should, in principle, be possible to identify submarkets with sufficient friction between the submarkets to justify the notion, there will probably always remain some friction within the submarket, no matter how narrowly it is delimited. If nothing else, it will at least take time for a worker to move from job to job within the submarket or for an employer to fill a vacancy. In practice, the friction between empirically identifiable submarkets will not be infinitely large, and the frictions within the submarkets not infinitely small, and this is actually what is presumed in setting up the concept of homogeneous frictionless submarkets. The implication is that an observable submarket will, for all practical purposes, have both unemployed men and vacant jobs, and that a change in the tightness of a particular submarket may show itself in

changes in both unemployment and vacancies.[12]

In terms of ordinary demand and supply theory, this means that actual employment is never *on* the supply curve (if the wage rate is below equilibrium) or the demand curve (when above equilibrium), but, let us assume, to the left of both the demand and supply curve.[13] Let us assume, therefore, that we can draw a curve, $E_i E_i$, in Figure II, showing actual employment at various wage rates, given the demand curve $D_i D_i$ and the supply curve, $S_i S_i$.[14]

In drawing $E_i E_i$ we assume that there are always, in a given short period, some employers who do not succeed in finding sufficient labor for satisfying their demands completely even though total supply in the submarket exceeds total demand. And there will always be some members of the labor force who do not succeed in getting a job

---

[12] It would seem that, for the United Kingdom a classification by industry would not be a classification by submarkets as defined here. This is borne out by the findings of Dicks-Mireaux and Dow (op. cit., pp. 162 ff.) that, for the individual industries, aggregate excess demand for all industries, rather than the "local" excess demand for the individual industry, serves to determine wage changes. For the British labor market, one would expect to find a classification on unions, or trades, more relevant for wage analysis, but it will presumably be difficult to obtain a classification of vacancies on unions, or trades. In general, the great problem in detailed excess-demand analysis is to obtain comparable, relevant classifications of vacancies and unemployment.

[13] E. S. Phelps, op. cit., p. 685, note 13.

[14] It cannot be excluded that $E_i E_i$ is to the right of the upper part of the demand and the lower part of the supply curve. In order to handle this case, we need the concepts of *overstaffing* (measured as the difference between $E_i E_i$ and $D_i D_i$ if it is positive) and *overemployment* (the difference between $E_i E_i$ and $S_i S_i$ if it is positive). We cannot even deny the possibility that a submarket is so broadly defined that we simultaneously find vacancies, overstaffing, unemployment, and overemployment. This more complicated situation, however, cannot be illustrated in a simple demand and supply diagram. Direct statistics on overstaffing and overemployment do not exist in any country (to my best knowledge), but overtime statistics could probably be used as a good proxy for overemployment. Overstaffing shows itself, *inter alia*, in the well-known short-term fluctuations of productivity, and this could, perhaps, somehow be used as a proxy for overstaffing.

FIGURE II

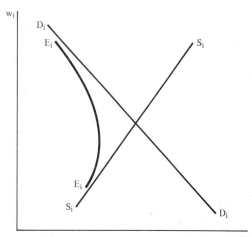

even though there is a more than sufficient number of jobs to employ the total supply. The horizontal distance between D_iD_i and E_iE_i measures the number of vacant jobs, q_i^v. The horizontal distance between S_iS_i and E_iE_i measures the number of unemployed, q_i^u. We have, of course, $q_i^x = q_i^v - q_i^u$. This relation holds true also for the rates of excess demand, r_i^x, the rate of vacancies, v_i, and the rate of unemployment, u_i, provided that all of them are measured on the same base, say on supply: $r_i^x = v_i - u_i$.[15]

Empirical application thus requires that in Equations (1) and (1') we interpret q_i^x as $= q_i^v - q_i^u$. But this changes nothing in the derivation of the macro relationship. In any case, we end up with (5''). It is only in the micro relationships that the difference between the two concepts of submarkets appear.

Dicks-Mireaux and Dow use vacancy and unemployment rates also for expressing excess demand, but instead of simply taking the

difference, $v_i - u_i$, they work with a somewhat complicated index of the excess demand based on vacancy and unemployment rates.[16] They do not really explain why this index of excess demand should be superior to the simple "common sense" definition, $v_i - u_i$. Our analysis has shown that if we follow the line of thought of neoclassical demand and supply theory, the simple definition, $v_i - u_i$, is the one which should be used in the wage-determining equation.[17]

IV. THE DERIVATION OF THE PHILLIPS RELATION

The Phillips curve expresses ΔW as a function of u alone. In order to transform (5'') into a Phillips relation, our problem is, therefore, to find a relation between v and u. For an individual submarket, we can obtain this relation directly from Figure II by dividing through pairs of q_i^v and q_i^u by the corresponding value of S_iS_i. As we have drawn E_iE_i, D_iD_i, and S_iS_i, the relation between v_i and u_i becomes a curve convex seen from the origin as depicted in Figure III, and asymptotic or not toward the axes, depending upon the convergence of E_iE_i toward D_iD_i and S_iS_i.

The u_iv_i curve in Figure III is derived from static assumptions concerning the demand,

---

[15] If a submarket simultaneously has vacancies, overstaffing, unemployment, and overemployment, we have excess demand = vacancies *minus* overstaffing *minus* unemployment *plus* overemployment. Four statistics are then necessary for describing exhaustively the disequilibrium situation. In what follows, we disregard overstaffing and overemployment. For some European countries this may be a serious omission.

[16] Dow and Dicks-Mireaux. op. cit., pp. 21–22. Their index is defined as $v - \sqrt{uv}$ (disregarding the problem of deficient or inflated "statements" of vacancies) for $u < v$ and $\sqrt{uv} - u$ for $u > v$.

[17] *Ibid.*, p. 22, Note 1 discusses briefly the "common-sense" definition, $v_i - u_i$, and presents figures for total annual excess demand on this definition.

Excess demand defined as $v - u$ was used by Bent Hansen and Gösta Rehn in "On Wage Drift. A Problem in Money Wage Dynamics," *25 Essays in Honour of Erik Lindahl* (Stockholm: Ekonomisk Tidskrift, 1957). The aim of this study was to explain wage drift (increase in earnings *minus* negotiated increase) only; hence prices were not used as an explanatory variable. Dicks-Mireaux and Dow, on the other hand, aimed only at explaining negotiated wage changes, which probably implies an underestimation of the role played by excess demand.

An index v/u has been used by L. Jacobson and A. Lindbeck, "Labor Market Conditions, Wages and Inflation—Swedish Experiences 1955–67," *Swedish Journal of Economics*, No. 2, 1969.

FIGURE III

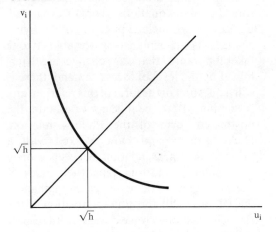

supply, and employment curves. It shows combinations of v_i and u_i at various wage levels. Changes in the labor market situation are, however, also related to shifts in the demand and supply curves. For the moment, let us assume that at shifts in D_iD_i and S_iS_i in Figure II, the position of E_iE_i always changes in such a way that the derived u_iv_i curve in Figure III remains unchanged. Theoretically, at least, this is not impossible, but it requires stationarity assumptions which cannot be upheld in a more realistic theory; we shall return to this in Section VI. The u_iv_i curve will then also show combinations of vacancies and unemployment at different demand and supply curves.

Furthermore, if all the individual submarkets happened to have the same "relative" position of their E_iE_i curve, their u_iv_i curves would coincide and the cross-sectional relation at any moment would be the same curve. Otherwise we cannot be sure that we will find any significant, systematic, cross-sectional relation; and if we do, it will not necessarily be identical with the time series curve(s) for the individual markets.

The macro relation, finally, between v and u should, in principle, be obtained through aggregation of all the individual u_iv_i relations. As long as we do not specify the individual relations, we can say nothing about what the aggregated relation would look like, but one would, of course, like to believe that it should

have a form similar to Figure III. Dow and Dicks-Mireaux suggested, on the basis of British time series data for 1950–1956, that the macro curve might be a simple rectangular hyperbola.[18] Cross-sectional data for Germany also point to this form.[19] And time series data (as published by the O.E.C.D.) for the Netherlands, Sweden, the United Kingdom, and a number of other countries, 1955–1968, point to the same form. Assume, therefore, that we have:

$$v = h\frac{1}{u}; \quad h > 0; \tag{6}$$

the coefficient h, or perhaps better, $\sqrt{h}$ has been suggested as a measure of the degree of structural disequilibrium in the labor market.[20]

In that case, the neoclassical relationship (5″) becomes:

$$\Delta W = kh\frac{1}{u} - ku + \omega \tag{7}$$

which is easily seen to be a curve which has all the properties of the Phillips curve (see Figure IV).

The form and position of the Phillips curve thus depend upon three basic factors:

(i) the *flexibility of money wages* with respect to excess demand (k),
(ii) the *degree of spontaneous wage increase* (ω) as defined in relation to (1′), and
(iii) the position of the uv curve (h) which shows the *degree of structural disequilibrium* in the labor market.

We notice that neither spontaneous wage increase nor structural disequilibrium are necessary conditions for a Phillips relation

---

[18] Dow and Dicks-Mireaux, op. cit., p. 22. Their index of excess demand was based on this assumption, among others.

[19] Gordon, op. cit., Ch. 4.

[20] Dow and Dicks-Mitreaux, *op. cit.*, p. 20, and Gordon, *op. cit.* Both define what they call "maladjustment" and "structural unemployment," respectively, as the amount of unemployment which exists when unemployment is equal to vacancies.

FIGURE IV

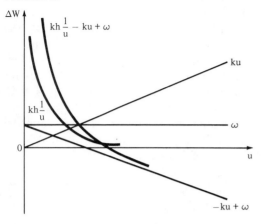

to exist. If $h = 0$, (7) becomes $-ku + \omega$, i.e., a straight line; with $\omega = 0$, the curve runs a bit lower, but preserves its form, $kh/u - ku$.

If other determinants—for instance, the rate of price change—enter the macro relation (5′), they will be carried over to the Phillips relation (7). Notice that the relationship we have derived may be considered a combination of the hyperbolic form which has been used, for instance, by Perry,[21] where unemployment enters as $1/u$, and the simple linear form used by, e.g., Klein and Bodkin,[22] where unemployment enters as $-ku$.

V. THE FORM OF THE PHILLIPS RELATION

In order to establish the Phillips relation (7), stable and convex seen from below, we have made use of a number of assumptions which deserve closer scrutiny.

[21] G. I. Perry, "The Determinants of Wage Rate Changes and the Inflation-Unemployment Trade-off for the United States," *Review of Economic Studies*, XXXI, 88 (Oct. 1964).

[22] L. R. Klein and R. G. Bodkin, "Empirical Aspects of the Trade-Offs among Three Goals: High Level Employment, Price Stability, and Economic Growth," in *Inflation, Growth, and Employment*, Commission of Money and Credit (Englewood Cliffs, N.J.: Prentice-Hall, 1964). Jan Tinbergen postulated and estimated a linear Phillips relation already in 1936! See his *Selected Papers* (Amsterdam: North-Holland, 1959), "An Economic Policy for 1936," p. 68.

(i) The individual submarkets were assumed to obey equations (1) or (1′), expanded, if necessary, to include price or cost-of-living changes as an explanatory variable. If one takes for granted that wage changes are determined by the level of excess demand, there is still a question of the form of this relationship. Assuming (1) to be linear, we obtain the postulated form of the Phillips relation. Dicks-Mireaux and Dow worked with a logarithmic linear relation between money wage changes and (one plus) their index of excess demand;[23] it preserves and enhances the curvature of the Phillips relation if the elasticity of money wage changes with respect to excess demand (on our definition) is larger than one. At an elasticity below one, the Phillips curve becomes flatter, and at a sufficiently low (positive) elasticity, it may even become concave seen from below.[24] A priori, there is nothing to prevent this elasticity from being smaller than one. Most of the wage elasticities with respect to excess demand (on their definition) found by Dicks-Mireaux and Dow were significantly larger than one, but for individual industries a few were actually below one.[25] If, moreover, trade unions behave in such a way that—*ceteris paribus* with respect to cost-of-living changes and other possible determinants of wage changes—they prevent money wages from falling no matter how large the excess supply of labor is, and prevent money wages from increasing faster than a certain maximum, irrespective of the size of excess demand (see note 8, page 4), we have an *S*-shaped relation between money wage change and excess demand and may then get a corresponding *S*-shaped Phillips relation.

The form of the Phillips curve depends, thus, upon the form of both the relation between excess demand and wage change, and

[23] With this relationship, money wages can never fall, no matter how big excess supply and unemployment are. For the postwar period, this is not very important, however.

[24] Assuming, of course, that the *uv* curve has the convex form of Figure III.

[25] Dicks-Mireaux and Dow, op. cit., pp. 153, 154, 158, 159, and 164.

the relation between the rates of unemployment and vacancies. The latter has been assumed to be convex seen from below, but
should it prove to be linear, the Phillips curve
might still become convex seen from below if
the relation between excess demand and wage
change is convex from below.[26]

(ii) In order to obtain (5), we assumed that
the units of measurement of labor were chosen
so that all $w_i = 1$. All the following equations
assume labor to be measured in this way. The
rate of excess demand is thus a weighted rate,
the weights being the money wages, and r^x
has to be interpreted as the ratio of the value
of excess demand to the value of total supply
of labor. It follows that the rates of vacancies
and unemployment relevant to the discussion
should also, in principle, be weighted rates.
This has obvious consequences for both the
uv curve and the Phillips relation, which
ought to be estimated on this basis.

(iii) We have assumed that the money
wage flexibility coefficients, k_i, are the same
for all submarkets. If this is not true—at
least approximately—the rate of excess demand appearing in the aggregate relations (5)
and (5') has to be a weighted average of the
individual submarkets' excess demands, the
weights being the individual wage flexibility
coefficients. The same applies, then, to the
rates of vacancies and unemployment in (5'')
and to the rate of unemployment in the
Phillips relation. Dicks-Mireaux and Dow's
estimates[27] indicate that the money wage
flexibilities are so different that we may not
be justified in assuming all $k_i = k$.

(iv) Fourth, for deriving the Phillips relation we needed a macro relation between
unemployment rate and vacancy rate; in

order to secure a convex Phillips relation it
should preferably, albeit not necessarily, have
a form similar to Figure III. Under what
conditions will such a stable macro relation
exist?

Here we shall first show that, even if there
is no friction within the individual submarkets
so that the employment curve, E_iE_i, in Figure II coincides with demand (above equilibrium) and supply (below equilibrium), we may
still be able to derive a macro uv curve like
Figure III. Without such frictions, there will,
at any given moment, exist a vector of money
wages which will clear the labor market completely so that both unemployment and vacancies are everywhere nil. Provided that the
actual money wages are rigid and deviate
from the equilibrium wages in the initial situation, changes in total demand may generate a
macro uv curve like Figure III.

Assume, for instance, that we have four
homogeneous submarkets, each with a constant supply of labor, a "normal" demand
curve, and a fixed wage rate, different from
the equilibrium rate; see Figure V. In the
initial situation we have excess demand and
vacancies in the first two markets, unemployment in the last two. Adding together the
vacancies in the first two markets and the
unemployment in the last two, and dividing
by total supply in all four markets, we obtain
a point, u^o, v^o, in Figure VI. If, then, we let the
demand curves shift simultaneously to the
right and left by the same constant amount,
the curve in Figure VI will be generated. It
has the same number of kinks as the number
of submarkets and coincides at the ends with
the axes. If we have a large number of submarkets, and if total demand never reaches
such extreme levels that all markets have unemployment or vacancies, the curve in Figure VI will approach the form of Figure III.

We have thus derived a macro uv curve
without assuming frictional unemployment
within the individual submarkets. It is easily
seen that we obtain the same curve if we shift
supply simultaneously to the right or left by
the same constant amount. The simultaneous
existence of vacancies and unemployment,
and of the uv curve, may, in this case, be

---

[26] In general: if $dw/dt = \dot{w} = f(v - u), f' > 0, f'' \gtreqless 0$,
$v = g(u)$ we have

$$\dot{w}' = d\dot{w}/du = f' \cdot (g' - 1), \text{ and}$$
$$\dot{w}'' = d^2\dot{w}/du^2 = f'' \cdot (g' - 1)^2 + g''f'.$$

With $g'' = 0$, the sign of $\dot{w}''$ depends upon the sign of
f''. With $f'' = 0$, $\dot{w}'' < 0$, provided that $g'' < 0$. In the
case without friction, i.e., g' and $g'' = 0$ for $u > 0$, we
have $\dot{w}'' < 0$ if $f'' < 0$.

[27] Dicks-Mitreaux and Dow, *op. cit.*, p. 164.

FIGURE V

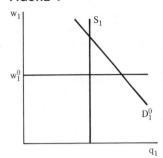
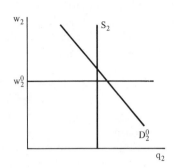

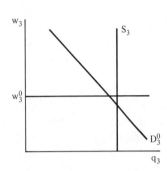
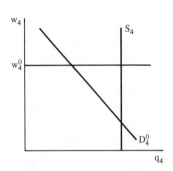

FIGURE VI

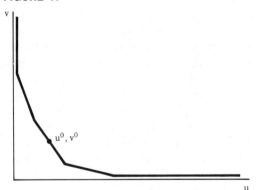

ascribed to a rigid ("wrong") wage structure and a rigid distribution of demand and supply by submarkets; the *uv* curve will obviously change position if either relative wages or the demand and supply structure changes. It may, on the other hand, also be maintained that the *uv* curve here only exists because labor does not move freely *between* the submarkets, and, in this sense, the simultaneous existence of vacancies and unemployment may even in this case be ascribed to labor market frictions. This is a matter of terminology. In any case,

we have found that even if we work with homogeneous submarkets a stable macro *uv* curve may exist.

If, on the other hand, the structure of relative wages and the distribution of demand and supply by submarkets are well matched, in the sense that there exists a level of demand where demand and supply of labor tally everywhere at the given wages, changes in the level of total demand may, nevertheless, generate a *uv* curve like Figure III if within each submarket actual employment is off the demand and supply curves in the way depicted in Figure II. We would then have a situation like Figure VII.

In the initial situation, with $w_i = w_i^o$, $D_i = D_i^o$, and $S_i = S_i^o$, demand and supply are equal in all (three) submarkets. But within all three submarkets, there are vacancies and unemployment, equal in size within the individual submarket. Adding together vacancies and unemployment, respectively, and dividing by total supply, we obtain point 0 in Figure VIII.

Let, then, total demand increase so that all individual demand curves shift to the right in the same proportion, or by the same amount

FIGURE VII

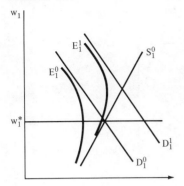 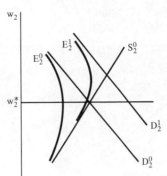 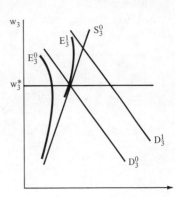

FIGURE VIII

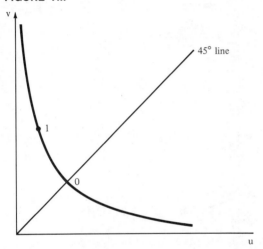

(in order to keep the demand structure unchanged). With the supply curves unchanged at S_i^0, the demand curves are now D_1^1. Our assumption is that the employment curves, E_i, also move to a new position, say E_i^1. The result is, as we have drawn the curves, an increase in total employment and in total vacancies, and a fall in total unemployment, and we move to point 1 in Figure VIII. In this way we can generate any number of points in Figure VIII. In the same way we can generate points by shifting the supply curves proportionately, or by the same amount. The whole family of such points can be said to have been generated on the assumption of an unchanged but well-balanced demand and supply structure. The problem is whether this family of points will lie on a single valued curve, and what form this curve will have. This, in turn, is a problem of the determinants of the position of the employment curve, E_iE_i. In the following section we shall show, at the macro level, that there are good reasons for expecting the short-term cyclical relationship between vacancies and unemployment to be somewhat more complicated than we have assumed so far.

VI. THE CYCLICAL CHARACTERISTICS OF UNEMPLOYMENT AND VACANCIES

In Graph I we have shown the *uv* curve for the United Kingdom for the two cycles 1953–1960 and 1960–1964 on quarterly, seasonally adjusted data. The graph shows a clear tendency for the downturn to take place at a lower level than the upturn, which suggests that the cyclical swings (at a given structural situation) take place in a counter-clockwise movement along a closed circuit. When one recalls the well-established tendency for employment to lag behind demand and output, it is not difficult to see why it should be like that. In a recession, a sudden upturn of demand does not affect employment, and thus unemployment, immediately; but it may work immediately on vacancies. At the lower turning point, the *uv* curve should thus tend to move vertically upward. As employment subsequently catches up, the curve will bend to the NW. When demand stagnates at the end of the upswing, vacancies will stop increasing and may even fall, with

GRAPH 1

United Kingdom quarterly data, seasonally adjusted. *Source*: *National Institute Economic Review* and Dow and Dicks-Mireaux, op. cit.

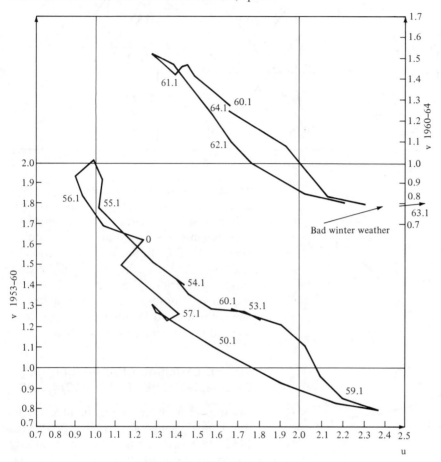

employment still increasing and unemployment falling. *Mutatis mutandis* for the downturn. It may be worthwhile to formalize this.

In their discussion of the concept of job vacancies in a dynamic setting, Holt and David[28] have argued that the stock of vacancies existing at any moment consists of the difference between desired employment (that is, short-term demand for labor) and

[28] Holt and David, op. cit., p. 83. Since the discussion here is concerned with the relation between neoclassic wage dynamics and the Phillips relation, I shall not take up the interesting theory of wage change which the authors formulate, but will just mention that there seems to me to be a basic difference between their theory and the Phillips relation (and neoclassical theory) in that the wage changes generated by the state of vacancies and unemployment is a transitory phenomenon only.

actual employment, *plus* the vacancies which it is already now necessary to announce because of expected future quits, retirements, and terminations, and expansion of output (demand). Measuring everything as rates (on total labor force), in addition to the definition of unemployment,

$$u(t) = 1 - e(t), \tag{8}$$

we have, therefore,

$$v(t) = [\delta(t) - e(t)] + \gamma \frac{d\delta(t)}{dt} T_v$$
$$+ [(\mu e(t) + \lambda)T_v], \tag{9}$$

where new symbols are δ, the rate of labor demand in terms of men to be employed (desired employment); e, the rate of actual employment; T_v, the average time necessary to fill a vacancy; and γ, μ, and λ, constants. Assuming that the expected rate of future expansion of desired employment is proportional to the current rate of change of desired employment, the present stock of vacancies necessary to procure a sufficient number of employees in time for expected future expansion becomes $\gamma\delta'T_v$, i.e., the second term on the right-hand side. Assuming, moreover, that the sum of expected quits, and so on, is linearly related to actual employment, we obtain the last term $(\mu e + \lambda)T_v$.

We shall then introduce a traditional employment adjustment mechanism,[29]

$$\frac{de(t)}{dt} = a(\delta(t) - e(t) - \mu e(t) - \lambda), \qquad (10)$$

it being noticed that, at time t, the gap between desired and actual employment is growing at the rate of quits, and so on, $\mu e + \lambda$. Instead of building up a complete model for labor demand, we shall impose an exogenous, cyclical fluctuation of demand for labor upon this system:

$$\delta(t) = \alpha \cos t + \beta. \qquad (11)$$

(10) and (11) together have the solution

$$e(t) = \frac{a\alpha}{a^2(1+\mu)^2 + 1}(a(1+\mu)\cos t + \sin t)$$

$$+ \frac{\beta - \lambda}{1+\mu} + Ce^{-a(1+\mu)t}. \qquad (12)$$

Since a and μ are positive, we can, for large values of t, ignore the last term (the initial conditions) and have in the limit

$$e(t) = \frac{a^\alpha}{a^2(1+\mu)^2 + 1}(a(1+\mu)\cos t + \sin t)$$

$$+ \frac{\beta - \lambda}{1+\mu}. \qquad (13)$$

[29] See, for instance, R. M. Solow and J. E. Stiglitz, "Output, Employment, and Wages in the Short Run," this *Journal*, LXXXII. 4 (Nov. 1968). p. 540, equation (4). See also C. Gillion, "Wage-Rates, Earnings, and Wage-Drift," *National Institute Economic Review*, 46 (Nov. 1968), p. 53. For a somewhat different approach, see E. S. Phelps, op. cit.

Insertion of (13) in (8) and (9) gives us u and v as functions of t. The solution has the property that the point (u, v) moves counterclockwise on a closed circuit in the uv space. The form and position of this circuit depend, of course, upon the value of the coefficients.

An obvious further dynamization of this model is to let T_v vary cyclically. It should be expected that the larger unemployment is, the shorter will become the time it takes to fill a vacancy. We might, then, for instance, have[30]

$$T_v = l\frac{1}{u}. \qquad (14)$$

It so happens that this does not change the characteristics of the cyclical behavior of u and v; they continue to rotate counterclockwise. A natural further extension would be to let a change cyclically, too. Indeed, a is inversely related to T_v. We could, for instance, put $a = a(1 - e(t))$. This leads to an expression which can only be integrated explicitly in terms of a rather complicated series, and we shall not work out the solution here. But it seems obvious that this does not change anything essential in the cyclical behavior of the model either.

From a short-run point of view, we have thus to admit that there may not exist a single valued uv curve along which the labor market moves up and down through the cycle—even given the structural disequilibrium in the labor market. This has consequences, not only for the measurement of the structural imbalance, but also for the Phillips relation. Using (14), and eliminating e in (9) by means of (8), we obtain from (5″), substituting dW/dt for ΔW,

$$\frac{dW}{dt} = kl[-\gamma\alpha \sin t + \mu + \lambda]\frac{1}{\mu}$$

$$+ k[a \cos t + \beta - 1 - \mu l] + \omega, \qquad (15)$$

which gives us a Phillips relation with the rate of change of money wages dependent upon $1/u$ plus some cyclical terms. Clearly,

[30] Holt and David, op. cit., pp. 96–97.

FIGURE IX

Cyclical (I) and stationary (II) relations between vacancies and unemployment, $a = 0.9$, $\mu = 0.02$, $\gamma = 1.0$, $\beta = 0.95$ and 0.99, $l = 0.01$, $\lambda = 0.02$, $t = 0 + n\pi/4$.

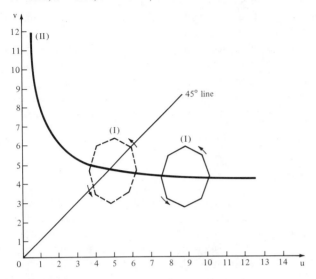

this relation will have a counterclockwise rotation, too, so that during the upswing, a given rate of unemployment is associated with a higher rate of money wage increase then during the downturn. Since $\alpha \cos t + \beta$ is total demand for labor, and $-\alpha \sin t$ is the rate of change of demand, which may be replaced, as a proxy, by $-u$ and du/dt, we find thus a sort of rationale for Phillips relations which includes both the level of unemployment and its rate of change as explanatory variables.[31] However, at least at the turning points this proxy may work badly.

It is interesting, though, to notice that the stationary solution to the dynamic model—(8), (9), (13), and (14)—leads us back to a single curve similar to Figure III. The cyclical counterclockwise movement takes place around this curve; see Figure IX. Assume, namely, that δ is kept constant at any arbitrary level, so that $d\delta/dt = 0$. We then have $\delta - e = \mu e + \lambda$. Inserting in (9), and eliminating e from (8) and (9), we obtain now, given (14),

$$v = \frac{l(\mu + \lambda)}{u} - \mu u + \mu(1 - l) + \lambda \qquad (15')$$

[31] R. G. Lipsey, op. cit., and E. S. Phelps, op. cit.

and, together with (5″), we obtain

$$\frac{dW}{dt} = \frac{kl(\mu + \lambda)}{u} - k(1 + \mu)u$$
$$+ k(\mu(1 - l) + \lambda) + \omega. \qquad (7')$$

Apart from the constants, this is exactly the same form of the Phillips relation which we derived in (7). All roads lead to Rome. But (15′) is to be conceived of as a longer-term relationship, and (7′), as well as (7), has to be interpreted in the same way. In the short term, we should expect the Phillips relation to rotate counterclockwise around this longer-term relationship,[32] as shown in Figure X, which is based on the same assumptions as Figure IX. Phillips' historical annual data persistently rotate this way for all cycles, 1861–1868, 1868–1879, 1879–1886, 1886–1893, 1893–1904, 1904–1909, and for 1920–1944.[33]

[32] F. Brechling, "The Trade-off between Inflation and Unemployment," *The Journal of Political Economy*, Vol. 76, No. 4, Part II (July/August 1968) has argued that expectations may produce a clockwise rotation in the Phillips relation.
[33] Phillips, op. cit., Figures 2, 3, 4a., 5, 6, 7, and 9. Our explanation of this phenomenon is obviously much simpler than the aggregation considerations of Lipsey, op. cit.

FIGURE X

Cyclical (I) and stationary (II) Phillips curves. Based on same assumptions as Figure IX plus $\omega = 0.07$ and $k = 1.00$, t all values.

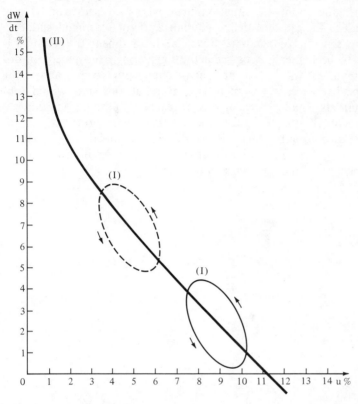

VII. VACANCIES, UNEMPLOYMENT, AND EQUILIBRIUM

It has been maintained, for instance by Arthur F. Burns,[34] that equality of vacancies and unemployment defines a zero-cyclical unemployment level; from an aggregate demand management point of view it should thus be particularly desirable to be on that point of the uv curve where it is cut by the 45° line through the origin (see Figure III). This idea has been strongly criticized by a number of authors.[35] We are now able to settle this issue.

It is seen that if the labor market is perfectly competitive and obeys equation (5)—that is, spontaneous wage changes are absent—and there are no changes in productivity, and, finally, the only aim of policy is to keep prices constant, then certainly equality of the (weighted) rates of vacancies and unemployment is an equilibrium condition. Under these heroic assumptions, Burns is right. But these assumptions are not likely to be fulfilled. Quite apart from the fact that economic policy is often interested in low unemployment for its own sake, or in maximizing production,[36] the society we live in is neither stationary nor perfectly competitive. Union activity and spontaneous wage increase cannot be ignored; technical change and productivity increase take place continuously.

[34] Arthur F. Burns, "Economics and Our Public Policy of Full Employment," in *The Nation's Economic Objectives*, ed. E. O. Edwards (Chicago: University of Chicago Press [for William Marsh Rice University, Texas], 1964).

[35] Jacob Mincer, "Comment" to Holt and David, op. cit.; N.B.E.R., op. cit., pp. 120 ff.; and Gordon, op. cit., pp. 74 ff.

[36] Abba P. Lerner, *The Economics of Employment* (New York: McGraw-Hill, 1951), Ch. 2, has in particular stressed this point.

Only by chance are spontaneous wage increases and productivity increases equal in size, unless a deliberate wage policy (union or government) is successful in bringing about this result. For wages to rise just at the rate needed to keep prices constant, the rate of vacancies, therefore, may have to be higher or lower than the rate of unemployment. And, if the wage flexibility with respect to excess demand varies as between submarkets, equality of vacancies and unemployment will not, even in the competitive case, secure a constant wage level.

Moreover, the equality of vacancies and unemployment will be reached at different levels of vacancies and unemployment on the downturn and in the upswing. Both of these situations are obviously transitive and do not define equilibria. If total demand suddenly were frozen at the moment the 45° line is passed in the downstring, a movement toward a stationary state would begin, and if the system is convergent, this state would subsequently be reached. But there is nothing to guarantee that here unemployment and vacancies would be equal, and that the economy thereafter would be in equilibrium in any sense of the word.

Money Wage Dynamics and Labor Market Equilibrium

Edmund S. Phelps

New York University

If the economy were always in macroeconomic equilibrium, then perhaps the full employment money-and-growth models of recent vintage would suffice to explain the time paths of the money wage and price level. But any actual economy is almost continuously out of equilibrium, so we need also to study wage and price dynamics under arbitrary conditions.

The Phillips curve studies of the past decade have done this with a vengeance, offering numerous independent variables in countless combinations to explain wage movements. But it is difficult to choose among these econometric models and rarely is there a clear rationale for the model used. This paper is a start toward a unified and empirically applicable theory of money wage dynamics. At the same time it tries to capture the role of expectations and thus to work into the theory the notion of labor-market equilibrium.

1. EVOLUTION OF THE PHILLIPS CURVE AND ITS OPPOSITION

Keynes' *General Theory*[1] and virtually all formal macroeconomic models of the postwar era postulated a minimum unemployment level—a full employment level of unemployment—which could be maintained with either stable prices or rising prices. In this happy state, additional aggregate demand would produce rising prices and wages but no reduction of unemployment. This residual unemployment was called "frictional" and "voluntary," and such unemployment was (mistakenly) assumed to be unresponsive to demand.[2] Hence there was no need to choose between low unemployment and price stability.

This doctrine depended on Keynes' notions of money wage behavior. At more than minimum unemployment, a rise (fall) of demand and employment would produce at most a once-for-all rise (fall) of the money wage, prices constant; any rise (fall) of the price level thereby induced would cause a rise (fall) of the money wage in smaller proportion. Hence, in a stationary economy at least, his theory did not predict the possibility of a secular rise of money wage rates at normal unemployment rates—let alone wage rises exceeding productivity growth—only the one-time "semi-inflation"[3] of prices and wages during the transition to minimum unemployment.

[1] J. M. Keynes, *The General Theory of Employment, Interest and Money* (The Macmillan Company, London, 1936).

[2] A monetary economy can choose among different levels of frictional unemployment that correspond to different levels of aggregate demand and job vacancies. Some of the mechanisms that enable demand to affect frictional unemployment are discussed below, especially in Section 3.

[3] Keynes, op. cit., p. 301.

This doctrine was quickly disputed by Robinson,[4] who wrote of a conflict between moderately high employment and price stability. Dunlop[5] suggested that the *rate of change* of the money wage depends more on the *level* of unemployment than upon the rate of change of unemployment, as Keynes had it. After the war, Singer,[6] Bronfenbrenner,[7] Haberler,[8] Brown,[9] Lerner,[10] and many others wrote that at low, albeit above-minimum, unemployment levels there occurs a process of "cost inflation," "wage-push inflation," "income inflation," "creeping inflation," "sellers' inflation," "dilemma inflation," or the "new inflation"—a phenomenon that was attributed to the discretionary power of unions or oligopolies or both to raise wages or prices or both without "excess demand."[11]

[4] Robinson, *Essays in the Theory of Unemployment* (The Macmillan Company, New York, 1937), pp. 30–31.
[5] J. T. Dunlop, "The Movement of Real and Money Wage Rates," *Economic Journal*, 48 (September 1938), pp. 413–434.
[6] H. W. Singer, "Wage Policy in Full Employment," *Economic Journal*, 62 (December 1947), pp. 438–455.
[7] M. Bronfenbrenner, "Postwar Political Economy: The President's Reports," *Journal of Political Economics*, 56 (October 1948), pp. 373–391.
[8] G. Haberler, "Causes and Cures of Inflation," *Review of Economics and Statistics*, 30 (February 1948), pp. 10–14.
[9] A. J. Brown, *The Great Inflation*, 1939–51 (Oxford University Press, New York, 1955).
[10] A. P. Lerner, "Inflationary Depression and the Regulation of Administered Prices," in *The Relationship of Prices to Economic Stability and Growth*, compendium of papers submitted to panelists appearing before the Joint Economic Committee, 85th Congress, 2nd session (U.S. Government Printing Office, Washington, 1958).
[11] Quite distinct from ordinary cost inflation, though often confused with it, is the Jimmy Hoffa theory of inflation which finds the source of most inflations in the animal spirits of the largest union and corporation leaders. Wage-push theorists like S. Weintraub in his *A General Theory of the Price Level, Output, Income Distribution and Economic Growth* (Chilton Co., Philadelphia, 1959) treat inflation as almost spontaneous, virtually independent of the unemployment rate over any relevant range, and hence not induced by aggregate demand. An early paper of mine, "A Test for the Presence of Cost Inflation in the United States, 1955–57," *Yale Economic Essays*, 1 (Spring 1960), tested the hypothesis that the 1955–1957 inflation was more of this character than were the two earlier postwar inflations, making the

The customary attribution of cost inflation to the existence of such large economic units is unnecessary and insufficient. Like the theory of unemployment, the theory of cost inflation requires a non-Walrasian model in which there is no auctioneer continuously equilibrating commodity and labor markets. Beyond that, it is not clear to me what monopoly power contributes. An increase of monopoly power—due, say, to increased concentration—will raise prices relative to wages at any given unemployment rate and productivity level; but once, at the prevailing unemployment rate, the real wage has fallen (relative to productivity) enough to accommodate the higher markup this process will stop and any continuation of inflation will depend on other sources.[12]

Similarly, the behavior of labor unions is not remotely sufficient to explain the cost inflation phenomenon. Whether the unions significantly exacerbate the problem—whether they increase that unemployment rate which is consistent with price stability—is, however, a difficult question. The affirmative answer frequently starts from the theory,

assumption that autonomous "wage push" or "profit push" would be uneven in its sectoral incidence, so that the coefficient of correlation between sector price changes and sector output changes would (if the hypothesis were true) be algebraically smaller in the 1955–1957 period than it was earlier. It was algebraically smaller, but the statistical significance of the decline was impossible to determine. Incidentally, the paper by R. T. Selden, "Cost-Push versus Demand-Pull Inflation, 1955–57," *Journal of Political Economy*, 67 (February 1959), pp. 1–20, wrongly attributes significance to the positivity of the coefficient in 1955–1957 instead of to the magnitude of the decline.
[12] The answer of Ackley [G. Ackley, "The Contribution of Guidelines," in G. P. Shultz and R. Z. Aliber, eds., *Guidelines, Informal Controls, and the Market Place* (University of Chicago Press, Chicago, 1966)] and Lerner [A. P. Lerner, "Employment Theory and Employment Policy," *American Economic Review: Papers and Proceedings*, 57 (May 1967), pp. 1–18] that, corresponding to every unemployment rate and productivity level, there is a natural real wage that is irreducible despite structural changes, so that money wages will keep pace with prices until unemployment is allowed to increase, seems to me to be terribly implausible. In any case, if this paper is right, cost inflation theory does not require any such "double monopoly" argument.

set forth by Dunlop,[13] that a union, to maximize its utility, seeks to "trade off" the real wage rate against the unemployment of its members, raising the former (relative to productivity) until the gain from a further real wage increase is offset by the utility loss from the increase in unemployment expected to result from it. At an unemployment level below the unions' optimum, the unions then push up wage rates faster than productivity. But firms pass these higher costs on to consumers, so the real wage gains are frustrated, and as long as the government maintains the low unemployment level the rounds of inflation will continue.

I have trouble applying such a model to the American economy. Almost three quarters of the civilian labor force do not belong to unions. This fact casts doubt on the quantitative importance of the model. And perhaps the fact goes much deeper. If the union members whom the unions make unemployed have no good prospect of future union employment, they will be inclined to seek employment elsewhere. If, at the other extreme, the union unemployment is shared in the form of a short workweek, this unemployment—although real enough to the extent that members do not "moonlight"—does not add to the official unemployment rate as it is measured. Certainly the unions *participate* in the cost inflation process, and they may even increase a little the volume of unemployment consistent with price stability. But I should think that a union must offer its membership a frequency of employment opportunities that is roughly comparable to that elsewhere in order to thrive and that appreciably reduced employment opportunities require a greater wage differential between union and other employment than is commonly observed.[14]

Phillips' successful fitting of what we now call the Phillips curve[15] to a scatter diagram of historical British data deprived the discussions of some of their institutional color but neatly epitomized the new concept of cost inflation—if by that term we mean (as I think most of the aforementioned writers intended) *that kind of inflation which can be stopped only by a reduction of the employment rate* through lower aggregate demand and which thus raises a cruel dilemma for fiscal and monetary policy.[16] The Phillips curve portrayed the rate of change as a continuous and decreasing function of the unemployment rate, with wage increases exceeding typical productivity growth at sufficiently low, albeit above-minimum, unemployment rates. Hence, if prices are tied to marginal or average costs, the smaller the level at which aggregate demand sets the unemployment rate, the greater is the *continuing* rate of inflation.

Strikingly, Phillips found that the nineteenth-century data pointed to a trade-off between wage increases and unemployment in the same way as contemporary data. Lipsey's sequel[17] showed a statistically significant

[13] J. T. Dunlop, *Wage Determination under Trade Unions* (A. M. Kelley, New York, 1950).

[14] It is certainly likely, however, that an *increase* of union power, even if localized, will raise the average money wage level at any constant unemployment rate. See A. G. Hines, "Trade Unions and Wage Inflation in the United Kingdom 1893–1961," *Review of Economic Studies*, 31 (October 1964), pp. 221–252.

[15] A. W. Phillips, "The Relation between Unemployment and the Rate of Change of Money Wage Rates in the United Kingdom, 1861–1957," *Economica*, 25 (November 1958), pp. 283–299.

[16] By contrast, in the pure "demand inflation" of Keynes and the classics, a reduction of the price trend could be achieved without cost to output and employment, because aggrement demand is necessarily superfluous to begin with. "Demand inflation" may be worth preserving, because a regime of "mixed inflation" is conceivable.

My earlier paper [E. S. Phelps, "A Test for the Presence of Cost Inflation in the United States 1955–57," *Yale Economic Essays*, 1 (Spring 1961), pp. 28–69] contains a fairly complete taxonomy of inflations [see also W. J. Fellner, "Demand Inflation, Cost Inflation, and Collective Bargaining," in P. D. Bradley, ed., *The Public Stake in Union Power* (University of Virginia Press, Charlottesville, Va., 1959)]. Incidentally, the occasional definition of cost inflation as an autonomous upward shift of the Phillips curve is very awkward and does not imply the "policy dilemma" with which inflation analysts were concerned in the 1950s.

[17] R. G. Lipsey, "The Relation between Unemployment and the Rate of Change of Money Wage Rates in United Kingdom, 1862–1957: A Further Analysis," *Economica*, 27 (February 1960), pp. 1–31.

Phillips curve relation for the subperiod 1861–1913. In fact, this early Phillips curve was *higher* (by about one percentage point) than the Phillips curve he fitted to the period 1929–1957.[18] Apparently the cost inflation tendency, if real, is not "new" in history; in Britain, anyway, it may be no worse than it used to be.

This paper will be addressed to two theoretical issues surrounding Phillips curves. The first topic is the microeconomic elaboration of the hypothesis that, *given expectations of general price and wage movements*, wage rates must *continue* to rise at a higher steady rate if a lower level of unemployment is to continue. It may be that such a theoretical contribution will swing the balance against neo-Keynesian (or more obscurely originating) contention that the steady-state Phillips "curve" is a flat line inasmuch as empirical investigations have not yet been widely persuasive. Though proponents of an American Phillips curve had tough sledding at first— numerous other variables were held to: be important[19]—Perry's synthesis[20] of much of this early work did leave a quantitatively important role for the unemployment rate (as well as for the profit rate and the rate of change of prices) in explaining money wage movements in U.S. manufacturing. But in 1963 Bowen and Berry[21] found that the *decrease* of the unemployment rate was far more important than the level of the unemployment rate in contributing to wage increases. The more recent study of annual long-term wage data by Rees and Hamilton[22] also showed a negligible (and statistically insignificant) relation between the steady-state unemployment rate and the rate of wage increase (though wage-change effects on prices feed back strongly on wages in their equation). This evidence strongly supports the neo-Keynesian revival led by Sargan[23] and Kuh,[24] who make the level of the unemployment rate, together with productivity and the price level, determine the *level* of the money wage.[25] The underlying theory is apparently that a rise of aggregate demand creates "bottlenecks" and hence a rise of wage rates in certain areas and skills at the same time that it increases employment; once these bottlenecks have melted away and employment has reached its new and higher level there is no longer upward wage pressure. On this theory, money-wage increases go hand in hand with employment growth and not intrinsically with a high level of the employment rate.

Less frontal in a way but having equally profound policy implications is the second issue of the so-called stability of the Phillips curve. Continental economists like von

---

[18] At a constant price level and an unemployment rate of 2 percent, Lipsey's (op. cit.) 1862–1913 regression (his equation [10]) predicts a 2.58 percent wage increase annually while the 1929–1957 regression (his equation [13]) predicts a 1.65 percent annual increase. At the same 3 percent productivity growth in both periods, for example, price stability would have permitted smaller unemployment in the latter period. But Lipsey's Table 2 (p. 30) is evidence of the early Phillips curve's underestimation of the wage increases after World War II.

[19] W. G. Bowen, *Wage Behavior in the Postwar Period* (Industrial Relations Sec., Princeton, N.J., 1960); R. J. Bhatia, "Profits and the Rate of Change of Money Earnings in the United States, 1935–1959," *Economica*, 29 (August 1962), pp. 255–262; and O. Eckstein and T. Wilson, "The Determinants of Money Wages in American Industry," *Quarterly Journal of Economics*, 70 (August 1962), pp. 379–414.

[20] G. L. Perry, "The Determinants of Wage Rate Changes and the Inflation-Unemployment Trade-off for the U.S.," *Review of Economic Studies*, 31 (October 1964), pp. 287–308.

[21] W. G. Bowen and R. A. Berry, "Unemployment Conditions and Movements of the Money Wage Level," *Review of Economics and Statistics.*, 45 (May 1963), pp. 163–172.

[22] A. Rees and M. T. Hamilton, "The Wage-Price-Productivity Perplex," *Journal of Political Economics*, 75 (February 1967), pp. 63–70.

[23] J. D. Sargan, "Wages and Prices in the United Kingdom: A Study in Econometric Methodology," in P. E. Hart, G. Mills, and J. K. Whitaker, eds., *Econometric Analysis for Economic Planning: Sixteenth Symposium of the Colston Research Society* (Butterworth, London, 1964).

[24] E. Kuh, "A Productivity Theory of Wage Levels— An Alternative to the Phillips Curve," *Review of Economic Studies*, 34 (October 1967).

[25] If the *real* wage rate were made a rapidly increasing function of the employment rate, the Kuh–Sargan model could then produce (cost) inflation at low, yet aboveminimum, unemployment rates.

Mises[26] always emphasized the role of expectations in the inflationary process. In our own day, Fellner and Wallich are most closely associated with the proposition that the maintenance of too low an unemployment rate and the resulting continued revision of disappointed expectations will cause a runaway inflation. These ideas are reflected in the modern-day models of steady, "anticipated" inflation, begun by Lerner,[27] which imply (or assume) that high inflation confers no benefits in the form of higher employment if (or as soon as) the inflation rate is fully anticipated by firms and workers.[28] Recently, Friedman[29] and I[30] have sought to reconcile the Phillips hypothesis with the aforementioned axiom of anticipated inflation theory. I postulated that the Phillips curve, in terms of percentage price increase (or wage increase), shifts uniformly upward by one point with every one point increase of the expected percentage price increase (or expected wage increase). Then the *equilibrium* unemployment rate—the rate at which the actual and expected price increases (or wage increases) are equal—is independent of the rate of inflation. If one further postulates, as Friedman and I did, an "adaptive" or "error-

correcting" theory of expectations, then the persistent underestimation of price or wage increases which would result from an unemployment level consistently below the equilibrium rate would cause expectations continually to be revised upward so that the rate of inflation would gradually increase without limit; correspondingly, an increase of the *constant* rate of inflation, while "buying" a very low unemployment rate at first, would require a gradual rise of the unemployment rate toward the equilibrium rate as expectations of that inflation developed. Therefore, society cannot trade between steady unemployment and steady inflation, on this theory; it must eventually drive (or allow) the unemployment rate toward the equilibrium level or force it to fluctuate around that equilibrium level.[31]

This paper is addressed primarily to these two issues. The next section sketches the microeconomic lines of a modified excess-demand theory of disequilibrium wage movements. This is subsequently coupled to a model of employment dynamics to show why, given expectations, both the level of unemployment *and* the rate of change of employment should be expected to be correlated with money wage movements. The last section introduces the influence of expected wage changes upon the Phillips curve.

[26] L. von Mises, *The Theory of Money and Credit* (Yale University Press, New Haven, 1953).

[27] A. P. Lerner, "The Inflationary Process—Some Theoretical Aspects," *Review of Economics and Statistics*, 31 (August 1949), pp. 193–200.

[28] Lerner ("Employment Theory and Economic Policy") now recants. My paper, "Anticipated Inflation and Economic Welfare," *Journal of Political Economy*, 73 (February 1965), pp. 1–17, contains many of the references. Two recent money-and-growth models which study the consequences of alternative anticipated price trends are those by J. Tobin, "Money and Economic Growth," *Econometrica*, 33 (October 1965), pp. 671–684, and M. Sidrauski, "Rational Choice and Patterns of Growth in a Monetary Economy," *American Economic Review: Papers and Proceedings*, 57 (May 1967), pp. 534–544.

[29] M. Friedman, "Comment," in G. P. Shultz and R. Z. Aliber, eds., *Guidelines, Informal Controls, and the Market Place* (University of Chicago Press, Chicago, 1966).

[30] E. S. Phelps, "Phillips Curves, Expectations of Inflation and Optimal Unemployment over Time," *Economica*, 34 (August 1967), pp. 254–281.

[31] On certain assumptions regarding preferences and other matters, I showed that society (or the world) would choose between an "overemployment" route *down* to the equilibrium employment rate (thus leaving a heritage of a high Phillips curve corresponding to inflationary expectations) and an "underemployment" route *up* to the equilibrium employment rate on the basis of "time preference." The role of time preference is illuminated by Friedman's characterization of "the true trade-off" (op. cit., p. 59) as one between "unemployment today and unemployment at a later date"; there is such an intertemporal trade-off in the model under discussion if one holds eventual inflation rates constant, in the same way that the Fisherian trade-off between consumption today and consumption tomorrow holds subsequent wealth or capital constant. But there remains at any moment of time a statical trade-off between unemployment and inflation (with the expected inflation rate a parameter), analogous to the statical trade-off between consumption and capital formation (with initial capital stock a parameter), which lies at the roots of the intertemporal trade-off.

2. TURNOVER AND "GENERALIZED EXCESS DEMAND"

For most of this section, until labor unions are fitted into the framework developed, the analysis will be confined to an "atomistic" labor market. This means that there is no collective bargaining between unions and firms. It will also be supposed that each worker is a "wage-taker."

But the labor market here is not perfectly competitive. I exclude any Walrasian auctioneer who, by collecting information on everyone's supply and demand data, might be capable of keeping the labor market in a full information, full employment equilibrium. Lacking anyone else to do so, each firm must set its own wage rates. Because suppliers of labor lack detailed information about each firm's wage rates, the individual firm has *dynamic monopsony power:* Given its other recruitment efforts, such as help-wanted advertising, the higher the wage rates it sets relative to other firms' wage rates, the faster will it attract labor. The effect of such a wage differential is "dynamic" and gradual because the diffusion of the wage information through the market takes time.[32] In a world where lives are short and information costs are high, the firm may have to pay a permanently higher wage differential the greater the employment force it wishes to sustain; but such *statical* monopsony power is not critical to the analysis that follows.[33]

The incompleteness of information arises partially from the diversity of economic experience. Even if jobs and workers were "technically" homogeneous—that is, even if every worker were to regard all firms and jobs as identical in their nonpecuniary rewards and every firm were to regard all workers as productivity equivalent—the presence of ever-changing product-demand shifts, nonuniform technological progress, or uneven labor-force growth would suffice to produce some dispersion in wage rates. Workers recognize, then, that their own experience with wage offers is not to be projected to other workers and other firms. Hence workers may reject wage offers, accepting unemployment in order more easily to search for better wage offers. The expectation of dispersion of wage rates by suppliers of labor causes positive unemployment to be normal.

The existence of unemployment need not spell deflation of this world. Because the demand for labor is normally growing, owing to productivity growth and because employed workers are always retiring, quitting, or dying, firms will normally be seeking to add new employees at some positive rate. When unemployment workers are sufficiently few, the firm cannot succeed in attracting new employees unless it keeps up its wage rate relative to workers' expectations of other wage rates. Only if there were complete information, so that unemployed workers would instantaneously find the best wage and in so doing bid it down, would positive unemployment—when it fleetingly appeared—necessarily drive money wage rates to lower levels.

The time that firms require to attract new employees, even when there is some unemployment, is reflected by the presence, normally, of job "vacancies." A firm may be said to have job vacancies when the quantity of labor that it would decide to employ (at the expected average wage) *if there were complete information*—i.e., no need for capital-type information outlays in the form of temporarily higher wage rates, help-wanted advertising, and so on for the acquisition of labor—exceeds the quantity of labor it in fact has on hand under the actual informational conditions. Where vacancies are especially large, firms will pay wage rates above the expected average rate elsewhere. The

---

[32] Somewhat similarly, if the firm allows its wage rates to fall relative to what workers believe average wage rates to be, it will not expect to lose all its workers instantaneously. Some employees may engage in on-the-job search for a better paid job before quitting. The expected duration of the fall of the differential is also a factor, one not included in the formal model.

[33] At one point, in the discussion of quit rates, it is useful to appeal to incomplete information in another dimension. Some firms may ration jobs much of the time, turning away workers who would be willing to accept jobs at wage rates below those paid to its employed workers. In this event, the worker will lack complete information not only about the wage rates that each firm is paying but also about the availability of jobs at each firm.

finding of these wage rates by some of the unemployed helps to remove workers from the unemployment pool as new workers enter it; unemployed workers are not systematically and invariably disappointed and thus not led invariably to revise downward their asking wage rates. Secondly, the firm that pays a wage equal to the expected average wage elsewhere, because it is "at rest," content with attracting its "fair share" from the unemployed pool and from other firms, also has vacancies on the above definition. When the firm is "at rest," it would still gain from the free delivery of some additional employees (up to the zero vacancy point) even if each had to be paid the firm's estimate of the average wage but it does not aim to fill those vacancies because of the interest cost of the capital-type outlays it believes to be required. Positivity of vacancies, even for the representative firm in normal times, like the positivity of unemployment in normal times, signalizes the cost to both employer and worker of reaching one another under incomplete information.[34]

Yet, if jobs and workers were technically homogeneous, information costs would be less important than this paper takes them to be. Firms could cheaply announce their daily wage rates in the "wage offers" section of the local newspaper. Workers could thus sample a great many wage rates each day without giving up employment to do so. At a small subscription fee, one could read weekly newsletter from employment advisory services that would digest regional wage movements and perhaps make "go," "leave," or "stay" recommendations about various regions. Information tends to be a great deal more imperfect when there is considerable

technical variety among jobs and among workers. The typical firm with heterogeneous labor requirements then has to generate more wage information to achieve the same recruitment performance. Moreover, wage information may travel more slowly if it is of only specialized interest.[35] A more important kind of heterogeneity is intra-"job." The nonpecuniary attributes of jobs in a certain category usually differ from firm to firm. In each job category, abilities and skills differ from worker to worker. As a consequence, interviewing is important and "search unemployment" is more valuable. Wage rates may be confidential, varying with the worker, so that the worker's information about alternative wage opportunities may be as seriously imperfect as his information about the nonpecuniary attributes of alternative jobs.

Analogous to the distinction between the "cost" and availability of credit is a distinction between the wage and the availability of jobs. "Job rationing" occurs when a worker is unable to find work at a firm despite his willingness to work for less than some already employed worker who is broadly like him in ability and skill. One reason, in part, why job rationing is prevalent is that workers want the promise of a degree of tenure in their jobs at the wage initially offered. They prefer this because there are frequently setup costs incurred by the individual in taking a new job, such as moving expenses; many, perhaps all, of these setup costs can be viewed as arising from the heterogeneity of jobs. By protecting workers from underbidding for the length of a "contract," the firm can normally enjoy wage savings, over the long run, compared to a

[34] One could, it is true, redefine vacancies in such a way that one nets out from marginal revenue productivity of labor the costs of holding employment at the firm constant relative to the firm's capital stock or to the total labor force so that vacancies are zero at the firm's "rest point," its steady-state target position. Similarly, one could define unemployment as the excess of unemployment above the "equilibrium" or "natural" level. For analyses of wage-marginal product relations at and away from the rest point, see the papers by Mortensen and by Phelps and Winter in original volume. See also Appendix 2.

[35] On the other hand, there may exist informational networks, formal or informal, among workers specializing in a certain job category; the sparseness of jobs in a certain category does not by itself raise the costs of sampling the corresponding wage offers to workers specializing in those categories, because the specialists may know where those offers are. But when rates are unacceptable in his otherwise preferred job category, many a worker will sometimes explore less familiar job categories where wage offers are not so easy for him to find.

policy that exposes its workers to the risk of wage fluctuations from underbidding. The second reason for job-rationing is the firm's preference for a predictable employment force (as distinct from the worker's preference for a more predictable wage). If the firm attempts to jiggle wage rates rapidly in accordance with changes in the supply of workers available to it or in its needs for workers, it will risk unexpectedly large quits in the case of wage reductions. The risk is costly because of the setup costs of hiring, rehiring, training, or retaining heterogeneous workers. The firm may find it expected-profit maximizing to delay the adjustment of its wage in response to changing supplies and demands, relying first, on refusal to hire and, second, on layoffs for "fine tuning" when buffer stocks of labor become too large.[36]

It is clear, then, that positive unemployment and positive vacancies can coexist and persist for every type of worker and job. In the more formal analysis that follows, I shall exclude serious bottlenecks in any job category in order to speak aggregatively of "the" wage rate, "the" unemployment rate, and "the" vacancy rate, as if these statistics were pretty much uniform over the categories of workers and jobs. The focus will be on the wage decisions and employment experience of "representative" firms—that is, some average of the population of firms.

The labor supply, L, is defined as the sum of unemployed and employed workers. Letting N denote the number of persons employed, and U the number of persons unemployed, we have

$$L = N + U. \qquad (1)$$

It will be supposed throughout that the size of this labor supply is a constant at each moment of time, independent of all prices, present and future, actual and expected, and independent of the availability of jobs. Because unemployed workers, by this supposition, prefer work to leisure whatever

the expected average real wage, we shall identify the unemployed as consisting of those actively searching for job offers acceptable to them.

Total labor demand, N_D, is defined as the number of workers that firms would accept for employment if an indefinitely large number of workers offered to work indefinitely at the wage rates that firms believe to be the going or average wage, given expected product prices, present and future, and expected real interest rates. N_D depends upon the technology, the currently expected "product wage" (net of interest and "depreciation" on the invesment outlays incurred in processing and training a new employee and calculated at the firm's planned product price), and, if the firm's price is fixed so as to generate inventories and queues, directly upon aggregate demand as well. Then, with jobs filled equal to the number of persons employed (no multiple job holding or part-time jobs), job vacancies, V, are given by

$$N_D = N + V. \qquad (2)$$

The concept of "excess demand" for labor, denoted X, is usually defined as

$$X = N_D - L. \qquad (3)$$

Hence, using (1) and (2),

$$X = V - U. \qquad (4)$$

The usual excess-demand theory of money wage dynamics states that the proportionate rate of change of the money wage is proportional to the excess demand *rate*, denoted x. The latter is excess demand per unit of labor supply, and hence equal to the excess of the vacancy rate, v, over the unemployment rate, u:

$$x = v - u, \quad x = \frac{X}{L}, \quad v = \frac{V}{L}, \quad u = \frac{U}{L}. \qquad (5)$$

A widespread rationale for the simple Phillips curve relation between wage change and the unemployment rate is that, at least in sectors or economies with little or no unionization, the unemployment rate is a good proxy for the excess-demand rate and that the latter largely explains wage movements (apart from aggregation phenomena

---

[36] In this variant of the non-Walrasian treatment of labor market, cyclical money wage increases represent to some degree the movement of workers to higher-paid (or, at any rate, preferred) job categories.

such as changes in the employment mix). Even if excess demand were the sole determinant of wage changes—this paper seeks to generalize that theory and to make it accommodate the influence of expectations— it is not obvious that the unemployment rate is a good proxy for it. What if, at times, the vacancy rate in (5) enjoys a life of its own, moving independently of the unemployment rate? (I shall later discuss the evidence on this.) Lipsey's paper brilliantly deduces from a model of employment dynamics a well-behaved relationship between the vacancy rate (hence the excess demand rate) and the *steady* unemployment rate. I shall show, however, using a similar model, that in the non-steady-state case the unemployment rate is an inadequate indicator of the excess-demand rate and that the rate of change of employment constitutes an essential additional indicator for inferring the excess-demand rate.[37]

[37] These two points can perhaps be understood simply from the following exercise: Draw a nonnegatively sloped labor-supply curve and a nonpositively sloped labor-demand curve in a Marshallian plane with the expected product wage on the vertical axis and units of labor on the horizontal axis. Consider now the locus of points corresponding to a given unemployment rate; this iso-unemployment-rate curve will lie to the left of the supply curve and will also be nonnegatively sloped. It is immediately obvious that if the demand curve is negatively sloped, or the supply curve positively sloped, then not all points on the locus represent equal algebraic excess demand; in particular, as we move down this locus from its intersection with the demand curve, vacancies and excess demand increase despite constancy of the unemployment rate. Thus the latter is not necessarily a sufficient proxy for excess demand. (This demonstration in no way contradicts the proposition that, *vacancy rate constant*, excess demand is decreasing in unemployment. The zero-vacancy, on-the-demand-curve case is a familiar example. This paper tries to get away from the supposition that we are always "on the demand curve," even the Keynesian demand curve arising from disequilibrium excess supply in commodity markets.)

As we consider situations of higher vacancies, the unemployment rate unchanged, we should expect the rate of increase of employment likewise to be higher, as employers seek to reduce vacancies through greater recruitment. The *two* pieces of information—the unemployment rate, and the rate of increase of employment— may together constitute a satisfactory proxy, or a better proxy, for excess demand.

The excess-demand explanation of wage movements calls for an underlying explanation. Why should it be expected that a one-unit increase of the vacancy rate always has the same wage effect as a one-unit decrease of the unemployment rate? Second, why should it be expected that most of the time, in the neighborhood of "equilibrium" (see Section 4), vacancies will equal unemployment and that a *disequilibrium* rise of wage rates requires vacancies to exceed unemployment? Why should unemployment have an effect? Why vacancies?

What follows is an attempt to rationalize a generalized excess-demand theory of money wage movements, one which is less restrictive than the simple excess-demand theory but which admits it as a special case, at least in steady states. It will be convenient to conduct the analysis in two stages: In the present section, "static" expectations of future money wage rates and product prices are postulated. By that is meant, loosely, that firms and workers expect that the average money wage prevailing in the near future will not differ from its present level or its level in the recent past, and similarly for prices. This does not mean, of course, that firms and workers do not revise over time their estimates of the past or present wage level as they observe or infer actual wage rates through time. In Section 4 the expected rate of change of the wage level will be allowed to differ from zero and to adapt to estimates of past rates of change.

We begin with the case in which each firm reviews its wage rate periodically—once a year, say. An equal number of firms, of the same average size, set wage rates each day throughout the year. This staggering of wage revisions makes the average wage move smoothly despite discrete changes in the determinants of each firm's optimal wage. The postulate that the "expected rate of wage change" is zero is most conveniently interpreted in this case as the proportionate difference between the expected average money wage one-half year hence (or over the next twelve months on average) and people's estimates of the average money wage one-half year ago (or over the past twelve months on average). The expected rate of change is thus "centered" on the current moment. In this model there is no need to suppose that events can cause people currently to mis-estimate the latter, past-average money wage level; even the current *average* money wage may be correctly estimated at the current time. But the possibility, in the model, that the average wage will steadily rise or steadily fall, together with the static expectations postulate, implies that the "expected rate of wage change" can differ from the actual rate of wage change.[38] The average wage six months hence may be misforecast. (I shall subsequently discuss briefly the case in which firms review wage rates continuously. In that limiting case, misestimation of the *current* average wage level does the work of mis-estimation of the average wage *one-half year hence* in the model with periodic wage setting.)

Consider the ith firm at wage-setting time. It will be convenient to express its optimal wage in terms of the proportionate differential it desires to have, say Δ_i^*, between its wage and the average money wage it expects to be paid elsewhere. That is,

$$\Delta_i^* \equiv \frac{w_i^* - w^e}{w^e}, \qquad (6)$$

where w_i^* is the firm's optimal wage and w^e is the average wage it expects to prevail one-half year hence. It will be supposed that workers and other firms, on average, have the same expectation of the future wage level, it being equal to their estimate of the mean wage one-half year ago.

One determinant of the desired wage differential is the firm's vacancies, V_i, cal-culated at the expected product wage, w^e/p, where p is the product price. An increase in the number of vacancies due either to a fall of the expected product wage or to a fall of the firm's current employment causes the firm to raise its desired differential in order to discourage quitting, to facilitate recruit-ment, and to encourage workers to seek

employment at the firm as they learn of the higher differential.[39] A larger proportion of those who sample the firm's wage are more likely to accept employment or to stay employed at the firm the higher is this differential; and a larger number of workers are likely to learn of the firm's wage and accept employment there the higher that differential. The magnitude of the desired differential corresponding to the number of vacancies depends upon the size of the unemployment rate, u, and the size of the total labor supply, L.

The role of the unemployment rate in the determination of the desired differential is more problematical. An increase of the un-employment rate eases recruitment at every wage differential the firm might set. This is because there will then be a larger flow to the firm of unemployed workers seeking acceptable employment; employed workers are not able to sample wage and employ-ment opportunities as intensively as the unemployed. Neglecting quit rates for the moment, we conclude that the firm can achieve the same rate of increase of employ-ment with a smaller wage differential the larger is the unemployment rate[40]; at the other extreme, the firm can have, for the same differential, a faster increase of its employment. It will be supposed that the firm "takes out" the gain part through a lower wage differential, though not so low that there is no increase in the current growth of the firm's employment.

When there is job rationing, the unemploy-ment rate will influence the quit rate expe-rienced by the firm, which, in turn, is likely to affect the firm's desired wage differential. A decrease of the unemployment rate, given the overall vacancy rate in the economy,

---

[38] This is the case studied in the previous version of this paper. See, especially, pages 688 and 698.

[39] It is supposed that new and old workers receive the same wage. The two sources of an increase of vacan-cies need not have precisely the same effect, so that the firm's current employment, N_i, should be allowed to have some effect, positive or negative, on the desired differential even for given V_i. This effect is neglected here.

[40] This is true for the indefinite future only to the extent that lifetimes are short enough that wage dis-crepancies can persist.

causes employees to expect to have to spend less time in the unemployment pool if they decide to seek a job opening elsewhere and thus encourages quitting. An increase of the quit rate corresponding to any wage will increase the wage differential the firm expects to require to maintain its employment force or to add to it at any given rate. It will be supposed that the firm responds to this situation with some increase of the wage differential, though not so much as to prevent some increase of quitting. Finally, the quit rate and, thereby, the wage differential will be affected in the same way by an increase of the overall vacancy rate in the economy, because the unemployment rate and vacancy rate together affect the mean duration of unemployment expected by anyone contemplating quitting and also the probability that employees will find job openings at other firms.

The above hypotheses state that

$$\Delta_i^* = j^i(u, v, V_i, L), \qquad j_1^i < 0,$$
$$j_2^i > 0, \quad j_3^i > 0. \tag{7}$$

It will be convenient to think of each firm as expanding its capital stock in proportion to the growing labor force in which case *relative* vacancies, v_i, indicates better the strength of the firm's desire for a faster (or slower) rate of growth of its employment force. If we neglect any informational economies of scale from a populous economy, we may then write

$$\Delta_i^* = k^i(u, v, v_i), \quad k_1^i < 0, \quad k_2^i > 0, \quad k_3^i > 0,$$
$$v_i = \frac{V_i}{L}. \tag{8}$$

If all firms are much alike, we can express the *average* desired wage differential, denoted Δ^*, as a function of the unemployment rate and of the aggregate vacancy rate, $v = \sum v_i$ [as given in (5)]:

$$\Delta^* = m(u, v), \qquad u, v > 0, \tag{9}$$

where

$$m_1 < 0, \qquad m_2 > 0 \tag{9a}$$

and, as conjectures,

$$m_{11} \gtreqqless 0, \quad m_{22} \gtreqqless 0, \quad m_{12} \lesseqqgtr 0. \tag{9b}$$

The restrictions on the second derivatives in (9b) are inessential; they affect only the curvature of the augmented Phillips curve to be derived. The inequality $m_{11} \geq 0$, meaning that Δ^* decreases with the unemployment rate at a nonincreasing rate, vacancy rate constant, is plausible if the quit rate is likewise convex with respect to the unemployment rate.[41] The inequality $m_{22} \geq 0$ is suggested by the hypothesis of "rising marginal costs" to the firm of filling vacancies by means other than raising its wage differential. Finally $m_{12} \leq 0$ makes sense if it takes a larger increase of the firm's wage differential to facilitate the filling of some fraction of a given increment in its vacancies the smaller is the unemployment pool from which workers can conveniently be drawn. The curve labeled $m(u, v) = 0$ in Figure 1 gives the combinations of u and v that makes $\Delta^* = 0$. Its slope, being $-m_2/m_1$, is necessarily positive, but the size of that slope and the curvature are indeterminate and of no qualitative consequence. To the right of this locus $\Delta^* > 0$, and to the left $\Delta^* < 0$.

Finally, it will be argued that, approximately, the rate of change of the average wage rate, w, is proportional to Δ^*:

$$\frac{\dot{w}}{w} = \lambda \Delta^*, \quad \lambda = \text{const.} > 0, \quad \dot{w} \equiv \frac{dw}{dt}. \tag{10}$$

It is clear that, in the present model of staggered wage setting, if Δ^* has been zero for some time and w has been level for some time, then w will go on being level if Δ^* remains equal to zero. If Δ^* should rise, then, with w^e the same as it was when firms last set their wage rates, firms setting wage rates today will raise their wage rates; the average wage will therefore gradually rise as more firms reach the respective dates of the year on which they reset their wage rates. At first the instantaneous rate of change of the average wage, expressed at an annual rate, will equal Δ^* (under uniform staggering). But soon resetting will be done by firms who have noticed the

[41] R. V. Eagly, "Market Power as an Intervening Mechanism in Phillips Curve Analysis," *Economica*, 32 (February 1965), pp. 48–64.

FIGURE 1

Relations between vacancy and unemployment rates.

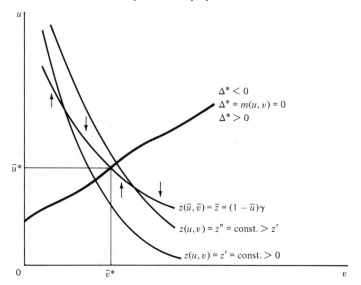

average wage at the midpoint of the expiring annual contract (i.e., the average wage six months ago) to be higher than the corresponding average wage when these firms previously set their wages, and *hence higher than these firms at that time expected the midcontract average wage would be.* Consequently, these firms must add a "catch-up" wage increase to the increase they would have otherwise found sufficient to obtain the increase in their desired wage differential. The average money wage will soon tend on this account to rise faster. But there is an offsetting and stabilizing tendency: The basic wage increases will have been completed by all the firms within a "year," so only the catch-up increases remain. As the current average wage grows faster, the catch-up wage increase by firms currently raising wages makes a smaller proportionate contribution to the rise of the current average wage because this increase is based on wage observations that are centered around some past time when the average wage was lower, and because the static-expectations assumption allows no extrapolation of the prevailing wage growth. Consequently, there exists a finite, asymptotic rate of wage increase corresponding to every positive Δ^*. Further, the asymptotic $\dot{w}/w$ is well approximated by (10) over the relevant range.

These propositions are demonstrated in Appendix 1. We will not go too far wrong in using (10) in and out of steady states in which u, v, and w/w^e are all constant.

One can explore the *dynamics* of the rate of wage change more conveniently if we consider a model of continuous wage setting. We retain the assumption of static expectations regarding the future trend of the average wage. Suppose, a little analogously to the staggered wage-setting model, that each firm's expectation of the current average wage level, denoted w^e, depends upon past actual values of the average wage, this time in the "adaptive" manner. Second, to maintain smoothness in wage behavior, let the ith firm adjust its wage in such a way that its expected wage differential, denoted by Δ_i^e, moves only gradually toward its "desired" differential, Δ_i^*.[42] Precisely, assume that

$$\dot{\Delta}_i^e = \mu(\Delta_i^* - \Delta_i^e), \qquad \mu > 0, \qquad \dot{\Delta}_i^e \equiv \frac{d\Delta_i^e}{dt}$$

$$(10'a)$$

---

[42] One defense of this device is that the firm may choose Δ_i^e according to estimates of the "permanent," "normal," or "near-term average," u^e, v^e, and v_i^e, and that the latter are revised adaptively in response to current u, v, and v_i.

FIGURE 2

Dynamics of expected wage differential and rate of wage change given Δ^*.

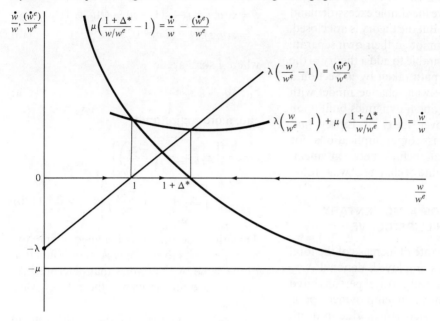

where

$$\Delta_i^e \equiv \frac{w_i - w_e}{w^e}, \qquad \Delta_i^* \equiv \frac{w_i^* - w^e}{w^e}$$

and assume that[43]

$$(\dot{w}^e) = \lambda(w - w^e), \qquad \lambda > 0. \qquad (10'b)$$

Then, upon expressing the derivative Δ_i^e in terms of $\dot{w}_i$ and $(\dot{w}^e)$ and solving for $\dot{w}_i$ we find

$$\frac{\dot{w}_i}{w_i} = \mu\left(\frac{\Delta_i^* - \Delta_i^e}{1 + \Delta_i^e}\right) + \frac{(\dot{w}^e)}{w^e},$$

where the last term is the continuous-time "catch-up" wage increase. For firms as a whole, using the adaptive-expectations relation, we then have

$$\frac{\dot{w}}{w} = \mu\left(\frac{\Delta^* - \Delta^e}{1 + \Delta^e}\right) + \lambda\Delta^e.$$

The dynamics of Δ^e, and hence of $\dot{w}/w$, is analyzed for a given Δ^* in Figure 2, where the

---

[43] The term $(\dot{w}^e)$ means the historical time rate of change of the expected (current) wage *level*, w_e. It must be distinguished from the currently *expected rate of change* over the future of the expected wage level. The latter is zero by virtue of the assumption of static expectations.

---

state variable is $w/w^e = 1 + \Delta^e$. From the relation

$$\frac{(w/w^e)}{w/w^e} = \frac{\dot{w}}{w} - \frac{(\dot{w}^e)}{w^e} = \mu\left(\frac{1 + \Delta^*}{w/w^e} - 1\right)$$

it follows that w/w^e approaches $1 + \Delta^*$ monotonically. In any steady state (constant Δ^e), therefore, $\Delta^e = \Delta^*$, which means that, in steady states, all the wage increases are purely "catch up." Denoting steady-state values of variables with a bar, we have

$$\frac{\overline{\dot{w}}}{w} = \lambda\overline{\Delta}^e = \lambda\Delta^*,$$

corresponding to any steady-state $m(\overline{u}, \overline{v})$. Out of the steady state, $\lambda\Delta^*$ may still be a good approximation. If $\mu = \lambda$, $\dot{w}/w$ varies little with Δ^e for small Δ^e. The direct influence of an increase of Δ^*, given Δ^e, upon the rate of wage increase wears off, but the resulting rise of Δ^e produces catch-up increases that replace that direct influence. Note, finally, that the finiteness of λ is crucial for the boundedness of $(\dot{w}/w)$. Section 4 will introduce a more general formulation of expectations.

Equations (9) and (10) constitute a generalized excess-demand theory of the rate of wage change when the expected rate of wage change is equal to zero. When $m(\cdot)$ takes the form $v - u$, we have the simple excess-demand theory: $\dot{w}/w = \lambda x$. But the theory is not closed, because u and v cannot go their own separate directions. It is desirable to add a theory of the effect of v on the path taken by u. Section 3 couples the above wage-change model with a theory of employment dynamics built upon some labor-turnover ideas of Lipsey (*loc. cit.*). The result is some implications for "momentary" relationships between unemployment and the rate of change of wage rates.

3. DERIVATION OF A MOMENTARY, AUGMENTED PHILLIPS CURVE

The absolute time rate of increase of the total number of persons employed, denoted $\dot{N} \equiv dN/dt$, consists of the number of persons hired per unit time from the unemployment pool, denoted R, less the departures (due to death and retirement) per unit time of employed persons from the labor force, denoted D, and the quitting of employees to join the unemployed in search of new jobs, denoted Q. This accounting ignores involuntary terminations and layoffs, which I shall not treat, and it assumes that entrants to the labor force first enter the unemployment pool before being hired. Of course, the accessions and separations of employed persons who transfer directly from one firm to another cancel out and do not add to $\dot{N}$. That is,

$$\dot{N} = R - D - Q. \tag{11}$$

I shall make the aggregate variables on the right-hand side of (11) depend only upon unemployment (or employment), vacancies, and the labor supply.

D will be made proportional to employment, δ being the factor of proportionality. To eliminate scale effects, I shall take new hires and quits to be homogeneous of degree one in unemployment, vacancies, and the labor supply. Hence

$$\dot{N} = R(U, V, L) - \delta N - Q(U, V, L),$$
$$R(U, V, L) = LR(u, v, 1), \tag{12}$$
$$Q(U, V, L) = LQ(u, v, 1).$$

Equivalently, defining $z \equiv \dot{N}/L$,

$$\begin{aligned} z &= R(u, v, 1) - \delta(1 - u) - Q(u, v, 1) \\ &= z(u, v), \qquad u, v > 0, \end{aligned} \tag{13}$$

where I shall argue

$$z_1 > 0, \qquad z_2 > 0 \tag{13a}$$

and, more conjecturally,

$$-z_2^{-2} \left\{ \left[z_{11} + z_{12}\left(\frac{-z_1}{z_2}\right) \right] z_2 \right.$$
$$\left. - \left[z_{21} + z_{22}\left(\frac{-z_1}{z_2}\right) \right] z_1 \right\} > 0. \tag{13b}$$

Thus the absolute rate of change of employment per unit labor supply is made a function of the same two variables that determine Δ^* and in so doing influence the rate of wage change.

What is the logic of the z function, in particular the role of the vacancy rate in that function? We ordinarily think of the level of labor input as determined by output, which in turn depends upon aggregate demand and productivity. There probably is a fairly tight relationship between man-hours and output (given productivity); but N is measured by the number of persons employed. In a labor market that is at least moderately tight, an increase of aggregate demand increases job vacancies. Firms respond initially to the increase of vacancies by lengthening hours worked per worker (including overtime), by more intensive use of "buffer" or "cushion" employees ("hoarded" labor), and by calls for extraordinary efforts on the part of employees. But these measures do not eliminate the job vacancies. Filling the additional vacancies requires finding additional employees, and finding new employees to fill new jobs takes time.[44] Firms will choose to take time for two reasons: because marginal recruit-

---

[44] Some of the new employees wanted can be acquired virtually instantaneously so that the response of N to aggregate demand is not entirely the gradual or continuous response that I have postulated.

ment costs are positive, it may pay the firm to wait for suitable persons to present themselves for employment; and because there may be "rising marginal recruitment costs,"[45] it will pay the firm to smooth its recruitment efforts over time.

Now the properties of the z function. In discussing the mechanisms by which u and v affect z, I shall rely primarily on the notion that firms, even in the aggregate, can shorten the duration of search unemployment, and thus add to employment, by intensifying non-wage recruitment efforts and by offering a larger "ration" of jobs.

It will be assumed that, the unemployment rate constant, the higher the vacancy rate, the greater is the rate at which firms will acquire unemployed workers; that is, $R_2 > 0$. A higher vacancy rate will induce more intensive recruitment, and it will increase the probability that any unemployed person contacting a firm will find a job open. This increase of accessions may itself induce more quits, as suggested in the paragraph preceding (6), so that $Q_2 > 0$ is possible. But it would be strange to find that the higher vacancy rate reduced employment growth on balance; any increase of quits will stimulate partially offsetting extra recruiting. Hence I postulate that $R_2 > Q_2 \geqq 0$, so that $z_2 = R_2 - Q_2 > 0$, for all u and v.

Clearly $R_1 > 0$ because, vacancy rate constant, the higher the unemployment rate, the greater is the flow to the firm of unemployed workers who can fill open jobs and the easier is recruitment. Since an increase of unemployment discourages quitting, $Q_1 < 0$. Hence $z_1 = R_1 + \delta - Q_1 > 0$.

Consider the dashed curves labeled $z =$ const. in Figure 1. Each depicts the locus of (u, v) combinations giving a particular value of z. The slope of such curves at any point is $-z_2/z_1 < 0$; as the unemployment rate is reduced, an increase of the vacancy rate is required to keep z constant. These z contours as drawn display strict convexity or "diminishing marginal rate of substitution," meaning that as the unemployment rate is reduced, the vacancy rate increases at an increasing rate along any contour. This convexity is the content of (13b).

The best rationale for this convexity is the presumption that $z_{21} = R_{21} - Q_{21} > 0$. This states that an increase of the vacancy rate has greater effect on employment growth the greater the unemployment rate. The primary basis for that assumption is that recruitment will be more difficult the smaller is unemployment (indeed, totally unsuccessful in the aggregate at zero unemployment), so that $R_{21} > 0$. It is plausible also that an increase of the vacancy rate has less effect, if it has any, upon quits the less tight the labor market, so that $Q_{21} \leqq 0$. (Since $z_{12} = z_{21}$, an equivalent view is that changes of the unemployment rate have greater impact upon z the greater the vacancy rate.) Second, we should expect that $z_{11} = R_{11} - Q_{11} \leqq 0$ on the two grounds that, vacancy rates constant, an increase of the *employment* rate reduces new hires at an increasing rate and that it increases quits at an increasing rate (or at least at nondecreasing rates).[46] Third, and most controversially, it might be argued that $z_{22} = R_{22} - Q_{22} \leqq 0$. $R_{22} < 0$ could result from a rising marginal recruitment cost schedule; given the unemployment rate, the new hire rate (R) might even approach an upper bound as the vacancy rate increased without limit. My guess is that $Q_{22} \geqq 0$, but, in any case, (13b) shows that the suggested signs here are merely sufficient for convexity.

It is possible to supplement the mechanism by which u and v control z somewhat along the lines suggested by Alchian[47] and

[45] That is, the additional recruitment or search costs necessary to increase by one the expected number of recruits per unit time may be greater if the firm is aiming at 500 recruits in a week than if it is aiming for only 10. This is a short-run cost curve in which we hold constant the size of the firm and its personnel office. Large firms are not implied to suffer disadvantages in recruitment.

[46] If quits *per employee* is linear in the employment rate, given the vacancy rate, then $Q(u, v, 1)$, that is, quits per unit labor supply, will be strictly convex with respect to the employment rate.

[47] "Information Costs, Pricing, and Resource Unemployment," this volume.

Mortensen.[48] Consider the staggered wage-setting model. Suppose that workers share the expectations of firms as to the average wage that will prevail one-half year hence, denoted $w^e(t)$. Then, in any steady state in which $\Delta^* > 0$, we have $w(t) > w^e(t)$; average wage offers at the current time will be regarded as higher than can be found, on the average, in months ahead; sampled wage rates will be regarded as abnormally and temporarily high, so that search unemployment will be shorter, quit rates smaller on that account, and the unemployment rate lower. Under continuous wage setting, $\Delta^* > 0$ also implies $w(t) > w^e(t)$, where the latter then means the expected *current* wage. In this case it is the underestimate by workers of the *current* average wage that lowers the unemployment rate, but in the same way. In steady states, therefore, one could write

$$Z(u, v) = R(u, v, 1, u \cdot \lambda m(u, v)) - \delta(1 - u)$$
$$- Q(u, v, 1, (1 - u) \cdot \lambda m(u, v)) \quad (13')$$

without necessarily jeopardizing (13a) and (13b). In particular, $R_4 > 0$ and $Q_4 < 0$ leaves the critical z_2 positive. I shall stick with (13) for the moment and discuss subsequently the outlines of a fuller dynamic model in which neither (10) nor (13) hold except in steady states.

We can now combine (9), (10), and (13) to obtain an augmented Phillips curve in terms of the easily observed variables u and z. Since z_2 is one-signed, (13) implicitly defines v as a single-valued function of u and z, say,

$$v = \psi(u, z), \quad (14)$$

whence

$$\frac{\dot{w}}{w} = \lambda m[u, \psi(u, z)] = f(u, z), \quad (15)$$

which is our augmented Phillips curve. Since to every (u, z) pair there corresponds a unique v, there exists a derived Phillips-like relation between $\dot{w}/w$ and (u, z) pairs.

We can establish the properties of f after determining how v varies with u and z.

[48] A Theory of Wage and Employment Dynamics," this volume.

$$\psi_1 = \frac{-z_1[u, \psi(u, z)]}{z_2[u, \psi(u, z)]} < 0,$$

$$\psi_2 = \frac{1}{z_2[u, \psi(u, z)]} > 0,$$

$$\psi_{11} = -z_2^{-2}\left\{\left[z_{11} + z_{12}\left(\frac{-z_1}{z_2}\right)\right]z_2\right.$$
$$\left. - \left[z_{21} + z_{22}\left(\frac{-z_1}{z_2}\right)\right]z_1\right\} > 0, \quad (16)$$

$$\psi_{22} = -z_2^{-3}z_{22} \gtreqless 0 \quad (?),$$

$$\psi_{21} = -z_2^{-2}\left[z_{21} + z_{22}\left(\frac{-z_1}{z_2}\right)\right] < 0 \quad (?)$$

The last two inequalities are based on the guesses discussed *in connection* with (13b), while the first three inequalities follow from (13a) and (13b).

Now we can deduce the following restrictions on the augmented Phillips curve:

$$f_1(u, z) = \lambda(m_1 + m_2\psi_1) < 0,$$
$$f_{11}(u, z) = \lambda(m_{11} + m_{12}\psi_1 + m_{22}\psi_1^2$$
$$+ m_{22}\psi_{11}) > 0,$$
$$f_2(u, z) = \lambda m_2 \psi_2 > 0, \quad (17)$$
$$f_{22}(u, z) = \lambda(m_{22}\psi_2^2 + m_2\psi_{22}) \gtreqless 0 \quad (?),$$
$$f_{21}(u, z) = \lambda[(m_{21} + m_{22}\psi_1)\psi_2$$
$$+ m_2\psi_{21}] < 0 \quad (?).$$

The first result states that every constant-z Phillips curve is negatively sloped: Decreased unemployment directly adds pressure on wage differentials, and this effect is reinforced by the concomitant increase of vacancies which is deducible from the constancy of z in the face of decreased unemployment. The second result states that this constant-z relation between the rate of wage change and the unemployment rate is strictly convex, as the Phillips curve is ordinarily drawn; as the unemployment rate is decreased by equal amounts the vacancy rate must increase at an increasing rate to keep z constant, by virtue of (13b), which implies $\psi_{11} > 0$, so that even in the simple excess-demand case [in which the second derivatives in (9b) are equal to zero] the rate of wage increase itself increases at an increasing rate. As for the third result, $f_2 > 0$, the higher is employment growth, the unemployment rate constant, the higher must be the vacancy rate and hence the greater the upward pressure on the money wage. Thus the association between high employment growth and high wage gains, known as the Phillips-Lipsey "loop," is consistent with the excess-demand or generalized excess-demand theory of the Phillips curve.[49] The convexity of this relation between wage change and z is not certain because it involves the problematical ψ_{22}. Finally, there is a negative interaction between u and z, meaning $f_{21} < 0$, if my guess is right that z_{21} is strongly positive; this interaction means that a given increase of z signifies a greater increase of the vacancy rate the smaller is the unemployment rate.

The variables u and z cannot go their own way for long since a high (low) z implies a falling (rising) u. There is, therefore, some interest in the "steady-state" Phillips curve that relates the rate of wage increase to alternative, *constant* values of the unemployment rate. Let us take the proportionate rate of growth of the labor supply to be a nonnegative constant, γ. Then, corresponding to any *steady-state* unemployment rate, to be denoted $\bar{u}$, there is a steady $\bar{z}$ and a steady $\bar{v}$ which obey the relation

$$\bar{z} = z(\bar{u}, \bar{v}) = \frac{N}{L}\frac{\dot{N}}{N} = \frac{N}{L}\frac{\dot{L}}{L} = (1 - \bar{u})\gamma, \quad \gamma \gtreqqless 0. \tag{18}$$

If $\gamma > 0$, then clearly $\bar{z}$ must be higher the smaller $\bar{u}$. This relation also yields a locus of steady-state $(\bar{u}, \bar{v})$ points, which is shown in Figure 1 by the solid, downward sloping curve intersecting (from below) the dashed-line iso-z contours. This locus is negatively sloped and flatter than the z contours, for as steady-state $\bar{u}$ is decreased, $\bar{v}$ must increase not only enough to keep z constant but to increase z to the required level implied by (18). Referred to the *vertical axis*, the slope is

$$\frac{d\bar{v}}{d\bar{u}} = \frac{-(z_1 + \gamma)}{z_2} < 0. \tag{19}$$

At least for sufficiently small γ, the locus will be convex like the z contours:

$$\frac{d^2\bar{v}}{d\bar{u}^2} = -z_2^{-2}\left\{\left[z_{11} + z_{12}\left(\frac{-z_1 - \gamma}{z_2}\right)\right]z_2\right.$$
$$\left. - \left[z_{21} + z_{22}\left(\frac{-z_1 - \gamma}{z_2}\right)\right](z_1 + \gamma)\right\}$$
$$> 0 \quad (?). \tag{20}$$

It is not surprising, therefore, that our steady-state Phillips curve, $f[\bar{u}, (1 - \bar{u})\gamma]$, is negatively sloped and steeper than the constant-z Phillips curves:

$$\frac{\partial f[\bar{u}, (1 - \bar{u})\gamma]}{\partial \bar{u}} = f_1 - f_2\gamma < 0. \tag{21}$$

Also we find

$$\frac{\partial^2 f[\bar{u}, (1 - \bar{u})\gamma]}{\partial \bar{u}^2} = f_{11} - f_{12}\gamma$$
$$- (f_{21} - f_{22}\gamma)\gamma > 0 \quad (?) \tag{22}$$

so there is some presumption of convexity (and certainly for small enough γ) in the steady-state curve as well as the constant-z-curve. These results are depicted in Figure 3,

FIGURE 3
Augmented Phillips curves and the steady-state equilibrium locus.

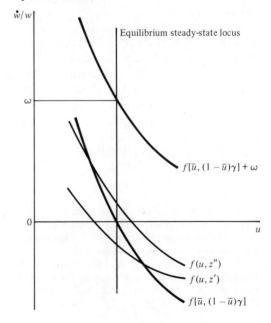

[49] The lagged response of u to an increase of v produces counterclockwise loops. But the analysis of wage expectations in Section 4 implies the possibility of clockwise loops.

which shows two constant-z Phillips curves and the steeper steady-state Phillips curve.

It might be noted that the steady-state Phillips curve is higher the greater the labor force growth rate; that is, $\partial f/\partial \gamma > 0$ for $\bar{u} < 1$. The reason is that faster growth of the labor supply requires a larger z and hence a larger vacancy rate to hold steady any given unemployment rate. This is an interesting testable implication of the theory.

Are there direct tests of the above theory of the augmented Phillips curve?[50] Quarterly British vacancy data have been prepared by Dow and Dicks-Mireaux.[51] Their study shows a scatter diagram of U and V points which, after 1950 or so, cluster around a convex, negatively sloped curve like the z contours or the steady-state locus in Figure 1. This is encouraging support for the *long-run* implications of (13) and (18). But my theory denies a strict and simple short-run relation between the unemployment rate *level* and the vacancy rate level. (Otherwise, the unemployment rate would suffice as an indicator of generalized excess demand.)

In its unadulterated form, the employment dynamics model here implies that unemployment and vacancy levels together determine the rate of change of employment and, hence, given γ, the *rate of change* of the unemployment rate. The differential equation is

$$-\dot{u} = z(u, v) - (1 - u)\gamma. \tag{23}$$

This says that if, at the prevailing u, v exceeds the corresponding $\bar{v}$ on the steady-state locus, so that $z > \bar{z} = (1 - u)\gamma$, then u will be falling (and vice versa if v is less than the corresponding $\bar{v}$). See the arrows in Figure 1.

The British data, despite being quarterly, offer a striking example that u can fall because v is high even though v is falling, which sup-

ports the emphasis on the level of v, rather than its rate of change, as a determinant of $\dot{u}$. After a sharp rise of vacancies that reduced unemployment, the latter went on falling in the second half of 1955 when vacancies had leveled off and proceeded to fall.[52] Indeed, the early postwar years in general showed a long-run trend of falling unemployment coinciding with falling vacancies. On the other hand, cyclical turning points usually occurred in the same quarter, so perhaps one should not totally neglect the rate of change of vacancies as a determinant of unemployment movements.

In the United States one has to make do with the Help-wanted Advertising Index in *Business Cycle Developments*.[53] In a recent study of this index, Cohen and Solow[54] in effect regressed the value of this index on the unemployment rate and the "new hire rate." Now (23) implies that v is a decreasing function both of u and $\dot{u}$, since points above the steady-state locus will be associated with falling u. It is of some interest, therefore, that the new hire rate, which may be a proxy for $-\dot{u}$, entered positively in that regression and the unemployment rate negatively; further, study of the residuals showed vacancies to be underestimated by this regression in cyclical phases of falling unemployment.[55]

A hasty study of the monthly data on aggregate unemployment and vacancies in Australia also appears to give some support

---

[52] *Ibid.*, p. 3, Fig. 1B.

[53] U.S. Department of Commerce. *Business Cycle Developments* (monthly).

[54] M. S. Cohen and R. M. Solow, "The Behavior of Help-Wanted Advertising," *Review of Economics and Statistics*, 49 (February 1967), pp. 108–110.

[55] Cohen and Solow (op. cit., *p.* 109) wrote: "The residuals [from this regression] progressively underestimated [the help-wanted index] in the course of upswings and overestimated during downswings, the error getting worse in the course of each one-way movement." Apart from the progressivity, this constitutes additional support for the theory. As for the progressivity, the authors suggest that "formal advertising is treated as something of a last-resort method of recruitment." This means, I take it, that the help-wanted advertising index is not a totally satisfactory measure of job vacancies.

---

[50] All the empirical evidence to be cited was consulted after I had arrived at an almost identical model in the first (unpublished) version of this paper, so that this evidence permits a real test of the model.

[51] J. C. R. Dow and L. A. Dicks-Mireaux, "The Excess Demand for Labor: A Study of Conditions in Great Britain, 1946–56," *Oxford Economic Papers*, 10 (February 1958), pp. 1–33.

FIGURE 4

Dynamics of expected wage differential and unemployment rate given the vacancy rate.

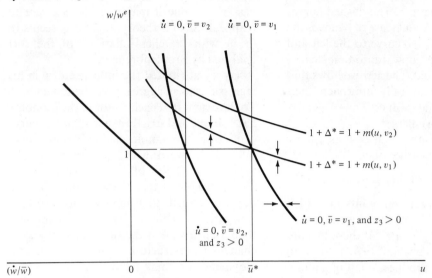

to the present model.[56] After dividing U and V by a geometrically rising series that approximates the growth of the labor supply, I used a standard program to deseasonalize the resulting unemployment and vacancy rates. One of the best regression results was the following:

$$\log v_t = 9.76 - 0.95 \log u_t - 0.35 \log\left(\frac{u_{t+1}}{u_t}\right),$$
$$\qquad\quad (44.10) \qquad\quad (2.40)$$

$$\bar{R}^2 = 0.925,$$
$$\text{DW} = 0.15, \qquad\qquad\qquad\qquad (24)$$

where the numbers in parentheses are t-ratios and v_t and u_t denote an average of the seasonally adjusted percentage vacancy rate and unemployment rate, respectively, in month t and month $t + 1$ (multiplied by 100). Both coefficients have the predicted signs and are highly significant. The serial correlation is fearsome, but that is due partially to the monthly averaging. When only even-numbered observations were run, the Durbin–Watson statistic rose to 0.35 and the t-ratio for $\log(u_{t+1}/u_t)$ rose to 3.17, with no appreciable change in the coefficients. On the

whole, these explorations offer hope of good results from a careful econometric analysis.[57]

Before we leave the analytics of the Phillips curve, let me sketch a more general analysis that (a) does not require the generalized excess-demand equation in (10) to hold out of steady states, and (b) allows w/w^e to influence z independently. The more general analysis is too complicated for any results as simple as (17), but it is more general!

Section 2 made w/w^e a "state variable" that responds gradually to Δ^*, hence to u and v. Section 3 makes u a state variable also responding to v. Figure 4 is a phase diagram in terms of both of these state variables, with $\bar{v}$ a parameter subject to the government's fiscal and monetary control.

Consider the flatter solid curves on the right-hand side of Figure 4, each one corresponding to a different value of $\bar{v}$. Each curve indicates, for every u, that value of $w/w^e = 1 + \Delta^*$ such that w/w^e is steady. The ordinate of this curve is therefore $1 + \Delta^* = 1 + m(u, v)$, so that the curve is negatively sloped on the assumption $m_1 < 0$. Each of the steeper curves indicates, for every value of w/w^e, that value of u such that u is steady. Now if z

---

[56] I am grateful to Peter Burley for providing me with these data and to Arthur Donner and Steven Salop for carrying out these calculations.

[57] When the regression is turned around to make $\log(u_{t+1}/u_t)$ the dependent variable, the t-ratios remained significant though the R^2 was much lower.

depends only upon v, as in (11), independently of $\dot{w}/w^e$, the latter curves are vertical with intercept decreasing in $\bar{v}$. The dashed curves illustrate this case. An increase of $\bar{v}$ moves the pertinent dashed $\dot{u} = 0$ curve to the left and the pertinent $1 + \Delta^*$ upward, so that steady-state w/w^e is increased. The arrow shows that u and w/w^e monotonically approach their respective steady-state values. Thus a steady-state Phillips curve emerges.

If z depends upon w/w^e as well as upon v and u, as discussed earlier, then

$$0 = -u = z(u, v, w/w^e) - (1 - u)\gamma \qquad (23')$$

gives the locus of $(\bar{u}, w/w^e)$ points for which $\dot{u} = 0$ for given v. Each such locus has the negative slope $- (z_1 + \gamma)/z_3$. If these loci are steeper than the constant (w/w^e) loci, an increase of $\bar{v}$ again produces a fall of u and a rise of w/w^e toward their new steady-state values. So, in this case, a steady-state Phillips curve once again emerges. It can be seen that if v has no influence upon the $\dot{u} = 0$ locus except through its eventual effect upon w/w^e, a "pure" Alchian–Mortensen view, a rise of $\bar{v}$ and hence Δ^* still reduces u and increases w/w^e, despite the absence of any accompanying leftward shift of the $\dot{u} = 0$ locus.

Let me now try informally and briefly to open the model to some other factors. The "bottleneck" theory also helps to explain why wage increases should be associated with rapidly *increasing* employment. An economy adjusted to one level of aggregate demand, with its peculiar structure, cannot adapt instantaneously to a higher aggregate demand level with its new structure; certain types of labor will be in excess demand, and this will drive up the general wage index. Hansen's model[58] emphasizes that excess supplies of other types of labor, even if they sum to a figure in excess of the total of excess demands, need not hold down the wage index if wages are stickier downward than upward. In the usual bottleneck theory, however, the resulting change in wage structure will dissolve the bottlenecks, so that a low *level* of unem-

ployment is not *ultimately* or *persistently* inflationary. It takes another slump and the passage of time if major bottlenecks are to reappear. Such a theory, therefore, seems to fit in with "ratchet inflation" of the sort analyzed by Bronfenbrenner.[59]

Lipsey attributed the influence of $\dot{u}$ in his regressions to an aggregation phenomenon.[60] To the extent that each sector of the economy has a simple and strictly convex Phillips curve of its own, the simple macro Phillips curve will shift upward with an increase in the sectoral inequality of unemployment rates. Lipsey suggested that these inequalities are worse in upturns than in downturns, so that a negative $\dot{u}$ tends to be more inflationary than a positive $\dot{u}$ at the same u. In any case, changes in the structure of vacancy and unemployment rates may be important.

What about unions? As a starting point, one might suppose the union to maximize the welfare of its members. In that case the union's wage objectives will be determined by real income opportunities outside the union. It will study and forecast the wage differential between union jobs and jobs that members could get elsewhere, weighing also the expected time required to get jobs elsewhere, hence unemployment rates and vacancy rates in the relevant areas and occupations. The average wage differential desired by unions thus depends upon our pervasive u and v. At sufficiently small unemployment rates or large vacancy rates, the unions, just like individuals and firms, desire incompatibly wage differentials, and the general index of wage rates will therefore rise.[61]

[58] B. Hansen, "Full Employment and Wage Stability," in J. T. Dunlop, ed., *The Theory of Wage Determination* (St. Martin's Press, New York, 1957).

[59] M. Bronfenbrenner, "Some Neglected Implications of Secular Inflation," in K. K. Kurihara, ed., *Post-Keynesian Economics* (Rutgers University Press, New Brunswick, N.J., 1954).
[60] Lipsey, op. cit., pp. 21–23.
[61] This ties in somewhat with Keynes' (op. cit., pp. 14–15) emphasis on the relative wage: "Every trade union will put up some resistance to a cut in money-wages [since such reductions 'are seldom or never of an all-round character']. But ... no trade union would dream of striking on every occasion of a rise in the cost of living." See also J. R. Hicks, "Economic Foundations of Wage Policy," *Economic Journal*, 65 (September 1955), pp. 389–404. I should think, however, that the desired relative wage is dependent on labor-market conditions.

4. EXPECTATIONS AND MACROEQUILIBRIUM

In Sections 2 and 3 it was postulated that each firm expects other firms to pay the same wage on the average over the future that was known (or believed) to have been paid in the recent past. In that case, it is natural for the firm to assume that an increase in its wage rates would attract more employees and discourage quitting, because it would expect any increase of its wage to increase its wage differential. But in the general case the firm may forecast wage changes elsewhere. How does this generalization affect the previous results?

Consider the following heuristic argument. Let each firm expect with certainty that the average wage paid elsewhere will change at a certain proportionate rate over the life of the firm's wage contract. Consider now a firm whose vacancy rate (v_i) in relation to labor-market conditions (u and v) is such that, in the absence of wage changes elsewhere, it would want to keep its present wage rate to maintain its expected wage differential at its present actual level; this firm is in equilibrium in the sense that its actual wage differential equals its desired differential. But if the firm in fact expects the average wage elsewhere to be increasing at the rate of 2 percent annually and it expects other firms to pass on the higher costs through a 2 percent rise of prices annually, then it will want to raise its wage rates by 2 percent annually; for it will calculate that it can raise its prices by 2 percent without loss of customers and thus leave unchanged its real position, that is, its real sales, its product wage and vacancy rate, and its competitiveness in the labor market. As for the disequilibrium case, if its vacancy rate and labor market conditions are such that in the absence of expectation of wage changes elsewhere it would want to raise its wage by 1 percent, say, it will, under the above expectations, want in fact to raise its wage by 3 percent for the next year. Upon averaging over firms we are then led to the proposition that we must add the expected rate of wage change, denoted $(\dot{w}/w)^e$, to the rate of wage change that would occur under static wage expectations, to determine the actual rate of wage change per annum:

$$\frac{\dot{w}}{w} = \lambda\Delta^* + \left(\frac{\dot{w}}{w}\right)^e = f(u, z) + \left(\frac{\dot{w}}{w}\right)^e. \tag{25}$$

The result is quite natural. By "equilibrium," following Hayek, Lindahl, Harrod, and others (using varied terminology), we generally mean a path along which the relevant variables work out as people think they will. A necessary labor-market condition for what might be called a *macroequilibrium* in terms of the relevant averages and aggregates is therefore equality of the expected and actual rate of change of the average wage rate:

$$\frac{\dot{w}}{w} = \left(\frac{\dot{w}}{w}\right)^e. \tag{26}$$

Hence macroequilibrium entails

$$f(u, z) = \Delta^* = m(u, v) = 0, \tag{27}$$

meaning that generalized excess demand for labor, as measured by $m(u, v)$, be equal to zero. Any other condition would be disturbing! Note that this equilibrium admits a rising or falling average money wage. It is an egregious error to say that rising wages, or rising anything else, implies excess demand.

The fundamental result in (25) needs further interpretation and defense. First there is a matter of dating the variables. Consider again the model in which wage negotiations are annual and are evenly staggered (across firms) over the year. Consider a firm negotiating at the beginning of the calender year. Suppose it expects average wage rates *in the future* to rise steadily at the rate of 2 percent per annum. Suppose the wage index is 100 at the beginning of the year and has been at 100 for a year. Then the firm will expect the index to stand approximately at 101 by midyear. By raising its wage by just 1 percent, the firm can expect to maintain on the average over its new contract its past average competitiveness with other employers over the old contract. We appear to get only a 1 percent wage rise resulting from a 2 percent expected rise of the index. The resolution of this puzzle already hinted at in Section 2, consists of defining $(\dot{w}/w)^2$ as the expected rate of change of the index from six months prior to the firm's wage negotiation to six months after the wage negotiation, so that it is centered on the date of the firm's wage decision. In our example, therefore, the "expected rate of wage change" so defined is really only 1 percent. If, in the following year, the expected rate of wage change (2 percent) is unaltered and this year's expectations are borne out—so that the index will next year be expected to rise from approximately 101 (at last midyear) to approximately 103 (at the next midyear)—our firm must then raise its wage by 2 percent if it expects to stay as competitive as before with other employers. This matter is possibly of some econometric significance; the above example suggests that a perfect proxy for the expected *future* rate of wage change will tend to enter a regression equation resembling (25) with a less-than-unitary coefficient; it is only the expected rate of wage change as defined here that is predicted to enter such an equation with a unitary coefficient.[62]

There is a question of why the expected rate of wage change should enter in (25) to the exclusion of the expected price change. As I shall shortly argue, the expectation of price increases affects money wages only *through* its effects on expected vacancy rates and the expected unemployment rate. *Given the latter*, a rise of the expected rate of inflation will have little or no effect upon the wage increase that a firm grants if it expects other firms to hold the line on the money wage rates they pay; in particular, the threat of an employee expecting a rise of the cost of

living to quit in search of another job will be empty if it is not expected that other firms' wages will rise with the cost of living. Whether Keynes was right that unions, too, are interested only in *relative* wages is hard to tell, but cost-of-living clauses are not very widespread in this country and have apparently never ranked very high among union objectives.

If the above result is to be really satisfactory, however, it must hold when the expected price trend is flat as well as in the case where producers can expect to pass on their wage increase in higher prices with impunity. Probably (25) *is* too simple; a full analysis requires a theory of the optimal price dynamics of the firm. Yet I am prepared to defend it as a tolerable approximation along the following lines. Continue to abstract from productivity growth and consider a firm at wage-setting time with flat price expectations. The vacancy rate of this firm, v_i, is to be calculated at a wage equal to the firm's expectation of the average money wage elsewhere at midcontract, six months hence. Imagine that *if the expected rate of wage change is zero*, the firm will find that its v_i, so calculated, would not prompt it to raise its wage. This means that its desired differential, $\Delta_i^* = k^i(u, v, v^i)$, is equal to its past wage differential at midcontract, Δ_i. As a second situation, suppose now that, *other things equal*, the firm expects a 1 percent rate of wage increase (as defined earlier, from midcontract to midcontract). Because its price expectations are flat, it does not expect to be able to raise its prices by an additional 1 percent without loss of customers. It will not raise its price that much. Therefore, when the firm evaluates its vacancy rate at the higher expected product wage, it will find its expected vacancy rate smaller in this second situation, so that its $\Delta_i^* = k^i(u^e, v^e, v_i^e)$ is less than its previous average wage differential, Δ_i. This means that while the firm may raise its wage it will raise it less than 1 percent in order to reduce its expected differential. To the extent that this second situation is general among firms, we will have a smaller $m(u, v)$. Firms will recruit less so that z and hence $f(u, z)$

[62] The left-hand-side variable is likewise the rate of change of the actual wage index expressed at annual rates. If wage negotiations are evenly distributed over the year, the firms setting wages in January, by raising their wage rates 1 percent, will raise the index by one-twelfth of 1 percent from its December level and hence by 1 percent at an annual rate. Where annual wage negotiations are unevenly distributed over the year (producing some seasonality), one may want to work with the actual one-year rates of change of the index (for example, January to January), in which case the "expected rate of wage change" is an average of twelve figures centered (respectively) on each of the twelve months in the one-year interval.

will both be smaller. Thus a *ceteris paribus* rise of $(\dot{w}/w)^e$ in (25), to the extent that businesses do not expect to be able to shift the expected wage costs onto buyers, will be partially offset by a resulting fall of z and $f(u, z)$, so that $\dot{w}/w$ is not implied to rise by an equal amount.

Of course other things need not be equal. Like the example earlier, if the firm expects to be able to raise its price in proportion to its wage rates without loss of prospective sales—because, say, other firms are expected to raise their prices in that proportion and demand per customer is not expected on balance to fall—then neither the expected product wage, the expected wage divided by the firm's planned price, nor the firm's vacancy rate will change; thus the firm will in this case match the expected rate of wage change, adding or substracting the wage change it would have chosen under stationary expectations. Another example of interest is the expectation by the firm of growth in the marginal and average productivity of its labor together with expected growth of its output demanded (at present prices) at a rate equal to the expected rate of wage change. Such a change in the firm's situation will leave its expected vacancy rate unchanged from its previous midcontract level, when this is evaluated at the wage expected to be necessary to keep its wage differential at its previous midcontract level. Hence the firm will raise its wage by just the amount of the expected rate of wage change if it likes its previous differential—by more (less) if that previous differential is too low (high).

In all cases, the firm is imagined notionally to increase its wage by the amount it expects is necessary to keep its past average competitiveness, to make an optimal price adjustment, and then to evaluate its expected vacancy rate at the implied product wage and expected demand for its product; if the desired differential calculated at that hypothetical vacancy rate is equal to its past average differential, it goes ahead with the "competitive" wage increase; if the desired differential is greater (less), the firm will increase its wage by more (less) than the expected or competitive amount. In mathematical terms, we can write the change in wage rate by firms currently resetting their wage rates as

$$
\begin{aligned}
w_t(t) - w_{t-1}(t) &= (1 + \Delta_t^*)w_t^e - w_{t-1}(t) \\
&= (1 + \Delta_t^*)(1 + \pi)w(t - \tfrac{1}{2}) \\
&\quad - w_{t-1}(t),
\end{aligned}
\tag{28}
$$

where π is the expected proportionate rate of wage change. Letting Δ_t denote $w_{t-1}(t)/\dot{w}(t - \tfrac{1}{2})$, we have

$$
\frac{w_t(t) - w_{t-1}(t)}{w_{t-1}(t)} = (1 + \pi)\left(\frac{1 + \Delta_t^*}{1 + \Delta_t} - 1\right), \tag{29}
$$

which may be approximated by $\pi + \Delta^* - \Delta$ for small magnitudes. In equilibrium the left-hand side must equal π, hence $\Delta_t^* = \Delta_t$. Since Δ_t must be approximately zero for firms as a whole, it follows that $\Delta^* = 0$ in equilibrium.

A rigorous argument is easier if we revert to the continuous wage-setting model together with adaptive expectations of the current wage level, as in (10′). We repeat, for the ith firm, the earlier (10′a):

$$
\dot{\Delta}_i^e = \mu(\Delta_i^* - \Delta_i^e), \tag{10′a}
$$

where

$$
\Delta_i^e = \frac{w_i - w^e}{w^e}, \qquad \Delta_i^* = \frac{w_i^* - w^e}{w^e}.
$$

But we now write in place of (10′b) the generalization:

$$
w^e = \lambda(w - w^e) + \pi w^e, \tag{10′b}
$$

π being the expected rate of wage change elsewhere, that is, the rate of change of the expected current wage that would be forecast in the absence of information on a discrepancy between the actual wage level elsewhere and the currently estimated average wage level. Then

$$
\frac{\dot{w}_i}{w_i} = \mu\frac{\Delta_i^* - \Delta_i^e}{1 + \Delta_i^e} + \frac{\dot{w}^e}{w^e},
$$

where the second term on the right includes the "catch-up" wage increase and π as well.

For firms as a whole, then,

$$\frac{\dot{w}}{w} = \mu \frac{\Delta^* - \Delta^e}{1 + \Delta^e} + \lambda\Delta^e + \pi.$$

The analysis of Figure 2 applies with slight change. In steady states we have $\Delta^e = \Delta^*$, so that

$$\frac{\dot{w}}{w} = \lambda\Delta^* + \pi,$$

which is (25). In this continuous-time model, "equilibrium" might be defined as "*ex post* $\dot{w}^e = \pi w^e$," meaning that the time change of the *estimate* (or expectation) of current w equals what was forecast for the estimate. Then, by (10'b'), $w = w^e$ is implied, whence $\Delta^e = 0$ and $\dot{w} = \dot{w}^e$. Then $\Delta^* = 0$ along any equilibrium path. If, alternatively, equilibrium were defined as *ex post* $\dot{w}/w = \pi$, so that expectations of the *level* of the current wage may be incorrect, then equilibrium implies only that $\Delta^* = 0$ when a steady state prevails. I prefer the former definition, though for steady-state analysis there is no need to choose.

The model, particularly (25) and (23), implies that there exists a unique steady-state equilibrium value of the unemployment rate, denoted by $\bar{u}^*$ and determined by the equation

$$f(\bar{u}^*, (1 - \bar{u}^*)\gamma) = 0. \tag{30}$$

This is because the steady-state $f(\bar{u}, (1 - \bar{u})\gamma)$ is strictly decreasing in $\bar{u}$ and $f(0, \gamma) > 0$, $f(1, 0) < 0$. At any other $\bar{u}$ there must be continuing, nonvanishing disequilibrium. Corresponding to $\bar{u}^*$ is some steady-state equilibrium vacancy rate, $\bar{v}^*$, given by the relation $m(\bar{u}^*, \bar{v}^*) = 0$.

The point about the result in (30) is that $\bar{u}^*$ is independent of π. In steady-state equilibrium the rate of wage increase is just the expected rate of wage increase, π. Hence a large $\dot{w}/w$ *in equilibrium* implies only a large π, not a small $\bar{u}$. This means that an economy that is in a steady state, and that is experiencing and expecting 10 percent money wage growth, would not have an unemployment rate different from what it would be if that economy were in a steady state and were

experiencing and expecting a much smaller rate of money wage growth. Figure 3 gives the diagrammatics: A shift of the expected rate of wage change from zero to ω produces a uniform upward displacement of the steady-state Phillips curve by the same amount. As a consequence, the (dashed) *locus of steady-state equilibrium points* is a vertical line, each point having the same abscissa, $\bar{u}^*$.

Before we question whether $\bar{u}^*$ is exactly independent of monetary factors, let us consider its "real" determinants.

What if higher money wage growth in steady states is matched by higher productivity growth? It is sometimes held that an economy can maintain a steady-state equilibrium—and thus a steady state with a stationary price trend (as well as any other trend)—with a smaller steady unemployment rate the faster its productivity growth. This is obvious on the usual Phillips curve analysis where no expectational variables are introduced; and it is also valid arithmetic if the expected rate of wage change in my model is replaced by the expected rate of price change. But our theory denies that formulation if it is assumed that steady wage growth eventually generates the expectation of that growth. Then the difference in rates of wage increase consistent with price stability between rapid-productivity-growth and slow-productivity-growth situations does not permit a favorable difference in steady unemployment rates, because the difference in $\dot{w}/w$ will be matched by an equal difference in $\dot{w}^e/w$. Indeed the proposition in question could be reversed in a more general model: If rapid productivity growth and resulting obsolescence of plants strike firms unevenly and thus make greater demands for labor mobility and flexible skills, the steady-state equilibrium unemployment rate may very well be higher the faster is the growth of productivity. (But *given* productivity growth, $\bar{u}^*$ is still independent of the expected nominal wage trend.)

A rise of the rate of growth of the labor force will increase the value of z and hence the vacancy rate needed to maintain any given unemployment rate. Equilibrium $\bar{u}^*$ must then rise to accommodate a higher $\bar{v}^*$.

From (30) we calculate that

$$\frac{d\bar{u}^*}{d\gamma} = \frac{-(1-\bar{u}^*)f_2}{f_1 - f_2\gamma} > 0. \qquad (31)$$

Thus rapid economic growth from any source appears to increase the equilibrium steady-state unemployment rate.

What are the implications of this theory for the consequences of policy decisions regarding $u(t)$ or, $\dot{w}(t)/w(t)$? Nil, until we specify a theory of π. Consider two examples. Let macro policy, through v, cause $\dot{w}/w$ to be constant. Then it is natural to suppose that, at least eventually, π will approach $\dot{w}/w$. Hence $u(t)$ will eventually approach $\bar{u}^*$ independently of the selected $\dot{w}/w$. An increase of $\dot{w}/w$ above current π will "buy" a *temporary* but not a *permanent* decrease of u. As a second example, let macro policy, through v, cause $u = \bar{u} < \bar{u}^*$. Then $f[\bar{u}, (1-\bar{u})\gamma] > 0$, so that $\dot{w}/w > \pi$ for all t. It is natural to suppose that, eventually, π tends toward $\dot{w}/w$. But each one-point increase of π makes $\dot{w}/w$ one point higher, given $u = \bar{u}$. Hence π and $\dot{w}/w$ will increase without limit. The result is hyper-inflation. The latter illustration shows, by the way, that the insidious Say's law has not returned. As long as the monetary system functions, the fiscal and monetary authorities can engineer departures from the equilibrium steady-state unemployment rate. Nor do we know at what speed a hyperinflation (or inperdeflation) would develop when disequilibrium was maintained.

Suppose we are convinced that steady, nonaccelerating inflation at some moderate rate is possible in this country at a steady unemployment rate of 4 percent. In the present model this implies that $\bar{u}^*$ equals 4 percent.[63] It is plausible that, as the above model predicts, wages and prices would spiral upward at an ever-accelerating rate if aggregate demand consistently maintained the unemployment rate at 3.5 percent. It is

time to qualify the contention that $\bar{u}^*$ is independent of π. There is a lot that is hidden in the m and z functions.

One might argue that an unemployment rate as high as 4 percent is consistent with a moderate and steady rate of inflation only because some of those firms that would like to reduce substantially their wage differentials prefer to accept below-optimal profits or even dismiss some employees rather than impose money wage cuts on their employees, and because some employees would rather quit than suffer the indignity of a money wage cut; this means that the average money wage can be rising at the expected rate of wage change even when the "true" average desired wage differential, Δ^*, is negative. But money wage cuts are occasionally appropriate for a firm that wants a lower wage differential only when the expected rate of wage change is moderately low. On this argument, therefore, a 3.5 percent unemployment rate might also be consistent with equilibrium if the expected rate of wage change were high enough that a firm could reduce its expected relative wage by the amount desired without having to impose a money wage cut.

This money-illusion variant of the model admits the possibility that a 3.5 percent unemployment rate may be sustainable equilibrium level, too, like 4 percent, though only at a higher rate of wage increase. The steady-state equilibrium locus will be negatively sloped at least over a range, because each steady-state curve in Figure 3 will shift up by less than one point for every one-point increase of π. Nevertheless, this variant does not deny that there exists some unemployment rate such that maintenance of the unemployment rate at a level below that rate would require a disequilibrium accelerating spiral of wages and prices. Such a revision of the model appears to reinforce the earlier hypothesis that faster labor growth worsens the unemployment-inflation tradeoff if the faster labor-force growth would tend to depress the rate of growth of real wage rates. It *could* reverse the earlier hypothesis that productivity growth increases the steady-state

---

[63] Note that the unemployment rate required to keep average money wage rates in pace with productivity in the American economy at present, will exceed the American $\bar{u}^*$ because the expected rate of change of the money wage surely exceeds the rate of growth of productivity.

unemployment rate necessary for price stability (or any steady-state equilibrium) if productivity growth tended to raise the rate of growth of real wage rates.

But "irrationality" is not the only ground for disclaiming any precise invariance of $\bar{u}^*$ to π. It is standard doctrine to acknowledge that an "anticipated inflation" *does* have real effects, especially through their effects upon fiscal and monetary efficiency. *If* the real rate of interest does not fall by a compensating amount, an anticipated inflation impairs the function of money as a *medium of exchange:* Nominal interest rates will be higher under anticipated inflation, and "liquidity" will thereby be reduced. This might affect $\bar{u}^*$, though it is hard to say in what way. Another effect is the impairment of money as a *unit of account*. It is harder to make intertemporal comparisons of wage offers when general wages are rising, even if rising at a known rate. It may be that, for small π, workers will neglect π in deciding to accept a job. Thus, up to a point, an increase of π may tend, comparing equilibrium steady states, to shorten the duration of search unemployment; supplies of labor may be content to use $\pi = 0$ as a convenient approximation for comparing wage offers over time even though, intellectually, they know that wage rates are trending upward. If a one-point increase of π produces a less-than-one point increase of the steady-state Phillips curve, then the equilibrium locus is negatively sloped. There may be a complementary tendency from the product side: If the real rate of interest is invariant to π, then nominal interest rates are higher. If expected inflation, like expected money wage growth, is neglected by workers for purposes of computational simplicity, then they will operate as if the real interest rate is higher when π is higher; this tendency may produce a shortening of job search, and thus a reduction of $\bar{u}^*$. Whether this alleged impairment of the money yard-stick is a Paretian improvement, in view of the many likely externalities, is beyond the scope of the present paper.

Symmetrically, the point might be made that anticipated inflation *enhances* fiscal efficiency by reducing the average tax rate necessary to induce any desired level of private consumption demand because expectations of inflation reduce the real value of the government's indebtedness. If the real rate of interest is constant, after-tax real wage rates and after-tax real interest rates will be higher, so that $\bar{u}^*$ may also change.

Enough has been said to convey the point that invariance of $\bar{u}^*$ to the rate of inflation is unlikely to be precise. But a very general theory seems to be ambiguous as to the nature of the relationship.

5. SUMMARY

A generalized excess-demand theory of the rate of change of the average money wage rate has been developed for frictional labor markets that allocate heterogeneous jobs and workers without perfect information. There are two explanatory variables: the vacancy rate and the unemployment rate. The unemployment rate and the rate of change of employment (per unit of labor supply) are shown to be joint proxies for the vacancy rate. Hence generalized excess demand can be regarded as a derived function of the unemployment rate and the rate of change of employment. This relationship is the augmented Phillips curve. Some of its properties are deduced. The steady-state Phillips curve that relates the rate of wage increase to the steady unemployment rate is also derived.

The expected rate of wage change is then added to the Phillips function—to the excess-demand term—to obtain the rate of wage increase under nonstatic expectations in a no-money-illusion world. Equilibrium entails equality between the actual and expected rates of wage change. The steady-state equilibrium locus is implied to be a vertical line at a unique-state equilibrium unemployment rate. This is consistent with the usual theory of anticipated inflation. But if there are downward money-wage rigidities or important considerations of monetary and fiscal efficiency, then no precise invariance of the equilibrium steady-state unemployment rate to the equilibrium inflation rate need hold.

APPENDIX 1
Mathematics of Wage Change Under Staggered Wage Setting

Let $w(t)$ denote the average wage paid at time t. Let $w_s(t)$ denote the (common) wage paid by firms whose most recent wage setting occurred at s. Resetting occurs "yearly" for each firm, so we need consider only $t - 1 \leq s \leq t$. If workers are distributed uniformly over firms and firms' wage-setting dates are distributed uniformly over the year, then

$$w(t) = \int_{t-1}^{t} w_s(t)\, ds \qquad (A1)$$

with $\partial w_s(t)/\partial t = 0$ for fixed s.

The model in the text hypothesizes

$$w_t(t) = h w_t^e, \qquad h > 0, \qquad (A2)$$

$$w_t^e = w(t - \tfrac{1}{2}), \qquad (A3)$$

where h signifies $(1 + \Delta^*)$ in the text and is here taken to be constant over time. Then we can derive

$$w(t) = h \int_{t - \frac{3}{2}}^{t - \frac{1}{2}} w(s)\, ds \qquad (A4)$$

or

$$w(t) = h \int_{\frac{1}{2}}^{\frac{3}{2}} w(t - \theta)\, d\theta. \qquad (A4')$$

For $h = 1$ it is clear that there exists just one steady-state growth rate, zero. For $h \neq 1$ we can find the steady-state growth rates, g, from

$$w'(t) = h[w(t - \tfrac{1}{2}) - w(t - \tfrac{3}{2})], \qquad (A5)$$

a mixed differential-difference equation whose characteristic equation [replace $w(t)$ by e^{zt}]

$$z = h(e^{-\frac{1}{2}z} - e^{-\frac{3}{2}z}) \qquad (A6)$$

every steady-state growth rate, $z \equiv w'/w$, must satisfy. It is easy to show that, outside $z = 0$, there exists just one steady-state growth rate, denoted g, with sgn $g = \text{sgn}(h - 1)$, and $g < \infty$ for $h < \infty$. There are a number of approximations of (A5), good for steady states, that are of use in describing the relation between g and h. One of them is

$$gw(t) = h[gw(t - 1)], \qquad (A7)$$

whence

$$e^g = h, \qquad \text{or, for small } g, g \doteq h - 1. \qquad (A8)$$

The question is now whether our equation exhibits relative stability in the sense that, as t goes to infinity, $w(t)/e^{gt}$ becomes constant; that is, does a limiting growth rate exist and equal g? [Note that $w(t)$, even so normalized, certainly does not seek any "equilibrium level" that is independent of past w.]

One approach, due to P. A. Samuelson, constructs a new variable,

$$u(t) = w(t)e^{-gt}, \qquad (A9)$$

which we desire to show tends to be constant asymptotically. Then, using (A4'),

$$u(t) = \int_{\frac{1}{2}}^{\frac{3}{2}} h e^{-g\theta} u(t - \theta)\, d\theta$$
$$= \int_{0}^{\infty} f(\theta) h e^{-g\theta} u(t - \theta)\, d\theta, \qquad (A10)$$

where

$$\int_{0}^{\infty} f(\theta) h e^{-g\theta}\, d\theta = \int_{\frac{1}{2}}^{\frac{3}{2}} h e^{-g\theta}\, d\theta$$
$$= \frac{h}{g}(e^{-\frac{1}{2}g} - e^{-\frac{3}{2}g}) = 1, \quad (A11)$$

by virtue of (A6). Hence (A10) shows u at each t to be a weighted average of its own past values. It is clear, therefore, that $u(t)$ approaches a constant as t goes to infinity. The value of that constant depends only upon $u(t)$ on the initial interval, $-\frac{3}{2} \leq t \leq 0$. The reason for this stability is that extreme values of u are averaged out, so that any past growth of u cannot be sustained.

There exists no steady-state relation giving a finite g for every $h > 0$ when the *growth* of wages tends to be extrapolated as well as the recent level. In that case we have

$$w_t^e = w(t - \tfrac{1}{2})e^{\pi}, \qquad \pi = g, \qquad (A12)$$

so a steady state requires

$$gw(t) = he^g[w(t - \tfrac{1}{2}) - w(t - \tfrac{3}{2})],$$
$$g = h(e^{\frac{1}{2}g} - e^{-\frac{1}{2}g}) \doteq hg, \qquad (A13)$$

which is impossible except when $h = 1$, in which case g is indeterminate.

APPENDIX 2
Nonwage Recruitment over Time

The analysis here will be confined to a fixed-wage firm that has committed itself to invest in such a way that its capital stock, K_t^i, will grow exponentially at rate $g \geq 0$. Its cash flow (abstracting from its investment) at any time t, in real terms, is

$$\frac{p_0^i}{p_0} F(N_t^i, K_0^i e^{gt}; \mu)$$

$$- \frac{w_0}{p_0} N_t^i - C(R_t^i, K_0^i e^{gt}; u) - hbK_0^i e^{gt} \quad \text{(A1)}$$

where its money product price, p_t^i, and its money wage rate, w_t^i, are both constant relative to the consumer price index, p_t, and to other wage rates. $F(\cdot)$ is the firm's output (produced and sold), homogeneous of degree one in capital and labor with diminishing marginal productivities, and hence $p_0^i F(\ )/p_0$ is its real value. The second term is the firm's real wage bill. $C(\cdot)$ is its real recruitment cost, also homogeneous of degree one in recruitment, denoted R, and K, with $C_R > 0$ and $C_{RR} > 0$ (rising marginal recruitment cost). The constant $h > 0$ denotes "volunteers" per unit capital whose unit processing cost is $b \geq 0$. By its homogeneity, we may write (A1) in the form (dropping unnecessary subscripts)

$$e^{gt} K_0 \left\{ \frac{p_0^i}{p_0} F(n_t, 1; \mu) \right.$$

$$\left. - \frac{w_0}{p_0} n_t - C(r_t, 1; u) - hb \right\}, \quad \text{(A1')}$$

where

$$r_t = \frac{R_t}{K_0 e^{gt}}, \qquad n_t = \frac{N_t}{K_0 e^{gt}}.$$

Letting R_t, H_t, D_t and Q_t denote the firm's recruits, volunteers, deaths, and quits, respectively, we have

$$\dot{N}_t = R_t + H_t - D_t - Q_t$$
$$= R_t + hK_0 e^{gt} - \delta N_t - q(u)N_t, \quad \text{(A2)}$$

where the quit ratio, $q(u)$, is a decreasing function of the unemployment rate, u. From

(A2) and differentiation of n_t we obtain

$$r_t = \dot{n}_t + \lambda(u)n_t - h,$$
$$\lambda(u) \equiv g + \delta + q(u) > 0. \quad \text{(A2')}$$

Now let us suppose that the firm maximizes, with respect to $r(t) \geq 0$, the improper integral of the discounted cash flow in (A1') subject to (A2'), where $e^{-\rho t}$ is the discount and ρ, the expected real rate of interest. I shall study only the borderline case in which $\rho = g$ and use the "overtaking principle," so that the firm maximizes the integral of the *excess* of cash flow over the exponentially rising "bliss level" of cash flow. The excess is

$$\int_0^\infty K_0 \left\{ \frac{p_0^i}{p_0} F(n, 1; \mu) - \frac{w_0}{p_0} n - C(r, 1; u) - hb \right.$$

$$- \frac{p_0^i}{p_0} F(n^*, 1; \mu) + \frac{w}{p} n^*$$

$$\left. + C(\lambda n^* - h, 1; u) + hb \right\} dt, \quad \text{(A3)}$$

where the constant (bliss-level) n^* is defined by

$$\frac{p_0^i}{p_0} F_n(n^*, 1; \mu) = \frac{w_0}{p_0} + \lambda C_R(\lambda n^* - h, 1; u) \quad \text{(A4)}$$

and $\lambda n^* - h > 0$ by assumption.

The optimal $\dot{n}(t)$ path satisfies $\dot{n}(t) \gtreqless 0$ according as $n(t) \lesseqgtr n^*$. The optimal path also satisfies

$$nC_R(\dot{n} + \lambda n - h, 1; u)$$

$$= \frac{p_0^i}{p_0} F(n^*, 1; \mu) - \frac{w_0}{p_0} n^* - C(\lambda n^* - h, 1; u)$$

$$- \left[\frac{p_0^i}{p_0} F(n, 1; \mu) - \frac{w_0}{p_0} n \right.$$

$$\left. - C(\dot{n} + \lambda n - h, 1; u) \right]. \quad \text{(A5)}$$

The level n^* is to be distinguished from the smallest "no-vacancy" level, say n^{**}, at which marginal (real) value productivity equals the real wage plus interest and "depreciation" on the sheer unit processing outlay, b:

$$\frac{p_0^i}{p_0} F_n(n^{**}, 1; \mu) = \frac{w_0}{p} + (\rho + \delta + q)b. \quad \text{(A6)}$$

Since $\rho = g$ and $b < C_R(r, 1; \mu)$ for all $r \geq 0$, $n^{**} > n^*$. Hence there are positive vacancies on the bliss path. Optimal $r = 0$ at some $\bar{n}$ between n^* and n^{**} and for all $n \geq \bar{n}$. Volunteers will be accepted if only $n < n^{**}$. It is supposed throughout that $n < \bar{n}$.

Given initial n, an increase of the technological shift parameter, μ, will increase n^{**} and hence vacancies if and only if $F_{n\mu}(n^{**}, 1; \mu) > 0$. Suppose that the technical change is *not* "very labor saving" at any n; i.e., $F_{n\mu}(n, 1; \mu) > 0$ for all n. Then we calculate from (A5) that

$$\frac{d\dot{n}}{d\mu} = \frac{\dfrac{p_0^i}{p_0}[F_\mu(n^*, 1; \mu) - F_\mu(n, 1; \mu)]}{\dot{n}C_{RR}(\dot{n} + \lambda n - h, 1; u)}, \qquad \text{(A7)}$$

which is positive since $F_{n\mu} > 0$ and $(n^* - n)$ and $\dot{n}$ have the same sign. By (A2′), $dr/d\mu = d\dot{n}/d\mu$, so recruitment increases along with vacancies when labor demand increases.

Vacancies decrease with n, *ceteris paribus*. From (A5) and (A2′) we find

$$\frac{dr}{dn} = \frac{-\dfrac{p_0^i}{p_0}\left[F_n(n, 1; \mu) - \dfrac{w_0}{p_0} - \lambda C_R(r, 1; u)\right]}{\dot{n}C_{RR}(r, 1; u)}. \qquad \text{(A8)}$$

The bracketed expression must have the sign of $\dot{n}$, so that $dr/dn < 0$ for all $n < \bar{n}$; hence r is monotone decreasing in n and therefore monotone increasing in vacancies. If for any n the bracketed expression were negative, then $dr/dn > 0$ for all greater n, and either the result $r = r^* \equiv \lambda n^* - h$ at $n = n^*$ or the result $r = 0$ at $n = \bar{n}$ would be contradicted.

Consider now an increase of the unemployment rate, u. This is postulated to make recruitment easier in the sense that $C_{Ru}(r, 1; u) < 0$. We calculate from (A5) that

$$\frac{d\dot{n}}{du} = \frac{\begin{bmatrix}\partial C(\dot{n} + \lambda n - h, 1; u)/\partial u \\ - \partial C(\lambda n^* - h, 1; u)/\partial u \\ - \dot{n}\partial C_R(\dot{n} + \lambda n - h, 1; u)/\partial u\end{bmatrix}}{\dot{n}C_{RR}(r, 1; u)}, \qquad \text{(A9)}$$

where it must be remembered that λ and h vary with u. If we take $\lambda'(u)$ and $h'(u)$ to be zero for the moment, the numerator can be approximated (for small $r - r^*$) by

$$C_{Ru}(r, 1; u) \cdot (r - r^*) - \dot{n}C_{Ru}(r, 1; u)$$
$$= \lambda(n - n^*) \cdot C_{Ru}(r, 1; u), \qquad \text{(A10)}$$

which has the sign of $\dot{n}$, so that $d\dot{n}/du > 0$ on this account. The other part of the numerator, due to the variation of λ and h with u, can be approximated by

$$[\lambda'(u)n - h'(u)]\{(r - r^*)C_{RR}(r, 1; u)$$
$$- \dot{n}C_{RR}(r, 1; u)\} + \lambda'(u)(n - n^*)C_R(r, 1; u)$$
$$= [\lambda'(u)n - h'(u)]\lambda(n - n^*)C_{RR}(r, 1; u)$$
$$+ \lambda'(u)(n - n^*)C_R(r, 1; u),$$

$$\text{(A11)}$$

where $\lambda'(u) < 0$, $h'(u) \geq 0$. This also has the sign of $\dot{n}$, so we find that $d\dot{n}/du > 0$ unambiguously.

But recruitment need not increase with u because less recruitment is needed for given $\dot{n}$ when quits fall and volunteers increase. Using (A2′), (A10), (A11), and the relation $\lambda(n - n^*) = -\dot{n} + r - \lambda n^* + h$, we have

$$\frac{dr}{du} = \frac{\lambda(n - n^*)C_{Ru}}{\dot{n}C_{RR}}$$

$$+ \frac{[\lambda'(u)n - h'(u)](-\dot{n} + r - \lambda n^* + h)}{\dot{n}}$$

$$+ \frac{\lambda'(u)(n - n^*)C_R}{\dot{n}C_{RR}}$$

$$+ [\lambda'(u)n - h'(u)]. \qquad \text{(A12)}$$

Although the troublesome last term (the reduction of quits) cancels with part of the second term, the remainder of the second term has the "wrong" sign, so dr/du *could* have the wrong sign. But $z_1 > 0$ of the text rather than $R_1 > 0$ is the interesting inequality, so it is $d\dot{n}/du > 0$ rather than $dr/du > 0$ that is important. The employment dynamics in the text can be modified considerably without loss of the end results.

Inflation and Unemployment

James Tobin*

Yale University

The world economy today is vastly different from the 1930's, when Seymour Harris, the chairman of this meeting, infected me with his boundless enthusiasm for economics and his steadfast confidence in its capacity for good works. Economics is very different, too. Both the science and its subject have changed, and for the better, since World War II. But there are some notable constants. Unemployment and inflation still preoccupy and perplex economists, statesmen, journalists, housewives, and everyone else. The connection between them is the principal domestic economic burden of presidents and prime ministers, and the major area of controversy and ignorance in macroeconomics. I have chosen to review economic thought on this topic on this occasion, partly because of its inevitable timeliness, partly because of a personal interest reaching back to my first published work in 1941.

I. THE MEANINGS OF FULL EMPLOYMENT

Today, as thirty and forty years ago, economists debate how much unemployment is

Reprinted from the *American Economic Review*, 62:1–18 (1972), by permission of the author and the publisher (copyright by the American Economic Association).

* Presidential address delivered at the eighty-fourth meeting of the American Economic Association, New Orleans, Louisiana, December 28, 1971.

voluntary, how much involuntary; how much is a phenomenon of equilibrium, how much a symptom of disequilibrium; how much is compatible with competition, how much is to be blamed on monopolies, labor unions, and restrictive legislation; how much unemployment characterizes "full" employment.

Full employment—imagine macroeconomics deprived of the concept. But what is it? What is the proper employment goal of policies affecting aggregate demand? Zero unemployment in the monthly labor force survey? That outcome is so inconceivable outside of Switzerland that it is useless as a guide to policy. Any other numerical candidate, yes even 4 percent, is patently arbitrary without reference to basic criteria. Unemployment equal to vacancies? Measurement problems aside, this definition has the same straightforward appeal as zero unemployment, which it simply corrects for friction.[1]

A concept of full employment more congenial to economic theory is labor market equilibrium, a volume of employment which is simultaneously the amount employers want to offer and the amount workers want to accept at prevailing wage rates and prices. Forty years ago theorists with confidence in markets could believe that full employment is whatever volume of employment the economy is moving toward, and that its achievement

[1] This concept is commonly attributed to W. H. Beveridge, but he was actually more ambitious and required a surplus of vacancies.

requires of the government nothing more than neutrality, and nothing less.

After Keynes challenged the classical notion of labor market equilibrium and the complacent view of policy to which it led, full employment came to mean maximum aggregate supply, the point at which expansion of aggregate demand could not further increase employment and output.

Full employment was also regarded as the economy's inflation threshold. With a deflationary gap, demand less than full employment supply, prices would be declining or at worst constant. Expansion of aggregate demand short of full employment would cause at most a one-shot increase of prices. For continuing inflation, the textbooks told us, a necessary and sufficient condition was an inflationary gap, real aggregate demand in excess of feasible supply. The model was tailor-made for wartime inflation.

Postwar experience destroyed the identification of full employment with the economy's inflation threshold. The profession, the press, and the public discovered the "new inflation" of the 1950's, inflation without benefit of gap, labelled but scarcely illuminated by the term "cost-push." Subsequently the view of the world suggested by the Phillips curve merged demand-pull and cost-push inflation and blurred the distinction between them. This view contained no concept of full employment. In its place came the tradeoff, along which society supposedly can choose the least undesirable feasible combination of the evils of unemployment and inflation.

Many economists deny the existence of a durable Phillips tradeoff. Their numbers and influence are increasing. Some of them contend that there is only one rate of unemployment compatible with steady inflation, a "natural rate" consistent with any steady rate of change of prices, positive, zero, or negative. The natural rate is another full employment candidate, a policy target at least in the passive sense that monetary and fiscal policy makers are advised to eschew any numerical unemployment goal and to let the economy gravitate to this equilibrium. So we have come full circle. Full employment is once again nothing but the equilibrium reached by labor markets unaided and undistorted by governmental fine tuning.

In discussing these issues, I shall make the following points. First, an observed amount of unemployment is not revealed to be voluntary simply by the fact that money wage rates are constant, or rising, or even accelerating. I shall recall and extend Keynes's definition of involuntary unemployment and his explanation why workers may accept price inflation as a method of reducing real wages while rejecting money wage cuts. The second point is related. Involuntary unemployment is a disequilibrium phenomenon; the behavior, the persistence, of excess supplies of labor depend on how large and how frequent the shocks are. Higher prices or faster inflation can diminish involuntary, disequilibrium unemployment, even though voluntary, equilibrium labor supply is entirely free of money illusion.

Third, various criteria of full employment coincide in a theoretical full stationary equilibrium, but diverge in persistent disequilibrium. These are 1) the natural rate of unemployment, the rate compatible with zero or some other constant inflation rate, 2) zero involuntary unemployment, 3) the rate of unemployment needed for optimal job search and placement, and 4) unemployment equal to job vacancies. The first criterion dictates higher unemployment than any of the rest. Instead of commending the natural rate as a target of employment policy, the other three criteria suggest less unemployment and more inflation. Therefore, fourth, there are real gains from additional employment, which must be weighed in the social balance against the costs of inflation. I shall conclude with a few remarks on this choice, and on the possibilities of improving the terms of the tradeoff.

II. KEYNESIAN AND CLASSICAL INTERPRETATIONS OF UNEMPLOYMENT

To begin with the *General Theory* is not just the ritual piety economists of my generation owe the book that shaped their minds. Keynes's treatment of labor market equilibrium and disequilibrium in his first chapter is remarkably relevant today.

Keynes attacked what he called the classical presumption that persistent unemployment is voluntary unemployment. The presumption he challenged is that in competitive labor markets actual employment and unemployment reveal workers' true preferences between work and alternative uses of time, the presumption that no one is fully or partially unemployed whose real wage per hour exceeds his marginal valuation of an hour of free time. Orthodox economists found the observed stickiness of money wages to be persuasive evidence that unemployment, even in the Great Depression, was voluntary. Keynes found decisive evidence against this inference in the willingness of workers to accept a larger volume of employment at a lower real wage resulting from an increase of prices.

Whenever unemployment could be reduced by expansion of aggregate demand, Keynes regarded it as involuntary. He expected expansion to raise prices and lower real wages, but this expectation is not crucial to his argument. Indeed, if it is possible to raise employment without reduction in the real wage, his case for calling the unemployment involuntary is strengthened.

But why is the money wage so stubborn if more labor is willingly available at the same or lower real wage? Consider first some answers Keynes did not give. He did not appeal to trade union monopolies or minimum wage laws. He was anxious, perhaps over-anxious, to meet his putative classical opponents on their home field, the competitive economy. He did not rely on any failure of workers to perceive what a rise in prices does to real wages. The unemployed take new jobs, the employed hold old ones, with eyes open. Otherwise the new situation would be transient.

Instead, Keynes emphasized the institutional fact that wages are bargained and set in the monetary unit of account. Money wage rates are, to use an unKeynesian term, "ad-ministered prices." That is, they are not set and reset in daily auctions but posted and fixed for finite periods of time. This observation led Keynes to his central explanation: Workers, individually and in groups, are more concerned with relative than absolute real wages. They may withdraw labor if their wages fall relatively to wages elsewhere, even though they would not withdraw any if real wages fall uniformly everywhere. Labor markets are decentralized, and there is no way money wages can fall in any one market without impairing the relative status of the workers there. A general rise in prices is a neutral and universal method of reducing real wages, the only method in a decentralized and uncontrolled economy. Inflation would not be needed, we may infer, if by government compulsion, economy-wide bargaining, or social compact, all money wage rates could be scaled down together.

Keynes apparently meant that relative wages are the arguments in labor supply functions. But Alchian (pp. 27–52 in Phelps et al.) and other theorists of search activity have offered a somewhat different interpretation, namely that workers whose money wages are reduced will quit their jobs to seek employment in other markets where they think, perhaps mistakenly, that wages remain high.

Keynes's explanation of money wage stickiness is plausible and realistic. But two related analytical issues have obscured the message. Can there be involuntary unemployment in an equilibrium, a proper, full-fledged neoclassical equilibrium? Does the labor supply behavior described by Keynes betray "money illusion"? Keynes gave a loud yes in answer to the first question, and this seems at first glance to compel an affirmative answer to the second.

An economic theorist can, of course, commit no greater crime than to assume money illusion. Comparative statics is a nonhistorical exercise, in which different price levels are to be viewed as alternative rather than sequential. Compare two situations that differ only in the scale of exogenous monetary variables; imagine, for example, that all such magnitudes are ten times as high in one situation as in the other. All equilibrium prices, including money wage rates, should differ in the same proportion, while all real magnitudes, including employment, should be the same in the two equilibria. To assume instead that workers' supply decisions vary with the price level is to say that they would behave differently if the unit of account were, and always had been, dimes instead of dollars. Surely Keynes should not be interpreted to attribute to anyone money illusion in this sense. He was not talking about so strict and static an equilibrium.

Axel Leijonhufvud's illuminating and perceptive interpretation of Keynes argues convincingly that, in chapter 1 as throughout the *General Theory*, what Keynes calls equilibrium should be viewed as persistent disequilibrium, and what appears to be comparative statics is really shrewd and incisive, if awkward, dynamic analysis. Involuntary unemployment means that labor markets are not in equilibrium. The resistance of money wage rates to excess supply is a feature of the adjustment process rather than a symptom of irrationality.

The other side of Keynes's story is that in depressions money wage deflation, even if it occurred more speedily, or especially if it occurred more speedily, would be at best a weak equilibrator and quite possibly a source of more unemployment rather than less. In contemporary language, the perverse case would arise if a high and ever-increasing real rate of return on money inhibited real demand faster than the rising purchasing power of monetary stocks stimulated demand. To pursue this Keynesian theme further here would be a digression.

What relevance has this excursion into depression economics for contemporary problems of unemployment and wage inflation? The issues are remarkably similar, even though events and Phillips have shifted attention from levels to time rates of change of wages and prices. Phillips curve doctrine[2]

is in an important sense the postwar analogue of Keynesian wage and employment theory, while natural rate doctrine is the contemporary version of the classical position Keynes was opposing.

Phillips curve doctrine implies that lower unemployment can be purchased at the cost of faster inflation. Let us adapt Keynes's test for involuntary unemployment to the dynamic terms of contemporary discussion of inflation, wages, and unemployment. Suppose that the current rate of unemployment continues. Associated with it is a path of real wages, rising at the rate of productivity growth. Consider an alternative future, with unemployment at first declining to a rate one percentage point lower and then remaining constant at the lower rate. Associated with the lower unemployment alternative will be a second path of real wages. Eventually this real wage path will show, at least to first approximation, the same rate of increase as the first one, the rate of productivity growth. But the paths may differ because of the transitional effects of increasing the rate of employment. The growth of real wages will be retarded in the short run if additional employment lowers labor's marginal productivity. In any case, the test question is whether with full information about the two alternatives labor would accept the second one—whether, in other words, the additional employment would be willingly supplied along the second real wage path. If the answer is affirmative, then that one percentage point of employment is involuntary.

For Keynes's reasons, a negative answer cannot necessarily be inferred from failure of money wage rates to fall or even decelerate. Actual unemployment and the real wage path associated with it are not necessarily an equilibrium. Rigidities in the path of money wage rates can be explained by workers'

---

[2] Phillips himself is not a prophet of the doctrine associated with his curve. His 1958 article was probably the most influential macroeconomic paper of the last quarter century. But Phillips simply presented some striking empirical findings, which others have replicated many times for many economies. He is not responsible for the theories and policy conclusions his findings stimulated.

preoccupation with relative wages and the absence of any central economy-wide mechanism for altering all money wages together.

According to the natural rate hypothesis, there is just one rate of unemployment compatible with steady wage and price inflation, and this is in the long run compatible with any constant rate of change of prices, positive, zero, or negative. Only at the natural rate of unemployment are workers content with current and prospective real wages, content to have their real wages rise at the rate of growth of productivity. Along the feasible path of real wages they would not wish to accept any larger volume of employment. Lower unemployment, therefore, can arise only from economy-wide excess demand for labor and must generate a gap between real wages desired and real wages earned. The gap evokes increases of money wages designed to raise real wages faster than productivity. But this intention is always frustrated, the gap is never closed, money wages and prices accelerate. By symmetrical argument, unemployment above the natural rate signifies excess supply in labor markets and ever accelerating deflation. Older classical economists regarded constancy of money wage rates as indicative of full employment equilibrium, at which the allocation of time between work and other pursuits is revealed as voluntary and optimal. Their successors make the same claims, for the natural rate of unemployment, except that in the equilibrium money wages are not necessarily constant but growing at the rate of productivity gain plus the experienced and expected rate of inflation of prices.

III. IS ZERO-INFLATION UNEMPLOYMENT VOLUNTARY AND OPTIMAL?

There are, then, two conflicting interpretations of the welfare value of employment in excess of the level consistent with price stability. One is that additional employment does not produce enough to compensate workers for the value of other uses of their time. The fact that it generates inflation is taken as prima facie evidence of a welfare loss. The alternative view, which I shall argue, is that the responses of money wages and prices to changes in aggregate demand reflect mechanics of adjustment, institutional constraints, and relative wage patterns and reveal nothing in particular about individual or social valuations of unemployed time vis-à-vis the wages of employment.

On this rostrum four years ago, Milton Friedman identified the noninflationary natural rate of unemployment with "equilibrium in the structure of real wage rates" (p. 8). "The 'natural rate of unemployment,'" he said, ". . . is the level that would be ground out by the Walrasian system of general equilibrium equations, provided that there is embedded in them the actual structural characteristics of the labor and commodity market, including market imperfections, stochastic variability in demands and supplies, the costs of getting information about job vacancies and labor availabilities, the costs of mobility, and so on." Presumably this Walrasian equilibrium also has the usual optimal properties; at any rate, Friedman advised the monetary authorities not to seek to improve upon it. But in fact we know little about the existence of a Walrasian equilibrium that allows for all the imperfections and frictions that explain why the natural rate is bigger than zero, and even less about the optimality of such an equilibrium if it exists.

In the new microeconomics of labor markets and inflation, the principal activity whose marginal value sets the reservation price of employment is job search. It is not pure leisure, for in principle persons who choose that option are not reported as unemployed; however, there may be a leisure component in job seeking.

A crucial assumption of the theory is that search is significantly more efficient when the searcher is unemployed, but almost no evidence has been advanced on this point. Members of our own profession are adept at seeking and finding new jobs without first leaving their old ones or abandoning not-in-labor-force status. We do not know how many quits and new hires in manufacturing are similar transfers, but some of them must be; if all reported accessions were hires of unemployed workers, the mean duration of unemployment would be only about half what it is in fact. In surveys of job mobility among blue collar workers in 1946–47 (see Lloyd Reynolds, pp. 214–15, and Herbert Parnes, pp. 158–59), 25 percent of workers who quit had new jobs lined up in advance. Reynolds found that the main obstacle to mobility without unemployment was not lack of information or time, but simply "anti-pirating" collusion by employers.

A considerable amount of search activity by unemployed workers appears to be an unproductive consequence of dissatisfaction and frustration rather than a rational quest for improvement. This was the conclusion of Reynolds' survey twenty-five years ago, p. 215, and it has been reemphasized for the contemporary scene by Robert Hall, and by Peter Doeringer and Michael Piore for what they term the secondary labor force. Reynolds found that quitting a job to look for a new one while unemployed actually yielded a better job in only a third of the cases. Lining up a new job in advance was a more successful strategy: two-thirds of such changes turned out to be improvements. Today according to the dual labor market hypothesis, the basic reason for frequent and long spells of unemployment in the secondary labor force is the shortage of good jobs.

In any event, the contention of some natural rate theorists is that employment beyond the natural rate takes time that would be better spent in search activity. Why do workers accept such employment? An answer to this question is a key element in a theory that generally presumes that actual behavior reveals true preferences. The answer given is that workers accept the additional employment only because they are victims of inflation illusion. One form of inflation illusion is over-estimation of the real wages of jobs they now hold, if they are employed, or of jobs they find, if they are unemployed and searching. If they did not under-estimate price inflation, employed

workers would more often quit to search, and unemployed workers would search longer.

The force of this argument seems to me diluted by the fact that price inflation illusion affects equally both sides of the job seekers's equation. He over-estimates the real value of an immediate job, but he also over-estimates the real values of jobs he might wait for. It is in the spirit of this theorizing to assume that money interest rates respond to the same correct or incorrect inflationary expectations. As a first approximation, inflation illusion has no substitution effect on the margin between working and waiting.

It does have an income effect, causing workers to exaggerate their real wealth. In which direction the income effect would work is not transparent. Does greater wealth, or the illusion of greater wealth, make people more choosy about jobs, more inclined to quit and to wait? Or less choosy, more inclined to stay in the job they have or to take the first one that comes along? I should have thought more selective rather than less. But natural rate theory must take the opposite view if it is to explain why under-estimation of price inflation bamboozles workers into holding or taking jobs that they do not really want.

Another form of alleged inflation illusion refers to wages rather than prices. Workers are myopic and do not perceive that wages elsewhere are, or soon will be, rising as fast as the money wage of the job they now hold or have just found. Consequently they under-estimate the advantages of quitting and searching. This explanation is convincing only to the extent that the payoff to search activity is determined by wage differentials. The payoff also depends on the probabilities of getting jobs at quoted wages, therefore on the balance between vacancies and job seekers. Workers know that perfectly well. Quit rates are an index of voluntary search activity. They do not diminish when unemployment is low and wage rates are rapidly rising. They increase, quite understandably. This fact contradicts the inflation illusion story, both versions. I conclude that it is not possible to regard fluctuations of unemployment on either side of the zero-inflation rate as mainly voluntary, albeit mistaken, extensions and contractions of search activity.

The new microeconomics of job search (see Edmund Phelps et al.), is nevertheless a valuable contribution to understanding of frictional unemployment. It provides reasons why some unemployment is voluntary, and why some unemployment is socially efficient.

Does the market produce the *optimal* amount of search unemployment? Is the natural rate optimal? I do not believe the new microeconomics has yet answered these questions.

An omniscient and beneficent economic dictator would not place every new job seeker immediately in any job at hand. Such a policy would create many mismatches, sacrificing efficiency in production or necessitating costly job-to-job shifts later on. The hypothetical planner would prefer to keep a queue of workers unemployed, so that he would have a larger choice of jobs to which to assign them. But he would not make the queue too long, because workers in the queue are not producing anything.

Of course he could shorten the queue of unemployed if he could dispose of more jobs and lengthen the queue of vacancies. With enough jobs of various kinds, he would never lack a vacancy for which any worker who happens to come along has comparative advantage. But because of limited capital stocks and interdependence among skills, jobs cannot be indefinitely multiplied without lowering their marginal productivity. Our wise and benevolent planner would not place people in jobs yielding less than the marginal value of leisure. Given this constraint on the number of jobs, he would always have to keep some workers waiting, and some jobs vacant. But he certainly would be inefficient if he had fewer jobs, filled and vacant, than this constraint. This is the common sense of Beveridge's rule—that vacanices should not be less than unemployment.

Is the natural rate a market solution of the hypothetical planner's operations research problem? According to search theory, an unemployed worker considers the probabilities that he can get a better job by searching longer and balances the expected discounted value of waiting against the loss of earnings. The employed worker makes a similar calculation when he considers quitting, also taking into account the once and for all costs of movement. These calculations are like those of the planner, but with an important difference. An individual does not internalize all the considerations the planner takes into account. The external effects are the familiar ones of congestion theory. A worker deciding to join a queue or to stay in one considers the probabilities of getting a job, but not the effects of his decision on the probabilities that others face. He lowers those probabilities for people in the queue he joins and raises them for persons waiting for the kind of job he vacates or turns down. Too many persons are unemployed waiting for good jobs, while less desirable ones go begging. However, external effects also occur in the decisions of employers whether to fill a vacancy with the applicant at hand or to wait for someone more qualified. It is not obvious, at least to me, whether the market is biased toward excessive or inadequate search. But it is doubtful that it produces the optimal amount.

Empirically the proposition that in the United States the zero-inflation rate of unemployment reflects voluntary and efficient job-seeking activity strains credulity. If there were a natural rate of unemployment in the United States, what would it be? It is hard to say because virtually all econometric Phillips curves allow for a whole menu of steady inflation rates. But estimates constrained to produce a vertical long-run Phillips curve suggest a natural rate between 5 and 6 percent of the labor force.[3]

So let us consider some of the features of an overall unemployment rate of 5 to 6 percent. First, about 40 percent of accessions in manufacturing are rehires rather than new hires. Temporarily laid off by their employers, these workers had been awaiting

[3] See Lucas and Rapping, pp. 257–305, in Phelps et al.

recall and were scarcely engaged in voluntary search activity. Their unemployment is as much a deadweight loss as the disguised unemployment of redundant workers on payrolls. This number declines to 25–30 percent when unemployment is 4 percent or below. Likewise, a 5–6 percent unemployment rate means that voluntary quits amount only to about a third of separations, layoffs to two-thirds. The proportions are reversed at low unemployment rates.

Second, the unemployment statistic is not an exhaustive count of those with time and incentive to search. An additional 3 percent of the labor force are involuntarily confined to part-time work, and another $\frac{3}{4}$ of 1 percent are out of the labor force because they "could not find job" or "think no work available"—discouraged by market conditions rather than personal incapacities.

Third, with unemployment of 5–6 percent the number of reported vacancies is less than $\frac{1}{2}$ of 1 percent. Vacancies appear to be understated relative to unemployment, but they rise to $1\frac{1}{2}$ percent when the unemployment rate is below 4 percent. At 5–6 percent unemployment, the economy is clearly capable of generating many more jobs with marginal productivity high enough so that people prefer them to leisure. The capital stock is no limitation, since 5–6 percent unemployment has been associated with more than 20 percent excess capacity. Moreover, when more jobs are created by expansion of demand, with or without inflation, labor force participation increases; this would hardly occur if the additional jobs were low in quality and productivity. As the parable of the central employment planner indicates, there will be excessive waiting for jobs if the roster of jobs and the menu of vacancies are suboptimal.

In summary, labor markets characterized by 5–6 percent unemployment do not display the symptoms one would expect if the unemployment were voluntary search activity. Even if it were voluntary, search activity on such a large scale would surely be socially wasteful. The only reason anyone might regard so high an unemployment rate as an equilibrium and social optimum is that lower rates cause accelerating inflation. But this is almost tautological. The inferences of equilibrium and optimality would be more convincing if they were corroborated by direct evidence.

IV. WHY IS THERE INFLATION WITHOUT AGGREGATE EXCESS DEMAND?

Zero-inflation unemployment is not wholly voluntary, not optimal, I might even say not natural. In other words, the economy has an inflationary bias: When labor markets provide as many jobs as there are willing workers, there is inflation, perhaps accelerating inflation. Why?

The Phillips curve has been an empirical finding in search of a theory, like Pirandello characters in search of an author. One rationalization might be termed a theory of stochastic macro-equilibrium: stochastic, because random intersectoral shocks keep individual labor markets in diverse states of disequilibrium; macro-equilibrium, because the perpetual flux of particular markets produces fairly definite aggregate outcomes of unemployment and wages. Stimulated by Phillips's 1958 findings, Richard Lipsey proposed a model of this kind in 1960, and it has since been elaborated by Archibald, pp. 212–23 and Holt, pp. 53–123 and 224–56 in Phelps et al., and others. I propose now to sketch a theory in the same spirit.

It is an essential feature of the theory that economy-wide relations among employment, wages, and prices are aggregations of diverse outcomes in heterogeneous markets. The myth of macroeconomics is that relations among aggregates are enlarged analogues of relations among corresponding variables for individual households; firms, industries, markets. The myth is a harmless and useful simplification in many contexts, but sometimes it misses the essence of the phenomenon.

Unemployment is, in this model as in Keynes reinterpreted, a disequilibrium phenomenon. Money wages do not adjust rapidly enough to clear all labor markets everyday. Excess supplies in labor markets take the form of unemployment, and excess demands the form of unfilled vacancies. At any moment, markets vary widely in excess demand or supply, and the economy as a whole shows both vacancies and unemployment.

The overall balance of vacancies and unemployment is determined by aggregate demand, and is therefore in principle subject to control by overall monetary and fiscal policy. Higher aggregate demand means fewer excess supply markets and more excess demand markets, accordingly less unemployment and more vacancies.

In any particular labor market, the rate of increase of money wages is the sum of two components, an equilibrium component and a disequilibrium component. The first is the rate at which the wage would increase were the market in equilibrium, with neither vacancies nor unemployment. The other component is a function of excess demand and supply—a monotonic function, positive for positive excess demand, zero for zero excess demand, non-positive for excess supply. I begin with the disequilibrium component.

Of course the disequilibrium components are relevant only if disequilibria persist. Why aren't they eliminated by the very adjustments they set in motion? Workers will move from excess supply markets to excess demand markets, and from low wage to high wage markets. Unless they overshoot, these movements are equilibrating. The theory therefore requires that new disequilibria are always arising. Aggregate demand may be stable, but beneath its stability is never-ending flux: new products, new processes, new tastes and fashions, new developments of land and natural resources, obsolescent industries and declining areas.

The overlap of vacancies and unemployment—say, the sum of the two for any given difference between them—is a measure of the heterogeneity or dispersion of individual markets. The amount of dispersion depends directly on the size of those shocks of demand and technology that keep markets in perpetual disequilibrium, and inversely on the responsive mobility of labor. The one increases, the other diminishes the frictional component

of unemployment, that is, the number of unfilled vacancies coexisting with any given unemployment rate.

A central assumption of the theory is that the functions relating wage change to excess demand or supply are nonlinear, specifically that unemployment retards money wages less than vacancies accelerate them. Nonlinearity in the response of wages to excess demand has several important implications. First, it helps to explain the characteristic observed curvature of the Phillips curve. Each successive increment of unemployment has less effect in reducing the rate of inflation. Linear wage response, on the other hand, would mean a linear Phillips relation.

Second, given the overall state of aggregate demand, economy-wide vacancies less unemployment, wage inflation will be greater the larger the variance among markets in excess demand and supply. As a number of recent empirical studies, have confirmed (see George Perry and Charles Schultze), dispersion is inflationary. Of course, the rate of wage inflation will depend not only on the overall dispersion of excess demands and supplies across markets but also on the particular markets where the excess supplies and demands happen to fall. An unlucky random drawing might put the excess demands in highly responsive markets and the excess supplies in especially unresponsive ones.

Third, the nonlinearity is an explanation of inflationary bias, in the following sense. Even when aggregate vacancies are at most equal to unemployment, the average disequilibrium component will be positive. Full employment in the sense of equality of vacancies and unemployment is not compatible with price stability. Zero inflation requires unemployment in excess of vacancies.

Criteria that coincide in full long-run equilibrium—zero inflation and zero aggregate excess demand—diverge in stochastic macroequilibrium. Full long-run equilibrium in all markets would show no unemployment, no vacancies, no unanticipated inflation. But with unending sectoral flux, zero excess demand spells inflation and zero inflation spells net excess supply, unemployment in excess of vacancies. In these circumstances neither criterion can be justified simply because it is a property of full long-run equilibrium. Both criteria automatically allow for frictional unemployment incident to the required movements of workers between markets; the no-inflation criterion requires enough additional unemployment to wipe out inflationary bias.

I turn now to the equilibrium component, the rate of wage increase in a market with neither excess demand nor excess supply. It is reasonable to suppose that the equilibrium component depends on the trend of wages of comparable labor elsewhere. A "competitive wage," one that reflects relevant trends fully, is what employers will offer if they wish to maintain their share of the volume of employment. This will happen where the rate of growth of marginal revenue product—the compound of productivity increase and price inflation—is the same as the trend in wages. But in some markets the equilibrium wage will be rising faster, and in others slower, than the economy-wide wage trend.

A "natural rate" result follows if actual wage increases feed fully into the equilibrium components of future wage increases. There will be acceleration whenever the nonlinear disequilibrium effects are on average positive, and steady inflation, that is stochastically steady inflation, only at unemployment rates high enough to make the disequilibrium effects wash out. Phillips tradeoffs exist in the short run, and the time it takes for them to evaporate depends on the lengths of the lags with which today's actual wage gains become tomorrow's standards.

A rather minor modification may preserve Phillips tradeoffs in the long run. Suppose there is a floor on wage change in excess supply markets, independent of the amount of excess supply and of the past history of wages and prices. Suppose, for example, that wage change is never negative; it is either zero or what the response function says, whichever is algebraically larger. So long as there are markets where this floor is effective, there can be determinate rates of economy-wide wage inflation for various levels of aggregate de-

mand. Markets at the floor do not increase their contributions to aggregate wage inflation when overall demand is raised. Nor is their contribution escalated to actual wage experience. But the frequency of such markets diminishes, it is true, both with overall demand and with inflation. The floor phenomenon can preserve a Phillips tradeoff within limits, but one that becomes ever more fragile and vanishes as greater demand pressure removes markets from contact with the zero floor. The model implies a long-run Phillips curve that is very flat for high unemployment and becomes vertical at a critically low rate of unemployment.

These implications seem plausible and even realistic. It will be objected, however, that any permanent floor independent of general wage and price history and expectation must indicate money illusion. The answer is that the floor need not be permanent in any single market. It could give way to wage reduction when enough unemployment has persisted long enough. But with stochastic intersectoral shifts of demand, markets are always exchanging roles, and there can always be some markets, not always the same ones, at the floor.

This model avoids the empirically questionable implication of the usual natural rate hypothesis that unemployment rates only slightly higher than the critical rate will trigger ever-accelerating deflation. Phillips curves seem to be pretty flat at high rates of unemployment. During the great contraction of 1930–33, wage rates were slow to give way even in the face of massive unemployment and substantial deflation in consumer prices. Finally in 1932 and 1933 money wage rates fell more sharply, in response to prolonged unemployment, layoffs, shutdowns and to threats and fears of more of the same.

I have gone through this example to make the point that irrationality, in the sense that meaningless differences in money values *permanently* affect individual behavior, is not logically necessary for the existence of a long-run Phillips tradeoff. In full long-run equilibrium in all markets, employment and unemployment would be independent of the levels and rates of change of money wage rates and prices. But this is not an equilibrium that the system ever approaches. The economy is in perpetual sectoral disequilibrium even when it has settled into a stochastic macro-equilibrium.

I suppose that one might maintain that asymmetry in wage adjustment and temporary resistance to money wage decline reflect money illusion in some sense. Such an assertion would have to be based on an extension of the domain of well-defined rational behavior to cover responses to change, adjustment speeds, costs of information, costs of organizing and operating markets, and a host of other problems in dynamic theory. These theoretical extensions are in their infancy, although much work of interest and promise is being done. Meanwhile, I doubt that significant restrictions on disequilibrium adjustment mechanisms can be deduced from first principles.

Why are the wage and salary rates of employed workers so intensive to the availability of potential replacements? One reason is that the employer makes some explicit or implicit commitments in putting a worker on the payroll in the first place. The employee expects that his wages and terms of employment will steadily improve, certainly never retrogress. He expects that the employer will pay him the rate prevailing for persons of comparable skill, occupation, experience, and seniority. He expects such commitments in return for his own investments in the job; arrangements for residence, transportation, and personal life involve set-up costs which will be wasted if the job turns sour. The market for labor services is not like a market for fresh produce where the entire current supply is auctioned daily. It is more like a rental housing market, in which most existing tenancies are the continuations of long-term relationships governed by contracts or less formal understandings.

Employers and workers alike regard the wage of comparable labor elsewhere as a standard, but what determines those reference wages? There is not even an auction where workers and employers unbound by existing relationships and commitments meet and determine a market-clearing wage. If such markets existed, they would provide competitively determined guides for negotiated and administered wages, just as stock exchange prices are reference points for stock transactions elsewhere. In labor markets the reverse is closer to the truth. Wage rates for existing employees set the standards for new employees, too.

The equilibrium components of wage increases, it has been argued, depend on past wage increases throughout the economy. In those theoretical and econometric models of inflation where labor markets are aggregated into a single market, this relationship is expressed as an autoregressive equation of fixed structure: current wage increase depends on past wage increases. The same description applies when past wage increases enter indirectly, mediated by price inflation and productivity change. The process of mutual interdependence of market wages is a good deal more complex and less mechanical than these aggregated models suggest.

Reference standards for wages differ from market to market. The equilibrium wage increase in each market will be some function of past wages in all markets, and perhaps of past prices too. But the function need not be the same in every market. Wages of workers contiguous in geography, industry, and skill will be heavily weighted. Imagine a wage pattern matrix of coefficients describing the dependence of the percentage equilibrium wage increase in each market on the past increases in all other markets. The coefficients in each row are non-negative and sum to one, but their distribution across markets and time lags will differ from row to row.

Consider the properties of such a system in the absence of disequilibrium inputs. First, the system has the "natural rate" property that its steady state is indeterminate. Any rate of wage increase that has been occurring in all markets for a long enough time will continue. Second, from irregular initial conditions the system will move toward one of these steady states, but which one depends on the specifics of the wage pattern matrix and the initial conditions. Contrary to some pessimistic warnings, there is no arithmetic compulsion that makes the whole system gravitate in the direction of its most inflationary sectors. The ultimate steady state inflation will be at most that of the market with the highest initial inflation rate, and at least that of the market with the lowest initial inflation rate. It need not be equal to the average inflation rate at the beginning, but may be either greater or smaller. Third, the adjustment paths are likely to contain cyclical components, damped or at most of constant amplitude, and during adjustments both individual and average wage movements may diverge substantially in both directions from their ultimate steady state value. Fourth, since wage decisions and negotiations occur infrequently, relative wage adjustments involve a lot of catching up and leap-frogging, and probably take a long time. I have sketched the formal properties of a disaggregated wage pattern system of this kind simply to stress again the vast simplification of the one-market myth.

A system in which only relative magnitudes matter has only a neutral equilibrium, from which it can be permanently displaced by random shocks. Even when a market is in equilibrium, it may outdo the recent wage increases in related markets. A shock of this kind, even though it is not repeated, raises permanently the steady state inflation rate. This is true cost-push—inflation generated neither by previous inflation nor by current excess demand. Shocks, of course, may be negative as well as positive. For example, upward pushes arising from adjustments in relative wage *levels* will be reversed when those adjustments are completed.

To the extent that one man's reference wages are another man's wages, there is something arbitrary and conventional, indeterminate and unstable, in the process of wage setting. In the same current market circumstances, the reference pattern might be 8 percent per year or 3 percent per year or zero, depending on the historical prelude. Market conditions, unemployment and va-

cancies and their distributions shape history and alter reference patterns. But accidental circumstances affecting stragetic wage settlements also cast a long shadow.

Price inflation, as previously observed, is a neutral method of making arbitrary money wage paths conform to the realities of productivity growth, neutral in preserving the structure of relative wages. If expansion of aggregate demand brings both more inflation and more employment, there need be no mystery why unemployed workers accept the new jobs, or why employed workers do not vacate theirs. They need not be victims of ignorance or inflation illusion. They genuinely want more work at feasible real wages, and they also want to maintain the relative status they regard as proper and just.

Guideposts could be in principle the functional equivalent of inflation, a neutral method of reconciling wage and productivity paths. The trick is to find a formula for mutual deescalation which does not offend conceptions of relative equity. No one has devised a way of controlling average wage rates without intervening in the competitive struggle over relative wages. Inflation lets this struggle proceed and blindly, impartially, impersonally, and nonpolitically scales down all its outcomes. There are worse methods of resolving group rivalries and social conflict.

V. THE ROLE OF MONOPOLY POWER

Probably the most popular explanation of the inflationary bias of the economy is concentration of economic power in large corporations and unions. These powerful monopolies and oligopolies, it is argued, are immune from competition in setting wages and prices. The unions raise wages above competitive rates, with little regard for the unemployed and under-employed workers knocking at the gates. Perhaps the unions are seeking a bigger share of the revenues of the monopolies and oligopolies with whom they bargain. But they don't really succeed in that objective, because the corporations simply pass the increased labor costs, along with mark-ups, on to their helpless customers. The remedy, it is argued, is either atomization of big business and big labor or strict public control of their prices and wages.

So simple a diagnosis is vitiated by confusion between levels and rates of change. Monopoly power is no doubt responsible for the relatively high prices and wages of some sectors. But can the exercise of monopoly power generate ever-rising prices and wages? Monopolists have no reason to hold reserves of unexploited power. But if they did, or if events awarded them new power, their exploitation of it would raise their real prices and wages only temporarily.

Particular episodes of inflation may be associated with accretions of monopoly power, or with changes in the strategies and preferences of those who possess it. Among the reasons that wages and prices rose in the face of mass unemployment after 1933 were *NRA* codes and other early New Deal measures to suppress competition, and the growth of trade union membership and power under the protection of new federal legislation. Recently we have witnessed substantial gains in the powers of organized public employees. Unions elsewhere may not have gained power, but some of them apparently have changed their objectives in favor of wages at the expense of employment.

One reason for the popularity of the monopoly power diagnosis of inflation is the identification of administered prices and wages with concentrations of economic power. When price and wage increases are the outcomes of visible negotiations and decisions, it seems obvious that identifiable firms and unions have the power to affect the course of inflation. But the fact that monopolies, oligopolies, and large unions have discretion does not mean it is invariably to their advantage to use it to raise prices and wages. Nor are administered prices and wages found only in high concentration sectors. Very few prices and wages in a modern economy, even in the more competitive sectors, are determined in Walrasian auction markets.

No doubt there has been a secular increase in the prevalence of administered wages and prices, connected with the relative decline of agriculture and other sectors of self-employment. This development probably has contributed to the inflationary bias of the economy, by enlarging the number of labor markets where the response of money wages to excess supply is slower than their response to excess demand. The decline of agriculture as a sector of flexible prices and wages and as an elastic source of industrial labor is probably an important reason why the Phillips trade off problem is worse now than in the 1920's. Sluggishness of response to excess supply is a feature of administered prices, whatever the market structure, but it may be accentuated by concentration of power per se. For example, powerful unions, not actually forced by competition to moderate their wage demands, may for reasons of internal politics be slow to respond to unemployment in their ranks.

VI. SOME REFLECTIONS ON POLICY

If the makers of macroeconomic policy could be sure that the zero-inflation rate of unemployment is natural, voluntary, and optimal, their lives would be easy. Friedman told us that all macroeconomic policy needs to do, all it should try to do, is to make nominal national income grow steadily at the natural rate of growth of aggregate supply. This would sooner or later result in price stability. Steady price deflation would be even better, he said, because it would eliminate the socially wasteful incentive to economize money holdings. In either case, unemployment will converge to its natural rate, and wages and prices will settle into steady trends. Under this policy, whatever unemployment the market produces is the correct result. No tradeoff, no choice, no agonizing decisions.

I have argued this evening that a substantial amount of the unemployment compatible with zero inflation is involuntary and nonoptimal. This is, in my opinion, true whether or not the inflations associated with lower rates of unemployment are steady or ever-accelerating. Neither macroeconomic policy makers, nor the elected officials and electorates to whom they are responsible, can avoid weighing the costs of unemployment against those of inflation. As Phelps has pointed out, this social choice has an intertemporal dimension. The social costs of involuntary unemployment are mostly obvious and immediate. The social costs of inflation come later.

What are they? Economists' answers have been remarkably vague, even though the prestige of the profession has reinforced the popular view that inflation leads ultimately to catastrophe. Here indeed is a case where abstract economic theory has a powerful hold on public opinion and policy. The prediction that at low unemployment rates inflation will accelerate toward ultimate disaster is a theoretical deduction with little empirical support. In fact the weight of econometric evidence has been against acceleration, let alone disaster. Yet the deduction has been convincing enough to persuade this country to give up billions of dollars of annual output and to impose sweeping legal controls on prices and wages. Seldom has a society made such large immediate and tangible sacrifices to avert an ill defined, uncertain, eventual evil.

According to economic theory, the ultimate social cost of anticipated inflation is the wasteful use of resources to economize holdings of currency and other noninterest-bearing means of payment. I suspect that intelligent laymen would be utterly astounded if they realized that *this* is the great evil economists are talking about. They have imagined a much more devastating cataclysm, with Vesuvius vengefully punishing the sinners below. Extra trips between savings banks and commercial banks? What an anti-climax!

With means of payment—currency plus demand deposits—equal currently to 20 percent of *GNP*, an extra percentage point of anticipated inflation embodied in nominal interest rates produces in principle a social cost of 2/10 of 1 percent of *GNP* per year. This is an outside estimate. An unknown, but substantial, share of the stock of money belongs to holders who are not

trying to economize cash balances and are not near any margin where they would be induced to spend resources for this purpose. These include hoarders of large denomination currency, about one-third of the total currency in public hands, for reasons of privacy, tax evasion, or illegal activity. They include tradesmen and consumers whose working balances turn over too rapidly or are too small to justify any effort to invest them in interest-bearing assets. They include corporations who, once they have been induced to undertake the fixed costs of a sharp-pencil money management department, are already minimizing their cash holdings. They include businessmen who are in fact being paid interest on demand deposits, although it takes the form of preferential access to credit and other bank services. But, in case anyone still regards the waste of resources in unnecessary transactions between money and interest-bearing financial assets as one of the major economic problems of the day, there is a simple and straighforward remedy, the payment of interest on demand deposits and possibly, with ingenuity, on currency too.

The ultimate disaster of inflation would be the breakdown of the monetary payments system, necessitating a currency reform. Such episodes have almost invariably resulted from real economic catastrophes—wars, defeats, revolutions, reparations—not from the mechanisms of wage-price push with which we are concerned. Acceleration is a scare word, conveying the image of a rush into hyperinflation as relentlessly deterministic and monotonic as the motion of falling bodies. Realistic attention to the disaggregated and stochastic nature of wage and price movements suggests that they will show diverse and irregular fluctuations around trends that are difficult to discern and extrapolate. The central trends, history suggests, can accelerate for a long, long time without generating hyper-inflations destructive of the payments mechanism.

Unanticipated inflation, it is contended, leads to mistaken estimates of relative prices and consequently to misallocations of resources. An example we have already discussed is the alleged misallocation of time by workers who over-estimate their real wages. The same error would lead to a general over-supply by sellers who contract for future deliveries without taking correct account of the increasing prices of the things they must buy in order to fulfill the contract. Unanticipated deflation would cause similar miscalculations and misallocations. Indeed, people can make these same mistakes about relative prices even when the price level is stable. The mistakes are more likely, or the more costly to avoid, the greater the inflationary trend. There are costs in setting and announcing new prices. In an inflationary environment price changes must be made more frequently—a new catalog twice a year instead of one, or some formula for automatic escalation of announced prices. Otherwise, with the interval between announcements unchanged, the average misalignment of relative prices will be larger the faster the inflation. The same problem would arise with rapid deflation.

Unanticipated inflation and deflation—and the unanticipated changes in relative prices—are also sources of transfers of wealth. I will not review here the rich and growing empirical literature on this subject. Facile generalization about the progressivity or equity of inflationary transfers are hazardous; certainly inflation does not merit the cliché that it is "the cruelest tax." Let us not forget that unemployment has distributional effects as well as dead-weight losses.

Some moralists take the view that the government has promised to maintain the purchasing power of its currency, but this promise is their inference rather than any pledge written on dollar bills or in the Constitution. Some believe so strongly in this implicit contract that they are willing to suspend actual contracts in the name of anti-inflation.

I have long contended that the government should make low-interest bonds of guaranteed purchasing power available for savers and pension funds who wish to avoid the risks of unforeseen inflation. The common objection to escalated bonds is that they would diminish the built-in stability of the

system. The stability in question refers to the effects on aggregate real demand, *ceteris paribus*, of a change in the price level. The Pigou effect tells us that government bond-holders whose wealth is diminished by inflation will spend less. This brake on old-fashioned gap inflation will be thrown away if the bonds are escalated. The considerations are only remotely related to the mechanisms of wage and price inflation we have been discussing. In the 1970's we know that the government can, if it wishes, control aggregate demand—at any rate, its ability to do so is only trivially affected by the presence or absence of Pigou effects on part of the government debt.

In considering the intertemporal trade-off, we have no license to assume that the natural rate of unemployment is independent of the history of actual unemployment. Students of human capital have been arguing convincingly that earning capacity, indeed transferable earning capacity, depends on experience as well as formal education. Labor markets soggy enough to maintain price stability may increase the number of would-be workers who lack the experience to fit them for jobs that become vacant.

Macroeconomic policies, monetary and fiscal, are incapable of realizing society's unemployment and inflation goals simultaneously. This dismal fact has long stimulated a search for third instruments to do the job: guideposts and incomes policies, on the one hand, labor market and manpower policies, on the other. Ten to fifteen years ago great hopes were held for both. The Commission on Money and Credit in 1961, pp. 39–40, hailed manpower policies as the new instrument that would overcome the unemployment-inflation dilemma. Such advice was taken seriously in Washington, and an unprecedented spurt in manpower programs took place in the 1960's. The Council of Economic Advisers set forth wage and price guideposts in 1961–62 in the hope of "talking down" the Phillips curve (pp. 185–90). It is discouraging to find that these efforts did not keep the problem of inflationary bias from becoming worse than ever.

So it is not with great confidence or optimism that one suggests measures to mitigate the tradeoff. But some proposals follow naturally from the analysis, and some are desirable in themselves anyway.

First, guideposts do not wholly deserve the scorn that "toothless jawboning" often attracts. There is an arbitrary, imitative component in wage settlements, and maybe it can be influenced by national standards.

Second, it is important to create jobs for those unemployed and discouraged workers who have extremely low probability of meeting normal job specifications. Their unemployment does little to discipline wage increases, but reinforces their deprivation of human capital and their other disadvantages in job markets. The National Commission on Technology, Automation and Economic Progress pointed out in 1966 the need for public service jobs tailored to disadvantaged workers. They should not be "last resort" or make-work jobs, but regular permanent jobs capable of conveying useful experience and inducing reliable work habits. Assuming that the additional services produced by the employing institutions are of social utility, it may well be preferable to employ disadvantaged workers directly rather than to pump up aggregate demand until they reach the head of the queue.

Third, a number of measures could be taken to make markets more responsive to excess supplies. This is the kernel of truth in the market-power explanation of inflationary bias. In many cases, government regulations themselves support prices and wages against competition. Agricultural prices and construction wages are well-known examples. Some trade unions follow wage policies that take little or no account of the interests of less senior members and of potential members. Since unions operate with federal sanction and protection, perhaps some means can be found to insure that their memberships are open and that their policies are responsive to the unemployed as well as the employed.

As for macroeconomic policy, I have argued that it should aim for unemployment lower than the zero-inflation rate. How much lower? Low enough to equate unemployment and vacancies? We cannot say. In the nature of the case there is no simple formula—conceptual, much less statistical—for full employment. Society cannot escape very difficult political and intertemporal choices. We economists can illuminate these choices as we learn more about labor markets, mobility, and search, and more about the social and distributive costs of both unemployment and inflation. Thirty-five years after Keynes, welfare macroeconomics is still a relevant and challenging subject. I dare to believe it has a bright future.

References

Beveridge, W. H., *Full Employment in a Free Society* (New York, 1945).

Doeringer, P., and Piore, M., *Internal Labor Markets and Manpower Analysis* (Lexington, 1971).

Friedman, M., "The Role of Monetary Policy," *American Economic Review*, 58:1–17 (1968).

Hall, R., "Why is the Unemployment Rate So High at Full Employment?" *Brookings Papers on Economic Activity*, 3:369–402 (1970).

Keynes, J. M., *The General Theory of Employment, Interest, and Money* (New York, 1936).

Leijonhufvud, A., *On Keynesian Economics and the Economics of Keynes* (New York, 1968).

Lipsey, R. G., "The Relation Between Unemployment and the Rate of Change of Money Wage Rates in the United Kingdom, 1862–1957: A Further Analysis," *Economica*, 27:1–31 (1960).

Parnes, H. S., *Research on Labor Mobility*, Social Science Research Council, Bull. 65 (New York, 1954).

Perry, G. L., "Changing Labor Markets and Inflation," *Brookings Papers on Economic Activity*, 3:411–441 (1970).

Phelps, E. S., et al., "Inflation and Optimal Unemployment Over Time," *Economica*, 34:254–281 (1967).

Phelps, E. S., et al., *Micro-economic Foundations of Employment and Inflation Theory* (New York, 1970).

Phillips, A. W., "The Relation Between Unemployment and the Rate of Change of Money Wage Rates in the United Kingdom, 1861–1957," *Economica*, 25:283–299 (1958).

Reynolds, L. G., *The Structure of Labor Markets* (New York, 1951).

Schultze, C. L., "Has the Phillips Curve Shifted? Some Additional Evidence," *Brookings Papers on Economic Activity*, 2:452–471 (1971).

Tobin, J., "A Note on the Money Wage Problem," *Quarterly Journal of Economics*, 55:508–516 (1941).

Commission on Money and Credit, *Money and Credit: Their Influence on Jobs, Prices, and Growth* (Englewood Cliffs, 1961).

Economic Report of the President 1962 (Washington, 1962).

U.S. National Commission on Technology, Automation, and Economic Progress, *Technology and the American Economy* (Washington, 1966).

Recent Developments in the Theory of Inflation and Unemployment

Robert J. Gordon

Northwestern University

1. INTRODUCTION AND BACKGROUND

Theoretical and empirical research on the causes, costs and cures of inflation and unemployment preoccupies a substantial portion of the economics profession. Any comprehensive survey of this body of work, while perhaps providing substantial revenue for the paper and ink industries, would be too indigestible to attract serious readers. Instead, this paper takes a selective rather than comprehensive approach and is concerned with the causes of inflation but not with its costs or cures; with theoretical developments but not with the results of empirical tests (except insofar as the empirical results bear on the relevance of theoretical assumptions); and with papers written during the last decade but not those written earlier.[1] The paper's scope includes the causes of unemployment as well as inflation, because the most interesting recent papers have treated both phenomena as part of a single analytical

Reprinted from the *Journal of Monetary Economics*, 2:185–219 (1976), by permission of the author and the publisher (copyright by the North-Holland Publishing Company).

[1] For a much more comprehensive approach, see the recent survey by Laidler and Parkin (1975) reprinted in this volume. This paper differs from theirs in its greater emphasis on the causes of unemployment and on microeconomic models of labor-market behavior, and in its relative lack of attention to empirical results, to the detailed specification of econometric wage-price models, and to the rates of inflation. For a more general, shorter and more readable introduction to the inflation literature, see Solow (1975).

problem, e.g., those which model the optimal adjustment by firms of employment and wage rates in response to unexpected changes in product demand.

The literature surveyed here spans the period since 1963, a starting point chosen not only because of the simultaneous appearance in that year of inflation surveys by Bronfenbrenner and Holzman (1963) and Johnson (1967), but also because 1963 antedated the late-1960s acceleration which so greatly influenced current views of the nature of inflation, and also because the span of roughly a decade makes this paper a companion piece to the survey of monetary theory by Barro and Fisher (1976).

Novel theoretical contributions of the past decade can be most easily distinguished from those repeating earlier themes, if we examine the reactions of a hypothetical modern-day Rip Van Winkle who had become well acquainted with the earlier inflation literature but who only recently awoke from a decade-long nap. What were the major elements in the body of inflation theory which Rip had assimilated when he fell asleep after reading the Johnson and Bronfenbrenner-Holzman survey articles?

2. WHAT RIP KNEW WHEN HE WENT TO SLEEP

2.1. Demand-Pull vs. Cost-Push Inflation

Theories of the causes of inflation were generally classified into two major groups,

FIG. 1

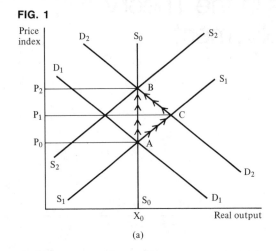

(a)

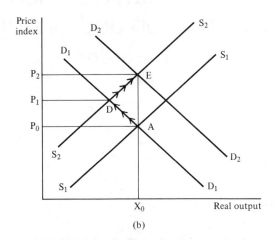

(b)

"demand-pull" and "cost-push," and can be distinguished with the aid of Fig. 1, where real output is plotted on the horizontal axis and an aggregate price index on the vertical. In each frame the aggregate demand curve DD is negatively sloped and represents those combinations of price and real output which clear *both* the commodity and money markets for a given level of the money supply, fiscal variables, and parameters in private spending functions. A higher price level reduces the real money supply and requires for money-market equilibrium a higher interest rate and hence lower level of real output to achieve a lower real demand for money.[2] An increase in the money supply or a fiscal stimulus, except in well-known extreme cases, shifts the DD curve rightward, e.g., from $D_1 D_1$ to $D_2 D_2$. The aggregate supply curves $S_0 S_0$ and $S_1 S_1$ represent alternative assumptions about the combinations of real output and the price level which keep factors of production (firms and workers) in equilibrium.

A "demand-pull" inflation was initiated by some event, whether a monetary or fiscal policy change or a change in private spending behavior, which shifted DD to the right. "Demand-pull" theories were divided between the quantity theory, which emphasized

the causative role of monetary changes, and Keynesian theories of inflation, which emphasized nonmonetary impulses. The quantity theory differed, first, in its dynamic setting, which attributed a steady inflation to a continuous upward shift in DD fueled by a continuous monetary injection. Keynesian inflation models, in contrast, could explain an increase in the price level from P_0 to P_1 or P_2 as initiated by fiscal or other nonmonetary disturbances if the dynamic process were stable, and explosive inflation with unstable parameters, but could not explain a continuing inflation without the implicit assumption of an unlimited supply of idle money balances or a passive monetary accommodation.

A second difference was the quantity theory assumption of a vertical supply curve, which, although not logically connected with the monetary source of the DD shift, had been part of the quantity theory tradition since Hume.[3] With the vertical supply curve $S_0 S_0$, a continuous money-fueled inflation shifted the economy in Fig. 1(a) from point A to B to further points directly north. The effect of a steady inflation on the real economy was limited to a redistribution from money holders to money issuers, especially the government, through the inflation tax. In contrast, Keynesian models emphasized shifts

---

[2] If the demand for real output is interest inelastic (the *IS* curve is vertical) then the *DD* curve will be vertical also. A complete development of the graphical apparatus is contained in Branson (1972).

[3] See Friedman's (1975) citations from Hume.

in the saving-investment balance as income was redistributed during the inflation process, through a wide variety of assumptions about the stickiness or constancy of some aspect of wage- or price-setting behavior, e.g., money illusion, lags, progressive taxation, differences in price-setting behavior between sectors, etc.[4] Since the very process of inflation generated real effects, a demand-induced price increase could be accompanied by an increase in real output, as along supply curve S_1S_1, in Fig. 1(a). Money illusion, for instance, might induce an increase in the price level, and allow the economy to move from point A to C. If workers were allowed to "learn," shifting the supply curve to S_2S_2, point B would eventually be reached, as in the quantity-theory approach.

"Cost-push" inflation was initiated in its various versions by a wage-push from small unions facing an inelastic demand curve for labor, rivalry among groups of unions, profit-push generated through administered pricing, or, more generally, a struggle for income shares among any set of subgroups in society. In fig. 1(b), S_1S_1 shifted to S_2S_2 as a result of the spontaneous increase in costs and, as most writers recognized, caused a reduction in output and employment unless the push was ratified by monetary accommodation, which could maintain the original output level if the money supply were increased sufficiently to shift aggregate demand from D_1D_1 to D_2D_2.

The distinction between cost-push and demand-push was largely spurious, because a one-shot spontaneous wage- or profit-push could only raise the *level* of prices, not permanently increase their *rate of change*, unless accompanied by faster monetary growth. If there were an existing state of union or firm monopolies, but the *degree* of monopoly had not been increasing, monopoly power could not be a source of continuing inflation. Thus, in retrospect any sustained inflation became

"always and everywhere a monetary phenomenon."[5] A demand-pull inflation initiated by a continuous monetary stimulus moved the economy from A to B to points further north in Fig. 1(a), while a cost-push inflation accommodated by monetary growth followed exactly the same path in Fig. 1(b) (A to E and points north). The two main types of inflation could be distinguished in retrospect only if adjustment speeds were slow. A demand inflation followed path ACB if lags or money illusion temporarily delayed the upward shift of supply curve S_1S_1 in Fig. 1(a), and a supply inflation followed path ADE in Fig. 1(b) if monetary accommodation were delayed.[6] In drawing a sharp line between demand and supply inflation, what people may have had in mind was a combination of slow adjustment speeds together with a succession of demand or supply shocks which occurred without enough pause between episodes to allow the dynamics to work themselves out.

Ruling out as implausible and empirically unproven an infinitely elastic supply of idle balances, a Keynesian demand inflation generated by shifts in fiscal policy or private spending propensities, or a cost-induced inflation generated by autonomous increases in wage or profit demands, had to be validated by the monetary authority. Could one therefore argue that a distinction should have been made *not* between demand-pull and cost-push inflation, but rather between inflations in which the role of money was active vs.

---

[4] Sections II, V, and VI of the Bronfenbrenner–Holzman Survey (1963) are all primarily devoted to innumerable assumptions which generate redistributions of income during an inflation.

[5] This phrase originated with Friedman (1966, p. 18), albeit in the post-1963 period. There have been exceptions, as he pointed out, including the 1933–37 period, during which the NRA and Wagner Act raised the level of firm and union monopoly power, and which can be cited as an instance of cost-push inflation.

[6] Empirical tests by Selden (1959), Attiyeh (1959) and Phelps (1961) attempted to distinguish supply from demand-induced inflations along these lines but were generally inconclusive, as one might expect either if the supply curve shifted up rapidly following an initial demand shift, or vice versa. Far better opportunities for such empirical tests have been provided by events during the past decade, during which the 1964–66 acceleration in inflation was unambiguously accompanied by an increase in output, while the 1973–74 inflation was accompanied by a pronounced decrease in output.

passive? Even this potential basis for classification became blurred when one recognized
that, even in most classic wartime or postwar
money-fueled inflations and hyperinflations,
the role of the monetary authority had been
passively to finance deficits resulting from the
unwillingness or inability of politicians to
finance expenditures through conventional
taxation. Keynesian fiscal-induced money-
accommodated inflation and quantity-theory
money-initiated inflation had, in almost all
actual cases, amounted to one and the same
thing.[7] Thus a more general view implicit in
pre-1963 developments, and explicitly set out
in Reder's (1948) classic analysis, attributed
inflation to the passivity of the monetary
authority in the face of a "tripartite" set of
pressures emanating from all groups in
society–labor, management and government.
A notable feature of the pre-1963 literature,
at least in the U.S., was the disproportionate
concern with unions and the bargaining process as the source of pressure, due presumably to the occurrence in the U.S. of the
1955–57 inflation during a period of government surplus.

Within this more general framework the
basic unsettled issues can be divided into two
basic categories:

1. Why do the pressures on the monetary
   authority from the private and public
   sectors differ across time within the same
   country, and differ across countries at any
   given time?
2. What structural features of the economy
   influence the ability of the monetary
   authority to resist pressure? In particular,
   what fraction of a monetary contraction
   takes the form of a reduction in output as
   compared to a reduction in prices, i.e. what
   is the slope of the short-run supply curve
   (e.g. $S_1 S_1$ in fig. 1 above) and under what
   conditions does the curve shift downward?

[7] Among the few U.S. examples of monetary growth
independent of government deficits were (1) 1919–20
in the U.S. when money expanded while the Federal
budget was in surplus, and (2) 1929–33 when money
contracted while the Federal budget was in deficit.

2.2. Where the Phillips Curve Fitted in

The Phillips Curve began as the result of an
empirical investigation of U.K. wage behavior by Phillips (1958), was extended and put
into a theoretical disequilibrium context by
Lipsey (1960), and was applied to the U.S.
and set in a policy context by Samuelson and
Solow (1960). The relationship had originally
been investigated by Irving Fisher thirty years
previously in a long-neglected and recently
rediscovered paper (1926). In Lipsey's version,
the rate of change of wages in a single labor
market was positively related to the excess
demand for labor, and the unemployment
rate was negatively related to the excess demand for labor. If one then aggregated and
added the assumption that the price level was
'marked-up' over the wage rate by a relatively
stable proportion, one obtained a negative
relationship between the rate of inflation and
the rate of unemployment. If by happy coincidence this negatively sloping Phillips
Curve crossed the zero-inflation point (on the
vertical axis) at an unemployment rate (on
the horizontal axis) generally regarded as
"full," or "optimal," no policy problem arose.
If, however, full employment and price stability were not compatible, policymakers were
forced to choose among a set of second-best
points along the Phillips Curve. It was common in the U.S. for economic advisers to
Democratic Presidents to recommend the
choice of a point on the curve northwest of
the target of Republican advisers.

As he fell asleep in 1963, Rip Van Winkle
was puzzled at the failure of either survey
author—Bronfenbrenner–Holzman or Johnson—to integrate the Phillips Curve with
Fig. 1, where a higher aggregate price level
could not induce a permanent increase in
output once workers and firms in individual
product markets had reevaluated their higher
wage offers and individual product prices in
terms of the higher aggregate price level.
Adjustment lags and/or money illusion were
required in fig. 1(a) for a demand shift to
increase output permanently, so Rip won-
dered how higher output and an excess demand for labor could persist permanently, as

implied by the immobile Phillips Curve. He was also disturbed by the absence of any rigorous theory explaining the determinants of the zero-inflation unemployment rate. Why was the "full-employment" unemployment rate so high, particularly in the U.S., and why was the zero-inflation rate even higher than that?

3. RIP AWAKES AND VIEWS THE PAST DECADE

Immediately after awakening, Rip rushed to the nearest good library to bring himself up to date on the development of inflation and unemployment theory.[8] His reactions follow and emphasize primarily those developments which he found surprising, novel and important: (1) the quantity theory resurgence (the natural rate hypothesis, the rise of monetarism, and the application of rational expectations to problems of monetary control); (2) the microeconomic theory of wage and employment adjustment (first as an explanation of voluntary unemployment, later as an explanation of layoffs and involuntary unemployment); and (3) the international transmission of inflation among open economies.

3.1. Revival and Extension of the Quantity Theory Approach to Inflation Theory

3.1.1. The Natural Rate Hypothesis: Implications and Critique

Early in the past decade, Rip was relieved to discover, the conflict between Fig. 1 and the Phillips Curve tradeoff was independently resolved by Friedman (1966, 1968) and Phelps (1967). Friedman was the first clearly to state that "there is no long-run, stable trade-off between inflation and unemployment" (1966, p. 60). Friedman's labor-market analysis (1968) differed from Lipsey's in its explicit assumption that both the demand for and supply of labor depended on the *real* wage rather than on the nominal wage. Since the

nominal wage was evaluated in terms of the current actual product price by employers and in terms of the expected average consumer price level by workers, employment could increase only as long as the expected price level lagged behind the actual level (thus simultaneously allowing a *lower* actual real wage to induce increased hiring by firms, and a *higher* expected real wage to induce a higher labor supply by workers). In equilibrium the expected and actual price level were equal, and so in equilibrium only one level of employment rate (given population, technology, and labor-force participation) as the "natural rate of unemployment," and later (1975) regarded his role as merely restating in dynamic form Hume's original proposition that a monetary expansion could "excite" real output only temporarily.

The "natural rate hypothesis" (NRH) completely changed the framework of optimum stabilization policy. Policymaker indifference curves drawn on the inflation-unemployment axes, which had formerly allowed the choice of an optimum point on a stable Phillips Curve, were now irrelevant.[9] The Council of Economic Advisers was now to be divided into two independent branches, one group of labor economists which would tally up the costs and benefits of manpower programs designed to shift the natural unemployment rate, on which monetary and fiscal policies by themselves had no effect, and a second group of monetary economists which determined the optimum rate of inflation as a function of the growth rate of real output and the interest rate paid on money, and the marginal costs of levying conventional taxes [see Bailey (1957), Friedman (1969) and Tower (1971)].

Phelps (1972) pointed out, however, and Hall (1976) later demonstrated in computer simulations, that this labor–money policy dichotomy implicitly assumed a zero rate of time preference, implying that if the economy was presently operating at an inflation rate

---

[8] The library was indeed a good one, since it contained many papers which, as of mid 1975, had scarcely been written, much less published.

[9] "Democratic" indifference curves were steep, with a point of tangency at a relatively high inflation rate and a low unemployment rate, whereas 'Republican' indifference curves were more gently sloped.

(p) above the optimum (p^*), a period of unemployment above the natural rate would be
suffered temporarily, but that this transition
cost had no bearing on the recommendation
that p should be reduced to p^* for the infinite
future. The policymakers' utility function re-
gained relevance, however, when their rate of
time preference was positive. Starting from a
position in which $p > p^*$, a deliberate 1970-
style recession might be rejected if the near-
term social cost of extra unemployment was
judged to exceed the long-term benefits of
reducing p to p^*. Similarly, even if $p = p^*$
initially, the benefit of sub-natural unemployment in the near future might outweigh the
permanent legacy of $p > p^*$ in the far future.

The Friedman–Phelps NRH was widely
misunderstood and continuously disputed
during most of the decade. A basic misunderstanding was the belief that the NRH had, in
and of itself, revived the quantity-theory
proposition that the rate of inflation (p) was
determined by the rate of growth of the money
supply (m). Consider the quantity identity

$$p = m + v - x, \qquad (1)$$

where lower-case letters represent proportional rates of growth, v is velocity growth,
and x is real-output growth. Whether or not
the Phillips Curve tradeoff is stable, a fixed
unemployment rate is associated with a given
rate of growth of "potential" output (the
growth in the labor force plus technical
progress). Assuming that velocity growth is
exogenous (determined by the income elasticity of money demand and the rate of introduction of money substitutes at any given
level of interest rates), the rate of inflation is
fundamentally determined by the rate of
monetary growth. This basic proposition was
not altered in the slightest by the NRH,
which was novel not by associating money
with inflation, but rather in its claim that
changes in the rate of monetary growth could
not cause the rate of unemployment permanently to diverge from its "natural rate"
without a continuously accelerating inflation
or deflation.

The initial reaction of U.S. mainstream
economists to the NRH was that the policy

implications of NRH could be safely ignored,
on the empirical grounds that U.S. price and
unemployment were inconsistent with it. In
the following inflation equation,

$$p_t = \alpha p_t^e + f(U_t - U_t^N), \qquad (2)$$

p_t^e is the expected rate of inflation (expected at
the beginning of period t), and U_t is the actual
and U_t^N the natural rate of unemployment
during that period. (2) is consistent with the
NRH, i.e., $U_t \neq U_t^N$ implies $p_t \neq p_t^e$, only if
$\alpha = 1$. Until 1971, published empirical tests
for the U.S., including those by Perry (1966,
1970), Solow (1968) and Gordon (1971),
yielded estimates of α which were significantly
less than unity. Two sets of influences gradually defused this line of criticism of NRH.
First, the gradual acceleration of inflation
during 1966–70 caused the computer to yield
ever higher values of α as the passage of time
provided additional observations until finally,
as demonstrated by Gordon (1972), tests with
a sample period including early 1971 were
unable to reject statistically the hypothesis
that $\alpha = 1$. Second, Lucas (1972a, 1976)
claimed that policy simulations with econometric models including fitted equations
like (2) above could not provide guidance for
policy decisions, because the fixed estimated
parameters were based on the particular
environment of the sample period, whereas
the true parameters might vary with each
alternative policy. Lucas' point had been
anticipated in Johnson's (1963) survey article
in a brief speculation that the Phillips Curve
might not prove to be stable "if an attempt
were made by economic policy to pin the
economy down to a point on it" (1963, p. 133).

Both Eckstein–Brinner (1972) and Gordon
(1972) developed models in which the α
parameter was allowed to vary in response
to changes in the inflationary environment.
Firms and workers might not have paid much
attention to the overall expected rate of inflation in setting wages and product prices if
the rate of inflation in the past had fluctuated
fairly randomly around a mean of zero, but
they would have an economic incentive to
adjust fully once the price level had developed
a noticeable positive trend which was not

expected to be reversed.[10] The "threshold" hypothesis allowed NRH to be reconciled with U.S. postwar data which had previously appeared to be in conflict with it.

A second criticism of the NRH has been its lack of validation in recession and depression episodes. When α equals unity, and when we add the additional hypothesis that expectations are formed adaptively, according to (2), a period when the unemployment rate remains above the natural rate for a substantial period should be characterized by an accelerating decline in the first derivative of prices and eventually in an accelerating deflation. During the Great Depression the unemployment rate remained above 8.5 percent for twelve straight years in the U.S. (between 1930 and 1941) without the slightest sign of an accelerating deflation.[11] This criticism, however, confuses two quite separate issues— the values in (2) of α and the shape of the $f(\ )$ function. It might be true that α equals unity but at the same time that $f'(U_t - U_t^N)$ equals zero for some range of unemployment rates, if, for instance, the short-run Phillips Curve $f(\ )$ were convex and became flat in the range of unemployment rates achieved during the 1930s. In this case the natural rate hypothesis would remain completely valid for all situations in which the unemployment rate remained outside of the flat range and, in particular, might have remained valid throughout the postwar period.

Nevertheless, a proper interpretation of the behavior of prices and unemployment during the Great Depression is crucial for the current formulation of anti-inflation policy. Even if the NRH remains valid when $f'(\ )$ is negative, an attempt to 'beat the inflation out of the system' by the deliberate creation of a major recession could be costly if $f'(\ )$ were very small in the range of unemployment rates above the natural rate and could be impossible if $f'(\ )$ were approxi-

mately equal to zero in that range. How strong is the evidence from the Great Depression that $f'(\ )$ is approximately equal to zero at "high" unemployment rates, and what are the precise unemployment numbers which we now define as "high"?

The basic fact of wage and price inflexibility during the last two-thirds of the Great Depression cannot be disputed. In 1940 the CPI was eight percent higher than in 1933, and average annual earnings per full time employee was 24 percent higher.[12] During the same 1933–40 interval the civilian unemployment rate did not fall below 14.3 percent. Two lines of argument are available to counter the conclusion that the $f(\ )$ function is virtually flat at high unemployment rates.

The first claims that the government encouraged price and wage increases during the 1930s, particularly through the NRA and the Wagner Act, and thus shifted the $f(\ )$ schedule upward, effectively disguising its negative slope. While the deliberate creation of a climate favorable to wage and price increases during the brief NRA period of 1933–34 cannot be denied, the attribution of post-1934 wage inflexibility to the Wagner Act is not convincing. Presumably the Wagner Act had its major effect on wages by encouraging the unionization of major industries, thus shifting workers from low-paid nonunionized activity to higher-paid unionized activity and raising the average level of earnings per worker in the economy. But available data indicate a uniform downward inflexibility of wage rates not only in the total private economy, which reflected the shift to unionized work, but within trades (e.g., printing and construction) which were already unionized before 1935, and in the market for hired farm labor, which was not unionized at all until the 1960s. Consider the percentage changes in wage rates between 1934 and 1940, the basic Wagner Act period (see table).[13]

---

[10] This hypothesis is developed more formally in my discussion of Lucas (1976).

[11] Between 1934 and 1940 the U.S. GNP deflator rested on a flat plateau, with a maximum deviation of only 2.5 percent above and below the mean.

[12] Darby (1976, table 4).

[13] *Sources:* Line 1, Darby (1976, table 4); lines 2–9, U.S. Bureau of Labor Statistics (1974, table 92); lines 10–11, U.S. Bureau of Labor Statistics (1974, table 46).

If high unemployment does reduce the rate of change of wages relative to the expected rate of inflation, adjusted for trend productivity growth, then an explanation of actual wage behavior during the late 1930s, particularly in the nonunionized farm labor sector, requires the assumption of a substantial positive expected rate of inflation.

(1) Average full-time earnings, all industries	19.2
(2) Union wage rates, all building trades	24.5
(3) Union wage rates, building journeymen	23.9
(4) Union wage rates, building laborers	31.0
(5) Union wage rates, all printing trades	15.6
(6) Union wage rates, printing book and job	14.1
(7) Union wage rates, newspapers	18.5
(8) Union wage rates, local trucking drivers	14.7
(9) Union wage rates, local transit	14.4
(10) Farm labor wage rates, with board	30.0
(11) Farm labor wage rates, without board	28.0

A second argument claims that the behavior of wage rates during the high unemployment period 1934–40 was not so surprising because the unemployment rate was actually not so high. Darby (1976) has recently pointed out that when unemployment during this period is recalculated excluding government employees in "emergency relief programs" (e.g., WPA, CCC), the minimum Depression unemployment rate reached during 1937, officially 14.3 percent, falls to 9.2 percent. At least three questions can be raised about the Darby attempt to explain 1934–40 wage behavior by redefining the unemployment data.

First, the minimum unemployment rate reached during 1937 still remains higher than the rate reached during any calendar quarter of the postwar era and so does not conflict with the standard impression that Depression unemployment was unusually high, that there was a substantial excess supply of labor, and that the wage rate should have exhibited some signs of downward flexibility if the $f(\ )$ function in (2) above is downward sloping. Second, the average wage received by government employees in the emergency relief programs during 1934–40 was 46.3 percent of the average private sector wage, virtually the same as the 48.6 percent ratio of unemployment compensation benefits to average after-tax earnings in 1971.[14] Since the relevant question in this context is the downward pressure placed on private sector wages by the "reserve army of the unemployed," a backward look from the present suggests that, since the employed government workers had the same incentive as today's insured unemployed to refuse private employment, those employed under government emergency stabilization programs should be counted as unemployed when compared with the postwar unemployed, who are largely insured, but should be counted as employed when compared to those unemployed before 1933, who are entirely uninsured (this argument assumes zero nonpecuniary benefits of leisure and becomes stronger if benefits are positive).

Third, while "Darby's millions" reduce the apparent size of the "reserve army" in the 1930s relative to the pre-1933 period (not relevant to the present period), "Lebergott's millions" work in the opposite direction. Lebergott's adjustment affects the denominator of the unemployment rate rather than the numerator. Since farmers and small business proprietors could be poor but never by definition unemployed without actually closing their businesses, the proper denominator for the unemployment rate consists of the civilian labor force minus farm and nonfarm business proprietors. An unemployment rate calculated with Lebergott's denominator differs from the official rate by a progressively greater amount for earlier years, e.g., the respective rates are 11.2 and 5.0 percent in

[14] Gordon (1973, pp. 152–153).

1900 but 6.1 and 5.6 percent in 1974. Even in the Depression years the nonfarm unemployment rate is substantially higher than the official rate, e.g., in 1937 the respective rates are 17.6 and 14.3.[15] A "fully adjusted' rate incorporating Darby's numerator and Lebergott's nonfarm denominator has a minimum Depression value of 11.3 percent in 1937 and is still as high as 13.2 percent in 1939.

A final problem in the recent development of NRH does not concern the validity of the basic proposition that the economy should be neutral in the long run to a change in the expected rate of inflation, but rather involves the assumption in the major theoretical papers which have popularized NRH that all changes in employment result from the voluntary choices of workers, without any role for layoffs or involuntary unemployment. In response to a decline in the expected real wage, Friedman's (1968) workers willingly reduce labor input by some combination of lower labor-force participation rates and fewer hours per week, and there is no mechanism to generate changes in unemployment. In the Lucas–Rapping model (1969) increases in unemployment occur when workers regard wage rates at which they could currently be employed as temporarily low; workers quit their jobs and voluntarily choose to wait or search for improved conditions. Other models developed by Phelps (1970) and Mortensen (1970a) in the tradition of the "new microeconomics" both incorporate the NRH and explain higher unemployment as the voluntary decision of workers to refuse job offers when falling product demand reduces wage offers relative to their "acceptance" or "refusal" wage.

In all of these models individual actors are induced to change their provision of labor input or output by prior changes in wages or prices relative to expectations. Unemployment and output fluctuations thus depend entirely on misinformation. This theoretical tradition based on the neoclassical price–output chain of causation has had a high fertility rate, spawning a literature on rational expectations which requires misinformation for output changes. But skeptics can question whether high unemployment in the 1930s or in 1975 was caused entirely by misinformation. This theme recurs below when we examine the rational expectations literature in more detail.

3.1.2. The Rise of Monetarism and Steps Toward Political Theories of Inflation

The popularization of the NRH and the rise of "monetarism" occurred simultaneously in the late 1960s, and the two have occasionally been considered as one and the same idea, partly as a result of Johnson's brilliant but misleading analysis (1971) of the monetarist counterrevolution, in which the success of monetarism is attributed to the acceleration of inflation in the late 1960s. Three separate statements must be distinguished:

(a) Monetary changes are the dominant cause of changes in nominal income, swamping the temporary and minor influence of fiscal changes.
(b) The NRH is valid.
(c) Wages and prices are relatively flexible, so that the short-run Phillips function [$f(\ )$ in (2)] is relatively steep.

Statements (a) and (b) constitute the essence of monetarism. The rise of monetarism was not due just to the acceleration of inflation in the late 1960s, which helped win converts to (b), but was due also to the evidence resulting from the 1966 monetary squeeze and 1968 tax surcharge that monetary effects on nominal income dominated fiscal effects when the two were operating in opposite directions, which helped win converts to (a).

Johnson's analysis becomes particularly misleading when he claims that "the triumph of monetarism has been short-lived . . . partly

---

[15] Lebergott (1964, p. 512). A comprehensive econometric study of twentieth century wage behavior using Lebergott's unemployment data was recently published by R. A. Gordon (1975); this study is not affected by Darby's data revisions, since it excludes the period 1930–53.

because ... the monetarists vastly exaggerated the potency ... of monetary restraint as a means of stopping inflation once inflation is well under way" (1971, p. 13). A rapid impact effect of a deceleration in monetary growth on the rate of inflation depends on the validity of proposition (c), which is logically separate from (a) and (b). Thus the evidence from the 1970–71 episode of a sluggish downward response of wage rates to high unemployment has not prevented a continued conversion of the economics profession to (a) and (b).[16] Nevertheless, given the importance of (c) for their standard policy recommendations of monetary restriction to fight inflation, it is surprising that monetarist authors have done so little empirical research on the short-run dynamics of wage and price behavior. This lack of interest in (c) can perhaps be explained by a low rate of time preference among monetarists, so that in the Phelps–Hall optimum policy framework the benefits in the far future of reducing the rate of inflation to the optimum rate outweigh the near-term costs of recession, whatever the time duration of the latter. In any case, work on Friedman's (1970) "missing equation" has been almost entirely in the hands of the nonmonetarists.

In addition to their lack of investment of research efforts in the short-run dynamics of wage and price adjustment, monetarist authors have been slow to shift their attention from the role of money as the basic determinant of income and price changes to the more fundamental underlying determinants of changes in money. Although Friedman and

Schwartz (1963) have informally discussed the motives of the monetary authorities in various episodes, and Barro (1975) has estimated econometric equations which describe the response of money to changes in the economic environment, there have been few other attempts to probe into the variety of economic and noneconomic factors which can affect monetary growth. Instead, monetarists have tended to regard any claim that inflation is caused by noneconomic factors, especially those generally falling under the label "cost push," as a *contradiction* of the monetary approach, a clear step backward from the 1963 environment in which there was widespread recognition [as reflected in Bronfenbrenner–Holzman's survey (1963, esp. p. 614)] that cost-push pressure causes a reduction in output unless accommodated by monetary expansion. The "hard-line" or "anti-cost-push" version of monetarism states, for instance, that the "basis of the world inflation is the expansion of the world money supply," and any attempt to bring in other factors, particularly those of the cost-push variety, represents a distressing resort to "amateur sociology and politics" which can play "no part whatsoever in the problem."[17]

A more general view [Gordon (1975b)] attempts to combine cost-push and political elements with the economic literature on optimum inflation. Too much money tends to be created when governments are faced with "a demand for inflation," i.e., pressure to raise the rate of money creation either when increased marginal benefits of government expenditures call for a spending increase which is best financed by a combination of conventional and inflation taxation, as during a war, or when pressure groups in society negotiate increases in wages or in other costs which raise the unemployment rate if not accommodated by more rapid money creation. The "supply of inflation," i.e., the extent to which the government bows to these pres-

---

[16] Regarding (a), a recent conference on monetarism (proceedings forthcoming in 1976 in a North-Holland conference volume edited by J. Stein) appeared to yield agreement by major monetarist authors that a change in government spending or tax rates could cause a one-time change in the level of velocity, and agreement by major nonmonetarist authors that deficits induced by fiscal policy must be continuously financed (until the economy raises tax revenues enough to eliminate the deficit), requiring attention to the stock effects of the continuous injection of money or bonds. Regarding (b), the leading nonmonetarist author Modigliani has implicitly adopted the validity of (b), at least for $U < U^N$, in his recent use of the concept "noninflationary rate of unemployment" ("NIRU") (1975).

[17] Johnson (1972a). See also Johnson (1972b). Typical of the refusal of monetarists to consider monetary and cost-push theories as complementary rather than competitive is Zis (1975).

sures, depends on the future electoral losses of resistance. When voters are sufficiently myopic, governments may regularly attempt to blow up the economy before elections and deflate it afterwards, and this policy, as Nordhaus (1975) and Sjaastad (1975) have shown, increases the mean inflation rate over the course of the political business cycle. An accommodative monetary policy may also yield a vote harvest when institutional arrangements minimize the political power of rentiers; when the incumbent party is one which relies on campaign contributions from groups which care more about taxes and unemployment than about inflation; when the perceived negotiation cost of "visible" compromise on tax changes is high relative to the "invisible" compromise available through monetary accommodation; and when wages are relatively rigid downward in the short run, which raises the unemployment cost and hence the vote cost of nonaccommodation.

3.1.3. Can the Impotent Policymaker Be Rejuvenated?—Searching for the Loophole in Rational Expectations[18]

While denying a permanent output-inflation tradeoff, the NRH allows the monetary authority to cause *temporary* deviations in the unemployment rate from the natural rate if it causes the actual rate of inflation during a given period of time (p_t) to diverge from the rate which is generally anticipated at the beginning of that period (p_t^e). When (2) is rewritten in a linear form with $\alpha = 1$, and when unemployment is also allowed to depend on a random term (γ_t^s) representing unanticipated changes in productivity, hours, or labor force participation, we have

$$U_t = U_t^N - \frac{1}{\beta}(p_t - p_t^e) + \gamma_t^s. \tag{3}$$

Since the γ_t^s term is assumed to be an exogenous "supply shock" (with mean zero) outside of the control of policymakers, a deviation of U_t from $U_t^N + \gamma_t^s$ requires the authorities to operate on p_t without simultaneously affecting p_t^e.

This may be difficult when the expectation of inflation is 'rational' in the sense of Muth (1961), i.e., an unbiased predictor of actual inflation (p_t) given all the information available just before the period begins, say I_{t-1}:

$$p_t^e = E(p_t|t_{t-1}), \tag{4}$$

where E is the expectations operator. This implies that p_t and p_t^e differ only by a random forecast error ϵ_t,

$$p_t - p_t^e = p_t - E(p_t|I_{t-1}) = \epsilon_t, \tag{5}$$

where ϵ_t is uncorrelated with everything known before the beginning of the period; any correlations which are present are part of I_{t-1} and can be exploited to improve the forecast value p_t^e. If, for instance, the structural relationship between the rate of inflation and the rate of growth of money (m_t) is

$$p_t = m_t + \gamma_t^d, \tag{6}$$

where γ_t^d is a random variable representing unpredictable demand shifts, then a rational expectation of the inflation rate would be

$$p_t^e = m_t^e.^{19} \tag{7}$$

How are expectations formed on the future growth rate of the money supply? Let us assume that the monetary authority follows a simple "proportional" feedback control rule for the growth rate of money:

$$m_t = \lambda_0 + \lambda_1(U_{t-1} - U_{t-1}^N) + \gamma_t^m. \tag{8}$$

Here the authority attempts to make money grow at a constant rate λ_0, plus some fraction λ_1 of last period's deviation of the unemployment rate from the natural rate. Monetary growth cannot be perfectly controlled by the authority's feedback rule, as indicated by the

---

[18] Readers are advised that this section overlaps with the section on 'Rational Expectations and the Phillips Curve' in the Barro-Fischer (1976) survey in this issue of the *Journal of Monetary Economics*. The treatment here is less comprehensive, more critical, and, perhaps, more accessible to readers who are new to this set of issues.

[19] (6) is the structural equation for prices assumed by Sargent and Wallace (1975b, p. 5).

random element γ_t^m (having a mean of zero), which causes monetary growth to deviate in an unpredictable way from the path intended by the authority. γ_t^m can also represent deliberate monetary "surprises" engineered by the authority. Individuals can use past observations on the behavior of the authority to form their expectation of current monetary growth,

$$m_t^e = \lambda_0 + \lambda_1(U_{t-1} - U_{t-1}^N). \tag{9}$$

The portion of monetary growth which cannot be predicted in advance is, from (8) and (9),

$$m_t - m_t^e = \gamma_t^m. \tag{10}$$

When (7) is subtracted from (6), we can substitute from (10),

$$p_t - p_t^e = m_t - m_t^e + \gamma_t^d = \gamma_t^m + \gamma_t^d. \tag{11}$$

Now (11) can be substituted back into the Phillips Curve (3), and we obtain

$$U_t - U_t^N = \gamma_t^s - \frac{1}{\beta}(\gamma_t^m + \gamma_t^d). \tag{12}$$

Since m_t does not appear in (12), but rather γ_t^m, we conclude that the monetary authority cannot cause even temporary changes in unemployment unless it does the unexpected, i.e., manipulates γ_t^m in a totally unpredictable way. Any systematic feedback-type monetary policy rule which incorporates past information becomes part of the information set I_{t-1}, is incorporated in p_t^e via eqs. (7) and (9), and hence cannot cause the deviation of p_t from p_t^e which is necessary (according to NRH in (3)) for unemployment to diverge from the natural rate.

This rather dramatic attack on policy activism has recently attracted considerable attention, as a result of innovative papers by Lucas (1972b) and Sargent and Wallace (1975a, 1975b), with recent extensions by Barro (1976). To put the point in a more general way, the monetary authority can change output only if it can find some handle which moves p while not simultaneously moving p^e by the same amount, but if the public can predict how money will behave in reaction to previous history, and knows the structural

connection between money and p, any predictable money change must simultaneously alter p, p^e, nominal income, the nominal interest rate, and other nominal magnitudes, and cannot alter unemployment, output, or other real magnitudes. Either the monetary authority can choose to follow Friedman's constant-growth-rate monetary rule, thus giving up the goal of controlling output, or it can choose to exercise its control in a totally unpredictable fashion (expanding money in reaction to some but not all increases in unemployment, chosen randomly). What it cannot choose is a systematic derivative or proportional "formula flexibility" feedback rule which reacts to past deviations of target variables from their desired values, of the type analyzed by Fischer and Cooper (1973) and others.

The Application of Rational Expectations to Economic Policy (AREEP) constitutes a major attack on policy activism, and a radical contribution to the theory of inflation and unemployment; any predictable change in the rate of monetary growth has 100 percent of its effect on inflation *even in the short run*, and zero percent of its effect on unemployment. Where can one find loopholes in the powerful logic? An easy criticism of AREEP is that a monetary feedback rule can affect real output if the monetary authority has superior information, so that its monetary changes in reaction to events unknown to individuals are treated by them as unexpected random events. But differential access to information is an implausibly weak reed upon which to rest a counterattack against AREEP in an economy like the U.S. in which government statistics are publicized in newpapers only a few days after they are compiled; there would be too great a payoff to close study by economic agents of the monetary authority's procedures.

My own preferred line of criticism questions the assumption of perfect price flexibility and the associated chain of causation from prior movements to subsequent output movements upon which most "new microeconomic" models incorporating NRH, as well as the more recent Lucas-Sargent-Wallace-Barro contributions, have been based. The entire thrust of AREEP requires that the effect of monetary changes reach real output by the route of changes in prices relative to expectations. Consider as an alternative extreme case a world of fixed wages and prices of the type analyzed by Barro and Grossman (1971). Starting from an equilibrium position at which firms and workers sell all they want, let us fix this wage and price level and reduce the money supply. Firms and workers now are able to sell less than they want at the going wage and price; they have been thrown off their voluntary "notional" supply schedules onto "effective" schedules constrained by the policy-imposed limit on sales. Any change in nominal income, whether engineered by monetary or fiscal policy, is completely reflected in a change in the sales constraint, output and employment. Once we discard the notional supply schedule relating output to the deviation of actual from expected prices, rational expectations become irrelevant to the output effect of systematic policy rules.

This criticism does not require the extreme assumption of completely rigid wages and prices, but is valid as long as wages and prices are less than perfectly flexible. Starting from an initial equilibrium set (W^*, P^*), a decline in the money supply requires a reduction to $(\hat{W}, \hat{P})$ if both firms and workers are to be able to sell all they want at that set of wages and prices. Any incomplete adjustment, for instance to (W', P'), where $\hat{W} < W' < W^*$ and $\hat{P} < P' < P^*$, will once again impose a sales constraint on firms and workers and prevent them from operating on their voluntary supply curves.

Faced with this criticism, the AREEP group might counterattack by denying the possibility of incomplete price adjustment to a preannounced monetary change. Rearrange (3) and write

$$p_t = p_t^e - \beta(U_t - U_t^N - \gamma_t^s). \tag{13}$$

Next, allow the change in the actual unemployment rate from one period to the next to be determined by deviations in the actual rate of growth of the money supply from the constant-unemployment monetary growth rate (m_t^*):

$$U_t = U_{t-1} - h(m_t - m_t^*), \tag{14}$$

where (6) above is modified to define

$$m_t^* = p_t + x_t^* - \gamma_t^d, \tag{15}$$

and x_t^* is the constant-unemployment rate of growth of "potential" real output (normal velocity growth is assumed equal to zero). Assuming that the economy starts in equilibrium with $U_{t-1} = U_t^N$, we substitute (14) and (15) into (13) to obtain

$$p_t = \frac{p_t^e + \beta[h(m_t - x_t^* + \gamma_t^d) + \gamma_t]}{1 + \beta h}. \tag{16}$$

A typical U.S. quarterly economic model with estimates of $\beta = 0.2$ and $h = 0.3$ would estimate a sluggish 0.057 (= 0.06/1.06) percent reduction in the quarterly rate of inflation in response to a 1.0 percentage-point reduction in the rate of growth of money, assuming that p_t^e is completely predetermined. The AREEP group, however, would point out that expectations must incorporate all available information, including (16). Setting $p_t^e = p_t$ in (16) yields

$$p_t = p_t^e = m_t - x_t^* + \gamma_t^d + \frac{\gamma_t^s}{h}, \tag{17}$$

in which a 1.0 percentage point reduction in monetary growth reduces the rate of inflation (and hence m_t^*) by a full 1.0 percent, averting in (14) *any change in unemployment*.

Thus rational expectations implies that prices *out of logical necessity* must be perfectly flexible following preannounced monetary changes. The debate on the relevance of AREEP thus raises once again the crucial issue of the short-run dynamics of price and wage adjustment. Four types of evidence are available which tend to point in the direction of sluggish price adjustment:

(a) Structural models of wage and price behavior, several of which are available in Eckstein (1972), indicate moderate lags in the response of prices to change in wages, but long lags in the response of wages to prices. Thus a change in aggregate demand takes a long time to work its way through the system.

(b) A reduced form relationship in Gordon (1975c) between inflation and the rate of change of money in the postwar U.S. has a mean lag of *four years*, and seven years are necessary for the total monetary effect to work itself out.

(c) Barro's (1975) tests indicate that the effect of monetary surprises on unemployment persists for three years.

(d) Hall (1975) has shown that only 1.7 percent of the quarterly variation in U.S. unemployment during 1954–74 remains unexplained in a simple two-quarter autoregression, in contrast to (11) above, in which the unemployment rate can differ from its equilibrium value only by a serially uncorrelated random disturbance.

It is important to recognize that sluggish short-term price adjustment is not "irrational" and does not in any way contradict the idea that expectations should be formed rationally. Recently theoretical developments, summarized below in section 3.2.2., have built a convincing case that there are some circumstances in which firms and workers optimize by fixing prices and wages (or by limiting their flexibility). If so, firms and workers may not calculate price expectations by reduced forms like (17) above, but instead may at least partly form their expectations adaptively by extrapolating recent events. First, they may not know enough about the structure of the economy to estimate the market-clearing $\hat{P}$ or the relative shares of the economy made up of "customer markets" with slowly changing prices vs. "auction markets" with flexible prices. Second, as demonstrated by B. Friedman (1975), if individuals gradually learn about the true structure of the economic system by a least-squares learning procedure, rational expectations closely approximate adaptive expectations. Finally, even if individuals do know the structure and do know the share (σ) of the economy made up of auction markets, a rational expectation of inflation will be a weighted average of (4) for auction markets, and adaptive expectations for customer markets.

When, for instance, expected inflation is a weighted average of a rational expectation and past inflation, the latter representing the simplest form of adaptive expectations, we have

$$p_t^e = \sigma E(p_t|I_{t-1}) + (1-\sigma)p_{t-1}. \qquad (18)$$

Substituting into (16), we obtain, in place of (17), the more general form

$$p_t = \frac{(1-\sigma)p_{t-1} + \beta[h(m_t - x_t^* + \gamma_t^d) + \gamma_t^s]}{1-\sigma+\beta h} \qquad (19)$$

(19) becomes (16) when $\sigma = 0$ and becomes (17) when $\sigma = 1$. In the general case ($0 < \sigma < 1$) output is once again determined by the Barro–Grossman sales constraint, and policy regains its short-run potency. The speed of adjustment of prices, and hence the persistence of unemployment, depends on the importance of long-term price and wage contracts, the average length of contracts, and the slope of the short-run Phillips Curve (β).[20]

3.2. Microeconomic Models of Voluntary Unemployment, Layoffs and Indexing

The preceding section reviewed, first, the NRH demonstration that the Phillips Curve is vertical in the long run, and the application of rational expectations to economic policy (AREEP), which makes the Phillips Curve vertical even in the short run. This line of theoretical development was criticized on the grounds that sticky price of adjustment throws economic agents off the voluntary output supply curves assumed in the AREEP

---

[20] Fischer (1975a), while accepting the flexible-price framework of AREEP, has shown that if long-term, e.g., two-period, wage contracts fix the wage rate one period ahead, the monetary authority can alter output by manipulating the price and through it the real wage which determines the voluntary notional supply decisions of firms. Phelps and Taylor (1977) reach essentially the same result by assuming, less plausibly, that both the wage rate and price level are fixed one period in advance.

literature, and that the weight of the past on the present through long-term contracts makes agents guess the prices which will be set by others at least partly by means of an adaptive rather than an extrapolative procedure. How convincing are recent theoretical models of wage and employment adjustment as explanations of imperfect wage and price flexibility, and what role is played in them by long-term contracts?

3.2.1. Voluntary Unemployment in the "New Microeconomics"

Soon after he and Friedman had proclaimed the NRH, Phelps and others produced a remarkable group of essays (1970) which collectively became known as the "new microeconomics" of inflation and employment theory.[21] With the single exception of Holt (1970), the contributing authors build models of wage and price adjustment which incorporate NRH. Beyond exploring the implications of NRH, the authors are mainly concerned with the factors which (1) make the natural unemployment rate greater than zero, and (2) explain the negative short-run Phillips curve relationship between wage change and actual unemployment.

Costly information and heterogeneous jobs and workers are sufficient to answer the first question. Workers sample from an array of job offers and firms sample from an array of workers. Both benefit by searching until it is no longer profitable to do so, where, for instance, workers apply the rule that a wage offer is refused unless it exceeds the "acceptance" wage, which in turn is set to equate the marginal cost of further search (costs of physical search plus foregone earnings net of unemployment benefits and taxes) with the marginal benefit of search (the expected value of further sampling from a known wage distribution).[22] Unemployment is a voluntary

activity, but all voluntary unemployment is not necessarily socially beneficial; in fact only a small portion of unemployed time is spent in actual search, and government unemployment benefits tend to stretch out the interval between searches, imposing a social cost through the taxes levied on some to support the idleness of others.[23]

The new microeconomic papers by Phelps (1970) and Mortensen (1970a) explain the second question, the causes of the relation between wage change and higher unemployment, as the result of a rational tendency of workers to quit their jobs more frequently and take up search activity when firms cut their wages in response to a decline in product demand. As in the above discussion of rational expectations models, the chain of causation is explicitly from prior wage change to subsequent quit decision and resulting increase in unemployment. The models strain reality by forcing all entry to unemployment through the mold of voluntary quit decisions, with no explanation for firing or layoffs.

The lack of reality in the standard "new microeconomics" model is vividly illustrated in Phelps' well-known "island parable" (1970a, pp. 6–7), in which individual firms are represented by separate islands lacking any inter-island communication links. Since an employee does not learn instantaneously of wage rates on other islands, but rather gains this information only after a slow trip by raft, individual firms face upward sloping rather than horizontal labor supply curves. When a firm suffers a decline in product demand during a recession, it reduces the wage rate to the level at which its demand for labor intersects its supply schedule. Some (but not all) employees quit on the assumption that the firm's behavior is unique, boarding their rafts to sample wage offers on other islands. Only after several inter-island voyages do they realize that the recession-induced decline in demand is universal, and that they will be

---

[21] Named after the title of Phelps' introduction to the volume.

[22] A clear and mercifully brief exposition of this approach is presented by Mortensen (1970b), who allows for differences in both wage offers and worker quality.

[23] Empirical estimates of time spent in search are contained in appendix C of Gordon (1973), and the adverse allocative effects of unemployment benefits have been most strongly criticized by Feldstein (1973, 1976).

no better off in a new job than with the original firm.

Real-world employees are not nearly as mindless as the parable suggests. We live in a world of underground telephone cables between desert islands, in which almost any white-collar worker can search for an alternative job using a company telephone on company time and without any prior need to quit. A blue-collar worker is only slightly less privileged and can substitute the neighborhood bar or the extended family gossip circle for the company phone, with ample opportunity to react to his wage cut by polling employees of other firms before he tenders his resignation. A cautious reaction is particularly probable when wages depend positively on seniority, e.g., when employees through learning-by-doing accumulate firm-specific skills over time, since quitting to search for a new job then involves a reduction in the employee's wage rate. As evidence that employees are in a position to acquire information on employment conditions in other firms before they depart, voluntary quits in the U.S. actually *decline* during recessions, whereas the parable implies countercyclical fluctuations in quits.

During a recession layoffs increase, but neither the parable nor any of the detailed formal models of the "new microeconomics" provide an economic explanation of layoffs. In these models economic booms and recessions are entirely symmetrical, in contrast to the real world where a firm has a single option in a boom, to attract more labor input by raising its wage offer, and two options in a recession, either to reduce the wage offer or to discharge employees.[24] The greater the

extent to which firms elect to react by discharging employees, the less flexible wages will be in a downward direction as compared to their flexibility in an upward direction. Because the "new microeconomic" models are symmetrical they yield a second counterfactual implication, that the long-run Phillips curve is vertical throughout, and hence a period when unemployment remains above the natural rate for a number of years will be characterized by an accelerating *deflation*.

The "new microeconomics" labor market models are not identical. In the "continuous auction market" models of Friedman (1968) and Lucas–Rapping (1970), a reduction in the wage rate relative to the expected price level causes an instantaneous withdrawal of workers from the labor force, whereas in the "search" model of Mortensen (1970a), a reduction in the wage rate relative to the acceptance wage of workers causes an increased flow of quits into unemployment and a reduced flow of hires out of unemployment. But there is no difference between the two approaches in their inability to explain layoffs and "no help wanted" signs and in their implication that the long-run Phillips curve is vertical throughout its range, and that the quit rate varies countercyclically. The major difference between the two approaches is in the ability of the search model rigorously to explain a positive rather than a zero "natural rate" of unemployment.

3.2.2. The "New–New" Microeconomics of Price and Wage Rigidity, Implicit Contracts and Layoffs

Very recently there have been signs that research resources are beginning to shift from model-building exercises in which output changes are caused by price "surprises," to those which attempt to explain price and wage contracts, and hence sluggish price adjustment, as the result of microeconomic optimizing behavior. The proponents of the contractual view do not claim that contracts are universal, but rather analyze factors which cause some product and labor markets to be governed by contracts and slow price ad-

---

[24] An additional choice, which is symmetrical in booms and recessions, must be made between changes in the number of employees and changes in hours worked per employee. It has been suggested that compulsory overtime is the reverse equivalent of layoffs in an economic boom, but the parallel is inexact because employees maintain the freedom to quit when compulsory overtime becomes objectionable, whereas in a recession there is no such alternative to an employee who is discharged. Compulsory overtime would be parallel to layoffs only in a society with slavery.

justment, while other "spot auction" markets are characterized by price flexibility and continuous market clearing.

Okun (1975) has provided the best rationale for long-term contractual arrangements in what he calls "customer" (product) markets. His essential hypothesis is an outgrowth of the search literature: costly search makes customers willing to pay a premium to do business with customary suppliers. Firms, in turn, have an incentive to maintain stable prices to encourage customers to return, using yesterday's experience as a guide. "A kind of intertemporal comparison shopping" discourages firms from changing price in response to short-run changes in demand in order to avoid giving customers an incentive to abandon the no-search relationships and to begin exploring.

Okun's model shares with several others examined below a reliance on negotiation and legal costs to explain why contracts remain implicit rather than formally spelled out in writing. Unwritten contracts only work if participants on both sides agree on conventions of fair play, in the style of the British unwritten constitution. Customers appear willing to accept as "fair" an increase in price based on a permanent increase in cost, since in the extreme few firms can stay in business when costs double while product prices are fixed. Transitory events, either an increase in demand or a reduction in productivity, are not generally expected to last long enough to cause bankruptcy and so are not considered sufficient justification for price increases, according to the rules of fair play.

Just as product heterogeneity and costly information can explain sluggish price adjustment in product markets, so can worker-job heterogeneity explain sluggish wage adjustment in labor markets when information is costly. Continuous recontracting in a spot auction labor market might occur if the unemployed were regarded by firms as perfect substitutes for incumbent workers. But, as Williamson, Wachter and Harris (1975) emphasize, building on the earlier work of Doeringer and Piore (1971), almost every job is 'idiosyncratic,' involving some specific

skills. "Incumbents who enjoy nontrivial advantages over similarly qualified but inexperienced bidders are well situated to demand some fraction of the cost savings which their idiosyncratic experience has generated."[25] Nor can incumbents be expected to capitalize prospective monopoly gains and make lump-sum payment bids to bribe firms to hire them into idiosyncratic on-the-job training ladders, because of liquidity constraints and negotiation and free-rider costs created by the interdependence with other workers. This analysis can be linked together with Okun's. Just as firms in customer product markets delay or avoid raising prices in response to higher demand, so firms avoid or delay raising wages, both because employees earn monopoly rents which would be lost by quitting, and because "fair play" leads to seniority rules which "pay back" the employee's high-demand wages lost by not quitting in the form of wages gained from the fixity or sluggishness of wage rates in recessions.

An interesting split has developed in the "new–new" microeconomics between the approach reviewed above, which relies on costly information and worker-job-product heterogeneity and uses relatively informal analytical tools, and a second more formal group of papers, which attempt to rationalize wage rigidity and layoffs without assuming heterogeneity or information costs.[26] Three simultaneously written and independent contributions by Azariadis (1975a), Baily (1974) and D. F. Gordon (1974) (A–B–G) share two common assumptions. First, employees are relatively more averse to risk than their employers, partly because of the limits on diversification in human capital imposed by the prohibition of slavery and, more important, because entrepreneurs are self-selected individuals who are relatively indifferent

[25] Iwai (1974) analyzes the effects on wage-setting behavior of uncertainty in a more general context.

[26] An exception is Bewley's (1975) study of transition costs as an explanation of discrete jumps in prices in a rather general context which does not analyze the source or determinants of the transactions' costs.

toward (or actually lovers of) risk. Second, A–B–G analyze contractual arrangements between firms and employees which may be implicit and unwritten but which nevertheless constrain behavior. Firms maximize profits by minimizing the variability of income to their workers, who dislike variability, thus in effect providing a compensation package which consists partly of pecuniary wage payments and partly of insurance services.

Up to this point, however, the theory justifies only a fixed-income contract (tenure), whereas an explanation is needed for contracts which call for rigidity of wages together with variability in man-hours, in contrast to the classical spot auction labor market, in which wages are perfectly flexible and all variations in man-hours, if any, are voluntary movements along notional supply curves. Firms find that workers are not indifferent between a fixed-wage-more-variable-man-hour contract and the spot auction outcome even when total pecuniary income paid out by firms under both has the same mean and variance, if employees can earn some positive income during periods of reduced man-hours which is not paid directly or indirectly by firms, particularly, the value of leisure (or the reduced disutility of work), and any unemployment benefits or welfare payments which are financed at least partly by general government revenues rather than being financed by firm contributions based on their past unemployment experience.

As I have pointed out [Gordon (1976a)], the A–B–G theory as initially developed is incomplete. In the absence of government-financed payments, the superiority of the fixed-wage-more-variable-man-hour policy compared to the spot auction outcome relies entirely on the value of employees of the extra leisure consumed during periods of low demand, a result which depends on an asymmetric analytical procedure in which demand can fall below normal but never rise above. When symmetric demand fluctuations are allowed, the hours of leisure foregone in high demand periods outweigh the less

valuable hours gained in low demand periods and tilt the balance back to a fixed-income (tenure) contract. Since the A–B–G theory cannot explain fixed-wage contracts without government payments, one can question its applicability to the period before the introduction of unemployment benefits in the late 1930s.

Two quite different considerations are capable of "rescuing" the fixed-wage contract. Grossman (1975b), working within the A B G risk aversion framework, argues that both agents entering into an implicit contract must weigh the risk of default by the other. A positive probability that a worker will default from a fixed-income contract by shifting to the spot auction market during high-demand periods will sufficiently reduce profits to force firms to eliminate from consideration the fixed-income option. The optimality of the fixed-wage contract as compared to the no-contract spot market alternative then depends positively on the degree of risk aversion and the size of the default penalty. The appeal of Grossman's approach is its ability to explain why three different arrangements are observed in real-world labor markets–spot auction markets (when workers perceive a low default penalty and are only mildly risk averse), tenure fixed income contracts (when the default penalty is high), and fixed-wage-rate contracts (in intermediate cases).

I have suggested (1976a) a second approach which is able to explain a fixed-wage policy without any consideration of risk aversion. Faced with the option of reducing wage rates or man-hours when the demand for its product declines, a firm may prefer the certain reduction in its wage bill which can be achieved by a fixed-wage, quantity-rationing policy. In contrast, a reduction in the wage rate may yield a highly uncertain reduction in the wage bill, because the number of employees who will quit depends on their subjective and unpredictable evaluation of alternative wage rates and employment opportunities open to them at that particular time.

These initial modelling efforts measure labor input along a single dimension, man-hours, and do not provide an explanation of the relative reliance on layoffs and reductions in hours per week when firms choose a fixed-wage policy. More recently both Baily (1976) and Feldstein (1977) have introduced hours per man and the number of men employed separately into firm production and worker utility functions; both illustrate the increased reliance of firms on layoffs as opposed to reductions in hours when there is an increase in unemployment benefits relative to the taxes a firm has to pay to finance benefits for its own employees.

The absence of any significant downward movement of wage rates during periods of high unemployment, e.g., 1934–40, 1958–64, and 1970–71, together with the rather rapid response of wage change to periods of low unemployment, e.g., 1955–57 and 1966–69, has stimulated interest in theoretical explanations of asymmetric wage adjustment. This theoretical effort may be largely unnecessary, since convexity in the $f(\ )$ function in (2) above appears adequate to explain wage behavior without recourse to discontinuous linked functions. More charitably, the asymmetry literature may be regarded as providing a rationalization for convexity. For instance, Tobin (1972) develops a model in which the NRH is valid only for downward departures of the unemployment rate below the natural rate, but his aggregate result depends on wage rigidity in individual micro labor markets which is assumed rather than deduced from maximizing behavior. Grossman (1975a) deduces asymmetry from the fact that in the spot market both man-hours and the wage rate are high in booms, which makes its superiority over the fixed-wage contract in periods of above-average demand exceed its inferiority when demand is low, so that the alternative of the spot market places relatively greater pressure for revision of the fixed contractual wage during boom periods. Azariadis (1975b) emphasizes the greater cost of default for employers than for employees as a source of asymmetry. While both

papers are suggestive, a more essential element of asymmetry needs to be incorporated: in a recession firms deal with an *existing* group of employees under an implicit or explicit contract, but if demand increases sufficiently in a boom, the potential for raising labor input by higher overtime hours from existing employees must eventually be exhausted, requiring firms to go outside and attract new employees at sufficiently appealing terms to lure them away from the spot market or from contracts at other firms.

3.2.3. Effect of Wage Indexing on Inflation and Unemployment

In the A–B–G work on labor contracts under risk aversion, firms sell insurance services to risk-averse employees. Since workers care about variance in real income, not just in nominal income, risk-neutral firms can profit by offering employees contracts which are 100 percent indexed to changes in the consumer price level, a point recently made by Fischer (1975a) and Feldstein (1976) but not brought out in the original A–B–G papers. The fact that wage indexation is only partial in real-world labor markets raises a question about the A–B–G assumption that workers are more risk averse than firms.

Full wage indexing would be optimal for the economy as a whole if prices were flexible and all disturbances were "nominal," i.e. caused by changes in the demand for commodities rather than the supply, leading wages and prices to change together but real output to remain unchanged following a disturbance. The greater instability of prices in the indexed economy would have no adverse welfare consequences if indexing were extended not only to wages but to financial assets, the tax system, and accounting rules. An indexed economy with flexible prices and nominal shocks is similar to a rational-expectations economy of the type described above.

As Gray (1976) and Fischer (1975b) have demonstrated, however, full wage indexing would increase the instability of real output if shocks were "real," i.e. changes in supply functions, since in that situation indexing would maintain a constant real wage instead of allowing the change in the real wage required to clear markets. If in 1974 U.S. wages had been totally indexed, the economy would have exhibited more inflation and greater unemployment in response to the food and oil supply shocks than actually occurred; as I showed in [Gordon (1975a)], a real "indexing recession" can be avoided only by monetary accommodation of higher prices, leading to a very rapid inflation, the rate of which would depend on the lag in the indexing formula between the change in prices and the correction in wages. Fischer (1975b) remarks that the payment of interest on money would amount to automatic monetary accommodation in this situation and would have to be counteracted by Central Bank open-market sales. If most real shocks tend to occur outside of the domestic nonfarm part of the economy (i.e. in the foreign and farm sectors) the adverse effects of indexing could be eliminated if the wage-indexing formula were based on the domestic nonfarm rather than the consumer price index.

3.2.4. Other Developments:
Markup Pricing and Taxes

Most of the recent microeconomic theory reviewed above attempts to explain the wage-setting behavior of competitive firms which are price *takers*. Very little innovative recent work has concerned the setting of prices. Econometric models have typically pegged the price level to wage rates (adjusted for some mixture of actual and normal productivity) by a "markup fraction" which in turn is a function of the excess demand for commodities. This is the "running man wearing a raincoat" view of inflation—price change can never get very far from wage change, even though the relationship may wiggle around a bit in response to demand movements, just as a raincoat can never get very far from the running man who wears it, even though the coat may ripple a bit in the wind.

Aside from Okun's (1975) informal discussion of customer markets, the most rigorous recent exposition of the markup approach to oligopolistic price behavior is presented by deMenil (1974), whose empirical work agrees with my conclusion (1971, 1975c) that the price–wage relationship is quite stable, and that the direct effect of demand on prices, as opposed to the indirect effect of demand on prices through the wage–unemployment relation, is minor but nevertheless perceptible. The major difficulty with the markup pricing approach is its insecure theoretical base. In his comprehensive survey of the markup literature, Nordhaus (1972) reached the surprising conclusion that markup pricing, which had been presumed to be justified only in noncompetitive industries, was actually optimal only under conditions of perfect competition and constant returns to scale. In general, price should not be set as a simple markup over labor cost, but should be a weighted average of labor plus capital cost (plus the prices of raw materials, if any). Clearly more work is required, perhaps building on Okun's, to explain why markup pricing appears to characterize some markets (automobiles, new houses) but not others (copper, wheat, plywood).

In recent years the analysis of tax effects on inflation has become much more sophisticated, perhaps stimulated in part by the failure of the 1968 U.S. tax surcharge to stem inflation, by the introduction of the value-added tax in the U.K., and by the growing importance of payroll taxes in all countries. The essential point is that higher taxes are a two-edged sword, on the one hand reducing aggregate demand, and on the other hand increasing the "wedge" between the market price of output and the after-tax income of factors of production. In principle all taxes—sales, excise, payroll, corporate income and personal income—may be shifted forward in varying degrees to output prices, and the net effect of higher taxation may be inflationary if after-tax wage rates are only partially flexible downward. The empirical contribution of higher tax rates to the late-1960s inflation was first pointed out in [Gordon (1971)], and formal analytical models were used by Blinder (1973) and Dernberg (1974) to derive the conditions under which the effect on prices of a tax increase goes in the opposite direction from the standard textbook analysis. Parkin–Summer–Ward (1976) and I (1976b) have derived econometric wage and price equations from explicit labor market models where taxes of various types enter into both supply and demand behavior. In the context of the first section of this paper, then, tax changes become another "cost-push" element which, while unable by themselves to generate a continuous inflation, add to the pressures for a higher rate of monetary expansion.

3.3. World inflation and the Transmission Mechanism

Almost all of the above literature, primarily developed by insular Americans, has concerned a closed economy. Three major questions immediately arise when one ventures beyond the national borders of the autarkic regime assumed explicitly or implicitly by most U.S. macro theorists: first, what determines the world rate of inflation; second, how are inflationary impulses transmitted from one open economy to another; and third, of what relevance for open economies is domestic price level if it is simply pegged to that of the world outside?

Two major frameworks for the analysis of open-economy inflation have developed in the past decade, the monetary approach to balance-of-payments theory, which claims to have an answer for all three basic questions, and the "Scandinavian" or Aukrust–EFO approach, which only claims to deal with the second and third.[27] The monetary approach (MA) was developed primarily by Mundell and Johnson and their remarkable group of graduate students at the University

of Chicago in the late 1960s. As summarized by Johnson (1972c), the MA answers the first question, the source of world inflation, essentially by repeating Friedman's dictum that "inflation is always and everywhere a monetary phenomenon," at least when the open economies of the world are linked by fixed exchange rates. This straightforward quantity-theory view is subject to the criticism as that directed above against domestic monetarism—most economists have long recognized that an inflation originating from any source must be ratified by monetary accomodation if it is to continue, so that a "theory" which links world inflation to the growth rate of world money simply describes the symptoms of the disease rather than its causes and cure. A shallow response would attribute the increase in world money to the creation of an excess supply of dollars in the U.S., together with the acceptance of those dollars by other nations in the form of international reserve accumulations in place of the inflation-fighting alternative of exchange-rate appreciations.

A deeper response would require the merging of the MA with the rudimentary theory of the politics of inflation, which accepts the basic premise of the quantity-theory approach as its point of departure and analyzes the pressure on the monetary authority from public and private sources. An international extension of the political approach to those economies which do not have independent control over the domestic money supply would presumably examine the political power of exporters and import-competitors to resist revaluation. The political approach counters the implicit or explicit MA recommendation of U.S. monetary restriction as a cure to world inflation by pointing to the real social costs of output reduction when wages are set according to slow-changing contractual arrangements, and when a positive political rate of time preference puts a positive weight on the near-term, albeit temporary, output loss (and, add the modelers of labor market asymmetry, "temporary" may be a very long time).

[27] See Aukrust (1975) and the "EFO" volume (Edgren, Faxen and Odhner) (1973).

Recent contributions on the international transmission mechanism are placed in perspective when contrasted with the alternative embedded in the large-scale econometric models of the mid-1960s, in which higher foreign demand reached the domestic price level by only two routes, the effect of higher exports on aggregate demand, both directly and via the Keynesian multiplier expansion, and through the appearance of import prices in the aggregate markup price equation. The MA added two additional channels, first in the "purchasing-power-parity" assumption that all goods, at least in the simple Johnson version, are tradeable with prices set in world markets, and, second, by allowing domestic holdings of foreign reserves to increase (raising the domestic monetary base and money supply), not just as the direct result of the export surplus, but more generally because the higher price level raises the demand for money relative to the initial supply.

The one-tradeable-good assumption focused attention on the neglect in previous econometric models of the direct effect of foreign prices on exports, and of the substitutability of domestic import-competing goods with imports. The critical contribution of the attention to money-market equilibrium was to focus on world capital markets rather than the trade surplus as the source of additional liquidity during an export-led expansion. Dornbusch (1973) extended the one-good model by allowing for both traded and nontraded goods. In his version domestic nontraded goods prices are perfectly flexible and the labor market always clears, requiring in response to a foreign demand stimulus an initial increase in the single nominal wage rate and a drop in the relative price of nontraded goods. Eventually the inflow of reserves raises the domestic money supply by enough to finance an increase in the relative price of nontraded goods to the initial level. In the final equilibrium all nominal magnitudes, including the domestic supply of money, are increased by the same proportion as the increase in the world price level.

The transmission mechanism in the Scandinavian model is essentially a Dornbusch-type, two-sector model without money. An initial increase in traded goods prices raises wages in that sector (the bargaining process maintains a constant rate of return in that sector), and nontraded sector wages rise in imitation, in turn pulling up nontraded sector prices (the latter are determined by a markup or are equal by definition to wages in many proprietor-owned service industries). In contrast to the Dornbusch monetary approach, there is no attention to the source of the extra money needed to finance the higher price level; it is implicitly provided as needed and its availability does not, as in the Dornbusch approach, constrain the speed at which nontraded goods prices can rise. A positive contribution, however, is made by the Scandinavian emphasis on differential productivity growth rates in the nontraded sector as sources of long-run differences in the growth of consumer price indexes across countries.

Turning to the third major question, both the Scandinavian and Dornbusch versions leave no room for the domestic Phillips curve approach to wage determination, since excess labor-market demand and supply plays no role in the process of adjustment. Both models are uncomfortable hybrids; in the Dornbusch model, for instance, the process of monetary expansion is explicitly short run in nature, but the labor market is ruled by the long run assumptions of perfect wage and price flexibility and full employment. Recent papers which attempt to merge together a short-run Phillips curve with these long-run theories include Calmfors' (1975) empirical demonstration that *both* the traded-goods price *and* excess labor demand determine Swedish wages in the short run, and my own theoretical analysis (1976b), which introduces imperfectly flexible price and wage adjustment and unemployment into the Dornbusch framework. But in the long run it is clear that the domestic Phillips curve approach will not do. Any econometric simulation (e.g., those regularly turned out by operation LINK) which yields a steady long-run divergence of domestic from world inflation rates when exchange rates are fixed (leaving aside differential nontraded-goods productivity growth rates) implicitly depicts an economy which eventually reaches complete specialization in traded or nontraded goods.

4. RIP VAN WINKLE'S CONCLUSION

Rip, breathless from his fast trip through a decade's literature, was extremely impressed at the progress made since 1963. The revival of the quantity theory and its application to both domestic and international problems had brought with it important insights on the role of expectations, the preconditions for inflation, and the international transmission mechanism. Financial unemployment had received a rigorous theoretical underpinning, and a healthy realism had more recently been evident in the increasing number of papers which had attempted to explain wage rigidity, layoffs and asymmetric adjustment from microeconomic behavioral postulates. A basic thrust of the labor market literature had been a questioning of the 1940s and 1950s emphasis on full employment as an overriding goal, by its shifting of a substantial share of the observed unemployment from involuntary in its motivation, explicitly in the case of the frictional unemployment analyzed in the search literature, and implicitly in the case of the temporary layoffs studied in the "new–new" contract literature.

The major remaining problems were, first, that too much attention was still being paid in popular and policy discussions to a simple-minded monetarist view which requires perfectly flexible prices for its validity. The extensive investment of resources in the flexible-price version of rational expectations had been carried too far, given the evidence on sluggish price adjustment provided by nonmonetarists. Some government agency needed to encourage a conference at which the AREEP group would be locked up in a room with the rigid-wage, implicit-contract theorists for a discussion of the conditions under which their conclusions remain relevant. Second, the recent theoretical discussions of "auction" and "customer" product markets, and "idiosyncratic" labor markets,

needed to be formalized and merged with the more formal but less comprehensive literature on implicit contracts and risk aversion. Finally, attention needed to be shifted from the effects of money on prices and income to the politico–economic determinants of the behavior of money. More work needed to be done to determine why the rate of monetary expansion differed across time and space, and to test empirically the validity of the conjectural explanations which had thus far been provided.

References

Attiyeh, Y., "Wage-Price Spiral vs. Demand Inflation: U.S. 1949–1957," unpublished Ph.D. dissertation (University of Chicago, 1959).

Azariadis, C., "Implicit Contracts and Underemployment Equilibria," Journal of Political Economy, 83:1183–1202 (1975).

Azariadis, C., "Asymmetric Wage Behavior," presented at the Third Reisenburg Symposium, On the Stability of Contemporary Economic Systems (July 1975).

Aukrust, O., "Inflation in the Open Economy: The Norwegian Model," Central Bureau of Statistics of Norway, working paper (March 1975).

Bailey, M. J., "The Welfare Cost of Inflationary Finance," Journal of Political Economy, 64:93–110 (1956).

Bailey, M. N., "Wages and Employment under Uncertain Demand," Review of Economic Studies, 41:37–50 (1974).

Baily, M. N., "On the Theory of Layoffs, and Unemployment," Econometrica, 45:1043–1063 (1977).

Barro, R. J., "Unanticipated Money Growth and Unemployment in the United States," American Economic Review, 67:101–115 (1977).

Barro, R. J., "Rational Expectations and the Role of Monetary Policy," Journal of Monetary Economics, 2:1–32 (1976).

Barro, R. J., and Fischer, S., "Recent Developments in Monetary Theory." Journal of Monetary Economics, 2:133–167 (1976).

Barro, R. J., and Grossman, H., "A General Disequilibrium Model of Income and Employment," American Economics Review, 61:82–93 (1971).

Bewley, T., "A Theoretical Study of Optimal Price Adjustment," unpublished (Harvard University, 1975).

Biacabe, P., *Analyses Contemporaines de l'inflation* (Paris: 1962).

Blinder, A., "Can Income Tax Increases Be Inflationary?" *National Tax Journal*, 26:295–301 (1973).

Branson, W., *Macroeconomic Theory and Policy* (New York: Harper & Row, 1972).

Bronfenbrenner, M., and Holzman, F. D., "Survey of Inflation Theory," *American Economic Review*, 53:593–661 (1963).

Cagan, P., "The Monetary Dynamics of Hyperinflation," in M. Friedman (ed.). *Studies in the Quantity Theory of Money* (University of Chicago Press, 1956).

Calmfors, L., "Swedish Inflation and International Price Influences," University of Stockholm Institute for International Economic Studies, Seminar Paper 45 (March 1975).

Darby, M. R., "Three-and-a-Half Million U.S. Employees Have Been Mislaid; or, An Explanation of Unemployment, 1934–1941," *Journal of Political Economy*, 84 (February 1976).

de Menil, G., "Aggregate Price Dynamics," *Review of Economics and Statistics*, 51:129–141 (1974).

Dernberg, T. F., "The Macroeconomic Implications of Wage Retaliation Against Higher Taxation," *International Monetary Fund Staff Papers*, 21:758–788 (1974).

Doeringer, P., and Piore, M., *Internal Labor Markets and Manpower Analysis* (Lexington, Mass.: Heath, 1971).

Dornbusch, R., "Devaluation, Money, and Nontraded Goods," *American Economic Review*, 53:871–880 (1973).

Eckstein, O. (ed.), *The Econometrics of Price Determination Conference* (Washington, D.C.: Federal Reserve Board, 1972).

Eckstein, O., and Brinner, R., "The Inflation Process in the United States," a study prepared for the use of the Joint Economic Committee, 92nd Congress, Second Session (Washington, D.C.: 1972).

Edgren, G., Faxen, K. O., and Odhner, C. E., *Wage Formation and the Economy* (London: 1973).

Feldstein, M.S., "Lowering the Permanent Rate of Unemployment," a study prepared for the use of the Joint Economic Committee, 93rd Congress, First Session (Washington, D.C.: 1973).

Feldstein, M. S., "Temporary Layoffs in the Theory of Unemployment," *Journal of Political Economy*, 84:937–957 (1976).

Fischer, S., "Long-Term Contracts, Rational Expectations, and the Optimal Money Supply Rule," *Journal of Political Economy*, 85:191–206 (1977).

Fischer, S., and Cooper, J. P., "Stabilization Policy and Lags," *Journal of Political Economy*, 81:847–877 (1973).

Fisher, I., "A Statistical Relation Between Unemployment and Price Changes," *International Labour Review*, 13:785–792 (1926); reprinted in *Journal of Political Economy*, 81:496–502 (1973).

Friedman, B., "Rational Expectations Are Really Adaptive After All," unpublished (Cambridge, Mass.: Harvard, 1975).

Friedman, M., "What Price Guideposts?" in Shultz, G. P., and Aliber, R. Z. (eds.), *Guidelines: Informal Controls and the Market Place* (University of chicago Press, 1966).

Friedman, M., "The Role of Monetary Policy," *American Economic Review*, 58:1–17 (1968).

Friedman, M., "The Optimum Quantity of Money," in *The Optimum Quantity of Money and Other Essays* (Chicago: Aldine, 1969).

Friedman, M., "Discussion," *American Economic Review*, 65:176–179 (1975).

Friedman, M., and Schwartz, A., *A Monetary History of the United States* (Princeton University Press, 1963).

Gordon, D. F., "A Neo-Classical Theory of Keynesian Unemployment," *Economic Inquiry*, 12:431–459 (1974).

Gordon, R. A., "Wages, Prices, and Unemployment, 1900–1970," *Industrial Relations*, 14 (October 1975).

Gordon, R. J., "Inflation in Recession and Recovery," *Brookings Papers on Economic Activity*, 2:105–158 (1971).

Gordon, R. J., "Wage-Price Controls and the Shifting Phillips Curve," *Brookings Papers on Economic Activity*, 3:385–421 (1972).

Gordon, R. J., "The Welfare Cost of Higher Unemployment," *Brookings Papers on Economic Activity*, 1:133–195 (1973).

Gordon, R. J., "Alternative Responses of Policy to External Supply Shocks," *Brookings Papers on Economic Activity*, 6:183–206 (1975).

Gordon, R. J., "The Demand for and Supply of Inflation," *Journal of Law and Economics* (December 1975).

Gordon, R. J., "The Effect of Aggregate Demand on Prices," *Brookings Papers on Economic Activity*, 6:613–662 (1975).

Gordon, R. J., "Aspects of the Theory of Involuntary Unemployment," *Journal of Monetary Economics*, 2:98–119 (1976).

Gordon, R. J., "Interrelations between Domestic and International Theories of Inflation," in Aliber, R. Z. (ed.), The *Political Economy of Monetary Reform* (London: Macmillan, 1976).

Gray, J. A., "Wage Indexation: A Macroeconomic Approach," *Journal of Monetary Economics*, 2:221–235 (1976).

Grossman, H. I., "Aggregate Demand, Job Search, and Employment," *Journal of Political Economy*, 81:1353–1369 (1973).

Grossman, H. I., "Is Wage Response Asymmetrical?" presented at the Conference on Inflation, Miami University (Oxford, Ohio: 1975).

Grossman, H. I., "The Nature of Optimal Labor Contracts: Towards a Theory of Wage and Employment Adjustment," presented at the Third Reisenberg Symposium, On the Stability of Contemporary Economic Systems (July 1975).

Hall, R. E., "The Rigidity of Wages and the Persistence of Unemployment," *Brookings Papers on Economic Activity*, 6:301–335 (1975).

Holt, C. C., "Job Search, Phillips Wage Relation, and Union Influence; Theory and Evidence," in Phelps (1970).

Iwai, K., "The Firm in Uncertain Markets and Its Price, Wage, and Employment Adjustments," *Review of Economic Studies*, 41:257–276 (1974).

Johnson, H. G., "The Keynesian Revolution and the Monetarist Counter-Revolution," *American Economic Review*, 61:1–14 (1971).

Johnson, H. G., "Panel Discussion: World Inflation," in Claasen, E., and Salin, P., *Stabilization Policies in Interdependent Economics* (London: George Allen and Unwin, 1972).

Johnson, H. G., "Inflation and the Monetarist Controversy," *Professor Dr. F. De Vries Lectures* (Amsterdam: North-Holland, 1972).

Johnson, H. G., "The Monetary Approach to Balance-of-Payments Theory," in *Further Essays in Monetary Economics* (London: George Allen and Unwin, 1972).

Laidler, D., and Parkin, M., "Inflation: A Survey," *Economic Journal*, 85:741–809 (1975).

Lebergott, S., *Manpower in Economic Growth* (New York: McGraw-Hill, 1964).

Lipsey, R. G., "The Relation between Unemployment and the Rate of Change of Money Wage Rates in the United Kingdom, 1862–1957; A Further Analysis," *Economica*, 27:1–31 (1960).

Lucas, R. E., Jr., "Testing the Natural-Rate Hypothesis," in Eckstein (1972).

Lucas, R. E., Jr., "Expectations and the Neutrality of Money," *Journal of Economic Theory*, 4:103–124 (1972).

Lucas, R. E., Jr., "Econometric Policy Evaluation: A Critique," *Journal of Monetary Economics*, 2:19–46 (1976).

Lucas, R. E., Jr., and Rapping, L. A., "Real Wages, Employment and Inflation," *Journal of Political Economy*, 77 (1969).

Modigliani, F., and Papademos, L. "Targets for Monetary Policy in the Coming Year," *Brookings Papers on Economic Activity*, 6:141–863 (1975).

Mortensen, D. T., "A Theory of Wage and Employment Dynamics," in Phelps (1970).

Mortensen, D. T., "Job Search, The Duration of Unemployment, and the Phillips Curve," *American Economic Review*, 60:847–862 (1970).

Muth, J. F., "Rational Expectations and the Theory of Price Movements," *Econometrica*, 29:315–335 (1961).

Nordhaus, W. D., "Recent Developments in Price Dynamics," in Eckstein (1972).

Nordhaus, W. D., "The Political Business Cycle," *The Review of Economic Studies*, 42:169–190 (1975).

Okun, A. M., "Inflation: Its Mechanics and Welfare Costs," *Brookings Papers on Economic Activity*, 6:351–390 (1975).

Parkin, J. M., Sumner, M. T., and Ward., R., "The Effects of Excess Demand, Generalized Expectations, and Wage-price Controls on Wage Inflation in the U.K., *Journal of Monetary Economics*, 2:191–219 (1976).

Perry, G. L., *Unemployment, Money Wage Rates, and Inflation* (Cambridge, Mass.: M.I.T. Press, 1966).

Perry, G. L., "Changing Labor Markets and Inflation," *Brookings Papers on Economic Activity*, 1:411–441 (1970).

Phelps, E. S., "A Test for the Presence of Cost Inflation in the United States, 1955–1957," *Yale Economic Essays*, 1:28–69 (1961).

Phelps, E. S., "Phillips Curves, Expectations of Inflation, and Optimal Unemployment Over Time," *Economica* (NS), 34:254–281 (1967).

Phelps, E. S., et al., *Microeconomic Foundations of Employment and Inflation Theory* (New York: Norton, 1970).

Phelps, E. S., "Money Wage Dynamics and Labor Market Equilibrium," in Phelps (1970).

Phelps, E. S., *Inflation Policy and Unemployment Theory* (New York: Norton, 1972).

Phelps, E. S., and Taylor, J. B., "Stabilizing Powers of Monetary Policy Under Rational Expectations," *Journal of Political Economy*, 85:163–190 (1977).

Phillips, A. W., "The Relation Between Unemployment and the Rate of Change of Money Wage Rates in the United Kingdom, 1862–1957," *Economica*, 25:283–299 (1958).

Reder, M. W., "The Theoretical Problems of a National Wage-Price Policy," *Canadian Journal of Economics and Political Science*, 46–61 (February 1948).

Samuelson, P. A., and Solow, R. M., "Analytical Aspects of Anti-Inflationary Policy," *American Economic Revue*, 50:177–194 (1960).

Sargent, T. J., and Wallace, N., "'Rational' Expectations, the Optimal Monetary Instrument, and the Optimal Money Supply Rule," *Journal of Political Economy*, 83:241–257 (1975).

Sargent, T. J., and Wallace, N., "Rational Expectations and the theory of Economic Policy," *Journal of Monetary Economics*, 2:169–183 (1976).

Selden, R. T., "Cost-push is Demand-Pull Inflation, 1955–1957," *Journal of Political Economy*, 67:1–20 (1959).

Sjaastad. L. A., "Why Stable Inflations Fail," in Parkin, J. M., and Zis, G., (eds.), *Inflation in the World Economy* (Manchester University Press, 1975).

Smithies, A., "Behavior of Money National Income Under Inflationary Conditions," *Quarterly Journal of Economics*, 56:113–129 (1942).

Solow, R. M., "Recent Controversy on the Theory of Inflation," in Rousseas, S. (ed)., *Proceedings of a Symposium on Inflation* (Wilton, Conn.: Kazanjian Economics Foundation, 1968).

Solow, R. M., "The Intelligent Citizen's Guide to Inflation," *The Public Interest*, 30–66 (Winter 1975).

Tobin, J., "Inflation and Unemployment," *American Economic Review*, 52:1–18 (1972).

Tower, E., "More on the Welfare Cost of Inflationary Finance," *Journal of Money, Credit, and Banking*, 3:850–860 (1971).

U.S. Bureau of Labor Statistics, *Handbook of Labor Statistics* (Washington, D.C.: U.S. Government Printing Office, 1974).

Williamson, O. E., Wachter, M. L., and Harris, J. E., "Understanding the Employment Relation: The Analysis of Idiosyncratic Exchange," *Bell Journal of Economics*, 6:250–278 (1975).

Zis, G., "Inflation, An International Monetary Problem or a National Social Phenomenon?" *Manchester Inflation Project, Working Paper 7508* (March 1975).

During the past decade there has been a tendency among macroeconomists to reevaluate the methodological and analytical foundations of the post-Keynesian macroeconomic orthodoxy. The orthodoxy, which Paul Samuelson had labeled "neoclassical synthesis," epitomized by Patinkin's book *Money, Interest, and Prices*, was a "synthesis" in that it combined the Keynesian income-expenditure approach with the neoclassical notion of general competitive equilibrium. However, it was the powerful methodology of general equilibrium theory, the Walrasian "tatonnement process," which dominated the synthesis and gave it a flavor that for some tastes was more neoclassical than Keynesian.

The "tatonnement" describes a hypothetical auction process, where prices are announced at random and an auctioneer registers the desired supplies and demands of each set of announed prices. If at a set of prices the desired supplies and demands are such that the markets are not cleared, the process will continue until a certain set of prices is reached at which the corresponding supplies and demands are such that all markets are cleared simultaneously. Only then are actual exchanges allowed to be carried out.

The system is not permitted to function at disequilibrium or "false" prices, and actual production and transactions can occur only at the set of market-clearing or equilibrium prices. Carrying over that methodology into macroeconomics, it is not surprising that a macroeconomic equilibrium has identical properties as a general competitive equilibrium.

The neoclassical synthesis is "equilibrium macroeconomics," a theoretical model concerned with proving that the economic system has an inherent tendency toward a full-employment equilibrium. As Patinkin summarized it, "Equilibrium means full employment, or, equivalently, unemployment means disequilibrium" (*Money, Interest, and Prices*, p. 328). If this equilibrium is perturbed by an exogenous shock, there will be unemployment, but merely as a transient and temporary phenomenon lasting only as long as it takes the economy to settle down again to its full employment state.

The neoclassical analysis, equipped with a methodology unsuitable for the study of disequilibrium situations, cannot describe what happens during this transitional phase of unemployment. The analysis of the dynamic

PART FOUR
Disequilibrium Macroeconomics

market responses to disequilibrium is carried out only in terms of "price adjustments," completely ignoring any "quantity adjustments," since such quantities as output and employment are by assumption fixed at full employment. It appears, therefore, that the interpretation of Keynesian doctrine embodied in the neo-classical synthesis is at odds with the central theme of *General Theory*.

According to Keynes, the economic system "seems capable of remaining in a chronic condition for sub-normal activity for a considerable period without any marked tendency either towards recovery or towards complete collapse" (*General Theory*, p. 249). If this quotation constitutes Keynes's "unem-ployment proposition," it apparently is opposed to the "full employment proposition" of the neoclassical theory. Those who agree with Keynes that unemployment is conceivably a "normal" situation find equilibrium economics unsuitable for the study of macroeconomic phenomena.[1] The explanation of unemployment requires a theory of disequilibrium and of disorder, one that is free from the limitations of the Walrasian methodology.

Disequilibrium macroeconomics started off as an attempt to reinterpret Keynes and to restore the orginality of his doctrine. As the protagonists of that school of thought argue, Keynes must have had in mind a non-Walrasian analytical scheme, otherwise his theory cannot be dis-tinct from the post-Keynesian neoclassical synthesis.[2]

Clower was the first to describe the economic agents' micro-behavior in disequilibrium. He introduced the "dual decision hypothesis," according to which a household's planned demand for commodities depends upon the planned supply of labor services. This is what he called a "notional" demand, based on a utility maximization process where the budget constraint consists of planned income, deriving from planned employment. In contrast to the "notional" demands, the "effective" demands are derived on the basis of realized income or employment, which can be less than the planned income or employment.

When the economy is in a full employment situation, all plans are realized, and thus notional and effective demands are identical. In cases of disequilibrium, when realized income can be less than planned, only the effective demands are relevant as intentions of purchase that can be validated by disposable income. The macroeconomic implications of the "dual decision hypothesis" are obvious. The economy may reach some sort of "equilibrium," with "effective" supplies and demands equalized at less than full employment. Any corresponding nonzero "notional" excess demands will fail to communicate themselves as signals, enabling the economy to escape from this under employment "equilibrium."

In the words of Clower, "The other side of involuntary unemployment would seem to be involuntary under-consumption." If the economic system is allowed to function when markets are not cleared, then we cannot assume that output and employment are fixed at their full employment level throughout the analysis, as in Patinkin's framework. The dynamic disequilibrium adjustments will involve both price adjustments and quantity adjustments. As a result, the existence, uniqueness, and stability of macroequilibrium no longer can be unequivocally established. The system may exhaust the possibilities of further adjustments and be "locked" in permanent disequilibrium before the disequilibrium can be resolved.

The abandonment of the Walrasian tatonnement market-clearing process greatly increases the analytical complexity of a macroeconomic model. Its stability analysis necessitates the use of the "temporary equilibrium" method, which divides the implicit continuous time of the analysis into arbitrary time intervals called "periods." The economic agents formulate, at the beginning of each period, their supply and demand plans on the basis of a given set of prices. To the extent that these plans are mutually inconsistent, an ex post equality between supplies and demands is established at the end of the period, by means of some sort of quantitative rationing. However, this is only a "temporary equilibrium," because the initial

[1] G. Shackle, *The Years of High Theory* (London: Cam-bridge University Press, 1967), esp. chaps. 11–13. P. Davidson, "A Keynesian View of Patinkin's Theory of Employment," *Economic Journal*, 77:559–578 (1967).

[2] A. Leijonhufund, *On Keynesian Economics and the Eco-nomics of Keynes* (New York: Oxford University Press, 1968). See also R. Clower, "Reflections on the Keynesian Perplex," *Zeitschrift für Nationalöl konomie*, 35:1–24 (1975).

inconsistency of the plans will cause changes in the set of prices taking place at the transition between two successive periods. The plans at the beginning of the following period will be modified due to the price changes and, if they are still mutually inconsistent, there will be further adjustments, and so on. Solow and Stiglitz were the first to explicitly use this method in discussing stability in a disequilibrium framework.

When non-zero "notional" excess demands persist while the "effective" excess demands are zero, it is said that the system has reached a state of "quasi-equilibrium." Bent Hansen[3] defined quasi-equilibrium as the situation where relative prices remain unchanged, although absolute prices are continuously changing, due to the nonzero notional excess demands (i.e., due to the mutual inconsistency of the various plans). Theoretically, the economy can settle down to either an inflationary or a deflationary quasi-equilibrium, which in the absence of any exogenous shock or policy intervention will have no tendency to change.

One can immediately see the relevance of the concept of quasi-equilibrium in explaining the Keynesian "underemployment proposition." A macroeconomic quasi-equilibrium, compared with the full employment general equilibrium, is certainly less than Pareto optimal. Whether inflationary or deflationary, and regardless of the existence or nonexistence of involuntary unemployment, any quasi-equilibrium implies less than the maximum output and employment levels which correspond to the market-clearing state. This situation is attributable to the imperfections and the inherent failure of the market mechanism, generally due to the lack of complete information and certainty.[4]

The articles by Solow and Stiglitz and by Barro and Grossman are representative of a tendency to focus on the interactions between the output and labor markets under nonmarket-clearing conditions. The mechanics of a model with a monetary sector are more complicated, and the paper by Korliras introduces a loanable funds market. Barro and Grossman have extended their basic model in several directions,[5] as they also have provided a more detailed characterization of the microeconomic behavior in disequilibrium situations.

Finally, the non-Walrasian methodology and the "dual decision hypothesis" have been extensively used in monetary general equilibrium theory,[6] where several fundamental theoretical issues are undecided, despite the fact that the nonmonetary general equilibrium theory has by now reached a level of maturity which allows for almost conclusive statements of that theory. For disequilibrium theory to become something other than an intellectual curiosity, at some point, one should be able to see what its concrete policy implications are. The growing econometric work on disequilibrium models[7] not only raises important problems of econometric methodology, but also promises to explore the possibility of using the disequilibrium approach for policy questions. As of today, however, to see what the policy implications of disequilibrium macroeconomics are remains a challenge for ongoing and future research.

[3] Bert Hansen, *A Survey of General Equilibrium Systems* (New York: McGraw-Hill, 1970), p. 111.

[4] T. Negishi, "Existence of an Under-Employment Equilibrium," in G. Schwödiauer, (ed.), *Equilibrium and Disequilibrium in Economic Theory* (Dordrecht: Reidel Publ. Co., 1977). P. Korliras, "On the Theory of Macroeconomic Quasi-Equilibria," *Zeitschrift für Nationalölkonomie*, 36:269–286 (1976).

[5] R. Barro and H. Grossman, *Money, Employment, and Inflation* (New York: Cambridge University Press, 1976).

[6] E. Glustoff, "On the Existence of a Keynesian Equilibrium," *Review of Economic Studies*, 35:327–334 (1968). P. Frevert, "On the Stability of Full Employment Equilibrium," *Review of Economic Studies*, 37:239–251 (1970). J.-P. Benassy, "Neo-Keynesian Disequilibrium in a Monetary Economy," *Review of Economic Studies*, 42:503–523 (1975). H. Varian, "Non-Walrasian Equilibria," *Econometrica*, 45:573–590 (1977).

[7] R. Fair and D. Jaffee, "Methods of Estimation for Markets in Disequilibrium," *Econometrica*, 40:497–514 (1972). G. Maddala, and F. Nelson, "Maximum Likelihood Methods for Markets in Disequilibrium," *Econometrica*, 42:1013–1030. R. Fair, *A Model of Macroeconomic Activity* (Cambridge, Mass.: Balinger Publ. Co., (1975, 1976). S. Goldfeld, "Estimation in a Disequilibrium Model and the Value of Information," *Journal of Econometrics*, 3:325–348 (1975).

The Keynesian Counter-Revolution: A Theoretical Appraisal

Robert W. Clower

University of California, Los Angeles

Twenty-five years of discussion and controversy have produced a large and surprisingly harmonious literature on Keynes and the Classics. Although the series still has not converged to a point of universal agreement, the domain remaining open to dispute has contracted steadily with the passage of time. On one essential issue, however, contemporary opinion is still largely undecided: precisely what are the purely formal differences, if any, between Keynes and the Classics? Perhaps the clearest symptom of our uncertainty is the continued lack of an explicit integration of price theory and income analysis. Equally significant, however, is the ambivalence of professional economists towards the Keynesian counter-revolution launched by Hicks in 1937 and now being carried forward with such vigor by Patinkin and other general equilibrium theorists.[1] The elegance and generality of this literature makes it most alluring. At the same time,

Reprinted from *The Theory of Interest Rates*, edited by F. H. Hahn and F. Brechling (1965), by permission of the author and the publisher (copyright by the International Economic Association, published by Macmillan Co., Ltd.). It includes corrections that were made by the author in *Monetary Theory* edited by Robert W. Clower (Penguin Books, New York, 1970).

[1] The 'counter-revolution' to which I refer is clearly not a conscious revolt against Keynesian economics, for all of the writers involved are, in a practical sense, strong supporters of what they conceive to be the Keynesian revolution. It is another question whether the same people are Keynesians in a theoretical sense. That is one of the issues on which this paper is intended to shed some light. See [10], [11], [17], [18], [20], and [21].

one can hardly fail to be impressed—and disturbed—by the close resemblance that some of its central doctrines bear to those of orthodox economics.

I do not presume at this late date either to improve the views of previous writers on Keynes and the Classics or to transform equivocations into certainties. Things are not that simple. However, I shall attempt to show that the same highly special theoretical presuppositions which led to Keynes' original attack on orthodox economics continue to pervade contemporary price theory and that the Keynesian counter-revolution would collapse without them. Unlike Keynes, who had to deal with doctrines of which no authoritative account had ever been given, we now have an extremely clear idea of the orthodox content of contemporary theory.[2] We thus have a distinct advantage over Keynes in describing what has been said. However, our basic problem is to discover and describe what has not but should have been said—and here we are on all fours with Keynes. Like Keynes, therefore, I must begin by asking 'forgiveness if, in the pursuit of sharp distinctions, my controversy is itself too keen' [13].

I. KEYNES AND TRADITIONAL THEORY

Our first task is to express in modern idiom those aspects of orthodox economics which

[2] For this, we have mainly to thank the counter-revolutionists, since it is their writings which have revived interest in general equilibrium theory.

were of special concern to Keynes. This may be accomplished most conveniently by considering a two-sector economy comprising households on one side and firms on the other. Corresponding to this division into sectors, we distinguish two mutually exclusive classes of commodities: (a) those which are supplied by firms and demanded by households; (b) those which are supplied by households and demanded by firms. Commodities in class (a) will be distinguished by numerical subscripts $i = 1, \ldots, m$, those in class (b) by numerical subscripts $j = m + 1, \ldots, n$. Thus, quantities supplied and demanded by firms are denoted, respectively, by variables $s_1, \ldots, s_m, d_{m+1}, \ldots, d_n$, while quantities demanded and supplied by households are denoted, respectively, by variables $d_1, \ldots, d_m$, $s_{m+1}, \ldots, s_n$. Prevailing market prices (expressed in units of commodity n) are then represented by symbols $\mathbf{p}_1, \mathbf{p}_2, \ldots, \mathbf{p}_{n-1}$ ($\mathbf{p}_n \equiv 1$), or, in vector notation, $\mathbf{P}$.[3]

For ease of exposition, we shall ignore aggregation problems and suppose that the preferences of all households in the economy are adequately characterized by a community utility function, $U(d_1, \ldots, d_m; s_{m+1}, \ldots, s_n)$. Similarly, we shall assume that technical conditions confronting all business firms in the economy are adequately characterized by an aggregate transformation function $T(s_1, \ldots, s_m; d_{m+1}, \ldots, d_n) = 0$. Needless to say, the functions U and T are assumed to possess all continuity and curvature properties needed to ensure the existence of unique extrema under circumstances to be specified below.

Dealing first with the orthodox theory of the firm, we obtain sector supply and demand functions, $\bar{s}_i(\mathbf{P})$, $\bar{d}_i(\mathbf{P})$ as solutions of the problem[4]:

maximize $\quad r = \sum_{i}^{m} \mathbf{p}_i s_i - \sum_{j}^{n} \mathbf{p}_j d_i$

subject to[5] $\quad T(s_1, \ldots, s_m; d_{m+1}, \ldots, d_n) = 0.$

Underlying both sets of solutions are transactor equilibrium conditions of the form

$$\mathbf{p}_k + \frac{\lambda \partial T}{\partial \bar{v}_k} = 0 \quad (\bar{v} = \bar{d}, \bar{s}; k = 1, 2, \ldots, n).$$

In particular, if $n = 2$ and we interpret s_1 as goods and d_2 as labor, we easily establish Keynes' classical postulate I, namely, 'the [real] wage is equal to the marginal product of labour'. ([13], p. 5.)

In a similar fashion, the demand and supply functions of the household sector are obtained as solutions, $\bar{d}_i(\mathbf{P}, \mathbf{r})$, $\bar{s}_i(\mathbf{P}, \mathbf{r})$, of the problem

maximize $\quad U(d_1, \ldots, d_m; s_{m+1}, \ldots, s_n),$

subject to $\quad \sum_{i}^{m} \mathbf{p}_i d_i - \sum^{n} \mathbf{p}_j s_j - \mathbf{r} = 0,$

the profit variable $\mathbf{r}$ being treated as a fixed parameter in this context.[6]

Underlying these solutions are transactor equilibrium conditions of the form

$$\frac{\partial U}{\partial \bar{v}_k} + \gamma \mathbf{p}_k = 0 \quad (\bar{v} = \bar{d}, \bar{s}; k = 1, \ldots, n).$$

Thus, if we consider the case $n = 2$ and adopt an appropriate interpretation of the variables d_1 and s_2, we readily derive Keynes' classical postulate II, namely, 'The utility of the [real] wage when a given volume of labor is employed is equal to the marginal disutility of that amount of employment.' ([13], p. 5)

So much for the basic ideas of the orthodox theory of transactor behavior. Let us turn

---

[3] Here and throughout the remainder of the paper, boldface symbols will invariably be used to refer to magnitudes that are to be regarded as given parameters from the standpoint of individual transactors.

[4] The symbols $\sum_{t}^{m}$ and $\sum_{i}^{n}$ denote, respectively, the operations $\sum_{i=1}^{m}$ and $\sum_{j=m+1}^{n}$.

[5] Since $\mathbf{p}_n \equiv 1$ by assumption, we have not shown it as an explicit divisor of the price variables included in the vector $\mathbf{P}$; but it is there all the same. Thus, the demand and supply functions of the business sector are homogeneous of order zero in the n price variables $\mathbf{p}_1, \ldots, \mathbf{p}_n$. Provided $d_n \not\equiv 0$, however, the same functions are not in general homogeneous in the $n - 1$ *numéraire* prices which are contained in the vector $\mathbf{P}$.

[6] The household demand-and-supply functions are homogeneous of order zero in the $n + 1$ variables $\mathbf{p}_1, \ldots, \mathbf{p}_n$ and $\mathbf{r}$, but not in the n variables $\mathbf{p}_1, \ldots, \mathbf{p}_{n-1}$ and $\mathbf{r}$ (provided $s_n \not\equiv 0$).

next to the theory of price formation, again seeking to express matters as Keynes might have expressed them had he been less steeped in Marshallian habits of thought.

At least since the time of Adam Smith, the market mechanism has been regarded by economists as an ingenious device for reconciling the freedom of individuals to trade as they please with the ultimate necessity for individuals in the aggregate to buy neither more nor less of any commodity than is offered for sale. To accomplish this feat, the mechanism must be supplied with information about individual sale and purchase plans, which is precisely what is supposed to be furnished by the supply-and-demand functions of orthodox theory.

Assuming that all business profits accrue to accounts in the household sector, we may assert first of all that the sale and purchase plans of individual transactors at any given instant of time[7] depend only on prevailing market prices.[8] We may then argue as follows.

If prevailing prices are such that demand differs from supply in any market, this means that individual trading plans, taken as a whole, are mutually inconsistent, which, in turn, means that at least some individual plans cannot be carried into effect at prevailing market prices. In these circumstances, it is plausible to suppose that prevailing prices tend to vary over time, rising in markets where demand exceeds supply, falling in markets where supply exceeds demand. Accord-

ingly, the economy may be said to be in a state of disequilibrium. On the other hand, if prevailing market prices at any given instant happen to be such that demand is equal to supply in every market simultaneously, this means that individual trading plans, considered as a whole, are mutually consistent; hence, that all transactions planned at prevailing prices can, in principle, actually be carried out. In these circumstances, it is plausible to suppose that there are no extraneous forces at work tending to alter either individual trading plans or prevailing market prices, and the economy may be said to be in a state of equilibrium.

The only snag in this argument is the familiar one about the number of equations being one greater than the number of prices to be determined. From the theory of household behavior, however, we know that

$$\sum_i^m \mathbf{p}_i \bar{d}_i - \sum_j^n \mathbf{p}_j \bar{s}_j - \mathbf{r} = 0, \tag{1}$$

and from the theory of business behavior, we know that

$$\sum_i^m \mathbf{p}_i \bar{s}_i - \sum_j^n \mathbf{p}_j \bar{d}_j - \bar{r} = 0. \tag{2}$$

Subtracting 2 from 1, therefore, we have

$$\sum_{k=1}^n \mathbf{p}_k [\bar{d}_k - \bar{s}_k] \equiv \mathbf{r} - \bar{r}. \tag{3}$$

Since in general the variables $\mathbf{r}$ and $\bar{r}$ refer to completely independent individual experiments, we cannot assume that $\mathbf{r} \equiv \bar{r}$.[8] In the case of market experiments, however, it does seem plausible to suppose that $\mathbf{r} = \bar{r}$ provided that the variables $s_1, \ldots, s_m$ and $d_{m+1}, \ldots, d_n$ have assumed their equilibrium values. If this is granted, then 3 leads immediately to Walras' law (in the sense of Lange, [16] pp. 49–68).[9]

$$\sum_{k=1}^n \mathbf{p}_k [\bar{d}_k(\mathbf{P}) - \bar{s}_k(\mathbf{P})] \equiv 0. \tag{4}$$

---

[7] I have chosen to regard 'time' as a continuous rather than a discrete variable, and to confine discussion to current values of all magnitudes, in order to discourage both myself and readers from playing meretricious games with alternative lag assumptions. No part of the present or subsequent argument is affected in any essential way if time is made discrete, lags are introduced, etc.

[8] Since we are performing market rather than individual experiments (Patinkin, [21], p. 15), the parameter $\mathbf{r}$ which appears in the household demand and supply functions is now replaced by the function value of

$$\bar{r} = \sum_i^m \mathbf{p}_i \bar{s}_i - \sum_j^n \mathbf{p}_j \bar{d}_j,$$

which depends only on the price vector $\mathbf{p}$.

[9] The distinction drawn by Lange between Walras' law and Say's law is not relevant here; from a formal point of view, the two propositions are equivalent.

Walras' law obviously implies that the *numéraire* value of one of the excess demands can be inferred from the values of the others, which rids us of the extra supply-and-demand equation. Rewritten in the form

$$\sum_k \mathbf{p}_k \bar{s}_k \equiv \sum_k \mathbf{p}_k \bar{d}_k,$$

Walras' law might also be said to assert that 'supply creates its own demand' (cf. [13], p. 18)—and we shall hear more of this in the sequel. For the time being, however, it may merely be remarked that Walras' law must be valid under the circumstances assumed here.

This account of orthodox doctrine accords well enough, I think, both with modern analysis and with Keynes' conception of classical theory. For the special case $n = 2$, in particular, it is apparent that Keynes' views, as expressed in chapter 2 of the *General Theory*, are exactly equivalent to what is presented above. Granted that this is so, we may reasonably assert that orthodox economics provides a general theory of equilibrium states—that is, an adequate account of the factors determining equilibrium prices and equilibrium transaction plans in a market economy. Moreover, the same analysis may be said to provide the beginnings of a theory of disequilibrium prices and disequilibrium transaction plans. Clearly, however, orthodox analysis does not provide a general theory of disequilibrium states: firstly, because it yields no direct information about the magnitude of *realized* as distinct from *planned* transactions under disequilibrium conditions; secondly, because it tacitly assumes that the forces tending at any instant to change prevailing market prices are independent of realized transactions at the same moment (this includes as a special case the assumption, made explicitly in all '*tâtonnement*', 'recontract' and 'auction' models, that no disequilibrium transactions occur).[10]

It is instructive to compare these views with those of Keynes, as represented by the

following assortment of quotations (not all of them torn out of context):

I shall argue that the postulates of the classical theory are applicable to a special case only and not to the general case . . . ([13], p. 3).

The question . . . of the volume of the *available* resources, in the sense of the size of the employable population, the extent of natural wealth and the accumulated capital equipment, has often been treated descriptively [in orthodox writings]. But the pure theory of what determines the *actual employment* of the available resources has seldom been examined in any detail. . . . I mean, not that the topic has been overlooked, but that the fundamental theory underlying it has been deemed so simple and obvious that it has received, at the most, a bare mention. ([13], pp. 4–5.)

A theory cannot claim to be a *general* theory unless it is applicable to the case where (or the range within which) money wages are fixed, just as much as to any other case. Politicians are entitled to complain that money wages *ought* to be flexible; but a theorist must be prepared to deal indifferently with either state of affairs ([13], p. 276).

. . . the classical theory . . . is wholly unable to answer the question what effect on employment a reduction in money wages will have. For it has no method of analysis wherewith to attack the problem ([13], p. 260).

Clearly, there is nothing very novel in any of this; up to this point, at least, the belief that Keynes is 'saying nothing new' need not be confined to those '. . . who are strongly wedded to . . . the classical theory' (cf. [13], p. v). Like us, Keynes does not in any way deny the generality of orthodox equilibrium analysis; he only denies that orthodox economics provides an adequate account of disequilibrium phenomena.

II. THE KEYNESIAN INDICTMENT OF ORTHODOX ECONOMICS

Grounds for theoretical controversy first begin to emerge when we come to the stage in Keynes' argument ([13], chapter 2) at which he seeks to isolate specific instances in orthodox economics of 'lack of clearness and of generality' ([13], p. v).

---

[10] J. R. Hicks [11], note to ch. 9, pp. 127 ff. Also Patinkin [21] supplementary note B, pp. 377–85.

The first item in his bill of particulars is embedded in a lengthy discussion of wage bargains between entrepreneurs and workers ([13], pp. 1–15). Outwardly, this item represents little more than a vigorous attack on orthodox preconceptions about the stability of a market economy. For the burden of his argument seems to be that if labor is ever forced to move 'off its supply curve' it may be unable to get back on again. If this is an accurate interpretation, we may say immediately that Keynes' criticisms are not of fundamental theoretical significance, for there is no reason to suppose that Keynes was more expert at stability analysis than his orthodox predecessors. However, the same argument might also be interpreted as a direct attack on the orthodox theory of household behavior. This would certainly put labor off its supply curve and would also explain Keynes' categorical rejection of classical postulate II. But if this is what Keynes intended, i.e., to deny the validity of the orthodox theory of household behavior, one can only say that he was singularly unsuccessful in providing a rationale for his attack.

The second item in Keynes' bill of particulars is essentially the same as the first: classical theory is charged with failure to recognize the existence of involuntary unemployment ([13], pp. 15–18). Again, the basic question is: Are 'involuntary unemployment' and 'chronic disequilibrium' synonymous terms for the same objective phenomenon, or is 'involuntary unemployment' a special kind of disequilibrium peculiarly associated with the breakdown of the orthodox theory of household behavior? Here there is somewhat clearer evidence that Keynes believes his objections to orthodox analysis go very deep indeed:

... if the classical theory is only applicable to the case of full employment, it is fallacious to apply it to the problems of involuntary unemployment—if there be such a thing (and who will deny it?). The classical theorists resemble Euclidean geometers in a non-Euclidean world who, discovering that in experience straight lines apparently parallel often meet, rebuke the lines for not keeping straight—as

the only remedy for the unfortunate collisions which are occurring. Yet, in truth, there is no remedy except to throw over the axiom of parallels and to work out a non-Euclidean geometry. Something similar is required today in economics. We need to throw over the second postulate of the classical doctrine and to work out the behavior of a system in which involuntary unemployment in the strict sense is possible ([13], pp. 16–17).

Again, however, we are given no compelling theoretical reason to think that the proposed reconstruction of orthodox economics is really necessary.

The third and final item in Keynes' indictment is a denial of the relevance of Walras' law ([13], pp. 18–21). Most later writers (e.g., Ohlin [20], p. 230, footnote; Goodwin [7], Patinkin [21], p. 249) have argued either that this portion of Keynes' indictment is wrong, or that the proposition which Keynes attacks is not in fact the one he thought he was attacking. Most economists have opted for the second explanation ([24], expecially p. 113),[11] partly in deference to Keynes' acknowledged intellectual powers, partly because they recognize that if Keynes seriously meant to question the validity or relevance of Walras' law, he would have to reject the orthodox theory of household behavior and propose an acceptable alternative—and the alternative would have to include orthodox theory as a special case, valid under conditions of full employment. Walras' law is not, after all, an independent postulate of orthodox analysis; it is a theorem which is susceptible of direct proof on the basis of premises which are typically taken as given in contemporary as well as classical price theory.

III. THE POST-KEYNESIAN DILEMMA

The conclusion which I draw from all this may be put in one phrase: *either Walras' law is incompatible with Keynesian economics, or Keynes had nothing fundamentally new to add*

---

[11] But see H. Rose's note on Walras' law and the reply by Patinkin [22], [25].

to orthodox economic theory. This may seem an unnecessarily brutal way to confront one sacred cow with another. But what other conclusion is possible? In Keynes' mind, at least, the three items in his bill of particulars 'all amount to the same thing in the sense that they all stand and fall together, any one of them logically involving the other two' ([13], p. 22). As we have already seen, he could hardly hold this view seriously unless he regarded each of the three items as an attack on the orthodox theory of household behavior. But suppose that this is not in fact Keynes' view; suppose that Walras' law is both unreservedly valid, relevant and compatible with Keynesian economics. In this event, the recent literature on monetary theory makes it perfectly evident that Keynes may be subsumed as a special case of the Hicks–Lange–Patinkin theory of *tâtonnement* economics, which differs from orthodox theory only in being more detailed and precise. We would then have to conclude that Keynes added nothing fundamentally new to orthodox economic theory.

Thus, we are caught on the horns of a dilemma. If Keynes added nothing new to orthodox doctrine, why have twenty-five years of discussion failed to produce an integrated account of price theory and income analysis? If Keynes did add something new, the integration problems becomes explicable; but then we have to give up Walras' law as a fundamental principle of economic analysis. It is precisely at this point, I believe, that virtually all previous writers have decided to part company with Keynes. I propose to follow a different course. I shall argue that the established theory of household behavior is, indeed, incompatible with Keynesian economics, that Keynes himself made tacit use of a more general theory, that this more general theory leads to market excess-demand functions which include quantities as well as prices as independent variables and, except in conditions of full employment, the excess-demand functions so defined do not satisfy Walras' law. In short, I shall argue that there has been a fundamental misunderstanding of the formal basis of the Keynesian revolution.

IV. DISEQUILIBRIUM SYSTEMS: A PRELIMINARY VIEW

Before attempting to deal directly with the issues raised above, we must say something more about the mechanics of disequilibrium states. In our earlier discussion of orthodox analysis, it was pointed out that the whole of traditional price theory rests on the tacit assumption that market excess demands are independent of current market transactions. This implies that *income magnitudes do not appear as independent variables in the demand or supply functions of a general equilibrium model;* for incomes are defined in terms of quantities as well as prices, and quantity variables never appear explicitly in the market excess-demand functions of traditional theory. To be sure, income variables could be introduced by taking factor supplies as given parameters; but this would preclude the formulation of a general equilibrium model containing supply functions of all marketable factor services.[12] The importance of these propositions for Keynesian economics can hardly be over-emphasized, for they imply directly that the Keynesian consumption function and other market relations involving income as an independent variable cannot be derived explicitly from any existing theory of general equilibrium.[13]

---

[12] This was apparently overlooked by Patinkin when he formulated his 'general theory' of macroeconomics ([21], ch. 9). It is instructive to notice that this chapter is not supplemented by a mathematical appendix. Some of the consequences of this oversight are evident in the later discussion, see especially the argument beginning at p. 216, including the footnotes to pp. 218 and 220. I do not mean to suggest that authors may not put such variables as they please into their models. My point is that such variables as can be shown to be functionally dependent on others should not then be manipulated independently.

[13] Cf. Lange, ([7], ch. 9, p. 53). Lange's usage of the phrase 'propensity to consume' is perfectly legitimate, but the concept invoked by him is not in any sense a consumption function of the sort Keynes worked with since, except on the Keynesian definition, it is not possible to talk about changes in consumption in reponse to changes in income without at the same time talking about changes in prices.

The most lucid account of the role which current transactions *might* play in general equilibrium theory has been presented by Professor Hicks in *Value and Capital* (pp. 119 ff.). The following passages are especially significant in the present connection (pp. 127–9):

Since, in general, traders cannot be expected to know just what total supplies are available on any market, nor what total demands will be forthcoming at particular prices, any price which is fixed initially can be only a guess. It is not probable that demand and supply will actually be found to be equated at such a guessed price; if they are not, then in the course of trading the price will move up or down. Now if there is a change of price in the midst of trading, the situation appears to elude the ordinary apparatus of demand-and-supply analysis, for, strictly speaking, demand curves and supply curves give us the amounts which buyers and sellers will demand and supply respectively at any particular price, if that price is fixed at the start and adhered to throughout. Earlier writers, such as Walras and Edgeworth, had therefore supposed that demand-and-supply analysis ought strictly to be confined to such markets as permitted of 'recontract'; i.e. markets such that if a transaction was put through at a 'false' price . . . it could be revised when the equilibrium price was reached. Since such markets are highly exceptional, their solution of the problem (if it can be called one) was not very convincing.

. . . in the general case . . . gains and losses due to false trading only give rise to income effects—effects, that is, which are the same kind as the income effects which may have to be considered even when we suppose equilibrium prices to be fixed straight away. We have seen again and again that a certain degree of indeterminateness is nearly always imparted by income effects to the laws of economic theory. All that happens as a result of false trading is that this indeterminateness is somewhat intensified. How much intensified depends, of course, upon the extent of the false trading; if very extensive transactions take place at prices very different from equilibrium prices, the disturbance will be serious. But I think we may reasonably suppose that the transactions which take place at *very false* prices are limited in volume. If any intelligence is shown in price-fixing, they will be.

It is heartening to know that income effects can be ignored if they are sufficiently unimportant to be neglected; but this is hardly a solution to the problem at issue. The essential question is whether the supply-and-demand functions of traditional analysis are in any way relevant to the formulation of market prices in situations where disequilibrium transactions *cannot* be ignored.

To answer this question, we must first define explicit theoretical measures of disequilibrium transaction quantities. Perhaps the simplest way to define such measures is to suppose that actual transactions in any given market are always dominated by the 'short' side of the market; that is to say, market transactions are equal to planned market supply if demand is greater than supply, to planned market demand if supply is equal to or greater than demand ([15], p. 203; [5]; [21], pp. 157–8). This is, of course, the procedure which has been followed by all previous writers, in so far as they have said anything at all on the subject.

Taken by itself, this addendum to traditional theory has no logical implications; but it opens the way for further analysis. For example, some writers have suggested the desirability of supposing that actual transactions exert a more or less direct influence on price adjustment via 'spillover' effects— changes in prevailing supply and demand conditions to reflect current discrepancies between planned and realized purchases and sales. The most recent expression of this view has been voiced by Patinkin ([21], p. 157).[14] His suggestion is to redefine the usual price adjustment functions to make the rate of change of price in one market a function not of excess demand in that market alone, but also of excess demand in all other markets. That this is not an entirely satisfactory vehicle for expressing his basic views, however, is indicated by three considerations.

Firstly, it is not consistent with established preference analysis to suppose that transactors alter their sale and purchase plans before prevailing market prices have already varied in response to the pressure of excess demand somewhere in the economy. Secondly, the

---

[14] Also see Hansen [9] and Enthoven [6].

supposition that price movements in one market are governed by excess-demand conditions in all markets is logically equivalent to the supposition that individual traders respond not merely to absolute levels of prevailing prices but also to current rates of change of prices. This implies some basic changes in established preference analysis to allow prices as seen by transactors to differ from current market prices [8]. Thirdly, from Walras' law (obviously applicable in this instance), the 'money' value of potential 'spillover' from any given market is measured by the aggregate 'money' value of the market excess supply of all other commodities. Thus, if 'spillover' effects from a given market are *fully* reflected in other markets, we are left with effective excess demand in the given market (and, by induction, in all other markets also) identically equal to zero; which is to say that prices never vary. Patinkin does not go to this extreme; he relies instead on a proposition of Samuelson ([26], p. 42)[15] and supposes that 'spillover' effects in any given market are only partially reflected in transfers of demand to other markets. But this is simply *ad hoc* theorizing—inventing a solution to a problem which has actually been evaded rather than resolved.

A more promising way to bring current transactions into general equilibrium theory is by way of so-called stock-flow models. Unless we suppose that all commodities traded in the economy are highly perishable, it is clearly plausible to argue that goods will accumulate or decumulate (or both) somewhere in the economic system during periods of market disequilibrium. This forces us to consider possible extensions of traditional theory to deal explicitly with asset-holding phenomena.

There is now a reasonably adequate theoretical literature on this subject, including a number of recent papers on monetary theory and at least one important book on the theory of investment.[16] I think it fair to say, however, that this literature has made little impression on the profession at large; which is perhaps another way of remarking that the equilibrium properties of stock-flow models are essentially the same as those of traditional pure-flow models and that few economists are deeply concerned with anything else. Here, therefore, I shall merely observe that the explicit introduction of asset-holding phenomena into traditional theory entails a redefinition of market excess-demand functions to include asset as well as price arrays among the relevant independent variables and, along with this, an extension of the usual equation systems to include stock-adjustment functions. As a consequence, actual transaction quantities influence market adjustment indirectly, via their impact on existing asset stocks—which creates certain new sources of potential instability ([13], [26], pp. 170–71). Even in this type of model, however, current transactions exercise an influence only after a certain time delay. As in more usual general equilibrium models, therefore, current incomes never appear as independent variables. Thus, this potential road to the *General Theory* also turns out to be a blind alley.

The preceding discussion probably does not exhaust the list of possible ways of introducing current transactions into excess-demand functions, but we have now gone far enough to appreciate that the problem is by no means so transparent as some writers might have us believe. At this point, therefore, let us return to the route which Keynes apparently travelled before us.

---

[15] In fairness to Samuelson, it should be added that his discussion does not refer to spillover effects, but instead to what I have elsewhere called 'dynamical interdependence' among market excess-demand functions. See Bushaw and Clower ([14], ch. 4, pp. 82 ff.).

[16] Vernon L. Smith, *Investment and Production* (20). This book includes a comprehensive bibliography on the 'real' part of the stock-flow literature. For further details of the 'monetary' part, see George Horwich, 'Money, prices and the theory of interest determination' [12]. The latest in this series is the article by Archibald and Lipsey, the related "Symposium on monetary theory' and Baumol's 'Stocks, flow and monetary theory'. The general theory underlying such models is developed at perhaps excessive length in Bushaw and Clower [4].

V. SAY'S PRINCIPLE AND WALRAS' LAW

In our earlier account of the theory of household behavior, we did not distinguish between planned and realized magnitudes because to have done so would not in fact have been a meaningful procedure in the context of orthodox equilibrium analysis. However, if we adopt the view that states of transactor disequilibrium are, in principle, just as admissible as states of transactor equilibrium (and how can we do otherwise?), the distinction between plans and realizations becomes both meaningful and theoretically relevant. In the discussion that follows, we shall adopt just this point of view; accordingly, we shall henceforth interpret boldface symbols $\mathbf{d}$, $\mathbf{s}$ and $\mathbf{r}$ as realized or actual magnitudes (hence, given parameters from the standpoint of individual transactors); planned or notional magnitudes will be denoted, as before, by such symbols as d, $\bar{s}$, r, etc.

For any individual household (here, we are informally modifying our discussion to recognize that the household sector comprises a multitude of independent decision units), we may clearly assume that the realized *numéraire* value of actual purchases during any given interval of time is identically equal to the aggregate *numéraire* value of realized sales and realized profit receipts during the same interval:

$$\sum_{k=1}^{n} \mathbf{p}_k [\mathbf{d}_k - \mathbf{s}_k] - \mathbf{r} \equiv 0. \qquad 5$$

Indeed, this is just a tacit definition of the concept of a transactor, since what it asserts is that commodities are acquired through market exchange rather than theft, gifts, heavenly favors, etc. The familiar household budget constraint, although similar in form to the truism, equation 5, asserts the rather different proposition that no transactor consciously *plans* to purchase units of any commodity without at the same time *planning* to finance the purchase either from profit receipts or from the sale of units of some other commodity. For later reference, I shall call

the last and very general proposition *Say's principle*. This is essentially a rational planning postulate, not a bookkeeping identity nor a technical relation. Unlike the market principle known as Walras' law, moreover, Say's principle does not depend on the tacit assumption that values are calculated in terms of current market prices, or on the equally tacit assumption that market prices are independent of individual purchases and sales. Neither does it presuppose that individual behavior is in any sense optimal. Thus, Say's principle may indeed be regarded as a fundamental convention of economic science, akin in all relevant respects to such basic ideas of physical science as the second law of thermodynamics. Say's principle is not true in the nature of things; but unless we presuppose something of the sort, we have absolutely nothing upon which to build an account of individual decision processes.

Suppose now that we carry through the usual utility maximization procedure to arrive at household demand and supply functions, $\bar{d}_i(\mathbf{P}, \mathbf{r})$, $\bar{s}_j(\mathbf{P}, \mathbf{r})$, interpreting Say's principle to mean what it usually means in this context, namely,

$$\sum_{i}^{m} \mathbf{p}_i d_i - \sum_{j}^{n} \mathbf{p}_j s_j - \mathbf{r} = 0.$$

Must we then assert that any reasonable definition of market demand and supply magnitudes will necessarily make use of the functions $\bar{d}_i$, $\bar{s}_j$ so defined? Not necessarily, for the definition of these functions tacitly presupposes something more than Say's principle, namely, that every household expects to be able to buy or sell any desired quantity of each and every commodity at prevailing market prices ([19], p. 232 ff.).

Now, the rationale of the last presupposition is hardly self-evident. Keynes has been scoffed at on more than one occasion for his dichotomized account of spending and saving decisions (see [13], p. 166). As far as I can see, the only reason for making humorous comments about this view is that established preference analysis tacitly presupposes that selling, buying and saving plans are all carried out simultaneously. But what if one does not happen to consider the presuppositions of established preference analysis, tacit or otherwise, to be the final word on this subject? [2, 28.] I suggest that the question will bear further examination.

The notion that all household decisions are accomplished at a single stroke seems to be an analytically convenient and intuitively plausible procedure as long as we consider each household to be an isolated performer of conceptual experiments. When households are considered to be part of a connected market system, however, the same notion assumes a rather different aspect. What is then presupposed about planned sales and purchases cannot possibly be true of realized sales and purchases, unless the system as a whole is always in a state of equilibrium; that is to say, not every household can buy and sell just what it pleases if supply exceeds demand somewhere in the economy. Do we nevertheless suppose that the facts of life never intrude upon the thought experiments of households?

The answer to this is, I think, that the matter is not of much theoretical significance if, as is usually true when we deal with competitive supply-and-demand models, we are primarily interested in comparative-statics propositions. In this event, differences between realized and planned purchases and sales of individual households may properly be supposed to occur more or less at random. If we entertain the notion of developing market models that will have practical application to situations of chronic disequilibrium, however, we must surely question the universal relevance of the 'unified decision' hypothesis and, by the same token, question whether the usual household supply and demand functions provide relevant market signals.

VI. THE DUAL-DECISION HYPOTHESIS

For the moment, let us imagine ourselves to be involuntarily unemployed in the sense of Keynes. Specifically, imagine that we have a strong wish to satisfy our champagne appetites but that the demand for our services as economic consultants does not in fact allow us to gratify this desire without doing serious damage to our household finances. How do we communicate our thirstiness to producers of champagne; how can they be made aware of our willingness to solve their market research problems in exchange for copious quantities of their excellent beverage?

The answer is that we do so indirectly. We offer more favorable terms to potential buyers of our services (these may include some champagne merchants), leaving it to the market to provide us more employment and income and, in due time, more booze. Do we also signal our craving directly by drawing on money balances and savings accounts and sending our children out to work? In short, do we drink more even before we work more? Or do we become, at least temporarily, involuntarily abstemious and postpone our satisfaction to financially more propitious times? Clearly, this is to pose the question in a highly misleading way, for the issue is not, 'Which do we do?', but 'How much do we do of each?'

But if even this much is granted, we thereby affirm that the demand functions of orthodox theory do not provide relevant market signals. For if realized current receipts are considered to impose any kind of constraint on current consumption plans, planned consumption as expressed in effective market offers to buy will necessarily be less than desired consumption as given by the demand functions of orthodox analysis.

A formal statement of the problem will clarify matters at this point. Following the usual procedure of traditional theory, suppose that the preference function $U(d_1, \ldots, d_m; s_{m+1}, \ldots, s_n)$ is maximized subject to the budget constraint

$$\sum_i^m \mathbf{p}_i d_i - \sum^n \mathbf{p}_j s_j - \mathbf{r} = 0,$$

and the resulting first-order conditions are used to define the notional demand and supply functions $\overline{d}_i(\mathbf{p}, \mathbf{r})$ and $\overline{s}_j(\mathbf{p}, \mathbf{r})$. Provided that realized current income is not less than notional current income, i.e. provided

$$\sum_{j}^{n} \mathbf{p}_j \mathbf{s}_j \geq \sum_{j}^{n} \mathbf{p}_j \bar{s}_j,$$

we may suppose that the functions $\bar{d}_i$ and $\bar{s}_j$ constitute relevant market signaling devices. For this is just to say that current income receipts do not impose an operative constraint on household spending decisions.[17]

In the contrary case, however, i.e. if

$$\sum_{j}^{n} \mathbf{p}_j \mathbf{s}_j < \sum_{j}^{n} \mathbf{p}_j \bar{s}_j,$$

a second round of decision making is indicated: namely, maximize

$$U(d_1, \ldots, d_m; \mathbf{s}_{m+1}, \ldots, \mathbf{s}_n),$$

subject to the modified budget constraint

$$\sum_{i}^{m} \mathbf{p}_i d_i - \sum_{j}^{n} \mathbf{p}_j \mathbf{s}_j - \mathbf{r} = 0.$$

Solving this problem, we obtain a set of *constrained* demand functions,

$$\hat{d}_i(\mathbf{P}, \mathbf{Y}) \quad (i = 1, \ldots, m),$$

where, by definition,

$$\mathbf{Y} \equiv \sum^{n} \mathbf{p}_j \mathbf{s}_j + \mathbf{r},$$

the values of the constrained functions, $\hat{d}_i$, will then be equal to those of the corresponding notional functions, $\bar{d}_i$, if and only if

$$\sum_{j}^{n} \mathbf{p}_j (\mathbf{s}_j - \bar{s}_j) \equiv 0.$$

Except in this singular case,[18] however, the constrained demand functions $\hat{d}_i(\mathbf{P}, \mathbf{Y})$ and

the notional supply functions $\bar{s}_j(\mathbf{P}, \mathbf{r})$, rather than the notional functions $\bar{d}_i$ and $\bar{s}_j$, are the relevant providers of market signals.

Here and elsewhere in the argument, it may be helpful if the reader imagines that a central 'market authority' is responsible for setting all prices (using the nth commodity as an accounting unit), and that this 'authority' maintains continual surveillance over all sale and purchase orders communicated to it by individual transactors to ensure that no purchase order is 'validated' unless it is offset by a sale order that has already been executed (i.e., purchase orders are simply 'cancelled' unless the transactor has a positive balance of 'book credit' with the market authority sufficient to cover the entire value of the purchase order). It must be assumed that the market authority communicates continuously with each transactor to inform it of the precise level of its current credit balance, and further informs each transactor of the precise rate at which previously validated purchase orders currently are being executed. Sale orders are 'validated' automatically, but the rate at which such orders are executed is governed by prevailing demand conditions. It is implicit in this entire line of argument that, at some 'initial' stage in the evolution of market trading arrangements, the market authority advances a nominal quantity of book credit to one or more transactors to set the trading process in motion (without such initial advances, no sale order could ever be executed since no purchase order would ever be validated).

Established preference analysis thus appears as a special case—valid in conditions of full employment—of the present *dual-decision theory*. Considered from this point of view, the other side of involuntary unemployment would seem to be involuntary under-consumption, which should have considerable intuitive appeal to those of us who really do have unsatisfied champagne appetites.

It is worth remarking explicitly that *the dual-decision hypothesis does not in any way flout Say's principle*. It would be more accurate to say that this hypothesis assigns greater

[17] More generally, we might argue that an excess of current income over desired income does affect current expenditure directly; compulsory overtime might be considered a case in point. But we shall not deal with situations of that kind here. In effect, we suppose that individuals are never forced to sell more factor services than they want to sell, though they may be forced for lack of buyers to sell less than they desire.

[18] The constrained demand functions are not even defined, of course, when realized income *exceeds* desired income.

force to the principle by recognizing that current income flows may impose an independent restriction on effective demand, separate from those already imposed by prevailing market prices and current transfer receipts. Indeed, it is this theory which is invariably presented in geometrical classroom expositions of the theory of consumer behavior. It is only in mathematical versions of preference analysis that we lose sight of realized current income as an operative constraint on effective demand.

It is another question whether Keynes can reasonably be considered to have had a dual-decision theory of household behavior at the back of his mind when he wrote the *General Theory*. For my part, I do not think there can be any serious doubt that he did, although I can find no direct evidence in any of his writings to show that he ever thought explicitly in these terms. But indirect evidence is available in almost unlimited quantity: in his treatment of the orthodox theory of household behavior, his repeated discussions of 'Say's law', his development of the consumption function concept, his account of interest theory, and his discussions of wage and price determination. It is also significant, I believe, that a year after the appearance of the *General Theory*, Keynes' own evaluation of the theoretical significance of the consumption function concept still differed sharply from that of his reviewers [14]:

This psychological law was of the utmost importance in the development of my own thought, and it is, I think, absolutely fundamental to the theory of effective demand as set forth in my book. But few critics or commentators so far have paid particular attention to it.

Finally, it is important to notice that unless the orthodox approach to household behavior is modified (tacitly if not explicitly) to recognize the dual-decision hypothesis, the Keynesian notion of an aggregate consumption function does not make sense, the distinction between transactions and speculative balances is essentially meaningless, the liquidity-preference theory of interest is indistinguishable from the classical theory of loanable funds, fluctuations in the demand for physical assets cannot be supposed to have more impact on output and employment than fluctuations in the demand for securities, and excess supply in the labor market does not diminish effective excess demand elsewhere in the economy. In short, Keynes either had a dual-decision hypothesis at the back of his mind, or most of the *General Theory* is theoretical nonsense.

VII. FROM THE CLASSICS TO KEYNES

We remarked above that the dual-decision hypothesis already has an established position in the oral tradition of established preference analysis. We have also argued that it plays an important (if tacit) role in income analysis. Thus, it is only when we turn to contemporary general equilibrium theory that no trace of the hypothesis is anywhere to be found. Yet it is precisely in this area that the dual decision approach is most clearly relevant—and most damaging to orthodoxy.

Referring to our previous account of traditional analysis (Part I, above), we recall that the business sector supply and demand functions may, from a market point of view, be so defined as to depend solely on the price vector **P**, permitting us to write Walras' law in the form

$$\sum_i^m \mathbf{p}_i[\overline{d}_t(\mathbf{P}) - \overline{s}_t(\mathbf{P})]$$
$$+ \sum_j^n \mathbf{p}_i[\overline{d}_j(\mathbf{P}) - \overline{s}_j(\mathbf{P})] \equiv 0.[19]$$

In the context of the present discussion, the most interesting implication of Walras' law is obtained by calling the commodities $1, \ldots,$ m 'goods' and the commodities $m + 1, \ldots, n$ 'factors'. We may then assert that excess supply of factors necessarily implies the simultaneous existence of excess demand for goods. More generally, we may assert that in any disequilibrium situation, there is always an element of excess demand working directly on the price system to offset prevailing elements of excess supply.

[19] Cf. equation 4, above.

FIGURE 1

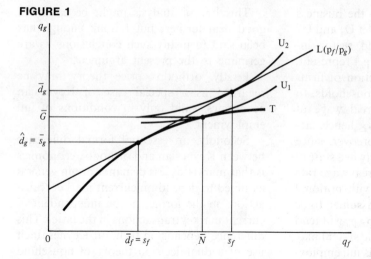

According to the dual-decision hypothesis, however, the market relevance of the household functions $\bar{d}_j(\mathbf{P})$ and $\bar{s}_j(\mathbf{P})$ is contingent on the satisfaction of the condition that realized current income be not less than planned income.[20] Suppose, however, that

$$\sum_{j}^{n} \mathbf{p}_j[\bar{d}_j - \bar{s}_j] < 0;$$

i.e. suppose that notational aggregate demand for factors is less than aggregate supply (in the sense indicated). Then involuntary unemployment may be said to exist since realized factor income cannot exceed the aggregate money value of planned demand for factor inputs, that is to say,

$$\sum_{j}^{n} \mathbf{p}_j[\bar{d}_j - \mathbf{s}_j] \geq 0.$$

In this situation, the dual-decision hypothesis requires that we replace the usual household demand functions, $\bar{d}_i$, by the constrained demand functions $\hat{d}_i(\mathbf{P}, \mathbf{Y})$, which, by defini-

tion, satisfy the condition

$$\sum_{i}^{m} \mathbf{p}_i \, \bar{d}_i(\mathbf{P}) \geq \sum_{i}^{m} \mathbf{p}_i \, \hat{d}_i(\mathbf{P}, \mathbf{Y});$$

i.e., the aggregate money value of constrained demand for goods is at most equal to the aggregate money value of planned demand for goods in the sense of traditional preference analysis. It follows immediately that, in a state of involuntary unemployment, Walras' law must be replaced by the more general condition

$$\sum_{i}^{m} \mathbf{p}_i[\hat{d}_i(\mathbf{P}, \mathbf{Y}) - \bar{s}_i(P)]$$
$$+ \sum_{i}^{n} \mathbf{p}_j[\bar{d}_j(P) - \bar{s}_j(\mathbf{P})] \leq 0;$$

i.e., *the sum of all market demands, valued at prevailing prices, is at most equal to zero.* Indeed, since the equality sign applies with certainty only in the absence of factor excess supply, the dual-decision hypothesis effectively implies that Walras' law, although valid as usual with reference to *notional* market excess demands, is in general irrelevant to any but full employment situations. *Contrary to the findings of traditional theory, excess demand may fail to appear anywhere in the economy under conditions of less than full employment.*

The common sense of the preceding analysis may be clarified by a simple geometrical illustration. See Figure 1. Let the

---

[20] Profit receipts do not concern us since we are still proceeding on the assumption that the condition $\mathbf{r} = \bar{r}$ is satisfied (this is no longer essential to the argument, but is very convenient). What we are supposing, in effect, is that household receivers of profit income have perfect information about profit prospects (they may even be producer-consumers) and react to this information precisely as if corresponding amounts of *numéraire* profit were actually being received.

curve T in the figure represent the business sector transformation function, let U_1 and U_2 represent alternative household sector indifference curves, and let $L(\mathbf{p}_f/\mathbf{p}_g)$ represent, simultaneously, the profit function of firms and the budget constraint of households. In the situation illustrated, the real wage at time t, $\mathbf{p}_f/\mathbf{p}_g$, is such that $\bar{s}_f > \bar{d}_f$; hence, factors are in excess supply. Moreover, since $\bar{d}_g > \bar{s}_g$, goods are simultaneously in a state of notional excess demand. If the real wage rate is assumed to vary inversely with notional excess demand for goods (as is assumed to be the case in orthodox analysis), $\mathbf{p}_f/\mathbf{p}_g$ will tend to fall over time at time t, and the system may therefore be said to tend towards full employment (defined by reference to the point $(\bar{N}, \bar{G})$). However, if the real wage rate is assumed to vary inversely with 'effective' excess demand for goods, no adjustment of the real wage rate will tend to occur at time t since, as indicated, constrained demand for goods, $\hat{d}_g$, is equal to planned supply of goods at prevailing price and income levels.[21]

This illustration of how effective excess demand may be insufficient to induce price adjustment, despite the obvious sufficiency of notional excess demand, says nothing, of course, about the stability of full employment equilibrium under alternative adjustment hypotheses. For example, if the real wage rate varies in response *either* to constrained excess demand for goods *or* excess demand for factors, then in the situation illustrated the system may still tend towards full employment equilibrium. The point of the example is merely to illustrate that, *when income appears as an independent variable in the market excess-demand functions—more generally, when transactions quantities enter into the definition of these functions—traditional price theory ceases to shed any light on the dynamic stability of a market economy.*[22]

This line of analysis might be carried a good deal further; but I think enough has been said to justify such conclusions as are germane to the present argument:

Firstly, orthodox price theory may be regarded as a special case of Keynesian economics, valid only in conditions of full employment.

Secondly, an essential formal difference between Keynesian and orthodox economics is that market excess demands are in general assumed to depend on current market transactions in the former, to be independent of current market transactions in the latter. This difference depends, in turn, on Keynes' tacit use of a dual-decision theory of household behavior and his consequent rejection of Walras' law as a relevant principle of economic analysis.

Thirdly, chronic factor unemployment at substantially unchanging levels of real income and output may be consistent with Keynesian economics even if all prices are flexible; this problem has yet to be investigated within the context of a Keynesian model of market price formation.

VIII. CONCLUSION

My original intention in writing this paper was simply to clarify the formal basis of the Keynesian revolution and its relation to

---

[21] Compare Keynes' discussion of the same model, [13], p. 261.

[22] In an unpublished article 'A Keynesian market equilibrium model', my colleague Mitchell Harwitz considers a more general version of the rigid wages case with results that go far to anticipate the dual-decision

hypothesis on which the present argument places so much weight. The following passage is particularly significant:

Suppose one market is permanently restrained from full adjustment. What does this mean in terms of the individual participants in the market? *It means that some or all of them face a binding constraint in addition to the budget constraint.* For concreteness, consider the Keynesian labor market. A worker, faced with a certain real wage, can sell *less* labor than is consistent with the usual constrained maximum. In effect, he is in equilibrium, but at a boundary [position] imposed by a quantity constraint on the labor he can sell.... It must be granted that these positions are equilibria by our definition; but their stability is a more delicate question.... A complete answer would require a theory of the dynamical behavior of economic units both in and out of equilibrium.

orthodox thought. This I think I have done. In a line, Keynesian economics brings current transactions into price theory whereas traditional analysis explicitly leaves them out. Alternatively, we may say that Keynesian economics is price theory without Walras' law,[23] and price theory with Walras' law is just a special case of Keynesian economics. The bearing of my argument on the Keynesian counter-revolution is correspondingly plain: contemporary general equilibrium theories can be maintained intact only if we are willing to barter Keynes for orthodoxy.

This is not the end of the matter, for there is a choice to be made. No one can deny that general equilibrium analysis, as presently constituted, is a useful instrument for thinking about abstract economic problems, and this would hardly be so if it did not omit many realistic frills. The danger in using this instrument to think about practical problems is that, having schooled ourselves so thoroughly in the virtues of elegant simplicity, we may refuse to recognize the crucial relevance of complications that do not fit our theoretical preconceptions. As Keynes has put it, 'The difficulty lies, not in the new ideas, but in escaping from the old ones, which ramify, for those brought up as most of us have been, into every corner of our minds' ([13], p. viii).

I shall be the last one to suggest that abstract theory is useless; that simply is not so. At the same time, I am convinced that much of what now passes for useful theory

is not only worthless economics (and mathematics), but also a positive hindrance to fruitful theoretical and empirical research. Most importantly, however, I am impressed by the worth of Keynesian economics as a guide to practical action, which is in such sharp contrast to the situation of general price theory. As physicists should and would have rejected Einstein's theory of relativity, had it not included Newtonian mechanics as a special case, so we would do well to think twice before accepting as 'useful' or 'general', doctrines which are incapable of accommodating Keynesian economics.

References

1. Archibald, G. C., and Lipsey, R. G., "Monetary and Value Theory: A Critique of Lange and Patinkin," *Review of Economic Studies*, 26:1–22 (1958), and "Symposium of Monetary Theory," 28:50–56 (1960).
2. Baumol, W. J., *Economic Theory and Operations* (Prentice-Hall, 1961).
3. Baumol, W. J., "Stocks, Flows, and Monetary Theory," *Quarterly Journal of Economics*, 76: 46–56 (1962).
4. Bushaw, D. W., and Clower, R. W., *Introduction to Mathematical Economics* (Irwin, 1957).
5. Clower, R. W., "Keynes and the Classics: A Dynamical Perspective," *Quarterly Journal of Economics* 74:318–320 (1960).
6. Enthoven, A. C., "Monetary Disequilibrium and the Dynamics of Inflation," *Economic Journal*, 66:256–270 (1956).
7. Goodwin, R. M., "The Multiplier as Matrix," *Economic Journal*, 59:537–555 (1949).
8. Hahn, F. A., "The Patinkin Controversy," *Review of Economic Studies*, 28:37–43 (1960).
9. Hansen, B., *A Study in the Theory of Inflation* (Allen and Irwin, 1951).
10. Hicks, J. R., "Mr. Keynes and the Classics: A Suggested Interpretation," *Econometrica*, 5: 147–159 (1937).
11. Hicks, J. R., *Value and Capital* (Clarendon Press, 1939).
12. Horwich, G., "Money, Prices, and the Theory of Interest Determination," *Economic Journal*, 67:625–643 (1957).
13. Keynes, J. M., *The General Theory of Employment, Interest, and Money* (Harcourt Brace, 1936).

[23] It is vacuously true, of course, that a proposition similar to Walras' law holds even in Keynesian economics if we *define* the difference between desired sales and realized sales as an excess demand for 'money income'. But the proposition then becomes an empirically meaningless tautology. In conventional value theory, the total value of commodities (goods and money) offered for sale is always equal to the total value of commodities (goods and money) demanded for purchase because all purchase orders are presumed to be effective regardless of prevailing demand-and-supply conditions. But in the present discussion, purchase orders are not validated automatically, sale orders thus do not necessarily generate effective demand for other commodities (effective demands are constrained by purchase orders *executed*, not purchase orders *placed*).

14. Keynes, J. M., "The General Theory of Employment," *Quarterly Journal of Economics*, 51:209–223 (1937).
15. Klein, L. R., *The Keynesian Revolution* (Macmillan, 1952).
16. Lange, O., "Say's Law: A Restatement and Criticism," in Lange, McIntyre, and Yntema (eds.), *Studies in Mathematical Economics and Econometrics*, (University of Chicago Press, 1942).
17. Lange, O., *Price Flexibility and Employment* (Principia, 1944).
18. Modigliani, F., "Liquidity Preference and the Theory of Interest and Money," *Econometrica*, 12:45–88 (1944).
19. Negishi, T., "General Equilibrium Models of Market Clearing Processes in a Monetary Economy," *The Theory of Interest Rates* (Macmillan, 1965).
20. Ohlin, B., "Some Notes on the Stockholm Theory of Savings and Investment," *Economic Journal*, 47:53–69, 221–240 (1937).
21. Patinkin, D., *Money, Interest, and Prices* (Row Paterson, 1956).
22. Patinkin, D., "Reply to R. W. Clower and H. Rose," *Economica*, 26:253–255 (1959).
23. Pearce, I. F., "A Method of Consumer Demand Analysis Illustrated," *Economica*, 28:371–394 (1961).
24. Rose, H., "Liquidity Preference and Loanable Funds," *Review of Economic Studies*, 24:111–119 (1957).
25. Rose, H., "The Rate of Interest and Walras' Law," *Economica*, 26:252–253 (1959).
26. Samuelson, P. A., *Foundations of Economic Analysis* (Harvard University Press, 1947).
27. Smith, V. L., *Investment and Production* (Harvard University Press, 1961).
28. Strotz, R. H., "The Empirical Implications of a Utility Tree," *Econometrica*, 25:269–280 (1957).

Keynes and the Keynesians: A Suggested Interpretation

Axel Leijonhufvud

University of California, Los Angeles

I

One must be careful in applying the epithet "Keynesian" nowadays. I propose to use it in the broadest possible sense and let "Keynesian economics" be synonymous with the "majority school" macroeconomics which has evolved out of the debates triggered by Keynes' *General Theory* (*GT*). Keynesian economics, in this popular sense, is far from being a homogeneous doctrine. The common denominator, which lends some justification to the identification of a majority school, is the class of models generally used. The prototype of these models dates back to the famous paper by Hicks [6] the title of which I have taken the liberty of paraphrasing. This standard model appears to me a singularly inadequate vehicle for the interpretation of Keynes' ideas. The juxtaposition of Keynes and the Keynesians in my title is based on this contention.

Within the majority school, at least two major factions live in recently peaceful but nonetheless uneasy coexistence. With more brevity than accurancy, they may be labeled the "Revolutionary Orthodoxy" and the "Neoclassical Resurgence." Both employ the standard model but with different specifications of the various elasticities and adjustment velocities. In its more extreme orthodox

Reprinted from the *American Economic Review*, 57:401–410 (1967), by permission of the author and the publisher (copyright by the American Economic Association).

form, the model is supplied with wage rigidity, liquidity trap, and a constant capital-output ratio, and manifests a more or less universal "elasticity pessimism," particularly with regard to the interest-elasticities of "real" variables. The orthodoxy tends to slight monetary in favor of fiscal stabilization policies. The neoclassical faction may be sufficiently characterized by negating these statements. As described, the orthodoxy is hardly a very reputable position at the present time. Its influence in the currently most fashionable fields has been steadily diminishing, but it seems to have found a refuge in business cycle theory—and, of course, in the teaching of undergraduate macroeconomics.

The terms of the truce between the two factions comprise two propositions: (1) the model which Keynes called his "general theory" is but a special case of the classical theory, obtained by imposing certain restrictive assumptions on the latter; and (2) the Keynesian special case is nonetheless important because, as it happens, it is more relevant to the real world than the general (equilibrium) theory. Together the two propositions make a compromise acceptable to both parties, permitting a decent burial of the major issues which almost everyone has grown tired of debating—namely, the roles of relative values and of money—and, between them, the role of the interest rate—in the "Keynesian system." Keynes thought he had made a major contribution towards a synthesis of the theory of money and "our fundamental theory of value" (*GT*, pp. vi-vii). But the truce between the orthodox and the neoclassicists is based on the common understanding that his system was *sui generis*—a theory in which neither relative values nor monetary phenomena are "important."

This compromise defines, as briefly as seems possible, the result of what Clower aptly calls the "Keynesian Counterrevolution" [4].

II

That a model with wage rigidity as its main distinguishing feature should become widely accepted as crystallizing the experience of the unprecedented wage inflation of the Great Depression is one of the more curious aspects of the development of Keynesianism, comparable in this regard to the orthodox view that "money is unimportant"—a conclusion presumably prompted by the worst banking debacle in U.S. history. The emphasis on the "rigidity" of wages, which one finds in the New Economics, reveals the judgement that wages did not fall enough in the early 1930's. Keynes, in contrast, judged that they declined too much by far. It has been noted before that, to Keynes, wage rigidity was a policy recommendation and not a behavioral assumption (e.g., [13]).

Keynes' theory was dynamic. His model was static. The method of trying to analyze dynamic processes with a comparative static apparatus Keynes borrowed from Marshall. The crucial difference lies in Keynes's inversion of the ranking of price- and quantity-adjustment velocities underlying Marshall's distinction between the "market day" and the "short run." The initial response to a decline in demand is a quantity adjustment. Clower's investigation of a system, which responds to deflationary disturbances in the first instance by quantity adjustments, shows that the characteristic Keynesian income-constrained, or "multiplier," process can be explicated in terms of a general equilibrium framework [4]. Such a model departs from

the traditional Walrasian full employment model only in one, eminently reasonable, respect: trading at "false prices"—i.e., prices which do not allow the realization of all desired transactions—may take place. Transactors who fail to realize their desired sales, e.g., in the labor market, will curtail their effective demands in other markets. This implies the amplification of the initial disturbance typical of Keynes' multiplier analysis.

The strong assumption of "rigid" wages is not necessary to the explanation of such system behavior. It is sufficient only to give up the equally strong assumption of instantaneous price adjustments. Systems with finite price velocities will show Keynesian multiplier responses to initial changes in the rate of money expenditures. It is not necessary, moreover, to rely on "monopolies," labor unions, minimum wage laws, or other institutional constraints on the utility maximizing behavior of individual transactors in order to explain finite price velocities. Keynes, in contrast to many New Economists, was adamantly opposed to theories which "blamed" depressions on such obstacles to price adjustments. The implied proposition that, if "competition" could only be restored, "automatic forces" would take care of the employment problem was one of his pet hates. Atomistic markets do not mean instantaneous price adjustments. A system of atomistic markets would also show Keynesian adjustment behavior.

In Walrasian general equilibrium theory, all transactors are regarded as price takers. As noted by Arrow, "there is no one left over whose job it is to make a decision on price" [2, p. 43]. The job, in fact, is entrusted to a *deus ex machina*: Walras' auctioneer is assumed to inform all traders of the prices at which all markets are going to clear. This always trustworthy information is supplied at zero cost. Traders never have to wrestle with situations in which demands and supplies do not mesh; all can plan on facing perfectly elastic demand and supply schedules without fear of ever having their trading plans disappointed. All goods are perfectly "liquid," their full market values being at any time instantaneously realizable. Money can be added to such models only by artifice.

Alchian has shown that the emergence of unemployed resources is a predictable consequence of a decline in demand when traders do not have perfect information on what the new market clearing price would be [1, Chap. 31]. The price obtainable for the services of a resource which has become "unemployed" will depend upon the costs expended in searching for the highest bidder. In this sense, the resource is "illiquid." The seller's reservation price will be conditioned by past experiences as well as by observation of the prices at which comparable services are currently traded (*GT*, p. 264). Reservation price will be adjusted gradually as search continues. Meanwhile the resource remains unemployed. To this analysis one need only add that the loss of receipts from its services will constrain the owner's effective demand for other products—a feedback effect which provides the rationale of the multiplier-analysis of a system of atomistic ("competitive") markets.

To make the transition from Walras' world to Keynes' world, it is thus sufficient to dispense with the assumed tatonnement mechanism. The removal of the auctioneer simply means that the generation of the information needed to coordinate economic activities in a large system where decision making is decentralized will take time and will involve economic costs. No other "classical" assumptions need to be relinquished. Apart from the absence of the auctioneer, the system remains as before: (1) individual traders still "maximize utility" (or profit)—one need not assume that they are constrained from bargaining on their own, nor that they are "money illusioned" or otherwise irrational; (2) price incentives are still effective—there is no inconsistency between Keynes' general "elasticity optimism" and his theory of unemployment. When price elasticities are assumed to be generally significant, one admits the potentiality of controlling the activities of individual traders by means of

prices so as to coordinate them in an efficient manner. It is not necessary to deny the existence of a vector of nonnegative prices and interest rates consistent with the full utilization of resources. To be a Keynesian, one need only realize the difficulties of finding the market clearing vector.

III

It is a widely held view that the main weaknesses of Keynesian theory derive from Keynes' neglect of the influence of capital and real asset values on behavior (e.g., [8, pp. 9, 11, 17]; [14, p. 636]). It is above all on this crucial point that the standard model has proved to be a most seriously misleading framework for the interpretation of Keynes' theory. This is readily perceived if we compare the "aggregative structures" of the standard model and the *General Theory* model. In either case, we are usually dealing with but three price relations, so that the relevant level of aggregation is that of four-good models:

Standard Model	*General Theory*
Commodities	Consumer goods
Bonds	Nonmoney assets
Money	Money
Labor services	Labor services

The aggregate production function makes the standard model a "one-commodity model." The price of capital goods in terms of consumer goods is fixed. The money wage is "rigid," and the current value of physical assets is tied down within the presumably narrow range of short-run fluctuations in the "real" wage rate. Relative prices are, indeed, allowed little play in this construction. "Money" includes only means of payment, while all claims to cash come under the heading of "bonds."

The four-good structure of the *General Theory* is a condensed version of the model of the *Treatise on Money* (*TM*) with its richer menu of short-term assets. All titles to prospective income streams are lumped together in "nonmoney assets." Bond streams and equity streams are treated as perfect substitutes, a simplification which Keynes achieved through some quite mechanical manipulations of risk and liquidity premia (*GT*, Chap. 17). The fundamental property which distinguishes nonmoney assets both from consumables and from money is that the former are "long" while the latter two are "short"—attributes which, in Keynes' usage, were consistently equated with "fixed" (or "illiquid") and "liquid," respectively (cf. *TM*, V:I, p. 248). The typical nonmoney assets are bonds with long term to maturity and titles to physical assets with a very long "duration of use or consumption." Basically, Keynes' method of aggregation differentiates between goods with a relatively high and a relatively low interest elasticity of present value. Thus the two distinctions are questions of degree. As a matter of course, the definition of money includes all types of deposits, since their interest elasticity of present value is zero, but "such instruments as treasury bills" can also be included when convenient (*GT*, p. 167 n.).

Keynes' alleged neglect of capital is attributed to his preoccupation with the short run in which the stock of physical capital is fixed. The critique presumes that Keynes worked with the standard model in which the value of such assets in terms of consumables is a constant. But in Keynes' two-commodity model, this price is, in principle, a short-run variable and, as a consequence, so is the potential command over current consumables which the existing stock of assets represents. The current price of nonmoney assets is determined by expectations with regard to the "stream of annuities" in prospect and by the rate at which these anticipated future receipts are discounted. The relevant rate is always the long rate of interest. In the analysis of short-run "equilibrium," the state of expectation (alias the marginal efficiency of capital) is assumed to be given, and the price of assets then varies with "the" interest rate.

In Keynes' short run, "a decline in the interest rate" and "a rise in the market prices of capital goods, equities, and bonds" are interchangeable descriptions of the same event. Since the representative nonmoney asset is very long-lived, its interest elasticity of present value is quite high. The price elasticity of the output of augmentable income sources is very high. The aggregative structure of this model leaves no room for elasticity pessimism with regard to the relationship between investment and the (long) rate of interest. It does not even seem to have occurred to Keynes that investment might be exceedingly interest inelastic, as later Keynesians would have it. Instead, he was concerned to convince the reader that it is reasonable to assume that "a moderate change in the prospective yield of capital-assets or in the rate of interest will not involve an indefinitely great change in the rate of investment" (*GT*, p. 252).

The relationship between saving and the interest rate is of less quantitative significance, but Keynes' ideas on the subject are of considerable interest and give some clues to his theory of liquidity preference. The criticisms of his supposed neglect of wealth as a variable influencing behavior have been directed in particular against the *ad hoc* "psychological law" on which he based the consumption-income relation. This line of criticism ignores the "windfall effect" which "should be classified amongst the major factors capable of causing short-period changes in the propensity to consume" (*GT*, pp. 92–94). This second psychological law of consumption states simply that the propensity to consume out of current income will be higher the higher the value of household net worth in terms of consumer goods. A decline in the propensity to consume may, therefore, be caused either by a decline in the marginal efficiency of capital (*GT*, p. 319) or by a rise in the long rate (*GT*, p. 94; *TM*, V:I, pp. 196–97). In the short run the marginal efficiency is taken as given and, so, it is the interest rate which concerns us.

The usual interpretation focuses on the passages in which Keynes argued that "changes in the rate of time-discount" will not significantly influence saving. In my opinion, these well-known passages express the assumption that household preferences exhibit a high degree of intertemporal complementarity, so that the intertemporal substitution effects of interest movements may be ignored. Consequently, the windfall effect of such changes must be interpreted as a wealth effect.

Hicks has shown that the wealth effect of a decline in interest will be positive if the average period of the income stream anticipated by the representative household exceeds the average period of its planned "standard stream" [7, especially pp. 184–88]. Households who anticipate the receipt of streams which are, roughly speaking, "longer" than their planned consumption streams are made wealthier by a decline in the interest rate. The present value of net worth increases in greater proportion than the present cost of the old consumption plan, and the consumption plan can thus be raised throughout.

This brings our discussion of the *General Theory* into pretty unfamiliar territory. But Keynes' "vision" was of a world in which the indicated conditions generally hold. In this world, currently active households must, directly or indirectly, hold their net worth in the form of titles to streams which run beyond their consumption horizon. The duration of the relevant consumption plan is sadly constrained by the fact "in the long run, we are all dead." But the great bulk of the "fixed capital of the modern world" is of a very long-term nature (e.g., *TM*, V:II, pp. 98, 364), and is thus destined to survive the generation which now owns it. This is the basis for the wealth effect of changes in asset values.

Keynes' *Gestalt*-conception of the world resembles Cassel's. Cassel used the wealth effect to argue the "necessity of interest" [3], an argument which Keynes paraphrased (*GT*, p. 94). The same conception underlies Keynes' liquidity preference theory of the term structure of interest. Mortal beings cannot hold land, buildings, corporate equities, British consols, or other permanent income sources "to maturity." Induced by the productivity of roundabout processes to invest his savings in such income sources, the representative, risk-averting transactor must suffer

"capital uncertainty." Forward markets, therefore, will generally show a "constitutional weakness" on the demand side [7, p. 146]. The relevance of the duration structure of the system's physical capital has been missed by the modern critics of the Keynes-Hicks theory of the term structure of interest rates [12, pp. 14–16] [9, pp. 347–48].

The recent discussion has dealt with the term structure problem as if financial markets existed in a vacuum. But the "real forces of productivity and thrift" should be brought in. The above references to the productivity of roundabout processes (*GT*, Chap. 16) and the wealth effect indicates that they are not totally ignored in Keynes' general theory of liquidity preference. The question why short streams should command a premium over long streams is, after all, not so different from the old question why present goods should command a premium over future goods. Keynes is on classical ground when he argues that the essential problem with which a theory of asset prices must deal derives from the postponement of the option to consume, and that other factors influencing asset prices are subsidiary: "we do not devise a productivity theory of smelly or risky processes as such" (*GT*, p. 215).

IV

Having sketched Keynes' treatment of intertemporal prices and intertemporal choices, we can now consider how "changing views about the future are capable of influencing the quantity of employment" (*GT*, p. vii). This was Keynes' central theme.

"It is by reason of the existence of durable equipment that the economic future is linked to the present" (*GT*, p. 146). The price of augmentable nonmoney assets in terms of the wage unit determines the rate of investment. The same price in terms of consumables determines the propensity to consume. This price is the focal point of Keynes' analysis of changes in employment.

If the "right" level of asset prices can be maintained, investment will be maintained and employment at the going money wage stabilized. If a decline in the marginal efficiency of capital occurs, maintenance of the prices of long-lived physical assets and equities requires a corresponding drop in the long rate and thus a rise in bond prices. To Keynes, "the sole intelligible explanation" (GT, p. 201) of why this will normally not occur is that bear speculators will shift into savings deposits. If financial intermediaries do not "operate in the opposite direction" (TM, V:I, pp. 142–43), bond prices will not rise to the full extent required and demand prices for capital goods and equities will fall. This lag of market rate behind the natural or "neutral" rate (GT, p. 243) will be associated with the emergence of excess demand for money—which always spells contraction. "The importance of money essentially flows from its being a link between the present and the future" (GT, p. 293).

Contraction ensues because nonmoney asset prices are "wrong." As before, "false prices" reveal an information failure. There are two parts to this information failure: (1) Mechanisms are lacking which would ensure that the entrepreneurial expectations guiding current investment mesh with savers' plans for future consumption: "If saving consisted not merely in abstaining from present consumption but in placing simultaneously a specific order for future consumption, the effect might indeed be quite different" (GT, p. 210). (2) There is an alternative "circuit" by which the appropriate information could be transmitted, since savers must demand stores of value in the present. But the financial markets cannot be relied upon to perform the information function without fail. Keynes spent an entire chapter in a mournful diatribe on the Casino-activities of the organized exchanges and on the failure of investors, who are not obliged to hold assets to maturity, to even attempt "forecasting the prospective yield of assets over their whole life" (GT, Chap. 12).

Whereas Keynes had an exceedingly broad conception of "liquidity preference," in the Keynesian literature the term has acquired the narrow meaning of "demand for money," and this demand is usually discussed in terms of the choice between means of payment and one of the close substitutes which Keynes included in his own definition of money. Modern monetary theorists have come to take an increasingly dim view of his speculative demand, primarily on the grounds that the underlying assumption of inelastic expectations represents a "special case" which is unseemly in a model aspiring to the status of a "general theory" [5, pp. 145–51] [15] [8, p. 10] [9, p. 344]. But it is only in the hypothetical world of Walrasian tatonnements that all the information required to coordinate the economic activities of a myriad of traders is produced de novo on each market day. In any other construction, traders must rely heavily on "memory" rather than fresh information. In the orthodox model, with its interest inelasticity of both saving and investment, there is admittedly no "real" reason why traders' past experiences should be of a narrow normal range of long rates. In Keynes' model, there are reasons. In imperfect information models inelastic expectations are not confined to the bond market. The explanation of the emergence of unemployed resources in atomistic markets also relies on inelastic expectations. To stress "speculative behavior" of this sort does not mean that one reverts to the old notion of a Walrasian system adjusting slowly because of "frictions." The multiplier feedbacks mean that the system tends to respond to parametric disturbances in a "deviation-amplifying" manner—behavior which cannot be analyzed with the pre-Keynesian apparatus.

A truly vast literature has grown out of the Pigou-effect idea, despite a most universal agreement on its "practical" irrelevance. The original reason for this strange development was dissatisfaction with Keynes' assertion that the only hope from deflation lies "in the effect of the abundance of money in terms of the wage-unit on the rate of interest" (GT, p. 253). This was perceived as a denial of the logic of classical theory. Viewing Keynes' position through the glasses of the standard one-commodity model, it was concluded that it could only be explained on the assumption that he had overlooked the direct effect of an increase in real net worth on the demand for commodities (e.g., [13, pp. 269–70] [14, Note K:1]). The one-commodity interpretation entirely misses Keynes' point: that the trouble arises from inappropriately low prices of augmentable nonmoney assets relative to both wages and consumer goods prices. Relative values are wrong. Absolute prices will "rush violently between zero and infinity" (*GT*, pp. 239, 269–70), if price-level movements do not lead to a "correction" of relative prices through either a fall in long rates or an induced rise in the marginal efficiency of capital (*GT*, p. 263). It is hard to see a denial of "our fundamental theory of value" in this argument.

V

We can now come back to the "terms of the truce" between the neo-classicists and the Keynesian orthodox. I have argued that, in Keynes' theory: (1) transactors do maximize utility and profit in the manner assumed in classical analysis, also in making decisions on saving and investment; (2) price incentives are effective and this includes intertemporal price incentives—changes in interest rates or expected future spot prices (*GT*, *loc. cit.*) will significantly affect present behavior; (3) the existence of a hypothetical vector of nonnegative prices and interest rates which, if once established, would bring full resource utilization is not denied.

The only thing which Keynes "removed" from the foundations of classical theory was the *deus ex machina*—the auctioneer which is assumed to furnish, without charge, all the information needed to obtain the perfect coordination of the activities of all traders in the present and through the future.

Which, then, is the more "general theory" and which the "special case"? Must one not grant Keynes his claim to having tackled the more general problem?

Walras' model, it has often been noted, was patterned on Newtonian mechanics. On the latter, Norbert Wiener once commented: "Here there emerges a very interesting distinction between the physics of our grandfathers and that of the present day. In nineteenth

century physics, it seemed to cost nothing to get information" [16, p. 29]. In context, the statement refers to Maxwell's Demon—not, of course, to Walras' auctioneer. But, *mutatis mutandis*, it would have served admirably as a motto for Keynes' work. It has not been the main theme of Keynesian economics.

References

1. Alchian, Armen A., and Allen, William R., *University Economics* (Belmont, California, 1964).
2. Arrow, Kenneth J., "Towards a Theory of Price Adjustment," in Abramowitz, M., et al., *The Allocation of Economic Resources* (Stanford, 1959).
3. Cassel, Gustav, *The Nature and Necessity of Interest* (1903).
4. Clower, Robert W., "The Keynesian Counterrevolution: A Theoretical Appraisal," in Hahn, F. H., and Brechling, F. P. R. (eds.), *The Theory of Interest Rates* (London, 1965).
5. Fellner, William, *Monetary Policies and Full Employment* (Berkeley, 1946).
6. Hicks, John R., "Mr. Keynes and the 'Classics': A Suggested Interpretation," *Econometrica*, 5: 147–159 (1937).
7. _____, *Value and Capital*, 2nd ed. (Oxford, 1946).
8. Johnson, Harry G., "The General Theory After Twenty-Five Years," *American Economic Review Proceedings*, 51:1–17 (1961).
9. _____, "Monetary Theory and Policy," *American Economic Review*, 52:335–384 (1962).
10. Keynes, John Maynard, *A Treatise on Money*, vols. I and II (London, 1930).
11. _____, *The General Theory of Employment, Interest, and Money* (London, 1936).
12. Meiselman, David, *The Term Structure of Interest Rates* (Englewood Cliffs, New Jesey, 1962).
13. Patinkin, Don, "Price Flexibility and Full Employment," *American Economic Review* (1948), as reprinted in Lutz, F. A., and Mints, L. M., (eds.), *Readings in Monetary Theory* (Homewood, Illinois, 1951).
14. _____, *Money, Interest, and Prices*, 2nd ed. (New York, 1965).
15. Tobin, James, "Liquidity Preferences as Behavior Towards Risk," *Review of Economic Studies*, 25:65–86 (1958).
16. Wiener, Norbert, *The Human Use of Human Beings*, 2nd ed. (New York, 1964).

Output, Employment, and Wages in the Short Run
Robert M. Solow and Joseph E. Stiglitz

M.I.T. and Stanford University

I. INTRODUCTION

This paper began as an attempt to clarify the relation between two alternative theories of distribution. One theory is usually, though not quite accurately, called the marginal productivity theory; it makes the distribution of income depend mainly, but not entirely, on technological conditions. The other theory we shall call the Cambridge theory because it has been argued, in slightly different ways, by Nicholas Kaldor,[1] Joan Robinson, and Luigi Pasinetti; in that theory the distribution of income is made to depend primarily or exclusively on the different propensities to spend and save wage income and profits.

It soon became clear to us that the essence of the relation between the two theories is this: in the marginal productivity theory the main function of the real wage is to clear the labor market, while in the Cambridge theory the main function of the real wage is to clear the commodity market. We were led, by this route, to a slightly novel theory of the determination of aggregate output and employment in the short run.[2] In particular, we pay

explicit attention to the nature of the aggregate supply of output; in this we are returning to the method of the *General Theory*. But we do not assume that the price level adjusts immediately to clear the market for goods, i.e., to equate aggregate supply and aggregate demand, any more than we assume that the money wage adjusts to clear the market for labor. Much does depend, however, on the character and speed of the reaction of prices and wages to disequilibrium in the goods market and to unemployment of labor.

The model we have constructed may help to elucidate two other questions about Keynesian economics. It permits a kind of underemployment equilibrium, although money wages have a certain amount of downward flexibility (thus suggesting that the operational significance of "rigid wages" is merely inability of the money wage to clear the labor market instantaneously). In addition it shows how the real wage may respond

Reprinted from the *Quarterly Journal of Economics*, 82:537–560 (1968), by permission of the authors and the publisher (copyright by the President and Fellows of Harvard College, published by John Wiley and Sons, Inc.).

[1] Nicholas Kaldor, "Alternative Theories of Distribution," *Review of Economic Studies*. XXIII (1955–56).

[2] Sen formulates the problem in a similar way, but goes in a different direction altogether. A. K. Sen, "Neo-

Classical and Neo-Keynesian Theories of Distribution," *Economic Record*, XXXIX (March 1963). Phelps explores yet another route. E. S. Phelps. "Short-Run Employment and Real Wage Rate Under Market-Clearing Prices." *International Economic Review*, forthcoming. Our approach has a lot in common with that of Rose and Williamson. Hugh Rose, "On the Non-Linear Theory of the Employment Cycle," *Review of Economic Studies*, XXXIV (April 1967). John Williamson, "The Price-Price Spiral," *Yorkshire Bulletin of Economic and Social Research*, Vol. 19 (1967), pp. 3–14. An earlier predecessor is Bent Hansen, *A Study in the Theory of Inflation* (London; Allen, 1951).

in either direction to fluctuations in effective demand, although production exhibits impeccable diminishing returns to labor in the short run.

Our analysis is limited strictly to the short run. Everything that happens is supposed to happen so quickly that the effects of current investment on the size and composition of the capital stock can be neglected. (Current investment is treated as exogenous.) The distributional impact of variations in effective demand can thus be studied in isolation. Moreover, any attempt at a *macroeconomic* application of marginal productivity theory in the long run is open to the usual criticism: except under the most stringent assumptions, there may not be any simply-defined "production function" whose partial derivatives can be interpreted as marginal productivities and related to factor prices. In the short run, with a given inventory of capital goods, this difficulty does not arise. If we think of labor as the only variable factor of production (which amounts to neglecting what Keynes called "marginal user cost"), no more than the usual aggregation problem is involved in treating aggregate output as a function of aggregate employment, whose slope is the short-run marginal product of labor. If the results of this investigation prove acceptable and interesting, then we are faced with the problem of extending them to the long run, i.e., of incorporating a reasonable representation of the way the short-run production function is shifted by current investment.

To simplify the analysis, we have ignored monetary factors. Thus the demand for goods and services is assumed not to depend on the rate of interest or on cash balances. This is odd in a theory in which money wages and prices play an important role; we hope the reader will see that the model could easily be extended to include the standard LM-IS apparatus. In the meanwhile, imagine that the monetary authorities follow the policy of maintaining a constant rate of interest, or a constant ratio of money supply to current-price value of output, or follow some other permissive policy.

II. BUILDING BLOCKS

Given the stock of capital goods inherited from the past, real output (Y) is a function of labor input (N) alone. The short-run marginal product of labor is positive. There are likely to be short-run diminishing returns to labor alone, because less efficient capacity must be drawn into use at higher levels of output. But the econometric indications on this point are unclear, perhaps because a component of overhead labor results in a phase of increasing average productivity of labor in the short run, along with decreasing marginal productivity, perhaps because of frictions in the adjustment of employment to changes in output. In any case, we assume that the marginal product of labor is lower at higher outputs. Thus for the short-run production function we have

$$Y = F(N), \quad F'(N) > 0, \quad F''(N) < 0. \tag{1}$$

Under more or less competitive conditions, the aggregate supply of output (Y^S) at any price level (p) and money wage (w) is the profit-maximizing output, or the output at which price equals marginal cost, or, *since labor is the only variable input, the output at which the marginal product of labor is equal to the real wage.* If we let $f(\cdot)$ stand for the inverse function of F', and let $v = w/p$ be the real wage, then

$$Y^S = F(f(w/p)) = G(v), \quad G' < 0; \tag{2}$$

aggregate supply at any real wage is the output corresponding to the employment at which the marginal product of labor equals the real wage, and is therefore a decreasing function of the real wage, because of diminishing returns.[3]

This is a conventional short-run supply curve, in the sense that the stock of capital goods is fixed while employment varies. But

---

[3] Under some market structures, naturally, no supply curve exists at all. One can imagine imperfectly competitive situations in which a curve like (2) makes sense, but with a fixed markup on marginal cost. Then the middle term in (2) would read $F(f(m\frac{w}{p}))$, where m is the markup.

there is strong econometric evidence that employment adjusts to changes in the demand for output only with a delay that presumably reflects both uncertainty and frictional costs. At any instant of time, therefore, employment, too, can be regarded as *fixed*, and the wage bill as a fixed cost. In other words, in the very short run, marginal cost is zero for outputs up to $F(N)$ and (as a simplification) prohibitively high for larger outputs. The momentary supply curve for output is thus completely inelastic at the level $F(N)$:

$$Y^* = F(N). \tag{3}$$

Employment does, however, adjust: toward what? Presumably it adjusts toward the level appropriate to an expected rate of output. A natural choice is the smaller of Y^D and Y^S, where Y^D is aggregate demand for output, to be discussed in a moment, and Y^S has already been defined. Given a going real wage and rate of employment, firms supply momentarily their current rate of output. They will wish to supply Y^S when they have had time to adjust employment appropriately. But this intention may be overriden if the limit to output is actually on the demand side. We adopt the simple linear adjustment process that moves employment each instant some part of the way from its current level toward its target level, $F^{-1}(min(Y^D, Y^S))$:

$$N' = \theta(F^{-1}(min(Y^S, Y^D)) - N); \tag{4}$$

where N' stands for dN/dt, $F^{-1}(\cdot)$ is the inverse function of F, and θ is a positive constant. For short-run analysis to make sense, θ must not be too small. The econometric evidence is that it is not.

On the side of aggregate demand (Y^D) we have nothing new to offer. We treat investment (I) as exogenous, and we ignore direct monetary influence on demand. To accommodate the Cambridge theory we allow for possibly different marginal propensities to consume $(1 - s_w$ and $1 - s_p)$ wage and profit incomes. Thus

$$Y^D = I + (1 - s_w)vN + (1 - s_p)(Y^D - vN). \tag{5}$$

Notice that aggregate demand is entirely in real terms. Notice also that we have inserted Y^D on the right-hand side of (5), and not Y; the aggregate demand function gives the sustainable real demand generated by any given rate of investment, wage bill, and propensities to save.[4] Then (3) can be solved to yield

$$Y^D = \frac{I}{s_p} + \frac{s_p - s_w}{s_p} vN, \tag{6}$$

so that, for given I and N, aggregate demand is an increasing function of the real wage, provided that $s_p > s_w$. Obviously, if $s_p = s_w = s$, then aggregate demand is simply I/s, investment times the ordinary multiplier. That traditional case is therefore included in the analysis that follows.

At the current moment, N is historically given. The momentary supply of output is Y^*; the demand for output, Y^D, is an increasing (or perhaps constant) function of v. There will usually be a positive real wage v_0 at which $Y^D = Y^*$; if the real wage happened to equal v_0, the goods market would be momentarily cleared. (Even so, the money wage and price level might be changing, as we will discuss soon.) If the current real wage is $v < v_0$, there is momentary excess supply of goods, $Y^* > Y^D$; if $v > v_0$, there is momentary excess demand for goods, $Y^* < Y^D$. We assume that

$$Y = min(Y^*, Y^D). \tag{7}$$

Remember the distinction between momentary and short-run equilibrium. At any given moment, wages, prices, and employment are given; all the firm has to decide is its output—hence (7). In the short run, both output and employment are variable. In full short-run macroeconomic equilibrium, with a given fixed level of investment, real wages are constant, and firms have no incentive to change either output or employment.

---

[4] It can be shown that inserting actual output on the right-hand side of (5) would not change the qualitative character of our results, but would create a peculiar simultaneity in a model with continuous time.

FIGURE 1

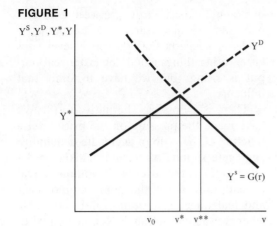

Whenever the real wage is such as to generate excess supply of goods, actual output limited by effective demand is, in fact, equal to effective demand.[5] When the real wage is such as to generate excess demand for goods, firms produce whatever their output of capital goods and current level of employment permit them to produce and sell.

At the same time, firms reduce or add to current employment, according to (4). If there is momentary excess supply, they lay off workers. If there is momentary excess demand they add workers, unless the going real wage is so high that it would be unprofitable to satisfy the demand or even to produce as much as is now being produced. In that case, they reduce employment (but they raise prices as well, only not all at once).

The picture is described in Figure I, drawn for the current level of N. If $v < v_0$, current output is given by the ordinate of Y^D; if $v > v_0$, $Y = Y^*$. Meanwhile employment is also changing. The direction of change can be traced in Figure I, in view of the monotone correspondence between Y and N via $Y = F(N)$. Employment falls from its current level, $F^{-1}(Y^*)$ whenever Y^* is above the inverted-V curve $min(Y^S, Y^D)$, and rises in the opposite case. Thus for $v < v_0$ *and for* $v > v^{**}$ employment falls, for, $v_0 < v < v^{**}$, it rises. At $v = v_0$ and $v = v^{**}$, employment is temporarily sta-

tionary; in the first case because there is no market for higher output, in the second case because at any higher output marginal cost would exceed price.

The situation of momentary excess demand, arising when $v > v_0$, or of short-run excess demand, arising when $v > v^*$, offers no special difficulty. We will, of course, assume that excess demand pulls up prices, only not so fast as to clear the market instantaneously.

The excess supply case is more of a problem. At a real wage less than v^*, or v_0, the market will take just so much. If producers produce just that much, price exceeds marginal cost. Each producer could increase his profits by selling more at the going price and, as a perfect competitor, he ought to try to do so, and he ought to succeed. But all producers together can sell no more than Y^D for the going real wage. The situation of excess supply seems to be incompatible with perfect competition. Arrow[6] has suggested that the way out of this dilemma is to recognize that markets necessarily become imperfectly competitive when sales are limited by inadequate effective demand, so that each producer sees himself as selling along a falling demand curve. That will do the trick formally, but the precise mechanism is far from clear. We do not try to settle the issue, if only because we would like the model to be compatible with a variety of market structures including, but not limited to, perfect competition. We simply assume, like Patinkin,[7] that, despite the excess of price over marginal cost, producers in the aggregate are restrained from increasing output beyond $Y = Y^D$ by the *force majeure* of effective demand. Under conditions of aggregate excess supply, however, there may be downward pressure on prices.

It only remains to formalize the dynamics of prices and money wages. As for prices, we

---

[5] This amounts to assuming away unintended inventory accumulation. To do otherwise would considerably complicate the later dynamic analysis.

[6] Kenneth J. Arrow, "Toward a Theory of Price Adjustment," in M. Abramovitz et al., *The Allocation of Economic Resources* (Stanford, Calif.: Stanford University Press, 1959), pp. 41–51.

[7] Don Patinkin, *Money, Interest, and Prices* (2d ed.: New York: Harper & Row, 1965).

make the natural assumption that the relative rate of change of the absolute price level is an increasing function of the proportional short-run excess demand. The price level may be constant if excess demand is zero, but we need not insist on it, especially since monetary policy is assumed to be permissive.

We would like also to allow prices to be partially cost-determined, under some mark-up formula. The natural hypothesis is that the rate of change of price depends on the rate of change of labor cost per unit of output. There is some recent evidence to suggest that prices do not respond to minor fluctuations in productivity, so that the relevant determinant is unit labor cost at some standard rate of output. In a short-run model, productivity can be appropriately treated as constant (or a trend only) at the standard output, so fluctuations in standard unit labor cost are proportional to fluctuations in the money wage. It is enough,[8] therefore, to add to the rate of change of prices a component proportional to the rate of change of the money wage:

$$p'/p = g(Y^D/Y^S) + jw'/w. \tag{8}$$

Here $g(\cdot)$ is an increasing function which may or may not have the property that $g(1) = 0$;

one would expect j to be between zero and one, and perhaps nearer one. Econometric evidence suggests that the price level rises faster, other things equal, the faster real output is rising; but we have to omit that influence.

There is a possible alternative to (8). We have made the pressure on the price level a function of the ratio of aggregate demand to aggregate supply. Aggregate demand is defined in (5) as the sustainable volume of real expenditures, given the going employment and real wage. That seems unobjectionable whenever actual output Y is in fact equal to aggregate demand, to the left of v_0 in Figure I. To the right of v_0, however, Y^D is a rather notional concept. One might argue that a better index of the pressure on prices is desired expenditure at the actual level of output, namely, $Y = Y^*$. Then the numerator of the argument of $g(\cdot)$ in (8) would be

$$I + (1 - s_w)vN + (1 - s_p)(Y - vN)$$
$$= I + (s_p - s_w)vN + (1 - s_p)Y$$
$$= X, \text{ say.}$$

To the left of v_0, (5) would hold as before; to the right, Y would be replaced by Y^*. This alternative formulation of demand pressure in the commodity market makes no qualitative difference to the results. The reason is the following. It is obvious that Y^D/Y^S is an increasing function of v. So is X/Y^S to the left of v_0, because $X = Y^D$. To the right of v_0, X is defined as above with Y replaced by Y^*, but obviously X/Y^S still increases with v. This is all we require for our analysis.

Money wages can be treated roughly symmetrically. We take the main influence on the rate of change of money wages to be the unemployment rate or, in our language, the ratio of current employment to the supply of labor (N^S). The supply of labor may have some elasticity with respect to the real wage even in the short run, but for simplicity we neglect that and think of N^S as a given constant. We also allow changes in the price level to react back on the rate of change of the money wage:

$$w'/w = h(N/N^S) + kp'/p. \tag{9}$$

<hr>

[8] We have also studied the behavior of this model under the strong assumption that prices are independent of the current state of demand: there is a target price, determined by a fixed markup on marginal cost at a standard output. Our impression is that this assumption causes no radical change in the behavior of the model, but that the version actually given in the text is both analytically richer and nearer the truth. For example, let $F(N^*)$ be the standard output, so $W/F'(N^*)$ and $WN^*/F(N^*)$ are standard marginal and average costs. Let the target price, p^*, be a fixed multiple, m of either, where m is presumably related to the subjective elasticity of demand in the usual way. We can replace the right-hand side of (8), or at least the second term, by $j\left(\dfrac{p^*}{p} - 1\right)$; so that p adjusts with a lag toward p^*. There remains the definition of N^*. At one extreme, we can take $N^* =$ constant; at the other, we can take $N^* =$ the short-run target employment (see (4)). In either case it is straightforward to verify that the resulting system is qualitatively unchanged; i.e., the partial derivatives of (8) with respect to N and v have the same sign pattern as in the text.

Undoubtedly $h(\cdot)$ is an increasing function, but where it crosses zero (or the long-run rate of productivity growth) is an empirical matter. The constant k is between zero and one; if it is very near one, the wage bargain is very nearly struck in real terms, and the expected rate of change of prices is very nearly accurate. A value of k closer to zero means more money illusion in the labor market or a stronger tendency to underestimate changes in the price level. Some econometric estimates suggest that k may be less than one-half.

In (2)–(5) and (7)–(9) we have seven equations in the seven unknown time functions Y^*, Y^D, Y^S, Y, N, p and w, with $v = w/p$. We turn now to the short-run flow equilibrium of this system and to its ultra-short-run dynamics.

III. THE WORKING OF THE MODEL

We study the trajectories of our system in the (N, v)-plane. The first step is to find, for each real wage, the short-run equilibrium level of employment. From (4), the answer is $F^{-1}(min(Y^S, Y^D))$. Thus the locus we seek is a transform of the solid inverted-V curve in Figure I. Along the falling branch of that curve, the construction is straightforward: $Y = Y^S = G(v)$ according to (2), and so equilibrium employment is simply $F^{-1}(G(v))$, a decreasing function of the real wage. Along the rising branch in Figure I, where $Y = Y^D$, the situation is less simple because—see (6)—the position of the aggregate demand curve itself depends on the current level of employment. We must find, for each real wage, a level of employment which will yield an aggregate demand at that real wage whose production will require the same amount of employment: that is to say, we must solve the equation $Y^D = A + BvN = F(N)$, where A and B are shorthand for the appropriate constants in (6).[9] Along this branch of the

[9] The equation will usually have two roots for a given real wage; it is the smaller root that counts because aggregate supply rather than aggregate demand will be binding at the higher N. To put it another way, at the higher N, the wage will be greater than the marginal product, a possibility we have already ruled out.

FIGURE II

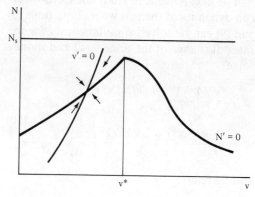

locus,

$$\frac{dN}{dv} = \frac{BN}{F'(N) - Bv} > 0 \text{ because } Y^D < Y^S$$

implies that the real wage, which is F' evaluated at $F^{-1}(Y^S)$, must be less than $F'(N) = F'(F^{-1}(Y^D))$, and B is between zero and one. So the transformed curve has positive slope all along this branch, and the picture is given by the inverted-V curve in Figure II. If the supply of labor places an absolute limit on employment and that limit is effective, then Figure III describes the situation. At any point in either diagram, the volume of unemployment is measured by the vertical distance to the line $N = N^S$.

At any point on the locus we have just constructed, N is constant, at least for the instant. At any point above the locus, N is decreasing; and at any point below it, N is increasing.

FIGURE III

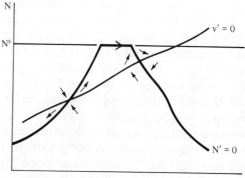

The next move is to study the ultra-short-run dynamics of the real wage. Equations (8) and (9) can be solved simultaneously for the rates of change of the price level and money wage:

$$p'/p = \frac{g(Y^D/Y^S) + jh(N/N^S)}{1 - jk}$$

$$w'/w = \frac{h(N/N^S) + kg(Y^D/Y^S)}{1 - jk} \tag{10}$$

and therefore

$$v'/v = w'/w - p'/p$$
$$= (1 - jk)^{-1} \left[(1 - j)h(N/N^S) \right.$$
$$\left. - (1 - k)g(Y^D/Y^S) \right]. \tag{11}$$

Since Y^D is a function of v and N, and Y^S a function of v alone, (10) permits us to calculate whether v is rising or falling at any point in the (N, v)-plane. The locus along which v is temporarily constant — with p and w rising or falling at the same proportional rate — is defined by

$$h(N/N^S) = \frac{1 - k}{1 - j} g \left(\frac{A + BvN}{G(v)} \right). \tag{12}$$

For the moment let us rewrite (11) and (12) to simplify notation:

$$v'/v = L(N) - C(N, v) \tag{11'}$$

$$v'/v = 0 \text{ whenever } L(N) = C(N, v). \tag{12'}$$

The natural presumption is that the locus defined by (12) or (12'), along which $v' = 0$, should be positively sloped in the (N, v) plane: a higher real wage strengthens the pressure of demand on supply in the commodity market and drives the price level up faster; the money wage can keep pace only at a lower unemployment rate. But from (11') it is seen that $dN/dv = C_v/(L' - C_N)$, and all three derivatives involved are positive. The sign of dN/dv is therefore the sign of $L' - C_N$. It can be negative. The economic reason is that an increase in employment at constant real wage adds to aggregate demand for goods. If it adds enough, the "natural presumption" is reversed. A higher real wage by itself always

tends to make the price level rise and the real wage fall; but higher employment might not only cause the money wage to rise but also stimulate demand enough to make the price level rise still faster and the real wage fall still faster. In that case it would take a reduction in employment to stabilize the real wage at a higher level. It is easy to show from (12) that the natural presumption is more likely to hold the larger is k and the smaller B is, i.e., the less *de facto* money illusion there is in the labor market, and the smaller the difference between s_p and s_w. (We shall allow for the possibility that the locus (12) should be downward sloping in the (N, v) plane, but this should be thought of as an unlikely case.)

It follows also from (11') that v is always increasing to the left of the locus (11'), and decreasing to the right.

We must now superimpose the curve defined by (12) on Figures II and III. In both diagrams we let the locus (12) slope upward; in Figure II it intersects the constant-N locus only on the branch where $Y = Y^D$ while in Figure III it intersects each branch once. Figures IV and V (the right-hand intersection) exemplify two other possibilities, when the constant-v locus slopes downward throughout. We mention, though we do not intend to pursue all logical possibilities, that the constant-v locus may in principle have several upward and downward sloping segments.[10] Whether it does so or not, it may intertwine with the constant-N locus and intersect any number of times, yielding alternately stable

---

[10] It is easily verified that, for any N, v' is a decreasing function of v so $v' = 0$ for only one v; but for given v there may be more than one N, v which $v' = 0$. We can, however, provide a condition which is sufficient to rule out there being more than one upward sloping segment and one downward sloping segment in the $v' = 0$ curve: if

$$\frac{h''}{Ns^2} - \left(\frac{1 - k}{1 - j} \right) \left\{ \frac{Bv}{G(v)} \right\}^2 g''$$

is one-signed, e.g., h'' is concave and g'' is convex, or vice versa. Note that (12') may not have solutions in the positive orthant for all values of v, although it will have solutions for all values of N.

FIGURE IV

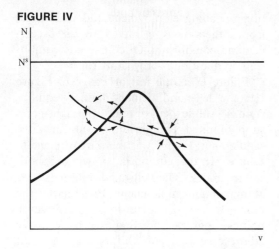

FIGURE VI

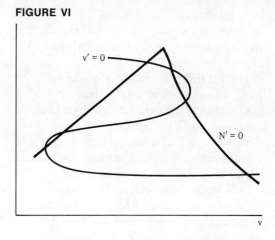

FIGURE V

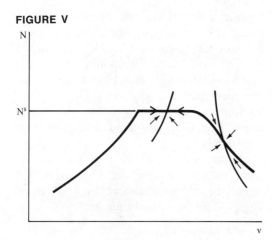

and unstable equilibria (see Figure VI). One could also discuss what happens at the axes, but neither case, zero real wages nor zero employment, seems worth the trouble.

Each intersection of the two curves represents a possible short-run equilibrium of the system. We are using the word "equilibrium" in a slightly extended sense.[11] At each intersection in Figures II–V, the real wage, the level of employment, and the level of real output are all constant,[12] and have no

[11] It is what Hansen, op. cit., calls a "quasi-equilibrium."

[12] It would be easy to introduce a steady trend increase in productivity, as in Williamson, op. cit. Then in a short-run equilibrium employment would be constant, but output and the real wage would rise at the trend rate.

inherent tendency to change. In that sense each intersection is a short-run equilibrium.

On the other hand, the money wage and the price level may both be rising or falling, so long as they are rising or falling at the same percentage rate. Moreover, except in the very special case that the intersection occurs right at the cusp of the constant-N curve, at $v = v^*$, the commodity market is not cleared at "equilibrium." In Figure II, or at the left-hand intersection in Figures III and IV, there is excess supply. Price exceeds marginal cost;[13] the marginal product of labor exceeds the real wage. But the special kind of market imperfection associated with inadequate effective demand keeps output from rising; the price level may be falling but, if it is, the money wage is falling at the same rate. Presumably, then, there is unemployment. If there were not, the money wage would not fall, the real wage would be rising and this could not be an intersection point.

In Figure V, or at the right-hand intersection in Figures III and IV, there is excess demand. There is no incentive to expand or contract output and employment because price is equal to marginal cost. The price level is inflating, but the money wage is just keeping pace, so that the real wage does not budge. Neither, therefore, does output or employment. There may be unemployment

[13] By more than the conventional fixed markup, if there is one.

in a short-run "equilibrium" with excess demand for goods, but only because the money wage is rising as fast as the price level despite the unemployment.

(It is at this point that our model calls out most obviously for an explicit monetary system. But if we were to introduce one, the economy could no longer be analyzed two-dimensionally; absolute prices and wages would enter. So we continue to assume monetary policy to be permissive.)

Not every intersection in Figures II–V represents a stable short-run equilibrium. Some are stable, but some are unstable. To distinguish, we can trace the motion of the system near each possible equilibrium point, using the rules already derived; N falls (rises) at any point above (below) the constant-N locus; v rises (falls) at any point to the left (right) of the constant-v locus. Arrows are sketched in each diagram to illustrate the character of the trajectories.

For example, the single equilibrium point in Figure II is a stable node. The rules of the game will carry any initial point into the equilibrium, and with very little in the way of fluctuation. Once a moving point enters the angular regions southwest or northeast of the equilibrium it can never again leave. The equilibrium itself is one in which output is limited by effective demand.

Figure III has two equilibrium points. The left-hand one is unstable. More precisely it is a saddlepoint. Trajectories approach it and then move away. (There are two singular motions which do approach the saddlepoint in infinite time, but they can be neglected—they represent the possibility of starting a pendulum so that it will just come to a dead stop in a vertical position, upside-down!) At the right-hand equilibrium the limit to output is on the supply side. It is a stable equilibrium, either a node or a focus. If it is a focus, trajectories will spiral in on it; employment and the real wage will converge in damped oscillations to their equilibrium values. Thus the configuration in Figure III offers the possibility that the ultimate outcome depends on initial conditions. From some starting points the economy gets trapped into a situa-

tion of falling employment and real wage; from others it is attracted to an excess-demand equilibrium. Of course, the equilibrium in question is only short-run.

Figure IV is the mirror image of Figure III: the left-hand demand-limited equilibrium is a stable focus or node. The right-hand supply-limited equilibrium is an unstable saddlepoint. Figure V is the mirror image of Figure II: the equilibria shown are both stable nodes. The left-hand alternative is at maximum employment. Presumably the money wage is rising, but so is the price level, because aggregate demand exceeds what the labor force is capable of producing. That configuration is not very plausible. If N^S represents the maximum possible employment, one would expect the constant-v locus to become horizontal as it approached $N = N^S$ from below. The money wage would always outstrip the price level as the unemployment rate fell near zero. The left-hand equilibrium point in Figure V would become more like the right-hand equilibrium in Figure III.

As an illustration we give the detailed local stability analysis for Figure III. The equations of motion near the right-hand (supply-limited) equilibrium are:

$$v' = v(L(N) - C(N, v))$$
$$N' = \theta(F^{-1}(G(v)) - N).$$

They have a linear approximation

$$v' = -v^* C_v^*(v - v^*) + v^*(L'^* - C_N^*)(N - N^*)$$

$$N' = \theta \frac{G'^*}{F'^*}(v - v^*) - \theta(N - N^*)$$

where the asterisk means evaluation at the equilibrium point. The character of the motion near (N^*, v^*) is determined by the roots Z of the characteristic equation

$$\begin{vmatrix} -v^* C_v^* - Z & v^*(L'^* - C_N^*) \\ \theta \dfrac{G'^*}{F'^*} & -\theta - Z \end{vmatrix}$$

$$= Z^2 + (\theta + v^* C_v^*)Z$$

$$+ \theta\left(v^* C_v^* - \frac{G'^*}{F'^*} v^*(L'^* - C_N^*)\right) = 0.$$

Thus

$$2Z = -(\theta + v^*C_v^*) \pm \Big((\theta + v^*C_v^*)^2$$
$$- 4\theta v^*C_v^* + 4\theta v^* \frac{G'^*}{F'^*}(L'^* - C_N^*)\Big)^{1/2}$$

If the discriminant is negative, the equilibrium point is a focus, but a stable focus because the real part of the characteristic roots is definitely negative. Output, employment, and real wages will approach $F(N^*)$, N^*, v^* in damped oscillations. The combination of employment lag, real-wage dynamics and different propensities to spend generates a kind of cycle. If the discriminant is positive, the equilibrium point is a node, but a stable node. The square root term must be between zero and $\theta + v^*C_v^*$ because the terms after the first are all negative ($G' < 0$ and $L' - C_N > 0$ in Figure III). Output, employment, and real wage approach their equilibrium values with at most one turning point.

It is possible to describe the dependence of the solution on θ, the speed of adjustment of employment to output. The discriminant is quadratic in θ. For $\theta = 0$, and therefore for small θ, the discriminant is positive and the solution nonoscillatory. The same is true for large θ. In between there may—or may not—be a range of θ for which the solution cycles.

At the left-hand equilibrium point in Figure III, the equation for v' is unchanged, but $N' = \theta(F^{-1}(A + Bv\dot{N}) - N)$. The characteristic equation of the linear approximation becomes

$$\begin{vmatrix} -v^*C_v^* - Z & v^*(L'^* - C_N^*) \\ \theta\dfrac{BN^*}{F'^*} & \theta\Big(\dfrac{Bv^*}{F'^*} - 1\Big) - Z \end{vmatrix}$$

$$= Z^2 + \Big(v^*C_v^* + \theta\frac{F'^* - Bv^*}{F'^*}\Big)Z$$

$$+ \theta\frac{(F'^* - Bv^*)}{F'^*}v^*C_v^*$$

$$- \frac{v^*\theta BN^*}{F'^*}(L'^* - C_N^*) = 0.$$

Since $v\theta/F' > 0$, the product of the roots has the sign of $(F'^* - Bv^*)C_v^* - BN^*(L'^* - C_N^*)$.

FIGURE VII

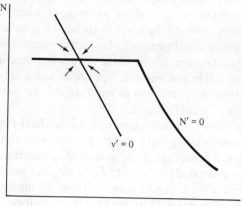

This number is negative when the v-stationary cuts the N-stationary from above. The roots must therefore be real and of opposite sign, so the equilibrium is a saddle-point and unstable.

The other configurations illustrated in Figures II, IV and V can be analyzed similarly. The only kinds of equilibria that can arise are stable foci and nodes, and (unstable) saddle-points. There are no unstable nodes or foci, and no centers (closed cycles). The equilibria in Figures II and V can only be nodes. Figure IV is like Figure III, with the right- and left-hand equilibria interchanged.

We make one further qualitative remark about dynamics. Suppose $s_p = s_w$, so $B = 0$. Then aggregate demand for goods is independent of the distribution of income and the picture is as in Figure VII. It is easily seen graphically that an equilibrium point at which output is limited by effective demand is necessarily a stable node. Indeed, with $B = 0$ the roots of the characteristic equation are simply $-v^*C_v^*$ and $-\theta$. No possibility of oscillations arises. Qualitatively, then, if the marginal propensities to spend wages and profits are nearly the same, the approach to a demand-limited equilibrium is essentially monotone.

IV. DISPLACEMENT OF SHORT-RUN EQUILIBRIUM

We turn next to the important question of comparative statics: what happens to the real wage, employment, the level of output—and therefore to the share of wages—when a short-run equilibrium is disturbed by a variation in investment, say? Not surprisingly, the qualitative character of the answer is different for stable and unstable equilibria. Since only stable equilibria are of real interest, we concentrate on that case.

There are two classes of stable short-run equilibrium points, and they have to be analyzed separately. Supply-limited equilibrium is illustrated by the right-hand singular point in Figure III and Figure V. Demand-limited equilibrium is illustrated by the equilibrium point in Figure II and the left-hand one in Figure IV. We take supply-limited equilibrium first, because it is somewhat simpler.

In any supply-limited equilibrium, $Y = Y^S = G(v)$. The equilibrium point is, therefore, determined by the two equations

$$G(v) = F(N) \tag{13}$$

$$L(N) = C(N, v; A, B). \tag{13'}$$

The second of these equations is simply (12') rewritten to display the parameters A and B; for the exact form of the equation see (12). A shift in investment amounts to a shift in $A(= I/s_p)$ in the same direction. If A changes, (13) is unaffected. The aggregate supply curve remains where it was. But (13'), the locus of constant real wages, does shift. One can see directly from (12) that it shifts to the left. Let A increase and consider any fixed N: the left-hand side of (12) is unchanged, so v must change to keep the argument of $g(\cdot)$ constant; a decrease in v increases the denominator and reduces the numerator, offsetting the initial change in A. It follows that an increase in investment will shift any stable supply-limited equilibrium upward and to the left along the aggregate supply curve. The real wage will fall; output and employment will rise; and the rate of inflation will also increase. The effect on relative shares will depend entirely on the "elasticity of substitution" associated with $F(N)$.[14] If it is less than one, the share

of wages falls; if it exceeds one, the share of wages rises.

It is important to understand the mechanism that leads to this result. The increase in aggregate demand accelerates the inflation of the price level; the money wage does not initially keep pace, so the real wage falls and permits an increase in employment. Employment rises until, for Phillips curve reasons, the money wage rises as fast as the price level and the real wage stabilizes. It is evident from (10) that the rate of inflation is faster in the new equilibrium. (Since we are dealing with a stable equilibrium, the new equilibrium will actually be approached.)

For completeness, we point out that a glance at Figure IV will show that if the equilibrium is unstable the results are just the opposite. An increase in A will increase the real wage and reduce employment, thus reversing the usual Keynesian proposition about the effect of an increase in the level of investment; but this is of no practical interest. The situation of equilibrium at maximum feasible employment, illustrated in Figure V, is very simple; the real wage falls, but employment and output do not increase because they cannot. The rate of inflation increases. But this situation is fundamentally implausible, as we mentioned earlier, because one would expect the money wage to rise fast enough at maximum employment to carry the real wage with it.

A shift in a demand-limited equilibrium is more complicated to analyze—and the results are less clear-out—because both curves shift when A changes. The equilibrium point is defined by (13') and

$$A + BvN = F(N). \tag{13''}$$

Just as before, the locus of constant real wages shifts to the left when investment increases. From (13''), the locus of constant employment shifts to the left too: for given N, a higher value of A must be offset by a lower v to

---

[14] The quotation marks are to remind the reader that there need not be any constant-returns-to-scale production function in labor and capital underlying $F(N)$. Even if there is not, for this calculation one pretends that there is.

preserve the equality. One cannot read the outcome unambiguously from the diagram, and we must make a closer analysis.

Total differentiation of (13′) and (13″) with respect to A yields

$$\begin{bmatrix} -C_v & L' - C_N \\ BN & Bv - F' \end{bmatrix} \begin{bmatrix} dv/dA \\ dN/dA \end{bmatrix} = \begin{bmatrix} C_A \\ -1 \end{bmatrix}$$

whence

$$dv/dA = D^{-1}(L' - C_N - C_A(F' - Bv)) \\ dN/dA = D^{-1}(C_v - C_A BN) \tag{14}$$

where $D = C_v(F' - Bv) - (L' - C_N)BN$ is known from earlier analysis to be negative if the equilibrium is unstable and positive if it is stable.

C_A is easily seen from (12) to be positive. Moreover, by partial differentiation of (11),

$$C_A = C_N/Bv = C_v/(BN - Y^D G'/G).$$

It follows at once that an increase in investment always increases employment and the rate of inflation if the equilibrium is stable. It is also true that $dN/dA < 0$ at an unstable equilibrium but this is less meaningful. As for the effect of an increase in investment on the real wage, one can show—by eliminating C_A in favor of C_v—that $dv/dA < 0$ at an unstable equilibrium. Unfortunately there is no unambiguous answer at a stable equilibrium. But one can show—by eliminating C_A in favor of C_N—that dv/dA is positive or negative at a stable equilibrium according as L' is greater or less than

$$C_N F'/Bv = \frac{1 - k}{1 - j} \frac{g'F'}{G(v)}.$$

Thus the real wage can go either way.

The other demand-side parameter that can vary is B. B rises with A constant if s_w falls, and falls if s_w rises. (A change in s_p changes both A and B.) It is straightforward that

$$dv/dB = D^{-1}(vN(L' - C_N) - C_B(F' - Bv)) \\ dN/dB = D^{-1}(C_v vN - C_B BN)$$

and $C_B = C_N N/B = C_v vN/(BN - Y^D G'/G) > 0$. A little more calculation shows that dv/dB and dN/dB have the same signs as dv/dA and dN/dA. So a fall in the propensity to save wages acts like an increase in investment.

We can also consider the displacement effects of changes in k and j. Those parameters affect the location of the constant-v locus only. It is clear from (12) that an increase in k, or a decrease in j, shifts the constant-v locus to the right. We see then from Figures II and IV that the effect on a stable demand-limited equilibrium is to increase the equilibrium employment and the real wage. (If $s_p = s_w$, the real wage rises but employment is unchanged.) Similarly, Figures III and V show that the effect on a stable supply-limited equilibrium is to increase the equilibrium real wage but to decrease equilibrium employment. (The effects at unstable equilibria are just the reverse.) In words, if money wages become more sensitive to changes in commodity prices or prices less sensitive to changes in standard unit labor costs, the equilibrium real wage will always be higher. In an excess-supply situation, employment will increase as well; if there is already excess demand, employment will fall.

V. EFFECTIVE DEMAND AND THE DISTRIBUTION OF INCOME

The theory presented here gives a determinate answer, though not a simple one, to the question: how does the share of wages in total income vary when effective demand varies in the short run? When output is limited by supply, the answer is the conventional one, depending on the "elasticity of substitution" or, more accurately, on the speed with which the short-run marginal product of labor falls as employment rises. When output is limited by effective demand, the answer is more complicated still. We observe that the share of wages is

$$vN/(A + BvN) = \frac{1}{A/vN + B}.$$

It follows that if investment (and therefore A) rises, the share of wages will rise or fall according as the sum of the elasticities of v and

N with respect to A exceed or fall short of one. This condition can be explored further with the aid of (14), but we have not been able to reduce it to any very simple form.

Indeed, we have already shown that the effect of shifts in aggregate demand on the real wage rate is ambiguous, depending on the money wage and price response mechanisms in an important way. It will be remembered that Keynes, in the *General Theory*, held that price was always equal (or proportional) to marginal cost, so that in the short run the real wage would always fall as employment rose and vice versa. The early empirical work of Dunlop[15] and Tarshis[16] seemed to subvert this idea. In reviewing the situation, Keynes[17] took a cautious view, apparently not quite convinced that the facts had been properly got at, but apparently willing to jettison that part of the theory if the data demanded it. Later statistical work, with better data and more appropriate concepts, appears to confirm Dunlop and Tarshis.[18] The real wage does not appear to fall, or fall relative to trend, in cyclical upswings. Nor does the real wage seem to have any other pronounced pattern in the course of short-run economic fluctuations. We are not unhappy, therefore, with a theory that permits the real wage to rise when effective demand increases and fall when effective demand falls, but does not require it. Since the outcome, in this theory, depends so much on the wage and price adjustment mechanism, and since those mechanisms must be expected to change from time to time, there is no reason to expect consistent behavior over long periods of time.

We come now to the relation between the Cambridge and marginal-productivity theories of distribution. There is a sense in which the marginal-productivity theory can be said

to hold at any supply-limited equilibrium, and the Cambridge theory can be said to hold at any demand limited equilibrium. At any supply-limited equilibrium, and only at supply-limited equilibria, the real wage is equal to the short-run marginal product of labor (perhaps modified by monopoly). At any demand-limited equilibrium, and only at demand-limited equilibria, it is true that

$$vN/Y = \frac{s_p}{s_p - s_w} - \frac{1}{s_p - s_w}\frac{I}{Y};$$

the standard equation of the Cambridge theory (although it is important to realize that Y and N are here *unknowns*, not given, as in Kaldor). If the economic system runs, or is run, in such a way as to keep it near the intersection of the aggregate supply and aggregate demand curves, then both theories can hold determinately and simultaneously. Under other circumstances, one or the other will be "true" at any time, but neither provides a complete or determinate theory unless supplemented by a market mechanism—the one we have described here, or some other.

The market mechanism described in this paper has an important asymmetry, with an important asymmetrical consequence. At a short-run equilibrium the real wage may equal the marginal product of labor (if the equilibrium is supply-limited) or fall short of the marginal product of labor (if the equilibrium is demand-limited). But the real wage can never exceed the marginal product of labor. This asymmetry arises because price may equal or exceed marginal cost, but cannot be less. Under conditions of inadequate demand, price may exceed marginal cost, but there is no tendency for output and employment to increase, precisely because demand is inadequate. The price level may fall, of course, but whether or not the price level falls relative to marginal cost depends on the behavior of the money wage. But there is no symmetrical situation. Marginal cost can never exceed price in short-run equilibrium because there is no hindrance to a reduction in output and employment under those circumstances. Output may be constrained by effective demand

[15] John T. Dunlop, "The Movement of Real and Money Wages," *Economic Journal*, XLVIII (Sept. 1938).

[16] Lorie Tarshis, "Changes in Real and Money Wages," *Economic Journal*, XLIX (Mar. 1939).

[17] J. M. Keynes, "Relative Movements of Real Wages and Output," *Economic Journal*, XLIX (Mar. 1939).

[18] See Edwin Kuh, "Unemployment, Production Functions, and Effective Demand," *Journal of Political Economy*, LXXXIV (June 1966), 238–49.

below the supply curve, but it cannot be dragged above the supply curve because there is no obligation to produce unprofitable items of output.

VI. NEXT STEPS

We have already mentioned some directions in which this theory needs to be extended. First and foremost, it needs a monetary mechanism. We have refrained from providing one in this exposition to keep the analysis two-dimensional. Under our assumptions, the dynamics and comparative statics could be analyzed in terms of the real wage and the level of employment. As soon as an explicit monetary system is introduced the analysis will have to be three-dimensional, in terms of the money wage, price level, and employment. We do not think that offers difficulties of principle, but there will be a loss of transparency. We intend later to extend the model in this direction.

Second, the model needs to be extended to the long run. The first requirement is to find a representation of the shift in short-run production possibilities brought about by current investment. The easiest course is to suppose that the short-run production function is simply a section of a long-run production function in capital and labor. If this is too great a stretch of the imagination, there are more plausible—but less maneuverable—alternatives; see, for example, Solow, Tobin, Weizsäcker, and Yaari[19] and Attiyeh.[20] Depending on how this task is accomplished, there may or may not arise the further question of the choice of labor-intensity for current investment. When a choice of technique is available, the current and prospective price configuration will have an influence on the labor-intensity selected for any given increase

in capacity. Moreover, since the price configuration has a lot to do with the profitability of any given investment, it will have an influence on the amount of capacity installed. In the long-run context, investment cannot be treated as exogenous, even as an approximation.

A third extension has to do with the equation (7), stating that actual output is the smaller of aggregate momentary supply and aggregate demand. This amounts to assuming away unintended inventory changes (intended inventory change is included in section I). It would be more realistic to suppose that when supply exceeds demand, actual output is somewhere between, and inventories are built up; and that, when demand exceeds supply, some of the excess demand is met out of inventories. By itself, that amendment might not be difficult. But as soon as one allows for an inventory policy, and the notion that some part of aggregate demand is intended to build stocks toward a target level, a new dynamic element is added to the model and it becomes much more complex.

Finally, we call attention to the price and wage adjustment equations (8) and (9). As they stand, especially the wage equation, they concede quite a lot to money illusion or systematic underextrapolation of price changes. That is not so bad in a short-run model, especially since the real wage does turn out to be constant in equilibrium. Most empirical studies of wage behavior suggest that k is considerably less than one. In a long-run context, however, one might prefer assumptions that guarantee that any prolonged rate of inflation will come to be expected, and built into money wage determination. One way to accomplish that would be to drop the last term in (9) and add instead a symbol representing the expected rate of inflation. The expected rate of inflation could then itself be governed by one of the usual differential equations for adaptive or extrapolative expectations. Such a model would behave in the short run much like (9) with $k < 1$, and in the long run much like (9) with $k = 1$, or at least nearer unity.

If, in fact, $k = 1$, (9) by itself determines the rate of change of the real wage. ("The wage

[19] R. M. Solow, J. Tobin, C. von Weizsäcker, M. Yaari, "Neo-classical Growth with Fixed Factor Proportions," *Review of Economic Studies*, XXXIII (Apr. 1966).
[20] Richard S. Attiyeh, "Estimation of a Fixed Coefficients Vintage Model of Production," *Yale Economic Essays*, Vol. 7 (Spring 1967), pp. 5–40.

bargain is in real terms.") The locus of constant real wage in our diagrams would be a horizontal line at a height corresponding to the employment at which $h(N/N^S) = 0$. The rest of the analysis would go pretty much as before; (8) would merely determine the rate of inflation. If, on the other hand, j were equal to one in (8), the locus of constant real wage would be a vertical line. If $g(1) = 0$, the only equilibrium point would be at the intersection of the aggregate demand and supply curves, with the rate of inflation determined by (9). The model will not function with $j = k = 1$.

A General Disequilibrium Model of Income and Employment

Robert J. Barro and Herschel I. Grossman

University of Chicago and Brown University

As is now well understood, the key to the Keynesian theory of income determination is the assumption that the vector of prices, wages, and interest rates does not move instantaneously from one full employment equilibrium position to another. By implication, Keynesian economics rejects the market equilibrium framework for analyzing the determination of quantities bought, sold, and produced. This framework is associated with Walras and Marshall, both of whom proceeded as if all markets were continuously cleared. Walras rationalized this procedure by incorporating recontracting arrangements, while Marshall did so by regarding price adjustments to be an instantaneous response to momentary discrepancies between quantities supplied and demanded.

By rejecting these rationalizations Keynesian theory proposes as a general case a system of markets which are not always cleared. Keynes was, tacitly at least, concerned with the general theoretical problem of the intermarket relationships in such a system. The failure of a market to clear implies that, for at least some individuals, actual quantities transacted diverge from the quantities which they supply or demand. Thus, the natural focus of Keynesian analysis is on the implications for behavior in one market of the existence of such a divergence in another market. Indeed, some recent writers,

Reprinted from the *American Economic Review*, 61:82–93 (1971), by permission of the authors and the publisher (copyright by the American Economic Association).

such as Robert Clower and Axel Leijonhufvud, have argued very convincingly that this focus is the crucial distinguishing feature of Keynesian economics.

Unfortunately, the evolution of conventional post-Keynesian macroeconomics failed to interpret the Keynesian system in this light.[1] Instead, conventional analysis has chronically attempted to coax Keynesian results out of a framework of general market equilibrium. The result has been to leave conventional macroeconomics with an embarrassingly weak choice-theoretic basis, and to associate with it important implications which are difficult to reconcile with observed phenomena.

A classic example of such a difficulty concerns the relationship between the level of employment and the real wage rate. In the conventional analysis, the demand for labor is inversely and uniquely related to the level of real wages. This assumption accords with Keynes; who, in this respect, had adhered to received pre-Keynesian doctrine.[2] Given this

---

[1] See Leijonhufvud.

[2] Keynes wrote:

> ... with a given organization, equipment and technique, real wages and the volume of output (and hence of employment) are uniquely correlated, so that, in general, an increase in employment can only occur to the accompaniment of a decline in the rate of real wages. Thus, I am not disputing this vital fact which the classical economists have (rightly) asserted.... The real wage earned by a unit of labor has a unique inverse correlation with the volume of employment [1936, p. 17].

assumption, cyclical variations in the quantity of labor demanded and the amount of employment must imply countercyclical variation in real wage rates. As is well known, however, such a pattern of real wages has not been observed.[3]

A few authors have pointed out the inappropriateness of attempts to force Keynesian analysis into a market equilibrium framework. Contributions by Don Patinkin (1956) and Clower, in particular, represent important attempts to reconstruct macroeconomic theory within an explicit disequilibrium context.

In the unfortunately neglected chapter 13 of *Money, Interest, and Prices*, Patinkin analyzed involuntary unemployment in a context of explicit market disequilibrium; and he showed that the misleading implications of the conventional analysis regarding the real wage are a direct consequence of its general equilibrium character.[4] Patinkin presented a theory in which involuntary unemployment of labor can arise as a consequence of disequilibrium, in particular, excess supply in the market for current output. In this theory, the inability of firms to sell the quantity of output given by their supply schedule causes them to demand a smaller quantity of labor than that given by their conventional (or notional) demand schedule. The immediate significance of this theory is that it is able to generate unemployment without placing any restrictions on the level or movement of the real wage.[5] Unemployment of

labor requires only that the vector of prices and wages implies a deficiency of demand for current output. As Patinkin suggests, this interpretation of the proximate cause of unemployment is more Keynesian than Keynes' own discussion.

The essence of Patinkin's theory is causality running from the level of excess supply in the market for current output to the state of excess supply in the market for labor. Patinkin thereby explains the proximate cause of cyclical unemployment, but his analysis involves only partial, rather than general, disequilibrium. At the least, a general disequilibrium model would, in addition, incorporate the possibility of a reverse influence of the level of excess supply in the labor market upon the state of excess supply in the market for current output.

Clower's important paper develops a theory emphasizing this causal relationship. He presents a derivation of the Keynesian consumption function in which he interprets the relationship between consumption and income as a manifestation of disequilibrium in the labor market. This approach to explaining household behavior is obviously similar to Patinkin's analysis of the firm. The only significant difference is that Clower's households have a choice between consuming and saving, so that his problem is explicitly choice theoretic. However, if Patinkin's approach were generalized to a multi-input production function, the resulting analysis would be formally analogous to Clower's.

The analysis in this paper builds on the foundations laid down by the Patinkin and Clower analyses of a depressed economy. Our purpose is to develop a generalized analysis of both booms and depressions as disequilibrium phenomena.[6] Section I sketches the

---

[3] The evidence has been recently reviewed by Edwin Kuh, esp. pp. 246–48; and Ronald Bodkin. Keynes (1939) recognized this discrepancy, and offered a rather contrived explanation for it in terms of monopoly and procyclical variation in demand elasticities. More recently, Kuh attempted to explain this discrepancy in terms of a fixed proportions production function in the short run.

[4] Chapter 13 also appears, apparently unchanged, in the second edition of *Money, Interest, and Prices* (1965). Patinkin had first presented some of the essentials of this analysis in an earlier article (1949). A similar formulation appears in Edgar Edwards.

[5] Patinkin's theory does not involve any restrictions either upon the substitutability among factors of production or upon demand elasticities. (See fn. 3.) Of

course, this theory does not deny that an excessive level of real wages can be an independent cause of unemployment. But, a clear analytical distinction is made between unemployment due to this cause, and unemployment which occurs even when the level of real wages is not excessive.

[6] The analysis by Robert Solow and Joseph Stiglitz, although they emphasize different questions, is somewhat similar to the present approach. However, their analytical

analytical framework employed. Section II reviews and generalizes Patinkin's analysis of the labor market and involuntary unemployment. Section III develops a distinction, implied by Patinkin's analysis, between two concepts of unemployment; one associated with excess supply in the labor market and the other associated with equilibrium in the labor market but with disequilibrium elsewhere in the system. Section IV reviews Clower's analysis and shows how it is formally analogous to Patinkin's. Section V joins the Patinkin and Clower analyses into a model of an economy experiencing deficient aggregate demand. Section VI formulates an analogous model of an economy experiencing excessive aggregate demand. Finally, Section VII summarizes the main results.

I. ANALYTICAL FRAMEWORK

The following discussion utilizes a simple aggregative framework which involves three economic goods—labor services, consumable commodities, and fiat money—and two forms of economic decision making unit—firms and households. Labor services are the only variable input into the production process. Other inputs have a fixed quantity, no alternative use, and zero user cost. Consumable commodities are the only form of current output; there is no investment.[7] Money is the only store of value, and it also serves as a medium of exchange and unit of account. The nominal quantity of money is exogenous and constant.

Firms demand labor and supply commodities. They attempt to maximize profits. Households supply labor and demand commodities and money balances. They also receive the profits of the firms according to a predetermined distribution pattern. Households attempt to maximize utility. Each firm and household is an atomistic competitor in the markets for both commodities and labor.

Following Patinkin (1956, 1965), each of the flow variables in the model—commodities, labor services, and the increment to money balances—is for simplicity expressed as the quantity which accrues over a finite unit of time, say a week, so that each assumes the dimensions of a stock. The model thus includes the following variables:

y = quantity of commodities
x = quantity of labor services
m = increment to real money balances (in commodity units)
π = quantity of real profits (in commodity units)
M = initial stock of nominal money balances
P = money price of commodities
w = real wage rate (in commodity units)

Throughout the following discussion, the method of analysis is to take a particular vector of the price level and real wage rate as given, and to work out the levels of income and employment implied by that vector. This procedure represents a non-Marshallian, or Keynesian, extreme, and following John Hicks may be denoted as the "fix-price method." The analysis does, of course, have implications for the appropriate specification of the forces making for changes in prices and wages. This paper does not explicitly investigate these implications, although we do consider a parenthetical example concerning the model's implications for the cyclical behavior of real wages.[8]

II. PATINKIN'S ANALYSIS OF THE LABOR MARKET

Consider the behavior of the representative firm under the provisional assumption that it regards profit maximization as being con-

format does differ from ours in at least three substantial respects: First, they do not discuss the choice-theoretic basis for the theory. Second, the equilibrium price level is indeterminate in their model. Third, by introducing restrictions on the rate of change of employment, they complicate matters and obscure what would seem to be essential in the intermarket effects of disequilibrium.

[7] It should be clear that the incorporation of investment and a market for securities would alter none of the conclusions advanced in this paper.

[8] Grossman develops a more general model of multi-market disequilibrium based on Clower's choice-theoretic paradigm, and focuses in detail on the implications of this model for the disequilibrium behavior of prices and interest.

strained only by the production function. In particular, the firm perceives that it can purchase all the labor which it demands and sell all the output which it supplies at the existing levels of w and P. Thus, profits are given by

$$\pi = y^S - wx^D,$$

where the superscripts indicate supply and demand quantities. Assuming the production function to be

$$y = F(x),$$

with positive and diminishing marginal product, profit maximization implies

$$x^D = x^D(w),$$

such that $\partial F/\partial x = w$, and

$$y^S = F(x^D).$$

Patinkin (1956, 1965) contrasts the above to a situation in which commodities are in excess supply. Voluntary exchange implies that actual total sales will equal the total quantity demanded. The representative firm will not be able to sell its notional supply y^S.[9] Let y represent its actual demand-determined sales, where $y < y^S$.[10] Then, the profit maxi-

mization problem becomes simply to select the minimum quantity of labor necessary to produce output quantity y.[11] In other words, the firm maximizes

$$\pi = y - wx^{D'},$$

subject to $y = F(x)$. The variable $x^{D'}$ may be denoted as the effective demand for labor. Profit maximization now implies

$$x^{D'} = F^{-1}(y) \quad \text{for } \frac{dF}{dx} \geq w. \tag{1}$$

The constraint of $y < y^S$ implies $x^{D'} < x^D$, with $x^{D'}$ approaching x^D as y approaches y^S.[12]

---

[9] We assume here that the firm would actually like to sell y^S. Such behavior may not always be optimal. For example, Section VI discusses a situation of excess demand for labor in which the firm's effective supply $y^{S'}$ is less than y^S. However, we assume for simplicity that excess demand for labor never coexists with excess supply of commodities and vice versa. Grossman presents a more general treatment of multi-market disequilibria which allows for the coexistence of excess supply in one market and excess demand in another, as well as excess supply or demand in both.

[10] In principle, y need not be less than y^S for every firm. The apportionment of the actual sales among the firms depends upon established queuing or rationing procedures. Grossman presents an explicit analysis of this apportionment within a framework of voluntary exchange.

The inability of a firm to sell its desired output at the going price violates an assumption of the perfectly competitive model. Kenneth Arrow has stressed this inconsistency of perfect competition with disequilibrium.

Essentially, he argues that economic units which act as perfect competitors in equilibrium must (at least in certain respects) perform as monopolists in disequilibrium. In this paper we focus on the reaction of economic units to given (equilibrium or disequilibrium) price levels. If, in addition, one wished to analyze explicitly the dynamics of price adjustment, it would be necessary to discard the perfectly competitive paradigm of the producer as a price taker. (In this regard, see Barro 1970, 1971.)

[11] This analysis abstracts from inventory accumulation or decumulation. For simplicity, we assume throughout that output always adjusts instantaneously to equal the smaller of supply and demand. Permitting inventory accumulation would not affect the essentials of the analysis, although it would introduce a complication analogous to the inclusion of an additional input. In general, we might obtain $dy/dt = k[\min(y^D, y^S) - yl$, where $k = k(w, y) > 0$. A similar gradual adjustment process for employment might also be possible, as in Solow and Stiglitz.

[12] The choice-theoretic nature of the problem becomes much more interesting when there is more than one form of input. Assume profits to be given by $\pi = y - w_1 x_1^{D'} - w_2 x_2^{D'}$, where the production function is $y = F(x_1, x_2)$, which has the usual convexity properties. Profit maximization now implies

$$x_1^{D'} = x_1^{D'}\left(\frac{w_1}{w_2}, y\right) \tag{1.1}$$

$$x_2^{D'} = x_2^{D'}\left(\frac{w_1}{w_2}, y\right) \tag{1.2}$$

such that at output y, $(\partial F/\partial X_1)/(\partial F/\partial X_2) = (w_1/w_2)$. In reducing output y^S to y, the firm must now make a decision regarding optimal input combinations. However, as y approaches y^S, $x_1^{D'}$ and $x_2^{D'}$ approach x_1^D and x_2^D.

The essential implication of equation (1) is that the effective demand for labor can vary even with the real wage fixed. Given voluntary exchange, employment cannot exceed the effective demand for labor. The quantity of employment thus is not uniquely associated with the real wage.

III. THE CONCEPT OF UNEMPLOYMENT

Figure 1 depicts the preceding analysis of the labor market. The notional demand schedule for labor x^D is downward sloping. If $y = y^S$, the effective demand for labor $x^{D'}$ coincides with the notional demand. If $y < y^S$, the effective demand is independent of the real wage and less than the notional demand. The (notional) supply schedule for labor x^S, which will be derived below, is shown as upward sloping.

Figure 1 suggests a distinction between two concepts of unemployment—involuntary unemployment associated with excess (effective) labor supply, and voluntary unemployment associated with equilibrium in the labor market, but with disequilibrium elsewhere in the system. Suppose that initially the commodity market is in equilibrium, so that $y = y^S$ and $x^{D'} = x^D$, and that initially the real wage is w^*. Thus, the labor market is in equilibrium at point A, which may be

denoted as full employment general equilibrium. Now suppose, say because the price level P is too high, that commodity demand is lower so that $y < y^S$ and $x^{D'} < x^D$. At the real wage w^*, excess supply of labor will amount to quantity AB. Failure of the price level to adjust to clear the commodity market leads to excess supply in the labor market. This excess supply represents what we usually refer to as involuntary unemployment. It is also what the Bureau of Labor Statistics ideally intends to represent by its statistical measure of unemployment—those seeking but not obtaining work at the going real wage. Involuntary unemployment clearly does not require a rise in the real wage above the level consistent will full employment equilibrium.

Now suppose that the real wage were to decline to w_C, so that the supply and effective demand for labor are equilibrated at point C. At point C, involuntary unemployment has vanished, but clearly this situation is not optimal. The reduced real wage has induced AB man-hours of labor to leave the labor force. Employment remains AB man-hours below the level associated with general equilibrium. Involuntary, i.e., excess supply, unemployment has been replaced by voluntary unemployment.[13]

The conclusion is that too high a real wage was not the cause of the lower employment, and a reduction in the real wage is only a superficial cure. The real cause of the problem was the fall in commodity demand, and only a reflation of commodity demand can restore employment to the proper level.

[13] In terms of the *BLS* unemployment statistic, it is not clear that "zero" unemployment would be measured at w_C. If the higher wage, w^*, were (at least for a time) viewed as "normal," a considerable proportion of job seekers at wage w_C would be those willing to work at w^*, but not at w_C. These people are in the labor market seeking information on possible employment opportunities at (or above) w^*, and would not actually be willing to work at the going wage (see Armen Alchain). To the extent that the *BLS* measure includes this type of frustrated job seeker, the index will be a better measure of the gap between actual and general equilibrium employment BA, while simultaneously being a poorer index of those seeking but not obtaining employment at the going wage w_C.

FIGURE 1

The labor market with excess supply of commodities.

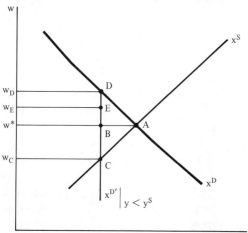

The above analysis suggests the following cyclical patterns of real wages and employment: A decline in commodity demand and output produces a decline in employment with a corresponding excess supply of labor (point B). To the extent that real wages decline in response to this excess supply, a fall in real wages toward w_C will accompany (follow upon) the decline in employment. If, at point C or at some intermediate point between B and C, some action is taken to restore effective commodity demand, excess demand for labor (or, at least reduced excess supply) will result. In that case, a rising real wage may accompany the recovery of output and employment. Thus, disequilibrium analysis of the labor markets suggests that real wages may move procyclically. This result differs from the conventional view that employment and real wages must be inversely related.

The present model can also be used to analyze involuntary unemployment which results from an excessive real wage. Clearly, if the real wage were above w^*, so stimulation of commodity demand could bring about full employment equilibrium, unless the real wage were reduced. This classical type of involuntary unemployment should be clearly distinguished from the type of unemployment discussed above, which arises, with the real wage at or below w^*, from a deficiency of demand for commodities.

IV. CLOWER'S ANALYSIS OF THE CONSUMPTION FUNCTION

In order to close the model, we must also analyze household behavior. Consider the behavior of the representative household under the provisional assumption that it regards utility maximization as being subject only to the budget constraint. In particular, the household perceives that it can sell all the labor which it supplies and purchase all the commodities which it demands at the existing levels of w and P. Assume the utility function to be

$$U = U\left(x^S, y^D, \frac{M}{P} + m^D\right),$$

with the partial derivatives $U_1 < 0$, $U_2 > 0$, and $U_3 > 0$. The budget constraint is

$$\pi + wx^S = y^D + m^D,$$

x^S, y^D, and m^D may be denoted as the notional supply of labor, the notional demand for commodities, and the notional demand for additional money balances. Utility maximization in general will imply that x^S, y^D, and m^D are each functions of w, M/P, and π. For simplicity, we shall assume that x^S depends only on the real wage. The important point is that the notional demand functions for commodities and additional money balances do not have the forms of the usual consumption and saving functions with income as an argument, because the household simultaneously chooses the quantity of labor to sell.

Clower contrasts the above notional process to a situation in which labor services are in excess supply. Given voluntary exchange, actual total employment in this situation equals the total quantity demanded. Thus, the representative household is unable to sell its notional labor supply x^S and obtain its implied notional labor income wx^S.[14] Labor income is no longer a choice variable which is instead exogenously given. We may assume that the representative household is able to obtain the quantity of employment x, where $x < x^S$, so that its total income is $wx + \pi$. In this case, the utility maximization problem amounts to the optimal disposition of this income.

In other words, the household maximizes

$$U\left(x, y^{D'}, \frac{M}{P} + m^{D'}\right)$$

subject to $\pi + wx = y^{D'} + m^{D'}$. The variables $y^{D'}$ and $m^{D'}$ may be denoted as the effective demands for commodities and additional money balances. Utility maximization now implies

$$y^{D'} = y^{D'}\left(\pi + wx, \frac{M}{P}\right), \tag{2}$$

---

[14] We assume that the household would actually like to sell x^S. As indicated in fn. 9, we assume for simplicity that excess demand for commodities never coexists with excess supply of labor.

and

$$m^{D'} = m^{D'} \left(\pi + wx, \frac{M}{P} \right). \tag{3}$$

Note that, in aggregate, $\pi + wx = y = F(x)$. Thus, since all income accrues to the households, consumption and saving demand depend ultimately only on the level of employment and real money balances and not on the real wage rate. The constraint $x < x^S$ would generally imply $y^{D'} < y^D$ and $m^{D'} < m^D$, but as x approaches x^S, $y^{D'}$ and $m^{D'}$ approach y^D and m^D.[15]

The important property of equations (2) and (3) is that they do have the form of the usual Keynesian consumption and saving functions. Labor income enters the consumption and saving functions as it represents the constraint upon the demand for current output imposed by the excess supply of labor.

The formal analogy between the Clower and Patinkin models should be apparent from the derivatives of equations (2), (3), and equation (1), or more particularly equations (1.1) and (1.2) in footnote 12. Patinkin's model involves profit maximization subject to an output constraint, whereas Clower's model involves utility maximization subject to an employment constraint.

V. GENERAL DISEQUILIBRIUM INVOLVING EXCESS SUPPLY

In Patinkin's analysis, the effective demand for labor was derived for a given level of demand for current output. To close this model, the demand for current output must be explained. In Clower's analysis, the effec-

tive demand for current output was derived for a given level of demand for labor. To close this model, the demand for labor must be explained. Thus, the Patinkin and Clower analyses are essential complements. When appropriately joined, they form a complete picture of the determination of output and employment in a depressed economy.

Figure 2 depicts Clower's analysis of the commodity market. The notional supply schedule for commodities is a downward sloping function of the real wage. The two notional demand schedules are upward sloping functions, reflecting the effect of substitutability between consumption and leisure as well as a positive income effect. As the real wage rate rises, leisure becomes relatively more expensive, and households tend to work and consume more. The schedule corresponding to the general equilibrium price level P^* passes through the point A. At point A, which corresponds to point A in Figure 1, P^* and w^* are consistent with simultaneous notional equilibrium in both the labor and commodity markets. The other notional commodity demand schedule in Figure 2 corresponds to the higher price level P_1. Because of the real balance effect, this curve lies to the left of the curve associated

.

[15] To the extent that long-run employment (income) exceeds current employment (income), a household may be more willing to maintain a higher demand for commodities at the expense of money balances. In this case effective commodity demand would remain closer to notional demand, and the "income multiplier" (as depicted later in Figure 4) would be smaller. In general, the size of the effect of quantity constraints on effective demands will depend on whether the constraint is viewed as "permanent" or "transitory."

FIGURE 2
The commodity market with excess supply of labor.

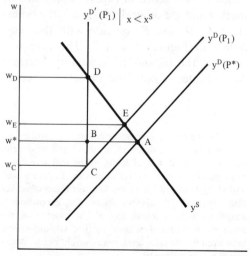

FIGURE 3

Interaction of excess supply on both markets.

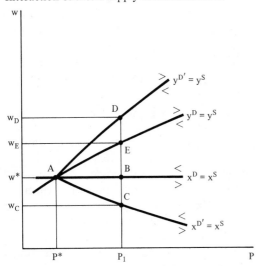

FIGURE 4

Output and employment with excess supply in both markets.

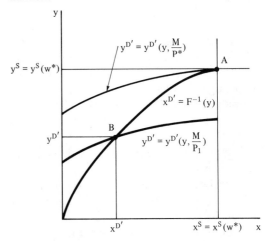

with P^*.[16] If $x = x^S$, the effective demand for commodities coincides with the notional demand. If $x < x^S$, the effective demand is independent of the real wage, as noted above, and is less than the notional demand. The effective demand schedule shown in Figure 2 corresponds to the higher price level P_1. Points B, C, D, and E also correspond to the same points in Figure 1. This correspondence can be seen most clearly by explicitly depicting the interaction between the two markets, as is done in Figures 3 and 4.

Figure 3 illustrates the relationship between the existence of excess supply in one market and the other. In Figure 3, the points A, B, C, D, and E coincide with the same points in Figures 1 and 2. The four loci separate the regions of inequality between the indicated supply and demand concepts.

The locus $x^D = x^S$ is horizontal because, by assumption, both x^D and x^S depend only on the real wage. The locus $y^D = y^S$ is upward sloping because as shown in Figure 2, y^S is a decreasing function of the real wage, whereas y^D is an increasing function of the real wage (substitution and income effect) and a decreasing function of the price level (real balance effect). These loci intersect at point A, which depicts full employment general equilibrium. Points B, C, D, and E are all associated with a price level P_1, which is higher than the equilibrium price level P^*.[17] Point B, for example, would be consistent with notional equilibrium in the labor market, but implies excess supply in the commodity market. The essential point of Patinkin's analysis is that the effective demand for labor is smaller than the notional demand when commodities are in excess supply. Thus, the locus $x^{D'} = x^S$ exists to the right of point A and lies everywhere below the locus $x^D = x^S$. The existence of excess supply in the commodity market enlarges the region of excess supply in the labor market. Similarly, according to Clower's analysis, the effective demand for commodi-

---

[16] As the model is constructed, only y^D and m^D of the five notional schedules; x^D, x^S, y^D, y^S, and m^D depend on the price level independently of the real wage. In a more general model, real balances would affect x^D, x^S, and y^S, and the price level would affect these schedules also. By ignoring this possibility, the exposition is simplified without losing any of the essence of the analysis. Of course, if none of the five schedules were influenced by the price level, prices would not be determined within the model.

[17] We could, of course, just as well think of these points as being associated with a nominal money supply which is too small.

ties is less than the notional demand when labor is in excess supply. Thus, the locus $y^{D'} = y^S$ exists to the right of point A and lies everywhere above the locus $y^D = y^S$. The existence of excess supply in the labor market also enlarges the region of excess supply in the commodity market.

Figure 4 illustrates the determination of the actual quantities of current output and employment when there is excess supply in both markets. In particular, Figure 4 has been drawn under the assumption that the existing wage-price vector is (w^*, P_1), that is that the economy is at point B of Figures 1, 2, and 3. Given voluntary exchange, x and y are determined by $x = \min[x^{D'}, x^S]$ and $y = \min[y^{D'}, y^S]$. The solid locus $x^{D'} = F^{-1}(y)$ describes firm behavior for values of y less than y^S. The solid locus $y^{D'} = y^{D'}(y, M/P_1)$ describes household behavior for values of x less than x^S. The intersection of these two loci determines the values of x and y corresponding to point B. Point A, full employment equilibrium, is at the intersection of y^S and x^S. Since at point B the real wage is consistent with full employment equilibrium, a movement from B to A involves on net only a fall in the price level from P_1 to P^*. In Figure 4, this fall in P is represented by an upward shift in $y^{D'}$ to the dashed locus $y^{D'}(y, M/P^*)$, which intersects $x^{D'}$ at point A. The income multiplier in this case is given by the ratio of the difference between y^S and $y^{D'}(B)$ to the vertical distance between the two curves $y^{D'}(P^*)$ and $y^{D'}(P_1)$. Figure 4 is simply the Keynesian cross diagram with employment replacing income on the horizontal axis.

VI. GENERAL DISEQUILIBRIUM INVOLVING EXCESS DEMAND

The preceding discussion has concentrated on the case of excess supply in the markets for both commodities and labor. However, analogous considerations clearly apply to the boom situation of excess demand for both commodities and labor.

First, consider the behavior of the representative firm when there is excess demand for labor. The representative firm will be able to obtain the quantity of labor x, where $x < x^D$. The firm then must maximize

$$\pi = y^{S'} - wx$$

subject to $y = F(x)$. The variable $y^{S'}$ may be denoted as the effective supply of commodities. The problem is simply to produce as much output as possible with the available labor. The solution is

$$y^{S'} = F(x) \quad \text{for } \frac{dF}{dx} \geq w. \tag{4}$$

Figure 5 depicts the commodity market in this situation, and is analogous to Figure 2. The price level P_2 is assumed to be below P^*.

Next, consider the behavior of the representative household when there is excess demand for commodities. The representative household will be able to obtain the quantity of commodities y, where $y < y^D$. The household then has to choose between either saving, i.e., accumulating as money balances the income which it cannot spend on consumption, or substituting leisure for the unobtainable commodities by supplying less labor, or some

FIGURE 5
The commodity market with excess demand for labor.

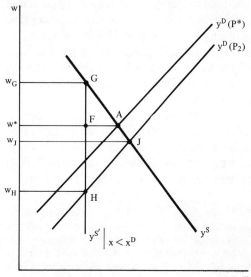

combination of the two. Formally, the household's problem is to maximize

$$U\left(x^{S'}, y, \frac{M}{P} + m^{D'}\right)$$

subject to $\pi + wx^{S'} = y + m^{D'}$.

The variable $x^{S'}$ may be denoted as the effective supply of labor. Utility maximization now implies

$$x^{S'} = x^{S'}\left(w, \frac{M}{P}, \pi, y\right), \tag{5}$$

and

$$m^{D'} = m^{D'}\left(w, \frac{M}{P}, \pi, y\right). \tag{6}$$

This theory stresses the fact that a household may react to frustrated commodity demand in two ways. First, the household may save the income which cannot be spent on consumption (in this model, solely by augmenting money balances). This option corresponds to the classical concept of forced saving, or, more precisely, what D. H. Robertson defined as "automatic lacking." Second, the household may increase leisure by reducing its supply of labor. The second option probably becomes more important when excess commodity demand is chronic, as in war-time or during other periods of rationing and price controls.[18] However, given that consumption, saving, and leisure in aggregate are substitutes, in general some combination of the two options will always be optimal. Excess demand will generally result in some fall in output.

Classical analysis, in which labor supply is solely a function of the real wage, assumes that households channel all frustrated commodity demand into forced saving. The possibility of reduced labor supply is ignored. However, the

inclusion of this option is especially interesting, since it has the apparently paradoxical implication that excess commodity demand can result in decreased employment and output.

Figure 6, which is analogous to Figure 1, depicts the labor market in this situation. Two important observations should be stressed. First, too low a real wage, that is a real wage below the level consistent with general equilibrium, is not a necessary condition for excess demand for labor, even though the notional demand and supply for labor are both assumed to depend only upon the real wage. This observation is obviously the converse of the earlier observation that the effective demand for labor is not uniquely associated with the real wage. If commodities are in excess demand so that, given voluntary exchange, $y < y^D$, which in turn implies $x^{S'} < x^S$, at real wage w^* excess demand for labor will amount to quantity AF.

Second, with commodities in excess demand, the quantity of employment will generally be below the full employment level. The explanation of this apparent paradox, as indicated above, is twofold: 1) the quantity of employment can be no greater than the quantity supplied; and 2) when their consumption

FIGURE 6
The labor market with excess demand for commodities.

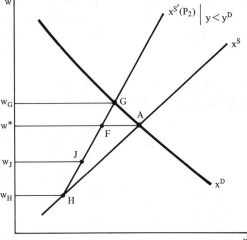

FIGURE 7

Interaction of excess demand in both markets.

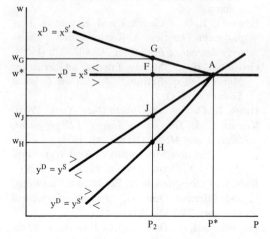

and 6. Figure 8 is drawn under the assumption that the existing wage-price vector is (w^*, P_2), that is, that the economy is at point F. The details of the construction of these diagrams are left as an exercise for the reader.

VII. SUMMARY

This paper describes the application of a general disequilibrium approach to familiar problems of macro-analysis. Some familiar results, such as the notion that insufficient commodity demand produces unemployment, are arrived at in a much more satisfactory manner than is possible under more conventional analysis. In addition, the specific inclusion of disequilibrium elements leads to some non-familiar results.

The impact of excess supply of commodities on labor demand removes the one-to-one classical relationship between real wage and employment. In a general disequilibrium situation, unemployment can coexist with "non-excessive" real wages, and a procyclical pattern of real wages is consistent with the theoretical model.

The disequilibrium analysis of the commodity market is formally parallel to the analysis of the labor market. The Keynesian consumption function emerges as a manifestation of the impact of excess labor supply on commodity demand. In this respect conventional macro-analysis is seen to be asymmetric. On the one hand, the disequilibrium impact of excess labor supply is implicitly recognized by entering income as a separate argument in the consumption function. However, on the other hand, the impact of excess commodity supply is neglected by adhering to the classical labor demand function which involves only the real wage. Because of this peculiar asymmetry, previous analyses of unemployment have had to rely on such contrived devices as a countercyclical pattern of real wages or fixed proportion production functions.

The framework for analyzing the excess supply, depression case is directly applicable to an analysis of sustained excess demand. The classical concept of forced saving is one

plans are frustrated households will generally substitute leisure and thus supply less labor at any given real wage. Notice that even if the real wage should rise sufficiently, i.e., to w_G, to eliminate the excess demand for labor, the level of employment would still be below that obtaining at general equilibrium.

Finally, Figures 7 and 8, which are analogous to Figures 3 and 4, depict the interaction between the two markets with excess demand in both. Points A, F, G, H, and J in Figure 7 coincide with the same points in Figures 5

FIGURE 8

Output and employment with excess demand in both markets.

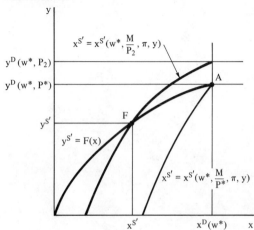

aspect of the impact of excess commodity demand on household decision making. The forced saving solution is, however, incomplete, since labor supply would also react inversely to a prolonged frustration of commodity demand. To the extent that labor supply declines in response to excess commodity demand, increases in commodity demand lead to reduced employment, rather than to increased (forced) saving.

References

Alchian, A. A., "Information Costs, Pricing, and Resource Unemployment," *Western Economic Journal*, 7:109–128 (1969).

Arrow, K. J., "Toward a Theory of Price Adjustment," in Abramowitz, M. (ed.), *The Allocation of Economic Resources* (Stanford, 1959).

Barro, R. J., "A Theory of Monopolistic Price Adjustment," read at Econometric Society Meeting (Detroit, 1970).

———, "A Theory of Optimal Adjustment," forthcoming 1971.

Bodkin, R. G., "Real Wages and Cyclical Variations in Employment," *Canadian Journal of Economics*, 2:353–374 (1969).

Clower, R., "The Keynesian Counter Revolution: A Theoretical Appraisal," in Hahn, F. H., and Brechling, F. P. R. (eds.), *The Theory of Interest Rates* (London, 1965). [Reprinted in this volume.]

Edwards, E. O., "Classical and Keynesian Employment Theories: A Reconciliation," *Quarterly Journal of Economics*, 73:407–428 (1959).

Grossman, H. I., "Money, Interest, and Prices in Market Disequilibrium," *Journal of Political Economy* (1971).

Hicks, J., *Capital and Growth* (New York, 1965).

Keynes, J. M., *The General Theory of Employment, Interest, and Money* (New York, 1936).

———, "Relative Movements of Real Wages and Output," *Economic Journal*, 49:34–51 (1939).

Kuh, E., "Unemployment, Production Functions, and Effective Demand," *Journal of Political Economy*, 74:238–249 (1966).

Leijonhufvud, A., *On Keynesian Economics and the Economics of Keynes* (New York, 1968).

Patinkin, D., "Involuntary Unemployment and the Keynesian Supply Function," *Economic Journal*, 59:360–383 (1949).

———, *Money, Interest, and Prices, 1956*, 2nd ed. (New York, 1965).

Robertson, D. H., *Banking Policy and the Price Level* (London, 1926).

Solow, R. M., and Stiglitz, J. E., "Output, Employment, and Wages in the Short Run," *Quarterly Journal of Economics*, 82:537–560 (1968).

Vicker, R., "USSR: Rising Income, Black Markets," *The Wall Street Journal* (April 21, 1970).

A Disequilibrium Macroeconomic Model

Panayotis G. Korliras

University of Pittsburgh

I. EQUILIBRIUM AND DISEQUILIBRIUM MODELS

The fundamental difference between equilibrium and disequilibrium macroeconomics is essentially the same as the difference between models that use the tâtonnement assumption and models that do not. In equilibrium-type theory the assumption is made that production and exchange take place only when the equilibrium price vector is reached. Production and exchange are not permitted at "false" prices, i.e., at prices corresponding to nonzero excess demands. This procedure of analysis is Walras' tâtonnement process, or Edgeworth's recontracting. In disequilibrium-type theory, on the other hand, production and exchange take place even when the economy is out of equilibrium.

Standard macroeconomic theory is dominated by equilibrium-type models. The equilibrium approach in macroeconomic theory is reflected mainly by the fact that, in the analysis of the stability of equilibrium, the two principal quantity variables, i.e., labor employment and income, are assumed to be given at the full employment level. Then the dynamic stability is analyzed with changes in the "price variables" involved in the markets for output, money, and loans. The plans of both the producers and the consumers are

formulated on the basis of full employment income, and the attainment of equilibrium (i.e., market clearance throughout) depends on changes in the price level and the rate of interest. The production-and-employment sector is almost completely separate, in the sense that it provides only the level of income as a datum to the rest of the economy.[1]

The macroeconomic model constructed in this paper is a disequilibrium model in the sense that production and exchanges take place even when the markets are not cleared. It thus involves both "price" and "quantity" adjustments because labor employment and income are true variables, since no market is cleared instantaneously. There has appeared recently a growing literature on disequilibrium models,[2] but the principle subject that

1. See, mainly, D. Patinkin, *Money, Interest, and Prices*, 2nd ed. (Evanston: Harper and Row, 1965), Part Two; and M. Bailey, *National Income and the Price Level*, 2nd ed. (New York: McGraw-Hill, 1970), esp. p. 34.

2. It seems that this body of literature has its beginning in R. W. Clower, "The Keynesian Counter-Revolution," in R. W. Clower, ed., *Monetary Theory* (Baltimore: Penguin Books, 1969), 270–97, originally published in F. Hahn and F. Brechling, eds., *The Theory of Interest Rates* (London: St. Martin's, 1965). The reinterpretation of Keynes along disequilibrium lines proceeded with A. Leijonhufvud, *On Keynesian Economics and the Economics of Keynes* (New York: Oxford University Press, 1968). See also P. Davidson, "A Keynesian View of Patinkin's Theory of Employment," *Economic Journal*, LXXVII (1967), 559–78. This is, however, still an unresolved issue. See H. I. Grossman, "Was Keynes a 'Keynesian'?" *Journal of Economic Literature*, X (1972), 26–30.

Reprinted from the *Quarterly Journal of Economics*, 89:56–80 (1975), by permission of the author and the publisher (copyright by the President and Fellows of Harvard College, published by John Wiley and Sons, Inc.).

339

most of the authors examined was solely the analytical structure of aggregative models whose dynamic adjustments include both "price" and "quantity" adjustments. Clower's "dual decision hypothesis" inspired the trend of thought that stresses the fact that, in conditions of disequilibrium, the quantity constraints imposed on the various participants in the markets are the result of the disequilibrium situation.[3] Thus, the dynamic adjustments become numerous, equal to the sum of "price" and "quantity" variables, which are, of course, interrelated. But in this case the analysis cannot proceed very easily beyond mere theoretical description. In particular, any stability analysis becomes virtually impossible in the context of an aggregative model with many differential equations describing the adjustment mechanisms. In this way, however, the disequilibrium models cannot be readily compared with the fully developed and completely analyzed equilibrium-type macro models, unless we arbitrarily reduce the model and thus the number of adjustments. There have been some attempts in constructing disequilibrium models whose adjustment mechanisms can be traced out. On the one hand, we have the Keynes-Wicksell monetary growth models, whose main content is the examination of the conditions and the stability of a steady-state growth equilibrium.[4] On the other hand, we have the Solow and Stiglitz model,[5] which is the only complete short-run disequilibrium model that fully analyzed its adjustment mechanisms. The Solow and Stiglitz model is of fundamental importance for the construction of a generalized disequilibrium macro model. The model developed in this paper can be thought of as an extension of theirs, with several crucial differences. First, our model is more easily comparable to the standard neoclassical macro model. Second, the independent quantity adjustments are eliminated. Third, the model does not include any formal Phillips curve assumption, which provides an inherent bias towards an unemployment quasi-equilibrium. Fourth, the present model includes a monetary or financial sector.

In this paper we shall examine a particular mechanism of disequilibrium adjustments. We shall express the quantity-cum-price adjustments by the price adjustments alone because the quantity adjustments are derived, i.e., the quantities demanded and supplied in each market are determined by the appropriate prices. The synchronous changes in both prices and quantities are clarified by adopting a seemingly discrete period analysis. Following the methodology of Solow and Stiglitz,[6] we distinguish between the momentary situations and the short run, which is defined as a sequence of momentary situations. The momentary situation is analogous to the Hicksian week or the Robertsonian day, and it can be thought of as being of infinitesimal duration so that the analysis is essentially continuous. During each momentary situation all prices are given, and on the basis of these prices all plans are formulated. If at the given prices there are nonzero excess demands, the actual quantities transacted in each market will be determined by a specific rule. For simplicity we shall ignore the unwanted increases in inventories when there is an excess supply situation, assuming that their influence will be reflected in the price changes. Nonzero excess demands generate changes in

3. See R. J. Barro and H. I. Grossman, "A General Disequilibrium Model of Income and Employment," *American Economic Review*, LXI (1971), 82–93; H. I. Grossman, "Money, Interest and Prices in Market Disequilibrium," *Journal of Political Economy*, LXXIX (1971), 943–96; D. P. Tucker, "Macroeconomic Models and the Demand for Money Under Market Disequilibrium," *Journal of Money, Credit and Banking*, III (1971), 57–83; and D. P. Tucker, "Patinkin's Macro-Model as a Model of Market Disequilibrium," *Southern Economic Journal*, XXXIX (1972), 187–203.

4. See H. Rose, "On the Non-Linear Theory of the Employment Cycle," *Review of Economic Studies*, XXXIV (1967), 153–73; H. Rose: "Real and Monetary Factors in the Business Cycle," *Journal of Money, Credit and Banking*, I (1969), 138–52; H. Rose, "Effective Demand in the Long Run," Harvard Institute of Economic Research, Harvard University, Discussion Paper No. 106, February 1970. See also J. Stein, *Money and Capacity Growth* (New York: Columbia University Press, 1971); and K. Nagatani, "A Monetary Growth Model with Variable Employment," *Journal of Money, Credit and Banking*, I (1969), 188–206.

5. R. Solow and J. Stiglitz, "Output, Employment, and Wages in the Short Run," this *Journal*, LXXXII (1968), 537–60.

6. Ibid.

the prices at the transition from one momentary situation to another. So in the next momentary situation a new set of prices will be given, and the various plans will change accordingly. These adjustments will stop only when the market forces that are responsible for them are neutralized. At this point the system will have attained a short-run equilibrium, which may be a quasi-equilibrium if not all the markets are cleared, but nothing changes at the same time.[7]

Here we shall have three markets: the market for labor, the market for output, and the market for loanable funds (i.e., bonds). Labor and output are homogeneous quantities, output being used either for consumption or for accumulation purposes. Bonds are also homogeneous, represented by a composite perpetuity of average risk, so that the price of bonds is the reciprocal of the bond interest rate. The nominal wage rate, the price level of output, and the bond interest rate are the three price variables, each determined primarily by the forces acting through the labor market, the output market, and the bonds market, respectively.

At the first stage of the analysis, we shall proceed with a model that does not contain a real balance or Pigou effect. Such a model highlights the repercussions of persistent inconsistencies among the various plans in such a way that they do not inherently tend to be resolved. The result is the possibility of a short-run quasi-equilibrium. At the second stage the real balance effect will be brought into the analysis, so that the short-run equilibrium is characterized by market clearance throughout. An interesting question concerning such a model is the stability of the short-run equilibrium, especially when our model is compared with other more conventional macro models.

II. THE STRUCTURE OF THE MODEL

In this section we examine the three markets mentioned previously and the nature of the adjustments taking place in each. As will become evident, the analysis of the labor and the output markets has a number of neoclassical features, but also one major Keynesian characteristic: the use of independent savings and investment functions.

The labor market is described by a demand function for labor, which specifies that the quantity of labor services demand (N^d) is a decreasing function of the real wage rate $\left(w = \dfrac{W}{P}\right)$:

$$N^d = h(w), \quad h'(w) < 0, \quad h''(w) \geqq 0, \tag{1}$$

and a supply function of labor, specifying that the quantity of labor services offered (N^s) is an increasing function of the real wage rate,

$$N^s = j(w), \quad j'(w) > 0, \quad j''(w) \leqq 0. \tag{2}$$

On the basis of equations (1) and (2), we can define the labor market clearing situation, which in turn defines full employment as

$$h(w_f) = j(w_f) = N_F. \tag{3}$$

At any momentary situation, however, there is a given real wage rate, which may not be equal to the full-employment real wage (w_f). In such a case, the demand for labor will not be equal to the supply of labor, so that at any momentary situation, the momentary level of labor employment (N^e) is determined by the rule,[8]

$$N^e = \min(N^d, N^s). \tag{4}$$

Obviously, equation (3) describes a particular case of the general rule defined by equation (4).

On the supply side of the output market, we have a production function that relates the momentary supply of output (Y^s) to the momentary level of labor employment, such that

$$Y^s = F(N^e), \tag{5}$$

---

7. The concept of the quasi-equilibrium, as well as the analytical framework of the disequilibrium approach, was part of the tradition of the Stockholm School. For a recent exposition see B. Hansen, *A Survey of General Equilibrium Systems* (New York: McGraw-Hill, 1970), Ch. 10. See also P. G. Korliras, "A Note on the Disequilibrium Method in Macroeconomics," *American Economist* (Winter 1972), pp. 79–82.

8. See F. H. Hahn and T. Negishi, "A Theorem on Nontâtonnement Stability," *Econometrica*, XXX (1962), 463–69, esp. p. 463.

with $F'(N^e) > 0$ and $F''(N^e) < 0$. On the basis of equations (1), (2), and (4), the supply function (5) may be written as

$$Y^s = f(w), \qquad (6)$$

such that

$$f'(w) > 0, \quad f''(w) < 0 \text{ for any } w < w_f \qquad (7)$$
$$f'(w) < 0, \quad f''(w) > 0 \text{ for any } w > w_f.$$

The aggregate demand for output (Y^d) consists of two components: the demand for investment (I), which is assumed to be a decreasing function of the bond rate of interest (r),

$$I = I(r), \quad I'(r) < 0; \qquad (8)$$

and the demand for consumption (C), which is assumed to be a constant fraction of disposable income (Y_{di}),

$$C = (1 - s)Y_{di}, \quad 0 < s < 1, \qquad (9)$$

where s is the average (and marginal) propensity to save. At this point we omit any direct influence of the interest rate on the consumption-saving decision, since the direction of the effect is likely to be uncertain. For the time being we also omit any real balance effect.

Disposable income, in this nontâtonnement context, consists of the wage bill actually paid and the profits that are realized in any momentary situation, so that

$$Y_{di} = wN^e + (Y^a - wN^e) = Y^a, \qquad (10)$$

where Y^a is the real value of the realized sales of output during the momentary situation. If at the momentarily given price level the demand for output is not equal to the supply of output, we assume that the actual sales of output are determined by the rule,

$$Y^a = \min(Y^d, Y^s). \qquad (11)$$

Thus, the aggregate demand for output is given by

$$Y^d = (1 - s)[\min(Y^d, Y^s)] + I(r). \qquad (12)$$

We then have the following possibilities:
If $Y^d > Y^s$, then

$$Y^d = (1 - s)Y^s + I(r), \qquad (13)$$

so that

$$E_y = Y^d - Y^s = (1 - s)Y^s + I(r) - \dot{Y}^s$$
$$= I(r) - sY^s = I(r) - s \cdot f(w) = E_y(w, r). \qquad (14)$$

If $Y^d < Y^s$,

$$Y^d = (1 - s)Y^d + I(r), \qquad (15a)$$

or

$$Y^d = \frac{I(r)}{s}, \qquad (15b)$$

so that

$$E_y = Y^d - Y^s = \frac{I(r)}{s} - f(w) = E_y(w, r). \qquad (16)$$

On that basis we can specify the following partial derivatives:

$$E_y(w, r)_1 = -s \cdot f'(w) \lessgtr 0 \text{ as } w \lessgtr w_f \ (Y^d > Y^s)$$
$$E_y(wr)_1 = -f'(w) \lessgtr 0 \text{ as } w \lessgtr w_f \ (Y^d < Y^s); \qquad (17)$$

$$E_y(w, r)_2 = I'(r) < 0 \ (Y^d > y^s) \qquad (18)$$
$$E_y(w, r)_2 = \frac{I'(r)}{s} < 0 \ (Y^d < Y^s).$$

Likewise, on the basis of (1) and (2), we can specify

$$E_N = h(w) - j(w) = E_N(w) \qquad (19)$$

and

$$\frac{dE_N(w)}{dw} = h'(w) - j'(w) < 0. \qquad (20)$$

Coming now to the analysis of the bonds market, we assume that the supply of bonds (B^s), as the flow supply of new bonds, consists of the demand for loanable funds in order to finance the investment plans, so that

$$B^s = I(r), \quad I'(r) < 0. \qquad (21)$$

The demand for bonds is related to the consumers' decisions to allocate their total savings between the two assets, bonds and money. According to equations (9)–(11), we can specify the following savings function:

$$S = s \cdot Y^a = s[\min(Y^d, Y^s)]. \qquad (22)$$

Then, the savings-allocation decision is such that

$$S = B^d + DH, \qquad (23)$$

where B^d is the net flow demand for bonds from the part of the households (consumers) and DH is the current desired change in the money hoardings, i.e., the change in the demand for money as an asset, such that

$$DH = l(w, r) \qquad (24)$$

with

$$l_1 \gtrless 0 \text{ as } w \lessgtr w_f$$
$$l_2 < 0.$$

In the demand-for-money-as-an-asset function, we assume a positive dependence on the real wage rate, which is used here as a proxy for an "income" variable, and a negative dependence on the bonds interest rate, assuming of course that money earns no interest.

In this model one could introduce commercial banks, whose business would be to absorb part of the supply of bonds from the part of the investors (firms). Then, the demand for bonds from the part of these commercial banks would amount to increases in the supply of inside money (deposits) that they create. For simplicity, we assume that the quantity of outside money is fixed and that a "strict" reserve-requirement ratio is observed by the banks, so that the total supply of money is also fixed. Then, the net flow demand for bonds is given by

$$B^d = S - DH. \qquad (25)$$

On this basis, we can specify E_B as the net excess supply of bonds (or net excess demand for loanable funds), such that if $Y^d > Y^s$ then

$$S = s \cdot Y^s = s \cdot f(w), \qquad (26)$$

and

$$E_B = B^s - B^d = I(r) - s \cdot f(w) + l(w, r)$$
$$= E_B(w, r), \qquad (27)$$

with

$$E_B(w, r)_1 = -s \cdot f'(w) + l_1 \lessgtr 0 \text{ as } w \lessgtr w_f \qquad (28a)$$

and

$$|l_1| < |s \cdot f'|.$$
$$E_B(w, r)_2 = I'(r) + l_2 < 0, \qquad (29a)$$

and if $Y^d < Y^s$ then

$$S = s \cdot Y^d = s \cdot \frac{I(r)}{s} = I(r), \qquad (30)$$

and

$$E_B = B^s - B^d = I(r) - I(r) + l(w, r) = l(w, r)$$
$$= E_B(w, r), \qquad (31)$$

with

$$E_B(w, r)_1 = l_1 \gtrless 0 \text{ as } w \lessgtr w_f \qquad (28b)$$
$$E_B(w, r)_2 = l_2 < 0. \qquad (29b)$$

We have in this model essentially two "price variables" that are endogenously determined: the interest rate and the real wage rate. From the definition of the real wage, we see that

$$w^* = W^* - P^*. \quad \text{(the asterisks signify relative rates of change)} \qquad (32)$$

The use of (32) is justified here because the price level has no other influence or effect on the other variables except insofar as it alters the real wage rate. Later on, we shall assume that the price level has an independent effect of its own, e.g., in the form of a real balance effect, in which case (32) cannot be rightly used. For now, however, we can specify that the nominal wage changes whenever there exists a nonzero excess demand in the labor market, such that

$$W^* = \lambda_N \cdot E_N(w). \qquad (33)$$

We also assume that the price level changes whenever there exists a nonzero excess demand in the output market, so that

$$P^* = \lambda_y \cdot E_y(w, r). \qquad (34)$$

Finally, the interest rate changes whenever there exists a nonzero excess supply in the bonds market, so that

$$r^* = \lambda_B \cdot E_B(w, r). \tag{35}$$

The λ_N, λ_y, and λ_B, which appear in the price adjustment equations, are constant positive and finite speeds of adjustment, meaning that, in the presence of nonzero excess demands, no price variable adjusts so fast as to clear the market instantaneously. We then have

$$w^* = \frac{\begin{aligned} &\lambda_N[h(w) - j(w)] \\ &\quad - \lambda_y[I(r) - s \cdot f(w)] \quad (Y^d > Y^s) \\ &\lambda_N[h(w) - j(w)] \\ &\quad - \lambda_y\left[\frac{I(r)}{s} - f(w)\right] \quad (Y^d < Y^s). \end{aligned}} \tag{36}$$

In short-run equilibrium we have

$$w^* = 0, \tag{37}$$

so that we can define the locus of combinations of real wages and interest rates that satisfy (37). The slope of such a locus in the (w, r) plane will be given by

$$\left.\frac{dw}{dr}\right|_{w^*=0} = -\frac{-\lambda_y \cdot I'(r)}{\lambda_N(h' - j') + \lambda_y s \cdot f'(w)} (Y^d > Y^s). \tag{38a}$$

The numerator is positive, so that the sign of the ratio is the opposite of the sign of the denominator. Therefore, given the specification of the various partial derivatives, we have the following possibilities:

denominator < 0 for any $w > w_f$;
denominator $\gtrless 0$ for any $w < w_f$,
    as $|\lambda_y \cdot s \cdot f'| \lessgtr |\lambda_N(h' - j')|$;

and by

$$\left.\frac{dw}{dr}\right|_{w^*=0} = -\frac{-\lambda_y \cdot I'(r)}{s \cdot \lambda_N(h' - j') + \lambda_y \cdot sf'(w)}$$
$$(Y^d < Y^s). \tag{38b}$$

Again, the sign of the ratio is the opposite of the sign of the denominator, the same as before, with the only difference that

denominator $\gtrless 0$ for any $w < w_f$,
    as $|\lambda_y sf'| \lessgtr |s \cdot \lambda_N(h' - j')|$.

From (35) we also have

$$r^* = \frac{\begin{aligned} &\lambda_B[I(r) - s \cdot f(w) + l(w, r)] \quad (Y^d > Y^s) \\ &\lambda_B[l(w, r)] \quad\quad\quad\quad\quad\quad (Y^d < Y^s). \end{aligned}} \tag{39}$$

In short-run equilibrium we have

$$r^* = 0, \tag{40}$$

so that we can specify in the (w, r) plane the locus of combinations of real wages and interest rates that satisfy (40). The slope of such a locus will be given by

$$\left.\frac{dw}{dr}\right|_{r^*=0} = -\frac{I'(r) + l_2}{l_1 - sf'(w)} \lessgtr 0 \text{ as } w \lessgtr w_f$$
$$(Y^d > Y^s) \tag{41a}$$

$$\left.\frac{dw}{dr}\right|_{r^*=0} = -\frac{l_2}{l_1} \gtrless 0 \text{ as } w \lessgtr 0 \text{ as } w \lessgtr w_f$$
$$(Y^d < Y^s). \tag{41b}$$

III. THE SHORT-RUN EQUILIBRIUM

The short-run equilibrium in this model is defined as the attainment of values (w^e, r^e) of the endogenously determined "price" variables, such that they satisfy system (42):

$$\begin{aligned} w^* &= \lambda_N \cdot E_N(w^e) - \lambda_y \cdot E_y(w^e, r^e) = 0 \\ r^* &= \lambda_B \cdot E_B(w^e, r^e) = 0. \end{aligned} \tag{42}$$

Then, this short-run equilibrium can be represented by the intersection point of the $w^* = 0$ and the $r^* = 0$ loci in the (w, r) plane. The preceding analysis, however, makes it clear that in any diagrammatic scheme of the adjustment process we must distinguish whether the disequilibrium position is a point where $Y^d < Y^s$ or $Y^d < Y^s$. The nature of the adjustment process depends crucially on this distinction. For the purpose we must insert in the (w, r) plane the locus of combinations of (w, r) for which $Y^d = Y^s$. Starting with any $w > w_f$, suppose that we are at a point (w_o, r_o), where $Y^d = Y^s$. Then, consider a point (w, r) on the $Y^d = Y^s$ locus with $w > w_o$. Now

FIGURE I

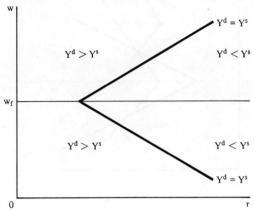

$f(w) < f(w_o)$, so that $Y^d(w, r) < Y^d(w^o, r_o)$. But when $Y^d = Y^s$, $I(r) = s \cdot Y^d(w, r)$. Thus, $I(r) < I(r_o), r > r_o$. So,

$$\left.\frac{dw}{dr}\right|_{p^* = 0} > 0 \text{ for } w > w_f. \tag{43a}$$

Similarly,

$$\left.\frac{dw}{dr}\right|_{p^* = 0} < 0 \text{ for } w < w_f. \tag{43b}$$

This result may be represented in the (w, r) plane as in Figure I.

Using (41a) and (41b), we observe that the slope of the $r^* = 0$ locus abruptly reverses if we cross over from the $Y^d > Y^s$ half plane to the $Y^d < Y^s$ half plane or vice versa. Two possibilities for the $r^* = 0$ locus are depicted in Figures IIa and IIb. Also, from (38a) and

(38b) we see that for $w > w_f$,

$$\left.\frac{dw}{dr}\right|_{w^* = 0} > 0 \text{ for both } Y^d < Y^s$$

and $Y^d < Y^s$ but for $w < w_f$,

$$\left.\frac{dw}{dr}\right|_{w^* = 0} \lesseqgtr 0,$$

as

$$s \cdot \lambda_y \cdot f'(w) \gtreqless - \lambda_N(h' - j') \quad \text{for } Y^d > Y^s,$$
$$\lambda_y \cdot f'(w) \gtreqless - \lambda_N(h' - j') \quad \text{for } Y^d < Y^s.$$

Thus, there are several possibilities concerning the slope of the $w^* = 0$ locus in the (w, r) plane. Some of the possibilities are depicted in Figures IIIa, IIIb, and IIIc. There, the insertion of both the $w^* = 0$ locus and the $r^* = 0$ locus reveals that a short-run equilibrium is likely to exist, but it may not be unique, since the $w^* = 0$ and $r^* = 0$ loci intersect more than once. Each short-run equilibrium is stable or not depending on whether the (local) stability conditions are satisfied. In general, we can take the linear term of a Taylor expansion of the solutions in the neighborhood of equilibrium and then form the matrix of the coefficients of the linear approximation. Thus, if the $w^* = 0$ and $r^* = 0$ loci intersect at point P, where $Y^d > Y^s$, then the matrix is

$$\begin{pmatrix} \lambda_N(h' - j') + \lambda_y s \cdot f' & - \lambda_y I' \\ \lambda_B(l_1 - s \cdot f') & \lambda_B(I' + l_2) \end{pmatrix} = A_1. \tag{44}$$

FIGURE IIa

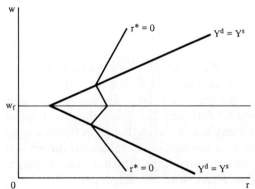

FIGURE IIb

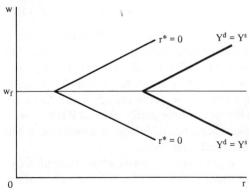

FIGURE IIIa

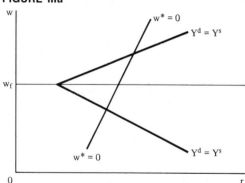

FIGURE IIIb

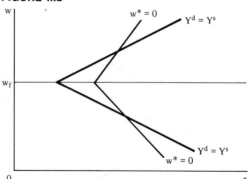

FIGURE IIIc

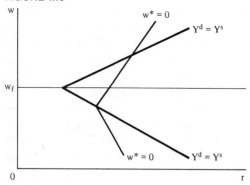

Then, the Ruth-Hurwitz conditions for stable equilibria are that

$$\det A_1 > 0$$
$$\text{trace } A_1 < 0 \tag{45}$$

or that

$$\frac{I' + l_2}{l_1 - s \cdot f'} > \frac{-\lambda_y I'}{\lambda_N(h' - j') + \lambda_y \cdot s \cdot f'} \tag{46a}$$

and

$$\lambda_N(h' - j') + \lambda_y \cdot s \cdot f' + \lambda_B(I' + l_2) < 0. \tag{46b}$$

Thus, P will be stable only if, to the left of the point of intersection, the $w^* = 0$ locus lies above the $r^* = 0$ locus for any $w > w_f$, and the $w^* = 0$ locus lies below the $r^* = 0$ locus for any $w < w_f$ (even though in this last case, (46b) is not necessarily satisfied if the $w^* = 0$ locus has a positive slope, in which case P will be an unstable focus).

If now the $r^* = 0$ and $w^* = 0$ loci intersect at a point P where $Y^d < Y^s$, the matrix of the

coefficients is

$$\begin{bmatrix} \lambda_N(h' - j') + \lambda_y \cdot f' & -\lambda_y \cdot \dfrac{I'}{s} \\ \lambda_B l_1 & \lambda_B l_2 \end{bmatrix} = A_2. \tag{47}$$

Then, the stability conditions are

$$\frac{l_2}{l_1} > \frac{-\lambda_y I'}{s \cdot \lambda_N(h' - j') + s \cdot \lambda_y \cdot f'} \tag{48a}$$

and

$$\lambda_N(h' - j') + \lambda_y \cdot f' + \lambda_B l_2 < 0. \tag{48b}$$

Thus, P will be stable only if, to the left of the point of intersection, the $w^* = 0$ locus lies above the $r^* = 0$ locus for any $w < w_f$ and the $w^* = 0$ locus lies below the $r^* = 0$ locus for any $w > w_f$ (even though in this last case, (48b) is not necessarily satisfied if the $w^* = 0$ has a positive slope, which it does, in which case P can be an unstable focus).

FIGURE IV

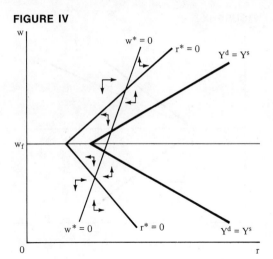

FIGURE VI

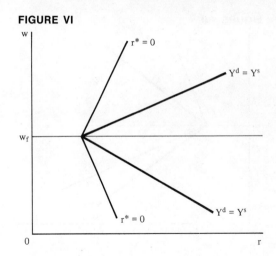

Figures IV and V depict some of the possible intersections of the $w^* = 0$ and $r^* = 0$ loci in both the $Y^d > Y^s$ and the $Y^d < Y^s$ half planes. Obviously, all these intersections define short-run equilibria that are really quasi-equilibria because the markets are not cleared. The only case where the short-run equilibrium would be not a quasi-equilibrium but a full market clearance equilibrium is when P lies on the $Y^d = Y^s$ locus. In this case, the real goods, the bonds, and hence the labor markets all clear, so that P must coincide with the intersection of $w = w_f$ and $Y^d = Y^s$ in the (w, r) plane. But then the stability conditions cannot be expressed in terms of the derivatives of the $w^* = 0$ and $r^* = 0$ loci because these derivatives do not exist. Instead we have

four separate sets of conditions corresponding to the four possible configurations of the $w^* = 0$ locus, while the $r^* = 0$ locus must look as it does in Figure VI.

Case 1 (the $w^* = 0$ locus appears as in Figure VII): P is stable $<=>$ there exist open intervals (w_1, w_f) and (w_f, w_2), such that

$$\frac{I'(r) + l_2(w, r)}{l_1(w, r) - s \cdot f'(w)}$$

$$> \frac{-\lambda_y I'(r)}{\lambda_N[h'(w) - j'(w)] + \lambda_y \cdot s \cdot f'(w)} \quad (49a)$$

and

$$\lambda_N[h'(w) - j'(w)] + \lambda_y \cdot s \cdot f'(w)$$
$$+ \lambda_B[I'(r) + l_2(w, r)] < 0, \quad (49b)$$

FIGURE V

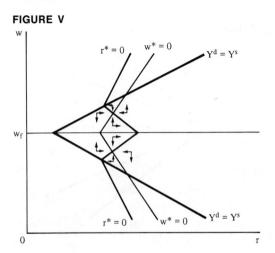

FIGURE VII

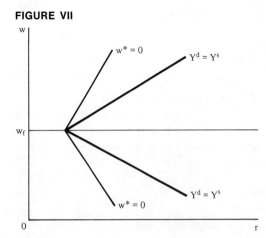

FIGURE VIII

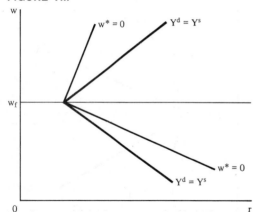

FIGURE IX

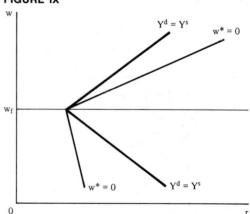

whenever $w_e(w_1, w_f) U(w_f, w_2)$ and $w^*(w, r) = 0$.

   Case 2 (the $w^* = 0$ locus appears as in Figure VIII): P is stable $<=>$ there exist open intervals (w_1, w_f) and (w_f, w_2), such that

$$\frac{I'(r) + l_2(w, r)}{l_1(w, r) - s \cdot f'(w)}$$

$$> \frac{-\lambda_y I'(r)}{\lambda_N[h'(w) - j'(w)] + \lambda_y s \cdot f'(w)} \quad (50a)$$

and

$$\lambda_N[h'(w) - j'(w)] + \lambda_y \cdot s \cdot f'(w)$$
$$+ \lambda_B[I'(r) + l_2(w, r)] < 0, \quad (50b)$$

whenever $w_e(w_f, w_2)$ and $w^*(w, r) = 0$; and

$$\frac{I'(r) + l_2(w, r)}{l_1(w, r) - s \cdot f'(w)}$$

$$> \frac{-\lambda_y I'(r)}{s \cdot \lambda_N[h'(w) - j'(w)] + s \cdot \lambda_y f'(w)} \quad (50c)$$

and

$$\lambda_N[h'(w) - j'(w)] + \lambda_y f'(w)$$
$$+ \lambda_B[I'(r) + l_2(w, r)] < 0, \quad (50d)$$

whenever $w_e(w_1, w_f)$ and $w^*(w, r) = 0$.

   Case 3 (the $w^* = 0$ locus appears as in Figure IX): P is stable $<=>$ there exist open intervals (w_1, w_f) and (w_f, w_2), such that

$$\frac{I'(r) + l_2(w, r)}{l_1(w, r) - s \cdot f'(w)}$$

$$> \frac{-\lambda_y I'(r)}{s \cdot \lambda_N[h'(w) - j'(w)] + s \cdot \lambda_y \cdot f'(w)} \quad (51a)$$

and

$$\lambda_N[h'(w) - j'(w)] + \lambda_y \cdot f'(w)$$
$$+ \lambda_B[I'(r) + l_2(w, r)] < 0, \quad (51b)$$

whenever $w_e(w_f, w_2)$ and $w^*(w, r) = 0$; and

$$\frac{I'(r) + l_2(w, r)}{l_1(w, r) - s \cdot f'(w)}$$

$$> \frac{-\lambda_y I'(r)}{\lambda_N[h'(w) - j'(w)] + \lambda_y s \cdot f'(w)}, \quad (51c)$$

and

$$\lambda_N[h'(w) - j'(w)] + \lambda_y s \cdot f'(w)$$
$$+ \lambda_B[I'(r) + l_2(w, r)] < 0, \quad (51d)$$

whenever $w_e(w_1, w_f)$ and $w^*(w, r_f) = 0$.

   Case 4 (the $w^* = 0$ locus appears as in Figure X): P is stable $<=>$ there exist open

FIGURE X

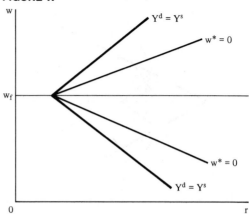

intervals (w_1, w_f) and (w_f, w_2), such that

$$\frac{I'(r) + l_2(w, r)}{l_1(w, r) - s \cdot f'(w)}$$

$$> \frac{-\lambda_y I'(r)}{s \cdot \lambda_N[h'(w) - j'(w)] + s \cdot \lambda_y \cdot f'(w)} \quad (52a)$$

and

$$\lambda_N[h'(w) - j'(w)] + \lambda_y \cdot f'(w)$$
$$+ \lambda_B[I'(r) + l_2(w, r)] < 0, \quad (52b)$$

whenever $w_e(w_1, w_f) U(w_f, w_2)$ and $w^*(w, r) =$ we have 0.

In view of the above conditions, we see that nothing can be said a prior whether the short-run equilibrium will be either unique or stable. Furthermore, the short-run equilibrium can be either a quasi-equilibrium or a full equilibrium. Obviously, this multiplicity of possibilities is a reflection of the non-tâtonnement structure of the model. In fact, in this model we have the possibility of a short-run quasi-equilibrium at which there exist unemployment $(w > w_f)$ and inflation (if P lies in the $Y^d > Y^s$ half plane). Not only the slopes of the $w^* = 0$ and $r^* = 0$ loci, but also their position in the (w, r) plane, are crucial. We do not have enough information about what determines their position. For example, the inclusion in the model of commercial banks tightly controlled by the Federal Reserve through a strictly observed reserve requirements ratio could explain shifts in the $r^* = 0$ locus because in that case changes in the supply of outside money would imply parametric (exogenous) changes in the demand for bonds (supply of loanable funds) by the commercial banks. If left by itself, however, the system may not stabilize at the full employment and price stability point. If there are inconsistencies to begin with, these inconsistencies may not be resolved, in the sense that the markets will not clear in the absence of outside intervention.

There is a sense in which the existence of these inconsistencies becomes meaningless. This happens when we assume that the inconsistencies are resolved instantaneously, as if in our model the speeds of adjustment are infinite. Thus, the basic characteristic of

Patinkin's equilibrium-type macro model[9] is that the labor market adjusts instantaneously, so that the system is always at full employment, or $w = w_f$ always. In this case, the adjustment mechanisms become

$$r^* = \lambda_B E_B(w_f, r)$$
$$P^* = \lambda_y E_y(w_f, r). \quad (53)$$

But since the influence of the price level is only through the real wage, the instantaneous adjustment in the nominal wage means that the real wage is fixed at w_f, so that the interest rate is the only "price" variable that remains to be determined. Thus, (53) collapses in

$$r^* = \lambda_B \cdot E_B(w_f, r). \quad (54)$$

But then we know that bonds (loanable funds) market equilibrium may not imply equilibrium in the output market as well. The excess demand for output is (for the $Y^d > Y^s$ case at least) included in the excess demand for loanable funds. This brings the analysis to the full employment Wicksellian loanable funds analysis, where the price stability condition can only be defined in a formal sense as

$$r^* = \lambda_B \cdot E_B(w_f, r_e) = 0$$
$$P^* = \lambda_y E_y(w_f, r_n) = 0 \quad (55)$$
$$r_e = r_n.$$

In the absence of further refinements in such a loanable funds formulation, there is nothing to guarantee that the loans market equilibrium interest rate (r_e) will be equal to the price stability natural interest rate (r_n). By fixing the real wage, we have severely limited the ability of the system to adjust in the presence of any given inconsistencies. Thus, system (53) is just a particular case of our more general formulation.

IV. THE REAL BALANCE EFFECT

We shall here amend the model of the previous sections by introducing a real balance effect in the consumption (and thus the saving) function. In this way the price level

9. Patinkin, op. cit.

has an independent effect of its own, apart from its influence on the real wage rate. In this way the endogenously determined "price" variables are now three: the nominal wage, the price level, and the interest rate. Although we continue to assume that

$$Y^a = C + S, \qquad (56)$$

the modified consumption and savings functions are now

$$C = C\left(\frac{W}{P}, \frac{M}{P}\right), \quad c_1 \gtrless 0 \text{ as } w \lessgtr w_f, c_2 > 0 \qquad (57)$$

$$S = S\left(\frac{W}{P}, \frac{M}{P}\right), \quad s_1 \gtrless 0 \text{ as } w \lessgtr w_f, s_2 < 0, \qquad (58)$$

where M is the fixed quantity of money. Thus, the excess demand for output can be formulated in the following way: If $Y^d > Y^s$, $Y^a = Y^s$, and so

$$E_y = Y^d - Y^s = I + C - Y^*$$
$$= I(r) - S\left(\frac{W}{P}, \frac{M}{P}\right) = E_y(W, P, r). \qquad (59)$$

If $Y^d < Y^s$, $Y^a = Y^d$, and so

$$E_y = Y^d - Y^s = I(r) + C\left(\frac{W}{P}, \frac{M}{P}\right) - f\left(\frac{W}{P}\right)$$
$$= E_y(W, P, r). \qquad (60)$$

For the net excess supply of bonds, we now have the following possibilities:

If $Y^d > Y^s$, $Y^a = Y^s$, and so

$$E_B = B^s - B^d = I(r) - S\left(\frac{W}{P}, \frac{M}{P}\right) + l\left(\frac{W}{P}, r\right)$$
$$= E_B(W, P, r). \qquad (61)$$

If $Y^d < Y^s$, $Y^a = Y^d$, so that from (56) $C + I = Y^d = Y^a$ or $Y^d - C = S = I$, and

$$E_B = B^s - B^d = I(r) - I(r) + l\left(\frac{W}{P}, r\right)$$
$$= l\left(\frac{W}{P}, r\right) = E_B(W, P, r). \qquad (62)$$

Then the adjustment mechanisms in this model, which includes the real balance effect in consumption (saving), will be

$$W^* = \lambda_N \cdot E_N(W, P)$$
$$P^* = \lambda_y \cdot E_y(W, P, r) \qquad (63)$$
$$r^* = \lambda_B \cdot E_B(W, P, r).$$

The short-run equilibrium is defined as the set of (W^e, P^e, r^e) such that

$$W^* = P^* = r^* = 0. \qquad (64)$$

It is obvious that such an equilibrium will not be a quasi-equilibrium but instead a full equilibrium with all the markets cleared. This reflects the theoretical importance of the real balance effect in establishing a full-employment and price stability short-run equilibrium in the context of an aggregate model. The original presentation of this result came first from Pigou and then from Patinkin. The existence of an inconsistency among planned savings and planned investment, such that planned savings are greater than planned investment at any positive interest rate, can be resolved through the real balance effect on savings (consumption). This result was strongly emphasized by Patinkin when he said that "there always exists a price decline such that its effect is stimulatory," and therefore "there always exists a sufficiently low price level such that full employment is generated."[10] Although there exists enough ambiguity concerning the empirical strength of the real balance effect, Patinkin built his general macroeconomic model on the basis of that assumption, in such a way that the short-run equilibrium that comes out of the structure of his model is a full-employment and price stability position. Then, unemployment and persistent price changes cannot be situations of quasi-equilibrium, but instead mere disequilibrium situations, temporary phenomena during the process towards the full market clearance equilibrium. The fact is,

10. D. Patinkin, "Price Flexibility and Full Employment," in F. Lutz and L. Mints, eds., *Readings in Monetary Theory* (Homewood, Ill. Irwin, 1951), 252–83, esp. p. 262.

however, that Patinkin was also able to establish that this equilibrium is also stable. But Patinkin, except for the brief and incomplete discussion in his Chapter 13,[11] does not in effect allow disequilibrium situations to exist. As it will be shown very shortly, his proof of the stability of equilibrium is due to a very simplifying assumption. In general, the stability of the short-run equilibrium in our model where disequilibrium situations are allowed for, in the fundamental sense that production and exchange take place at them, can be examined if we linearize the system around its equilibrium solutions and form the matrix of the coefficients of the linearized system. The coefficients are the following:

$$E_{YW} = \begin{cases} -\dfrac{S_1}{P} \lessgtr 0 \text{ as } w \lessgtr w_f \ (Y^d > Y^s), \\ \\ \dfrac{1}{P}(C_1 - f') \lessgtr 0 \text{ as } w \lessgtr w_f \\ \\ \quad (Y^d < Y^s), |C_1| < |f'| \end{cases} \tag{65}$$

$$E_{YP} = \begin{cases} \dfrac{1}{P^2}(S_1 W + S_2 M) \gtrless 0 \text{ as } w \lessgtr w_f \\ \\ \quad (Y^d > Y^s), |S_1| > |S_2| \\ \\ -\dfrac{1}{P^2}(C_1 W + C_2 M - f'W) \gtrless 0 \\ \\ \quad \text{as } w \lessgtr w_f \ (Y^d < Y^s) \end{cases} \tag{66}$$

$$E_{Yr} = I' < 0 \tag{67}$$

$$E_{BW} = \begin{cases} -\dfrac{1}{P}(S_1 + l_1) \lessgtr 0 \text{ as } w \lessgtr w_f \\ \\ \quad (Y^d > Y^s), |S_1| > |l_1| \\ \\ \dfrac{l_1}{P} \gtrless 0 \text{ as } w \lessgtr w_f \ (Y^d < Y^s) \end{cases} \tag{68}$$

$$E_{BP} = \begin{cases} \dfrac{1}{P^2}(S_1 W + S_2 M - l_1 W) \gtrless 0 \text{ as } w \lessgtr w_f \\ \\ \quad (Y^d > Y^s), |S_1| > |S_2| + |l_1| \\ \\ -\dfrac{l_1 W}{P^2} \lessgtr 0 \text{ as } w \lessgtr w_f \ (Y^d < Y^s) \end{cases} \tag{69}$$

$$E_{Br} = \begin{cases} I' - l_2 < 0 \ (Y^d > Y^s), \\ \\ \quad\quad\quad |I'| > |l_2| \\ \\ l_2 < 0 \ (Y^d < Y^s) \end{cases} \tag{70}$$

$$E_{NW} = \frac{1}{P}(h' - j') < 0; \tag{71}$$

$$E_{NP} = -\frac{W}{P^2}(h' - j') > 0; \tag{72}$$

$$E_{Nr} = 0. \tag{73}$$

Then, the matrix of the coefficients is

$$A = \begin{bmatrix} E_{NW} & E_{Nr} & E_{NP} \\ E_{YW} & E_{Yr} & E_{YP} \\ E_{BW} & E_{Br} & E_{BP} \end{bmatrix}. \tag{74}$$

The short-run equilibrium is stable only if the following conditions are satisfied:

$$a_1 = [-\text{trace of } A] > 0$$

$$a_2 = \begin{bmatrix} \text{sum of the second-order} \\ \text{principal minors} \end{bmatrix} > 0 \tag{75}$$

$$a_3 = [-\text{determinant of } A] > 0$$

$$(a_1 a_2 - a_3) > 0.$$

In view of the difficulty in specifying the sign of many of the coefficients (65)–(73) and also in view of the fact that here again the nature of the adjustment process depends crucially on whether the disequilibrium position is a point where $Y^d > Y^s$ or $Y^d < Y^s$, we cannot a priori know whether the stability conditions (75) are satisfied or not. Furthermore, we are also uncertain about the existence and the uniqueness of the short-run equilibrium. This ambiguity is, of course, due to the nontâtonnement assumption, i.e., to the disequilibrium nature of the model. This model is essentially the same as Patinkin's[12] macro model, but under the nontâtonnement assumption. By comparing the two models, we see therefore that although Patinkin's

---

11. Patinkin, *Money, Interest, and Prices.*

12. Ibid.

tâtonnement model has a stable equilibrium and all sorts of nice properties, the same model but without the tâtonnement assumption has an uncertain stability and, in general, its simplicity is destroyed.

In his book Patinkin,[13] does not examine the stability of his model by analyzing simultaneously the three markets that we see here, although his model contains a labor market. The reason is that a mathematical treatment of the stability conditions with all three markets is not needed because he assumes that the labor market is always cleared. Indeed, if nominal wages adjust with an infinite speed, then the level of labor employment is always at the full employment level, so that the real wage rate is essentially fixed at w_f. If, in other words,

$$h(w_f) \equiv j(w_f) = N_f, \qquad (76)$$

then the supply of output is fixed through the production function at the full employment level (Y_0). By assuming an infinite speed of adjustment in the labor market, we assume away a lot of potential inconsistencies in the model, and the system's adjustment mechanisms are reduced to the adjustment of the interest rate and the price level only. Furthermore, since the equilibrium position is such that $Y^d = Y^s = Y_0$, Patinkin uses Y_0 in his consumption (saving) function and the demand for money as an asset function. We can thus have the following system:

$$0 \equiv h\left(\frac{W}{P}\right) - j\left(\frac{W}{P}\right) = E_1 \qquad (77)$$

$$r^* = \lambda_B\left[I(r) - S\left(Y_0, \frac{M}{P}\right) + l(Y_0, r)\right] = E_2 \qquad (78)$$

$$P^* = \lambda_y\left[I(r) - S\left(Y_0, \frac{M}{P}\right)\right] = E_3, \qquad (79)$$

and the short-run equilibrium is now defined as

$$r^* = P^* = 0. \qquad (80)$$

13. Ibid.

Patinkin has examined the stability of such a system,[14] which is essentially a tâtonnement model. The biggest source of inconsistencies in a nontâtonnement model is that current spending is limited and depends on current realized disposable income, but this is eliminated by the assumption that the labor market is always cleared. It is not surprising, then, that such a model does not have an ambiguous answer to the question of stability of the short-run equilibrium. Now, the matrix of the coefficients is

$$\begin{bmatrix} \frac{1}{P}(h'-j') & 0 & -\frac{W}{P^2}(h'-j') \\ 0 & \lambda_B(I'+l_2) & \lambda_B\frac{M}{P^2}S_2 \\ 0 & \lambda_y I' & \lambda_y\frac{M}{P^2}S_2 \end{bmatrix} = A',$$

$$(81)$$

so that the stability conditions (75) are now satisfied because

$$-a_1 = \frac{1}{P}(h'-j') + \lambda_B(I'+l_2) + \frac{\lambda_y M}{P^2}S_2 < 0; \qquad (82)$$

$$a_2 = \frac{1}{P}(h'-j')\left[\lambda_B(I'+l_2) + \frac{\lambda_y M}{P^2}\cdot S_2\right] + \left(\lambda_y\lambda_B\frac{M}{P^2}\right)S_2 l_2 > 0; \qquad (83)$$

$$a_3 = \frac{1}{P}(h'-j')\left(\lambda_y\lambda_B\frac{M}{P^2}S_2 l_2\right) < 0; \qquad (84)$$

and it can also easily be established that

$$(a_1 a_2 - a_3) > 0. \qquad (85)$$

We see, therefore, that starting from a general model with three markets adjusting at finite speeds and, as a consequence, with disposable income as a variable, if we impose the assumption that the labor market alone adjusts at an infinite speed, we fix disposable income at the

14. D. Patinkin, "Keynesian Economics and the Quantity Theory," in K. Kurihara, ed., *Post-Keynesian Economics* (New Brunswick, N.J.: Rutgers University Press), 1954), 123–52, esp. pp. 151–52.

full employment level, exactly as Patinkin does in his equilibrium model. As a result, we transform the original model, with an uncertain stability of the short-run equilibrium, into a model whose stability of the short-run equilibrium is certain. The mere comparison of the two models reveals how crucial is the assumption that the labor market is always cleared. It is an assumption that greatly simplifies the analysis and permits the establishment of easier conclusions. We thus conclude that Patinkin's equilibrium-type model is a special and simple case of a generalized disequilibrium-type model.

Monetary growth theory is concerned with the influence of money on the rate of growth and the steady-state characteristics of a growing economy. Following the path-breaking analyses of R. Harrod and E. Domar, who extended the Keynesian theory to a growing economy, most of the economic growth models either ignored or underestimated the role and importance of monetary factors in the growth process. Only the rate of interest was occasionally discussed, to the extent that it—together with the state of long-term expectations or the entrepreneurs' "animal spirits"—affected planned investment decisions. The role of monetary policy in such a "Keynesian" framework, as represented by Harrod and Joan Robinson, was bound to be limited, either because investment was interest-inelastic or because of the presupposition of a liquidity trap.

On the other hand, the impact of R. Solow's model heralded a genuine neoclassical revival, leading to a great variety of growth models based upon the assumption that the rate of capital accumulation is fundamentally deter-mined by the propensity to save. Needless to say, the postulated identity between ex ante savings and investment constitutes a denial of the most interesting questions raised by Keynes in macroeconomic theory, as well as of the knife-edge cyclically unstable properties of Harrod–Hicks-type of macrodynamic models.[1]

The origin of monetary growth theory can be found in the specification of those short-run macroeconomic models which stressed the implications of the so-called "Pigou effect" on the execution of monetary policy. Lloyd Metzler[2] demonstrated, in a two-asset model, that if wealth affects savings, the monetary authority by affecting the stock of net private wealth may affect the rate of interest and thereby the rate of economic growth. Tobin[3] generalized Metzler's wealth effect into a theory of portfolio balance, in which the rate of interest equates the public's desire to hold monetary and nonmonetary wealth with the existing stocks of monetary and nonmonetary wealth. As a consequence,

PART FIVE
Monetary Growth Models

[1] R. Eisner, "On Growth Models and the Neoclassical Resurgence," *Economic Journal*, 68:707–721 (1958).

[2] L. Metzler, "Wealth, Saving, and the Rate of Interest," *Journal of Political Economy*, 59:93–116 (1951). Reprinted in R. Thorn, (ed.), *Monetary Theory and Policy*, rev. ed (New York: Praeger, 1976).

[3] J. Tobin, "A Dynamic Aggregative Model," *Journal of Political Economy*, 63:103–115 (1955). Reprinted in R. Thorn, op. cit.

portfolio balance became the necessary and sufficient condition for price stability and macroeconomic equilibrium in general.

Tobin considers money to be an alternative asset or a partial substitute for real capital for the wealth-portfolio holders. It follows that part of total savings which might otherwise be channeled into capital formation can be absorbed by changes in cash balances. Since money and capital are competing assets in satisfying the public's desire for wealth, portfolio balance requires that their respective rates of return be equal. As a result a monetary growth model admits a variety of steady-state capital-labor ratios, since the rate of return on capital (equal to its marginal productivity in a neoclassical production model) has to adjust to the rate of return on money. This rate, in a steady state, is determined by the difference between the rate of growth of the money supply and what Harrod has labeled the natural rate of growth, that is, the economy's maximum feasible growth rate determined by population growth and technical progress. In the case of money being government debt, or "outside money," the monetary authority, by controlling its rate of growth, can thus affect the economy's steady-state properties.[4]

Retaining Tobin's basic assumptions, a whole class of "neoclassical" monetary growth models developed. Their common character, apart from the use of portfolio balance as the mechanism that may explain such a "non-neutrality of money in the long run," consisted by assuming the following: First, that money is strictly of the "outside" type. Second, that such money is injected in the economy by means of unspecified transfers, comparable to Patinkin's "manna from heaven." Third, that people suffer from a "money or wealth illusion"—in believing that their real wealth can be augmented by "paper manufactured by the government from thin air" (Tobin). In fact, neoclassical growth models invariably assume that savings depend on a measure of disposable income that includes capital gains or losses, such as (unanticipated?) changes in the real

value of the private sector's cash balances.[5] Finally, the neoclassical monetary growth models assume that all markets are always in equilibrium. This pervasive sense of equilibrium, expressed by the portfolio-balance requirement and the identity between planned savings and investment, not only eliminates Harrod's difficulties in achieving stable growth, but also is incapable of examining the question of unemployment in the longrun.

Opposed in many ways to the neoclassical approach were the so-called "Keynes-Wicksell" monetary growth models. Initially conceived as an extension in the long run of the IS-LM model, the Keynes-Wicksell models have the following distinguishing features: First, they postulate an independent investment function, ruling out the identity between planned savings and investment. Second, they rely on dynamic market adjustments in case of disequilibrium in order to trace out the effect of monetary factors on the growth process. At the steady state, ex post or realized investment and savings are equal, but capital accumulation may be financed both by planned and "forced" savings. These forced savings are the result of the inflationary consequences of disequilibrium created by a monetary disturbance. By partially frustrating planned consumption, these forced savings represent funds transferred to financing investment.

The excess of realized investment over planned savings reflects a macroeconomic disequilibrium. The market interest rate, determined by the equality between ex post savings and investment, will be below that interest rate which corresponds to the equality between ex ante savings and investment. This latter rate is what Wicksell has called the "natural rate of interest." When the market and the "natural" rates are equal, we have price stability. If, instead, the market rate is below the "natural" rate, we have what is known as the Wicksellian inflationary cumulative process, which generates "forced savings." The source of such a disequilibrium is an excessive money or credit creation, and the monetary authorities can employ this mechanism in order to raise the rate of capital accumulation. When the system finally converges to a new state, the

[4] A similar conclusion was reached in an earlier study by R. S. Thorn, "Long-Run Adjustments to changes in the Capital-Output Ratio and the National Debt," *Yale Economic Essays*, 3:247–299 (1962). See pp. 298–299.

[5] K. Shell, M. Sidrauski, and J. Stiglitz, "Capital Gains, Income, and Saving," *Review of Economic Studies*, 36:15–26 (1969).

capital-labor ratio will be higher than it initially was, due to the diminishing marginal productivity of capital.

In the Keynes-Wicksell models the issue of the nonneutrality of money in the long run is examined in terms of a concrete transmission of monetary diturbances via the loanable funds market. In that respect the Keynes-Wicksell approach has some advantages over the neoclassical approach. First, by admitting the possibility of disequilibrium, it can analyze the problem of unemployment in the long run. Second, the analysis can include both "outside" and "inside" money. Third, the Keynes-Wicksell approach can be reconciled with several traditional business cycle theories.

Concerning both the neoclassical and the Keynes-Wicksell models, it has been asked exactly what are the implied short-run dynamics of the analysis and the stability conditions of the steady-state equilibrium.[6] Several economists have attempted a synthesis of the two approaches,[7] while others maintain that monetary growth theory, in general, has been unsuccessful in capturing the fundamental role of money and finance in the process of economic growth.[8] This criticism points to the fact that most models have not examined the role of financial intermediaries in the process of economic growth, although it is evident that the issue of the nonneutrality of money in the long run has to be analyzed by taking into account the behavior of both the monetary authorities and the financial intermediaries.[9]

Finally, monetary growth has provided a new analytical framework for, and raised some new issues relating to, the discussion of the optimal rate of monetary expansion and the effectiveness of stabilization policies.[10]

The core of the neoclassical monetary growth theory, that is, the notion of portfolio balance and its implied assumption that money and real capital are substitutes as assets, has been recently criticized by Shaw and McKinnon. Based on observations concerning less-developed economies, these authors believe that any positive correlation among the propensity to save, stocks of monetary assets, and rates of growth necessitates a reconstruction of monetary growth theory along lines that view money and real capital as complements rather than substitutes.[11]

It may be argued that even in the neoclassical framework the substitutability between these two assets cannot exceed certain limits. The economy cannot operate with a very large capital stock and extremely low cash balances, and vice versa. By further restricting, or even eliminating, the possibility of substituting money for real capital, we are effectively down-playing their role as assets, and instead the emphasis is put on the role of money (and finance) as a medium of transactions and of deferred payments. The assumption that money and capital are complements rather than substitutes may be a realistic one not only for less-developed economies, but also perhaps for industrialized economies with insufficiently developed capital markets, where the financing of investment relies heavily on bank credit extensions. The futher formalization and extension of this approach appears to be a promising direction of future research, together with the need to see the empirical relevance of monetary growth theory as a whole.

[6] M. Hadjimichalakis, "Equilibrium and Disequilibrium Growth with Money—The Tobin Models," *Review of Economic Studies*, 38:457–479 (1971); D. Purvis, "Short-Run Dynamics in Models of Money and Growth," *American Economic Review*, 63:12–23 (1973).

[7] J. Stein, "*Money and Capacity Growth* (New York: Columbia University Press, 1971); S. Fischer, "Keynes-Wicksell and Neoclassical Models of Money and Growth," *American Economic Review*, 62:880–890 (1972); W. Ethier, "Financial Assets and Economic Growth in a 'Keynesian' Economy," *Journal of Money, Credit, and Banking*, 7:215–233 (1975).

[8] P. Davidson, "Money, Portfolio Balance, Capital Accumulation, and Economic Growth," *Econometrica*, 36:291–321 (1968); G. Pierson, "The Role of Money in Economy Growth," *Quarterly Journal of Economics*, 86:383–395 (1972).

[9] F. Takahashi, "Money Supply and Economic Growth," *Econometrica*, 39:285–303 (1971); P. Korliras, "A Model of Money, Credit, and Economic Growth," *Kyklos*, 27:757–776 (1974).

[10] P. Diamond, "National Debt In a Neoclassical Growth Model," *American Economic Review*, 55:1126–1150 (1965); J. Tobin, "Notes on Optimal Monetary Growth," *Journal of Political Economy*, 76:833–859 (1968); S. C. Tsiang, "A Critical Note on the Optimum Supply of Money," *Journal of Money, Credit, and Banking*, 1:266–280 (1969).

[11] E. Shaw, "Financial Deepening in Economic Development (New York: Oxford University Press, 1973); R. McKinnon, *Money and Capital in Economic Development* (Washington, D.C.: Brookings Institution, 1973).

Money and Economic Growth[1]

James Tobin

Yale University

Reprinted from *Econometrica*, 33:671–684 (1965), by permission of the author and the publisher (copyright by the Econometric Society).

[1] The Fisher Lecture presented at the Joint European Conference of the Econometric Society and The Institute of Management Sciences in Zurich, September 11, 1964.

In nonmonetary neoclassical growth models, the equilibrium degree of capital intensity and correspondingly the equilibrium marginal productivity of capital and rate of interest are determined by "productivity and thrift," i.e., by technology and saving behavior. Keynesian difficulties, associated with divergence between warranted and natural rates of growth, arise when capital intensity is limited by the unwillingness of investors to acquire capital at unattractively low rates of return. But why should the community wish to save when rates of return are too unattractive to invest? This can be rationalized only if there are stores of value other than capital, with whose rates of return the marginal productivity of capital must compete. The paper considers monetary debt of the government as one alternative store of value and shows how enough saving may be channeled into this form to bring the warranted rate of growth of capital down to the natural rate. Equilibrium capital intensity and interest rates are then determined by portfolio behavior and monetary factors as well as saving behavior and technology. In such an equilibrium, the real monetary debt grows at the natural rate also, either by deficit spending or by deflation. The stability of the equilibrium is also considered.

1. The purpose of this paper is to discuss the rôles of monetary factors in determining the degree of capital intensity of an economy. The models I shall use in discussing this question are both aggregative and primitive. But I believe they serve to illuminate the basic points I wish to make. At any rate, I have taken the designation of this talk as a "lecture" as a license to emphasize exposition rather than novelty and sophistication. And my subject falls naturally and appropriately in the tradition of Irving Fisher of my own university.

Fisher and Keynes, among others, have drawn the useful and fruitful analytical distinction between choices affecting the disposition of income and choices affecting the disposition of wealth. The first set of choices determines how much is saved rather than consumed and how much wealth is accumulated. The second set determines in what forms savers hold their savings, old as well as new. Considerable economic discussion and controversy have concerned the respective rôles of these two kinds of behavior, and their interactions, in determining the rate of interest.

2. Most models of economic growth are nonmonetary. They offer no place for significant choices of the second kind—portfolio choices. They admit only one type of asset that can serve wealth owners as a store of value, namely reproducible capital. It is true

that some of these models, particularly dis-aggregated variants, may allow savers and owners of wealth to choose between different kinds or vintages of capital. But this is the only scope for portfolio choice they are permitted. Different questions arise when monetary assets are available to compete with ownership of real goods. I shall proceed by reviewing how the intensity and yield of capital are determined in a typical aggregative nonmonetary model of economic growth, and then indicating how their determination is modified by introducing monetary assets into the model.

3. In a nonmonetary model of growth and capital accumulation, so long as saving continues it necessarily takes the form of real investment. And so long as saving and investment augment the capital stock faster than the effective supplies of other factors are growing, nothing prevents the yields on capital investment from being driven to zero or below. Of course, low or negative yields may cause people to reduce or discontinue

their saving or even to consume capital. This classical reaction of saving to the interest rate may help to set an upper limit to capital deepening and a lower bound to the rate of return on capital. But clearly this kind of brake on investment causes no problems of underemployment and insufficiency of aggregate demand. Increased consumption automatically replaces investment.

4. I can illustrate in Figure 1 the manner in which saving behavior determines capital intensity and the rate of interest in a non-monetary growth model. (For the basic construction of the diagram I am indebted to my Yale colleague, John Fei, but he is not responsible for my present use of it.)

In Figure 1 the horizontal axis measures capital intensity k, the quantity of capital (measured in physical units of output) per effective manhour of labor. The significance of the term "effective" is to allow for improvements in the quality of labor inputs due to "labor-augmenting" technological progress. Thus, if a 1964 manhour is equivalent

FIGURE 1

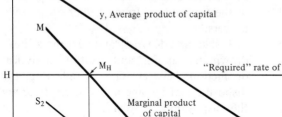

as input in the production function to two manhours in the base period, say 1930, then k measures the amount of capital per man half-hour 1964 or per manhour 1930.

The vertical axis measures various annual rates. Curve AA' represents y, the average annual product of capital. Since output and capital are measured in the same physical units, this variable has the dimension, pure number per year. It is the reciprocal of the famous capital-output ratio. In accordance with usual assumptions about the production function, y is shown to decline as capital intensity k becomes deeper.

Curve MM' represents the corresponding marginal product of capital. In Figure 1 this becomes zero or negative for sufficiently intense use of capital. There are, of course, some technologies—Cobb-Douglas, for example—in which this cannot occur.

For present purposes it will be convenient to regard the average product y, shown by AA', and the corresponding marginal product of capital MM', as referring to output net of depreciation. If depreciation is a constant proportion δ of the capital stock, the average gross product of capital would simply be $y + \delta$, and the marginal gross product would likewise be uniformly higher than MM' by the constant δ.

Even after this allowance for depreciation, the yield on durable capital relevant to an investment-saving decision is not always identical with the marginal product of capital at the time of the decision. The two will be identical if the marginal product is expected to remain constant over the lifetime of the new capital. But if it is expected to change because of future innovations or because of future capital deepening or capital "shallowing" in the economy, the relevant marginal efficiency of current new investment is a weighted average of future marginal products. I shall, however, ignore this distinction in what follows and use the marginal product in Figure 1 as at least an indicator of the true rate of return on capital. For the most part I shall be concerned with equilibrium situations where the two are stationary and therefore identical.

A curve like $S_1 S_1'$ reflects saving behavior. It tells the amount of net saving and investment per year, per unit of the existing capital stock. Therefore it tells how fast the capital stock is growing. In Harrod's terminology, this is the "warranted rate of growth" of the capital stock. The particular curve $S_1 S_1'$ is drawn so that its height is always the same proportion of the height of $A_1 A_1'$. This represents the common assumption that net saving is proportional to net output.

The effective labor force, in manhours, is assumed to grow at a constant rate n, independent of the degree of capital intensity. The "natural rate of growth" n depends on the natural increase in the labor force and on the advance of labor-augmenting technology. This conventional growth-model assumption is indicated in Figure 1 by the horizontal line NN'.

5. So much for the mechanics of Figure 1. Now what determines the development and ultimate equilibrium value, if any, of capital intensity? A rate of growth of capital equal to n will just keep intensity constant. If the "warranted" rate of growth of capital exceeds the "natural" rate of growth of labor n, then capital deepening will occur. If capital grows more slowly than labor, k will decline. These facts are indicated in the diagram by the arrows in curve $S_1 S_1'$. With the saving behavior assumed in $S_1 S_1'$, the equilibrium capital intensity is k_1. The corresponding stationary marginal product is M_1. To emphasize the point suggested above, M_1 in the diagram is negative.

A different kind of saving behavior is depicted by $S_2 S_2'$. Here the ratio of net investment to output declines with k. This decline could be the result of one or both of two factors which have played a rôle in the theory of saving. One factor is that capital deepening lowers the yield on saving and therefore increases the propensity to consume. The other is that capital deepening implies an increase in wealth relative to current income; according to some theories of consumption, this should diminish the saving ratio quite apart from any accompanying decline in the rate of return. With saving behavior S_2S_2', the ultimate equilibrium has a capital intensity k_2 and a marginal product M_2.

6. The theory of interest sketched in Section 5 is classical. The rate of return on capital, in long-run equilibrium, is the result of the interaction of "productivity" and "thrift," or of technology and time preference. To dramatize the conflict of this theory and monetary theories of interest, I shall begin with an extreme case—so extreme that the crucial monetary factor is not even specified explicitly.

Some growth models assume a lower limit on the marginal product of capital of quite a different kind from the limit that thrift imposed in Section 5. Harrod, for example, argues that investors will simply not undertake new investment unless they expect to receive a certain minimum rate of return. Savers, on the other hand, are not discouraged from trying to save when yields fall to or below this minimum. The result is an impasse which leads to Keynesian difficulties of deficient demand and unemployment. In Harrod's model these difficulties arise when the warranted rate of growth at the minimum required rate of profit exceeds the natural rate. The rate of saving from full employment output would cause capital to accumulate faster than the labor force is growing. Consequently, the marginal product of capital would fall and push the rate of return on investment below the required minimum.

In Figure 1, suppose HH to be the required minimum. Then, correspondingly, k_H is the maximum capital intensity investors will tolerate. Yet the saving behavior depicted in the diagram would, if it were actually realized, push marginal product toward M_1 and capital intensity toward k_1, given saving behavior S_1S_1' (or M_2 and k_2, given saving behavior S_2S_2'). It is this excess of ex ante S over I which gives rise to the Keynesian difficulties.

The opposite problem would arise if there were a *maximum* return on investment *below* the equilibrium return (M_1 or M_2) to which saving behavior by itself would lead. At this maximum, the warranted rate of growth would fall short of the natural rate. So long as actual yields on investment exceeded the critical maximum, investment demand would be indefinitely large. In any event it would exceed saving.

The consequences of this impasse in Harrod's model are less clear than the events that follow the deflationary or Keynesian impasse. At this stage the two cases lose their symmetry, though it is possible for output to fall short of the technologically feasible, when *ex ante* investment is less than *ex ante* saving, it is not possible for output to surpass its technological limits in the opposite case. Presumably an excess of *ex ante* investment is an "inflationary gap," and its main consequence is a price inflation which somehow—for example, through forced saving—eliminates the discrepancy. But this only makes the point that monetary assets had better be introduced explicitly. For it is scarcely possible to talk about inflation in a nonmonetary model where there is no price level to inflate.

7. I have spoken of Harrod's model, but I have the impression that the concept of a required rate of profit plays a key rôle in other theories of growth, notably those of Mrs. Robinson and Mr. Kaldor. Indeed I understand one of the key characteristics of their models—one of the reasons their authors consider them "Keynesian" growth models in distinction to classical models of the type sketched in Section 5 above—is that they separate the investment decision from saving behavior.

A minimal rate of return on capital (a required rate of profit) cannot exist in a vacuum, however. It must reflect the competition of other channels for the placement of saving. For a small open economy, a controlling competitive rate might be set by the yield available on investment abroad. This would, however, leave unexplained the existence of such a limit for a closed economy, whether a national economy or the world as a whole. In any case the growth models under discussion are closed economy models.

In a closed economy clearly the important alternative stores of value are monetary assets. It is their yields which set limits on the acceptable rates of return on real capital and on the acceptable degree of capital intensity. To understand these limits, both how they are determined and how they may be altered, it is necessary to introduce monetary assets into the model explicitly. It is necessary to examine the choices of savers and wealth owners between these assets and real capital. I continue, I remind you, to make the useful distinction between saving-consumption choices, on the one hand, and portfolio choices on the other. The choices I am about to discuss are portfolio choices; that is, they concern the forms of saving and wealth rather than their total amounts.

8. The simplest way to introduce monetary factors is to imagine that there is a single monetary asset with the following properties:

(a) It is supplied only by the central government. This means that it represents neither a commodity produced by the economy nor the debts of private individuals or institutions.

(b) It is the means of payment, the medium of exchange, of the economy. And it is a store of value by reason of its general acceptability in the discharge of public and private transactions.

(c) Its own-yield (i.e., the amount of the asset that is earned by holding a unit of the asset a given period of time) is arbitrarily fixed by the government. This may, of course, be zero but is not necessarily so.

Furthermore, it will be convenient for expository reasons to introduce money in two stages, avoiding in the first stage the complications of a variable value of money, a variable price level. Suppose, to begin with, that the value of money in terms of goods is fixed. The community's wealth now has two components: the real goods accumulated through past real investment and fiduciary or paper "goods" manufactured by the government from thin air. Of course the nonhuman wealth of such a nation "really" consists only of its tangible capital. But, as viewed by the inhabitants of the nation individually, wealth exceeds the tangible capital stock by the size of what we might term the fiduciary issue. This is an illusion, but only one of the many fallacies of composition which are basic to any economy or any society. The illusion can be maintained unimpaired so long as the society does not actually try to convert all of its paper wealth into goods.

9. The simplest kind of two-asset portfolio behavior is the following: If the yields of the two assets differ, wealth owners will wish to place all of their wealth in the asset with the higher yield. If they are the same, wealth owners do not care in what proportions they divide their wealth between the two assets. Evidently, if there are positive supplies of both assets, they can be willingly held in portfolios only if the two yields are equal. On this assumption about portfolio behavior, it is easy to see how the institutionally determined rate of interest on money controls the yield of capital. In particular, it is this rate of interest which is the minimal rate of profit that leads to the deflationary impasse discussed in Section 6 above.

At the same time, we can see two ways in which government policy can avoid this impasse. Returning to Figure 1, suppose that HH is the yield on money and therefore the minimal yield acceptable to owners of capital. The corresponding capital intensity is k_H. One measure the government could take is to reduce the yield on money, say to M_1. Such a reduction might—and in Figure 1 it does—entail a negative rate of interest on money, reminiscent of the "stamped money" proposals of Silvio Gesell. Manipulation of interest rates on monetary assets within more normal limits is, in more realistically complex models, accomplished by the usual instruments of central banking.

Alternatively, the government could channel part of the community's excessive thrift into increased holdings of money. Thus, let us now interpret S_1S_1' to measure the amount by which the public wishes to increase its total wealth relative to its existing holdings of capital. This leads to the Harrod impasse if all the saving must take the form of capital.

But if only part of it goes into capital accumulation, if in particular the rate of increase of the capital stock can be lowered to S_3S_3', then all will be well. Equilibrium capital intensity will be k_H, consistent with maintaining the marginal product of capital at the required level HH. This can be done if the government provides new money to absorb the saving represented by the difference between S_1S_1' and S_3S_3'.

The only way for the government to achieve this is continuously to run a deficit financed by issue of new money. The deficit must be of the proper size, as can be illustrated by Figure 2. Here saving is measured vertically, and output and income horizontally. Both are measured in proportion to the capital stock, as in Figure 1. y_H is the output per unit of capital corresponding to the required equilibrium capital intensity k^H. Government purchases of goods and services are assumed to be a fraction g of output. Consequently, $y_H(1 - g)$ is output available for private use, and if the budget is balanced it is also the disposable income of the population. Taking S_1S_1' as the function relating saving to disposable income, S_H is the amount of private saving, (relative to the capital stock) when the budget is balanced. By assumption, however, this is too much investment—it causes the warranted rate to exceed the natural rate. Now n is the natural rate of growth; it is therefore the "right" amount of investment relative to the capital

stock. A deficit of d_H (per unit of capital) will do the trick. It increases disposable income to $y_H(1 - g) + d_H$, and this raises total saving to S_H'. But of this, d_H is acquisition of government debt, leaving only n for new tangible investment.

The arithmetic is simple enough: Since

$$S = s[\,y(1 - g) + d\,] = d + n, \qquad (1)$$

$$\frac{d}{y} = \frac{s(1 - g) - n/y}{1 - s} \quad \begin{array}{l}\text{gives the deficit as a}\\ \text{fraction of income.}\end{array} \quad (2)$$

On these assumptions about portfolio choice, the size of the government debt, here identical to the stock of money, does not matter. The deficit must absorb a certain proportion of income, as given in (2). But since wealth owners will hold money and capital in any proportions, provided their yields are in line, the size of the cumulated deficit is immaterial.

The opposite case would correspond to Harrod's inflationary impasse. Just as there is a deficit policy that will resolve the deflationary impasse, so there is a surplus policy that will remedy the opposite difficulty. In this case a balanced budget policy would leave the yield on capital so high that no one wants to hold money. To get the public to hold money it is necessary to increase capital intensity and lower the marginal product of capital. But a higher capital intensity takes more investment relative to output. To achieve a higher investment ratio, the resources that savers make available for capital formation must be supplemented by a government budget surplus. The mechanics of this can be seen by operating Figure 2 in reverse.

10. The portfolio behavior assumed in Section 9 is too simple. A more realistic assumption is that the community will hold the two assets in proportions that depend on their respective yields. There is a whole range of rate differentials at which positive supplies of both assets will be willingly held. But the greater the supply of money relative to that of capital, the higher the yield of money must

FIGURE 2

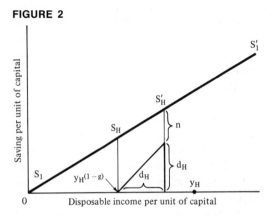

Saving per unit of capital

S_1'

S_H'

S_H

n

d_H

S_1

$y_H(1 - g)$

d_H

y_H

0   Disposable income per unit of capital

be relative to that on capital. I shall not review the explanations that have been offered for this kind of rate-sensitive portfolio diversification. One explanation runs in terms of risk-avoiding strategy where one or both yields are imperfectly predictable. Other explanations are associated with the specific functions of money as means of payment. Yield differentials must compensate for the costs of going back and forth between money and other assets. They must also offset the value of hedging against possible losses in case of unforeseen and exigent needs for cash.

The demand for money, presumably, depends also on income. Other things equal (i.e., asset yields and total wealth), more money will be required and less capital demanded the higher the level of output.

11. One implication of the assumption about portfolio behavior made in Section 10 can be stated very simply. Capital deepening in production requires monetary deepening in portfolios. If saving is so great that capital intensity is increasing, the yield on capital will fall. Given the yield on money, the stock of money per unit of capital must rise. Provided the government can engineer such an increase, capital deepening can proceed. There is a limit to this process, however. As in the previous cases discussed, there is an equilibrium capital intensity. Monetary deepening cannot push capital intensity beyond this equilibrium because the deficit spending required would leave too little saving available for capital formation.

In such an equilibrium, the shares of money and capital in total wealth must be constant so that their yields can remain constant. To maintain the fixed relation between the stocks, money and capital must grow at the same rate. That is, new saving must be divided between them in the same ratio as old saving.

Let $m(k, r)$ be the required amount of money per unit of capital when the capital intensity is k and the yield of money is r. We know that m is an increasing function of r: more money is demanded when its yield is higher. At the moment, we are taking r as fixed. I take m to be also an increasing function of k because an increase in k lowers the yield of capital. It is true that an increase in k also lowers y and therefore reduces the strict transactions demand for means of payment. But I assume the yield effects of variations in capital intensity to be the more powerful.

Let w (for "warranted") be the rate of growth of the capital stock, and let d represent, as before, the deficit per unit of existing capital. Then, constancy of amount of money per unit of capital at $m(k, r)$ requires that $d = m(k, r)w$. Assuming as before that saving is a constant proportion of disposable income, the basic identity is essentially the same as (1) above:

$$S = s(y(1 - g) + d) = d + w.$$

Using the fact that $d = m(k, r)w$, we have

$$w(k, r) = \frac{sy(k)(1 - g)}{1 + (1 - s)m(k, r)}. \tag{3}$$

In equilibrium $w = n$: the warranted and natural rates must be equal. The equilibrium degree of capital intensity is the value of k that equates $w(k, r)$ in (3) to n. I have written w and y in (3) as functions of k as a reminder that these variables, as well as m, depend directly or indirectly on capital intensity. Since y is a decreasing and m an increasing function of k, it is clear that w declines with k. Moreover, the amount by which w in (3) falls short of the hypothetical w for $m = 0$ $(sy(1 - g))$ increases with k.

This analysis may be presented diagrammatically, following the format of Figure 1. In Figure 3, $S_1 S_1'$ reflects, as before, the balanced budget $(d = 0)$ saving function, with saving a constant fraction of disposable income. This would be the warranted rate of growth of capital if m were zero. $W_1 W_2'$ represents for every capital intensity the warranted rate of growth of capital, assuming that the stock of money is adjusted to that capital intensity and maintained in that adjustment by deficit spending. The intersection of $W_1 W_2'$

with NN', the natural rate of growth, gives the equilibrium capital intensity k_1. As before, the equilibrium yield on capital is M', its marginal product at k_1. This yield, however, is not necessarily equal to the yield on money r.

The curve $W_1W'_2$ is drawn for a particular yield on money $\bar{r}_1$. Lowering the yield on money, say to $\bar{r}_2$, would shift the curve to the right, to $W_2W'_1$—increasing equilibrium capital intensity and lowering the equilibrium rate of return on capital.

12. I turn now to the more interesting and realistic case where the value of money in terms of goods is variable. Its variability has two important consequences. The real value of the monetary component of wealth is not under the direct control of the government but also depends on the price level. And the real return on a unit of money—a favorite concept of Fisher—consists not only of its own yield but also of the change in its real value.

Once again, we may ask whether there is an equilibrium capital intensity and, if so, how it is determined. The analysis of Section 11 tells us that there is an equilibrium capital intensity associated with a stable price level. But this requires a particular fiscal policy that maintains through deficit spending of the right magnitude just the right balance between stocks of money and capital. Now what happens when fiscal policy is determined independently so that a stable price level cannot necessarily be maintained?

In particular, suppose that a balanced budget policy is followed and the nominal stock of money remains constant. Real capital gains due to deflation play the same rôle as deficits did in Section 11. That is, they augment real disposable income and they absorb part of the propensity to save. Therefore, we can use the same apparatus as before, illustrated in Figure 3, to find the equilibrium capital intensity.

There is, however, one important difference. In the equilibrium the real stock of money must be increasing as fast as the capital stock, namely at the natural rate n. In the present instance this can happen only if the price level falls at rate n. If so, the real return on money r is not simply the nominal yield $\bar{r}$ but $\bar{r} + n$. Consequently the demand for money will be larger than if prices were

FIGURE 3

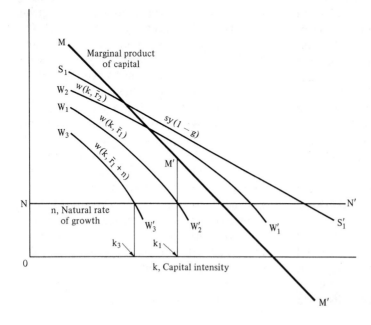

expected to remain stable. Equilibrium will require a greater stock of money per unit of capital and a lower capital intensity if deflation is substituted for money creation. This is indicated in Figure 3 where W_3W_3' is the curve corresponding to a yield on money n points higher than the yield behind W_1W_2'.

13. It is natural to ask whether there are symmetrical *equilibrium* situations in which a budget surplus or inflation is called for. The most obvious symmetrical case occurs when the natural rate of growth of the effective labor force is negative. But this is not a very interesting case of "growth."

The Harrod inflationary impasse, discussed above, would mean that at the hypothetical equilibrium capital intensity and rate of profit achievable when 100 per cent of saving goes into capital formation there is zero demand for money. Any money in existence, therefore, would have to be wiped out by surpluses or price increases; but these would be temporary rather than permanent.

One might, I suppose, imagine the public to desire a negative monetary position, i.e., to be net debtors to the government. Then there would be an equilibrium in which the public's net debt to the government grows in real value at the natural rate, thanks either to budget surpluses (with which the government acquires IOU's from its citizens) or to price inflation. In either case capital formation exceeds normal saving because the public saves extra either through taxes and the government budget or through the necessity to provide for the increased real burden of its debt to the government.

A negative monetary position is not as far-fetched as it sounds, if "money" is interpreted in a broad sense to connote the whole range of actual fixed-money-value assets, not just means of payment. It is quite possible, then, for the government to be a net creditor over this entire category of assets, while still providing a circulating medium of exchange.

14. So far only the existence of an equilibrium path of the kind described in Section 12 has been discussed. Its stability is something else again. I can only sketch the considerations involved.

What happens when the community is thrown out of portfolio balance either by some irregularity in technological progress, labor force growth, saving behavior, change in yield expectations, or portfolio preferences? If the result of the shock is that the public has too much capital and too little money for its tastes, goods prices will fall faster or rise more slowly than before. In the opposite case, the public will try to buy capital with money and will push prices up faster or retard their decline.

Evidently there are two effects, at war with each other. One we might call the Pigou effect, the other the Wicksell effect. The Pigou effect is stabilizing. Consider the case of a deflationary shock. The accelerated decline in prices, by augmenting the real value of existing money balances, helps to restore portfolio balance. Moreover, by increasing total real wealth it retards the flow of saving into capital formation. The Wicksell effect is destabilizing. An accelerated decline in prices means a more attractive yield on money and encourages a further shift in portfolio demand in the same direction as the original shock.

There is no *a priori* reason why one effect should be stronger than the other in the neighborhood of equilibrium. In the model under discussion, the Pigou effect will eventually win out, but only after what may be a prolonged period of deflation, zero or negative capital formation, and retarded growth.

Figure 4 concerns the question of stability. Here the vertical axis measures the rate of price deflation, $-\dot{p}/p$, and the horizontal axis the rate of capital accumulation, $\dot{K}/K$. On each axis the natural rate of growth n is shown. On the horizontal axis, a rate of capital accumulation larger than n means capital deepening and a decline in yield, while capital accumulation at a rate slower than n means the opposite. It is assumed that a balanced budget policy is being followed so that the nominal stock of money is constant. The real value of this stock increases at the

FIGURE 4

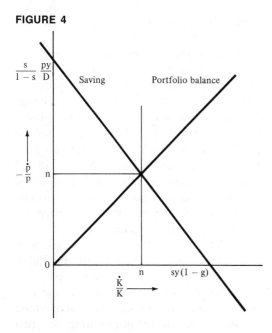

rate of deflation. It is, furthermore, assumed that existing real money balances and capital are in equilibrium; that is, their relative supplies are adjusted to the prevailing rate of profit on capital and to a real rate of return on money equal to n, the natural rate. The 45° line from the origin, labeled "portfolio balance," shows the combinations of price deflation and capital formation that will preserve portfolio balances at the existing rates of return. The negatively sloped line labeled "saving" shows the combination of $-\dot{p}/p$ and $\dot{K}/K$ that exhausts saving, assuming once again the saving behavior of Figure 2. The values of the intercepts on both axes are indicated. On the horizontal axis, $sy(1 - g)$ is the rate of capital growth if all saving goes into capital. On the vertical axis, $s/(1 - s) \cdot py/D$ (where D is the nominal stock of money per unit of capital) measures a rate of price deflation at which the entire propensity to save would be satisfied by capital gains on monetary assets. The "saving" line crosses the "portfolio balance" line at the point (n, n). This is another representation of the equilibrium of Section 12. At this point, new saving will be divided so as to maintain both portfolio balance and capital intensity.

But suppose the rate of deflation were to exceed n. The point describing the division of saving would move to the northeast along the saving line. This means that the yield on money is higher—too high for the initial portfolio balance. Portfolio behavior may not reflect this rise in yield at once, since it will take time for the new rate of deflation to register in expectations and for wealth owners to try to adjust to new expectations.

Meanwhile, the yield on capital will be rising because capital accumulation is falling short of the natural rate. Moreover, via the Pigou effect the price decline is increasing the stock of money relative to the stock of capital. These two effects take time and increase in strength with time. They tend to satisfy or offset the increased demand for money due to the rise in yield on money, but they may do so too little and too late. If so, the rate of deflation will increase even further, and the point describing the course of the economy moves even further northeast on the saving curve. But the further it moves and the longer this process goes on, the smaller becomes capital's share in wealth and the higher its yield. The stabilizing effects become stronger, destabilizing effects weaker. As the ratio of income to money stock (py/D) declines, the vertical intercept of the saving line moves down. That is, the rate of deflation that would divert all saving away from capital formation becomes smaller and smaller. So the yield on money declines, the yield on capital rises, while the relative supplies are moving in the opposite direction. Eventually the rate of deflation will fall to n again, and we know that this is compatible with balanced growth.

This mechanism contains some cyclical possibilities. The cycle would be one in prices and in the composition of output as between consumption and investment. More realistic is the familiar possibility which I do not consider here, i.e., that downward stickiness of money wages prevents or limits deflation and substitutes underproduction and underemployment. In that case, capital formation is shut off, not because saving is diverted into government deficits or into real capital gains on monetary assets but because saving is curtailed by reduction of income and employment. The interruption of capital formation and growth is qualitatively the same either way, but the real losses of welfare during the process are of course much greater when employment rather than prices bears the brunt of adjustment.

15. In classical theory, the interest rate and the capital intensity of the economy are determined by "productivity and thrift," that is, by the interaction of technology and saving propensities. This is true both in the short run, when capital is being accumulated at a rate different from the growth of the labor force, and in the long-run stationary or "moving stationary" equilibrium, when capital intensity is constant. Keynes gave reasons why in the short run monetary factors and portfolio decisions modify, and in some circumstances dominate, the determination of the interest rate and the process of capital accumulation. I have tried to show here that a similar proposition is true for the long run. The equilibrium interest rate and degree of capital intensity are in general affected by monetary supplies and portfolio behavior, as well as by technology and thrift.

Monetary Growth Theory in Perspective

Jerome L. Stein

Brown University

"The rivalry of scholars increases wisdom . . ." *Babylonian Talmud*

Monetary growth theory is concerned with the role of money in a growing economy. Money is a medium of exchange and store of value which may or may not be costless to produce, and which is a liability of either the government or a private banking system. Monetary policy is concerned with the management of these types of money. Several questions immediately arise. To what extent can financial policies and institutional arrangements affect the time profiles of the capital-labor ratio $k(t)$, the real wage $w(t)$, and the rent per unit of capital $r(t)$? It is obvious that the growth of a commodity money (e.g., gold) will affect the real variables in the system, because resources (labor, capital) are required for the production of gold. Can variations in the rate of growth of a type of money which is costless to produce affect the time profiles, and steady state solutions, of these real variables? Is there an optimum growth of the various types of money? What are the most desirable stabilization policies in a growing economy?[1] These are some of the central issues in monetary growth theory.

There are several different ways of analyzing the effects of monetary policy in a growing economy. First, why restrict the analysis to a money which is costless to produce? Jürg Niehans considered the case where some fraction of the stock of money consists of monetary gold. The opportunity cost of producing gold (or exports to purchase gold) is output which is no longer available for consumption and investment. The realism of this assumption is unquestionable and paves the way for a discussion of growth in an open economy which uses money.[2] Second, there is the neoclassical approach taken in the papers by James Tobin, David Levhari and Don Patinkin, Miguel Sidrauski, and Duncan Foley. They assume that: (a) the rate of capital formation is identically equal to planned savings, and (b) markets are always in equilibrium regardless of the rate of price change. Third, the Keynes-Wicksell approach, taken by Hugh Rose, Jerome Stein (1966, 1969), Keizo Nagatani, and Sho Chieh Tsiang assumes that: (a) prices are changing if, and only if, there is market disequilibrium and (b) there are independent savings and investment functions. During inflationary periods, when all demands cannot be satisfied, capital formation may differ from planned savings.

The aim of this essay is to discuss the following topics in monetary growth theory where attention is focused upon aggregative variables. What are the relations among the

Reprinted from the *American Economic Review*, 60:85–106 (1970), by permission of the author and the publisher (copyright by the American Economic Association).

[1] This topic is discussed in Stein and Nagatani and Stein (1971, chap. 6) but is ignored here.

[2] This is the subject of Mrs. Allen's Ph.D. thesis at Brown University.

different approaches? What are the relative strengths and weaknesses of the various models? What are the substantive differences among models and which differences are inconsequential? To what extent is the distinction between outside and inside money crucial to the analysis? My main conclusion is that equally plausible models yield fundamentally different results. Recourse to models derived from the theory of rational behavior does not resolve the ambiguities, since there are several different plausible utility maximizing models.[3] This subject is now ready for sophisticated hypothesis testing. Since I am a proponent of the Keynes-Wicksell approach, it is possible that the other protagonists would not subscribe fully to the point of view expressed in this critical essay.[4]

Underlying the various approaches is a simple framework for the analysis of economic growth in a single sector economy. Assume that full employment always prevails and the labor force $N(t)$ grows exponentially at rate n. If technological change is of the Harrod-neutral type, then n may be interpreted as the growth of "effective" labor: the natural rate of growth plus the rate of Harrod-neutral technical change. Then output, $Y(t)$, depends upon the inputs of capital services, which are assumed to be positively related to the stock, $K(t)$, and of effective labor services, $N(t) = N(O)e^{nt}$. Output per unit of effective labor, $y(t) = Y(t)/N(t)$, is assumed to depend upon the ratio of capital per effective worker, $k(t) = K(t)/N(t)$, equation (1).[5]

$$y(t) = f[k(t)]. \tag{1}$$

[3] For lack of space, two major topics were omitted from the final version of this paper: (a) the optimal monetary policy in a growing economy and (b) the implications of different utility maximization models. They are discussed in Stein (1971). Relevant references are D. Cass and M. Yaari, P. Diamond, M. Friedman, M. Sidrauski, J. Stein, J. Tobin (1968), S. C. Tsiang, and H. Uzawa.

[4] In many respects, the views expressed are consistent with Alvin Marty's penetrating analyses (1968, 1969) of the neoclassical model. There are also substantial differences between our points of view.

[5] Not only is this production function assumed to be smooth and concave, but capital and labor are assumed to be essential for the production of output.

Investment per worker can be considered as the sum of two parts: the investment per worker required to maintain the current capital-labor ratio, nk, plus the time rate of change of the capital-labor ratio, Dk (where $D \equiv d/dt$). Only if investment per worker exceeds the amount required to provide the new workers with the existing ratio of capital per worker will the amount of capital per worker rise. From the definition of $k \equiv K/N$ we derive:

$$DK/N = nk + Dk. \tag{2}$$

Output per worker is divided between consumption per worker c and investment per worker DK/N. Therefore:

$$y = c + nk + Dk \quad \text{or} \tag{3}$$

$$Dk = (y - nk) - c. \tag{4}$$

Figure 1 graphs equation (4). The curve $y - nk$ represents the amount of output per worker available for consumption per worker

FIGURE 1

The neoclassical growth model. A rise in the rate of monetary expansion shifts the equilibrium from E to E'. $Dk = y(k) - nk - C[k + \theta L(k, \mu - n)]$.

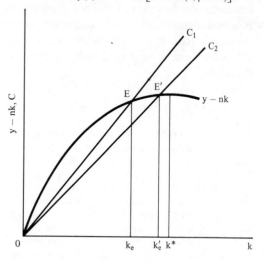

Output per unit of capital Y/K would fall to zero, if the capital intensity grew infinitely large. Assume also that the marginal product of capital is larger than the growth rate when the capital-labor ratio is zero.

plus the change in the ratio of capital to labor. The previous assumptions imply the shape of $y - nk$.

Assume that consumption per worker C_1 is positively related to the capital intensity, k. This assumption seems safe since a rise in k raises both output per worker and wealth per worker. At present, disregard the consumption function C_2.

When the capital intensity $k(t)$ is below k_e then $y - nk$ exceeds c. Some output per worker is available to raise the capital intensity; and $k(t)$ rises. If $k(t)$ exceeded k_e, then the capital intensity would decline since c exceeds $y - nk$. Equilibrium capital intensity k_e is stable in Figure 1. At k^*, the output per worker available for consumption per worker and for a rise in the capital intensity is maximal. Obviously $y'(k^*) = n$ at this "Golden Rule" value.

In this exposition, it is assumed that there is no commodity money: i.e., all money is costless to produce.[6] Moreover, for the sake of simplicity, only a single sector will be considered.[7]

Monetary policy can affect the time profile of the capital intensity, as well as its steady state solution k_e, if it can shift either the consumption function or the net production function (defined as) $y - nk$. The neoclassical monetary growth model considers how these shifts can occur within a fully employed economy.

Accordingly, a dichotomy is made concerning the role of real balances in the neoclassical model. First, under what conditions will variations in the rate of monetary expansion (and hence in real balances per worker) shift the consumption function? Second, under what conditions will the net production $y - nk$ be affected by variations in the rate of monetary expansion? The first question is usually subsumed under the heading: real balances as a consumer good, and is discussed in part C of Section I. The second question is usually subsumed under the heading: real balances as a producer's good, and is discussed in part B below.

I. NEOCLASSICAL MONETARY GROWTH MODELS

A. The Logical Structure

The neoclassical monetary growth model was first presented by Tobin (1965), and was a development made possible by the pioneering work of Robert Solow and T. W. Swan. It assumes that the rate of capital formation is identically equal to planned savings and all markets are always in equilibrium, regardless of the rate of price change.

Monetary policy affects the consumption function in this model, even in the steady state.[8] In this manner, monetary policy could affect the equilibrium capital intensity. Tobin assumed that consumption of goods per worker is a constant fraction of "disposable income" per worker. The latter is the sum of output per worker $y(k)$ and the increment of real balances per worker[9] $D(M/p)/N$. The

---

[6] See Niehans for the case where there is a commodity money.

[7] What is the role of money in such an economy? To avoid the complications of a multi-sector model, assume that the relative prices of a vector of goods are fixed. Thereby, we act as if the economy produced a single good. Insofar as the elements of the composite good are produced in different plants or firms, there is a need for a medium of exchange to avoid paying the workers in kind. The output produced by a worker consists of an element of the composite good, but his consumption consists of the composite good. Assume that each household, firm or plant is directly aware of the advantages of having the medium of exchange. The microeconomic foundation of the role of money (which is not interest bearing) in macroeconomic models is based upon the transactions demand and the precautionary demand for the medium of exchange. We shall assume that there is always less risk involved in holding money than there is in holding real capital.

[8] Sidrauski derived a long-run consumption function which is independent of monetary influences. His conclusion was based upon two assumptions: (a) the economic unit is an immortal family maximizing utility over an infinite horizon and (b) the marginal rate of time preference is constant. The relaxation of either of these assumptions could change his results drastically.

[9] Tobin assumed that total consumption C depended upon total real disposable income Y'. The latter is the sum of (a) total real output Y and (b) the change in the real value of the claims of the private sector upon the public sector $D(M/p)$, where M is outside money and

stock of money consists of the claims of the private sector upon the public sector which varies as a result of net transfer payments to or from the public. There is no other type of public debt or type of money. Assume that M grows exponentially and exogenously at rate μ; and define the proportionate rate of change of the price level $\pi = D \ln p$, where p is the absolute price level. Then his consumption function is (5).

$$C/N = C[\,y(k) + D(M/p)/N\,] \qquad (5)$$

$$C/N = C[\,y(k) + (\mu - \pi)m\,] \qquad (5a)$$

where $m = M/pN$ is real balances per worker.

It would have been simpler, more general and more amenable to a dynamic analysis had Tobin used consumption function (6), which he suggested in an earlier paper in 1955. Let consumption (of goods) per worker depend upon wealth per worker where wealth consists of real capital per worker, k, plus the real public debt per worker. It is not necessary to assume that the real public debt per worker is M/p. We could assume that it is $\theta M/p$, where θ represents the ratio of the nominal public debt to the stock of money M. Variable θ would be equal to unity if there were neither government bonds nor inside money. We may simply assume that θ is a positive constant. Then:

$$c = C/N = C[k + \theta m]. \qquad (6)$$

is the consumption function.[10]

Monetary policy will be able to shift the consumption function if it can vary m real balances per worker held, given the capital intensity.

The demand for real balances per worker is a function of transactions requirements

per worker reflected by y; the stock of the complementary asset per worker, k; and the opportunity cost of holding real balances. Capital yields an expected return equal to its expected rent; and real balances yield an expected return equal to the negative of the expected rate of price change π^*. It is generally assumed that the expected rent is equal to the current level $r(k)$. The demand for real balances per worker can be written as equation (7).

$$m = L(k, \pi^*). \qquad (7)$$

Clearly, $L_2 < 0$, since a rise in the expected rate of price change decreases the quantity of real balances demanded per worker at any given capital intensity. The sign of L_1 is positive since a rise in k raises the transactions demand for real balances and also reduces the opportunity cost (the yield on real capital) of holding real balances.

The stability of the system is profoundly affected by the price expectations function. In the steady rate, real balances per worker $m = M/pN$ are constant. Therefore, the price level eventually grows at a rate, π_e, equal to the growth of the money supply per worker. Let μ be the growth of the money supply. Then the steady state rate of price change π_e is equal to:

$$\pi_e = D \ln(M/N) = \mu - n. \qquad (8)$$

A simple[11] price expectations function, which is both a stabilizing influence and is consistent with the steady state solution, is:

$$\pi^* = \mu - n. \qquad (9)$$

Therefore, the consumption function is:

$$C/N = C[k + \theta L(k, \mu - n)]; \qquad (10)$$

and the time rate of change of the capital intensity is:

$$Dk = y(k) - nk - C[k + \theta L(k, \mu - n)]. \qquad (11)$$

---

there are no government bonds. Deflate by the size of the labor force N to obtain the measure of real disposable income per work: $y(k) + D(M/p)/N$.

[10] If the equilibrium $\mu - \pi = n$ is always positive, then it really does not matter in the steady state solution whether (5) or (6) is used. I shall use (6) rather than (5) in describing the neoclassical approach, since it is analytically more appealing and much simpler to use in a dynamic analysis. Tobin's 1965 paper was concerned with steady state solutions rather than a dynamic analysis.

[11] Alternatively, adaptive expectations function $D\pi^* = b(\pi - \pi^*)$ could be used. This function is not simple insofar as it adds a differential equation to the model. Moreover, the system will explode for a sufficiently high value of b, the adaptive expectations coefficient. If we assume that π^* is always equal to π, for all $D\pi^*$, then $D\pi^*/b = \pi - \pi^* = 0$ implies that b would be infinite. Such a model would not be stable.

Figure 1 graphs this fundamental differential equation of neoclassical monetary growth theory.

A rise in the rate of monetary expansion shifts consumption function C downwards. Why? The rise in $\mu - n$ raises the expected rate of price change $\pi^* = \mu - n$. Thereby, there is a decline in the quantity of real balances demanded $L_2(k, \pi^*) < 0$ at any capital intensity $k > 0$. Since wealth per worker is $k + m$ (when $\theta = 1$ in most models), the decline in $L(k, \pi^*) = m$ reduces real wealth per worker.

Consumption per worker is positively related to wealth per worker. Consequently, the rise in μ lowers the consumption function from C_1 to C_2. The dynamics of this situation raises[12] the equilibrium capital intensity from k_e to k'_e. Monetary policy is able to affect the time profile of the capital intensity and its steady state solution, even if money is costless to produce.

B. Real Balances as a Producer's Good in a Neoclassical Economy

Two conclusions, which have been questioned recently, seem to emerge from the previous model. First, it would appear that inflation is conducive to economic development. A rise in the rate of growth of the money supply lowers the consumption function and raises the capital intensity. The average productivity of labor and the real wage are positively related to the capital intensity. Therefore, should developing countries, which want to raise real per capita income, be advised to inflate the growth of the money supply? Second, monetary policy was able to affect the time profile of the capital intensity because there was a real balance effect in the consumption function. If, however, all money were "inside" money, i.e., liabilities of a regulated but privately owned banking system, would there be a real balance effect in the consumption function? In that case, would monetary policy be able to affect the time profile of the capital intensity[13] in this model?

Whether or not money is of the "inside" or the "outside" type, real balances may be viewed as generating a productive service, complementary with labor and capital. If there were no medium of exchange, then the inefficiencies of a barter economy would result. Labor and capital would have to be diverted from the production of goods to their "distribution" in order to achieve the "double coincidence of wants." Firms would be established to act as brokers between potential buyers and sellers of goods and services; and the open book credit of those broker firms would undoubtedly develop as an inefficient money supply. What makes such a situation inefficient is that these firms use labor and capital to distribute goods and services which would otherwise be available for the production of goods and services. An explicit medium of exchange which is costless to produce increases the productivity of the economy by permitting a more efficient means of distribution and hence a greater rate of production of goods and services with given aggregate inputs of capital and labor.

There may be a real loss to society resulting from a reduction in real balances below a certain level. Either there must be more frequent payments, involving additional bookkeeping and other administrative expenses, or part of one's wage will be paid in kind entailing the use of some barter. For these reasons, aggregate output may be a monotonic nondecreasing function of real balances, regardless of whether money is of the inside or the outside type. We continue to assume that fiat money is used which is costless to produce.

If real balances are productive services, then the neoclassical model should be re-

---

[12] Stability requires that, at the equilibrium, the C function be steeper than the $y - nk$ function. At this stage of the argument, the C function could cut the $y - nk$ function above or below the Golden Rule level of k.

[13] If the banking system uses a commodity money as reserves, then we must use something similar to Niehans' model.

vised.[14] Output per worker should depend upon[15] both capital per worker k and real balances per worker m, as described in equation (12).

$$y = y(k, m); \quad y_k > 0, \quad y_m \geqq 0. \tag{12}$$

A limiting case that may occur with fully developed financial institutions is $y_m = 0$, i.e., an increment of real balances does not liberate any perceptible amount of resources. Assume however, that $y_m > 0$ for a sufficiently small m. Otherwise, why would money be used?

The private sector is assumed to allocate its wealth between the two assets: capital and real balances. In equilibrium, the net expected yields from each type of wealth will be equal. The anticipated return on capital is its expected rent, which is assumed to be equal to its current marginal product $y_k(k, m)$. The anticipated return on real balances has three components. First, there is the anticipated marginal product of real balances, which is assumed to be equal to its current level, $y_m(k, m)$. Second, there is the anticipated appreciation $-\pi^*$ in terms of its command over goods. Third, there is the "liquidity" yield of money $Z(k, m)$ which reflects the feeling that usually real balances are safer to hold real capital. Real balances are not treated here as a consumer good which yields utility directly. The liquidity yield reflects the price that asset holders are willing to pay, in terms of yield sacrificed, to hold an asset which may fluctuate less in real value. Assume that the liquidity yield is positively related to

k and negatively related to m, i.e., $Z_k > 0$ and $Z_m < 0$. It is, of course, possible that $Z(k, m)$, the relative liquidity of money compared to real capital, is negative; but that would be unusual. In any case, $Z(k, m)$ reflects the relative variances of the expected returns on capital and real balances.

Equilibrium requires that equation (13) be satisfied: the net yields of the two assets must be equal when the risk factor is taken into account.

$$y_k(k, m) = y_m(k, m) - \pi^* + Z(k, m). \tag{13}$$

Differentiate equation (13) and solve for dm in terms of dk and $d\pi^*$. Equation (14a) is derived; and equation (14b) is a more compact version of the same thing. If there are diminishing returns to substitution ($y_{ii} < 0$) and if the two inputs are complementary or independent ($y_{km} \geq 0$), then the denominator in equation (14a) is positive.

$$dm = \frac{(y_{mk} - y_{kk} + Z_k)}{(y_{km} - y_{mm} - Z_m)} dk \tag{14a}$$

$$- \frac{1}{(y_{km} - y_{mm} - Z_m)} d\pi^*. \tag{14b}$$

$$dm = L_1 \, dk + L_2 \, d\pi^*.$$

Solving explicitly for the desired quantity of real balances per unit of effective labor, equation (14c) is derived. This is just the familiar portfolio balance equation.

$$m = L(k, \pi^*); \quad L_1 > 0, \quad L_2 < 0. \tag{14c}$$

Equation (14c) can be derived regardless of whether money is a liability of the public sector or of the private sector. The significant features of money, insofar as (14c) was concerned, are that it is a medium of exchange and a store of value.

An interesting and important question arises concerning the role of real balances as an argument in the consumption function. Continue to assume that consumption depends upon wealth. Should real balances be considered part of wealth if money is a liability of the public sector, but excluded from a definition of wealth if money is a liability of the private sector? The question

---

[14] This aspect of the role of money has been stressed by Marty (1969), and Levhari and Patinkin. J. Niehans commented on this approach as follows: "While treating money as a 'productive service' may be better than neglecting it, it is still in the tradition of 'solving' problems of monetary theory by metaphor instead of analysis. In fact, money is quite unlike the usual factors of production." We shall confine our attention to the aggregate level, and not try to answer Niehan's profound comment.

[15] It is an oversimplification to assume that the production function $Y = Y[K, N]$, where N is effective labor, is unchanged during the process of economic development. For example, the allocation of resources between sectors has been improved during the process of economic development. See George Borts and Stein.

takes on added significance if real balances, regardless of who issues the money, affect the productive capacity of the economy.

In a barter economy, wealth (per effective worker) is k. What happens to wealth when an explicit medium of exchange is introduced and the inefficiencies of a barter economy are eliminated? Boris Pesek and Thomas Saving and Harry Johnson (1969) have asked whether there is an essential difference between outside and inside money. Does it make sense to say that wealth (per effective worker) is $k + m$ if the pieces of paper which serve as the media of exchange are liabilities of *all* of the people (the government), but that wealth (per effective worker) remains at k if the pieces of paper are liabilities of *some* of the people (a privately owned banking system)? Both types of money serve equally as well as media of exchange. The m in the production function $y(k, m)$ applies equally to outside and inside money. In view of this assumption, how should the consumption function be analyzed? We now discuss the implications of this issue for the neoclassical monetary growth model.

1. *Wealth consists of capital and real balances.* Suppose that consumers, in the aggregate, consider a dollar of outside money to be a larger increment to private wealth than a dollar of inside money, because there is a private liability associated with the latter but not with the former. Let M' represent outside money and M'' inside money. Nominal private wealth may be considered to be equal to $pK + \theta_1 M' + \theta_2 M''$, where $1 > \theta_1 > \theta_2 > 0$ represents the fraction of each type of money which the public considers to be private wealth. The conventional assumption is that $\theta_2 = 0$, but it is quite unnecessary for purposes of analysis. Let $M' = \xi M$ and $M'' = (1 - \xi)M$ be the division of the total money supply between outside and inside money, respectively. Private nominal wealth is: $pK + [\theta_1 \xi + \theta_2(1 - \xi)]M$. If the weights θ_i and the division of the money supply ξ are constant, then $\theta = [\theta_1 \xi + \theta_2 (1 - \xi)]$ will be constant. Real private wealth (per effective worker) would be $k + \theta m$. If all money were inside money, then real wealth

per worker would be $k + \theta_2 m$; if all money were outside money, then real wealth per worker would be $k + \theta_1 m$.

Using consumption function (6), price expectations function (9), and production function (12), the basic differential equation for the time path of k can now be derived: equation (15). It is graphed in Figure 2.

$$Dk = y[k, L(k, \mu - n)] - nk \\ - C[k + \theta L(k, \mu - n)]. \qquad (15)$$

Equation (15) is more general than equation (11) for we allow for the possibility that $y_m > 0$, i.e., that the loss of real balances will adversely affect the production of output with given total supplies of labor and capital.

Let the rate of monetary expansion rise from μ_1 to μ_2. When money is of the outside type, then a rise in μ entails a rise in the growth of the volume of net transfer payments. If money is of the inside type, then the liabilities of a privately owned banking system rise at a faster rate than before.[16] There are now two effects. First, there may be an effect upon the demand for consumption per worker at any given capital intensity. A rise in μ raises

FIGURE 2

Real balances are productive services. A rise in the rate of inflation affects both the production function and the consumption function.

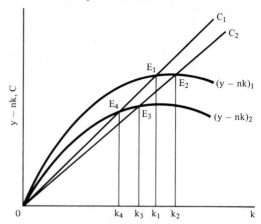

[16] See Section II A for a brief discussion of the determinants of μ in an inside money system, where a group received a franchise to print currency.

the expected rate of price change π^* (equation (9)) and reduces the quantity of real balances demanded per worker ($L_2 < 0$ in equation (14)). If money is purely of the inside type, $\theta = \theta_2$, then wealth will be affected by $\theta_2 L_2$, and there will be an effect upon the consumption function equal to $C'\theta_2 L_2$. On the other hand, if money were of the outside type then there will be a larger effect upon wealth equal to $\theta_1 L_2$ and the consumption function will shift by $C'\theta_1 L_2$. The magnitude of the downward shift of the consumption function, given k, is:

$$\frac{\partial C}{\partial \mu} = C'[\theta_1 \xi + \theta_2(1 - \xi)]L_2 = C'\theta L_2,$$

and is described by the shift of the consumption function from C_1 to C_2 in Figure 2.

Second, the decline in the quantity of real balances demanded per worker may affect output per worker, i.e., $y_m L_2$ may be substantial (especially in an economy whose financial institutions are not fully developed). This means that the function $y - nk$ declines at the same time that the consumption function declines from C_1 to C_2.

What will be the effect of a rise in the rate of monetary expansion upon the equilibrium capital intensity k? It depends upon which effect dominates. In the original neoclassical model, the decline in the quantity of real balances per worker at any capital intensity did not affect output. This means that, in effect, a fully developed financial economy was considered where $y_m(k, m)$ was approximately zero. Hence, the $y - nk$ function did not shift. However, the economy contained outside money: i.e., real balances are considered part of wealth. The decline in m reduced wealth, and thereby lowered the consumption function. The rise in the rate of monetary expansion, in that case, raised the steady state capital intensity from k_1 to k_2.

In the more general case analyzed here, it is not clear that inflation should be recommended as an aid to economic development. If real balances are highly productive (i.e., y_m is large), the decline in $y - nk$ could exceed the decline in C. The magnitude of the decline in C depends upon the division of

the money stock between inside and outside money (ξ) and the different weights attached to each other form of wealth. If θ_2 is small, i.e., there is a weak real balance effect in the consumption function derived from inside money, and most of the money consists of inside money, i.e., ξ is close to zero, then there will be a small decline in the consumption function. Then a rise in the rate of inflation would lower the $y(k, m) - nk$ curve to $(y - nk)_2$ and lower the consumption function to C_2. As a result of the rise in the rate of inflation, the equilibrium capital intensity would be *lowered* from k_1 to k_3. In this formal but general case, it was shown that inflation can lower output per capita and consumption per capita. A variety of results can be obtained from this model.

2. *Wealth consists of capitalized output.* Instead of considering wealth as the stock of capital plus some function of real balances per worker, why not consider wealth as the capitalized flow of output? If a medium of exchange enables the economy to produce more output with the same expenditure of effort and the same rate of utilization of its equipment, then that medium of exchange is part of the nation's wealth. What difference does it make whether it is a liability of all of the people (the government) or of some of the people (a privately owned banking system)?

For simplicity, assume that (i) current output per worker $y(k, m)$ is expected to remain constant and (ii) the discount factor is the marginal product of capital $y_k(k, m)$. Then wealth per worker, a, is capitalized output per worker.

$$a = y(k, m)/y_k(k, m); \tag{16a}$$

and consumption per worker, c, depends upon wealth per worker, a.

With competitive pricing, the share of output earned by capital is β where:

$$\beta = y_k(k, m) \cdot k/y(k, m) = \beta(k, m). \tag{16b}$$

Therefore, wealth per worker is simply:

$$a = k/\beta(k, m). \tag{16c}$$

Empirically, the elasticity of substitution is equal to or less than unity which implies that $\beta_k \leq 0$. Therefore, the consumption function becomes:

$$c = C[k/\beta(k, m)], \tag{16d}$$

and c is positively related to k as before.

The remaining question is whether the share of capital β is affected by the quantity of real balances. Suppose that the share β were not affected by m. Under these assumptions, the growth model is described by equations (16), (14), and (8).

$$Dk = y(k, m) - nk - C[k/\beta(k)]; \quad \beta' \leqq 0. \tag{16}$$

$$m = L(k, \pi^*). \tag{14}$$

$$\pi^* = \mu - n. \tag{8}$$

No distinction whatsoever is made between inside and outside money if they are indistinguishable as media of exchange and as productive services. There is no real balance effect in the consumption function if the share of output earned by capital is independent of the quantity of real balances. On the other hand, there is a real balance effect in the net production function.

No ambiguity exists in this model concerning the effect of a rise in the rate of monetary expansion upon the steady state capital intensity: it must *decline*.

A rise in the rate of monetary expansion lowers the quantity of real balances demanded at any given capital intensity: $L_2 < 0$. Real balances are productive services and therefore output per unit of effective labor changes by $y_m L_2 < 0$. The net production function declines from $(y - nk)_1$ to $(y - nk)_2$ in Figure 2. Consumption per effective worker is unaffected by a change in the quantity of real balances per worker, if capital's share of output is independent of the quantity of real balances per worker. As a result of the rise in the rate of monetary expansion, the steady state capital intensity *declines* from k_1 to k_4.

No ambiguity exists here. A rise in the rate of inflation *lowers* the steady state capital intensity, when wealth is measured as capitalized output. Inflation (in Figure 2) lowers the steady state output, and consumption, per unit of effective labor.

C. Real Balances as a Consumer Good

The analysis underlying equation (13) can be used to explain the derivation of equation (7): why real balances may be held even if they are not productive services on the margin (i.e., if $y_m = 0$). The answer would be that there is a liquidity yield $Z(k, m)$ derived from holding real balances rather than capital. This yield is positively related to transactions $y(k)$ and to wealth k; and is negatively related to the quantity of real balances held. The optimum stock of real balances per worker will be held when the liquidity yield $Z(k, m)$ is equal to the opportunity cost $y_k(k) + \pi^*$. In this manner, equation (7) is derived when on the margin real balances are not a producer's good. But there does exist (m, k) such that $y_m > 0$.

Johnson (1967) and Levhari and Patinkin take a different approach and view the services of real balances as an addition to produced output, just as the services of owner occupied houses is part of national income. They view the services of real balances as a component of disposable real income which is consumed.

"Disposable real income" per worker in this framework is equal to output per worker $y(k)$ plus the real transfers per worker from the public sector $(\mu - \pi)\theta m$ plus the value of the services of real balances per worker. Most authors assume $\theta = 1$. How should the value of the services of real balances per worker be measured?

One approach, taken by Levhari and Patinkin, measures the value by the opportunity cost of holding real balances: the yield on capital less the yield on real balances. Assume that the expected yield on real capital is equal to its current rental r. What is the return derived from holding real balances? There may be a positive nominal interest rate paid on money i. Then, the expected yield on real balances is $i - \pi^*$, the nominal interest rate less the expected rate of price change. Therefore, the opportunity cost of holding real balances relative to capital is $r + \pi^* - i$, which is equal to the marginal utility of real balances as a consumer good. The value of the services of real balances is the quantity m multiplied by the opportunity cost $r + \pi^* - i$. Disposable real income, according to this approach, would be Y_d' (equation (17)).

$$\frac{Y_d'}{N} = y(k) + (\mu - \pi)m + (r + \pi^* - i)m.$$

$$(17)$$

Another approach, taken by Johnson (1967), measures the value of the services of real balances, a component of disposable real income, as the integral under the demand curve for real balances per worker. Let $U(m)$ be the total utility per worker associated with the possession of real balances per worker of quantity m. Function U is monotonic non-decreasing. Then disposable real income per worker is (18).

$$\frac{Y_d''}{N} = y(k) + (\mu - \pi)m + U(m). \qquad (18)$$

There are serious criticisms which can be levied at each approach. First, the usual definitions of real national income accounting are violated. Real output y is presumably measured in constant prices. Each item in the bundle of outputs is valued at constant prices, and the total is summed. This was not done for the services of real balances. In equation (17), the real value of the services of real balances is measured in current prices since $r + \pi^* - i$ is not constant during the analysis. A paradox would arise if the demand for real balances had an inelastic section. A rise in the quantity m would be associated with a decline in $(r + \pi^* - i)m$, the total real value. The value of real output y is not measured this way. Why treat the value of the services of real balances in an asymmetrical way?

Equation (18) is not much better in this respect. The real value of the services of output consumed, a component of y, is not measured as an integral under a demand curve reflecting the total utility associated with the given quantity. Why measure the services of real balances as an integral under a demand curve? There is no justification for the asymmetry of treatment between currently pro-

duced output and the services of real balances, in a measure of disposable real income.

Second, there is a difficulty in interpreting the real balance effect in this approach. There are two components of consumption: the consumption of goods and the consumption of the services of real balances. These models generally assume that total real consumption of goods and real balances is a constant fraction $1 > c > 0$ of real disposable income. Therefore, the consumption of goods per worker C/N is derived from each definition of real disposable income.

Using the definition of disposable income in (17), the demand for consumption of goods per worker can be derived. Assume that $\theta = 1$ and there is no interest on money $i = 0$. Consider the steady state solution $\pi^* = \pi = \mu - n$. Then:

$$C/N = cY_d'/N - (r + \mu - n)m.$$
$$C/N = cy(k) + cnm - (1 - c)(r + \mu - n)m.$$

$$(19)$$

Suppose population were constant, $n = 0$. Then, the consumption function for goods is:

$$C/N = cy(k) - (1 - c)(r + \mu)m. \qquad (19a)$$

A *negative* relation exists between real balances held per worker m and the consumption of goods per worker. This is an unusual result.

Definition (18) yields the same paradox. This is described by equations (20) and (20a).

$$C/N = cY_d''/N - U(m), \; U' > 0.$$
$$C/N = cy(k) + cnm - (1 - c)U(m).$$

$$(20)$$

$$C/N = cy(k) - (1 - c)U(m), \quad \text{when} \quad n = 0.$$

$$(20a)$$

Again C/N and m are *negatively* related when population is constant.

When the services or real balances are regarded as a component of disposable income which yields utility directly, many paradoxes arise.

D. How Money Enters the Economy

All of the neoclassical models are very sensitive to the manner in which the money supply grows. It has hitherto been assumed in the outside money models that the money stock grows exclusively because of net transfer payments to or from the public. Therefore, wealth is affected by the rate of monetary expansion. Relax this assumption and suppose that the medium of exchange is a liability of the government which grows *exclusively* because it bears an interest rate i. Then, the growth of the money supply $D \ln M \equiv \mu$ is equal to i. Consider (for the sake of simplicity) the case where money is a producer's good, though similar results occur in the case where m yields utility directly. The steady state rate of price change $\pi - \mu - n$. Therefore, the expected real rate of interest on money is $i - \pi^* = \mu - \pi^* = n$. The interest rate paid on money $i \equiv \mu$ offsets completely, in the steady state, the effects of changes in the rate of price change $\mu - n$.

When both k and m are held as producers' goods, their marginal returns must be equal. The yield on capital, $y_k(k, m)$, must be equal to the real yield on money $y_m(k, m) + n + Z(k, m)$. The demand for real balances per worker in the steady state must satisfy:

$$y_k(k, m) = y_m(k, m) + n + Z(k, m) \qquad (21)$$

$$m = L(k, n), \quad L_2 > 0 \qquad (22)$$

for the reasons discussed earlier. Real balances demanded per worker will be independent of monetary influences.

As long as real balances have some productivity $y_m > 0$, or are considered to offer a convenience or liquidity yield $Z > 0$, the marginal product of capital $y_k(k, m)$ must exceed the growth rate n. Otherwise, people would not wish to hold capital. If that occurred, $r < n$, capital decumulation would result; and the marginal product of capital would rise. There could occur no equilibrium with a positive capital stock if the marginal product of capital were less than the growth rate.

A simple institutional change, whereby the growth of the money supply results exclusively from the payment of interest on money, makes monetary policy neutral. Variations

in the rate of monetary expansion cannot affect the steady state capital intensity.

E. The Instability Elements in the Neoclassical Model

In the neoclassical model, the supply of and demand for real balances are always equal, i.e., portfolio balance is always assumed to prevail. This assumption will lead to the instability of the model, unless frictions are introduced.

Suppose that the expected rate of price change π^* were always equal[17] to the rate currently experienced π. Then, the equality of the supply of and demand for real balances per worker implies that:

$$m = L(k, \pi); \quad L_2 < 0, \qquad (23)$$

based upon equation (7) and the assumption that $\pi^* = \pi$. To induce people to hold a larger quantity of real balances, given k, the rate of price change must decline. Solving explicitly for π, we derive:

$$\pi = \pi(k, m); \quad \pi_2 < 0. \qquad (24)$$

This is a condition for portfolio balance; but it does not explain what causes the price level to change.

The growth of real balances per worker $D \ln(M/pN)$ is the growth of the money supply per worker $\mu - n$ less the growth of the price level π. Since portfolio balance is always assumed to prevail, the growth of the price level is given by (24). We, therefore, derive:

$$D \ln M/pN = Dm/m = \mu - \pi(k, m) - n. \quad (25)$$

Instability is quite apparent. Say that k is given and m is displaced above its equilibrium value. Will m return to its equilibrium? The answer is: No. Why? To induce people to hold the larger stock of real balances, the rate of price change must *decline*. Therefore, real balances per worker *rise* at a *faster* rate than before; and m deviates further away from

---

[17] Or, suppose it were positively related to the current rate.

equilibrium. Formally,

$$\frac{\partial}{\partial m}(Dm/m)\big|_k = -\pi_2 > 0, \tag{26}$$

which is instability in the m direction. Equations (25), (4), and (6) imply saddle point stability.

This source of instability is the same as the paradox that Hahn develops in his 1966 paper. The trouble with this neoclassical model is that: "... the price of money was changing because this was required for asset equilibrium and not because any reason was adduced why, in fact, it should change" (Hahn 1969, p. 183).

Stability of the neoclassical monetary growth model can be guaranteed[18] if a sufficiently sluggish price expectations function is introduced. Price expectations function (9) was excellent for this purpose: it was constant at $\mu - n$, the steady state rate of price change. That is why we did not encounter any instability earlier. The adaptive expectation equation can also be stabilizing if the value of coefficient b in $D\pi^* = b(\pi - \pi^*)$ is sufficiently small.[19] When portfolio balance is always assumed to prevail, frictions in the formation of price expectations are necessary for stability of the neoclassical model.

II. KEYNES-WICKSELL MONETARY GROWTH MODELS

In sharp contrast to the neoclassical model is a set of models which assumes that: (a) prices are changing if, and only if, the goods market is not in equilibrium and (b) there are independent savings and investment functions.[20]

[18] Assume that in $y = f(k)$, $f'(0) = \infty$ and $f'(\infty) = 0$.
[19] This assumption is made in Sidrauski, Foley and Sidrauski.
[20] This Keynes-Wicksell approach was taken independently in 1966 by Rose and Stein and is similar to early work by Hahn (1960, 1961). This method has been developed in 1969 in subsequent papers by Rose, Stein, Nagatani and Tsiang. As a result of his criticisms of the neoclassical model, Hahn (1969) also seems to lean in a Keynes-Wicksell direction. Cagan (1969) implicitly thinks along these lines in the short run, but not in the long run.

My aim in 1966 and 1969 was to formulate a general macroeconomic model which contains money in an essential way regardless of whether it is inside or outside money. If the inputs of labor and capital were arbitrarily fixed, then it would look like a dynamic version of Patinkin's 1965 short-run aggregative model. Alternatively, this growth model would be the generalization of post-Keynesian macroeconomics to the problems of a growing economy: where the input of capital is endogenously determined and growing over time. Long-run equilibrium is nothing other than the steady state solution of the short-run dynamic model with endogenous capital. Or, the short-run dynamic model is a special case of the general growth model. It has been used both in a full employment context by Stein, Tsiang and Hahn and in the case of unemployment by Rose and Nagatani.

There are two essential differences between the neoclassical and Keynes-Wicksell monetary growth models. They concern the dynamics of price change and the existence of independent savings and investment functions.

A. The Dynamics of Price Change

The fundamental assumption, which distinguishes between the two classes of models, concerns the determinants of price change in continuous time. In the Keynes-Wicksell model prices are changing if, and only if, aggregate demand for goods differs from aggregate supply. Excess aggregate demand is planned consumption C plus planned investment I less output Y. Since planned saving is $Y - C$, excess aggregate demand is $I - S$. Assume that the rate of price change $\pi = D \ln p$ is proportional to excess demand (deflated, for convenience,[21] by the stock of capital). The price change equation is:

$$Dp/p = \pi = \lambda(I/K - S/K). \tag{27}$$

Such an approach was taken by Tobin in 1955, but clearly not in his subsequent work

[21] In Tsiang's adaptation of Stein's 1966 model, he deflates I and S by effective labor.

on growth. He considered a model where money and capital were the only stores of value (i.e., there were no bonds). Portfolio balance was defined as a condition where the supply of, and demand for, real balances are equal. The demand for real balances per worker was similar to that used in Section I above. He wrote:

Portfolio balance is assumed to be the necessary and sufficient condition for price stability $(Dp = 0)$. If, instead, owners of wealth desire to hold more goods and less currency, they attempt to buy goods with currency. Prices are bid up $(Dp > 0)$. If they desire to shift in the other direction, they attempt to sell goods for currency $(Dp < 0)$ [p. 105].

The mathematical formulation of this statement would be equation (28). The rate of price change is positively related to the excess supply of real balances per worker. Use the same demand for real balances function as was used in the neoclassical model. Then:

$$Dp/p = \pi = h[m - L(k, \pi^*)]. \quad (28)$$

According to the usual version of Walras' Law (in a two-asset model), the excess demand for goods $C + I - Y$ is equal to the flow excess supply of real balances. If the excess flow supply of real balances is positively related to the excess stock supply $m - L$, then equation (28) states that the rate of price change is positively related to excess aggregate demand per worker. Except for the arbitrary deflator, equations (27) and (28) are very similar.

An example of the implications of the dynamic Walrasian equation (27) or (28) will be helpful seeing: (a) the difference in point of view between the Keynes-Wicksell and the neoclassical monetary growth model; and (b) why monetary nonneutrality can occur even if there is no real balance effect in the savings function.

Suppose that a group was given the franchise to print the medium of exchange (currency).[22] The output produced by the owners of the franchise (which shall be called the bank) is DM in nominal terms and DM/p

in real terms.[23] Nominal output DM is exchanged for DM/p of goods with the nonbank public, which desires currency for the usual reasons.

The real value of the flow of output per worker produced by the bank is:

$$DM/pN = (DM/M)M/pN = \mu m, \quad (29a)$$

where m is real balances per worker and μ is the rate of monetary expansion. If people were always holding their desired stocks of real balances (an assumption which will be dropped very shortly):

$$m = L(k, \pi^*), \quad (29b)$$

where L is the quantity of real balances demanded per worker. Continue to assume that the expected rate of price change π^* is equal to the steady state rate of price change $\pi_e = \mu - n$. Then, the real value of the output per worker produced by the bank would be:

$$DM/pN = \mu L(k, \mu - n). \quad (29c)$$

If the marginal cost of producing currency is zero, then the rate of monetary expansion $\mu = \mu_0$ will maximize the real revenue (per worker) per unit of time of the bank (DM/pN) will be such that:

$$\mu_0 \frac{L_2(k, \mu_0 - n)}{L(k, \mu_0 - n)} = -1. \quad (29d)$$

At the maximum profit rate of monetary expansion μ_0, the demand for real balances per worker will have a unit elasticity. If there is a strictly positive marginal cost of currency creation then the rate of monetary expansion will differ from μ_0. In either case, μ_0 is the rate of monetary expansion produced by the owners of the franchise. Its derivation is not essential to my argument.

The franchise owners produce the currency and try to exchange it for goods produced by the nonbank public. There are only two ways in which the bank can sell its output: by demanding goods in exchange for currency, or by demanding nonbank debt in exchange for currency. The first case will be considered here, and the second in the next section. When

---

[22] This example was inspired by Cagan in his unpublished 1969 paper, who must be absolved from any responsibility for the views expressed here.

[23] $D \equiv d/dt$.

the owners of the franchise demand goods (in exchange for their currency) aggregate demand is directly affected. There is no reason why the nonbank public should always wish to give up the goods demanded by the owners of the franchise, at the given price level and capital intensity. This is the point of divergence between the Keynes-Wicksell and the neoclassical models. A market mechanism must be operative. What is its nature?

At any time the stock of money (currency) is $M(t) = M_0 \exp \mu_0 t$, based upon the desire of the bank to maximize its profits. The nonbank public desires to hold $p(t)L(k_t, \mu_0 - n)$ $N(t)$ of nominal balances. Alternatively, the nonbank public wishes to hold $L(k_t, \mu_0 - n)$ of wealth per worker in the form of real balances; but $M(t)/p(t)N(t)$ of real wealth per worker in the form of currency is in existence. The gap $M(t)/p(t)N(t)$ less $L(k_t, \mu_0 - n)$ may arise because the franchise owner has been demanding goods at a faster rate than the nonbank public has been willing to give them up; or the latter may have decided to switch from real balances to goods. In either case, the gap $M(t)/p(t)N(t) - L$ represents an excess demand for goods.

If the rate of price change Dp is proportional to the level of excess demand, i.e., the difference between the stock of money in existence $M(t)$ and the quantity demanded by the nonbank public $p(t) L(\cdot)N(t)$, then equation (30) or (28) follows.

$$Dp = h\left[\frac{M(t)}{N(t)} - p(t)L(k, \mu_0 - n)\right], \qquad (30)$$

where $M(t)/N(t) = (M_0/N_0) \exp(\mu_0 - n)t$.

To illustrate the importance of this key assumption, assume that k_t is at its equilibrium level $k(t) = k$. Then $p(t)$, the solution of differential equation (30), will eventually grow at rate $\mu_0 - n$. In the steady state:

$$\mu_0 - n = \pi = \pi^*$$

$$= h\left[\frac{M(t)}{p(t)N(t)} - L(k, \mu_0 - n)\right]. \qquad (31)$$

A permanent gap $(\mu_0 - n)/h$ will exist between the stock of real balances in existence $M(t)/p(t)N(t)$ and the quantity demanded $L(k,$

$\mu_0 - n)$. It is this inflationary gap that is the driving force behind the rise in prices in the short run, in almost all dynamic models. Solution of differential equation (30) shows that a similar situation exists in the steady state. Long-run inflation, at a rate $\pi = \mu_0 - n = \pi^*$, implies long-run excess demand.

Expectations of the rate of price change enter via the demand for real balances; and we have assumed that people always act as if the expected rate of price change were equal to its steady state value. The long run (steady state) is consistent with the price expectations function. What must be stressed is that the steady state represents the asymptotic solution of the model; and is not a condition that is imposed upon the model regardless of its consistency with short run dynamics. The short run is a special case of the steady state.

The neoclassical model assumes that portfolio balance always exists, regardless of the rate of price change: i.e., $m = L(k, \pi^*)$. This crucial neoclassical assumption would make sense if (a) the speed of adjustment h were assumed to be infinite or (b) a discrete period, rather than a continuous time, analysis were used. In the latter case, no contracts would be binding until all markets were cleared; and the market would then be closed until the following day. If equation (28) were used instead of equation (7), then very different results would be obtained from the neoclassical model. A real balance effect in the savings function would not be necessary for the rate of monetary expansion to affect the steady state capital intensity.

B. Independent Saving and Investment Functions

Suppose that the franchise owners try to sell their output in exchange for interest bearing debt; and they plan to use their future interest receipts to purchase consumer goods. The original sellers of the debt are business firms who would use the acquired currency to demand output in the form of investment goods. The investment demand function may be of the form described by equation (32). The desired proportionate rate of change of the ratio of capital per effective worker $I/K - n$ (where I is desired investment) is assumed to be proportional[24] to the difference between the expected yield on capital $r + \pi^*$ and the nominal rate of interest ρ on debt.

$$I/K - n = r + \pi^* - \rho$$
$$= r - (\rho - \pi^*). \qquad (32)$$

Alternatively we could say that the desired proportionate rate of change of the ratio of capital per unit of effective labor is proportional to the difference between the rent[25] per unit of capital and the expected real rate of interest $\rho - \pi^*$. If the rent per unit of capital r were equal to the real rate of interest $\rho - \pi^*$, then equation (32) states that firms would desire a constant *ratio* of capital per unit of effective labor. Hence, desired capital would grow at rate n. This equation is the generalization of the short-run investment functions to a growing economy, and is consistent with marginal productivity theory.

The franchise owners use their newly produced money to purchase debt in the market, thereby lowering the nominal interest rate on debt. At this lower nominal rate of interest, there will be a rise in planned investment by firms since the expected yield on capital $r + \pi^*$ has risen relative to ρ the nominal rate of interest.

The decline in the nominal rate of interest ρ leads to an excess demand for goods: planned investment has increased without a corresponding decline in the demand for consumption! In the neoclassical model, on the other hand, there is no independent investment function, and planned investment is identically equal to planned savings by consumers. Monetary changes can only affect the real variables; in the neoclassical model, by working through the consumption function. It is not easy to reconcile the neoclassical model with the example of the franchise owners presented here.

There is an excess demand for goods resulting from the attempt of the franchise owners to sell their output. What will happen to the rate of capital formation? The Keynes-Wicksell model shows how the rate of monetary expansion, produced by the franchise owners or the monetary authority, will affect the capital intensity $k(t)$ in both the short run and in the long run (steady state). No real balance effect in the savings function is necessary for this result.

There are (at least) two versions of the Keynes-Wicksell model. In one, there is forced savings during inflationary periods: the actual rate of capital formation exceeds planned savings but is less than planned investment. In the other, the rate of utilization varies positively with the rate of price change.[26] Both versions imply monetary nonneutrality, even if there is no real balance effect in the savings function. Only a sketch of the first version will be presented here.

C. A Heuristic Exposition of the Keynes-Wicksell Model

1. *The possibility of forced savings during inflationary periods.* During inflationary periods, the demand for output $C + I$ exceeds the capacity of a fully employed economy $Y = F(N, K)$ where N and K are the currently available input quantities, and the rate of utilization of K and N is constant. Since $C + I - Y = I - (Y - C) = I - S$ is positive, the question arises: how much of output will actually be allocated for consumption and how much will be allocated for investment. Clearly both consumers and firms cannot be satisfied simultaneously during periods of excess aggregate demand. Will the actual rate of capital formation be equal to planned savings, i.e., output less planned consumption? Or will the actual rate of capital formation be equal to planned investment? We assume that the actual rate of capital formation DK, during periods of excess aggregate

---

[24] For simplicity, the factor of proportionality is assumed equal to unity.

[25] Assume that the expected rent is equal to the current rent.

[26] See Council of Economic Advisers and *Studies by the Staff of the Cabinet Committee on Price Stability* for some evidence consistent with this assumption.

demand, will be less than firms desire (I) but more than consumers plan to save (S). Neither investment plans nor consumption plans are fully realized in periods of excess aggregate demand. Everyone is partially frustrated. The actual rate of growth of capital DK will be such that $I > DK > S$. Specifically, assume that the actual rate of growth of capital DK will be a linear combination of planned savings and planned investment, equation (33).

$$DK/K = aI/K + (1 - a)S/K. \tag{33}$$

Coefficient a is institutionally determined such that $1 > a > 0$ during periods of excess aggregate demand. Even if there were perfect foresight that $C + I$ exceeded Y, not everyone could be satisfied. Which demands are frustrated and which demands are satisfied has to be determined by the institutional structure. No such problem exists during deflationary periods when there is sufficient output such that consumption plans can be and are fully realized. Then $a = 0$, and there is more capital formation than is desired by firms. Firms find that they have not been operating on their investment demand schedules since I differs from DK in periods of price change. During deflationary periods, the full employment assumption may be questionable. Hence, we shall confine our analysis to inflationary periods.

Using equation (27), which states that the rate of price change π is proportional to excess demand per unit of capital, the rate of capital formation is:

$$DK/K = a\pi/\lambda + S/K;$$
$$1 > a > 0 \quad \text{when} \quad \pi > 0 \tag{34}$$
$$a = 0 \quad \text{when} \quad \pi \leqq 0.$$

Forced savings per unit of capital $a\pi/\lambda$ occurs during inflationary periods and reflects the fact that consumers acquire less output than they planned. It is based upon the assumption that if $C + I > Y$, then consumers will find that their actual consumption-income ratio is less than their desired consumption-income ratio. To be sure, firms

will find that the actual rate of capital formation is less than the planned rate.

The proportionate rate of change of the ratio of capital to labor Dk/k is DK/K less n the growth of effective labor. Variables π and S/K are endogenous[27] and contain k and m as arguments.

$$Dk/k = a\pi/\lambda + S/K - n. \tag{35}$$

The growth of real balances per worker Dm/m is equal to the growth of the money supply per worker ($\mu - n$) less the growth of the price level π.

$$Dm/m = \mu - \pi - n. \tag{36}$$

In the steady state, k and m are constant at k_e and m_e respectively. Therefore: (a) capital and labor grow at exogenous rate n and (b) the equilibrium rate of price change π_e is equal to the proportionate rate of change of the money supply per effective worker.

$$(DK/K)_e = n. \tag{37}$$
$$\pi_e = \mu - n. \tag{38}$$

Figure 3a describes the steady state when planned savings per unit of capital is primarily a function of output per unit of capital. Then, the S/K function is negatively sloped[28] and is not very sensitive to monetary disturbances. If there were price level stability, then there would be no forced savings. Planned savings per unit of capital would be equal to the growth of effective labor, at capital intensity k_0.

What will be the effects of a rise in the rate of monetary expansion? Consider the inflationary case ($\mu - n > 0$) where forced savings occur. Figure 3a describes this situation. At capital intensity k_0, capital and labor grow at the same rate; and the rate of capital formation is equal to planned savings. Inflation raises the rate of capital formation above the rate of desired savings, since it is assumed

---

[27] See Stein (1966, 1969) for this derivation.

[28] For example, if $S = sY$ then $S/K = sY/K$. But Y/K is negatively related to the capital intensity k. Therefore, S/K is negatively related to k. In general, $S/K = S(Y/K), S' > 0$ and $Y/K = f(k), f' < 0$. Therefore, S/K and k are negatively related.

that the driving force behind inflation is excess aggregate demand, i.e., the difference between planned investment and planned savings. (Recall our example where the franchise owners are purchasing debt with their output of currency.) The curve DK/K shifts to $S/K + a\pi/\lambda$.

The capital intensity is raised above k_0. As the capital intensity rises, the average productivity of capital Y/K declines. Therefore, planned savings per unit of capital also declines. Equilibrium is attained when planned savings per unit of capital declines by the amount of forced savings per unit of capital $a(\mu - n)/\lambda = a\pi_e/\lambda$. Here, the equilibrium capital intensity is positively related to the rate of monetary expansion. The original neoclassical result was obtained in a different manner. However, if S/K depended upon m and k, but $a = 0$ (i.e., consumption plans are always realized) a rise in $\mu - n$ can lower the steady state capital intensity, in a dynamically stable model.

2. *Reverse results when savings plans are realized.* If saving plans are realized ($a = 0$), then the growth of capital DK/K is equal to planned savings per unit of capital: equation (39).

$$n = S(k, m); \quad S_1 < 0, \quad S_2 < 0. \tag{39}$$

In the Keynes-Wicksell framework, the money market need not always be in equilibrium. If the bond market has a very rapid speed of adjustment, then disequilibrium in the goods market is offset by disequilibrium in the money market. Equation (28), which was used by Tobin in 1955, states that the rate of price change is proportional to excess supply of real balances per worker. Rewriting (28), we obtain an expression for m the quantity of real balances per worker in existence, equation (40).

$$m = \frac{\pi}{h} + L(k, \pi^*). \tag{40}$$

In the steady state $\pi = \pi^* = \mu - n$. Using this relation in (40), and substituting (40) into (39) we obtain equation (41).

$$n = S\left[k, \frac{\mu - n}{h} + L(k, \mu - n) \right] = \frac{DK}{K}.$$

$$\tag{41}$$

When equation (41) is satisfied, then both capital and labor grow at rate n. This is graphed in Figure 3b, where again S/K is negatively related to k, since $S_1 + S_2L_1 < 0$.

A rise in the rate of monetary expansion $\mu = \pi_e + n$ is associated with a rise in the

FIGURE 3a

A rise in the rate of monetary expansion raises the steady state capital intensity. Inflation is associated with excess aggregate demand and forced savings per unit of capital.

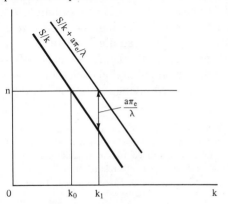

FIGURE 3b

A rise in the rate of inflation lowers the steady state capital intensity. Savings plans are always realized, but the supply of real balances exceeds the demand for real balances.

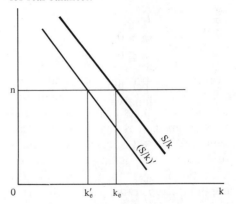

excess supply of real balances per unit of capital, equation (28) in the steady state. At any given capital intensity, the quantity demanded will decline, i.e., $L_2 < 0$. But the actual quantity of real balances per worker in existence will change by:

$(1/h + L_2)\Delta\mu$.

With a slow speed of response of price, the rise in the rate of monetary expansion will raise $M(t)$ faster that $p(t)$; and, therefore, m rises. If m rises, then S/K declines to $(S/K)'$ in Figure 3b. The decline in savings per unit of capital reduces the steady state capital intensity from k_e to k'_e.

Analytically, this result is obtained by differentiating (41) with respect to μ and solving for $dk_e/d\mu$.

$$\frac{dk_e}{d\mu} = (-S_2)\frac{(1/h + L_2)}{(S_1 + S_2 L_1)},\qquad(42)$$

where $S_1 < 0$, $L_1 > 0$ and $L_2 < 0$. If $(1/h + L_2) > 0$, then a rise in μ raises m and lowers S/K. Hence, $dk_e/d\mu < 0$, i.e., equilibrium shifts from k_e to k'_e in Figure 3b. The neoclassical model assumes that h is infinite; but that is an abitrary assumption and is counter to the usual practice in short-run dynamics. An important conclusion that emerges from the Keynes-Wicksell model is that a rise in the rate of monetary expansion can either raise, lower, or keep the steady state capital intensity constant, in a dynamically stable system (see Stein 1969).

It is implicitly assumed that the rate of inflation is not sufficiently great as to interfere with the productivity of the economy; hence, the effects of inflation upon capacity output are ignored.

D. Conclusion and a Possible Synthesis of Neoclassical and Keynes-Wicksell Models.

Monetary growth theory can be made to yield a variety of qualitatively different results, depending upon which model is used. Both the neoclassical and the Keynes-Wicksell model imply that in the steady state: the ex-

pected and actual rates of price change are equal $(\pi_e^* = \pi_e)$; and the actual rate of price change π_e is equal to the growth of the money supply per worker $\mu - n$. For expository purposes, assume that there is secular inflation in the steady state. The models differ with respect to the underlying *short-run* dynamic models, and this difference carries over to the steady state characteristics of the model. The steady state must be the asymptotic solution of the short-run dynamic model: it cannot be brought in as *deus ex machina*.

Instantaneous equilibrium in all markets at all times is implied by the *neoclassical* model. As the excess demand curves shift, the equilibrium prices change immediately. During an inflationary process, everyone is always holding his desired real balances, and there is no excess demand for goods. Prices always rise instantly by the amount required to clear all markets. No sooner is the market cleared than the excess demand curve rises again, and a new and higher equilibrium price is established instantly. Stability in the neoclassical model requires that price expectations change sluggishly: e.g., a sufficiently low adaptive expectations coefficient must be assumed.

A very different approach is taken in the first version of the Keynes-Wicksell model. It is assumed that prices rise if, and only if, there exists excess demand. Expectations by themselves do not raise prices, but expectations working through excess demands produce price changes. Markets are not always cleared. At any time, rising prices imply disequilibrium, i.e., unsatisfied demands. A Walraisian dynamic price adjustment process is postulated, and there is no presumption that prices move in precisely the manner postulated by the neoclassical model. Prices do not change too rapidly in response to changes in excess demand. A stable economy converges to a steady state in terms of variables deflated by the growing stock of capital or the growing size of the labor force. In this steady state, there is inflation which is anticipated $\pi_e^* = \pi_e = \mu - n$. Prices do not rise just because people expect them to do so, in a dynamically stable model. They rise steadily because there is permanent excess demand. A natural bridge is created between the short run and the steady state in this set of models. The Patinkin model is a special case of the Keynes-Wicksell model developed here.

A possible synthesis of the neoclassical and Keynes-Wicksell models could be made[29] if the price change equation were:

$$\pi = Dp/p = \pi^* + \lambda(I/K - S/K). \qquad (43)$$

In a perfectly competitive market, firms must take the market price as a datum, and production is adjusted accordingly. If there is excess demand (i.e., $I > S$) then there is some market bidding process that produces a rise in prices. Expectations of rising prices affect $I - S$ and only thereby affect the rate of price change. This was the rationale underlying equation (27). On the other hand, it is possible that firms may have some power to set prices, or that markets are organized by specialists who take the expected rate or price change into account in setting prices. The actual rate of price change may be the sum of two elements: the specialists' expectations of price changes and the actual state of excess demand, as described by equation (43).

If equation (43) were the correct price determination equation, then the Keynes-Wicksell model would describe the growing economy outside of the steady state. As the economy approaches the steady state, π approaches π^* and I/K approaches S/K. Then (a) all markets would be in equilibrium and (b) the actual rate of growth of capital will be equal to S/K. Monetary policy would be able to affect the steady state capital intensity, with this synthesis, only if there were a real balance effect in the consumption (savings) function or in the net production function. The crucial question is: which is the correct monetary growth model?

References

Borts, G. H., and Stein, J. L., *Economic Growth in a Free Market* (New York, 1964).

Cagan, P., "The Non-Neutrality of Money in the Long Run," *Journal of Money, Credit, and Banking*, 1:207–227 (1969).

——, "The Revenue From Money Creation and its Disposition—A Theoretical Analysis," unpublished (1969).

Cass, D., and Yaari, M., "Individual Saving, Aggregate Capital Accumulation and Efficient Growth," in Shell, K. (ed.), *Essays on the Theory of Optimal Economic Growth* (Cambridge, Massachusetts, 1968).

Diamond, P., "National Debt in a Neoclassical Growth Model," *American Economic Review*, 55:1126–1150 (1965).

Foley, D., and Sidrauski, M., "Portfolio Choice, Investment, and Growth," *American Economic Review*, 59:44–63 (1969).

Friedman, M., *The Optimum Quantity of Money* (Chicago, 1969).

Hahn, F., "The Stability of Growth Equilibrium," *Quarterly Journal of Economics*, 74:206–226 (1960).

——, "Money, Dynamic Stability and Growth," *Metroeconomica*, 13:57–76 (1961).

——, "Equilibrium Dynamics with Heterogeneous Capital Goods," *Quarterly Journal of Economics*, 80:633–646 (1966).

——, "On Money and Growth," *Journal of Money, Credit, and Banking*, 1:172–187 (1969).

Johnson, H. G., *Essays in Monetary Economics* (Cambridge, Massachusetts, 1967).

——, "Inside Money, Outside Money, Income, Wealth, and Welfare in Monetary Theory," *Journal of Money, Credit, and Banking*, 1:30–45 (1969).

Levhari, D., and Patinkin, D., "The Role of Money in a Simple Growth Model," *American Economic Review*, 58:713–753 (1968).

Marty, A., "Some Notes on Money and Economic Growth," *Journal of Money, Credit, and Banking*, 1:252–265 (1969).

——, "The Optimal Rate of Growth of Money," *Journal of Political Economy*, 76:860–873 (1968).

Nagatani, K., "A Monetary Growth Model with Variable Employment," *Journal of Money, Credit, and Banking*, 1:188–206 (1969).

Niehans, J., "Efficient Monetary and Fiscal Policies in Balanced Growth," *Journal of Money, Credit, and Banking*, 1:228–251 (1969).

Patinkin, D., *Money, Interest, and Prices*, 2nd ed. (New York, 1965).

Pesek, B., and Saving, T., *Money, Wealth, and Economic Theory* (New York, 1967).

Rose, H., "Unemployment in a Theory of Growth," *International Economic Review*, 7:50–58 (1966).

---

[29] Stein (1971, chaps 5 and 6) discusses this type of model in detail.

———, "Real and Monetary Factors in the Business Cycle," *Journal of Money, Credit, and Banking*, 1:138–152 (1969).

Samuelson, P. A., "An Exact Consumption Loan Model of Interest with or without the Social Continuance of Money," *Journal of Political Economy*, 66:467–482 (1958).

Sidrauski, M., "Rational Choice and Patterns of Growth in a Monetary Economy," *American Economic Review*, 57:534–544 (1967).

Solow, R., "A Contribution to the Theory of Economic Growth," *Quarterly Journal of Economics*, 70:65–94 (1956).

Stein, J. L., "Money and Capacity Growth," *Journal of Political Economy*, 74:451–465 (1966).

———, "Rational Choice and Patterns of Growth in a Monetary Economy: Comment," *American Economic Review*, 58:944–950 (1968).

———, "Neoclassical and Keynes-Wicksell Monetary Growth Models," *Journal of Money, Credit, and Banking*, 1:153–171 (1969).

———, and K. Nagatani, "Stabilization Policies in a Growing Economy," *Review of Economic Studies*, 36:165–183 (1969).

———, "A Minimal Role of Government in Achieving Optimal Growth," *Economica*, 36:139–150 (1969).

———, "The Utility Yield of Real Balances in an Intergeneration Neoclassical Monetary Growth Model," unpublished (1969).

———, *Money and Capacity Growth* (Columbia University Press, 1971).

Swan, T. W., "Economic Growth and Capital Accumulation," *Economic Record*, 32:334–361 (1956).

Tobin, J., "A Dynamic Aggregate Model," *Journal of Political Economy*, 63:103–115 (1955).

———, "Money and Economic Growth," *Econometrica* 33:671–684 (1965).

———, "Notes on Optimal Monetary Growth," *Journal of Political Economy*, 76:833–859 (1968).

Tsiang, S. C., "A Critical Note on the Optimum Supply of Money," *Journal of Money, Credit, and Banking*, 1:266–280 (1969).

Uzawa, H., "On a Neoclassical Model of Economic Growth," *Economic Studies Quarterly*, 17:1–14 (1966).

U.S. Council of Economic Advisors, *Economic Report of the President*, with the annual report of the Council of Economic Advisors, transmitted to the Congress (Washington, D.C., January 1969).

———, *Studies by the Staff of the Cabinet Committee on Price Stability* (Washington, January 1969).

Effective Demand in the Long Run

Hugh Rose

Johns Hopkins University

I. INTRODUCTION

The idea of a general macro-dynamic theory of money, growth and fluctuations is appealing but probably chimerical, if only because choice must be made between alternative hypotheses for expectations and speeds of adjustment. But the rather bewildering variety of views about the long run is, I believe, only superficially connected with expectational hypotheses. Most of the theories that have been offered us retain their distinctiveness when recast so as to eliminate differences from this source. Speeds of adjustment, on the other hand, are frequently a defining characteristic.

By adhering to a particular set of expectational assumptions chosen for their convenience, and employing the usual principle of rational microeconomic behavior, one might hope to construct a reasonably general framework within which the various models, neo-Keynesian, neo-classical and hybrids, can be fitted and brought into relation with one another. In view of the importance of the adjustment speeds, one should resolve to postulate only those lags that are implied by rational conduct, at least when allowance is made for uncertainty and imperfect knowledge.

Reprinted from *Models of Economic Growth*, edited by J. A. Mirrlees and N. H. Stern (1973), by permission of the author and the publisher (copyright by the International Economic Association, published by Macmillan Co., Ltd.).

In this paper I have tried to construct such a framework for the inside-money economy, and have then used it to derive and compare two theories of monetary growth. The first is the 'neo-Swedish' or Wicksellian model which I myself favor [and which I have analyzed more fully elsewhere (Rose, 1967, 1969)], and the second an inside-money version of the full-employment monetary growth model proposed by Tobin (1965). They provide a useful illustration of the crucial role of adjustment rates. As a further illustration I give a revision of my previous formalization (Rose, 1957) of the issue between the liquidity-preference and loanable-funds theories of interest.

II. PRODUCTION, INVESTMENT DEMAND AND THE BUSINESS DEMAND FOR MONEY

The aggregate supply function, the demand for labor, investment demand and the business sector's demand for money are to be derived from the intertemporal profit maximization of the representative firm. We shall exploit recent developments in the intertemporal theory of the firm[1] in combination with convenient assumptions about expectations. In this section the 'state of expectations' is a datum.

---

[1] See Arrow (1968) and Treadway (1969) and their references.

(1) Costs and Profit

The firm is assumed to maximize the discounted excess of its expected 'proceeds' (= planned net value added) over the factor cost.[2] The factor cost of any period is the lowest expectation of proceeds which would contribute to the firm's survival in the long run. (The decision to survive, however, does not require that expected proceeds cover factor cost at all dates. The long-period supply price of the factors is the discounted integral of factor costs over the whole future.)

Factor cost is the sum of wage cost and normal profit. Define net profit as proceeds minus wage cost. Then the maximand is alternatively expressed as the present value of expected surplus profits (or net revenues), where surplus profit is the excess of net profit over normal profit.

(2) Expectations

At time t the firm plans for all times $s \geq t$, given its initial command of capital services and its expectations. As t increases the expectations are revised, and a new plan is made at each t, given the new initial capital and the new expectations.

We denote by $X(s, t)$ the value of X planned or expected at t for $s \geq t$, and for $X(t, t)$ we write X_t. The dating will, however, be omitted wherever possible. In this section and the following one X stands for $X(s, t)$.

The functions introduced are assumed to be continuously differentiable as many times as the argument requires.

Let $x(s, t)$ be the employment–capital ratio planned for s. Both employment and capital are the amounts commanded by the firm, not the amounts utilized, i.e. they include spare capacity, in so far as it is under contract. Expected real proceeds, or planned net value added, is

$$Y = Kf(x) \tag{2.1}$$

and K is planned capital. Y is a flow per unit of time. Technical progress is expected to be

labor-augmenting, and will in fact be so, and x is measured in efficiency units. $f(x)$ is positive and increasing. The marginal productivity of labor, $f'(x)$, is eventually diminishing. The marginal productivity of capital, $f(x) - xf'(x)$, may be negative for small x, but it eventually increases with x and is positive. It does not change sign or direction more than once.[3]

Demand at each price is a random variable. The firm's expected demand function is defined as its real expected proceeds at each selling price. It is (the inverse of)

$$p = Au(Y/B). \tag{2.2}$$

p is selling price, u is a positive, decreasing function, and A and B are expectational parameters. Marginal revenue is positive and strictly decreasing. The firm is a price-maker on its selling side.

The state of demand expectations is given by the positive functions $A(s, t)$ and $B(s, t)$, $s \geq t$. B represents the expected trend of demand, the relevance of which disappears as the elasticity of demand, η, approaches infinity. A represents all other influences on demand expectations.

Define the planned ratio of capital to (the trend of) expected demand:

$$k = K/B \tag{2.3}$$

and use it, with (2.1), to write (2.2) in the form

$$p = Au\{kf(x)\}. \tag{2.4}$$

The firm expects a constant exponential growth of B at the rate β,[4] but the trend level at t, B_t, reflects the influence of aggregate wealth at t on expected demand. The simplest assumption is to make B_t proportional to aggregate capital at t, which in turn is a constant multiple of the representative firm's capital at t, K_t. Since the size of the representative firm in relation to the economy is

---

[2] Cf. Keynes (1936) pp. 23–5.

[3] We are allowing for the possibility of constant or falling short-run marginal and average costs. But both are eventually increasing.

[4] β represents Keynes' 'animal spirits.' There is some attractiveness in equating it with the economy's natural growth rate, for in that case the representative firm's expectations of trend will be confirmed on the average.

immaterial, we can simply choose to make $B_t = K_t$. Thus

$$B(s, t) = K_t e^{\beta(s-t)} \qquad (2.5)$$

and

$$k_t = 1. \qquad (2.6)$$

The demand expected for t is then independent of k, being

$$p_t = A_t u\{f(x_t)\}. \qquad (2.7)$$

The other parameter, $A(s, t)$, together with the expected money wage rate of an efficiency unit of labor, $w(s, t)$, the expected general price level of goods, $q(s, t)$, and expected rates of interest, complete the description of the state of expectations. The only non-stationary element affecting A, w and q as functions of s is the expected percentage rate of inflation, λ, which is itself independent of s. Hence

$$q(s, t) = q_t e^{\lambda(s-t)}, \quad A(s, t) = A_t e^{\lambda(s-t)},$$
$$w(s, t) = w_t e^{\lambda(s-t)} \qquad (2.8)$$

and the ratios A/q, w/q and w/A are independent of s.

w_t and q_t are the actual wage and price levels at t. The firm is a price-taker on the buying side. A_t and λ are also data at t. The behavior of these variables as functions of t will be described in due course.

Two rates of interest are distinguished, the (real) rate on illiquid claims, r, and the (real) rate on money, ρ. They are data to the firm at t and are independent of s. r is the rate at which real surplus profits are discounted, for we must have $r \geq \rho$ if the banks are to supply any money at all.

(3) Maximum Net Profit, Given k

The real net profit expected for s, $P = (pY - wxK)/q$, is a function of x and k, by (2.1) and (2.3)–(2.6):

$$P = \frac{A}{q} K_t e^{\beta(s-t)} y\left(x, k; \frac{w}{A}\right) \qquad (2.9)$$

where

$$y = \left[u\{kf(x)\} f(x) - \frac{w}{A} x \right] k. \qquad (2.10)$$

We assume that y is bounded above, and that for every positive k and w/A the partial derivative y_x, which is proportional to the excess of labor's marginal revenue productivity over the wage rate, is decreasing,[5] and goes to $-k(w/A)$ as $x \to \infty$ and to infinity as $x \to 0$.

A necessary condition for a maximum of discounted surplus profit is that, whatever k is chosen for s, x should be chosen to maximise $P(s, t)$. The vanishing of y_x, or

$$u\{kf(x)\} f'(x) \left(1 - \frac{1}{\eta}\right) = \frac{w}{A} \qquad (2.11)$$

is necessary and sufficient for this.

Particular interest attaches to the short-run plan for t, found by putting $k = 1$ in (2.11):

$$u\{f(x_t)\} f'(x_t) \left(1 - \frac{1}{\eta_t}\right) = \frac{w}{A}. \qquad (2.12)$$

It gives w/A as a decreasing function of x_t only, the inverse of which is the demand for labor per unit of capital at t.

Equation (2.11) can be solved for x as a function of k and w/A, and therefore, by means of (2.12), as a function of k and x_t (x decreases with k and increases with x_t.) Hence y in (2.10) becomes a function of k and x_t,

$$\hat{y} = \hat{y}(k, x_t) \qquad (2.13)$$

where $\hat{y}$ denotes $\max_x y$.

The partial derivative $\hat{y}_k$ is proportional to the marginal revenue productivity of capital. We assume that it is a decreasing function of k when k is small, and that $\lim_{k \to 0} \hat{y}_k = \infty$ and $\lim_{k \to \infty} \hat{y}_k \leq 0$. Thus $\hat{y}_k$ is both positive and decreasing for small k, but our assumptions about $f(x)$ allow it to become, and remain, negative when k is large.[6]

---

[5] The condition for this is that $\epsilon + \mu\theta > 0$, where $\epsilon = -(xf''(x))/(f'(x))$ is the elasticity of marginal cost with respect to x, μ is the elasticity of marginal revenue, $p[1 - 1/\eta]$, with respect to Y, and $\theta = (xf'(x))/(f(x))$ is the elasticity of Y/K with respect to x. The condition is therefore that marginal cost falls less rapidly as Y/K increases than does marginal revenue.

[6] The assumption that y_k is positive and decreasing for small k is equivalent to the assumption that, when k is small, x (which rises as k falls) enters the region of increasing marginal and average cost, $\epsilon > 0$, $\theta < 1$.

Finally, we assume that capital and labor are 'co-operant',[7] which implies that $\hat{y}_k$ increases with x_t.

Now the general price level at t is simply the price set by the representative firm,

$$q_t = p_t = A_t u\{(x_t)\} \qquad (2.14)$$

and so

$$A/q = 1/u\{f(x_t)\}. \qquad (2.15)$$

Net profit, P, is therefore a function only of k, x_t and K_t, viz.,

$$P(s, t) = e^{\beta(s-t)} K_t \hat{y}(k, x_t)/u\{f(x_t)\}. \qquad (2.16)$$

As a function of k and x_t, P has the same qualitative properties as $\hat{y}$.

(4) Normal Profit: (i) Capital Cost and the Business Sector's Demand for Money

Normal profit consists of three elements: illiquidity cost, forgone interest on capital disposal, and adjustment cost. It is convenient to lump together the first two under the title of capital costs, in contrast to the third, which is an investment cost.

Illiquidity cost measures the trouble and expense of raising and retiring money with every fluctuation in the need for immediate purchasing power, whether in the normal course of transactions or in unknown contingencies. It increases in proportion to the size of the firm, as measured by physical capital. In addition it is a decreasing function of the 'state of confidence', which we shall measure by the parameter A/w: business confidence increases as expected demand rises in relation to cost of production.

Planning a larger average real money balance per unit of capital reduces illiquidity cost per unit of capital, up to a point at least. 'Money' is interpreted broadly as liquid claims. Let $L(s, t)$ be the average real balance (per unit of capital) planned for the receipts-payments interval in which (or at the beginning of which) date s occurs, and let $h(L, A/w) \geq 0$ be real illiquidity cost per unit of capital. We assume that h_L is negative for small L, given A/w, but is strictly increasing and eventually becomes positive. (There are diminishing returns to increased liquidity and too much of it is an actual embarrassment.)[8] Also $\lim_{L \to 0} h_L = -\infty$. Both h and h_L are increasing functions of A/w.

In real terms (and given that $r \geq \rho$) the interest forgone on real capital and on the money balance is (per unit of real capital) $r + (r - \rho)L$.

Let $c(s, t)$ be capital cost per unit of planned capital. Then

$$c = r + (r - \rho)L + h(L, A/w). \qquad (2.17)$$

Now for maximum discounted surplus profit it is necessary to choose L to minimize c; and since the parameters of c are independent of s, the same L will be chosen for all s. It will be the solution to

$$-h_L(L, A/w) = r - \rho. \qquad (2.18)$$

Consequently

$$L = L(x_t, r - \rho) \qquad (2.19)$$

for $r \geq \rho$ and $x_t > 0$, with both partial derivatives negative. (x_t has been introduced in lieu of A/w, using (2.12) above.) (2.19) is the firm's (average) demand for money.

Write $\hat{c}$ for $\min_L c$. Evidently

$$\hat{c} = \hat{c}(x_t, r, r - \rho). \qquad (2.20)$$

It increases with r and decreases with ρ and x_t.

(5) Normal Profit: (ii) Adjustment Cost

Is investment demand a decreasing function of r? Or is it perfectly elastic at a critical r? The theoretical answer turns on the presence

---

[7] Capital is co-operant with labor if a rise in employment with capital constant increases the marginal revenue productivity of capital. The condition is $\epsilon > \mu(1 - \theta)$. In the range where θ is < 1 it can be written as $\mu\sigma < 1$, where σ is the elasticity of substitution; for $\epsilon = (1 - \theta)/\sigma$ when $\theta \neq 1$.

[8] The assumption that h_L becomes positive is merely a convenience to avoid the awkwardness of an indeterminate demand for money at $r = \rho$, which would be implied by the alternative (probably more sensible) assumption that h_L is zero for $L \geq$ some L^*. But in any case the problem of what happens where $r = \rho$ is really an artificial one, arising only because we intend to abstract from banking costs. If they were included, $r - \rho$ would have to be sufficiently positive to cover them.

of rising marginal adjustment costs of expansion or contraction. If they exist, they set a margin to investment demand at each r. If not, demand is perfectly elastic. We may capture both cases by assuming either rising marginal adjustment costs or no adjustment costs at all.

We shall confine our attention to subjective adjustment costs,[9] in the spirit of the principle of increasing risk (Kalecki, 1937). There is a risk of marginal loss due to precipitate expansion or contraction, a risk that can be alleviated by circumspection. The marginal expected loss from malinvestment increases when planned investment per unit of capital (which we write I) is above or below the expected growth of demand, β.

Thus if $g(I - \beta)$ is the expected loss from malinvestment, per unit of planned capital, either $g \equiv 0$ (no adjustment cost); or $g(0) = 0$, sign $g'(I - \beta) = \text{sign}(I - \beta)$, and $g''(I - \beta)$ is > 0, and remains so as $I - \beta$ approaches the end-points of the interval on which g is defined.

(6) Investment Demand at t

Real discounted surplus profits are

$$V_t = K_t \int_t^\infty e^{-(r-\beta)(s-t)} \left[\frac{\hat{y}(k, x_t)}{u\{f(x_t)\}} \right. $$
$$\left. - \{\hat{c}(x_t, r, r - \rho) + g(I - \beta)\}k \right] ds. $$

$$(2.21)$$

The market will ensure that r exceeds β. The representative firm cannot have infinitely valuable prospects.

(a) *Increasing Marginal Adjustment Cost.*

V_t is maximized by choosing $I(s, t)$ subject to $\dot{k} = (I - \beta)k$ and the initial condition $k_t = 1$. (The dot means differentiation with respect to s.)

The optimum plan for $k(s, t)$ must, with increasing s, approach the 'desired' capital–demand ratio, k^*, whose marginal revenue productivity equals marginal capital cost, i.e. such that

$$\hat{y}_k(k^*, x_t)/u\{f(x_t)\} = \hat{c}(x_t, r, r - \rho). \quad (2.22)$$

Solving for k^* as a function of the parameters

$$k^* = k^*(x_t, r, r - \rho) \quad (2.23)$$

we could show that k^* must increase with x_t and ρ and decrease with r.

Optimum investment at t is likewise a function of these parameters, and of β. But we can suppress β since we shall not allow it to vary.[10] Thus

$$I_t = I(x_t, r, r - \rho). \quad (2.24)$$

The partials of I_t with respect to x_t and ρ have the signs of the corresponding partials of k^*, i.e. they are positive. But the situation with regard to sign $(\partial I_t/\partial r)$ is slightly more complicated. Given x_t and ρ, I_t must be a decreasing function of r for all r at which k^* is ≥ 1 and, by continuity, for some values of r above this. But for high enough values of r, I_t may begin to increase with r.[11]

---

[9] Many of the objective costs that have been suggested can be circumvented by buying extra (services of) capital already in existence, and hardly any seem to be applicable to contraction. Moreover, the increasing supply price of rapid delivery, which has been suggested as an objective cost, is not really relevant. The requirement of rapid delivery would arise from an *unexpectedly* high rate of planned investment, not from a high rate as such. If plans are laid sufficiently in advance no such costs are incurred, and unless expectations at t differ radically from those of the immediate past, the investment planned at t will consist mainly of projects planned before t.

[10] It can be shown that sign $I_t - \beta = \text{sign } k^* - 1$. Therefore if β is > 0, planned investment can be positive even when the desired capital-demand ratio is less than the actual ratio at t.

[11] These propositions are based on the elegant proof by Treadway (1969) pp. 237–8, which, however, contains one error. His claim that sign $(\partial I_t)/(\partial r) = \text{sign } (\partial k^*)/(\partial r)$ (< 0), regardless of whether desired capital is greater or less than actual capital, is invalid. A rise in r has a twofold effect on I_t. By reducing k^* it tends to reduce $I_t - \beta$. But by lessening the importance of later marginal profits in comparison with earlier marginal profits it tends to reduce the *absolute* value $|I_t - \beta|$. When k^* exceeds k_t both factors pull together, and $(\partial I_t)/(\partial r)$ is < 0, as Treadway shows. But when k_t exceeds k^* the factors are pulling in opposite directions. (There is, however, a limit on the rise in investment that can be induced by high values of r. For with $k^* < 1$ we must have $I_t < \beta$. Cf. note 1 above.)

(b) No Adjustment Cost.

The optimum solution is to choose $k(s, t) = k^*$ for all s, jumping initially to it if $k^* \neq k_t \equiv 1$. Thus $I_t = \pm\infty$ according as $k^* \gtrless 1$. When $k^* = 1$, however, I_t is indeterminate. It can be any quantity without penalty of adjustment cost. And although $k(s, t) = k^*$ implies $I(s, t) = \beta$ almost everywhere on s, it does not preclude isolated departures from β, so long as they have a negligible effect on $k(s, t)$, i.e. so long as I is finite. Thus when $k^* = 1$ the firm can be persuaded to take any finite flow of disposal over capital that the market is supplying at t. In short, investment demand is perfectly elastic at the value of $\hat{c}$ which makes $k^* = 1$.

The critical value of $\hat{c}$ is the marginal revenue productivity of $k^* = 1$, i.e. of initial capital

$$\hat{c}^* = \{f(x_t) - x_t f'(x_t)\}\left(1 - \frac{1}{\eta_t}\right). \qquad (2.25)$$

It is an increasing function of x_t. It follows, via (2.20) above, that the critical rate of interest

$$r^* = r^*(x_t, \rho) \qquad (2.26)$$

at which I_t is perfectly elastic is an increasing function of x_t and a decreasing function of ρ.[12,13]

---

[12] For the case of zero adjustment cost the marginal revenue productivity of capital must be positive and decreasing at $k = 1$. Thus the short-run plan for t must be characterized by increasing marginal and average costs, and since this must be true for all values of w/A, we are forced to assume uniformly increasing costs for all x, implying that $\hat{y}_k$ is everywhere a positive, decreasing function of k and an increasing function of x_t.

[13] Can we say that *aggregate* investment demand is perfectly elastic at a critical r when this is true for the representative firm? It would seem that those who make this assumption are implicitly assuming that all firms are alike. If they are not alike, it may be possible to justify the notion that aggregate I_t will decrease with r despite investment's being perfectly elastic for some proportion of the firms at every r. (This conjecture was suggested to me in conversation by K. J. Arrow.) However, in what follows we shall take it that r^* is the critical rate for aggregate investment.

III. CONSUMPTION, SAVING AND THE AGGREGATE DEMAND FOR MONEY

(1) The Household Plan

The representative household chooses consumption $C(s, t)$, and wealth, $W(s, t)$, to maximize the integral of utility subject to initial wealth, W_t, and a budget constraint.[14] For brevity we consider only the case of an infinite horizon. Utility depends only on consumption, and marginal utility has a constant elasticity, κ. There is a positive subjective time discount, δ. The real interest rates, r and ρ, are expected to be constant.

The choice of a liquid reserve is decided much as it was by the firm. The average money balance does not enter the utility function, but reduces illiquidity cost. It is chosen to maximize the overall rate of return on wealth. If π is this return,

$$\pi = r - (r - \rho)m - h(m, x_t) \qquad (2.27)$$

in which m is the ratio of the average balance to wealth and h is illiquidity cost defined analogously to the firm's h, and endowed with the same properties. The inclusion of x_t is to capture the effect of 'confidence', which increases with x_t. m is chosen to maximize π, so that

$$-h_m(m, x_t) = r - \rho \qquad (2.28)$$

from which the liquidity ratio is a decreasing function of x_t and $r - \rho$:

$$m = m(x_t, r - \rho). \qquad (2.29)$$

$\text{Max}_m \pi = \hat{\pi}$ is

$$\hat{\pi} = \hat{\pi}(x_t, r, r - \rho). \qquad (2.30)$$

It increases with x_t and with both r and ρ.

Utility is maximized subject to the budget equation

$$\dot{W} = \hat{\pi}W - C. \qquad (2.31)$$

---

[14] The 'public household' is like the private sector, we assume, in choosing rationally public consumption subject to its initial wealth and a budget constraint reflecting the current tax laws. For present purposes the two sectors are consolidated, and the 'representative household' plans total consumption, private and public.

The optimum consumption is

$$C = \frac{\delta - (1 - \kappa)\hat{\pi}}{\kappa} \cdot W \qquad (2.32)$$

provided that $\delta > (1 - \kappa)\hat{\pi}$. C/W is a decreasing function of x_t, r and ρ, if κ is <1, but an increasing function of all three if κ is >1.[15]

(2) Aggregate Prospective Wealth at t

The wealth of the community as a whole is the present value of its expected receipts from work and property. We adopt a simple assumption about these expectations: the ratio, R_t, of aggregate prospective wealth to real capital at cost value (which we may identify with the ratio of the representative household's initial wealth to the initial capital of the representative firm) is an increasing function of current business activity,[16] measured by x_t, and a decreasing function of r.

$$R_t = R(x_t, r) \qquad (2.33)$$

$$R_t = W_t/K_t. \qquad (2.34)$$

(3) Aggregate Consumption and Saving Planned for t

Substituting (2.33) and (2.34) into (2.32) we obtain C_t/K_t as a function of x_t, r and ρ. If κ is <1 it is a decreasing function of r and ρ, but the effect of x_t is ambiguous. The liquidity effect, via $\hat{\pi}$, tells against the positive wealth effect. If κ is >1, C_t/K_t increases with x_t and ρ, but the effect of r is ambiguous.

Define planned saving as the value of the planned increase in wealth. Planned household saving for t is therefore expected cash income ($\hat{\pi}W_t$ minus expected capital gains) less consumption. To this must be added the planned retained profits of business. We assume that households' expected cash income

for t is what firms (including the financial sector) are planning to distribute in wages and profits at that time. Let it be D_t. Then planned real saving per unit of capital is

$$S_t = \frac{(Y_t - D_t) + (D_t - C_t)}{K_t} = \frac{Y_t - C_t}{K_t}$$

so that

$$S_t = f(x_t) - C_t/K_t = S(x_t, r, r - \rho). \qquad (2.35)$$

If κ is <1, S increases with r and ρ, and there is a strong presumption that S_{x_t} is >0 (positive marginal propensity to save). The presumption is weaker if κ is >1. Moreover, in this case S_ρ is <0 and sign S_r is ambiguous.

(4) The aggregate Demand for Money

The household sector's demand for money per unit of real capital is mR_t, the product of (2.29) and (2.33). Adding it to business demand (2.19) and letting L now stand for total demand per unit of capital, we get

$$L = L(x_t, r, r - \rho). \qquad (2.36)$$

It decreases with r and increases with ρ. But there is now uncertainty about the effect of x_t. The positive wealth effect on household demand could possibly outweigh the negative confidence effect on total demand.

IV. MONEY AND CREDIT FLOWS

From now on we shall be concerned only with the plans and expectations for t and their revision. Accordingly we shall change the notation, using x, A, etc., to stand for x_t, A_t, etc., and letting a dot mean differentiation with respect to t.

(1) The Flow Excess Supply of Money

The demand for money, L, is for an average balance over a receipts-payments interval. The real supply (per unit of capital), M, is similarly an average planned over an interval. If there were no uncertainty about cash inflows and outflows, and about the fluctuating recourse to and repayment of bank[17] loans, both demanders and suppliers would adjust

---

[15] The clear-cut negative interest elasticity when κ is <1 should not be taken too seriously. If the horizon were finite the commonly recognized ambiguity could emerge.

[16] For (i) employment prospects improve with x_t, and (ii) a rise in x_t (which must be due to a rise in A/w) raises the present value of the representative firm relative to its cost value, K_t.

[17] By 'banks' we mean the suppliers of liquid assets generally.

instantaneously at t to remove any discrepancy between the planned average and the observed average. But since random flows are anticipated, the rate of adjustment will not be instantaneous. Instead there will be planned hoarding and money creation at a finite rate per unit of time to counter the discrepancy. Therefore the excess flow supply of money, X_M, per unit of capital, is assumed to be

$$X_M = \gamma(M - L) \qquad (2.37)$$

with γ a positive constant.[18]

(2) 'Loanable Funds': The Flow Excess Supply of Capital Disposal

This consists of planned household (including public) and business saving plus the excess flow supply of money, minus investment demand.[19] Per unit of capital it is

$$X_{CD} = \gamma(M - L) + S - I. \qquad (2.38)$$

V. THE DYNAMICS OF SUPPLY AND THE PRICE LEVEL

(1) The Dynamic Multiplier

In the short-run plan for t:

$$u\{f(x)\}f'(x)\left(1 - \frac{1}{\eta}\right) = w/A \qquad (2.12)$$

---

[18] Properly, the flow should be derived from inventory theory, and would be a more general expression, no doubt.

[19] If households expected full employment at t, instead of the employment planned by business, their expected cash income would exceed the planned disbursements of the business sector by the value of the excess supply of labor. If v is the ratio of the supply of labor to the stock of capital, we should have

$$S = (Y - C)/K + \frac{w}{p}(v - x),$$

so that in (2.38):

$$X_{CD} = \gamma(M - L) + \frac{Y - C}{K} - I + \frac{w}{p}(v - x).$$

The excess supply of capital disposal would be the sum of the excess supplies of money, goods and *labor* (Walras' Law *stricto sensu*). Our exclusion of the excess supply of labor seems to be for much the same reason as Clower's (1965). But we are not sure that we can agree with him in the importance he attaches to the omission.

the employment–capital ratio, x, is a decreasing function of w/A. Its percentage rate of change with t is

$$\dot{x}/x = \phi(x)(\dot{A}/A - \dot{w}/w) \qquad (2.39)$$

with $\phi > 0$.[20] (2.39) is the basis for the long-run extension of the dynamic multiplier. To complete the picture the determinants of $\dot{A}$ and $\dot{w}$ must be specified.

Expected demand depends on the expected general price level, on the expected prices of the firm's close competitors, and on previous experience of actual demand. (There is also the trend factor, but we have already accounted for that.) Accordingly, we assume for the representative firm

$$\dot{A}/A = \lambda + E(I - S, \dot{w}/w) \qquad (2.40)$$

in which

$$E(0, 0) = 0, \quad \frac{\partial E}{\partial(I - S)} > 0, \quad 0 \le \frac{\partial E}{\partial \dot{w}/w} < 1.$$

The expected demand curve rises over time (a) by the expected rate of inflation, (b) by an amount depending on the excess of actual over expected demand (which for the representative firm is $I - S$), and perhaps on a 'cost push' element, in so far as a rise in w induces the expectation that competitors will raise their prices. Cost push is, however, unlikely to raise demand in proportion to w. For wages do not rise all together, and even if they did the reaction of other firms would be shrouded in uncertainty. In many contexts we may simplify by omitting cost push, writing

$$\dot{A}/A = \lambda + E(I - S). \qquad (2.41)$$

With zero excess demand for labor, w rises at the expected rate of inflation.[21] In an imperfect market it is imperfectly flexible in some neighborhood of zero excess demand, for unemployment and vacancies are each

---

[20] ϕ is the reciprocal of $\epsilon + \mu\theta$.

[21] This means that effort-wages rise with productivity. It need not indicate union power, since the commodity traded is an efficiency unit of labor. The rise with λ reflects the fact that rational bargaining is about the expected *real* wage.

acting as restraints on competition. But both employment and vacancies rise with excess demand. When the unemployment pool becomes negligible, perfect upward flexibility is approached; and similarly perfect downward flexibility as vacancies disappear. Thus

$$\dot{w}/w = \lambda + F(z) \tag{2.42}$$

where z is the ratio of the demand to the supply, $F(1) = 0$, $F'(z) > 0$, and $\lim_{z \to a} F = -\infty$, $\lim_{z \to b} F = +\infty$ ($0 < a < 1 < b < \infty$). (a and b are the values of z at which vacancies and unemployment are respectively zero.)[22]

When (2.41) and (2.42) are substituted into (2.39), we get

$$\dot{x}/x = \phi(x)\{E(I - S) - F(z)\} \tag{2.43}$$

for the long-run dynamic multiplier process.

(2) The Mechanism of Inflation

The behavior of the price level $p(=q)$ follows from the log derivative of

$$p = Au\{f(x)\} \tag{2.7}$$

with respect to t, together with (2.43) to eliminate $\dot{x}/x$:

$$\dot{p}/p = \{1 - \xi(x)\}E + \xi(x)F + \lambda. \tag{2.44}$$

ξ must be non-negative.[23] It goes to zero as $\eta \to \infty$, when (unexpected) inflation depends only on the excess demand for goods (and cost push, if any). It is unity when both η and marginal cost are constant, and then (unexpected) inflation depends only on the excess demand for labor. (Under decreasing marginal cost ξ can exceed unity. The influence of E is then deflationary.)

Evidently $E = F = 0$ is insufficient to remove inflation unless λ is always zero in these circumstances.

(3) The Dynamics of Factor Supply

(a) Capital

When there is, for example, an excess demand for goods, firms may respond either by releasing stocks or by working longer hours. In the latter case actual production is greater than planned, and there are unexpected disbursements of cash income or unexpected retained profits. Since consumption depends on prospective wealth only, there is unintended saving. In practice firms are apt to respond in both ways. Let α be the proportion of $I - S$ which is satisfied by unplanned production ($0 \le \alpha \le 1$). Then $\alpha(I - S)$ is unplanned production = unplanned saving; and *ex-post* accumulation, $\dot{K}/K$, as the sum of planned and unplanned saving, is

$$\dot{K}/K = S + \alpha(I - S). \tag{2.45}$$

We shall assume that α is a constant.

(b) The Labor–Capital Ratio.

Let v be the ratio of the (efficiency) supply of labour to the stock of capital and n the percentage growth rate of the (efficiency) supply of labor. By definition

$$\dot{v}/v = n - [S + \alpha(I - S)]. \tag{2.46}$$

Finally, also by definition,

$$z = x/v. \tag{2.47}$$

VI. A 'Neo-Swedish' Theory of Growth, Inflation and the Cycle

(1) The General Framework

We have constructed a set of relations referring to time t:

The demand for goods:

Investment demand	(2.24)	$I = I(x, r, r - \rho)$
or I perfectly elastic at	(2.26)	$r = r^*(x, \rho)$
Planned saving	(2.35)	$S = S(x, r, r - \rho)$

---

[22] In a perfect market $a = b = 1$, and w is perfectly flexible at $z = 1$.

[23] $\xi = \theta/\eta/(\epsilon + \mu\theta)$. (It can be shown that $\mu = 1/\eta$ when η is constant.)

The demand for money: (2.36) $L = L(x, r, r - \rho)$

Flow excess supplies:

     Money   (2.37) $X_M = \gamma(M - L)$

     Capital disposal   (2.38) $X_{CD} = \gamma(M - L) + S - I$

Dynamics:

     The multiplier   (2.43) $\dot{x}/x = \phi(x)\{E(I - S) - F(z)\}$

         where   (2.47) $z = x/v$

     Factor supplies   (2.46) $\dot{v}/v = n - [S + \alpha(I - S)]$

     Inflation   (2.44) $\dot{p}/p = \{1 - \xi(x)\}E + \xi(x)F + \lambda.$

To obtain from them a closed dynamic system it is necessary to specify the determinants of the natural rate of growth, n, the expected rate of inflation, λ, the real supply of money per unit of capital, M, and the interest rates, r and ρ.

(2) The Neo-Swedish Model

Let n be a constant and λ a non-decreasing function of the level of activity, x. Assume that, given x, r is determined competitively so that $X_{CD} = 0$, but that the nominal rate on money is linked to the discount rate of the central bank, which is a non-decreasing function of x. Wicksell (1936) apparently assumed this to be the only control exerted by the central bank. Consequently, with free entry prevailing in banking, the supply of money would be perfectly elastic at $r = \rho(x)$,[24] and the market rate of interest would always equal the money rate, with M determined passively to satisfy $X_{CD} = 0$. More generally, however, we may assume that the central bank determines the banks' (real) cash supply in proportion to the size of the economy, as measured by real capital. If the banks' desired cash–deposit ratio decreases with $r - \rho$ and also with the state of confidence, we shall have M as an increasing function of x and $r - \rho$,

$$M = M(x, r - \rho). \tag{2.48}$$

(Stabilization policy could be built into (2.48) by assuming that the ratio of cash reserves to total capital determined by the central bank is itself a function of x, etc. This could reduce

the magnitude, even alter the signs, of the partials of M.)

With $X_{CD} = 0$ and investment demand subject to adjustment costs, r will be the solution to

$$I[x, r, r - \rho(x)] - S[x, r, r - \rho(x)]$$
$$= \gamma\{M[x, r - \rho(x)] - L[x, r, r - \rho(x)]\}. \tag{2.49}$$

Thus

$$r = r(x) \quad \text{and} \quad \rho = \rho(x). \tag{2.50}$$

Neither r nor ρ depends on the price level. For (2.48) preserves a distinguishing feature of the Wicksellian assumption, that the suppliers of money have no money illusion.

When (2.50) is substituted into I, S, M and L they become functions of x only, $\hat{I}(x)$, $\hat{S}(x)$, $\hat{M}(x)$ and $\hat{L}(x)$. Moreover $\hat{I}(x) - \hat{S}(x) \equiv \gamma\{\hat{M}(x) - \hat{L}(x)\}$ identically in x. E in (2.43) and (2.44) may therefore be regarded equally as a function of $\hat{I} - \hat{S}$ or of $\gamma(\hat{M} - \hat{L})$. Let this function be

$$H = E(\hat{I} - \hat{S}) = H(x). \tag{2.51}$$

It sums up the influence of 'effective demand' on the economic system. When it is substituted into (2.43) and (2.44) we obtain the dynamic system

$$\left.\begin{array}{l} \dot{x}/x = \phi(x)\{H(x) - F(z)\} \\ \dot{v}/v = n - G(x) \\ \dot{p}/p = \{1 - \xi(x)\}H(x) + \xi(x)F(z) + \lambda(x) \end{array}\right\} A$$

in which

$$z = x/v \tag{2.47}$$

$$G(x) \equiv \hat{S} + \alpha(\hat{I} - \hat{S}) \equiv \hat{S} + \alpha\gamma(\hat{M} - \hat{L}). \tag{2.52}$$

---

[24] We are abstracting from banking costs.

In the case of zero adjustment costs $r(x)$ in (2.50) is the solution to (2.26) with $\rho = \rho(x)$. The equation $X_{CD} = 0$ then determines $\hat{I}$ as $\hat{S}(x) + \gamma\{\hat{M}(x) - \hat{L}(x)\}$.

The first two equations of system A are a self-contained sub-system in x and v, independent of ρ. Having previously examined many of its properties, we shall do not more than summarize them here. It is necessary to assume that there is an $\bar{x} > 0$ such that $G(\bar{x}) = n$, and that $G'(x)$ is > 0; also that the sub-system is twice continuously differentiable and structurally stable.

There is a unique growth equilibrium $(\bar{x}, \bar{z})$, determined by $G(\bar{x}) = n$, $F(\bar{z}) = H(\bar{x})$. Long-run inflation is $H(\bar{x}) + \lambda(\bar{x})$. The equilibrium is globally stable if

$$xH'(x) < zF'(z) \tag{2.53}$$

for all $x > 0$ and z in (a, b), but there may be damped oscillations in response to shocks. If, however, $\bar{x}H'(\bar{x}) > \bar{z}F'(\bar{z})$ the equilibrium is unstable, and every motion tends to a limit cycle around it. No shocks are needed to keep a cycle alive.

(3) Long-Run Inflation and Employment

Apart from the effects of 'cost push', long-run inflation is independent of the excess demand for labor.[25] The F function determines only the $\bar{z}$ corresponding to $F = H(\bar{x})$, and since, as we shall see, there are practical limits to the variation in $\bar{z}$ achievable by altering the parameters of H, long-run employment depends more on the structure of the labor market than on effective demand.

(4) Wage Flexibility and the Cycle

The degree of wage flexibility is of prime importance for the cycle, which could not occur if wages were sufficiently flexible. Given

[25] Cost push, whereby $\dot{w}/w$ becomes an argument in the E function (2.40) above, and therefore in H, raises the rate of inflation corresponding to a given $\bar{x}$. Even so, since its partial derivative is < 1, a positive excess demand for labor cannot alone sustain inflation in the long run.

$H'(x)$, with $F'(z)$ large enough, the equilibrium must be stable and non-oscillatory.[26]

(5) Say's Law and Effective Demand

The significance of the effective demand factor, $H(x)$, is best appreciated by assuming its absence. Suppose that $\rho(x)$ is determined not by the central bank but by competition,[27] so that $X_M = 0$. Then Say's Law of Markets is established.[28] $\hat{I}(x) \equiv \hat{S}(x)$ and $H(x) \equiv 0$ identically in x.

The equilibrium rate of inflation is then $\lambda(\bar{x})$, the expected rate. Now even though Say's Law is not fulfilled exactly even in the long run, there must be some tendency keeping long-run inflation close to $\lambda(\bar{x})$, i.e. keeping $|H(\bar{x})|$ small. For there is likely to be an adaptive element in λ which will take over if $|H(\bar{x})|$ is large enough. This would induce a cumulative rise (or fall) of the long-run actual rate. System A is applicable only if $|H(\bar{x})|$ does not cross the threshold. This is the practical limitation on achieving high long-run employment by means of inflation.

[26] With perfect wage flexibility the path to equilibrium must be monotonic. The system essentially becomes the Solow growth model in that case. See below, section VII.

[27] To ensure a stable adjustment of both interest rates to their market equilibrium, without regard to the relative adjustment rates, it is necessary and sufficient to assume both $S_r > I_r$ and $S_\rho - I_\rho / S_r - I_r > M_\rho - L_\rho / M_r - L_r$.

[28] If, in addition, there is free entry into private banking, so that M is perfectly elastic at $r = \rho$, it might be thought that money would be completely neutral, in the sense that the configuration of the economy would be exactly like that of an ideal 'barter' system which needs no special monetary assets because it encounters no illiquidity costs. (The ideal system has costless clearing arrangements, and in effect every good and claim is a generally acceptable medium of exchange. It is the world of non-monetary economic theory, not the world of primitive barter.) But in general this not so. For although with $r = \rho$ marginal illiquidity costs are zero, average illiquidity costs (h in (2.17) and (2.27) above) may still be positive. (Cf. Friedman and Schwartz (1969) p. 5.) Thus even with Say's Law and $r = \rho$, money is not neutral. The yield on household wealth, $\hat{\pi}$, is $< r$, and r is $< \hat{c}$, the cost of capital to firms, whereas in the ideal system they are all equal. However, neutrality is not necessarily a desideratum, unless the 'barter' configuration is a Pareto optimum.

The tendency whereby hyperinflation[29] is avoided may be automatic—market forces may operate, though tardily, on ρ; or monetary policy may move it in the right direction on the average.[30]

Contrary to a popular impression, Say's Law does not necessarily eliminate cycles. As we have shown elsewhere (Rose, 1969), a damped cycle, due, for example, to unsteady technical progress, may be generated if wages are sticky, which has a strong resemblance to those actually observed. Nevertheless the movements of demand in relation to supply greatly enrich the theory. Although the 'over-investment' element of the real cycle must always be present,[31] and the existence of turning-points is ultimately ensured by the behavior of money wages, yet (i) the actual turning-points can be brought about by non-linearity of $H(x)$, due either to an investment ceiling and floor or to alterations of active and passive monetary control in response to movements of $\lambda(x)$; (ii) the cumulative process may predominantly reflect either the multiplier–accelerator interaction or the effect of confidence on the excess demand for money, depending on the interest elasticities of the excess demands for goods and money; (iii) shocks, if they are needed, may come from the parameters of effective demand; and finally (iv) the parameters of H provide a lever for stabilization policy. In fact we have here a very general theory of fluctuations.

We have attributed the failure of Say's Law to inflexibility of ρ. This is, of course, an over-simplification. The same results can, and no doubt in practice do, flow from rigidity of interest rates on certain illiquid claims,[32] such as bank advances and trade credit.

Should its failure be ascribed in part to the zero nominal yield on currency? Probably not. The supply of currency is usually passively adapted to the demand for it.

VII. STOCKS, FLOWS, AND THE 'NEO-CLASSICAL' THEORY OF MONEY AND GROWTH

The neo-Swedish model takes a large step back from Keynes towards neo-classicism. At the beginning of the *General Theory*[33] Keynes criticized classical economics for supposing that labor can directly influence its employment by accepting reduced money wages, thereby reducing costs. Equation (2.43) tells us that in general the classical supposition is correct.[34]

The problem of the incompatibility of the warranted rate of growth, $\hat{I}(x) = \hat{S}(x)$, with the natural rate, $G(\bar{x}) = n$, which has beset neo-Keynesian growth theory and, in view of its reluctance to rely on real balance effects, necessitated the introduction of v as an argument in $\hat{I}$ or $\hat{S}$ (autonomous investment or consumption), is the direct result either of accepting Keynes' critique or of his other anti-classical postulate, complete wage inflexibility. The problem simply does not arise in the Wicksellian model. A discrepancy (in equilibrium) between the two rates is just a reflection of the inflationary gap.

On the other hand, our theory is obviously at variance with the monetary growth theory of the so-called neo-classical revival. Because the suppliers of money have no money illusion, the price level is 'indeterminate', just as it is in Wicksell. An initial value of it must be stipulated, and if the equilibrium is one

---

[29] By hyperinflation we mean not a high rate but an increasing one.

[30] Of course other steps will also normally be taken to guard against a breakdown of the monetary system.

[31] Accumulation (G) in the boom exceeds what can be permanently sustained (n).

[32] Cf. Tobin (1969) p. 26.

[33] Keynes (1936) pp. 11–13. But the denial of a direct effect via costs actually dates from the *Treatise*. See Keynes (1930) vol. I, pp. 160, 167.

[34] There are only two assumptions under which Keynes would be right. One is if there is an extreme form of cost push, whereby in (2.40) $(\partial E)/(\partial \dot{w}/w) \equiv 1$. Every wage change leads the firm to *expect* a proportional change in all prices, hence a proportional change in its own demand curve. The other is if the firm's short-run expectations adjust instantaneously (in the face of excess demand) in relation to the rate of change of money wages. Neither of them has much to recommend it as a foundation for a general theory.

with p constant it is, for p, a neutral equilibrium. In contrast, the revivalists have resuscitated (under perfect wage flexibility) an extreme form of the Quantity Theory of Money, in which p is always such as to make the real value of the *given* nominal stock of money equal to the demand for it. In fact, despite its name, their theory is essentially Keynesian: whatever the degree of wage flexibility, wages affect the economy only via real balances, and when they are perfectly flexible the quantity equation determines the price level at each t.

Our comparison of the two theories is confined to the case of perfect wage flexibility. Consider the Wicksellian model under this assumption. The second equation of system A becomes

$$\dot{x}/x = n - G(x) \qquad (2.54)$$

and in the first equation $\lambda + E - \dot{w}/w$ must replace $E - F$, by (2.39) and (2.41). Since (2.54) above determines the course of $x = v$, the revised first equation now tells us how w must move to sustain full employment. Together with various substitutions it enables us to derive this expression for the rate of inflation:

$$\dot{p}/p = E\{\gamma[\hat{M}(x) - \hat{L}(x)]\} + \frac{\theta}{\eta}\{\hat{S}(x) +$$

$$+ \alpha\gamma[\hat{M}(x) - \hat{L}(x)] - n\} + \lambda. \qquad (2.55)$$

In one variant of the revivalists' theory, at every t there is a stock equilibrium established both for money and for real capital.[35] This would require both that adjustment costs are zero and that $\gamma \to \infty$. There is, in effect, no uncertainty either about investment prospects or about cash flows.

Now our theory can absorb either of these assumptions on its own, but in general not

both together.[36] We have already allowed for the case of zero adjustment costs. The case $\gamma \to \infty$ (but increasing marginal adjustment cost) merely implies a 'liquidity preference' theory of interest in place of our 'loanable funds' theory. The flow excess supply of money, $\lim_{\gamma \to \infty} \gamma(M - L)$, is perfectly elastic at the r which equates M and L. (It is not zero, however, nor infinite, but equals $I - S$ in market equilibrium; cf. (2.49) above.)[37]

If, however, adjustment costs are zero, r must satisfy equation (2.26), and as γ goes to infinity r is unaffected. Instead $\lim_{\gamma \to \infty} \gamma[\hat{M}(x) - \hat{L}(x)] \equiv \hat{I}(x) - \hat{S}(x)$ will become infinitely positive or negative. Assuming, as seems reasonable, that E goes to $\pm\infty$ when its argument does so, we find that $\dot{p}/p$ in (2.55) must tend to $\pm\infty$, unless by a fluke $\hat{M}(x) = \hat{L}(x)$. The price level is either zero or infinite.

This kind of 'indeterminacy' is, of course, intolerable. It is plausible to say that in these circumstances the nominal money supply would have to be a datum at each t, since it could not be planned to keep pace with the price level. In any case, if it is a datum the indeterminacy is removed. The price level will be instantaneously adjusted to eliminate the infinite flow excess supply, i.e. so that

---

[35] It is often assumed for simplicity that money and goods are the only assets. There is no market for capital disposal. This means that every wealth-holder with goods in his portfolio must be an entrepreneur. For if there is a market for the services of capital there is, indeed, a market for loans. To sell a good's services is to lend the good, i.e. to part with its use for a time.

[36] This is true whatever the degree of wage flexibility. There is one exception, namely when ρ is flexible. Under Say's Law the stock-equilibrium postulate presents no problem.

[37] The paradox (that with stock equilibrium the flow excess supply is non-zero) is resolved by the consideration that when, e.g., $I > S$, those tending to accumulate unwanted money balances are dishoarding them at a rate, $\lim_{\gamma \to \infty} \gamma(M - L)$; that is, just sufficient to obviate the unplanned hoarding, $I - S$, which would otherwise occur. Thus the tendency is never actualized.

In a previous attempt to formalize the liquidity preference theory (Rose, 1957), I claimed that in it unintended disinvestment $(I - S)$ should be subtracted from the demand for funds, so that the flow excess supply of funds equals the flow excess supply of money. I was criticized by Patinkin (1959) for mixing in *ex post* with *ex ante* ingredients. Although not convinced of the decisiveness of this criticism, I am now inclined to prefer an explanation that avoids it.

$\lim_{\gamma \to \infty} \gamma[M - \hat{L}(x)] = 0$, where $M = N/pK$ and N is the nominal supply of money. Thus we have

$$\left. \begin{array}{l} \hat{L}(x) = N/pK \\ \dot{x}/x = n - \hat{S}(x) \end{array} \right\} B$$

[for when the supply and demand for money are equal, $G(x) (\equiv \dot{K}/K) = \hat{S}(x)$].

System B is an inside-money version of the 'monetary growth' theory. It can be completed by assuming, e.g., constant exponential growth of N. If the nominal rate of interest on money is constant, $\hat{S}$ will depend on λ, the behaviour of which must also be specified (see Tobin, 1965).

In another variant of the theory, perfect wage flexibility is combined not with stock equilibrium but with the Keynesian postulate of instantaneous adjustment of short-run expectations. There is correct anticipation of short-run demand or price, presumably through a Walrasian auction. Here again in (2.55) $\dot{p}/p = \pm\infty$, this time because E is 'perfectly elastic' at $I = S$. In this variant r will depend not only on x but also on M. In general, therefore, so will $\hat{S}$ and $\hat{L}$.

There is, incidentally, one further case in which system B must replace A, namely if, although marginal adjustment costs may be increasing and the derivative of E is finite, (i) neither L nor M depends on interest rates and (ii) $\gamma \to \infty$. [Once again $\lim_{\gamma \to \infty} \gamma[\hat{M}(x) - \hat{L}(x)]$ would be $\pm\infty$.] It establishes the 'crude' quantity theory of money.

The revivalists' monetary recommendations do not, of course, stand or fall with the acceptability of their assumptions. The prima facie attractiveness of the constant-growth-of-money proposal is that it may be easier to to guess the natural rate of growth than the natural rate of interest. But if the general framework is completed by this assumption in place of (2.48), the system contains three interlocking differential equations, and if moreover λ is believed to be adaptive whenever it differs from $\dot{p}/p$, a fourth is added. The crucial stability question remains an open one.[38]

References

Arrow, K. J., "Optimal Capital policy with Irreversible Investment," in Wolfe, J. N. (ed.), *Value, Capital, and Growth* (Edinburgh U.P., 1968).

Clower, R. W., "The Keynesian Counterrevolution: A Theoretical Appraisal," in Hahn, F. H., and Brechling, F. P. R. (eds.), *The Theory of Interest Rates* (London: Macmillan, 1965) [reprinted in this volume].

Friedman, M., and Schwartz, A. J., "The Definition of Money: Net Wealth and Neutrality as Criteria," *Journal of Money, Credit, and Banking*, 1 (1969).

Kalecki, M., "The Principle of Increasing Risk," *Economica*, 4 (1937).

Keynes, J. M., *A Treatise on Money* (London: Macmillan, 1930).

———, *The General Theory of Employment, Interest, and Money* (London: Macmillan, 1936).

Patinkin, D., "Reply to R. W. Clower and H. Rose," *Economica*, 26 (1959).

Rose, H., "Liquidity Preference and Loanable Funds," *Review of Economic Studies*, 24 (1957).

———, "On the Non-Linear Theory of the Employment Cycle," *Review of Economic Studies*, 34 (1967).

———, "Real and Monetary Factors in the Business Cycle," *Journal of Money, Credit, and Banking*, 1 (1969).

Stein, J. L., and Nagatani, K., "Stabilization Policies in a Growing Economy," *Review of Economic Studies*, 36 (1969).

Tobin, J. "Money and Economic Growth," *Econometrica*, 33 (1965) [reprinted in this volume].

———, "A General Equilibrium Approach to Monetary Theory," *Journal of Money, Credit, and Banking*, 1 (1969).

Treadway, A. B., "On Rational Entrepreneurial Behaviour and the Demand for Investment," *Review of Economic Studies*, 36 (1960).

Wicksell, K., *Interest and Prices* (London: Macmillan, 1936).

[38] Stein and Nagatani (1969) have considered a special case, eliminating two equations by assuming instantaneous adjustment of λ and perfect wage flexibility. Personally I doubt whether this throws much light on the general case.

Money, Growth, and the Propensity to Save

Ronald I. McKinnon

Stanford University

INTRODUCTION

In his famous paper, "Wealth, Saving, and the Rate of Interest" [9], Metzler followed the classical tradition of Pigou in assuming that the stock of privately held wealth—an important part of which was real cash balances—was negatively correlated with the aggregate propensity to save. However, Metzler's model was mainly in the static Keynesian mold where the rate of growth did not enter explicitly, and a generation of graduate students has come to associate an increase in the net wealth of the household sector with an upward shift in the aggregate consumption function (unless the marginal propensity to save is arbitrarily assumed to be a fixed parameter). Indeed, the proposition must be true in certain disequilibrium situations where wealth holdings are deemed to be too large relative to current income flows, and individuals increase their current consumption in order to reduce stocks of money, bonds, or commodities to desired levels.

Once equilibrium growth is taken into account, however, there is an important sense in which this standard proposition drawn from static macroeconomic theory should be reversed. Instead, large holdings of private wealth, particularly in the form of real cash

balances, can increase the propensity to save when income itself is growing rapidly. Hence, monetary policy that induces individuals to increase their stock of financial assets, relative to the flow of current income, can encourage private saving and so increase the rate of accumulation of physical capital. On the one hand, a higher yield on liquid assets, including money, rewards saving directly while increasing desired stocks of financial assets.[1] On the other hand, the desire to maintain large stocks of assets in portfolio balance induces a further increment to saving once growth begins.

This latter "portfolio effect" of growth on the propensity to save is emphasized in this chapter, and related to the monetary system's role as a financial intermediary in the accumulation of physical capital. This portfolio effect can help explain the relationship between saving and financial structure in high growth economies such as Japan and Taiwan, both of which have unusually high

[1] As is well known, this direct impact of higher interest rates is subject to an ambiguous income effect that makes it unclear theoretically as to whether current saving (and presumably stocks of financial assets) would actually increase. However, the present author has convinced himself [8, Chapter 8], that, as an empirical matter, stocks of financial assets can be expected to increase when the reward for holding them rises. If desired stocks of financial assets do not increase in response to interest rate stimuli, this does not invalidate my thesis about wealth effects in the presence of growth; but it does make the implications for economic policy considerably less interesting.

Reprinted from *Trade, Stability, and Macroeconomics: Essays in Honor of Lloyd Metzler*, edited by G. Horwich and P. A. Samuelson (1974), by permission of the author and the publisher (copyright by Academic Press, Inc.).

saving rates and high money/GNP ratios for their level of development and per capita income. Elements of the model are also applicable to more mature economies, although the degree of applicability will have to be decided by each reader for himself, since this chapter is oriented toward the less-developed countries.

Metzler's remarkable contribution was written well over twenty years ago. Since then, there has been a plethora of articles, first on growth and accumulation alone, and then on money and growth, mainly within a neoclassical framework.[2] If real cash balances do indeed exert a strong positive influence on saving propensities and the accumulation of physical capital, as claimed here, should this portfolio effect not have been picked up in the literature now extant? Unfortunately, most contributors to the neoclassical literature on economic growth assume that the private propensity to save is fixed irrespective of the return on saving, the size of wealth holding, and the rate of growth; or they assume that real money balances, while useful as a means of facilitating current transactions, are substitutes for physical capital in the asset portfolios of the private sector. As we shall see, both of these neoclassical postulates tend to vitiate one's understanding of the nexus between growth and the propensity to save—particularly in less-developed countries.

The neo-Keynesian approach to equilibrium growth is no better. For example, Williamson [13] specifies that monetary policies that increase desired real cash balances also shift the aggregate consumption function upward. In contrast, the model outlined herein is designed to avoid these pitfalls that seem to be inherent in the neoclassical and Keynesian approaches to monetary policy and the rate of accumulation. I hypothesize that large real cash balances, held in portfolio equilibrium, enhance rather than retard the rate of growth in physical

capital over the time horizon relevant for economic development.

I. FINANCIAL STRUCTURE AND MONETARY POLICY

In analyzing poor countries, it is sometimes quite reasonable to suppose that "money," broadly defined to include time and savings deposits, is virtually the only financial asset available to savers that is at all liquid (see Goldsmith [3]). Open markets for primary securities such as bonds, mortgages, and common stock are usually quite moribund or very small. Hence there is no uniform rate of interest on "bonds" that represents the opportunity cost of holding money.

For analytical convenience, therefore, I assume that each year saver can hold only money, whose return is heavily influenced by the State, or can hold physical commodities whose return will vary with the use that he himself in his household or firm can find for them.[3] Thus money has considerable importance as a store of value as well as a medium of exchange, and there is *no* market in primary securities for fully equalizing the returns on physical capital, much of which is self-financed. Private capital markets are highly imperfect.

A concomitant of restricting the asset portfolios of savers to money or commodities is that the role of the monetary system as a financial intermediary must be specified explicitly.[4] Hence I assume that the net

---

[2] Some principal authors in this monetary tradition are Friedman [2], Johnson [5], Levhari and Patinkin [7], Tobin [12], and Mundell [10].

[3] In contrast, the prevailing assumption in the neoclassical and Keynesian models is a "perfect" market in primary securities, so that a uniform rate of interest is established on "bonds" as well as on physical capital. This perfect capital-market assumption is no less extreme than to assume that individual savers simply do not have the chance of holding "bonds"—or indeed any primary security which is a claim on enterprises other than their own.

[4] With a perfect market for primary securities in the neoclassical world, the monetary system's role as a financial intermediary is redundant. Hence, money is usually created by "outside" means within traditional economic models, and the demand for money is justified purely on the grounds of improving the efficiency with which current transactions are conducted.

acquisition of real cash balances, M/P, by the private sector is channeled via bank credit either to industrial and agricultural borrowers, who wish to accumulate physical capital rather than consume, or to the government for current public consumption.[5] For simplicity, assume that the real rate of interest paid by private borrowers to the banking system fully reflects the scarcity value of total bank credit allocated to the private sector; and assume that the government consciously appropriates its own share of bank credit at a zero interest cost. In effect, the government determines the amount of seigniorage it wishes to extract from the monetary system, and the real bank credit remaining is allocated to the private sector at equilibrium rates of interest.[6]

For illustrative purposes, our model views the banking system—central bank, commercial banks, savings banks, and so on—as being completely integrated with only private depositors (inclusive of currency holders) on the liabilities side of its balance sheet (no bank ownership or equity capital), and the two classes of borrowers, private and public, on the asset side. Let L be the loans outstanding to the private sector at high equilibrium rates of interest. Let us further suppose that seigniorage is appropriated through government sales of noninterest bearing securities, denoted by S_g, to the banking system in return for deposits that are immediately spent for current goods and services. The relevant T account (balance sheet) for the banking system at any point in time is

Assets	Liabilities
L	M
S_g	

[5] Of course, there can also be real accumulation in the public sector or consumption loans in the private one. This sharp distinction is made for reasons of analytical convenience.

[6] The government can always allocate some of its seigniorage outside the public sector by designating certain private borrowers to receive low cost loans. Again, for simplicity, I omit this possibility because it does not affect the analysis in any essential way.

To put the balance sheet in real terms, the stocks L, S_g, and M can be divided through by P.

What then are the relevant instruments of monetary policy open to the authorities? In a relatively early paper [11], Tobin noted many of the subtle difficulties in using data on liquid assets – including real cash balances—as an "explanation" of consumption or spending behavior by economic units. As long as economic units attain portfolio equilibrium in the sense that they jointly determine both their average real cash balances and their level of consumption, cash balances cannot be used to "explain" consumption or saving behavior. One must look for explanatory variables that are outside the direct control of households and firms, and in this chapter I focus on the real return on holding money as the control variable that may be manipulated by the monetary authority.

First let us define an appropriate time horizon. Only alternative "balanced-growth" paths will be considered. Along any such path, I assume that the holders of real cash balances (and the private recipients of bank credit) fully and accurately anticipate the actual percentage rate of inflation $\dot{P}$. The model is Fisherian in this respect. Now suppose that the composition of cash balances— various classes of deposits and currency—is determinate for given deposit rate(s) of interest and the relative liquidity values of hand-to-hand currency, demand deposits, and time deposits.[7] We can then define d to be the *average nominal* interest rate on deposits and currency. Hence $d - \dot{P}$ is a primary determinant of the private sector's willingness to hold real money balances M/P. Insofar as government monetary policy operates on the private demand for real money balances at any given level of income Y, such policy must influence $d - \dot{P}$.

The demand for money that reflects these assumptions can then be written as a function

[7] The problems involved in defining an optimal monetary portfolio are not pursued here. They have been discussed by Johnson [6].

of the real deposit rate $d - \dot{P}$ and real income Y:

$$M/P = f(d - \dot{P}, Y)$$

where $f_1 > 0$ and $f_2 > 0$.   (1)

Implicit in (1) would be the variance in future expectations regarding $\dot{P}$, and absent from (1) is a uniform market rate of interest on primary securities that simply does not exist in most of the underdeveloped world.

While the government cannot determine $d - \dot{P}$ directly, its own policies regarding the collection of seigniorage as related to the percentage rate of issue of nominal money $\dot{M}$ will eventually determine $d - \dot{P}$. For any nominal return d to the holders of money, $\dot{M}$ will ultimately govern the percentage rate of change in the price level $\dot{P}$. In the neo-classical tradition, we are assuming that the price level rises at a rate equal to the rate of issue of nominal money less the rate of growth in the demand for real cash balances. Hence, by controlling d and $\dot{M}$, the monetary authority ultimately controls $d - \dot{P}$, the real return on holding money. Accepting this, our principal task is to show how the selection of $d - \dot{P}$ is related to (or jointly determined with) seigniorage, investment in physical capital I, and the rate of growth in real output $\dot{Y}$.[8]

If $\dot{M}$ is increased while d is fixed, higher price inflation ensues and the real return to the holders of money is decreased. They respond by reducing M/P, and the economy moves to a new growth path with a higher rate of price inflation coupled with a *lower rate of investment*. This last effect is a direct consequence of the banking system's diminished role as a financial intermediary between private savers and private investors as M/P declines. Essentially, the reduction in $d - \dot{P}$ associated with the increase in $\dot{M}$ (with d fixed) has led to an increase in government seigniorage (real revenue from the banking system) which reduces and diverts private saving from investment in physical capital.

Similar disintermediation would occur if d were lowered when $\dot{M}$ was held constant.

To see the disintermediation effect of increasing $\dot{M}$ most clearly, let us start from a growth path in which the government extracts no explicit or implicit[9] seigniorage. Then the real return to the holders of money, $d - \dot{P}$, will fully reflect the returns on physical investment less the real costs of providing bank intermediation and transactions services. (The monetary system will be relatively large in real terms.) Consequently, any additions to the stock of real cash balances in the portfolios of private savers—due either to an increase in $d - \dot{P}$ or to an increase in income Y—will be fully reflected by the accumulation of a like amount of physical capital. Hence the government's budget must be balanced in the sense that it is not using the monetary system for financing unrequited deficits. There are an infinite number of combinations of d and $\dot{P}$ (as determined by $\dot{M}$) that are consistent with this situation of no seigniorage.

Now suppose that the government runs a current account deficit for consumption, and finances it through the sale of interest-free securities to the banking system, causing $\dot{M}$ to rise. The d is kept constant so that money holders are not compensated for the increased price inflation. The real return on holding money falls and disintermediation occurs. Two effects now operate so as to squeeze the flow of real bank credit to private investment. For a given flow of private saving and bank lending based on it, an increased share is appropriated by the government. But in addition, the fall in the real return to the holders of money causes a reduction in M/P, at any given level of income, that reduces the total flow of private saving and of real bank credit available to all borrowers. Hence, lending to the private sector for investment in physical capital will have fallen more than proportionately than real cash balances, once

---

[8] Throughout, the superscript dot is used to denote proportional growth. For example, $\dot{Y} = (dY/dt)/Y$.

[9] There are no usury restrictions and the banks are efficient and competitive—or at least simulate a competitive structure of interest rates for depositors and borrowers.

the new equilibrium growth path is achieved. The influence of bank disintermediation on investment can be very strong if private firms cannot sell their own primary securities to the general public because capital markets are imperfect.

II. THE SAVING FUNCTION

Corresponding to the simplified financial structure just sketched, there exists a social saving function that can be partitioned conveniently in the following manner:

$$s = \frac{\text{saving}}{Y} = \frac{d(M/P)/dt}{Y} - \frac{G}{Y} + s' \qquad (2)$$

where G is the real flow of government seigniorage and s' is the ratio of self-financed investment to income. The s is defined as the realized propensity to save socially, and need not be equal to the purely private propensity to save as long as opportunities exist for the government to extract seigniorage from the banking system. Our concern in this section is to show how monetary policy, as it operates through the government's choice of $d - \dot{P}$, influences s.

The first term in (2) is that portion of private saving that goes to acquire real cash balances; the remainder of private saving goes into self-financed investment as represented by s'. If we differentiate the money demand function (1) with respect to time, and remember that $d - \dot{P}$ must be constant on a balanced inflation path, then

$$d(M/P)/dt = f_2 \, dY/dt. \qquad (3)$$

Substituting (3) back into the first term of (2) yields

$$s = f_2 \dot{Y} - (G/Y) + s'. \qquad (4)$$

To demonstrate the positive influence of an increase in the real return from holding money on s, take the partial derivative of s with respect to $d - \dot{P}$, with $\dot{Y}$ and Y held constant, to yield

$$\frac{\partial s}{\partial (d - \dot{P})} > 0$$

because

$$f_{21} = \frac{\partial f_2}{\partial (d - \dot{P})} > 0, \qquad \dot{Y} > 0, \qquad (5)$$

$$\frac{\partial (G/Y)}{\partial (d - \dot{P})} < 0, \qquad (6)$$

and

$$\frac{\partial s'}{\partial (d - \dot{P})} \simeq 0. \qquad (7)$$

Let us discuss in turn the economic rationale for the signs of each of the partial derivatives (5)–(7). Consider the importance of f_{21}. The positive coefficient f_2 of $\dot{Y}$ in (5) reflects the private incremental demand to hold money as income grows. This incremental demand will be higher, the higher are desired real cash balances at any given level of income as influenced positively by the real return on holding money, $d - \dot{P}$. Hence $f_{21} > 0$. Increases in $d - \dot{P}$ operate through the monetary system to stimulate greater private saving—an effect which is particularly important in a world where money is the only financial asset.

The other embodiment of private saving is the rate of self-financed investment in physical capital s'. What is the economic rationale for assuming that $\partial s'/\partial (d - \dot{P})$ is approximately zero? McKinnon [8] devotes a whole chapter to showing why real money balances M/P and physical capital K are likely to be complementary in private portfolios over some relevant ranges of $d - \dot{P}$, although the more conventional relationship of substitutability becomes important over other ranges. Since my principal concern is to demonstrate that $\partial s/\partial (d - \dot{P}) > 0$ in financially repressed economics, let me sketch briefly the rather unconventional argument that self-financed investment in physical capital might actually be augmented as the real return on holding money increases.

Since money is the only financial asset in our less-developed economy, self-financed investment is important. But the process of saving through time for internal investment is facilitated if real cash balances can be used as a convenient store of value. Then small enterprises will simply build up and then draw down their owned real cash balances as a means of "financing" their internal investments. But if real cash balances are unattractive to hold because $d - \dot{P}$ is, say, negative, such patterns of self-financed investment will be discouraged. That is, price inflation that heavily taxes holders of real cash balances also taxes the process of self-financed saving and investment. Therefore, if we begin from a situation where $d - \dot{P} < 0$, and the monetary authority takes steps to reduce $\dot{M}$ and raise $d - \dot{P}$, self-financed investment may well increase, i.e., $\partial s'/\partial(d - \dot{P}) > 0$.

Finally, the negative sign of the "seigniorage" term in our saving function needs justification. Equation (6) specifies that the flow of government seigniorage rises as $d - \dot{P}$ declines, which is consistent with the argument provided in Section I that extraction of seigniorage is associated with a decline in the real return to the holders of money.

We have, therefore, shown in that $\partial s/\partial(d - \dot{P}) > 0$ in all three terms—(5), (6), and (7)—assuming that the economy moves from one equilibrium growth path to another when $d - \dot{P}$ is changed. If we also associate an increase in M/P—an endogenous variable—with a policy shift upward in $d - \dot{P}$, then investment in physical capital (realized social saving) and higher real cash balances are *positively* related. This is the "intermediation effect" of raising $d - \dot{P}$.

In the history of economic thinking on the subject, however, a *negative* wealth effect on saving has been posited (as in Metzler's "disequilibrium" static model [9]) in equilibrium growth theory in a Keynesian context as given by Williamson [13], and in the equilibrium neoclassical investment function as typified by Levhari and Patinkin [7]. Traditional theory ignores the intermediation role of the monetary system and essentially views real cash balances as competitive with, or a liquidity trap for, the accumulation of physical capital. This conventional approach is wanting generally, but it is peculiarly deceptive when applied to less-developed countries.

But there is another interesting aspect of our partitioned saving function as given by (4). From the first term $f_2\dot{Y}$, we see that,

ceterus paribus, an increase in the growth rate in real income will itself increase the private propensity to save, at least in the form of owned cash balances! For convenience, call the positive influence of an increased $\dot{Y}$ on s the "portfolio effect" of growth on saving. The strength of this portfolio effect is also influenced by monetary policy because f_2 is derived from the money demand function and is positively related to $d - \dot{P}$. In contrast, the private propensity to save is usually specified independently of the rate of growth in both Keynesian and neoclassical models.

The economic rationale for this portfolio effect is simple enough. In an interdependent economy, an innovation that increases the aggregate rate of growth will spread its dividends to most firms and households—even those that were not directly affected by the initial innovation. Many workers find that their wages simply begin to grow fortuitously. But income and consumption cannot grow efficiently without asset accumulation. The "convenience" yield—transactions, liquidity and store-of-value services—of monetary assets induces firms and households to keep stocks of these assets in a certain balanced relationship with current income flows. Even households who are quite insensitive to interest rates find that they are induced to save—i.e., not to consume all their incremental income—in order that their stocks of money and commodities rise commensurately with their growing income. That is, $\partial s/\partial\dot{Y} > 0$ as we can see by noting that $f_2 > 0$ in Eq. (4).

This portfolio effect can be seen most clearly by starting from a stationary state where there is, by definition, no net saving. Now suppose there is continuous innovation that costlessly induces growth in aggregate income. Then individuals must begin to save to allow their net wealth—inclusive of M/P—to accumulative *pari passu* with $\dot{Y}$.[10] The

[10] There is a rather weak constraint that the desired net wealth position of the private sector rises with income. As a general proposition, I think this is empirically self-evident. But in the constrained world of imperfect capital markets used here, it would be virtually impossible for households or firms to issue primary securities so as to make their net wealth position negative.

propensity to save goes from zero to some positive number. But simply moving from a lower to a higher rate of growth will be sufficient for this portfolio effect to operate—an effect that will be accentuated the higher is the ratio of money to GNP. For example, suppose the desired money/GNP ratio is 0.5, and growth suddenly increases from 5 to 10% per year. Just to maintain their money/GNP ratios, individuals will have to increase their propensity to save out of current income from 2.5 to 5%. (Insofar as some physical assets also have a convenience yield to households, saving may rise even further to maintain portfolio balance.)

The preceding discussion of the intermediation and portfolio effects allows us to write down a more general and somewhat simpler version of the function describing the social propensity to save:

$$s = s(\dot{Y}; d - \dot{P}) \tag{8}$$

where

$$s_1 = \frac{\partial s}{\partial \dot{Y}} > 0 \quad \text{and} \quad s_2 = \frac{\partial s}{\partial(d - \dot{P})} > 0.$$

The real return on holding money, and the rate of growth itself, each influence positively the social propensity to save out of current income. This saving function, as described by (8), is the basis for the modified Harrod–Domar model developed in Section III within which $\dot{Y}$ is endogenously determined and $d - \dot{P}$ can be exogenously manipulated as the instrumental variable of monetary policy.

III. A HARROD–DOMAR GROWTH MODEL WITH A VARIABLE PROPENSITY TO SAVE

The original Harrod–Domar model [4, 1] made no reference to money and finance; and intended saving was automatically transformed into investment at a uniform rate of return along the equilibrium growth path. Correspondingly, the output/capital ratio—denoted by σ—was taken as given, and the aggregate production function was written as

$$Y = \sigma K \tag{9}$$

where K is the stock of physical capital.

The omission from (9) of a separate labor constraint on aggregate output has been justified in two ways. Technical change is sufficiently labor augmenting so that the effective labor force grows at the same rate as aggregate output. Alternatively, one can assume the existence of a residual unemployed or underemployed labor force that requires new investment to bring it into "organized" economic activity. The former explanation applies mainly, although not exclusively, to mature economies; whereas the latter is more readily associated with less-developed countries.

Financial innovation could conceivably increase the output/capital ratio if new saving and investment were accompanied by increased intermediation through the monetary system. In the algebraic development to follow, however, I shall forgo this possibility and simply follow tradition by assuming that σ is constant—that is, diminishing returns are absent. Furthermore, M/P is omitted from the aggregate production function in order to emphasize the "intermediation" rather than the "transactions" role of money. Inclusion of real cash balances as a current factor of production in (9) would not alter the qualitative nature of any conclusions.

In the unmodified Harrod–Domar model, the propensity to save—as denoted by s—is simply a fixed proportion of income. Moreover, private saving is fully reflected in the accumulation of physical capital. That is,

$$I = dK/dt = sY. \tag{10}$$

Hence, one can easily solve (9) and (10) within the traditional framework to obtain the percentage rate of growth in aggregate income as simply the product of the output/capital ratio and the marginal propensity to save:

$$\dot{Y} = \sigma s. \tag{11}$$

Now, let us reinterpret s as the social propensity to save—private saving minus government seigniorage—in the mode of our analysis of financial structure in Section II. Hence s is now endogenous and is a function of the real return on holding money, $d - \dot{P}$, and the rate of growth itself, $\dot{Y}$. Combining Eqs. (8) and (11), we have $\dot{Y}$ defined by the

FIG. 1

The intermediation and portfolio effects of monetary policy.

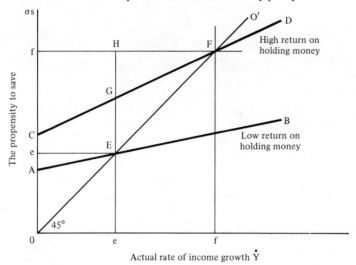

implicit equation

$$\dot{Y} = \sigma s(\dot{Y}; d - \dot{P}) \qquad (12)$$

where $d - \dot{P}$ is an exogenous variable under the policy control of the government.

The solution to (12) is portrayed graphically in Fig. 1 in a manner that visually distinguishes the intermediation effect from the portfolio effect on the variable saving propensity. In reading Fig. 1, the vertical axis should be interpreted as measuring the right-hand side of Eq. (12)—the product of the *ex ante* propensity to save s and the constant output/capital ratio σ. The *actual* rate of growth is plotted on the horizontal axis. Hence equilibrium, where *ex ante* saving matches the rate of investment necessary to support the existing rate of growth, holds only along the 45° line from the origin.

AB and *CD* are alternative saving functions plotted so as to show saving increasing with $\dot{Y}$—their slopes representing the portfolio effect. (The saving function in the traditional Harrod–Domar model would simply be a fixed horizontal line.) By raising the real return on holding money, the monetary authority can raise the whole saving schedule from *AB* to *CD*—the shift representing the intermediation effect. The *AB* is associated with a "low" or negative return on money, and *CD* is associated with a high positive return. Correspondingly, the equilibrium rate

of growth increases from E on AB to F on CD.

In Fig. 1, the buoyant impact of making money more attractive to hold by raising d or reducing $\dot{M}$ can be partitioned into two stages. When $d - \dot{P}$ increases, but before growth in aggregate income responds, private saving moves upward from E to G. Hence EG measures the pure intermediation effect, which is the rise in the private propensity to save at a given rate of growth in aggregate income. However, aggregate income will be induced to grow faster as realized saving and investment rise. In order to maintain portfolio balance in the face of this general economic progress, individuals will be induced to save still more with a further impact on growth that is measured by the distance GH—the portfolio effect.[11] I hypothesize that the two effects together can be a powerful and positive influence on saving and growth.

Those with a penchant for pedantry will be worried, justifiably, about the stability of the model just outlined. Without pretending to specify completely the dynamics of adjustment, let us consider the case of the saving function AB and the existence of the equilibrium position E. If the actual growth were

---

[11] One should note that the upward slope of CD is steeper than that of AB because an increase in M/P strengthens the influence of $\dot{Y}$ on the propensity to save.

"arbitrarily" set at zero so as to eliminate the portfolio effect, then the saving propensity would still be positive and equal to OA (divided by σ). If these savings were successfully translated into net investment, the rate of growth would be driven upward toward E—as measured by e on either axis. However, to ensure that AB intersects the $45°$ line so that an equilibrium such as point E exists and the rate of growth does not become arbitrarily large, AB must be constrained to having a slope of less than unity. That is, to prevent explosive growth in the context of the model it is necessary that

$$\partial s/\partial \dot{Y} < 1/\sigma. \tag{13}$$

Intuitively, it is easy to see that this last condition, which puts an upper bound on the portfolio effect, is not very stringent. Suppose that the output/capital ratio σ is $1/3$—a commonly assumed number. Then condition (13) implies that a one percentage point increase in $\dot{Y}$ can increase the propensity to save as much as three percentage points without inducing explosive growth. Hence, the portfolio effect of growth on saving can be quite large and still be consistent with the existence of equilibrium in our Harrod–Domar economy.

IV. CONCLUDING NOTES AND EMPIRICAL OBSERVATIONS

Across diverse countries, the observed high and positive correlation among saving propensities, stocks of monetary assets, and rates of growth must seem puzzling to economists steeped in the conventional theory that associates the real balance effect with a high social propensity to consume. Without pretending to be comprehensive empirically,[12] let me be merely provocative by providing fragmentary information on Taiwan and Japan, two countries that are well known to have experienced unusually high economic growth during the decade of the 1960's. Tables 1 and 2 display money/GNP ratios—where money is broadly

[12] An attempt to be somewhat more comprehensive can be found in the book by McKinnon [8, Chapter 8].

TABLE 1

The Ratio of Money (M_2) to GNP in Selected Less-Developed Countries[a]

Country	1960	1965	1970
Taiwan	0.20	0.36	0.46
Argentina	0.30	0.26	0.35
Brazil	0.31	0.26	0.32
Chile	0.12	0.16	0.18
India	0.23	0.25	0.25
Ceylon	0.30	0.34	0.29
Turkey	0.20	0.24	0.30
Philippines	0.23	0.24	0.32
Colombia	0.21	0.22	0.24[b]

[a] Source: International Financial Statistics, published by the International Monetary Fund. M_2 is generally calculated from lines 34 and 35 of the IFS, unless additional data are available.
[b] Data for the year 1969 were used because data from 1970 were not available.

defined to include time and saving deposits—for the benchmark years 1960, 1965, and 1970.

The data on Taiwan are presented together with a "peer" group of less-developed economies, which have per capita real incomes comparable to the Taiwanese, but rates of growth that are much lower. Similarly, the data on Japan are presented together with a peer group of developed industrial economies—although in this case the peer group had generally much higher per capital income, particularly in 1960. Comparing the two

TABLE 2

The Ratio of Money (M_2) to GNP in Selected Industrial Countries[a]

Country	1960	1965	1970
Japan	0.88	0.98	0.97
Belgium	0.60	0.60	0.59
France	0.47	0.55	0.59
Germany	0.36	0.42	0.52
United Kingdom	0.52	0.50	0.56
United States	0.63	0.71	0.70

[a] Source: International Financial Statistics, published by the International Monetary Fund. M_2 is generally calculated from lines 34 and 35 of the IFS, unless additional data are available.

groups, per capita income is strongly related to financial maturity as measured by the money/GNP ratio.

For 1970, the relative size of the banking system in Taiwan was much higher, i.e., the money/GNP ratio was 0.46, than in the peer group of developing countries, where the average money/GNP ratio was 0.30. My theoretical model of equilibrium growth only compares economies along balanced growth paths after full adjustment to any discrete change in the real return on holding money has been made. Hence the model does not directly reflect the period of financial transition that Taiwan was going through in the 1960's, when the money/GNP ratio more than doubled—in large measure reflecting a dampening of inflationary expectations that had been built up in the 1950's. In a more general sense, however, the extraordinary growth in M/P seems quite consistent with the high saving that one would expect from the intermediation and portfolio effects conceptualized in the theoretical model.

Japan is not so much of a transitional case because it had been maintaining a very high rate of growth for many years prior to 1960. Hence, it had already reached the level of monetary development associated with a high rate of saving and growth at the beginning of the 1960's. Still, the Japanese money/GNP ratio moved up from 0.88 in 1960 to 0.97 in 1970, levels that were much higher than the average of 0.59 in the group of industrial countries (Table 2)—despite the greater wealth per capita of the peer group. Again, the Japanese data are consistent with my view of the importance of real cash balances for saving and growth, although the direction of causation can never be proved by simply observing statistical correlations.

The policy implications of the above theoretical and empirical analysis are obvious. Money and finance are important in the development process despite the short shrift they have been given in the development literature. Moreover, the extraction of seigniorage by inflation or other financial devices necessarily lowers the real return on holding money and shrinks the money/GNP ratio in a way which is very damaging to private saving and investment propensities. The tranditional monetary literature, neoclassical or Keynesian, fails to reflect the extent of the damage because it is exclusively concerned with the transactions motive for holding money and assumes that private capital markets operate perfectly without bank intermediation.

References

1. Dommar, E., "Capital Expansion, Rate of Growth, and Employment," *Econometrica*, 14: 137–147 (1946); reprinted in Stiglitz, J,, and Uzawa, H., (eds). *Readings in the Modern Theory of Economic Growth* (MIT Press, 1969).
2. Friedman, M., *The Optimum Quantity of Money and Other Essays* (Chicago, 1969).
3. Goldsmith, R., *Financial Structure and Development* (Yale University Press, 1969).
4. Harrod, R. F., "An Essay in Dynamic Theory," *Economic Journal*, 49:14–33 (1939); reprinted in Stiglitz, J., and Uzawa, H., (eds). *Readings in the Modern Theory of Economic Growth* (MIT Press, 1969).
5. Johnson, H., "Money in a One-Sector Neoclassical Growth Model," in *Essays in Monetary Economics* (Harvard University Press, 1967).
6. Johnson, H., "Problems of Efficiency in Monetary Management," *Journal of Political Economy*, 76:971–990 (1968).
7. Levhari, D., and Patinkin, D., "The Role of Money in a Simple Growth Model," *American Economic Review*, 58:713–753 (1968).
8. McKinnon, R. I., *Money and Capital in Economic Development* (Washington, D.C., The Brookings Institution, 1973).
9. Metzler, L., "Wealth, Saving, and the Rate of Interest," *Journal of Political Economy*, 59: 93–116 (1951) [reprinted in R. Thorn, *Monetary Theory and Policy* (Praeger, 1977)].
10. Mundell, R., *Monetary Theory* (Pacific Palisades, California: Goodyear Publication, 1971).
11. Tobin, J., "Asset Holdings and Spending Decisions," *American Economic Review*, 42: 109–133 (1952).
12. Tobin, J., "Money and Economic Growth," *Econometrica*, 33:671–684 (1965) [reprinted in this volume].
13. Willamson, J., "A Simple Neo-Keynesian Growth Model." *The Review of Economic Studies*, 37:157–171 (1970).

78 79 80 81 82 9 8 7 6 5 4 3 2 1